TERRORISM

Documents of International and Local Control

VOLUME 89

TERRORISM

Documents of International and Local Control

VOLUME 89

EUROPE'S APPROACH TO TERRORISM

Douglas C. Lovelace Jr., Esquire
Senior National Security Strategist

Oceana®
NEW YORK

OXFORD
UNIVERSITY PRESS

Oxford University Press, Inc., publishes works that further Oxford University's objective of excellence in research, scholarship, and education.

Published by Oxford University Press, Inc.
198 Madison Avenue, New York, New York 10016

Cataloging-in-Publication information is available from the Library of Congress.

ISSN 1062-4007
Terrorism: Documents of International and Local Control

ISBN: 978-0-19-537691-3 (v. 89)

Note to Readers:

This publication is designed to provide accurate and authoritative information in regard to the subject matter covered. It is based upon sources believed to be accurate and reliable and is intended to be current as of the time it was written. It is sold with the understanding that the publisher is not engaged in rendering legal, accounting, or other professional services. If legal advice or other expert assistance is required, the services of a competent professional person should be sought. Also, to confirm that the information has not been affected or changed by recent developments, traditional legal research techniques should be used, including checking primary sources where appropriate.

(Based on the Declaration of Principles jointly adopted by a Committee of the American Bar Association and a Committee of Publishers and Associations.)

TABLE OF CONTENTS

VOLUME 89

DOCUMENTS

A. IN GENERAL

B. TERROR FUNDING AND FINANCIAL RECORDS

E. RELIGIOUS EXTREMISM

F. SPECIAL TOPICS

A. IN GENERAL

DOCUMENT NO. 1

EUROPEAN PARLIAMENT RESOLUTION OF 12 DECEMBER 2007 ON THE FIGHT AGAINST TERRORISM

The European Parliament,

– having regard to the Presidency conclusions of the Brussels European Council of 25 and 26 March 2004, in particular the European Council Declaration of 25 March 2004 on combating terrorism, which included a solidarity clause,

– having regard to the Report of the High-Level Group of the 'Alliance of Civilisations' presented to the UN Secretary-General on 13 November 2006,

– having regard to its resolution of 14 February 2007 on the alleged use of European countries by the CIA for the transportation and illegal detention of prisoners,[1]

– having regard to Rule 108(5) of its Rules of Procedure,

A. whereas:

- the terrorist threat not only has a direct impact on the security of citizens of the countries that are victims of terrorist attacks, but also has the potential to undermine the security of everyone else; for this reason, a global response is required in order to meet the need for security, giving law enforcement authorities the necessary resources and legal framework while fully respecting fundamental rights, and also ensuring adequate data protection,
- terrorism is a common threat to democracy, the rule of law and human rights, as well as the safety of Union citizens and should therefore be firmly resisted, while the most scrupulous respect should, at the same time, be shown for fundamental rights,
- by virtue of Articles 2 and 6 of the EU Treaty, the Union should be an area of freedom, security and justice according with the principles underlying the Union of democracy, the rule of law and protection of

[1] OJ C 287 E, 29.11.2007, p. 309.

fundamental rights, and by virtue of Article 29 of that Treaty 'the Union's objective shall be to provide citizens with a high level of safety', in particular by preventing and combating terrorism,

- the EU firmly intends to assess the achievements, limits and prospects of the Union's anti-terrorism policy after the attacks of 11 September 2001, 11 March 2004 and 7 July 2005, at a time when the terrorist threat has acquired a global dimension and accordingly calls for a response at the same level,
- the Union is committed to the fight against terrorism in all its dimensions, whether its origin lies or its activities occur inside or beyond its borders, while acting within the limits defined by the rule of law and respect for fundamental rights, and in the fight against terror in particular there must be no areas in which fundamental rights are not respected,
- any limitation on fundamental rights and freedoms in the fight against terrorism must be limited in time and scope, prescribed by law, subject to full democratic and judicial scrutiny, and be necessary and proportionate in a democratic society,
- terrorism can be eradicated, and the threat of terrorism can be reduced by tackling its causes,

B. regretting that the EU institutions have responded to the exceptional pressures resulting from terrorist attacks by adopting acts that have not been thoroughly discussed with Parliament and with national parliaments and that have been in violation of the rights to a fair trial, to data protection or to access to the documents of the EU institutions connected with the fight against terrorism, and as a consequence have been rightly annulled by the Court of Justice of the European Communities,

C. having very particular regard for the victims of terrorism and their agonising experience and for the need to give priority to upholding their rights and to measures seeking to afford them protection and recognition, ever bearing in mind that the terrorists begin to lose ground when their victims speak out and society gives them a hearing,

D. D concerned about the far-reaching consequences of using large-scale immigration and asylum databases at the EU level in the fight against terrorism and in particular about giving access to the Eurodac database to Member States' police and law enforcement authorities as well as Europol in the course of their duties in relation to the prevention, detection and investigation of terrorist offences and other serious criminal offences, as called for in the conclusions of the Justice and Home Affairs Council of 12 and 13 June 2007,

E. conscious, therefore, that the fight against terrorism is a very complex matter and requires, now more than ever, a multi-level and multi-disciplinary strategy as planned at international level:-

- by the UN Counter-Terrorism Strategy adopted on 8 September 2006[2] and the Council of Europe Convention on the Prevention of Terrorism concluded on 16 May 2005,[3]
- by the European Council when it adopted a Counter-Terrorism Strategy[4] in December 2005, unfortunately without any substantial involvement by Parliament and by national parliaments,
- and by the Commission which presented its counter-terrorism package on 6 November 2007,

F. F considering that each one of the aspects of the EU strategy—prevention, protection, pursuit, response—requires the full involvement of Parliament and of national parliaments, which should be fully and regularly informed through evaluations carried out by the Commission every two years and enabled to verify the real effectiveness of the measures taken, including the impact on fundamental rights, whether the initial objectives have been implemented and the actual cost of the initiatives,

G. regretting that there is a substantial lack of transparency, democratic oversight, accountability and judicial review, and noting that the EU institutions and agencies such as Europol and Eurojust are just starting to collect the information required for their activities in a more structured way,

H. dismayed at the refusal of some governments of the Member States and the Council to answer to allegations of abuse of powers under the pretext of counter-terrorism, in particular in the case of CIA extraordinary renditions and 'black sites',

I. concerned that extreme interrogation techniques have been applied on terror suspects,

J. taking the view that cross-border cooperation of intelligence and security services must be subject to more thorough and systematic scrutiny,

K. deeply concerned at the function creep of many measures introduced under the counter-terrorism label, but which in practice are used for a wide range of purposes,

L. emphasising the need to pay considerably more attention in the EU counter-terrorism strategy to the causes of terrorism and the EU's role therein,

---

[2] See http://www.un.org/terrorism/strategy-counter-terrorism.html

[3] See http://conventions.coe.int/Treaty/Commun/QueVoulezVous.asp?NT=196&CM=2&DF=&CL=ENG(already ratified by BG, DK, RO, SL, SK).

[4] See http://register.consilium.eu.int/pdf/en/05/st14/st14469-re04.en05.pdf

M. recalling that the Treaty of Lisbon should also make it possible to frame in a transparent, simpler and accountable way the Union's role in the fight against terrorism, to strengthen solidarity between the Member States and to associate Parliament and national parliaments in the evaluation of AFSJ-related policies, while regretting that for these policies there will be no full judicial control at EU level for legislation adopted prior to the entry into force of the Treaty of Lisbon,

1. Warmly welcomes the signing of the Treaty of Lisbon, and calls on the Member States to ratify it so as to make the Charter of Fundamental Rights of the European Union binding, which is a necessary complement to the EU strategy for combating terrorism;

As Far as 'Prevention' is Concerned:

2. Considers that the EU should support actions at EU, national and local level aimed at preventing violent radicalisation, by fostering the integration of people through intercultural dialogue and the promotion of democracy and human rights as the universal values underpinning our society, avoiding social exclusion; also considers it necessary to combat violent radicalisation, including incitement to commit violent acts;

3. Demands that there be, at long last, a Europe-wide ban on any apology for terrorism;

4. Believes, further, that an important element in preventing terrorism is an EU and Member State development aid policy that also functions as a security policy; considers that promoting civil society and helping to achieve social peace and prosperity are a suitable means of showing people their opportunities and restricting the spread of fundamentalist ideologies; believes, therefore, that the development of education, health and social security systems in countries often identified as the origin of terrorist activities should be made a much greater priority than before in development aid policy;

5. Deems, in this respect, that the EU should favour best practices and their dissemination within the EU, and notes that Parliament will shortly be making recommendations in this area, while taking of account the contributions of the Council and the Commission;

6. Believes that cases such as the US Supreme Court's dismissal of Khalid Al-Masri torture appeal tend to reinforce the impression, particularly among Muslim minorities in the EU, that anti-terror measures create double standards; calls, therefore, on the EU to engage more forcefully in the struggle to uphold the rule of law within the EU and in the international context, in particular by defending its own citizens in prosecutions in third countries in which citizens of Muslim descent are disproportionately concerned;

7. Considers that the prevention of terrorism requires an EU foreign policy that promotes democracy, the rule of law and respect for human rights both in the EU's neighbourhood and beyond;

8. Calls on the Commission and the Council to launch an initiative at the European and international levels for the resettlement of Guantánamo prisoners from third states who cannot be returned to their country of origin because they risk being persecuted or tortured;

9. Reaffirms the importance of police and judicial cooperation at EU level, especially as far as exchanges of information and analysis are concerned, and calls on the Member States to reinforce their cooperation, with the coordination and support of Europol;

10. Demands that Europol's role be strengthened and reaffirms that, in the fight against terrorism, Europol needs its own investigative powers; further demands in this connection that Europol set up its own task force and staff it with national experts;

11. Considers that, in order to increase the EU's effectiveness in the fight against terrorism, the Commission and the Member States should put in place a permanent network of information exchange between EU anti-terrorist centres;

12. Reiterates the importance of sharing intelligence information, both at EU level and among Member States' services, and reaffirms the need for uniform rules at EU level to ensure the necessary democratic and parliamentary control and scrutiny;

As Far as 'Protection' is Concerned:

13. Considers that, in order to protect citizens, fundamental rights, human rights, democracy, and infrastructure and to reduce the EU's vulnerability to attack, including through improved security of borders, transport and critical infrastructure, it is essential that the EU:

a) establish, with the cooperation of the Member States, an EU-wide

- crisis-alert and—detection system, based also on national protection schemes operational seven days a week and round-the-clock for disasters caused by nature or human activity,
- map of critical and strategic infrastructures and networks, taking into account the future Council Directive on the identification and designation of European Critical Infrastructure and the assessment of the need to improve their protection,
- effective solidarity mechanism between Member States which can give immediate access to rare resources available at national level (so-called 'assets' such as vaccines or sophisticated technologies);

b) render the SIS II and VIS databases fully operational, including provisions regarding the access of law enforcement authorities; points out that these databases have no primary law enforcement purpose and that access for law enforcement purposes has thus been limited to specific cases, when necessary and proportionate in a democratic society; considers that mass collection of personal data and data processing in order to create profiles through data-mining techniques, as envisaged in the recent proposal for a directive on an EU-PNR system, are not allowed at EU level

c) coordinate better, through the Member States, the work of its intelligence services to ensure that existing obstacles to the exchange of information, such as a lack of trust, are swiftly removed, as individual 'information islands' and the sealing off of information by national intelligence services run counter to the Community approach to fighting terrorism;

d) rationalise and improve the clarity, transparency and applicability of its counter-terrorism legislation;

14. Emphasises that any monitoring of the internet in order to prevent terrorist attacks should under no circumstances entail restrictions on free speech that is not intended to incite terrorist acts and cannot reasonably in itself lead to such acts;

15. Reminds the Council of its promises to Parliament, and calls on it finally to adopt the framework decision on the protection of personal data processed within the framework of police and judicial cooperation in criminal matters providing for an adequate level of data protection, and the framework decision on certain procedural rights in criminal proceedings throughout the EU before introducing any further measures relating to the fight against terrorism;

16. Recalls that the primary purpose of Eurodac as a first pillar database is to facilitate the application of the Dublin II Regulation to establish the Member State responsible for examining an asylum application, and that any proposal to transform it into a security measure and criminal investigation tool would be unlikely to be legal under EU or international law;

17. Notes with concern that access by law enforcement authorities and Europol to the Eurodac database could lead to stigmatisation of, discrimination against, and possible danger to, asylum seekers;

18. Calls on its Committee on Civil Liberties, Justice and Home Affairs to organise, in cooperation with the national parliaments, a hearing before June 2008 on measures proposed and adopted at EU level in the fight against terrorism and on their application and effectiveness;

19. Considers that any form of 'profiling' in counter-terrorism measures is unacceptable; regards it as unacceptable to pursue an EU-PNR system without a complete evaluation of the EU-US and EU-Canada PNR agreements, in particular their impact on reducing the threat and increasing security as well as their impact on privacy and civil liberties;

20. Expresses concern that access by law enforcement authorities and Europol to the Eurodac database could diminish the effectiveness of the principal purpose of the Eurodac database;

As Far as 'Pursuit' is Concerned:

21. Urges the Member States to cease to hesitate and enhance judicial and police cooperation at EU level in the fight against terrorism; asks to be informed without delay of the effectiveness of current cooperation and what results have emerged from the mutual evaluation mechanism between the Member States and the EU institutions;

22. Emphasises the need to strengthen the coordination and operational role of Eurojust and Europol, that are essential tools for real and effective cooperation in prosecution and pursuit at EU level; at the same time reaffirming the need to ensure full democratic control at EU level;

23. Firmly reiterates the urgent need to adopt a framework decision on data protection in the third pillar, ensuring a high level of safeguards for EU citizens, which is now lacking at EU level;

24. Therefore asks,

a) the Commission to refer to Parliament before the end of the year the answers obtained to its questionnaires on the implementation at national level of the counter-terrorism legislation, in particular the framework decision on terrorism and on the European arrest warrant, and the directive on data retention, and its impact on fundamental rights and on any differences in implementation in the Member States, along with an assessment and any proposals with regard to how a better implementation and use of existing legislation on the fight against terror can be ensured;

b) the Commission to inform Parliament whether all anti-terrorism acts adopted have been implemented by the Member States and, if this is not the case, to inform Parliament which countries are lagging behind, and for what reason;

c) the Commission to carry out an overall evaluation of the consequences of the anti-terrorism legislation, by measuring the effectiveness of the legislation, and by investigating its positive and negative effects, both in terms of security and in terms of citizens' rights;

d) the Commission to inform Parliament whether all the laws that infringe citizens' rights give citizens the possibility of correcting their data, of challenging the facts and of complaining about the proportionality of the measures;

e) the Counter-Terrorism Coordinator to report to Parliament before June 2008 on the effectiveness of the measures taken by the Member States and by Europol and Eurojust; considers that it is also essential to examine what kind of measures could be best suited to cooperation between a limited number of Member States and what measures should be applied by all the Member States in conformity with the solidarity principle;

f) the Council to act on Parliament's recommendations regarding the CIA rendition programme;

g) the Commission and the Council to carry out an overview, which has been repeatedly requested by Parliament, of companies that are being forced by third countries (notably the US) to submit their customer data to the authorities;

25. Asks the Council and the Commission to cooperate in establishing a real feedback mechanism regarding the effectiveness of European and national measures in this field by progressively defining neutral indicators in relation to the development of the terrorist threat to the EU (e.g. statistics on number of inquiries and judicial proceedings, analysis of possible regional crises, evidence of successful/unsuccessful cooperation, etc.) so as to provide Parliament and national parliaments with a clearer picture at least of the effectiveness and any shortcomings or positive features of public policies in these areas;

26. Proposes that the Member States should concentrate their resources in the area of police cooperation and, instead of taking the technical approach favoured so far, stress the importance of individual and staff cooperation; considers, in this regard, that there should be a greater drive to encourage exchanges between national emergency services and to eliminate obstacles, e.g. as a priority, the removal of linguistic barriers through language courses; considers, moreover, that police training measures should be adapted to the realities of European society, so that, for example, teaching about all the different cultures composing the European reality should be included in such training in the future;

27. Takes note of the adoption by the Commission of new measures concerning, in particular, an amendment to the framework decision on terrorism and a proposal for an EU-PNR system; expresses its desire to attentively examine these measures and reiterates its concerns on the proposal

for EU-PNR system, especially concerning the necessity and proportionality of the proposed profiling scheme on which it seems to be based;

28. Calls on the Commission and the Council to ensure more effective use of existing mechanisms for cross-border cooperation between Member States, such as the European arrest warrant;

29. Reminds the Commission of the importance of evidence-based policy making; therefore calls on the Commission to ensure that all future counter-terrorism proposals are accompanied by a thorough impact assessment or evaluation which demonstrates the necessity and usefulness of the measures to be taken;

30. Reaffirms the importance of cooperation with third countries in the prevention of and the fight against terrorism, and observes that the US is an essential partner in this field; considers that a common legal framework for police and judicial cooperation, with special emphasis on the protection of fundamental rights, especially of personal data, should be defined between the EU and the US, via an international agreement, ensuring appropriate democratic and parliamentary scrutiny at national and EU level;

31. Is concerned at Member States" knee-jerk reaction to anti-terror legislation, in which the desire to send a political message often takes priority over serious and conscientious consideration of the boundaries of the possible and the useful, including the increasingly inadequate consideration of rule of law principles, such as the proportionality principle and the presumption of innocence;

As Far as 'Response' is Concerned:

32. Considers it to be of the utmost importance that, in the event of a terrorist attack, Member States should show an effective spirit of solidarity, by managing and minimising the consequences of the attack, in particular for EU countries which do not have sufficient human, financial or technological resources to manage the aftermath, coordinate the response and help victims;

33. Recalls the importance of unity between all democratic forces in the fight against terrorism;

34. Considers that a key element in the response to terrorist attacks should be to put in place the necessary, effective and proportionate instruments to support the overall fight against terrorism, and considers it equally important to protect all aspects of the rule of law, citizens' civil rights, judicial and legal safeguards for suspects, and democratic control and scrutiny over all legislation introduced, both at EU level and in relations with third countries;

35. Urges the Commission to come forward with a proposal to ensure Parliamentary control over joint and coordinated intelligence activities at EU level;

As Far as the 'Roots' of Terrorism are Concerned:

36. Calls on the Council and the Commission to draw up an action plan for spreading democracy throughout the world and strengthening economic and political cooperation with Islamic countries by

a) supporting democracy movements,

b) promoting student exchanges and other forms of education,

c) funding media stations which spread democratic ideas and bring to light terrorist activities and those who support them;

37. Calls on the Commission to define measures to ensure protection of and support for the victims of terrorism, including the promotion of exchanges of best practices and a uniform set of guarantees at EU level;

The Need for Stronger and More Effective Interparliamentary Cooperation for the New Counter-Terrorism Strategy:

38. Considers that, immediately following the signature of the Treaty of Lisbon, Parliament and national parliaments should start a joint evaluation exercise of the European Counter Terrorism Strategy, in order to prepare a new form of 'high-level dialogue' in this sphere, associating citizens' representatives at EU and national levels;

Cooperation with the Commission and the Council

39. Considers, bearing in mind that the Lisbon Treaty is expected to enter into force in 2009 and that the EU institutions should already in 2008 create the conditions for its entry into force, that any proposals which come under the codecision procedure and are not adopted before the entry into force of the Lisbon Treaty, should be treated as 'quasi-codecision';

40. Notes the new package of counter-terrorism legislative proposals comprising the Council framework decision on the use of Passenger Name Records (PNR) for law enforcement purposes, the directive on explosives and the evaluation report on the implementation of the framework decision on combating terrorism; and is determined to carry out an evidence-based assessment of the proposals;

41. Believes that the EU anti-terrorism coordinator should play an important role in the Community's approach and wishes to clarify his responsibilities and structures of accountability;

42. Expects a strategy for an EU anti-terror policy to be developed in cooperation with Parliament that not only displays an integrated approach and central theme but, above all, sets out distinct, short-, medium—and long-term measures;

43. Instructs its President to forward this resolution to the Council, the Commission, the Council of Europe, and the governments and parliaments of the Member States.

DOCUMENT NO. 2

COUNCIL DECISION 2007/124/EC OF 12 FEBRUARY 2007 ESTABLISHING FOR THE PERIOD 2007 TO 2013, AS PART OF GENERAL PROGRAMME ON SECURITY AND SAFEGUARDING LIBERTIES, THE SPECIFIC PROGRAMME 'PREVENTION PREPAREDNESS AND CONSEQUENCE MANAGEMENT OF TERRORISM AND OTHER SECURITY RELATED RISKS'

THE COUNCIL OF THE EUROPEAN UNION,

Having regard to the Treaty establishing the European Community, and in particular Article 308 thereof,

Having regard and to the Treaty establishing the European Atomic Energy Community, and in particular Article 203 thereof,

Having regard to the proposal from the Commission,

Having regard to the opinion of the European Parliament,[1]

[1] Opinion delivered on 14 December 2006 (not yet published in the Official Journal).

Whereas:

(1) Prevention, preparedness and consequence management of terrorism and other security related risks are essential aspects of the protection of people and critical infrastructure within the area of freedom, security and justice.

(2) The revised European Union Plan of Action on Combating Terrorism as adopted by the European Council of 17–18 June 2004, identified as priority issues, *inter alia,* the prevention and consequence management of terrorist attacks, and the protection of critical infrastructures.

(3) On 2 December 2004, the Council adopted the revised European Union Solidarity Programme on the Consequences of Terrorist Threats and Attacks, highlighting the importance of risk and threat assessments, protection of critical infrastructure, mechanisms for the detection and identification of terrorist threats, and the political

and operational preparedness and capability for consequence management.

(4) The Council in December 2005 decided that the European Programme for Critical Infrastructure protection (EPCIP) will be based on an all hazards approach while countering threats from terrorism is regarded as priority. New Counter Terrorism Strategy which contains four strands: Prevent, protect, pursue and respond, was also adopted at December 2005 European Council.

(5) The Community mechanism to facilitate reinforced cooperation in civil protection assistance interventions, established by Council Decision 2001/792/EC, Euratom[2] of 23 October 2001, addresses immediate response to all major emergencies, but has not been designed specifically for prevention, preparedness and consequence management of terrorist attacks.

[2] OJ L 297, 15.11.2001, p. 7.

(6) The Hague Programme,[3] set up by the European Council in November 2004, has called for integrated and coordinated management of crises within the EU with cross-border effects.

[3] OJ C 53, 3.3.2005, p. 1.

(7) Within the scope of its competence the Community shall contribute to taking the necessary measures to prevent terrorists from attacking the values of democracy, the rule of law, open society and the freedom of our citizens and societies, and to limit the consequences of any attack wherever possible.

(8) In the interest of efficacy, cost-efficiency and transparency, the specific efforts on prevention, preparedness and consequence management of terrorism should be streamlined and financed by one single programme.

(9) With regard to legal certainty and coherence, and to the complementarity with other financial programmes, the terms 'prevention and preparedness', 'consequence management' and 'critical infrastructure' should be defined.

(10) The primary responsibility for protecting critical infrastructures falls on the Member States, owners, operators and users (users being defined as organisations that exploit and use the infrastructure for business and service provision purposes). Member States authorities will provide leadership and coordination in developing and implementing a nationally consistent approach to the protection of critical infrastructure within their jurisdictions, taking into account existing

Community competences. The responsibility for carrying out risk and threat assessments therefore lies primarily with the Member States.

(11) Commission actions, together with transnational projects where appropriate, are essential to achieve an integrated and coordinated EC approach. In addition, it is useful and appropriate to support projects within Member States to the extent that they can provide useful experience and knowledge for further actions at Community level, in particular risk and threat assessments. In this regard it is appropriate to adopt all hazards approach while considering the terrorist threat as a priority.

(12) It is also appropriate to provide for third countries and international organisations to participate in transnational projects.

(13) Complementarity needs to be ensured with other Community and Union programmes such as the European Union Solidarity Fund and the Civil Protection Financial Instrument, the Community mechanism to facilitate reinforced cooperation in civil protection assistance interventions, Seventh Framework Programme for Research, Technological Development and Demonstration Activities and the Structural Funds.

(14) Since the objectives of this Decision cannot be sufficiently achieved by the Member States and can therefore, by reason of the scale or impact of the programme, be better achieved at the Community level, the Community may adopt measures in accordance with the principle of subsidiarity as set out in Article 5 of the Treaty. In accordance with the principle of proportionality, as set out in that Article, this Decision does not go beyond what is necessary to achieve those objectives.

(15) The expenditure of the programme should be compatible with the ceiling under Heading 3 of the financial framework. It is necessary to foresee flexibility in the definition of the programme to allow for eventual adjustments in any envisaged actions, in order to respond to the evolution of needs in the course of the period 2007–2013. The decision should, therefore, be limited to the generic definition of envisaged actions and their respective administrative and financial arrangements.

(16) Appropriate measures should also be taken to prevent irregularities and fraud and the necessary steps should be taken to recover funds lost, wrongly paid or incorrectly used in accordance with Council Regulations (EC, Euratom) No 2988/95 of 18 December 1995 on the protection of the Communities' financial interests,[1] (Euratom, EC) No 2185/96[2] of 11 November 1996 concerning on-the-spot checks and inspections carried out by the Commission and Regulation (EC) No 1073/1999 of the European Parliament and of the Council of 25

May 1999 concerning investigations conducted by the European Anti-Fraud Office (OLAF).[3]

[1] OJ L 312, 23.12.1995, p. 1.

[2] OJ L 292, 15.11.1996, p. 2.

[3] OJ L 136, 31.5.1999, p. 1.

(17) Council Regulation (EC, Euratom) No 1605/2002 of 25 June 2002 on the Financial Regulation applicable to the general budget of the European Communities[4] and Commission Regulation (EC, Euratom) No 2342/2002[5] of 23 December 2002 laying down detailed rules for the implementation of Council Regulation (EC, Euratom) No 1605/2002, which safeguard the Community's financial interests, apply, taking into account the principles of simplicity and consistency in the choice of budgetary instruments, a limitation on the number of cases where the Commission retains direct responsibility for their implementation and management, and the required proportionality between the amount of resources and the administrative burden related to their use.

[4] OJ L 248, 16.9.2002, p. 1. Regulation as amended by Regulation (EC, Euratom) No 1995/2006 (OJ L 390, 30.12.2006, p. 1).

[5] OJ L 357, 31.12.2002, p. 1. Regulation as last amended by Commission Regulation (EC, Euratom) No 1248/2006 (OJ L 227, 19.8.2006, p. 3).

(18) The measures necessary for the implementation of this Decision should be adopted in accordance with Council Decision 1999/468/EC of 28 June 1999 laying down the procedures for the exercise of implementing powers conferred on the Commission,[6] with a distinction being made between those measures which are subject to the management committee procedure and those which are subject to the advisory committee procedure, the advisory committee procedure being in certain cases, with a view to increased efficiency, the more appropriate.

[6] OJ L 184, 17.7.1999, p. 23. Decision as amended by Decision 2006/512/EC (OJ L 200, 22.7.2006, p. 11).

(19) The Treaty establishing the European Community and the Treaty establishing the European Atomic Energy Community provide for no powers, other than those in Articles 308 and 203, respectively, for adopting this Decision.

(20) The European Economic and Social Committee has delivered an opinion.[1]

[1] OJ C 65, 17.3.2006, p. 63.

(21) In order to ensure the effective and timely implementation of the programme, this Decision should apply from 1 January 2007,

HAS DECIDED AS FOLLOWS:

Article 1
Subject Matter

1. This Decision establishes the Specific Programme 'Prevention, Preparedness and Consequence Management of Terrorism and other Security related risks', hereinafter referred to as 'the Programme', in order to contribute to supporting Member States' efforts to prevent, prepare for, and to protect people and critical infrastructure against risks linked with terrorist attacks and other security related risks, as part of the General Programme on Security and Safeguarding Liberties.

2. The Programme shall cover the period from 1 January 2007 to 31 December 2013.

3. This Decision shall not apply to matters that are covered by the Civil Protection Financial Instrument.

Article 2
Definitions

For the purposes of this Decision, the following definitions shall apply:

(a) 'prevention and preparedness' refers to measures aimed at preventing and/or reducing risks linked to terrorism and other security related risks;

(b) 'consequence management' refers to the coordination of measures taken in order to react to and to reduce the impact of the effects of a security related incident, in particular resulting from terrorist attacks in order to ensure a smooth coordination of crisis management and security actions;

(c) 'critical infrastructure' includes in particular those physical resources, services, information technology facilities, networks and infrastructure assets which, if disrupted or destroyed, would have a serious impact on the critical societal functions, including the supply chain, health, safety, security, economic or social well-being of people or of the functioning of the Community or its Member States.

Article 3
General Objectives

1. The Programme shall contribute to support Member States' efforts to prevent, prepare for, and to protect people and critical infrastructure against terrorist attacks and other security related incidents.

2. The Programme is intended to contribute to ensuring protection in the areas such as the crisis management, environment, public health, transport, research and technological development and economic and social cohesion, in the field of terrorism and other security related risks within the area of freedom, security and justice.

Article 4
Specific Objectives

1. Within the general objectives, and unless covered by other financial instruments, the Programme shall stimulate, promote and develop measures on prevention, preparedness and consequence management based, *inter alia,* on comprehensive threat and risk assessments, subject to the supervision by the Member States and with due regard to existing Community competence in that matter, and aiming to preventing or reducing risks linked with terrorism and other security related risks.

2. With regard to prevention and preparedness of risks linked with terrorism and other security related risks the Programme aims at protecting people and critical infrastructure, in particular by:

(a) stimulating, promoting, and supporting risk assessments on critical infrastructure, in order to upgrade security;

(b) stimulating, promoting, and supporting the development of methodologies for the protection of critical infrastructure, in particular risk assessment methodologies;

(c) promoting and supporting shared operational measures to improve security in cross-border supply chains, provided that the rules of competition within the internal market are not distorted;

(d) promoting and supporting the development of security standards, and an exchange of know-how and experience on protection of people and critical infrastructure;

(e) promoting and supporting Community wide coordination and cooperation on protection of critical infrastructure.

3. With regard to consequence management the Programme aims at:

(a) stimulating, promoting and supporting exchange of know-how and experience, in order to establish best practices with the view to coordinate the response measures and to achieve cooperation between various actors of crisis management and security actions;

(b) promoting joint exercises and practical scenarios including security and safety components, in order to enhance coordination and cooperation between relevant actors at the European level.

Article 5
Eligible Actions

1. With a view to pursuing the general and specific objectives set out in Articles 3 and 4, the Programme shall provide under the conditions set out in the annual work programme financial support for the following types of action:

(a) projects initiated and managed by the Commission with a European dimension;

(b) transnational projects, which shall involve partners in at least two Member States, or at least one Member State and one other country which may either be an acceding or a candidate country;

(c) national projects within Member States, which:

(i) prepare transnational projects and/or Community actions ('starter measures');

(ii) complement transnational projects and/or Community actions ('complementary measures');

(iii) contribute to developing innovative methods and/or technologies with a potential for transferability to actions at Community level, or develop such methods or technologies with a view to transferring them to other Member States and/or other country which may either be an acceding or a candidate country.

2. In particular, financial support may be provided for

(a) actions on operational cooperation and coordination (strengthening networking, mutual confidence and understanding, development of contingency plans, exchange and dissemination of information, experience and best practice);

(b) analytical, monitoring, evaluation and audit activities;

(c) development and transfer of technology and methodology, particularly regarding information sharing and inter-operability;

(d) training, exchange of staff and experts; and

(e) awareness and dissemination activities.

Article 6
Access to the Programme

1. Access to the Programme shall be opened to bodies and organisations with legal personality established in the Member States. Bodies and organisations which are profit oriented shall have access to grants only

in conjunction with non-profit oriented or State organisations. Non-governmental organisations may apply for funding of the projects referred o in Article 5(2) provided that they ensure sufficient level of confidentiality.

2. As regards transnational projects, third countries and international organisations may participate as partners but are not permitted to submit projects.

Article 7
Types of Intervention

1. Community financial support may take the following legal forms:

(a) grants;

(b) public procurement contracts.

2. Community grants shall be awarded further to calls for proposals, save in duly substantiated exceptional cases of urgency or where the characteristics of the beneficiary leave no other choice for a given action, and shall be provided through operating grants and grants for actions.

The annual work programme shall specify the minimum rate of the annual expenditure to be awarded to grants. This minimum rate shall be at least 65%.

The maximum rate of co-financing of the costs of the projects shall be specified in the annual work programme.

3. Expenditure is foreseen for accompanying measures, through public procurement contracts, in which case Community funds shall cover the purchase of services and goods. This shall cover, *inter alia,* expenditure on information and communication, preparation, implementation, monitoring, checking and evaluation of projects, policies, programmes and legislation.

Article 8
Implementing Measures

1. The Commission shall implement the Community financial support in accordance with Regulation (EC, Euratom) No 1605/2002, hereinafter referred to as 'the Financial Regulation'.

2. To implement the Programme, the Commission shall, within the limits of the general objectives defined in Article 3, adopt an annual work programme, by the end of September specifying its specific objectives, thematic priorities, a description of accompanying measures envisaged in Article 7(3) and if necessary a list of other actions.

The annual work programme for 2007 shall be adopted three months after taking of effect of this Decision.

3. The annual work programme shall be adopted in accordance with the procedure referred to in Article 9(3).

4. The evaluation and award procedures relating to grants for actions shall take into account, *inter alia,* the following criteria:

(a) conformity with the annual work programme, the general objectives as specified in Article 3 and measures taken in the different domains as specified in Articles 4 and 5;

(b) quality of the proposed action regarding its conception, organisation, presentation and expected results;

(c) amount requested for community financing and its appropriateness as to expected results;

(d) impact of the expected results on the general objectives defined in Article 3 and on measures taken in the different domains as specified in Articles 4 and 5.

5. Decisions related to actions submitted under Article 5(1)(a) shall be adopted by the Commission in accordance with the management procedure referred to in Article 9(3). Decisions related to actions submitted under Article 5(1)(b) and (c) shall be adopted by the Commission in accordance with the advisory procedure referred to in Article 9(2).

Decisions on applications for grants involving profit-oriented bodies or organisations shall be adopted by the Commission in accordance with the management procedure referred to in Article 9(3).

Article 9
Committee

1. The Commission shall be assisted by a committee (hereinafter referred to as the Committee).

2. Where reference is made to this paragraph, Articles 3 and 7 of Decision 1999/468/EC shall apply.

3. Where reference is made to this paragraph, Articles 4 and 7 of Decision 1999/468/EC shall apply.

The period laid down in Article 4(3) of Decision 1999/468/EC shall be set at three months.

4. The Committee shall adopt its rules of procedure.

Article 10
Complementarity

1. Synergies, consistency and complementarity shall be sought with other Union and Community instruments, *inter alia,* with the specific programmes 'Prevention of and Fight against Crime' and 'Criminal Justice', the Seventh Framework Programme for Research, Technological Development and Demonstration Activities, the European Union Solidarity Fund and the Civil Protection Financial Instrument.

2. The Programme may share resources with other Community and Union instruments, in particular the 'Prevention of and Fight against Crime' programme, in order to implement actions meeting the objectives of both the Programme and other Community/Union instruments.

3. Operations financed under this Decision shall not receive financial support for the same purpose from other Union/Community financial instruments. It shall be ensured that the beneficiaries of the Programme shall provide the Commission with information about funding received from general budget of the European Union and from other sources, as well as information about ongoing applications for funding.

Article 11
Budgetary Resources

The budgetary resources allocated to the actions provided for in the Programme shall be entered in the annual appropriations of the general budget of the European Union. The available annual appropriations shall be authorised by the budgetary authority within the limits of the financial framework.

Article 12
Monitoring

1. The Commission shall ensure that, for any action financed by the Programme, the beneficiary submits technical and financial reports on the progress of work and that a final report is submitted within three months of the completion of the action. The Commission shall determine the form and structure of the reports.

2. The Commission shall ensure that the contracts and agreements resulting from the implementation of the Programme provide in particular for supervision and financial control by the Commission (or any representative authorised by it), if necessary by means of on-the-spot checks, including sample checks, and audits by the Court of Auditors.

3. The Commission shall ensure that for a period of five years following the last payment in respect of any action, the beneficiary of the Community

financial support keeps available for the Commission all the supporting documents regarding expenditure on the action.

4. On the basis of the results of the reports and on-the-spot checks referred to in paragraphs 1 and 2, the Commission shall ensure that, if necessary, the scale or the conditions of allocation of the financial support originally approved and also the timetable for payments is adjusted.

5. The Commission shall ensure that every other step necessary to verify that the actions financed are carried out properly and in compliance with the provisions of this Decision and the Financial Regulation be taken.

Article 13
Protection of Community Financial Interests

1. The Commission shall ensure that, when actions financed under this Decision are implemented, the financial interests of the Community are protected by the application of measures to prevent fraud, corruption and any other illegal activities, by effective checks and by the recovery of the amounts unduly paid and, if irregularities are detected, by effective, proportional and dissuasive penalties, in accordance with Regulations (EC, Euratom) No 2988/95, (Euratom, EC) No 2185/96 and (EC) No 1073/1999.

2. For the Community actions financed under this Decision, Regulations (EC, Euratom) No 2988/95 and (Euratom, EC) No 2185/96 shall apply to any infringement of a provision of Community law, including infringements of a contractual obligation stipulated on the basis of the Programme, resulting from an act or omission by an economic operator, which has, or would have, the effect of prejudicing the general budget of the European Union or budgets managed by it, by an unjustified item of expenditure.

3. The Commission shall ensure that the amount of financial assistance granted for an action is reduced, suspended or recovered, if it finds irregularities, including non-compliance with the provisions of this Decision or the individual decision or the contract or agreement granting the financial support in question, or if it transpires that, without Commission approval having been sought, the action has been subjected to a change which conflicts with the nature or implementing conditions of the project.

4. If the time limits have not been observed or if only part of the allocated financial support is justified by the progress made with implementing an action, the Commission shall ensure that the beneficiary is requested to submit observations within a specified period. If the beneficiary does not give a satisfactory answer, the Commission shall ensure that the remaining financial support might be cancelled and repayment of sums already paid demanded.

5. The Commission shall ensure that any undue payment is repaid to the Commission. Interest shall be added to any sums not repaid in good time under the conditions laid down by the Financial Regulation.

Article 14
Evaluation

1. The Programme shall be monitored regularly in order to follow the implementation of activities carried out hereunder.

2. The Commission shall ensure regular, independent and external evaluation of the Programme.

3. The Commission shall submit to the European Parliament and the Council:

(a) an annual presentation on the implementation of the Programme;

(b) an interim evaluation report on the results obtained and the qualitative and quantitative aspects of the implementation of the Programme no later than 31 March 2010;

(c) a communication on the continuation of the Programme no later than 31 December 2010;

(d) an *ex-post* evaluation report no later than 31 March 2015.

Article 15
Publication of Projects

Each year the Commission shall publish the list of actions financed under the Programme with a short description of each project.

Article 16
Taking of Effect and Application

This Decision shall take effect on the day of its publication in the *Official Journal of the European Union*.

It shall apply from 1 January 2007.

Done at Brussels, 12 February 2007.

For the Council

The President

F.-W. STEINMEIER

DOCUMENT NO. 3

EUROPEAN COUNCIL: IMPLEMENTATION OF THE STRATEGY AND ACTION PLAN TO COMBAT TERRORISM

Report 15411/1/07 Rev 1
Council of the European Union

Brussels, 28 November 2007

from: Counter-terrorism Coordinator
to: COREPER/Council/European Council

Subject: Implementation of the Strategy and Action Plan to Combat Terrorism

1. This report responds to the European Council's request for a report every six months on the implementation of the Action Plan to combat terrorism adopted in June 2004.[1] The report summarizes progress since June 2007 and indicates the state of play regarding ratification of the conventions and implementation of the legislative acts regarded as having priority, the details of which are set out in ADD 1.

[1] The latest version of the Action Plan to Combat Terrorism is contained in 7233/1/07 REV 1

2. In December 2005 the European Council adopted the European Counter-terrorism Strategy,[1] which has provided the framework for EU activity in this field. The strategic commitment of the Union is to combat terrorism globally while respecting human rights and to make Europe safer, allowing its citizens to live in an area of freedom, security and justice. The Strategy groups all actions under four headings—PREVENT, PROTECT, PURSUE, RESPOND. The Revised Action Plan follows this pattern with the objective of setting out clearly what the EU is trying to achieve and the means by which it intends to do so. The present report covers progress on the individual actions within this same framework.

[1] 14469/4/05 REV 4

Introduction

3. To combat terrorism effectively all Member States must ensure that all their relevant national services coordinate their activities and operate on the basis of sufficient capabilities. With regard to this, the Council has launched a number of evaluation exercises over the last few years.

4. After the peer evaluation of national anti-terrorist arrangements yielded positive results, the Member States agreed to launch the next exercise focusing on preparedness and consequence management, covering three main topics: arrangements in the event of a terrorist attack, training/exercises for testing national crisis centres and communication systems in the event of a terrorist attack. The preparatory phase of the exercise has been completed and on-site visits will start at the beginning of 2008. The exercise should be completed and results presented by the end of 2009.

5. In order to succeed in fighting terrorism and organized crime, which are sometimes interconnected, a sufficient flow of information at national and international level has to be ensured. As one way of addressing this issue, the Council has completed the third round of mutual evaluations focusing on the 'Exchange of information and intelligence between Europol and the Member States and among the Member States respectively'. The final report[2] has been presented and includes a number of recommendations on strengthening national coordination in Member States and on intensifying cooperation with Europol.

[2] 13321/2/07 REV 2

6. This round of mutual evaluation has highlighted, however, that considerable deficiencies remain in sharing information at national level. Despite a general trend among the Member States in favour of a "multi-agency" approach, those deficiencies constitute one of the main obstacles to cooperation at European level. They relate chiefly to the lack of platforms bringing together the different agencies (police, customs, FIU, etc.) and to insufficient links between the agencies' databases.

7. Precise recommendations along these lines have been made to each Member State, taking account of its specific situation: 2008 should provide the opportunity for making an initial evaluation of the follow-up to those recommendations.

Prevent

8. The first objective of the Counter-terrorism Strategy is to prevent people from turning to terrorism by tackling the factors or root causes which can lead to radicalisation and recruitment, in Europe and internationally. To attain this objective, in December 2005 the Council adopted a Strategy and an Action Plan to counter radicalisation and recruitment.

9. The Counter-terrorism Coordinator has separately reported on the implementation of the strategy on Radicalisation and Recruitment Strategy.[1]

[1] 15443/07

10. The internet has been identified as a key vector for the spread of terrorist propaganda and recruitment. Germany has launched an initiative ('Check the Web') to tackle terrorist incitement on the Internet. At the end of the German Presidency a handbook of "Check the Web" expert meetings was distributed to Member States giving a detailed overview of these meetings. An information portal was launched at Europol which serves as a technical platform for information exchange among Member States. This project is currently in its second phase, to be completed by the end of 2008, which will allow more data, including restricted materials, to be uploaded and access for more users.

11. The Commission has addressed the issue of the Internet in its proposal for a revised Framework Decision on Combating Terrorism in the three main areas: bomb making instructions on the Internet, incitement to terrorism and law enforcement requirements for more technologies, training and language equipment to monitor the Internet. The proposal[1] was presented by the Commission in November 2007.

[1] 14960/07

12. During the Portuguese Presidency a number of seminars have been held in cooperation with the European Commission and the Member States, mainly addressing the radicalisation of youth. On the basis of these discussions the Action Plan on combating Radicalisation and Recruitment will be revised.

13. The Commission has set up an expert group on violent radicalisation and intends to present a report on the state of play of research in the field by the end of this year. Based on the outcome of these initiatives, among others, the Commission plans to issue a communication on violent radicalisation in the course of 2008.

14. A Media Communication Strategy, approved by the Council in July 2006, aims to challenge inaccurate depictions of EU policies and to undermine terrorist propaganda which distorts conflicts around the world as supposed proof of a clash between the West and Islam. The Counter-terrorism Coordinator has separately reported on the implementation of the Media Communication Strategy.[2]

[2] 15445/07 RESTREINT UE

15. A strategic cooperation agreement between the European Police College (CEPOL) and Europol has been signed. The purpose of this agreement is to

enhance cooperation between Europol and CEPOL in strengthening the training of senior police officers, in particular by organising courses, seminars and conferences and developing and implementing common curricula and course material.

16. In external relations, the EU has continued to engage with international partners on radicalisation and recruitment. Sharing experience and best practices is an important part of tackling this global phenomenon. Examples of this can be found in the context of Euromed, Asean Regional Forum and ASEM. In addition, the EU has worked to reinforce the international consensus on respect for human rights in the fight against terrorism and has continued its efforts to address the international conflicts which facilitate radicalisation and recruitment into terrorism.

Protect

17. The second objective of the Counter-terrorism Strategy is to protect citizens and infrastructure and reduce vulnerability to attacks, *inter alia* through improved security of borders, transport and critical infrastructure.

18. With the adoption of the Council Decision on the establishment, operation and use of the second generation Schengen Information System (SIS II), the legal basis for the SIS II has been completed. The Commission has confirmed that the technical part of the SIS II project should be finalised by December 2008.

Following the extension of the current SIS (SISone4all project) and the successful evaluation of nine Member States that joined the EU in 2004, the abolition of border checks (land and sea borders) for the new Schengen Members will take place in December 2007 and the abolition of air borders in March 2008.

19. A Council Decision concerning access to the Visa Information System (VIS) by designated authorities and Europol for the purposes of the prevention, detection and investigation of terrorist offences and of other serious criminal offences was agreed by the Council in June 2007.[1]

[1] doc. 11077/1/07 REV 1

20. Following the conclusion of the EU-US Agreement on the processing and transfer of passenger name record (PNR) data by air carriers to the US department of Homeland Security, the Commission has prepared a draft Framework Decision on the use of PNR data for law enforcement purposes,[1] the so called EU PNR, which forms part of the counter-terrorism measures presented by the Commission in November 2007.

[1] 14922/07

21. Following the submission by the Commission of the first elements of the European Programme on Critical Infrastructure Protection (EPCIP) policy package, the Council has started examination of the proposal for a Directive of the Council on the identification and designation of European Critical Infrastructures and an assessment of the need to improve their protection.

22. One of the difficulties within the negotiations appears to be that some Member States would prefer there to be no legal obligation for the owners/operators of European Critical Infrastructures to establish Operator Security Plans and to identify Security Liaison Officers. It was also agreed that the cross-cutting and sector-specific criteria should be annexed to the proposed Directive to clarify the impact of the Directive. The Commission has already presented its ideas on cross-cutting as well as on the sector specific criteria for the energy, transport, and information and technology sectors.

23. In the absence of an agreed EU position on EPCIP, formal cooperation with third countries has not yet been initiated. However, the Presidency, together with the Commission, has invited delegations from the EFTA countries, Russia, the United States and Canada to an informal update on the state of play of EU work on EPCIP. The practice will continue in the future.

24. With regard to security research and enhanced public-private partnership, the European Security Research and Innovation Forum (ESRIF) has recently been set up. It brings together EU stakeholders in security research and has as its main task the design of the Joint Security Research Agenda and the monitoring of its implementation. This ensures higher visibility of security research in the EU as well as greater dissemination of relevant information.

Pursue

25. The third objective of the European strategy against terrorism is to pursue and investigate terrorists across EU borders as well as globally; to impede planning, travel and communications; to disrupt support networks; to cut off funding and access to attack materials and to bring terrorists to justice.

Terrorist Financing

26. The Counter-terrorism Coordinator reported separately on the implementation of the strategy against terrorist financing in October 2007.[1]

[1] 11948/2/07 REV 2

27. Progress has continued in transposing the nine FATF Special Recommendations into Community law and the main instruments will be finalised in 2007. The *Payment Services Directive* completing the implementation of FATF Special Recommendation VI on alternative remittances has been adopted and is expected to enter into force before the end of 2007.

28. The Commission envisages issuing a report on the implementation of the *Framework Decision on confiscation of crime-related proceeds, instrumentalities and property* (deadline for transposition 15.3.2007) by the end of 2007.

It is envisaged that the Council will adopt a Council Decision on cooperation between Asset Recovery Offices before the end of 2007.

29. Development of the European network *of Financial Intelligence Units* is still incomplete. All Member States need to be connected operationally and FIUs need to use the platform in order to establish the FIU.NET as a viable EU-wide network. The informal FIU Platform has continued its activities. This platform was established by the Commission to provide EU FIUs with a forum for discussing practical issues affecting their activities, with a view to the implementation of the third Anti-Money Laundering Directive and to ensure its uniform implementation. Key issues have been selected for ad-hoc analysis, in order to identify practical problems and solutions to be incorporated in reports.

30. The Commission has also begun its evaluation of the implementation by EU Member States of the Council Decision of 17 October 2000 concerning arrangements for cooperation between FIUs. A report is expected by the end of 2007.

31. There has still not been much progress on the abuse of the non-profit sector by terrorist financers. At the current stage of discussions, it appears that there are significant differences between practices in the Member States, allowing limited scope for comprehensive EU level legislation in this area. However, while implementing their own rules individually according to the FATF criteria, Member States could continue to explore further the scope for a common EU approach to certain aspects of reducing NPO vulnerabilities to criminal (terrorist) infiltration. The five principles, decided by the JHA Council in December 2005, could function as a general guideline for this. Building on the Communication of November 2005 [COM (2005) 620], the Commission has launched a study assessing the extent of the abuse of non-profit organisations for criminal, including terrorist financing purposes at EU level. Results are to be presented at a meeting of experts hosted by the Commission in the first half of 2008.

32. Given the fact that several recommendations of the current Strategy have been implemented and on other recommendations progress has been made, decisions on a follow-up to the Strategy are necessary. Countering terrorist financing is an evolving process. Terrorist financing typologies

are constantly changing, as are the methods and tools for countering them. Two years after the adoption of the strategy, this would be the right time to update and, where appropriate, revise the strategy on the basis of proposals made jointly by the Secretary General/High Representative and the Commission. EU policies and practices must be kept under constant scrutiny to ensure that they continue to be appropriate in the face of current terrorist financing trends.

33. An exchange of views with the Member States will start in December 2007 and a final decision is expected in the first half of 2008. In the interim and until this decision has been taken, a proposal will be made to transform the current strategy into an implementation plan, focusing on those elements that have not yet been implemented. This implementation plan needs to set out specific target dates and indications of responsibility for taking action.

Operational Cooperation

34. At the end of the German Presidency the Council reached political agreement on a Decision on the stepping up of cross-border cooperation, particularly in combating terrorism and cross-border crime.[1] This Decision contains provisions based on the essential parts of the Prüm Treaty (originally signed by 7 Member States in 2005) and is designed to improve the exchange of information between authorities responsible for the prevention and investigation of criminal offences. The Council reached agreement on a general approach on the implementation of the relevant Decision[2] in November.

---

[1] 11896/07
[2] 14611/07

35. In November the Council also reached agreement on a general approach on the Draft Council Decision on the improvement of cooperation between the special intervention units of the Member States of the European Union in crisis situations.[1] This Decision lays down general rules and conditions to allow for special intervention units of one Member State to provide assistance and/or operate on the territory of another Member State in cases where they have been invited by the latter Member State and have agreed to do so in order to deal with a crisis situation.

---

[1] 14312/07

36. The Council has continued its discussions on replacing the Europol Convention by a Council Decision. A general approach has been reached on Chapters I, II and III of the draft Council Decision establishing the European Police Office (Europol). An implementation plan for the

draft Council Decision was endorsed by the JHA Council at its meeting on 8 and 9 November 2007. The draft Council Decision is expected to be finalised by June 2008.

37. The Commission issued a communication[2] on the role of Eurojust and the European Judicial Network in the fight against organised crime and terrorism, proposing steps which would enable Eurojust to develop its potential for cooperation and to establish itself further as a vital player in the fight against organised crime and terrorism in Europe.

[2] 14253/07

38. During the Portuguese Presidency, work in the area of explosives has been taken forward. The Commission adopted Communication on enhancing the security of explosives on 6 November 2007, which contains an EU Action Plan for Enhancing the Security of Explosives. Further to this communication, Council conclusions will be agreed on 6 and 7 December 2007 adopting Strategic Orientations and Priorities on the security enhancement of explosives. The Priorities include the establishment of an Early Warning System, of a network of EOD units, of a Standing Committee on precursors and of a European bomb database. Negotiations with a view to adopting a full EU Action Plan for Enhancing the Security of Explosives will continue under the Slovenian Presidency and will *inter alia* cover issues such as public security, precursors to explosives, storage, transport, traceability and detection of explosives.

39. SitCen has continued to provide the Council and the Commission with regular analyses of developments in relation to the terrorist threat. Joint analyses with Europol have also been presented.

Legislative Agenda

40. The Council reached agreement on a general approach on the Framework Decision on taking into account convictions in the course of new criminal proceedings last year. However, there are parliamentary reservations outstanding.

41. According to The Hague Programme, the Framework Decision on the European Evidence Warrant should have been adopted by the Council at the end of 2005. The Council reached political agreement in June 2006. However, since several parliamentary scrutiny reservations remain, the text will probably not be formally adopted by the end of 2007. The issue of parliamentary reservations from some Member States is continuing to slow down the adoption of instruments in the Third Pillar.

42. Discussions about the Framework Decision on the protection of personal data processed in the framework of police and judicial cooperation in

criminal matters have continued. As the scope of the Draft Framework Decision has been limited to cross-border data, a general approach was reached in November 2007.

43. The draft Framework Decision on organisation and content of the exchange of information extracted from criminal records between Member States is nearly finalised in the Council and the European Parliament. It became apparent, however, that a new instrument will have to be created before it can become operational. A pilot project is on-going between 12 MS and the Commission is expected to come forward with a new proposal for a second instrument in the first semester of 2008.

44. In the Hague Programme (item 3.3) the European Council called for the adoption of a Framework Decision on certain procedural rights in criminal proceedings by the end of 2005. After long discussions, the Council has noted that no agreement can be found among the Member States.

International Cooperation

45. In its political dialogue with international partners, the EU continued to promote the role of the UN in the fight against terrorism. In particular, the EU played a key role in supporting the implementation of the UN Counter-terrorism Strategy which reflects the priorities of the EU's own strategy. Dialogue with the US and Russia was maintained in several fora. A high-level political dialogue on counter-terrorism took place with Pakistan. In its dialogue with partners, bilaterally and multilaterally, the EU has continued to emphasize that the fight against terrorism must be conducted in full respect of the rule of law and human rights.

46. In line with UNSCR 1373 (2001), the EU has continued to offer technical assistance to many countries so as to enhance their counter-terrorism capacity. Special cooperation and assistance programmes in the area of counter-terrorism are in place with Morocco and Algeria. The EU has convened ad hoc troika meetings with Algeria in order to assess cooperation to date and exchange views on a possible next phase. Cooperation has also been launched with Indonesia. The EU's support for the Jakarta Centre for Law Enforcement (JCLEC) has yielded practical results and assistance to the African Union Counter-terrorism Centre in Algiers is under consideration. The lack of appropriate funding has been a major obstacle on the EU side. The EU should therefore continue to make sure that existing funds, such as the Stability Instrument or the CFSP budget, are used efficiently for counter-terrorism cooperation. The lack of availability of experts for carrying out concrete projects is also a matter of concern.

47. In bilateral and multilateral meetings, the EU continues to raise the issue of ratification and full implementation of the 16 counter-terrorism UN Conventions and Protocols. With regard to the implementation of

the UN Global CT Strategy, the EU is conducting a stocktaking exercise in order to assess its own achievements so far. The EU will also examine further possibilities to develop its activities in this respect, to cooperate with relevant UN agencies and to share its experience and best practices with partners. The EU has also continued its diplomatic efforts to achieve an international consensus on the Comprehensive Convention on International terrorism.

Respond

48. The fourth priority of the EU's Counter-terrorism strategy is to prepare the EU, in a spirit of solidarity, to manage and minimize the consequences of a terrorist attack, by improving capabilities to deal with the aftermath, the coordination of the response, and the needs of victims.

49. In November, the Council adopted the Decision establishing a Community Civil Protection Mechanism (recast). The Mechanism itself is a system for preparedness, mutual assistance and coordination in the response to disasters. The recast will make the Mechanism more robust, especially by the use of a "modular approach" which will enhance interoperability among EU teams. It will also make the Monitoring and Information Centre more proactive, mainly in the areas of assessment of the situation and of the provision of transport for civil protection interventions. Account has also been taken of the immediate sharing of medical resources in the event of disasters such as CBRN attacks.

50. In parallel, the Council adopted, in June 2007, conclusions on enhancing the coordination capacity of the Civil Protection Monitoring and Information Centre (MIC), which invites the Commission to develop that Centre as a user-friendly platform for information, communication, analysis, advice and practical assistance.

51. Also in June the Council adopted conclusions on preparedness for the decontamination of casualties following chemical, biological, radiological and nuclear incidents (CBRN) which advocate, in the framework of the Financial Instrument and the Mechanism, precautionary measures to avoid primary or secondary contamination, exercises, training and the spread of best practices.[1]

[1] 10015/07

52. The Commission submitted to the Council in July a Green Paper on Bio-Preparedness[2] that started a wide consultation among the Institutions, industry, Member States and third countries about ways and means to protect populations, life and the environment against all biological hazards

[2] 11951/07

such as diseases, accidents, crimes and terrorism, in particular in the event of multiple incidents.

53. The Green Paper suggested the creation of a pro-active safety culture in a public-private partnership, using the existing Community tools such as the many EU rapid alert systems (RAS) and the EU strategy and programme on weapons of mass destruction. Elements for special attention could be controls on the dissemination of bio-agents and of relevant information, the creation of a network of experts, the listing of bio-agents, the analysis and classification of bio-risks, vaccine-banks, improved surveillance, detection, laboratory capacity and expertise.

54. For its part, the Council is likely to adopt in December 2007, in reaction to the Green Paper, conclusions on addressing Chemical, Biological, Radiological and Nuclear Risks and on Bio-preparedness, which aim at improving the quality and interoperability of threat assessments, detection, preparedness and response in the EU, using the existing Community Programmes, Strategies and instruments, as well as public-private partnerships.

55. Following approval of the Emergency and Crisis Coordination Arrangements in Brussels by the Council in 2006, the Council in cooperation with the Commission and the Member States, held, in September, a second crisis exercise. The scenario envisaged a near-simultaneous terrorist attack using a biological agent.[1]

[1] report in 14650/1/07 REV 1

ESDP

56. Work continued on the Headline Goal 2010, where the terrorist threat was included in all relevant scenarios in 2005 in the framework of the definition of military requirements leading to completion of the Progress Catalogue 2007. Required military capabilities include Command and Control, Intelligence, Survivability, Readiness, Deployability, Force and Mission Protection, and CBRN Defence. The key military tasks to be investigated include preventive measures such as Embargo Operations, Secure Lines of Communications, Fight against the Proliferation of WMD, and protective/reactive measures such as Consequence Management.

57. The database of military assets and capabilities (originally created for dealing with the consequences of terrorist attacks) is under expansion to cover all natural and man-made disasters. The database is a compilation of voluntary contributions from Member States.

58. Helping citizens in an emergency situation requires rapid and effective delivery of assistance. Military means may be essential to complement civilian capabilities. Detailed procedures concerning military-owned and

military-chartered transportation have been developed with the Member States, the relevant Commission departments (DG ENV-MIC and DG ECHO), and the Multi-National Movement Coordination Centres in Athens and Eindhoven. A tabletop exercise with the Commission's department for humanitarian aid (ECHO) to test transport procedures took place in May 2007. A similar event with the Monitoring and Information Centre (MIC) is also scheduled to take place by the end of 2007. The framework for military support for EU disaster response developed in 2006 will be revised in the light of experience gaine d.

DOCUMENT NO. 4

IMPLEMENTATION OF THE EU COUNTER-TERRORISM STRATEGY—DISCUSSION PAPER

Discussion Paper 15448/07
Council of the European Union

Brussels, 23 November 2007

from: Counter-terrorism Coordinator
to: COREPER/Council/European Council

Subject: Implementation of the EU Counter-terrorism strategy—Discussion paper

This note covers five subjects which the Counter-terrorism Coordinator wishes to draw to the Council's attention:

- information sharing and special investigative methods;
- radicalisation and recruitment;
- financing of technical assistance to third countries;
- organisation of work within the Council; and
- implementation of EU instruments.

Other aspects of the fight against terrorism will be the subject of special reports over the coming months, to cover transport security, the protection of critical infrastructure, the financing of terrorism, and crisis management in particular.

In separate documents drawn up by the Counter-Terrorism Coordinator, the Council will find reports on the state of implementation of the various strategies which have been adopted in relation to the fight against terrorism:

- the EU's overall Counter-Terrorism Strategy (15411/07)
- the Radicalisation and Recruitment Strategy and Action Plan (15443/07)
- the Media Communication Strategy (15445/07 RESTREINT UE)
- the strategy on terrorist financing (11948/2/07 REV 2)

1. Information Sharing and Special Investigative Methods

1.2. Information Sharing

Considerable efforts have been made since 2001 in the sector of processing and exchange of information. New rules will soon improve the exchange of data on requests[1] and work is progressing on direct access to national databases in the context of police cooperation (Decision incorporating the Prüm Convention into Union law) or judicial cooperation (direct access to criminal records). Access to data contained in European databases (SIS, VIS and Eurodac) is improving gradually. The Directive on the retention of telecommunications data and the Commission's recent initiative on PNR data aim at increasing the availability of data which is produced by private players but is crucial for investigations into terrorism. Finally, a general framework for the protection of data in this sector is being finalised.

All this work must be continued in order to ensure practical implementation. The consistency of all the work must be seen to, at both technical level (ensuring the compatibility of the information systems set up) and legal level (in particular defining the scope of the various instruments and guarantees in terms of data protection). For historical reasons, the different files are currently being negotiated and discussed in different working parties, depending on diverse elements such as the legal basis but also the workload of the working parties or the timing of the negotiations. However, the multiplication and growing importance of files in this area require enhanced coordination as there are more and more links and sometimes overlaps between projects, which are not properly or promptly identified in the current Council structures. The principle of availability has many aspects but its implementation or translation into policy proposals and/or legislative texts is not coordinated, sometimes leading to illogical results[2] that demonstrate the lack of a consistent and global view of the principle of availability. To improve this as soon as possible, it is therefore proposed to

- conduct an assessment of the practical use of EU instruments related to information exchange in order to identify gaps and further specific needs of law enforcement bodies, with regard to categories of data to be shared, as well as consultation technologies and procedures; this assessment should also consider judicial cooperation needs and lead to the adoption by the Council of a common EU Policy on Information Sharing;
- mandate a single Council Working Party/Committee to reflect on, prepare, develop and monitor the implementation of this common EU

[1] Framework Decision of 18 December 2006 on simplifying the exchange of information.

[2] Different constraints in the negotiations on the SIS II and the VIS with the EP have now led to the situation that certain intelligence services will have access, under certain conditions, to the (non-criminal) VIS data but not to the data on criminals entered in the SIS.

Policy on Information Sharing to ensure coordination at an early stage and supervise work at technical level so that all the details of the different instruments are coordinated and overlaps or gaps can be identified.

In the coming months stress should be laid on the specific dimension of sharing information and principally on the following aspects:

1.2.1. Sharing Information at European Level:

Pooling information at European level makes it possible to carry out strategic and operational analyses which are not made possible merely by ad hoc cooperation between Member States in specific cases. A priority for the near future in this field should be the monitoring of implementation of Decision 2005/671/JHA of 20 September 2005, which provides for the systematic transmission of information to Europol and Eurojust.

With regard to Europol, and although this is a long-standing concern, the impression remains that there is too great a disparity in the way Member States treat this obligation: the situation remains largely unsatisfactory for certain Member States. The situation is currently that Europol itself identifies ongoing terrorism cases in the Member States using open sources and contacts the State concerned in order to be sure of receiving the relevant operational information. By June 2008, the Council should be provided with a qualitative and quantitative evaluation carried out by Europol concerning inputs into its information system and analysis files in the terrorist sector by the various Member States. It is time for such evaluations to be submitted at political level.

The situation concerning implementation of the 2005 Decision is different with regard to Eurojust, for which the question of systematic transmission and processing of information is quite recent. In addition to reminding Member States of the obligations resulting from the 2005 Decision, three aspects should be emphasised: the establishment of the necessary procedures at national level for ensuring systematic transmission (such procedures exist in only a few Member States), the provision of technical means by Eurojust so that this transmission can be carried out in a structured way and finally a clear definition by Eurojust of the practical purposes of using the mass of information resulting from systematic transmission.

The latter aspect prompts the question of the interaction between Eurojust and Europol. Criminal analysis is the main reason for Europol's existence: Eurojust should not have to develop the same kind of activities. This means that Eurojust must be able to benefit fully from Europol's capacity in this context. However, the legal frameworks of the two bodies keep them radically separated. In the last stage of negotiation of a new legal framework for Europol, Eurojust therefore continues to be regarded merely as a third party. Structural links must urgently be created between these two agencies, which form part of the same *continuum* in coordinating criminal investigations.

1.2.2. Sharing Information at National Level

The first round of evaluation in the context of terrorism revealed a trend towards setting up central bodies at national level with the task of coordinating the sharing and analysis of information concerning terrorism. These national central bodies could explore how to develop reciprocal cooperation. An initial meeting is being considered for the first half of 2008.

1.2.3. Sharing Internet-Related Information

The "check the web" project carried out by Europol is a natural consequence of the need to pool resources with regard to the surveillance of websites advocating terrorism. Because it is so obviously useful and because it is relatively simple, a lack of participation by Member States would be difficult to justify. Member States must contribute intensively to the project, keeping in mind the possibilities it offers through its intranet portal, managed by Europol, and its sub-projects. The carrying out of sub-projects should be multiplied, such as the ongoing project on the media wing of Al-Qaeda, As-Sahab.

Furthermore, the development of the second phase of "Check the Web" (wider number of user accounts in EU Member States, several technical improvements and opening to third parties), planned for 2008, should be accelerated.

1.2.4. Sharing Information with Third Countries

Sharing of information with third countries, in particular with the United States, is vital to effectively combating terrorism. At the same time, care must be taken to ensure that personal data transferred to third countries are sufficiently protected and are not used for unacceptable purposes or procedures. The draft Framework decision on data protection in the context of police and judicial cooperation, on which the Council reached a general approach at its meeting of 7 and 8 November 2007, lays down certain data protection requirements with regard to onward transfer of personal data received from another Member State to a third State. One of these requirements is that the third country concerned must have an adequate data protection regime.

With regard to the United States, concerns have sometimes been voiced over the US data protection regime and more particularly over the use that is made of personal data obtained from European citizens. This debate has been sparked, in part, by a lack of understanding of US data protection principles. The ongoing exercise, in the context of the EU-US High Level

Contact Group on Data Protection and Data Sharing, to draft common data protection principles on the adequacy of these principles is potentially very helpful. Not only could it lead to a better mutual understanding, but if it results in comprehensive data protection principles to which both the EU and the US can adhere, it can foster mutual trust between the EU and the US and lead to an increased exchange of data between EU and US law enforcement authorities. In that perspective, it would be preferable for the proceedings of the EU-US High Level Contact Group on Data Protection and Data Sharing to result in a document, irrespective of its legal status, to which both parties could at least politically sign up. In the context of transatlantic cooperation against terrorism, it seems essential that all Member States take the same position with regard to data protection issues, including the question of the adequacy of the US data protection regime.

1.3. Special Investigative Methods

One of the major specific features of investigations into terrorism cases, particularly with a proactive approach, is the need for frequent recourse to special investigation methods such as the interception of telecommunications, the use of undercover agents, recourse to surveillance devices placed inside buildings, etc.

The legal framework for transnational cooperation in this type of measures is not non-existent (mainly the Convention of 29 May 2000) but it is either too complicated (in particular for the interception of telecommunications) or largely insufficient to solve the problems resulting from differences between national laws and practices. In such a sensitive sector, these differences have a major impact: frequently they obstruct cooperation and, when they do not obstruct it, they are likely to lead to the invalidity of evidence in the State of prosecution.

Initial work was carried out under the German Presidency in the context of undercover activities and is being continued. These efforts should be extended to other special investigation methods. A working method and a programme should be adopted to structure the work.

Mere recourse to the principle of mutual recognition does not enable difficulties in this sector to be resolved, given the extreme sensitivity of the measures concerned. The first stage should be learning about other Member States' systems by means of questionnaires, as is already done for undercover activities, and an in-depth discussion of the results by the competent working parties. This learning process would concern solutions found at national level for making measures sufficiently effective and making recourse to them subject to appropriate guarantees concerning fundamental rights.

2. Radicalisation and Recruitment

Over the last twelve months, the Council and the Commission have made some progress in the implementation of the Strategy for Combating Radicalisation and Recruitment. As was already mentioned in last year's implementation report, the adoption of the Strategy has ensured that the issue of prevention is now a very prominent feature of the EU's counter-terrorism agenda. Follow-up discussions about the implementation of the Strategy have led to an exchange of Member States' experiences and best practices in the framework of COTER and TWG (the Terrorism Working Group). The development and implementation of the Strategy have also compelled national experts to look more broadly at the European dimension of processes of radicalisation.

Overall, however, implementation has been uneven. While in some areas new initiatives have been launched, in others there has been no action.

An impetus for new work in the field of justice and home affairs came from the Commission which developed a number of initiatives to carry out the recommendations of the Strategy. To pull some of these activities together (studies, seminars, questionnaires), the Commission is preparing a communication for mid-2008 which will identify good practices on how to address violent radicalisation within the EU and make concrete recommendations to the Member States.

For both Council working parties, a major challenge is the identification of funds for the implementation of various aspects of the Strategy. The funding tends to be either national or from the Community budget. The Commission is responsible for various financial programmes, both within the EU and for third countries, which support many activities and projects in the fight against terrorism. It is essential that Community funds are allocated in line with the Council's political priorities. To this end, relevant Council working parties should be duly informed about the Commission's intentions and where appropriate given sufficient opportunity to make recommendations with regard to the allocation of these funds.

Finally, EU policy in the field of radicalisation and recruitment, particularly in the area of integration, is the result of a compromise between Member States whose traditions and policies are sometimes divergent. In consequence, the wording of some of the recommendations in the Strategy and the classified Action Plan attached to it is vague and difficult to translate into operational action. Attempts at implementation sometimes give rise to additional political debate where one would expect a mere technical discussion.

If the European Union wishes to supplement Member States' efforts in the field of prevention, then fresh ideas for implementation of the Strategy for Combating Radicalisation and Recruitment need to be developed.

The Council (Presidency and Counter-Terrorism Coordinator) ought to step up efforts to implement the Strategy for Combating Radicalisation and Recruitment. They need to continue to seek cooperation with other relevant actors in the area, including Council working parties that do not deal with counter-terrorism, and encourage them to work on the various aspects of the Strategy where counter-terrorism officials do not have primary competence.

The Council and the Commission could consider setting targets for the implementation of the Strategy in areas where progress has to be made within the next twelve months. These targets may include the enhancement of EU capacity to communicate its policies in Arabic and the development of instruments for de-radicalisation on the Internet. Of course, close coordination between the EU Presidency and future Presidencies would be indispensable for such a course of action. The EU Counter-Terrorism Coordinator could facilitate discussion between the Member States and the Commission on targets and present proposals to the Council.

With the exception of some Commission initiatives in the internal field, there has been too little involvement of experts (such as integration officials at local level, youth workers, teachers, management of penitentiary institutions, development assistance practitioners, etc.) in the implementation of the Strategy, which has been largely left to the generalists responsible for COTER and TWG. In order to generate greater "ownership" among experts, the Council may wish to entrust informal groups of experts from Member States and the Commission with the implementation of various aspects of the Strategy. Of course, it would be important to reflect thoroughly on the institutional challenges such a course of action would entail.

Alternatively, individual Member States could be asked to take the lead in implementing various aspects of the Strategy. The EU Counter-Terrorism Coordinator intends to invite national coordinators or equivalents (and as appropriate other high-ranking national officials responsible for counter-terrorism) to a meeting in the first half of 2008 to discuss a division of labour and targets for future action. A debate among high-level officials would have the additional benefit of enhancing awareness of the Strategy within Member States' administrations.

Finally, COTER and TWG should develop closer cooperation in the area of radicalisation and recruitment.

3. Technical Assistance to Third Countries

On the basis of the Declaration on Combating Terrorism of 25 March 2004, namely objective 7, the Council (COTER) has selected priority countries for enhanced counter-terrorism cooperation, both in terms of political dialogue and provision of technical assistance.

As regards technical assistance, the process has not been able to provide the full leverage for maximising global EU counter-terrorism assistance to third countries. Experience to date shows that the major obstacles are the limited financial resources available at the EU level for purely counter-terrorism external relations activities and the availability of experts to carry out assessment missions and specific projects. Those issues need to be addressed at an early stage so as to avoid a loss of credibility with our external partners for not being able to deliver on our commitments.

With respect to financing, the new Stability Instrument under Community funding and the CFSP budget could represent viable solutions. It is important however that when engaging in dialogue with third countries, we know that we can count on a certain amount of funds which could be specifically devoted to counter-terrorism cooperation. This should be duly taken into account when discussing yearly priorities for the CFSP budget or when drafting the Indicative Programme and Action Plan for the implementation of the Stability Instrument Strategic Framework. Obviously, the approach needs to be flexible and realistic. Some reflection would also be needed on how to enhance the EU angle as against bilateral projects, possibly through enhanced cooperation among Member States and between Member States and the Commission.

The issue of expertise will also be crucial. The need for experts is expected to increase in the future and engagement of Member States in this respect is essential.

Another path that deserves to be explored is the interaction between security and development. Although the respective objectives and responsibilities under security and development differ, we need to take into account their increasing interdependence. It is important to underline that full respect of the internationally agreed framework for development cooperation should be the starting point for this debate.

The European Security Strategy recognises that security is a precondition for development and identifies terrorism as one of the main global challenges to security. The Joint Statement by the Council and the representatives of the governments of the Member States meeting within the Council, the European Parliament and the Commission on the EU Development Policy, "The European Consensus", highlights the fact that development and poverty eradication are not possible without peace and security. Terrorism, as one of the most serious threats to security, causes loss of human life, imposes high costs in the short term and in the long term. It also undermines societies and disrupts economies. The EU should therefore include terrorism in the ongoing debate on Security and Development.

In this context, we should reflect on the specific relation between terrorism and development and explore ways to ensure complementarity and coherence of policies and actions in these fields. The reflection could address both the short term (assistance in implementing commitments pursuant to relevant international legal instruments) and the long term (addressing conditions that lay the ground for radicalisation and recruitment into terrorism). Development assistance and the countering of terrorism are not competing policies but can be mutually reinforced.

4. Organisation of Work within the Council

Three Council working parties work exclusively on preparations for the Council's proceedings on preventing and fighting terrorism: the Working Party on Terrorism (TWG), for internal aspects, the Working Party on Terrorism (International Aspects) (COTER) for external aspects and the CP 931 Working Party for the designation of organisations and individuals involved in terrorist acts. Since 2005 a network of contact points (consisting of one representative in each Permanent Representation) has served as a channel of communication between Commission and Council staff and capitals, and has exceptionally been examining the updating of the action plan implementing the Union's counter-terrorism strategy.

For reasons to do with the composition of these three groups and the existence of groups formed for other purposes, several aspects of the fight against terrorism are not satisfactorily covered by the Council's preparatory bodies.

Four recent subjects illustrate the difficulty of drawing up integrated policies on terrorism; the updating of the strategy on terrorist financing, the drawing up of an action plan to increase the security of explosives, the drawing up of conclusions on CBRN and bio-preparedness and the protection of critical infrastructures. In many of these cases, the Presidency has had to set up "friends of the Presidency" groups to coordinate the efforts of several working parties.

It is proposed that this question should be looked at in more detail over the coming months and that, in the second half of 2008, the Council's structures relating to the fight against terrorism should be reorganised, in the more general framework of preparations for the entry into force of the Reform Treaty.

5. Implementation of EU Instruments

Adequate implementation of EU instruments at national level is still among the main challenges (see tables of implementation, 15411/07 ADD 1). For some instruments, continuous follow-up in the competent Council working parties is necessary, not only to increase awareness but also to share good practices and identify possible problems.

The situation is particularly alarming for the following instruments:

- the Convention of 29 May 2000 on mutual assistance in criminal matters and its protocol of 2001: no progress has been made compared to last year as five ratifications for the convention and seven ratifications for the protocol ratifications are still lacking.
- Framework Decision 2003/577/JHA on mutual recognition of judicial decisions on the freezing of assets: implementation is still lacking for 12 Member States. Regular discussions should take place in the COPEN Working Party, as was done for the European Arrest Warrant.
- Decision 2005/671/JHA on the exchange of information and cooperation concerning terrorist offences: as mentioned above, Europol and Eurojust should produce a report for June 2008 and thorough evaluation should take place in the competent working parties.
- Framework Decision 2005/222/JHA on attacks against information systems: only 12 Member States have implemented the Framework Decision. The next step will be the report of the European Commission, which was due to be issued before September 2007.

Furthermore, it should be noted that only four Member States have so far ratified the Council of Europe Convention on the prevention of terrorism of 16 May 2005. It is relatively recent convention but ratification should be considered as a priority given its importance for this sector.

Conclusions

1. Information Sharing and Investigative Methods

Objective 1: to ensure consistency and efficiency of the work carried out in the Council with regard to information exchange.

Proposal: task a single Working Party / Committee with all the preparatory work on information exchange within Justice and Home Affairs, on the basis of a comprehensive report identifying the needs of law enforcement authorities, the types of information concerned and the methods and technology for accessing that information.

Objective 2: to ensure implementation of Decision 2005/671/JHA with regard to the transmission of information to Europol.

Proposal: that Europol in June 2008 submit to the Council, for discussion, a qualitative and quantitative report concerning inputs into its information system and analysis files in the terrorist sector by the various Member States.

Objective 3: to ensure implementation of Decision 2005/671/JHA with regard to the transmission of information to Eurojust.

Proposal: that Eurojust submit to the Council, in June 2008, a report on procedures set up at national level for transmitting information to Eurojust, on measures taken by Eurojust to enable structured transmission, and on the practical purposes of the use of such information.

Objective 4: to create structural links between Europol and Eurojust, enabling Eurojust to benefit fully from Europol's capacity in terms of criminal analysis.

Proposal: amend the draft Decision on Europol, especially with regard to the relationship between Eurojust and Europol's Analytical Workfiles.

Objective 5: to enhance cooperation and mutual learning between national bodies created to coordinate the sharing and analysis of terrorism-related information.

Proposal: organise a meeting of such national bodies during the first half of 2008.

Objective 6: to enhance surveillance of websites advocating terrorism.

Proposal: speed up the completion of phase 2 of "check the web".

Objective 7: to foster mutual trust between the EU and the US regarding exchange of information.

Proposal: speed up the work of the EU-US High Level Contact Group on Data Protection and Data Sharing so as to determine common principles and to consider what legal form it should be given.

Objective 8: to facilitate the use of special investigative methods in trans-national cases.

Proposal: define a common method of work on this issue, starting with mutual learning on legislation and practice in the Member States.

2. Radicalisation and Recruitment

Objective 9: to facilitate the identification of proper Community and EU funding for the implementation of the Strategy for Combating Radicalisation and Recruitment.

Proposal: ensure effective communication with regard to possibilities for Community funding to relevant Council working parties.

Objective 10: to increase monitoring of the implementation of the Strategy.

Proposal: set targets in areas of the Strategy where progress has to be made within the next twelve months and consider including among these targets issues such as (1) the EU 's capacity to communicate its policies in Arabic and (2) the further development of instruments to counter radicalisation on the Internet.

Objective 11: to generate "ownership" of the Strategy among experts and practitioners (such as integration officials at local level, youth workers, teachers, management of penitentiary institutions, development assistance practitioners, etc.).

Proposal: entrust informal groups of experts from Member States and the Commission with the implementation of various aspects of the Strategy.

Objective 12: to identify areas where individual Member States could be asked to take the lead in implementing various aspects of the Strategy.

Proposal: invite national coordinators or equivalents (and as appropriate other high-ranking national officials responsible for counter-terrorism) to a meeting in the first half of 2008 to discuss a division of labour and targets for future action.

Objective 13: to develop closer cooperation between COTER and TWG in the area of radicalisation and recruitment.

Proposal: make better use of the joint meeting between COTER and TWG and involve TWG in work on project proposals and the implementation of the Media Communication Strategy.

3. Technical Assistance to Third Countries

Objective 14: to secure appropriate financial resources at EU level for counter-terrorism activities in the area of external relations, *inter alia* with regard to radicalisation and recruitment in external relations.

Proposal: take due account of counter-terrorism when discussing yearly priorities for the CFSP budget or when drafting the Indicative Programme and Action Plan for the implementation of the Stability Instrument.

Objective 14a: to explore the interactions between policies and actions related to terrorism, as part of the security framework, and development, taking into account their respective objectives and responsibilities.

Proposal: include terrorism in the ongoing debate on security and development.

4. Organisation of Work in the Council

Objective 15: to improve the preparatory work of the Council with regard to the fight against terrorism.

Proposal: discuss the working structure of the Council during the second half of 2008 in the context of preparations for the entry into force of the Reform Treaty.

5. Implementation of EU Instruments

Objective 16: to increase monitoring of the implementation of EU instruments relevant for the fight against terrorism.

Proposal: discuss regularly in the competent working parties the state of play, good practice and problems in the implementation of Framework Decision 2003/577/JHA on mutual recognition of judicial decisions on the freezing of assets.

DOCUMENT NO. 5

STEPPING UP THE FIGHT AGAINST TERRORISM

Communication from the Commission of the European Communities to the European Parliament and the Council COM(2007) 649

Burssels, 6 November 2007

I. The Threat

Terrorism today is international in nature. While substantial progress has been made against terrorist threats worldwide and in the EU, there remains a global threat from international terrorism. Terrorist structures continue to adapt to global counter-terrorist efforts. Terrorist groups can be scattered in different countries and work across traditional country borders, exploiting the great potential of communications technologies such as the internet and mobile telephony for their own malicious purposes. The internet is commonly used by terrorist for propaganda communication, training, indoctrination, recruitment, and fund-raising. Certain terrorist organisations also use the Internet to plan operations and publicize claimed attacks.

This threat poses a significant challenge to the European Union and its Member States. Europol and Eurojust can—and should—play a role in addressing this threat, but cooperation between the Member States and their national services is crucial. Such cooperation has improved enormously in the last years as a result of the shared common threat.

Terrorists will strike whenever, wherever and with whatever they think they will have the most impact. Today chemical, biological, radiological and nuclear weapons exist. Apart from nuclear material, these are relatively inexpensive and traditional military machinery is largely ineffective to counter them.

We cannot be complacent. The behaviour of the inhabitants of our cities where terrorists have struck in recent years is an example for us all. By remaining resilient they are continuing to enjoy and uphold the fundamental rights on which our societies are based while knowing that radical elements might be plotting an attack. We have to find a balance between being aware of this risk, taking adequate and proportionate measures to prevent it from materialising, and not letting it overwhelm our daily lives. Causing disruptions to society is a key aim of terrorists.

II. The Context of EU Action: Key Measures

The European Union supports the Member States in facing the global threat. Protecting our citizens can succeed only by acting together to deal with this common concern. We should not expect to feel secure without taking some responsibility for providing security.

Europe has therefore been a producer of security and can, and should, continue to do more. We cannot take our values and our way of life for granted—they are a delicate fabric that has to be continuously safeguarded. Terrorism must be fought in full respect of fundamental rights. Terrorists threaten our fundamental rights. The Commission is fully committed to protecting and promoting fundamental rights. Within their scope, we should develop necessary and lawful security measures.

Across the EU we must unite against terrorism. We must work in solidarity. Terrorism threatens us all—our security, way of life and ideals. We need a common response to a shared challenge.

Terrorist threats should mostly be addressed at national level—even in the knowledge that the current threat is mostly international. Work at EU level complements these efforts and is built around prevention, protection, prosecution and responding if an attack occurs. These four elements form the core of the EU Counter terrorism strategy, which was adopted first in 2001 and updated most recently in December 2005. The Action Plan to implement on the strategy was updated last in the spring of 2007.

Since terrorism is a global phenomenon, the EU also cooperates closely with partner countries and international organisations regarding counter-terrorism legislation, law enforcement and judicial cooperation. The fight against terrorism in its various facets is a standing agenda item in Justice and Home Affairs Ministerial meetings with strategic partners and in other fora such as the UN and the G8. This cooperation has notably resulted in agreements with the United States and Canada on the transfer of Passenger Name Record data allowing to better identify terrorism treats to security, while ensuring protection of personal data. The EU is a major provider of technical assistance to third countries world wide helping them to implement the UN Security Council Resolution 1373 (2001).

The EU Counter Terrorism Strategy defines the way in which the EU can contribute to the fight against terrorism. Key measures identified in the Strategy include:

- Stopping violent radicalisation;
- Protecting our critical infrastructure;
- Improving the exchange of information between national authorities and cooperation between all stakeholders when appropriate;
- Reacting to non conventional threats;
- Improving the detection of threats;
- Depriving terrorists of financial resources;
- Supporting victims;
- Research and technological development.

The Commission has suggested a framework in June 2006 on how to evaluate the policies in the field of Freedom, Security and Justice.[1] Evaluating counter-terrorism policies is particularly decisive given the possibility of changed threat assessments and the impact of policy on fundamental rights and operation of markets. The Commission will continuously evaluate adopted counter-terrorism policies and the measures put forward in the package adopted today.

1. Violent Radicalisation

Understanding the motivations behind terrorist activity is a key part of prevention. The Commission is in the process of developing a policy on identifying and addressing the factors contributing to violent radicalisation.[2] Research into this complex area is important and the Commission funds studies, conferences, and projects to share experience and better understand the issue. For example studies on the factors triggering violent radicalisation, the ideologies of radicals and the recruiting methods used to mobilise support for terrorism have been commissioned this year. All these activities takes place within the context of the specific EU Anti-radicalisation Strategy and Action Plan. The Strategy recalls that "The Commission supports this through channelling its policies effectively, including through the investment of funds for research, the organisation of conferences, support for education and inter-cultural engagement, and monitoring at the pan-EU level".

---

[1] Communication on evaluation of EU policies in the area of Freedom, Security and Justice—COM(2006) 332, 28.6.2006.

[2] See for example the September 2005 Communication COM(2005) 313.

2. Critical Infrastructure Protection

Protecting our critical infrastructure, such as our roads, railways, bridges, information and communication infrastructures and power stations, is crucial. Such infrastructure is highly interdependent within the EU and globally: the level of security of any individual State depends on the security provided by others.

The EU adds value by establishing minimum standards for security and eliminating, as far as possible, weak links and vulnerabilities.[3] Action at EU level supports Member States, while respecting the principle of subsidiarity. Ultimately it is the responsibility of each Member State to manage arrangements for the protection of critical infrastructures within their national borders.

A proposal for a general policy framework on Critical Infrastructure Protection is being discussed in Council and the Commission is hopeful that results will be achieved soon. This should allow us to focus on the assets and sectors that need greater attention.

3. Urban Transport Security

In reply to the call by EU Heads of State and Government,[4] the Commission has assessed how the European Community can best contribute towards securing European urban transport[5] from terrorist attacks.

Improving security in urban transport systems, whilst maintaining a full and unrestricted service, is extremely challenging. With very few exceptions, the equipment and infrastructure supporting urban transport were not originally selected or constructed with security considerations in mind. To reach improved security levels for European urban transport systems, a close cooperation between Member States and all the national authorities and operators involved is necessary at a European level. To facilitate such cooperation, the Commission will set up a specific Urban Transport Security Expert Working Group, which will work in close association with other specific workgroups set up under the general policy framework on Critical Infrastructure Protection. The background to this particular action can be found in the Annex to this Communication.

---

[3] The Commission adopted on 12 December 2006 a Communication on a European Programme for Critical Infrastructure Protection (EPCIP)—COM(2006) 786—and a proposal for a Directive on the identification and designation of European Critical Infrastructure and the assessment of the need to improve their protection—COM(2006) 787.

[4] The Council of the European Union—Declaration on combating terrorism of 29 March 2004 (Document 07906/04).

[5] Defined as collective passenger land transport carried out by buses, surface and underground trains and trams ('light railways').

4. Exchange of Information

Exchange of information—in compliance with fundamental rights including data protection—is essential. The PNR proposal which is part of this package demonstrates it. Much has been done by the Commission. Telecom and internet service providers now have to retain their data, as a consequence of the Data Retention Directive. The principle of availability has made its first step with the Prüm Treaty: soon, all Member States' databases on fingerprints, DNA and vehicle registration will be accessible to the authorities of other Member States.

The Commission plans to fund activities aimed at making this work or making it work better. Agreement has been reached to give law enforcement authorities access to the Visa Information System (VIS) once it becomes operational. Access to the VIS will allow police and other law enforcement authorities, as well as Europol, to consult data in the Visa Information System. It will store data on up to 70 million people concerning visas for visits to, or transit through, the Schengen Area. These data will include the applicants' photograph and their ten fingerprints. The VIS will become the largest ten finger print system in the world.

All these developments need to be underpinned by a robust framework on data protection. The Council is expected to satisfactorily conclude its discussions on the Commission's proposed Framework Decision in this respect by the end of this year.

5. Chemical, Biological, Radiological and Nuclear ("CBRN") Weapons

Although explosives are the weapons most frequently used by terrorists, it is also essential that we stop terrorists from having access to CBRN weapons. Some of these have the capacity to infect thousands of people, contaminate soil, buildings and transport assets, destroy agriculture and infect animal populations and affect the food supply chain. A green paper on bio-preparedness was adopted in July 2007.

Workshops with practitioners on law enforcement, health and science are being held to develop a guide to best practices on preparedness and response. The challenge is to bring together authorities active in many different fields: customs, police, the military, bio-industry, health communities, academic institutions and bioresearch institutes. The Commission is also gathering expertise in the radiological and nuclear field. The fear of dirty bombs and nuclear terrorism continues to trouble our society and those responsible for its protection. Terrorists and other criminals have already shown an interest in this. Today's interconnected economies and societies not only provide the basis for global development and cooperation, they also facilitate the illicit trafficking of radioactive and nuclear materials. The Commission intends to submit a package of policy proposals on CBRN in early 2009.

6. Detection Technologies

Sound, tested, accessible, affordable and mutually recognised detection technologies are an indispensable asset in counter-terrorism work. New technologies should not just be the preserve of the terrorists. Detection tools play a crucial role in the work of security authorities. Working with the private sector is crucial and the Commission is facilitating this. A green paper on detection technologies was published in 2006, and the responses are in the process of being analysed. Detection issues also feature prominently in the EU Action Plan on Explosives, adopted as part of the current package.

7. Depriving Terrorists of Financial Resources

Efforts have to be maintained, strengthened to deprive terrorists of financial resources. By now, EC legislation is in place, but increasingly there is a need to address broader non-legislative actions, such as transparency measures, to ensure that EU Member States have the tools to fight terrorist financing. The Commission is continuing to work with Member States to improve ways of freezing and confiscating terrorist assets and crime related proceeds, as well as to establish common minimum training standards for financial investigators, and is promoting efficient cooperation among Financial Intelligence Units at EU level.

8. Victims of Terrorism

The Commission is committed to promoting solidarity with, and assistance to, victims of terrorism.

The Commission provides financial assistance[6] to organisations which represent victims' interests. It has financed innovative and cross-border projects with the aim of helping victims get their lives back to the way they were before the terrorist attack—as much as possible.

9. Research and Technological Development

In 2004 the Commission launched a three-year "Preparatory Action for Security Research (PASR)" in the field of Security Research. With three annual budgets of € 15 million, the Preparatory Action was a first step towards a new Security theme in the 7th RTD Framework Programme (FP7).

Under PASR, 39 projects[7] have been funded. Building on PASR, the 7th RTD Framework Programme (FP7, 2007–2013) saw a substantial increase

[6] Council Decision of 12 February 2007 establishing for the period 2007 to 2013, as part of the General Programme on Fundamental Rights and Justice, the Specific Programme 'Criminal Justice'.

[7] A description of the 39 PASR research projects, including final and intermediate results, can be found on: http://ec.europa.eu/enterprise/security/articles/article_2007-02-23_en.htm

of the budget for Security Research to 1,4 billion € including covering topics such as the detection of explosives, the protection against CBRN terrorism, crisis management and the protection of critical infrastructure. In parallel, a European Security Research and Innovation Forum (ESRIF) has been created.[8] ESRIF will build on the work already done by the Group of Personalities[9] and the European Security Research Advisory Board (ESRAB).[10]

The objective of the ESRIF is to support civil security policy-making with the appropriate technology and knowledge base by establishing a mid—and long-term Joint Security Research Agenda that will involve all European stakeholders from both the supply and the demand sides. This agenda should contain a research roadmap based on the future needs of the public and private end-users and the state-of-the-art security technologies.

The Joint Security Research Agenda will aim to be the reference document for security research programming for the next coming years, at national, regional and industrial level, taking into account the research that will be carried out at European level as decided in the 7th RTD Framework Programme. The Commission will ensure that the necessary links will be established between the different counter-terrorism activities and the appropriate ESRIF Working Groups.

III. A New Package of Proposals: Stepping up the Fight Against Terrorism

The different elements of the package all respond to clear calls for action by the Commission—mostly from the European Council or JHA Council meetings. The measures proposed are the result of carefully prepared work involving extensive consultations with stakeholders, including member States representatives, NGOs and other public and private bodies. The recent foiled attacks in Germany, Denmark and Austria serve to remind us all that the terrorist threat is unfortunately still real and that further

[8] The creation of ESRIF was announced in the Commission Communication on a public/private dialogue in the field of European security research and innovation—COM(2007) 511, 11.9.2007.

[9] The 'Group of Personalities' (GoP) was set up in 2003. In its final report (Research for a Secure Europe: Report of the Group of Personalities in the field of Security Research, 15 March 2004, http://ec.europa.eu/enterprise/security/doc/gop_en.pdf.), the GoP recommended the launch of a security research theme in FP7 with a minimum threshold of € 1 billion per annum as well as the creation of the 'European Security Research Advisory Board' (ESRAB).

[10] The ESRAB Board was created by Commission Decision 2005/516/EC on 22 April 2005 and published its final report on 22 September 2006. It recommends that multidisciplinary mission-oriented research should be undertaken. It should combine end-users and suppliers in project definition and execution. The report identified a number of areas, including security of infrastructures, to stimulate innovation and improve the use of research in procured products and services. Finally, the ESRAB report also suggested 'the creation of a European Security Board (the later ESRIF), to foster greater dialogue and a shared view of European security needs. The board should bring together, in a non-bureaucratic manner, authoritative senior representatives from the public and private communities to jointly develop a strategic security agenda and act as a possible reference body for the implementation of existing programmes and initiatives'.

measures are required. In addition to implementing the EU Counter-terrorism strategy, the measures envisaged also contribute to the implementation of the general United Nations Global Counter-terrorism strategy, as adopted by the General Assembly in September 2006.

This security package aims to improve the security of Europe and face the terrorist threat by:

- ***Dealing with those who support terrorism.*** The dissemination of terrorist propaganda, training of terrorists, financing of terrorism, circulation of information on bomb-making and explosives and public provocations to commit terrorist offences should be recognised as crimes and subject to appropriate criminal penalties across the European Union. The proposed amendment of the 2002 Framework Decision will ensure that all Member States define these activities as crimes and apply criminal sanctions, including imprisonment, to their perpetrators. The European Arrest and Evidence Warrants will also have to be used to the full for this purpose.
- ***Practical action to stem the use of explosives.*** A large number of different actions will be pursued aimed at making it more difficult for terrorist to have access to explosives or precursors to explosives and to enhance the tools available to law enforcement authorities to prevent terrorist attacks using explosives, either commercial or improvised. This includes rapid alert systems on lost and stolen explosives and suspicious transactions, a network of experts on bomb-disposal and de-activation, and the vetting of personnel involved in the explosives industry. Co-operation between the public and private sectors is crucial.
- ***Establishing a European system for the exchange of Passenger Name Records ("PNR").*** Member States must collect these records, process them and, where appropriate, exchange them with others. PNR has been associated mostly with negotiations outside the EU in particular the United States. The Union is at least as much a potential target as the United States. Passenger Name Records are important because past experience shows that many terrorist plots involve travel between the EU and a third country at some stage.
- The Commission is also adopting its ***report on the implementation of the present Framework Decision on terrorism.*** Member States need to act more decisively to put the regime adopted in 2002 into their law to support the work of their police forces, prosecutors and judges.

Conclusion

We must continue to work at EU level to counter the threat of terrorism, while also duly developing the external dimension of this policy. There is no choice but to do so due to the international and cross border nature of the threat and common interests across the EU as a result of successful EU development. The EU adds value by supporting Member States and addressing cross border issues. It is the Member States which are ultimately responsible for protecting their citizens. Security policy must both seek to protect EU citizens and go hand in hand with respecting fundamental rights. Terrorism is a multifaceted and complex challenge. Work at EU level therefore seeks to address all aspects of the challenge—prevention, protection, prosecution and responding if an attack occurs. The current package demonstrates the European Commission's commitment to continue addressing these challenges and puts another building block in place to strengthen our defences against terrorism.

Annex: Tackling Urban Transport Security

Urban transport is highly complex, involving numerous transport providers, local service industries and millions of daily passengers. It is easily accessible, with multiple stops and interchanges. In terms of security, there is generally no passenger screening and little, if any, access control. In addition, there is a wide variation in terms of threat assessment and vulnerability of different transportation modes. The result of this complexity means that a "one size fits all" approach to security is not appropriate.

Currently, security for urban transport is provided by transport operators, and local and national authorities. Whereas European measures are in place for aviation, maritime transport and international transport of goods, no comparable measures exist for urban transport. In addition, whereas aviation and maritime transport measures can build on rules established in international organisations, neither international organisations nor rules exist for urban passenger transport.

As indicated under point 3 of this Communication, the Commission will set up an Urban Transport Security Expert Working Group to deal with these issues. This will enable an exchange of best practice and lessons learnt—positive and negative—in four key areas: *organisational measures; surveillance and detection; more resilient equipment and installations;* and *incident management.* In the longer term, this could lead to commonly agreed security criteria and benchmarks, allowing authorities and operators to carry out self-assessments and to develop security plans.

The Commission invites each Member State to nominate a national Focal Point who will facilitate the work of the Urban Transport Security Expert Working Group, ensuring its clarity of purpose and the consistency of national contributions, as well as monitoring progress. The Focal Point should be a representative of the Member State's appropriate transport security authority.

Member States, authorities and operators alike are encouraged to introduce and test new security concepts, technologies and hardware and software solutions. All the lessons learnt can be of greater benefit to the Community if they are shared through the Urban Transport Security Expert Working Group and a European technology ledger or through on-the-job learning initiatives as a result of cooperation between operators. In addition, the Commission will establish a permanent list of on-going publicly-financed research and development projects in this area, encouraging a special emphasis on human factors and new technologies. Representatives will be encouraged to get involved and identify, where appropriate, new security-related research needs.

Finally, the Commission will take appropriate steps to encourage that EU funded urban transport projects contain, where deemed necessary, an adequate security dimension.

DOCUMENT NO. 6

PREVENTION, PREPAREDNESS AND CONSEQUENCE MANAGEMENT OF TERRORISM

European Parliament Legislative Resolution on the Proposal for a Council Decision Establishing the Specific Programme 'Prevention, Preparedness and Consequence Management of Terrorism' P6_TA(2006)0584

14 December 2006

The European Parliament,

- having regard to the Commission proposal to the Council (COM (2005)0124),[1]
- having regard to Article 308 of the EC Treaty, pursuant to which the Council consulted Parliament (C6–0241/2005),
- having regard to Rule 51 of its Rules of Procedure,
- having regard to the report of the Committee on Civil Liberties, Justice and Home Affairs and the opinion of the Committee on Budgets (A6–0390/2006),

1. Approves the Commission proposal as amended;
2. Considers that the indicative financial reference amount indicated in the legislative proposal must be compatible with the ceiling of heading 3 A of the new multi-annual Financial Framework and points out that the annual amount will be decided within the annual budgetary procedure in accordance with the provisions of point 38 of the Interinstitutional Agreement between the European Parliament, the Council and the Commission on budgetary discipline and sound financial management of 17 May 2006;[2]

[1] Not yet published in OJ.
[2] OJ C 139, 14.6.2006, p. 1.

3. Calls on the Commission to alter its proposal accordingly, pursuant to Article 250(2) of the EC Treaty;
4. Calls on the Council to notify Parliament if it intends to depart from the text approved by Parliament;
5. Asks the Council to consult Parliament again if it intends to amend the Commission proposal substantially;
6. Instructs its President to forward its position to the Council and Commission.

DOCUMENT NO. 7

REVISED ACTION PLAN ON TERRORISM

Commission of the European Community
Working Document SEC(2006) 686

Brussels, 24 May 2006

Introduction

Prevention

- Prevent people turning to terrorism within the EU and internationally;
- Identify and address the factors which can contribute to radicalisation and recruitment to terrorism;
- Prevent terrorists from gaining access to finance
- Promote use of financial intelligence to disrupt terrorist activity

Protection

- Protect citizens;
- Protect infrastructures;
- Address vectors of threats to both citizens and infrastructures;
- Protect borders;

Prosecution

- Establish EU and international legal framework for fighting terrorism;
- Sustain international consensus on fighting terrorism and support third countries;
- Enhance law enforcement, intelligence and customs cooperation;
- Enhance judicial cooperation

Response

- Enhance EU's crisis and consequence management;

Action Plan

	Measure/Action	Competent Body	Deadline	Status/Observations
1. PREVENT				
1.1. DISRUPT THE ACTIVITIES OF THE NETWORKS AND INDIVIDUALS WHO DRAW PEOPLE INTO TERRORISM				
1.1.1	Effective action against misuse of the Internet, inter alia, by sharing expertise, and exchanging national assessments and analyses and, where relevant, acting in common against extremist websites.	MS Commission/ Europol/ Council	Ongoing	Contained in the policy recommendations drawn up on the basis of SitCen reports.
1.1.2	Promote community policing including through improved training.	MS/ CEPOL/ Council	Ongoing	Task undertaken by CEPOL.
1.1.3	Put in place a legal framework to prevent individuals from inciting violence and exchange information on incitement.	MS/ Council/ Commission	Ongoing	Obligation according to UNSC 1624 as well as under the European Convention on the Prevention of terrorism
1.1.4	Enhance political dialogue and technical assistance including police training to help others outside the EU to disrupt the activities of networks and individuals who draw people into terrorism.	MS/CTC/ Council/ Commission	Ongoing	Terrorism is at the center of political dialogue with third countries. Police training has been provided at regional level (by CEPOL to Balkans and Mediterranean countries).
1.1.5	Tackle radicalization in particular in key environments, for example prisons, places of religious training or worship.	MS/Council	Ongoing	
1.1.6	Measures against illegal extremist literature and other media.	MS/ Commission	Ongoing	

	Measure/Action	Competent Body	Deadline	Status/Observations
1.1.7	Implementation of the Council strategy and action plan on radicalisation and recruitment.	Council/ MS/ Commission/ Commission	Ongoing	Deadlines are set according to the individual measures in the R&R action plan. Commission is now working on: – First report on the state of play of research in the field expected for June 2006; – organising conference on role of media in countering violent radicalisation; – journalist training programmes and, regional language broadcasts of European television and radio news in Middle Eastern and North African countries. A research project on Transnational terrorism and rule of law-funded within the 6th Framework Programme for RTD, to start in June 2006 will address radicalization.
1.1.8	Make more efficient use of relevant external assistance programmes including in particular support for good governance and the rule of law to address factors which can contribute to the support for terrorism.	MS/ Council/ Commission	Ongoing	EC assistance mainly consists of capacity building assistance in the fields of good governance and the rule of law thus addressing factors contributing to the support for terrorism. Examples of this work can be foundin Euromed, Western Balkans and ASEM context or with Morocco and Algeria.

	Measure/Action	Competent Body	Deadline	Status/Observations
1.2. ENSURE THAT MODERATE VOICES PREVAIL OVER THOSE OF EXTREMISM				
1.2.1	Empower moderate voices by engaging with the different religions practiced in the EU and providing support for their communities.	MS/ Commission/ Council	Ongoing	
1.2.2	Support the availability of moderate religious literature.	MS/ Commission	Ongoing	
1.2.3	Encouraging religious communities to embrace the fundamental norms and values of European society including through training of religious leaders.	MS	Ongoing	
1.2.4	Develop a non-emotive lexicon for discussing radicalization.	Commission/ Council/ CTC	June 2006	
1.2.5	Develop a comprehensive communication strategy to explain EU policies and hold a conference with media professionals and terrorist experts to discuss radicalisation. Put in place funding for journalist training programmes and regional language broadcasts of European television and radio news and other initiatives in ME and North African countries.	MS/ Commission/ Council/ CTC	June 2006	Commission to start work on eg organizing a conference on role of media in countering violent radicalisation.

	Measure/Action	Competent Body	Deadline	Status/Observations
1.3. PROMOTE SECURITY, JUSTICE, DEMOCRACY AND OPPORTUNITY FOR ALL				
1.3.1	Target inequalities and discrimination where these exist within the EU and promote long-term integration where appropriate.	MS/ Commission	Ongoing	
1.3.2	Make proposals for enhancing inter-cultural dialogue.	Commission	Ongoing	Ongoing dialogue in e.g. Euromed. Research projects funded under the 6th Framework Programme for RTD address inter-cultural dialogue (e.g. RAMSES project in the Mediterranean area) and more research is planned in the 7th Research Framework Programme (2007–2013).
1.3.3	Promote good governance, democracy, education and economic prosperity outside the EU.	MS/ Commission/ Council	Ongoing	
1.4. ASSESSMENTS AND ANALYSIS				
1.4.1	Annual Review of the Radicalisation Strategy assisted by Strategic analysis of the radicalization process.	Council/ SitCen	Annual (end 2006)	Gathering of best policy practices in fighting radicalization.
1.4.2	Enhance co-operation between research institutions in the context of the EU multi-annual research programme.	Council/ Commission	Mid-2006	Expert network and research project launched.
1.4.3	Conduct more detailed studies, including academic studies, of recruitment in specific contexts such as	Council/ Commission		

	Measure/Action	Competent Body	Deadline	Status/Observations
	prisons, schools, places of religious worship; studies in the role of the media, including the internet.			
1.4.4	Continue to investigate the links between extreme religious or political beliefs, as well as socio-economic and other factors, and support for terrorism, building on work already undertaken in this area, and identify response measures.	Council/ Commission		Sitcen to include relevant material in assessments. Working Groups to make policy recommendations as appropriate. Research projects ongoing in the 6th Framework Programme include research on links between socio-economic and other factors contributing to terrorism.
1.5. TERRORIST FINANCING (see also Strategy Terrorist Financing (16089/04) and its updates (11325/05 and 14349/05)				
1.5.1	Review the EU's performance on Terrorist Financing in particular in respect of FATF special recommendations and act on recommendations.	Council/ Commission	End 2006	Commission has awarded a Study to assess EU performance against the nine Special Recommendations of the FATF. Study will complete before end 2006.
1.5.2	Take forward national codes of conduct for Non-Profit Organisations (implementation FATF SR VIII).	MS/ Commission	June 2006	Council Declaration of July, 13th 2005 called for agreement on a code of conduct for non-profit organizations (doc. 11158/1/05 REV 1) Council agreement on principles on 1–2 December 2005. Commission communication in November 2005.
			Middle of 2007	FATF members agreed on an Interpretative Note to SR VIII in February 2006. Produce a public version of the two Commission Internal reports: Analysis of the non

	Measure/Action	Competent Body	Deadline	Status/Observations
				profit sector in the EU10/15 for Monitoring and Control. Work to be coordinated by JRC with JLS and MSs
1.5.3	Conduct research on risk indicators to identify vulnerable entities in the non profit sector for terrorist financing	Commission	End 2007	A questionnaire has been created after full discussions with JLS and the process of validation of the questionnaire is underway. The validated questionnaire will be sent out to all MSs for their input that will help extract risk indicators. This research outcome will be useful to law enforcement authorities, the FIU net and the donor community.
1.5.4	Adopt Regulation on information on the payer accompanying transfers of funds (FATF SR VII).	Council/EP	June 2006	Council general approach agreed on 6 December 2005. Discussions underway in Parliament.
1.5.5	Improve the effectiveness of EU asset freezing procedures, including non-financial economic resources, in accordance with UN obligations and the need to respect due process and rule of law.	Council/ Commission/ CTC	2006	Coreper noted a revised Best Practices paper on restrictive measures including on the application of Community freezing measures.
1.5.6	Ensure national asset freezing capability and improve implementation of freezing procedures.	MS	End 2006	Guidelines on sanctions and Best Practices Paper under constant review. Latest updates adopted in December 2005. Various seminars organised by Presidencies and will continue. FATF start in 2006 discussion on implementation of SR III among its members.

	Measure/Action	Competent Body	Deadline	Status/Observations
1.5.7	Adopt Directive on regulating the alternative remittance system (inter alia, implementation FATF SR VI).	Council/EP/ Commission	End 2006	Commission proposal for a draft Directive on a New Legal Framework for Payments in the Internal Market was adopted in December 2005.
1.5.8	Improve co-operation between investigation/law enforcement community including FIUs and financial supervisory authorities, including through the use of FIU.Net.	MS/ Commission	Ongoing	Commission assessed the best practices in EU in the communication adopted on 29th November 2005 which contain a series of recommendations. Follow-up could take place in context of new Peer Evaluation round. 3rd AML/CTF Directive provides strong basis for cooperation.
1.5.9	Ensure that financial investigation is a core part of all terrorist investigations.	Commission/ MS		Commission organized an EU Forum meeting in March 2006 to which EU 25 and Candidate Countries were invited on Commission/Europol project to promote use of FI. Common training standards in Financial Investigation under elaboration in conjunction with Member State stakeholders.
1.5.10	Implement the Third Money Laundering Directive.	MS/ Commission	December 2007	Directive entered into force on 15 December 2005. Implementation by MS before mid-December 2007. Commission to adopt the implementing Directive by mid-June 2006, pending vote by Committee on the Prevention of Money Laundering and Terrorist Financing in May 2006.

	Measure/Action	Competent Body	Deadline	Status/Observations
1.5.11	Initiate outreach programmes to EU financial private sector to coordinate procedures to combat terrorist financing.	Council/ Commission		The Commission Communication adopted on 29 November 2005 addresses various ways in which public and private sector cooperation should be enhanced to ensure more effective fight against the financing of terrorism.
1.5.12	Implement Regulation (EC) No. 1889/2005 of 26 October 2005 on controls of cash entering or leaving the Community	MS	15 June 2007	Regulation entered into force in December 2005. It shall apply from mid-June 2007.
1.5.13	Ratification and full implementation of the 1999 UN Convention for the Suppression of the Financing of Terrorism and to give increased effect to the provisions of UNSCR 1373 directed to the freezing of assets.	MS	1 January 2005	All Member States have ratified the 1999 UN Convention for the Suppression of the Financing of Terrorism.
1.6. LIMIT TERRORISTS' ACCESS TO WEAPONS AND EXPLOSIVES				
1.6.1	Action on explosives, detonators, bomb-making equipment and fire arms in the context of the Commission Communication.	MS/ Commission/ Europol/ Council		Discussed in TWP during UK Presidency with policy recommendations agreed by Council. Next steps are for Commission to organize conference of all major stakeholders in first half of 2006. Analyse possibilities of making transmission of bomb-making expertise a crime under the Framework Decision on Combating Terrorism. Examine modification of related directives, eg Fertilizer regulation.

	Measure/Action	Competent Body	Deadline	Status/Observations
				Consideration of a monitoring regime regarding the precursors for home-made explosives. Consideration of improving the exchange of information on lost and stolen explosives.
1.6.2	Control of access by terrorists to dual use items relevant to the production, development, handling and dissemination of weapons of mass destruction.	Commission	Mid 2006	Modification of Regulation 1334/2000 setting up the community regime for export control of dual use items. Proposal to the Council is foreseen in mid 2006.
1.6.3	Raise the importance of the adoption and enforcement of rigorous security regimes relating to weapons and explosives in bilaterals with third parties.	MS/Council	Ongoing	Addressed in the policy recommendations based on the SitCen reports.
1.6.4	Improve control over illicit arms and explosives in the Balkans.	MS/ Commission/ Council	Ongoing	
2. PROTECT				
2.1. THREAT AND RISK ASSESSMENTS				
2.1.1	Carry out strategic assessments of terrorist threat	SitCen/ Europol/MS	Regular	
2.1.2	Make structured use of threat assessment and analysis for the risk assessment, prevention and consequence management, Stimulate, where necessary and through the appropriate channels,	Council/ Council Secretariat/ Cion/ Europol and MS	Ongoing	Undertake expert meetings with a view to developing a common understanding of the methodologies of risk assessment.

	Measure/Action	Competent Body	Deadline	Status/Observations
	improved cooperation between intelligence services, national authorities and relevant emergency services such as civil protection, health and police. Improve the bilateral exchange of information on cross-border risks			.
2.1.3	In the framework of the Conceptual Framework on the ESDP dimension of the fight against terrorism: – Elaboration of a report on interoperability between military and civilian capabilities. – Consolidate ongoing work in view of deepening and widening the content of the military database of military assets and capabilities relevant to the protection of civilian populations against terrorist attacks, including CBRN.	Council	ongoing	In this framework, a bidding process to incorporate Member States voluntary contributions in an addendum to the current Force Catalogue has been launched.
2.2. SECURITY OF THE SUPPLY CHAIN				
2.2.1	Reinforce security of the global supply chain	MS/ Commission	June 2006	Adoption of the Implementing Regulation to the security amendments of the Community Customs Code (Regulation EC no. 648/2005).
2.2.2	Reinforce security of the global supply chain	MS	Ongoing	Implementation of the security amendments to the Community Customs Code that relate to checks on the flow of goods by introducing a

	Measure/Action	Competent Body	Deadline	Status/Observations
				system of pre-arrival and pre-departure declarations and by using an improved system of data communication and information sharing between Member States.
2.2.3	Modernisation of the customs code/ Decision on e-customs	Commission	Ongoing	Proposals for a complete modernisation of the customs code and a Decision on e-customs—ongoing discussion in Council and EP. Aim i.a. to further strengthen and structure the measures to secure the supply chain and to speedily introduce the supporting IT systems.
2.2.4	Bilateral and multilateral activities reinforcing supply chain security.	Commission/ Presidency/ MS	Ongoing	EC-US Expanded Customs cooperation on maritime container transport, WCO SAFE framework for securing and facilitating trade;, multi-agency Joint Customs Operation ("Protect"), CCWG's informal counter-terrorism project group "second action plan to take forward customs counter-terrorism initiatives" (14054/05).
2.3. PROTECTION OF CRITICAL INFRASTRUCTURE				
2.3.1	Establish a European Programme for Critical Infrastructure protection (EPCIP), including the Critical Infrastructure Warning and Information Network (CIWIN).	Council/ Commission	Mid 2006.	See Council conclusions of EPCIP of 1/12/2005 (14766/05), which set out the key principles for this purpose. See Commission Green Paper, introducing a consultation phase until February 2006. Task of ProCiv in a special composition. Commission plans to draft a proposal on the establishment of CIWIN by end 2006.

	Measure/Action	Competent Body	Deadline	Status/Observations
2.3.2	Put in place adequate protective measures against electronic attack on key computer systems.	MS	16 March 2007	Council Framework Decision 2005/222/JHA of 24 February 2005, 01 L 69, 16.3.2005, p. 67 sets a deadline for 16 March 2007.
2.3.3	Continue to improve security of networks and information systems. In this context and under the umbrella of EPCIP, launch a multi-stakeholder dialogue to develop an ICT sector specific approach to enhancing the security and the resilience of networks and information systems.	Commission	Ongoing	A Communication from the Commission on a strategy for a secure Information Society is scheduled for adoption by the end of May 2006.
2.3.4	A Communication from the Commission on a strategy for a secure Information. The Communication sets out a policy approach for identifying and meeting security challenges through an open and inclusive multi-stakeholder dialogue.		Ongoing	
2.3.5	Ensure full implementation of the EU Health Security Strategy and CBRN programs.	Council/ Commission/ MS	Continuous action	Partially Achieved The 2002 CBRN-programme (Doc. 14627/02) was replaced by the 2004 Solidarity Programme.
2.4. TRANSPORT SECURITY				
2.4.1	Implement provisions of Regulation 2320/02 establishing common standards on civil aviation security, including staff	MS/ Commission	Ongoing	Ongoing legislative work to develop detailed implementing legislation (by comitology) to complement Regulation 2320/2002.

	Measure/Action	Competent Body	Deadline	Status/Observations
	screening, baggage, cargo and aircraft security.			Two implementing Regulations were adopted in 2004: - Commission Regulation (EC) N°68/2004 of 15 January 2004 amending Commission Regulation (EC) N°622/2003 - Commission Regulation (EC) N° 1138/2004 of 21 June 2004 establishing a common definition of critical parts of security restricted areas at airports. In 2005 - Commission Regulation (EC) N°781/2005 of 25 May 2005 amending Commission Regulation (EC) N°622/2003 Commission Regulation (EC) N°857/2005 of 6 June 2005 amending Commission Regulation (EC) N°622/2003
2.4.2	Reinforce common standards on aviation security by adopting revised common rules in the field of civil aviation security (12588/05). Revision of Regulation 2320/2002.	Commission/ Council/ EP	Mid 2006	A revised Reg.2320/2002 is in the process of co-decision. After deadline continuing action is expected.
2.4.3	Implement agreed EU standards on maritime security (Regulation) and security in ports (Directive).	MS/ Commission	Ongoing	a) Regulation (EC) No 725/2004 of the European Parliament and of the Council 2004 on enhancing ship and port facility security,

	Measure/Action	Competent Body	Deadline	Status/Observations
				b) Directive 2005/65/EC of 26.10.2005 of the European Parliament and of the Council on enhancing port security.
2.4.4	Report on transport security and its financing	Council/ Commission		Commission to publish a report on transport security, including financing issues.
2.5. BORDER CONTROL				
2.5.1	Council Decision and Regulations on the SIS II.	Commission/ Council/ EP	July 2006	Presently being discussed by Schengen Acquis working party and the European Parliament. Question of wider access for other authorities are under discussion.
2.5.2	Regulation of the European Parliament and of the Council concerning the VIS and the exchange of data on short stay-visas	Council/EP/ Commission	July 2006	Under negotiation in Council and EP. SCIFA reviewed the proposal and agreed on a number of PRES amendments. LIBE will review the amendments submitted by MEPs.
2.5.3	(Technical) Establishment of the VIS Roll out the use of biometrics under the VIS to countries/ regions of high risk.	Council/ Commission	Begin operational End 2006	As regards VIS, there are two different actions: 1) Implementation of the central VIS; this is for COM to do. 2) Roll-out: This is for MS to do, following a coherent approach on the consular roll-out agreed in council.
2.5.4	(Technical) Establishment of the SIS II	Council/ Commission/ MS	Begin operational March 2007	As regards SIS II, there are two different actions: 1) Implementation of the central SIS; this is for COM to do. 2) National Projects: This is for MS to do. Beware: SIS II can only get operational if all MS completed their projects in due time.

	Measure/Action	Competent Body	Deadline	Status/Observations
2.5.5	Improve security of EU passports by use of biometrics, including facial image and fingerprints in order to prevent identity fraud.	MS	August 2006 (facial image)	The introduction of biometrics in all relevant ID documents. 36 months after the adoption of the technical specification (fingerprints).
2.5.6	Develop and implement a common EU approach to the exchange and analysis of passenger information: agree Directive on airline passenger name records.	Commission/ Council/EP	End 2006	The Court of Justice will issue a judgment on the applicable legal framework on the European level regarding an obligation on air carriers to provide passenger information, including PNR. The future initiative from the Commission will depend on the outcome of the judgment. The Commission will ensure an appropriate follow-up on this matter.
2.5.7	Feasibility Study on appropriate measures to register entries and exits of third country nationals at the common external border, and developing the use of biometrics at entry and exit controls of third country nationals at the Schengen borders.	Commission	June 2007	As set out in doc 11910/1/05 Commission is undertaking this feasibility study taking into account the proportionality and practicality of additional checks at the borders against the potential advantages of recording and using the resulting information.
2.5.8	Effective risk analysis of the EU external border, discussion of the contribution which border security makes to the CT effort, and effective information exchange with Europol.	Frontex/ SitCen	Regularly	
2.5.9	Prevention of illicit trafficking of dual use items	Commission/ MS		In line with the UN Resolution 1540, the Commission has made an impact assessment on the possibilities to allow

	Measure/Action	Competent Body	Deadline	Status/Observations
	.			MS competent authorities to stop dual use items in transit when they are aimed at WMD weapons in third countries.
2.6. PROTECTION OF OTHER POTENTIAL TARGETS				
2.6.1	Improve protection of other potential targets of terrorist attack, other than critical infrastructures (ie soft targets, crowded places, public transport) on the basis of relevant research.	MS/ Council/ Commission	Ongoing	
2.7. RESEARCH				
2.7.1	Make best use of EU research level activity, and in particular the 6th and 7th R&D Programmes, including the Security Research Programme (8087/05).	Council/ Commission	2007–13	The three-year Preparatory Action (2004–2006) will lay the ground for a fully fledged "European Security Research Programme" in 2007 being proposed by the Commission one of the research themes in the 7th Framework Programme for research.
2.7.2	Develop a consistent research activity in the field of trust and security.	Commission	2007–2013	In addition and in continuation of the 6th Framework Programme, ICT for trust and security is proposed to be an important priority in the IST theme of the 7th Framework programme. This includes ICT for CIP, information and network security, digital identity management and biometrics
2.7.3	Scientific Support to Policies.	Commission/ MS	6th Frame-work Programme for	In the field of biological and chemical terrorism, the 6th Framework Programme's Scientific

	Measure/Action	Competent Body	Deadline	Status/Observations
			Research (2002–2006)	Support to Policies activities covers "Civil protection (including biosecurity and protection against risks arising from terrorist attack) and crisis management". Research is currently ongoing on biological agents, risk assessment, crop bioterrorism and modelling the propagation of bioterrorist agents. In addition, nanotechnological approaches for the detection of harmful substances in water, air and with persons are developed.
2.8. INTERNATIONAL DIMENSION				
2.8.1	Deliver assistance on protective security as a component of technical assistance to priority third countries.	MS/ Commission	Ongoing	Border Security a component of proposed assistance to a number of third countries in particular to priority country Morocco.
2.8.2	Implement the Economic Initiative of the June 2005 EU-US Summit: Joint EU-US Work Programme (PDBTS).	Commission/ MS/Council	Ongoing	Continue the implementation of the various actions e.g. dialogue on AML/CFT issues, enhancing Trade, Travel and Security. Prepare implementation report for the 2006 Summit.
2.8.3	Raise the importance of responsible and robust aviation security in bilaterals with third parties.	MS/ Commission/ Council		Contained in the policy recommendations drawn up on the basis of SitCen reports.
2.8.4	Work to develop further EU transport security standards, in coordination with relevant international organizations and third countries.	Council/ Commission		On 11 March 2004 the Council agreed to submit to ICAO a Working Paper on PNR on behalf of the European Community and its MS, thereby initiating multilateral

	Measure/Action	Competent Body	Deadline	Status/Observations
				work on this subject. On 22 September 2004 the Presidency submitted a working paper on establishing an international framework for the transfer of PNR data to the ICAO 35th Assembly (28/09–8/10/04).
2.8.5	Encourage and support non-EU states to comply fully with the ICAO and IMO standards.	Council/ Commission/ MS		In the field of maritime security, the Community has launched a review of the implementation of the IMO's security measures for the EUROMED partners through a program called SAFEMED (2006/2008). Morocco is benefiting from a twinning program financed by the Community for the enhancement of maritime safety and security. Member States support the EU's multinational initiative on PNR at ICAO with a view to promoting the development of global standards.
2.8.6	Follow up to U.S. Container Security Initiative (CSI) Examination of extension to other regions.	Commission/ MS	Phase I has been concluded on 31/1/2006 Phase II until 31/12/ 2006	EC/US Agreement allows for co-operation on exchange of advance cargo information and creation of equal levels and standards of controls for US and EC operators. At the 5th EU-US Joint Customs Cooperation Committee, the EC and the US agreed to implement the recommendations elaborated by the Working Group and to continue work in the areas that need further deliberations.

	Measure/Action	Competent Body	Deadline	Status/Observations
				The Working Group Action Plan indicates the different actions for further implementation of the ten recommendations, providing operational standards and working methods which will enable the EU and U.S. customs services to improve the controls on security in the transatlantic maritime transport and also provides possibilities to closely study each other's trade partnership programs. At the 6th EU-US Joint Customs Cooperation Committee, the results and recommendations of the working group were endorsed. In the second phase of the action plan EU feeder ports will implement minimum requirements for container security to participate in the US CSI. A joint set of risk rules will be finalized and tested. A common list of advanced cargo data requirements should be agreed.
2.8.7	Strengthen international cooperation at the level of WCO. Encourage and support non-EU states to comply fully with the Framework of Standards from WCO.	Commission		The WCO adopted in July 2005 a framework of standards with the objective of increasing the supply chain security. Adoption of the implementing provisions of the Community customs code that are in principle in line with these standards Provide support on capacity building to priority non-EU members.

	Measure/Action	Competent Body	Deadline	Status/Observations
2.8.8	Strengthen international cooperation in R&D between developed countries on Critical Infrastructures Protection, and other fields of common interest	Commission/ MS	2006 and further	Cooperation started in 2006 between research teams funded by IST programme and NSF in EU and US on CIP and related issues.
2.8.9	Improve the role of international export control regimes in particular with the view to prevent access by terrorists to WMD weapons via the acquisition of dual use items. Enhance information sharing in those regimes and within the EU.	Commission/ MS		Reference to the Thessaloniki Action Plan.
3. PROSECUTE				
3.0.1	Implementation of Framework Decision on Combating Terrorism.	Commission/ MS	End 2006	Partially achieved 20 Member States have reported completion of implementation measures. The Council has adopted the Presidencies report on the implementation (11687/2/04 DROIPEN 40 REV 2) which is based on the report from the Commission. The Commission plans to submit a new report by the end of 2006.
3.0.2	MS to report on how they have responded to the recommendations of the Peer Evaluation process to strengthen national CT arrangements and—assess need for further evaluation once MS have reported on follow up to recommendations during 2006.	MS/CTC	2006/7	Member States to report in the Working Party on Terrorism how they have responded to the recommendations of the relevant country report and, where appropriate, the recommendations of the final report.

	Measure/Action	Competent Body	Deadline	Status/Observations
3.1. INFORMATION GATHERING, ANALYSIS, AND EXCHANGE				
3.1.1	Framework Decision on simplifying the exchange of information and intelligence between law enforcement authorities of the MS (Swedish proposal).	Council	achieved	General approach at 1–2 December 2005 Council.
3.1.2	Framework Decision on the principle of availability.	Council	End 2006	Presently being discussed in the MDG/ Article 36 Committee
3.1.3	Framework Decision on Data Protection.	Council	End 2006	Presently being discussed in the MDG.
3.1.4	Ensure access of authorities competent for internal security matters and Europol to VIS.	Council	End 2006	Commission proposal on access to VIS by authorities competent for internal security matters and Europol (COM (2005) 600) tabled on 24 November 2005 and is presently being discussed in the PCWG.
3.1.5	Enhancing the interoperability of VIS, SIS II, and EURODAC	Commission/ Council/ EP	As soon as possible	Commission Communication was presented in Council December 2005.
3.1.6	Improve information sharing on lost and stolen passports.	MS	December 2006	Common Position adopted 24-05-05, report on implementation December 2006.
3.1.7	Implement Directive on the retention of data generated or processed in connection with the provision of publicly available electronic communications services or a public communication network and amending Directive 2002/58/EC.	MS		Adopted in February 2006.
3.1.8	Ensuring that Europol is provided by MS law enforcement	MS/CTC	Ongoing	Second CTTF evaluation report was endorsed by the Council. Only a few Member States

	Measure/Action	Competent Body	Deadline	Status/Observations
	authorities with all relevant terrorist related criminal information as soon as it is available and that Eurojust is provided with all relevant prosecutorial information, in the context of the Council Decision on the exchange of information concerning terrorist offences adopted in September 2005.		Ongoing	exchange information on terrorism matters with Eurojust regularly and in a structured way, according to Eurojust annual report for 2005.
3.1.9	Work to improve the exchange of information on convictions.	Council/ Commission	ongoing	On 25 January 2005 the Commission presented a White Paper analysing the main difficulties in exchanging information on convictions and making proposals for a computerised information exchange system COM (2005) 10. 25.1.2005. The Commission presented in October 2004 a first proposal on criminal records, adopted by the Council in November 2005 (Council Decision 2005/876/JHA of 21 November 2005 on the exchange of information extracted from the criminal record). Following discussions on the White Paper, the Justice and Home Affairs Council of 14 April 2005 agreed on a way forward. On that basis, the Commission adopted on 22 December 2005 a proposal for a Council Framework. Decision COM (2005) 690 2005/0267 (CNS) on the organisation and content of the

	Measure/Action	Competent Body	Deadline	Status/Observations
				exchange of information extracted from criminal records between MS. Further proposals will be made to improve access to information on convictions handed down in the European Union against third country nationals (a Commission Working Paper should be adopted in May-June 2006). The work to improve the exchange of information on convictions shall take into account the results of the German-French-Spanish-Belgian pilot project of interconnection of their national judicial registers. See also Commission Communication on measures to be taken to combat terrorism and other forms of serious crime, in particular to improve exchanges of information [COM (2004) 221] Discussion by Council on 2 June 2005.
3.1.10	Identify legal and practical blockages to the co-operation between Eurojust and Europol, in particular regarding the exchange of information and the full involvement of Eurojust in Analytical Work Files of Europol, with a view to finding practical solutions.	Europol/ Eurojust	December 2006	Despite the agreement concluded on 9 June 2004, the exchange of information with Europol is limited by its legal framework. Europol and Eurojust should present proposals in due course.
3.1.11	Make full use of Europol analysis capability (including CTTF).	Europol/MS	Ongoing	

	Measure/Action	Competent Body	Deadline	Status/Observations
3.1.12	Developing a common approach to the exchange of information on deportations and expulsions related to terrorism, including radical imams.	Council	2006	
3.1.13	Enhance information sharing, as to action 2.8.9.	Commission/ MS		Reference to the Thessaloniki Action Plan.
3.1.14	Ensure the setting up of a secure network between Eurojust and MS for the exchange of information in the field of terrorism.	MS/Eurojust		
3.2. IMPEDING TERRORISTS' MOVEMENTS AND ACTIVITIES				
3.2.1	Monitor travel to and from conflict zones.	MS	Ongoing	SitCen to draw up report.
3.2.2	Prevent individuals from gaining access to terrorist training.	MS/Europol	Ongoing	Addressed in the policy recommendations based on the SitCen reports.
3.2.3	Maximise the capacity of existing border systems to monitor, and, where relevant, counter the movement of suspected terrorists across our internal and external borders (see also Protect).	Frontex	Ongoing	FRONTEX Agency will: 1) set up centralised records of technical equipment and 2) launch joint operations at the borders.
3.3. POLICE CO-OPERATION				
3.3.1	Develop the European Crime Intelligence Model with the assistance of the Police Chiefs Task Force.	PCTF/ Council	OCTA April 2006.	Europol will present 1st OCTA in April 2006.
3.3.2	Review how operational capacity of the PCTF can be reinforced.	PCTF/ Council	Ongoing	PCTF set up 6 action plans under COSPOL one of which on terrorism. Continuation of this action plan will be decided upon in connection with OCTA.

	Measure/Action	Competent Body	Deadline	Status/Observations
3.3.3	Report on enhancing mutual trust between law enforcement authorities.	CEPOL/ Europol, with input from Sitcen	Mid 2006	CEPOL and Europol to produce joint report on what CT related training they have so far provided and what more could be done.
3.3.4	Proposal for a Council Decision on the improvement of police cooperation between the Member States of the European Union, especially at the internal borders, including proposals to improve police co-operation on cross border hot pursuit, and amending the Convention implementing the Schengen Agreement.	Council	End 2006	Currently being discussed in PCWG and Article 36 Committee.
3.3.5	Member States to consider their participation in the Treaty of Prum; consideration to be given to implementation of its provisions, eg on exchange of information on potential terrorists.	MS	Ongoing	Details of this issue are included in doc 11910/1/05. Decisions are for individual Member States to be taken. 7 MS have so far signed the Treaty.
3.3.6	Enhanced co-operation against terrorist use of the internet.	MS/Europol	June 2007	Addressed in the policy recommendations based on the SitCen reports.
3.3.7	Further develop legal framework to remove illegal material from the internet.	Council/ Commission/ MS	June 2007	Subject of concern are e.g. manuals or instructions for homemade explosives or bombs. Commission is preparing seminars on legal and practical possibilities of regulations.

	Measure/Action	Competent Body	Deadline	Status/Observations
3.4. JUDICIAL CO-OPERATION				
3.4.1	Framework Decision on a European Evidence Warrant.	Council	As soon as possible	Further work by Coreper.
3.4.2	Enhance use of Eurojust and consider measures to improve its capacity, to enable more effective cooperation in terrorist investigations and prosecutions including through the practical application of relevant Council Decisions.	MS/CTC/ Eurojust		The obstacles identified in the letter Eurojust sent to the Council in May 2004 still exist. Eurojust faces ongoing challenges, relating to the lack of information conveyed to it, due to organizational and legal barriers, traditional approaches to co-operation, a lack of human and technical resources, and inertia in Member States. On the Council's request, Eurojust has examined and defined the scope of measures to improve its capacity to contribute to the fight against terrorism (see Eurojust's report: Council Document of 01/06/04 No. 10008/04). Thus: – Need for more and complete, updated information – Need for more budgetary support MS are obliged to taker the necessary measures to comply with the provisions of Council Decision 2005/671/JHA of 20 September 2005 on the exchange of information and co-operation concerning terrorist offences by 30 June 2006 at the latest. This will significantly broaden the scope of information which must be transmitted to Eurojust

	Measure/Action	Competent Body	Deadline	Status/Observations
3.4.3	Draft Framework Decision on the application of the principle of mutual recognition to Confiscation Orders.	Council	As soon as possible	General approach reached mid 2004, awaiting lifting of one parliament reservation.
3.4.4	Develop best practice in witness protection programmes, including the issue of granting residence permits to foreign nationals who co-operate with CT investigations. European Protection Programme for the protection of witnesses in terrorist cases.	Commission	As soon as possible	Commission Communication on witness protection is planned.
3.4.5	Make use of Joint Investigation Teams, when appropriate involving Europol and Eurojust, and consider options for funding JITs.	MS	Ongoing	Network of national experts on JITs established. First meeting took place on 23 November 2005. Funding issues to be considered in the context of discussions on the Security Framework Programme (prevention and fight against crime) and of the Justice framework programme (Criminal Justice).
3.5. INTERNATIONAL DIMENSION				
3.5.1	Support the key role of the United Nations and its sub-organisations in sustaining the international consensus and mobilizing the international community.	Presidency/ Council/ CTC/ Commission	Ongoing	In light of GAER conclusions of November 2005 and April 2006, it might be useful to add at the end, after "Summit": "which it continues to emphasize during ongoing Summit implementation process".
3.5.2	Ratification of 13 UN legal instruments against Terrorism and continue to lobby for this in third countries	MS	End 2006	Partially Achieved Not all Member States yet have a full record on ratification/ implementation.

	Measure/Action	Competent Body	Deadline	Status/Observations
	both bilaterally and at EU level.			To do: Work to ensure early ratification and implementation of the UN Convention on the Suppression of Acts of Nuclear Terrorism, which was adopted on 13 May 2005. This convention was signed by all EU MS on 14 September 2005.
3.5.3	Support the adoption of a Comprehensive Convention on Terrorism including through proactive outreach.	Council/ Commission /MS	Ongoing	The EU has been actively arguing in the UN and in its meetings with key third countries in favour of the adoption of the UN Comprehensive Convention on International Terrorism.
3.5.4	Support the adoption of a United Nations Counterterrorism Strategy.	Council/ Commission MS	Ongoing	The EU has already sent information and some initial thoughts about this Strategy and stands ready to work further on this issue.
3.5.5	Sign and ratify Council of Europe Convention on prevention of acts of terrorism.	Council/ Commission MS		Work to ensure early ratification and subsequent implementation. Lobby for signature and ratification in third countries. Support the Council of Europe's work on combating terrorism in general.
3.5.6	Further develop contacts with the UNODC, UN CTC, the UN CTED, the 1267 Committee, including sharing of information on EU assistance programs and further develop contacts with the UN Special Representative for Human Rights and Terrorism.	Council/ EUCTC/ Commission/ MS	Ongoing	EU participation on CTED missions to Morocco, Kenya, Albania, Algeria, Tanzania and FYROM. Systematic contacts with the UNODC.

	Measure/Action	Competent Body	Deadline	Status/Observations
3.5.7	Continue to make available voluntary contributions for the UNODC's Global Programme against Terrorism.	MS	Ongoing	
3.5.8	Identify and demarche, third countries which are failing to meet their commitments under UNSCR 1373.	Council/ HR/EU CTC/ Commission	Ongoing	
3.5.9	Further develop dialogue, including aspects on terrorist financing, with, and provision of technical assistance to, regional and sub-regional organizations.	Council/EU CTC/ Commission/ MS	Ongoing	(i) Commission has been providing support to JCLEC and is working on the provision of assistance to the AU centre in Algiers and to ASEAN. Council, Commission and Member States to develop proposals for assistance to such organisations [For the ACP countries this kind of measures cannot be financed over the EDF, see footnote 1] (ii) MS to supply expertise and funding to the maximum extent possible (iii) a network of experts has been set up (iv) EU organized the 4th seminar on financing of terrorism with Gulf Cooperation Council in April 2006. (v) EU organized an expert-level seminar on terrorism financing with Israel (March 2006) The Revised Cotonou Partnership Agreement and the Joint Council-Commission Declaration on financial and technical assistance in the area of cooperation in the fight against

	Measure/Action	Competent Body	Deadline	Status/Observations
				terrorisms stipulate that targeted assistance to strengthen ACP countries' ability, applies both to national and regional level, to counter terrorism must be financed by resources other than those intended for the financing of ACP-EC development cooperation. See also art. 11 a, the counterterrorism clause inserted in the Revised Coutonou Partnership Agreement
3.5.10	Enhance co-ordination between Member States and the Commission, on technical assistance projects, working closely with the United Nations and other donors.	MS/ Commission/ EU CTC/ Council	Ongoing	See observations in action 3.5.9
3.5.11	Deliver technical assistance to Morocco and Algeria in order to build their CT capacity, working closely with UN and other donors.	MS/ Commission	June 2006 On going	Morocco: project on training for judges launched by Sweden (study visit/workshop); twinning on financing of terrorism/money laundering launched by the Commission; visit of Moroccan officials to Spanish FIUs by Spain. Algeria: Training course for police on Cyber terrorism organised by the Commission and Malta but Algerian officials cancelled at the last minute
3.5.12	Develop and implement technical assistance programmes to other priority countries in order to build their CT capacity, in	MS/ Commission		Partially achieved (i) Commission has been providing support to around 80 third countries and to a number of international organizations.

	Measure/Action	Competent Body	Deadline	Status/Observations
	co-ordination with the UN and other donors and review existing projects in priority countries to identify duplication. Further develop political dialogue with priority countries in order to strengthen political capacity in the fight against terrorism.			(ii) MS to supply expertise and funding to the maximum extent possible (iii) a network of experts has been set up (iv) EU organised the 4th seminar on financing of terrorism with Gulf Cooperation Council in April 2006 See observations in action 3.5.9
3.5.13	Cooperate closely with the Financial Action Task Force (FATF) on all issues regarding the financing of terrorism.	All		
3.5.14	Take into account CT objectives into the work of geographical working groups and external assistance country strategies to formulate the appropriate policy mix including through the insertion of counter-terrorism clauses into agreements with third countries.	Council/ Commission	Ongoing	Partially achieved. Commission is taking CT objectives into account in external country assistance strategies. CT clauses prepared for insertion into agreements. Terrorism covered in all ENP action plans
3.5.15	Produce country and thematic CT threat assessments as the basis for policy development.	SitCen	Ongoing	First nine reports drawn up by SitCen and presented to the Working Party on Terrorism. The Article 36 Committee has equally dealt with a number of reports. Policy recommendations based on six reports to be endorsed by the Council.
3.5.16	Develop technical capacity for monitoring and	SitCen/MS/ Commission	Ongoing	

	Measure/Action	Competent Body	Deadline	Status/Observations
	analysing open source information relevant to third country CT activities.			
3.5.17	Coordinated EU position on reservations to Conventions should be encouraged.	Commission/ Council/MS	Ongoing	This issue is regularly discussed in COTER and COJUR.
3.5.18	Develop dialogue with the OSCE in the fight against terrorism.	Commission	Ongoing	The Commission and the OSCE had an informal meeting in April 2006.
3.5.19	Negotiations between Eurojust and the United States of America on a co-operation agreement.	Eurojust	Autumn 2006	Eurojust is currently negotiating with the US a co-operation agreement aimed at improving judicial co-operation in order to facilitate the co-ordination of investigations and prosecutions covering the territory of the USA and one or more EU MS.
3.5.20	Organize regular tactical meetings with the countries most concerned with terrorism, with a view to strengthen co-operation between the MS and to establish a network between magistrates dealing with terrorist matters.	Eurojust	Immedi-ately	The main objective of these meetings is to provide a platform for Leading Magistrates dealing with terrorist cases, to discuss terrorist matters, exchange information and experiences and to build up a network.
4. RESPOND				
4.1. CIVILIAN RAPID EU RESPONSE CAPABILITY TO DEAL WITH THE AFTERMATH OF A TERRORIST ATTACK				
4.1.1	Strengthen the Community Civil Protection Mechanism on the basis of the Commission's proposal for a recast	Council/ Commission	Council negotia-tions ongoing	

	Measure/Action	Competent Body	Deadline	Status/Observations
	of the Council Decision establishing the Mechanism (COM(2006) 29 of 26/01/06)			
4.1.2	Agree a proposal for a Council regulation establishing a Rapid Response and Preparedness Instrument for major emergencies ("financial instrument") (12827/05).	Council	End 2006	
4.1.3	Follow up the Commission report on the assessment of civil protection assistance through the Mechanism in case of major terrorist attack in the EU, including the medical resources required to respond to a bio-terrorist attack.	Commission/ Council	Mid 2006	Within the framework of the Community Mechanism, the Commission has developed response scenarios to identify the assistance available in case of terrorist attacks. All Member States have contributed to the database and an assessment of the available capabilities has been finalized. Through its Communication SEC(2005) 1406), the Commission has alerted the Council to a number of possible shortfalls that could undermine the effectiveness of mutual civil protection assistance in the event of major terrorist attacks. The Commission report was noted by the JHA December 2005 Council; no specific follow-up has been agreed by the Council. The report will be taken into account in the framework of the examination of the proposals on a Rapid

	Measure/Action	Competent Body	Deadline	Status/Observations
				Response Instrument and on a revision of the civil protection mechanism.
4.1.4	Improve the ability of MS to use a risk based approach to develop their capabilities to respond to national emergencies and those of their neighbours in a spirit of solidarity.	Council	Mid 2006	Two expert seminars were held in September and December 2005.
4.1.5	Develop the concept of Civil Protection Modules, capable of rapid reaction, interoperable and trained to work together.	Commission/ Council	Mid 2006	
4.1.6	Carry out training and exercises directed at interoperability in coping with terrorist attacks.	Commission/ Council	Ongoing	1) The Commission has launched a call for proposals for major simulation exercises in the field of civil protection, including exercises focusing on the response to terrorist attacks. 2) Training activities in the framework of the Civil Protection Mechanism help preparing first responders for assistance in case of major emergencies, including terrorism. 3) Joint Training Programme of Commission with EUROPOL on interaction between Law Enforcement and Public Health (April 2004)
4.1.7	Agree common insignia for EU intervention teams.	Commission	End 2005	Common vests with European insignia have been developed and are

	Measure/Action	Competent Body	Deadline	Status/Observations
				being distributed to Member States' experts participating in EU civil protection assistance interventions in order to increase the visibility of EU assistance.
4.1.8	Improve exchange of information on victim identification	Council	Ongoing	Council in dialogue with Interpol on the use and further development of Interpol's database.
4.1.9	Ensure appropriate consideration is given within Civilian Headline Goal 2008 to the deployment and further development of civilian capabilities (in particular Police, Rule of Law, Civilian Administration and Civil Protection), in order to prevent as well as counter the terrorist threats within the limitations of the mandate.	Council	Ongoing	
4.1.10	Protect minority communities which may be at risk of a backlash in the event of a major attack.	Council/ Commission		Continued monitoring by the European Monitoring Centre on Racism and Xenophobia of racial violence and discrimination.
4.1.11	Ensure full implementation of the EU Health Security Strategy and Solidarity Programme.	Council/ Commission /MS		
4.2. MILITARY RAPID RESPONSE CAPABILITY TO DEAL WITH THE AFTERMATH OF A TERRORIST ATTACK				
4.2.1	Adapt the military database of assets and capabilities relevant to the protection of civilian populations against the effects of	Council/ Commission	First half 2006.	Develop co-operation between relevant Council and Commission bodies as appropriate.

	Measure/Action	Competent Body	Deadline	Status/Observations
	terrorist attacks (including CBRN) to reflect its expansion to all types of natural and man-made disasters.			
4.2.2	Elaboration of a detailed report on modalities procedures and criteria to develop the appropriate level of interoperability between military and civilian capabilities in the framework of protection of civilian populations following a terrorist attack, including in crisis management operations under Title V of the TEU.	Council	Mid 2006	
4.2.3	Follow-up the "trilateral initiative" at NATO in the framework of civil emergency planning in crisis management (cf. 14797/04 sub 19.1).	Council/ Commission	Soonest possible	The EU will continue to seek ways to cooperate with NATO in the context of the "trilateral initiative". The Secretariat, with the participation of the Commission, will continue to maintain the necessary contacts with the IS to ensure the exchange of information and to enable PSC-NAC and PMG-PCG meetings to be held with all the Member States.
4.2.4	Ensure the terrorist threat is incorporated into the illustrative scenarios of the Headline Goal 2010.	Council	Ongoing	
4.2.5	Improve protection of all personnel, material and assets deployed for crisis management operations under Title V of the TEU,	Council/MS	Ongoing	

	Measure/Action	Competent Body	Deadline	Status/Observations
	including, as appropriate, the ability to protect possible key civilian targets, including critical infrastructure, in the area of operations within available means and capabilities and on a case by case basis based on the threat analysis.			
4.3. EARLY WARNING OF TERRORIST ATTACKS				
4.3.1	Timely analysis of attacks carried out by terrorists.	Sitcen		
4.4. CAPABILITIES TO COORDINATE EFFECTIVELY THE MANAGEMENT OF THE RESPONSE				
4.4.1	Implement EU Crisis Coordination arrangements to share information, ensure coordination and enable collective decision-making at politico-strategic level in the event of an emergency.	Council/ Commission	Ongoing Report in June 2006	Agreed by the Council in December 2005.
4.4.2	Agree Integrated Crisis Management Arrangements which develop the necessary procedures for the above EU Crisis Coordination arrangements.	Council/ Commission	Mid 2006	
4.5. ASSISTANCE TO VICTIMS				
4.5.1	Ensure that support and assistance is provided to the victims of terrorism.	MS/ Commission	Ongoing	Commission will launch in 2006 a call for proposals in the framework of a preparatory action in favour of victims and will evaluate the pilot project run in 2004 and 2005

	Measure/Action	Competent Body	Deadline	Status/Observations
4.6. INTERNATIONAL DIMENSION				
4.6.1	Establishing working and cooperation methods, concepts and procedures between the EU and the UN.	Council/ Commission	Ongoing	
4.6.2	Deliver technical assistance on consequence management as a component of technical assistance to priority third countries.	MS/ Council/ Commission	Ongoing	
4.6.3	Reinforce the protection of European citizens in third countries.	Commission/ MS		In April 2005, the Commission proposed to make the MIC available to facilitate and support consular cooperation in the event of major emergencies in third countries, affecting EU citizens. This was welcomed by the GAERC on 18.07.05.
4.7. RESEARCH				
4.7.1	Implementation of the 6th Framework Programme for Research and Development.	Commission/ MS		Research should, in particular, aim at promoting interoperability.
4.7.2	The Cooperation part of the Commission proposal for the 7th RTD Framework Programme (FP7), will include a Security and Space theme. After more than a year work, ESRAB (the European Security Research Advisory Board) is finalizing its report. The final report is expected in September 2007.	Commission		In the proposal for the 7th Framework Programme the Commission proposes to include Security as one of the research themes in order to develop multidisciplinary technologies and knowledge for building capabilities needed to ensure the security of citizens from threats such as terrorism and crime. In addition ICT

	Measure/Action	Competent Body	Deadline	Status/Observations
	It will advise the Commission on the content and the implementation of security research within FP7, more particularly, the 1st workprogramme of FP7.	ESRAB, the European Security Research Advisory Board to the Commission		for Trust and Security will remain a priority in the IST programme of the 7th Framework programme. Following the agreement on the next financial perspectives, the Commission will table a revised proposal for FP7, end of April early May 2006.
4.7.3	Scientific support to policies.	Commission/ MS		In the field of biological and chemical terrorism, the 6th Framework Programme's Scientific Support to Policies activities cover "Civil protection (including biosecurity and protection against risks arising from terrorist attack) and crisis management". Research is currently ongoing on biological agents, risk assessment, crop bioterrorism and modelling the propagation of bioterrorist agents.

ANNEXES

Annex 1: Implementation of the legislative Instruments

listed in the Declaration on terrorism of the European Council of 25 March 2004—state as on 13 February 2006

AT	BE	CY	CZ	DE	DK	EE	ES	FIN	FR	GR	HU	IE	IT	LV	LT	LU	MT	NL	PL	PT	SE	SI	SK	UK
1. INSTRUMENTS OF THE EUROPEAN UNION[1]																								
a) Framework Decision of 13 June 2002 on the European Arrest Warrant (initial deadline for old Member States: 31 December 2003; for new Member States: date of accession; deadline set by the Declaration of the European Council: June 2004)[2]																								
y	y	y[3]	y	p[4]	y	y	y	y	y	y	y	y	y	y	y	y	y	y	y	y	y	y	y	y

[1] y = in case of a Framework Decision: implementation completed, legislation has entered into force; - = implementation not completed; c = implementation completed, legislation has not entered into force; p = implemented in part; in case the Commission has already submitted a report on the implementation of an instrument (by the old Member States), the report is taken account of;

y = in case of a Convention or a Protocal: notified the general Secretariat of the Council that the Member State has ratified the instrument, — = no notification;

°= Member State has informed General Secretariat of the Council that the instrument has been implemented, but legislation has not been sent to the Council Secretariat;

[2] In February 2005, the Commission submitted a report on the implementation of the FD on the EAW (doc. 6815/05 COPEN 42 + ADD 1) and in January 2006 a revised report taking account of the implementation by IT (doc. 5706/06 COPEN 5 EJN 2 EUROJUST 6 + ADD1). According to this report, the legislation of in particular CZ, DK, EE, IE, IT, LU, MT, NL, SI and UK does not fully comply with the FD.

[3] Following a decision taken by the Supreme Court of Cyprus on 7 November 2005, Cyprus will not be in a position to execute European Arrest Warrants against Cypriot nationals until its Constitution has been changed.

[4] On 18 July 2005 the German Constitutional Court declared the German law to implement the execution of the EAW null and void. During the transitional period until a new German act has been enacted and entered into force, Germany will apply extradition arrangements; the extradition of German nationals to other Member States is not possible during that provisional period. However, German judicial authorities can continue to issue European arrest warrants.

AT	BE	CY	CZ	DE	DK	EE	ES	FIN	FR	GR	HU	IE	IT	LV	LT	LU	MT	NL	PL	PT	SE	SI	SK	UK
b) Framework Decision of 13 June 2002 on Joint Investigation Teams (initial deadline for old Member States: 1 January 2003; for new Member States: date of accession; deadline set by the Declaration of the European Council: June 2004)[5]																								
y	y	y	y	-	y	-	y	y	y	-[6]	y	y	-[7]	y	y	-[8]	y	y	y	y	y	-	y	y
c) Framework Decision of 13 June 2002 on Combating Terrorism (initial deadline for old Member States: 31 December 2002; for new Member States: date of accession; deadline set by the Declaration of the European Council: June 2004)[9]																								
y[10]	y	-[11]	p[12]	p[4]	y	y	y	y	y	y	y	y	y	y	y	y	y	y	y	y	y	y	p[13]	y

[5] In January 2005, the Commission submitted a report on national measures taken to comply with the FD on JITs (doc. 5448/05 COPEN 10 + ADD 1). According to this report, only the legislation of ES (out of the 19 Member States whose legislation was examined) fully complies with the FD.

[6] GR has indicated that its draft legislation to implement the FD on Joint Investigation Teams has been submitted to the Greek Parliament.

[7] IT has indicated that its draft legislation to implement the FD on Joint Investigation Teams is currently pending before its Parliament and that no estimate can be given as to when the Parliament will approve it.

[8] LU has indicated that its draft legislation to implement the FD on Joint Investigation Teams is currently pending before its Parliment.

[9] On 8 June 2004 the Commission submitted a report on the implementation of the FD on Combating Terrorism by the 15 old Member States (doc. 10528/04 DROIPEN 28 CATS 30 + ADD 1 issued on 15 June 2004). According to this report, only FIN, FR and PT appear to have fulfilled entirely the obligations emerging from the FD on Combating Terrorism except Article 9(2) of the FD. The latter provision appears to have been incorporated, according to the aforementioned report, by none of the Member States. This report is the basis for a note from the Presidency to the Council (doc. 11687/2/04 DROIPEN 40 REV 2). The legislation of the 10 new Member States as well as further progress in implementing this Framework Decision and additional information provided for by the old Member States will be examined in a second report from the Commission (to be submitted to the Council by 30 June 2005).

[10] According to the aforementioned report from the Commission (doc. 10528/04 DROIPEN 28 CATS 30 + ADD 1), AT did not entirely comply with the Framework Decision at the time of the drafting of the report. Since then, AT has introduced further legislative procedures so as to enact supplementary legislation.

[11] CY has indicated that new counter terrorism legislation is in preparation.

[12] CZ has indicated that it has implemented the FD on Combating Terrorism with the exception of the provisions on liability of legal persons.

[13] SK has informed the General Secretariat of the Council that it has implemented the FD on Combating Terrorism with the exception of the provisions on liability of legal persons. Criminal liability of legal persons will be established in the framework of the new Criminal Code which is currently in preparation.

AT	BE	CY	CZ	DE	DK	EE	ES	FIN	FR	GR	HU	IE	IT	LV	LT	LU	MT	NL	PL	PT	SE	SI	SK	UK
d) Framework Decision of 26 June 2001 on money laundering, the identification, tracing, freezing, seizing and confiscation of instrumentalities and the proceeds of crime[14] (initial deadline for old Member States: 31 December 2002; for new Member States: date of accession; deadline set by the Declaration of the European Council: June 2004)																								
y[15]	y	°	p[16]	y	y	y	y[17]	y	y	y	y	y	y[18]	°	y	-	-	y	y	y[19]	y	y	y	y

14 The report from the Commission on the implementation of this Framework Decision (doc. 9251/04 DROIPEN 14) which is the basis for the Presidency's note to Council (doc. 10369/2/04 DROIPEN 24 REV 2 + COR 1) examines only the legislation of the 15 old Member States. The legislation of the 10 new Member States as well as further progress in implementing this Framework Decision and additional information provided for by the old Member States will be examined in a second report from the Commission (to be submitted to the Council by 30 June 2005). According to the report from the Commission on the implementation of this Framework Decision (doc. 9251/04 DROIPEN 14), ES, IT and LU were, at the time of the drafting of the report, preparing legislation that had not yet entered into force, and a special legislative drafting committee was producing national transposing provisions in GR. Since then, GR has enacted legislation to implement the Framework Decision.

15 According to the aforementioned report from the Commission (doc. 9251/04 DROIPEN 14), AT did not entirely comply with the Framework Decision at the time of the drafting of the report. Since then, AT has notified the COM and the GSC of legislation that was enacted in order to comply with the Framework Decision.

16 CZ has indicated that draft legislation to fully implement the Framework Decision is being discussed in Parliament.

17 According to the aforementioned report from the Commission (doc. 9251/04 DROIPEN 14), ES did not entirely comply with Articles 1 and 3 of the Framework Decision at the time of the drafting of the report. Since then, ES has enacted new legislation in order to transpose the Framework Decision. These provisions are applicable to offences committed after 1 October 2004.

18 According to the aforementioned report from the Commission (doc. 9251/04 DROIPEN 14), IT did not inform on provisions implementing Article 2 of the Framework Decision. Since then, IT has notified the COM and the GSC of legislation that was enacted in order to comply with the Framework Decision.

19 According to the aforementioned report from the Commission (doc. 9251/04 DROIPEN 14), PT did not entirely comply with the Framework Decision at the time of the drafting of the report. Since then, PT has enacted new legislation in order to transpose the Framework Decision.

AT	BE	CY	CZ	DE	DK	EE	ES	FIN	FR	GR	HU	IE	IT	LV	LT	LU	MT	NL	PL	PT	SE	SI	SK	UK
e) Decision of 28 February 2002 establishing Eurojust[20] (initial deadline: 6 September 2003; deadline set by the Declaration of the European Council: June 2004)																								
y	y	y	-	y	y	y	-[21]	y	y	-[22]	y	y	y	°	y	y	y	y	y	y	y	y	y	y
f) Decision of 19 December 2002 on the implementation of specific measures for police and judicial cooperation to combat terrorism[23] (deadline set by the Declaration of the European Council: June 2004)																								
y	y	y	y	y	y	y	y	y	y	y	y	y	y	y	y	y	y	y	y	y	y	y	y	y
g) Convention of 29 May 2000 on Mutual Assistance in Criminal Matters between the Member States of the European Union (deadline set by the Declaration of the European Council: December 2004); entry into force on 23 August 2005																								
y	y	y	-[24]	y	y	y	y	y	y	-[3]	y	-[25]	-[26]	y	y	-	-	y	y	y	y	y	-[27]	y

20 The information refers to the question whether Member States have enacted legislation or take the view that they comply with the Council Decision on the basis of existing provisions (=y) or not (= -). As to the appointment of national members of Eurojust, all (old and new) Member States have notified the General Secretariat of the Council of the EU of their decisions. On 6 July 2004 the Commission submitted a report on the legal transposition of the Council Decision setting up Eurojust by the 15 old Member States (doc. 11280/04 EUROJUST 66 + ADD 1). According to this report from the Commission, FIN, UK, IE, GR, SE and DK still had to bring, at the time of the drafting of the report, their national legislation into conformity with the Eurojust Decision.

21 ES has indicated that the draft legislation to implement the Eurojust Decision has been submitted to Parliament.

22 GR has indicated that its legislation to implement the Eurojust Decision has been submitted to the Greek Parliament.

23 Designation of a Eurojust national correspondent for terrorism matters by each Member State.

24 CZ has indicated that the MLA Convention and the Protocol thereto were approved by its Government and Parliament and have been submitted to the President in order to complete the ratification process.

25 IE has indicated that legislation to implement the MLA Convention is in preparation.

26 IT has indicated that a draft law to ratify the MLA Convention is currently pending before its Parliament.

27 SK has indicated that it is preparing its accession to the MLA Convention and the Protocol thereto.

AT	BE	CY	CZ	DE	DK	EE	ES	FIN	FR	GR	HU	IE	IT	LV	LT	LU	MT	NL	PL	PT	SE	SI	SK	UK
h) Protocol of 16 October 2001 to the Convention on Mutual Assistance in Criminal Matters between the Member States of the European Union (deadline set by the Declaration of the European Council: December 2004); entry into force on 5 October 2005																								
y	y	y	-[28]	y	y	-[29]	y	y	y	-[30]	y	-[31]	-[32]	y	y	-	-	y	y	-[33]	y	y	-[34]	-[35]
i) Protocol of 30 November 2000 amending the Europol Convention (deadline set by the Declaration of the European Council: December 2004)																								
y	y	y	y	y	y	y	y	y	y	y	y	-[4]	y	y	y	-[36]	y	-[37]	y	y	y	y	y	y

28 CZ has indicated that the MLA Convention and the Protocol thereto were approved by its Government and Parliament and have been submitted to the President in order to complete the ratification process.

29 EE has indicated that a draft act will be submitted to the Ministry of Foreign Affairs in February 2006. Thereafter it will be sent to the Government for approval and to the Parliament for ratification.

30 GR has indicated that an ad hoc committee of the Ministry of Justice has prepared draft laws to implement the FD on JITs, the Eurojust Decision, the 2000 MLA Convention and the 2001 Protocol thereto as well as the FD on freezing orders. Their submission to the Parliament is imminent.

31 IE has indicated that legislation to implement the instrument is in preparation.

32 IT has indicated that a draft bill to ratify the 2001 Protocol is being prepared.

33 PT has indicated that the ratification process has been delayed by the elections of the Parliament.

34 SK has indicated that it is preparing its accession to the MLA Convention and the Protocol thereto.

35 UK has indicated that it is in a position to ratify the 2001 Protocol.

36 LU has indicated that its draft legislation to implement the Protocols to the Europol Convention is currently pending before its Parliament.

37 NL has indicated that it does not intend to ratify the 2000 Protocol since that Protocol will become obsolete when the 2003 Protocol will enter into force.

j) Protocol of 28 November 2002 amending the Europol Convention and the Protocol on the privileges and immunities of Europol (deadline set by the Declaration of the European Council: December 2004)																								
y	y	y	y	y	y	y	y	y	y	y	y	-[4]	-[38]	y	y	-[9]	y	y	y	-[6]	-[39]	y	y	y
k) Protocol of 27 November 2003 amending the Europol Convention (deadline set by the Declaration of the European Council: December 2004)																								
y	y	y	y	-[40]	y	y	y	y	-	y	y	-[4]	-[41]	y	y	-[9]	y	y	y	-[6]	-[12]	y	y	y

AT	BE	CY	CZ	DE	DK	EE	ES	FIN	FR	GR	HU	IE	IT	LV	LT	LU	MT	NL	PL	PT	SE	SI	SK	UK
l) Framework Decision of 22 July 2003 on the execution of orders freezing property or evidence (initial deadline for Member States (and current Acceding States): 2 August 2005; deadline set by the Declaration of the European Council: December 2004)																								
y	y	y	y	y	y	y	y	y	y	y	y	y	y	y	y	y	y	y	y	-[42]	y	-	-[43]	po[44]

AT	BE	CY	CZ	DE	DK	EE	ES	FIN	FR	GR	HU	IE	IT	LV	LT	LU	MT	NL	PL	PT	SE	SI	SK	UK

38 IT has indicated that a draft bill to ratify the protocal was examined by the Senate on 30 November 2005.

39 SE has indicated that the ratification procedure is expected to be completed by spring 2006.

40 De has indicated that its draft legislation to ratify the 2003 Protocol is expected to be sent to the Parliment (Bundestrat) once the new government is in place. The ratification process is expected to be concluded early 2006.

41 IT has indicated that a draft billto ratify the Protocal was approved by the Council of Ministers and will now be submitted to the Italian Parliment.

42 PT has indicated that a draft bill which is currently being finalised, will soon be submitted to the government and the Parliment for approval.

43 SK has indicated that its draft legislation to implement the FD on freezing orders is currently in preparation.

44 UK has indicated that it has implemented the FD on freezing orders insofar as terrorist assets are concerned. UK is making progress towards full implementation.

2. INSTRUMENTS OF THE UNITED NATIONS[45]																								
a) Convention on Offences and Certain Other Acts Committed on Board Aircraft of 14 September 1963																								
r	r	r	r	r	r	r	r	r	r	r	r	r	r	r	r	r	r	r	r	r	r	r	r	r
b) Convention for the Suppression of Unlawful Seizure of Aircraft of 16 December 1970																								
r	r	r	r	r	r	r	r	r	r	r	r	r	r	r	r	r	r	r	r	r	r	r	r	r
c) Convention for the Suppression of Unlawful Acts against the Safety of Civil Aviation of 23 September 1971																								
r	r	r	r	r	r	r	r	r	r	r	r	r	r	r	r	r	r	r	r	r	r	r	r	r
d) Convention on the Prevention and Punishment of Crimes against Internationally Protected Persons, including Diplomatic Agents of 14 December 1973																								
r	r	r	r	r	r	r	r	r	r	r	r	r	r	r	r	-[46]	r	r	r	r	r	r	r	r
e) International Convention against the Taking of Hostages of 17 December 1979																								
r	r	r	r	r	r	r	r	r	r	r	r	r	r	r	r	r	r	r	r	r	r	r	r	r
f) Convention on the Physical Protection of Nuclear Material of 3 March 1980																								
r	r	r	r	r	r	r	r	r	r	r	r	r	r	r	r	r	r	r	r	r	r	r	r	r

[45] r= ratification (or accession or succession or accession); s= signature (without ratification);

[46] LU has indicated that the draft law to ratify the Convention was submitted to the Luxembourg Parliment in October 2005.

g) Protocol for the Suppression of Unlawful Acts of Violence at Arports Serving International Civil Aviation, supplementary to the Convention for the Suppression of Unlawful Acts against the Safety of Civil Aviation of 24 February 1988																								
r	r	r	r	r	r	r	r	r	r	r	r	r	r	r	r	r	r	r	r	r	r	r	r	r
h) Convention for the Suppression of Unlawful Acts against the Safety of Maritime Navigation of 10 March 1988																								
r	r	r	r	r	r	r	r	r	r	r	r	r	r	r	r	r	r	r	r	r	r	r	r	r

AT	BE	CY	CZ	DE	DK	EE	ES	FIN	FR	GR	HU	IE	IT	LV	LT	LU	MT	NL	PL	PT	SE	SI	SK	UK
i) Protocol for the Suppression of Unlawful Acts against the Safety of Fixed Platforms Located on the Continental Shelf of 10 March 1988																								
r	r	r	r	r	r	r	r	r	r	r	r	r	r	r	r	-	r	r	r	r	r	r	r	r
j) Convention on the Marking of Plastic Explosives for the Purpose of Detection of 1 March 1991																								
r	s	r	r	r	r	r	r	r	r	r	r	r	r	r	r	-[47]	r	r	-[48]	r	s[49]	r	r	r
k) International Convention for the Suppression of Terrorist Bombings of 15 December 1997																								
r	r	r	r	r	r	r	r	r	r	r	r	r	r	r	r	r	r	r	r	r	r	r	r	r
l) International Convention for the Suppression of the Financing of Terrorism of 9 December 1999																								
r	r	r	r	r	r	r	r	r	r	r	r	r	r	r	r	r	r	r	r	r	r	r	r	r

47 LU has indicated that the draft law to ratify the Convention was submitted to the Luxembourg Parliament in October 2005.

48 PL has indicated that the ratification procedure has been initiated.

49 SE has indicated that work on the ratification of the Convention is ongoing. It is expected that the Parliament will deal with the ratification in spring 2006.

Annex 2: List of Achieved Measures in the Fight Against Terrorism

General

- The EU Action Plans (June 2004, December 2004, June 2005 and February 2006)
- Communication on prevention, preparedness and response to terrorist attacks
- Communication establishing a framework programme on "Security and Safeguarding Liberties" for the period 2007–2013": Proposal for a Council decision establishing the specific programme "Prevention, Preparedness and Consequence Management of Terrorism" for the period 2007–2013
- Commission financing decision — Pilot Project 'Fight against terrorism
- The EU Counter-Terrorism Strategy

I. Prevent

1.1 Disrupt the Activities of the Network and Individuals who Draw People into Terrorism

Communications

- Communication addressing radicalisation and recruitment of terrorists

Report

- Report on "The Impact of 7 July 2005 Bombs Attack on Muslim Communities in the EU" by the European Monitoring Centre (EUMC)
- Report on recruitment to terrorism including the possible adoption of an agreed set of recommendations

Other

- EU Strategy for Combating Radicalisation and Recruitment to Terrorism
- Coordinated long-term strategy based on the report on recruitment to terrorism
- Establishment of an Expert Group on Violent Radicalisation
- Establishment of the High Level Group on Minorities
- Research Projects in the 6th Framework Programme, key action "Citizens and governance"

1.2 Terrorist Financing

Communications

- Communication on Organised Financial Crime
- Communication on the prevention of and the fight against terrorist financing
- EU Joint Strategy Paper on Terrorist Financing
- Communication setting out (i) best practice advice in cooperation structures and the exchange of financial intelligence and (ii) putting forward a Recommendation to the MS and a framework for a Code of Conduct for NPOs to enhance transparency within the non-profit sector

Adopted Legislation

- Framework Decision of 26 June 2001 on money laundering, the identification, tracing, freezing, seizing and confiscation of instrumentalities and the proceeds of crime[50]
- Council Act of 16 October 2001 establishing, in accordance with Article 34 of the Treaty on European Union, the Protocol to the Convention on Mutual Assistance in Criminal Matters between the Member States of the European Union
- Directive amending Council Directive 91/308/EEC on prevention of the use of the financial system for the purpose of money laundering
- Council Decision extending Europol's mandate to deal with serious forms of international crime listed in the Annex to the Europol Convention
- Council Common Position on combating terrorism
- Council Common Position on the application of specific measures to combat terrorism
- Council Regulation on specific restrictive measures directed against certain persons and entities with a view to combating terrorism
- Council Decision establishing the list provided for in Article 2(3) of Council Regulation (EC) No 2580/2001 on specific restrictive measures directed against certain persons and entities with a view to combating terrorism

---

[50] [the state regarding implementation as on 3 March 2006 is that in two Member States implementation is not completed (LU, MT), two Member States have informed the General Secretariat of the Council that the instrument has been implemented, but legislation has not been sent to the Council Secretariat (CY, LV), and one Member State has implemented the instrument partially (CZ)]

- Council Common Position concerning restrictive measures against Usama bin Laden, members of the Al-Qaida organisation and the Taliban and other individuals, groups, undertakings and entities associated with them and repealing Common Positions 96/746/CFSP, 1999/727/CFSP, 2001/154/CFSP and 2001/771/CFSP
- Council Regulation imposing certain specific restrictive measures directed against certain persons and entities associated with Usama bin Laden, the Al-Qaida network and the Taliban, and repealing Council Regulation (EC) No 467/2001 prohibiting the export of certain goods and services to Afghanistan, strengthening the flight ban and extending the freeze of funds and other financial resources in respect of the Taliban of Afghanistan
- Directive on Insider Trading and Market Manipulation (Market Abuse)
- Council Framework Decision on the execution in the European Union of orders freezing property or evidence
- Directive on a New Legal Framework for Payments in the Internal Market (regulating inter alia alternative remittance systems, in compliance with FATF SR VI)
- Framework Decision of 20 September 2005 on the exchange of information and cooperation concerning terrorist offences (2005/671/JHA)
- Regulation on controls on cash entering or leaving the Community (Regulation (EC) No. 1889/2005)
- Directive on the prevention of the use of the financial system for the purpose of money laundering, and terrorist financing (also known as the Third Money Laundering Directive) (entered into force 15 December 2005)

Other

- Project to design common minimum financial investigation training standards in EU. The Commission organised a meeting in March 2006 to which all Member States were invited, the purpose being to raise awareness of the Commission / Europol initiated project and to explain and disseminate a questionnaire to participating Member States and Candidate Countries. A Working Group was established in 2005 to elaborate common minimum training standards in FI. This work is still in progress. The Commission, in partnership with the four European credit sector federations established in June 2004 an electronic database containing all relevant data concerning persons, groups and entities which are subject to European Union financial sanctions

- Completion of a scoping study on the capacity of EU institutions and legal instruments to respond to the problem of aliases/front organisations and to apply sanctions against leaders of terrorist organisations
- Establishment of intelligence capacity in relation to terrorist financing within SitCen to inform the work of relevant bodies
- Informal EU-US ad-hoc Troika meetings on terrorist financing
- Practitioners' seminar on financial investigation
- Study on EU's performance on Terrorist Financing in particular in respect of FATF special recommendations and act on recommendations awarded in April 2006. Study will be completed before end 2006.

1.3 Limit Terrorists' Access to Weapons and Explosives

Communications

- Communication on ensuring greater security of explosives, detonators, bomb-making equipment and fire-arms

Adopted Legislation

- Council Directive on the supervision and control of shipments of radioactive waste and spent fuel

2. Protect

2.1 Security of the Supply Chain

Communications

- Communication and a possible proposal for a legal instrument on supply chain security

Adopted Legislation

- Security amendments to the Community Customs Code that relate to checks on the flow of goods by introducing a system of pre-arrival and pre-departure declarations and by using an improved system of data communication and information sharing between Member States (adopted in April 2005 – Regulation (EC) No. 648/2005).

Proposed Legislation

- Implementing regulation to the Security amendments to the Community Customs Code.
- Proposals for a complete modernisation of the customs code and a Decision on e-customs

Other

- The World Customs Organisation adopted a framework of standards with the objective of increasing the supply chain security

2.2 Protection of Critical Infrastructure

Communications

- Communication on Critical Infrastructure Protection in the fight against terrorism
- Green paper on European Programme for Critical Infrastructure Protection (EPCIP)

Adopted legislation

- Council Framework Decision on Attacks against Information Systems
- Framework Decision on Attacks against Information Systems

Other

- The Commission has organised three EU Critical Infrastructure Protection Seminars

2.3 Transport Security

Adopted Legislation

- Regulation n° 68/2004 amending Regulation (EC) n° 622/2003 laying down measures for the implementation of the common basic standards on aviation security (January 2004)
- Regulation (EC) n° 724/2004 amending Regulation (EC) No 1406/2002 establishing a European Maritime Safety Agency
- Regulation (EC) n° 725/2004 on enhancing ship and port facility security
- Council Directive 2004/82/EC on the obligation of carriers to communicate passenger data
- Commission Regulation (EC) n° 1138/2004 establishing a common definition of critical parts of security restricted areas at airports
- Commission Regulation EC 884/2005 laying down procedures for conducting Commission inspections in the field of maritime security
- Commission Regulation (EC) n° 781/2005 amending Regulation (EC) n° 622/2003 laying down measures for the implementation of the common basic standards on aviation security
- Commission Regulation (EC) N°781/2005 amending Commission Regulation (EC) N°622/2003 Commission Regulation (EC) N°857/2005 of 6 June 2005 amending Commission Regulation (EC) N°622/2003

laying down measures for the implementation of the common basic standards on aviation security

- Commission Regulation (EC) N°857/2005 amending Regulation (EC) n° 622/2003 laying down measures for the implementation of the common basic standards on aviation security

Proposed Legislation

- Proposal for a Directive on enhancing port security

2.4 Border Control

Adopted Legislation

- Council regulation (EC) n° 871/2004 concerning the introduction of new functions for the Schengen Information System
- Council decision n° 2004/512/EC establishing the Visa Information System (VIS)
- Council Regulation (EC) n° 2007/2004 establishing a European Agency for the Management of Operational Cooperation at the External Borders of the Member States of the European Union
- Regulation (EC) n° 648/2005 amending Council Regulation (EEC) No 2913/92 establishing the Community Customs Code

Proposed Legislation

- Proposal for a Regulation of the European Parliament and of the Council concerning the Visa Information System (VIS) and the exchange of data between Member States on short-stay visas
- Proposal for a Council decision on the establishment, operation and use of the second generation Schengen Information System (SIS II)
- Proposal for a regulation on the establishment, operation and use of the second generation Schengen Information System (SIS II)
- Proposal for a Regulation regarding access to the Second Generation Schengen Information System (SIS II) by the services in the Member States responsible for issuing vehicle registration certificates
- Proposal for a regulation laying down provisions for the implementation of Council Regulation (EEC) No 2913/92 establishing the Community Customs Code. The recently published preliminary draft proposal aims at defining the necessary amendments that must be made to Commission Regulation (EEC) No 2454/93, consequent to the amendments made to Council Regulation 92/2913 (EEC), by Regulation (EC) 648/2005 of the European Parliament and Council, OJ L 117, 04.05.2005,

p. 13. The deadline for response to the open consultation related to the above mentioned proposal was 16th September 2005.

Report

- Report from study of the role of Customs in the Member States in relation to security/anti-terrorism at EU Borders (approved by CCWG, 10238/04)

Other

- Strategy for Customs Cooperation and related work plan
- Statement of support for the Proliferation Security Initiative
- The Borders Code

2.5 Protection of Other Potential Targets

Adopted Legislation

- Commission Regulation (EURATOM) 302/2005 on the application of EURATOM safeguards

Report

- Report to the Council on modalities procedures and criteria to develop the appropriate level of interoperability between military and civilian capabilities in the framework of protection of civilian populations following a terrorist attack, including in crisis management operations under Title V of the TEU

2.6 Research

Other

- Inventory and analysis of on-going research activities in the field of biological and chemical terrorism and identification of gaps and needs in scientific knowledge and research priorities which contribute to define annual research work programmes and priorities made in collaboration with the R&D Expert Group on Countering the Effects of Chemical and Biological Terrorism set up by the European Commission following a decision of Council of Research Ministers of 30th October 2001 (updated 2005)
  - Funding of eight projects (Scientific Support to Policies) in the area of biological and chemical terrorism within the scope of the 6th Framework Programme for RTD (2002–2006), and one additional project open for funding in 2006"

- Protection against terrorism and crime: delivering technology solutions for threat (e.g. CBRN) awareness, detection, prevention, identification, protection, neutralisation and containment of effects of terrorist attacks and organised crime.
- Security of infrastructures and utilities: analysing and securing existing and future public and private critical/networked infrastructure (e.g. in transport, energy, ICT), systems and services (including financial and administrative services)
- Border security: focusing on technologies and capabilities to enhance the effectiveness and efficiency of all systems, equipment, tools and processes required for improving the security of Europe's land and coastal borders, including border control and surveillance issues
- The preparatory action in the field of security research 2004–2006
- Commission proposal to incorporate Security Research in the 7th Framework Programme for RTD in (FP7) with an appropriate budget

2.7 International Dimension

Other

- Reinforcement of the protection of European citizens in third countries — in April 2005, the Commission proposed to make the MIC available to facilitate and support consular cooperation in the event of major emergencies in third countries, affecting EU citizens.
- The follow up to the Container Security Initiative (CSI)
- EC/US Agreement concluded expanding customs co-operation to cover CSI and related matters in order to cover transport security aspects
- Joint EC/US JCCC Working Group — comprised of customs exports — is established under the agreement to examine and make recommendations to be adopted by the EU. US Joint Customs Cooperation Committee in November 2004
- The EC and the US agreed to implement the recommendations elaborated by the Working Group and to continue work in the areas that need further deliberations (minimum CSI requirements for feeder ports; Joint Threat Assessment, a mechanism to exchange control information and a comparison of trade partnership programs on supply chain security) at the 6th meeting of the ECUS Joint Customs Cooperation Committee (31/1/2006)

3. Prosecute

3.1 Information Gathering, Analysis, and Exchange

Communications

- Communication on Information Policy for Law Enforcement Purposes
- Communication on measures to be taken to combat terrorism and other forms of serious crime, in particular to improve exchanges of information
- Communication on improved effectiveness, enhanced interoperability and synergies among European databases in the area of Justice and Home Affairs

Adopted legislation

- Framework Decision on combating terrorism[51]
- Framework Decision to replace Joint Action 1998/733/JHA on Criminal Organisations
- Council Decision on the exchange of information and co-operation concerning terrorist offences
- Framework Decision on simplifying the exchange of information and intelligence between law enforcement authorities of the Member States, in particular as regards serious offences including terrorist acts
- Directive on the retention of telecommunications traffic data

Proposed legislation

- Draft Framework Decision on information exchange under the principle of availability
- Draft Framework Decision on the processing of personal data in the framework of police and judicial cooperation
- Draft Framework Decision on Data Protection
- Proposal for a Council Decision on the implementation of specific measures for the transmission of information concerning and resulting from the activities of security and intelligence services with respect to terrorist offences

Report

- Interim report on the outcome of the process of peer evaluation on national arrangements in the fight against terrorism in the 15 Member States

[51] [22 Member States have reported that implementation is completed. The Commission plans to submit a report on the implementation by the end of 2006.]

- Final report on the outcome of the process of peer evaluation on national arrangements in the fight against terrorism covering the new Member States

Other

- The drawing up of common lists containing the most significant terrorists and terrorist organisations, which are regularly and appropriately updated
- All Member States are connected to the BDL

3.2 Impeding Terrorists' Movements and Activities

Adopted Legislation

- Council Framework Decision on the European arrest warrant and the surrender procedures between Member States (June 2002)

Other

- SitCen reports addressing among other issues preventing individuals from gaining access to terrorist training

3.3 Police Co-operation

Communications

- Communication: Towards enhancing access to information by law enforcement agencies

Adopted Legislation

- Council Decision on the implementation of specific measures for police and judicial cooperation to combat terrorism in accordance with Article 4 of Common Position 2001/931/CFSP
- Council Common Position on exchanging certain data with Interpol
- Council Decision establishing the European Police College (CEPOL)
- Framework Decision on Joint Investigation Teams[52]
- Council Decision of 20 September 2005 establishing the European Police College (CEPOL)

[52] According to a Commission report of January 2005, only the legislation of one Member State fully complies with the Framework Decision.

Proposed Legislation

- Proposal for a Council decision on the improvement of police cooperation between the Member States of the EU, especially at internal borders, and amending the Convention implementing the Schengen agreement
- Proposal for a Council Decision imposing on Member States specific obligations on the supply of information on terrorist organisations to Europol and Eurojust
- Proposal on the protection of personal data in the third pillar
- Proposal on the exchange of information under the principle of availability

Report

- Report from the Commission on the legal transposition of Council Decision of 28 February 2002 setting up Eurojust, with a view to reinforcing the fight against serious crime
- Report on the Terrorist attacks in Madrid from a law enforcement perspective
- Report on the implementation of the Framework decision on Joint Investigation Teams
- Joint report by CEPOL and Europol on what Counter-Terrorism related training they have so far provided and what more could be done

Other

- Europol/Eurojust Agreement (effective from 10 June 2004)
- Setting up of the Counter-Terrorism Task Force (CTTF) (Europol)
- Establishment of links between SitCen and Europol
- All Member States have designated their Eurojust national correspondent for terrorist matters
- Implementation of the Europol Information System (available in the 25 Member states since 10 October 2005)
- Development of the European Crime Intelligence Model with the assistance of the Police Chiefs Task Force

---

[53] According to a Commission report of January 2006, the legislation in Member States does not fully comply with the framework decision.

[54] OJL322, 9.12.2005, p. 33.

3.4 Judicial Co-operation

Communications

- White Paper on exchanges of information on convictions and the effect of such convictions in the European Union

Adopted Legislation

- Council Decision setting up Eurojust with a view to reinforcing the fight against serious crime
- Framework Decision on the European Arrest Warrant[53]
- Framework Decision on the Confiscation of crime related proceeds, instrumentalities and property
- Council Decision 2005/876/JHA of 21 November 2005 on the exchange of information extracted from the criminal record[54]

Proposed Legislation

- Proposal for a framework decision on the fight against organised crime to replace joint action 1998/733/JHA.
- Proposal for a Council framework decision on taking account of convictions in the Member States of the European Union in the course of new criminal proceedings.
- Draft Framework Decision on the application of the principle of mutual recognition to Confiscation Orders (when the remaining national parliamentary reservation is lifted).
- Draft Framework Decision on a European Evidence Warrant was proposed by COM in November 2003 and has not been decided, notwithstanding the Hague Programme deadline for adoption of December 2005.
- Proposal for a Council framework decision on the organisation and content of the exchange of information extracted from criminal records between Member States.

Reports

- Report by Eurojust on the measures the unit has implemented since December 2004 in the fight against terrorism
- Report on the transposition by the Member States of the Framework Decision on the Execution in the EU of orders freezing Property or Evidence

[55] This measure is partially achieved, as 13 Member States ratified the 2001 Protocol, which entered into force on 5 October 2005.

Other

- Convention on Mutual Assistance in Criminal Matters and its Protocol[55]
- All Member States have designated their Eurojust national correspondent for terrorist matters
- Network on national experts on Joint Investigation Teams established

3.5 International Dimension

Adopted Legislation

- Council Common Position on the transfer of certain data to Interpol

Other

- The UN Convention on the Suppression of Acts of Nuclear Terrorism was adopted 13 May 2005, and signed by all EU MS on 14 September 2005
- Establishment and development of contacts between the CFSP Working Group on Terrorism and the Counter-Terrorism Committee
- Establishment and development of contacts between the CFSP Working Group on Terrorism and the 1267 Committee
- Meeting at the Troika level with the US in order to enhance counter terrorism dialogue at political and official level
- The SG/HR document on integrating the fight against terrorism into EU external relations policy identifies additional concrete steps to enhance effectiveness of troika dialogues.
- Delivering of technical assistance to Morocco, Algeria and other countries in order to build their Counter-Terrorism capacity, working closely with UN and other donors

4. Respond

4.1 Civilian Rapid EU Response Capability to Deal with the Aftermath of a Terrorist Attack

Communications

- Communication on preparedness and consequence management in the fight against terrorism
- Communication on improving Community Civil Protection Mechanism
- Communication on Building Solidarity Through Mutual Assistance: Report on the assessment of civil protection assistance available through

the Community Civil Protection Mechanism in case of major terrorist attacks in the Union (EU Restricted)

Proposed Legislation

- Proposal for a regulation establishing a rapid response and preparedness instrument for major emergencies
- Proposal for a Council Decision establishing a Community Civil Protection Mechanism (recast)

Other

- Commission Matrix on deciding on health system vulnerabilities, prioritising and resource allocation for facing up to attacks and threats using particular pathogens
- A network of high-level of safety laboratories has been formed to provide quality-assured diagnostics for high-risk pathogens and for mutual assistance between all Member States to allow quick introduction of counter-measures
- Guidance on use of vaccines, antidotes and dilution of vaccinia immunoglobulins has been issued and negotiations on vaccines and anti-virals for pandemic influenza have started
- The 2002 CBRN-programme was replaced by the 2004 Solidarity Programme. The implementation of the programme is a continuous process
- The 2004 solidarity programme contains a report on the implementation of the 2002 CBRN-Programme

4.2 Military Rapid Response Capability to Deal with the Aftermath of a Terrorist Attack

Other

- Adaptation of the military database of assets and capabilities relevant to the protection of civilian populations against the effects of terrorist attacks (including CBRN) to reflect its expansion to all types of natural and man-made disasters
- The database of military assets and capabilities relevant to the protection of civilian population against the effects of terrorist attacks, including CBRN, has been made available to the Community Civil Protection Mechanism.

4.3. Early Warning of Terrorist Attacks and Capabilities to Coordinate Effectively the Management of the Response

Adopted Legislation

- Council Decision approving the conclusion of the Convention on Early Notification of a Nuclear Accident
- Commission Decision for accession to the Convention on Early Notification of a Nuclear Accident

Other

- The Programme on Health, Security aims at setting up EU cooperation and mutual assistance against biological or chemical attacks
- Establishment by the Community Civil Protection Mechanism of procedures for early warning, alert and activation of response through the central MIC
- RAS-BICHAT rapid alert system for deliberate releases of biological and chemical agents, improved co-operation with other alert mechanisms
- Set up of a RASCHEM — exchange of information and warnings between Poison Control Centres
- MediSYS, monitoring of Web-based information to provide advance, real-time, warning of suspicious circumstances or outbreaks
- Guidance on General preparedness and response planning and integration of EU dimension in all national health emergency plans is being prepared
- HEOF — Health emergency operations facility: improvement of the current crisis and communication centre
- Establishment of a secure general rapid alert system (ARGUS)

4.4 Assistance to Victims

Adopted Legislation

- EU Directives 2000/43/EC and 2000/78/EC protect people against discrimination on grounds of race, ethnic origin, religion and belief
- Council Directive on Compensation to crime victims

Report

- A memorial report dedicated to the victims of terrorism

Other

- A pilot project approved by the EP, allowing the Commission to spend respectively 1 and 2M€ in 2004 and in 2005 on projects aimed at raising public awareness and at improving the situation of victims of terrorism (7 projects for an amount of 1,1 M€ were granted)
- Declaring 11 March as a European day commemorating the victims of terrorism

4.5 International Dimension

Communications

- The Communication on preparedness and consequence management in the fight against terrorism

Other

- Sponsoring of an ISS seminar on the ESDP contribution to the fight against terrorism in the wider context of the EU approach in this field

4.6 Research

Other

- Restoring security in case of crisis: focusing on technologies in support of diverse emergency management operations (such as civil protection, humanitarian and rescue tasks, support to CFSP), and on issues such as inter-organisational co-ordination and communication, distributed architectures and human factors.

DOCUMENT NO. 8

THE EUROPEAN UNION COUNTER-TERRORISM STRATEGY

Report 14469/4/05 REV 4
Council of the European Union

Brussels, 30 November 2005

from:	Presidency and CT Co-ordinator
to:	Council/European Council
No. prev. doc.:	14469/3/05 REV 3 JAI 423 ECOFIN 353 TRANS 234 RELEX 639 ECO 136 PESC 1010 COTER 72 COSDP 810 PROCIV 174 ENER 172 ATO 103
Subject:	The European Union Counter-Terrorism Strategy

This document is being forwarded to the Council for agreement and will then be transmitted to the European Council for adoption.

* * *

THE EUROPEAN UNION COUNTER-TERRORISM STRATEGY

PREVENT PROTECT PURSUE RESPOND

The European Union's strategic commitment:
To combat terrorism globally while respecting human rights, and make Europe safer, allowing its citizens to live in an area of freedom, security and justice

The EU's Counter-Terrorism Strategy covers four strands of work, fitting under its strategic commitment:

STRATEGIC COMMITMENT

To combat terrorism globally while respecting human rights, and make Europe safer, allowing its citizens to live in an area of freedom, security and justice

PREVENT	PROTECT	PURSUE	RESPOND
To prevent people turning to terrorism by tackling the factors or root causes which can lead to radicalisation and recruitment, in Europe and internationally	To protect citizens and infrastructure and reduce our vulnerability to attack, including through improved security of borders, transport and critical infrastructure	To pursue and investigate terrorists across our borders and globally; to impede planning, travel, and communications; to disrupt support networks; to cut off funding and acccess to attack materials, and bring terrorists to justice	To prepare ourselves, in the spirit of solidarity, to manage and minimise the consequences of a terrorist attack, by improving capabilities to deal with: the aftermath; the co-ordination of the response; and the needs of victims

Member states have the primary responsibility for combating terrorism, and the EU can add value in four main ways:

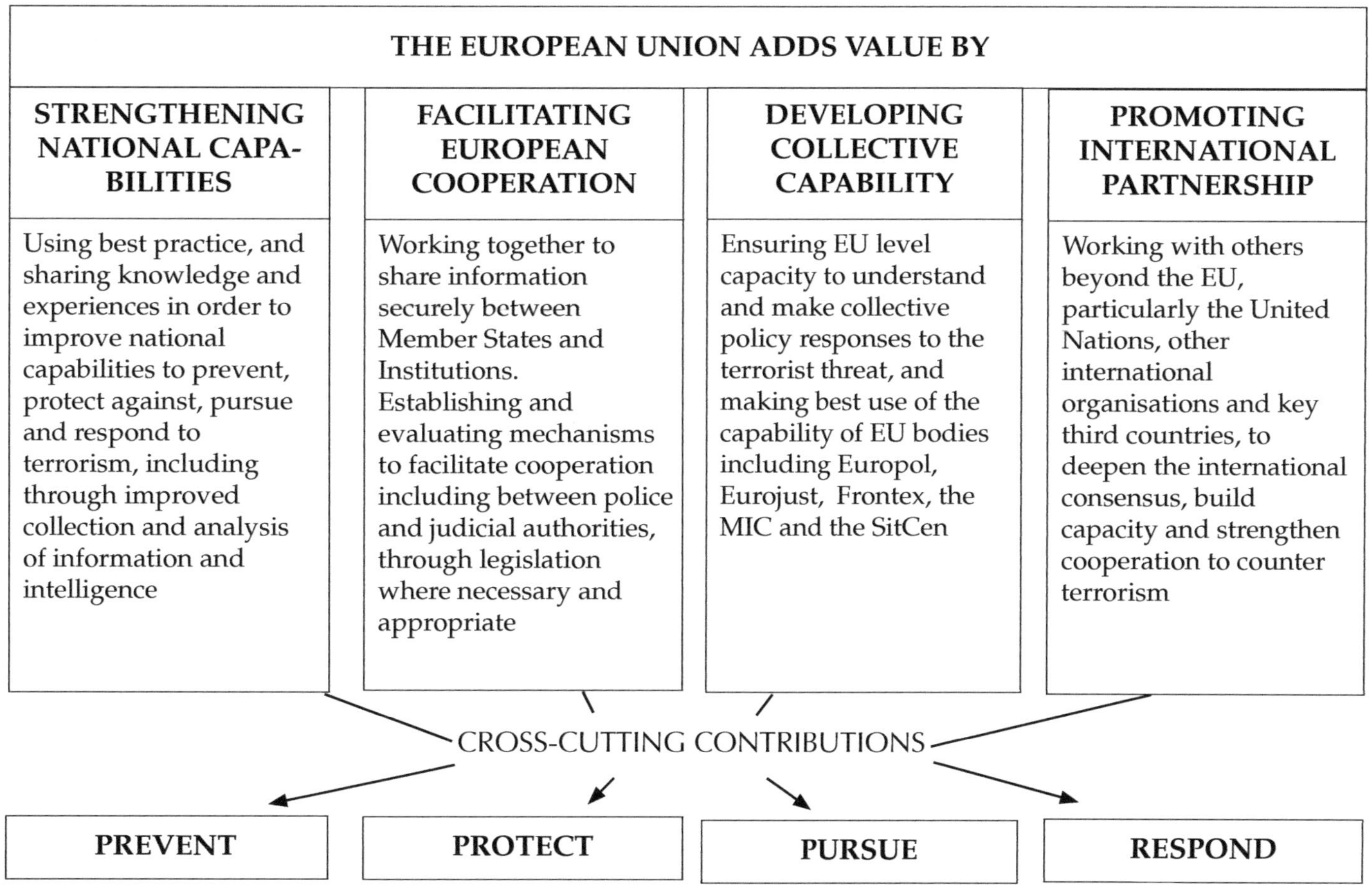

The EU should pursue its goals in a democratic and accountable way. Political oversight of the Strategy and regular follow-up will be essential:

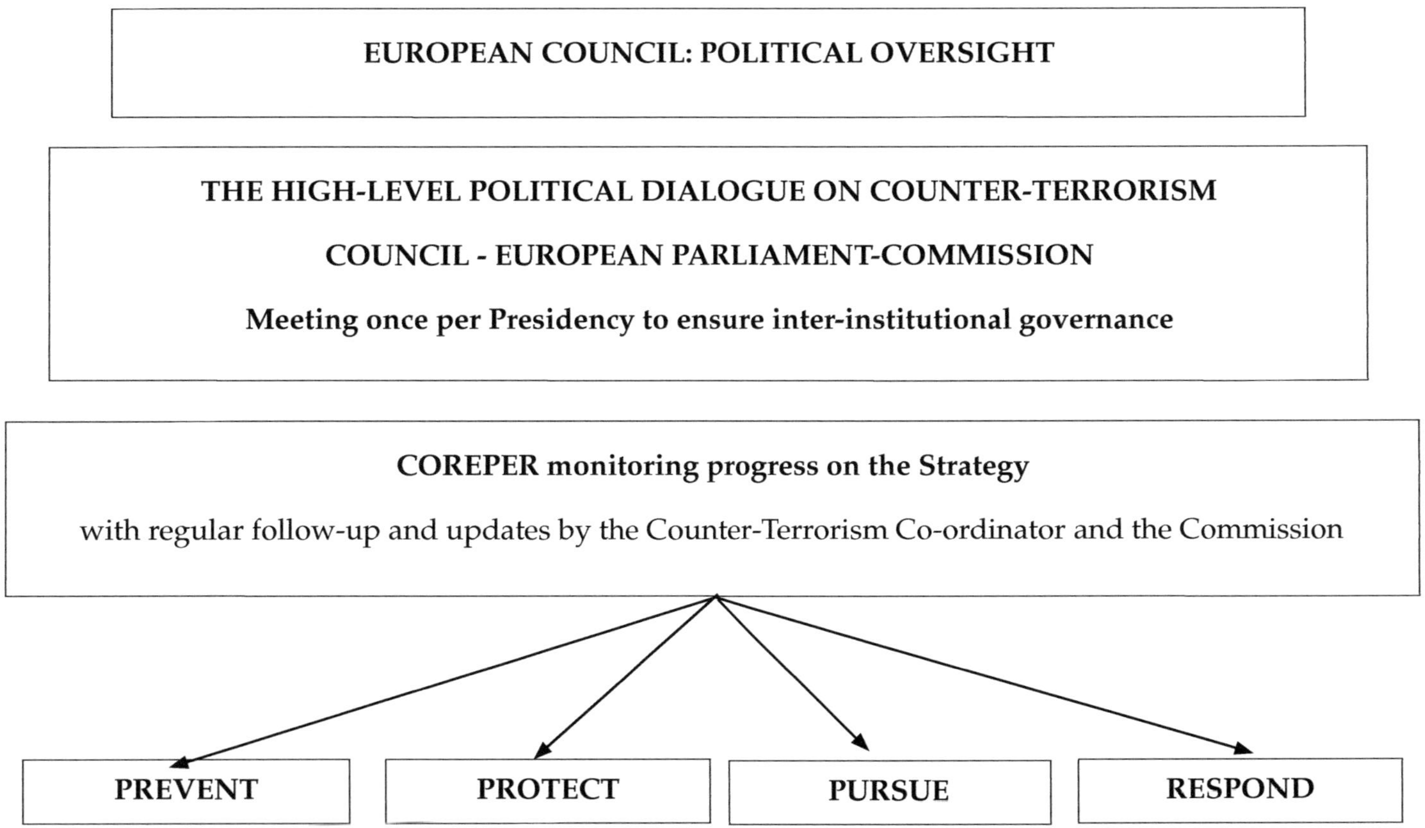

THE EU COUNTER-TERRORISM STRATEGY

PREVENT PROTECT PURSUE RESPOND

Strategic Commitment

To combat terrorism globally while respecting human rights, and make Europe safer, allowing its citizens to live in an area of freedom, security and justice

Introduction

1. Terrorism is a threat to all States and to all peoples. It poses a serious threat to our security, to the values of our democratic societies and to the rights and freedoms of our citizens, especially through the indiscriminate targeting of innocent people. Terrorism is criminal and unjustifiable under any circumstances.

2. The European Union is an area of increasing openness, in which the internal and external aspects of security are intimately linked. It is an area of increasing interdependence, allowing for free movement of people, ideas, technology and resources. This is an environment which terrorists abuse to pursue their objectives. In this context concerted and collective European action, in the spirit of solidarity, is indispensable to combat terrorism.

3. The four pillars of the EU's Counter-Terrorism Strategy—prevent, protect, pursue, and respond—constitute a comprehensive and proportionate response to the international terrorist threat. The Strategy requires work at national, European and international levels to reduce the threat from terrorism and our vulnerability to attack. The Strategy sets out our objectives to prevent new recruits to terrorism; better protect potential targets; pursue and investigate members of existing networks and improve our capability to respond to and manage the consequences of terrorist attacks. This Strategy takes into the next phase the agenda of work set out at the March 2004 European Council in the wake of the Madrid bombings.

4. Across the four pillars of the Union's Strategy a horizontal feature is the Union's role in the world. As set out in the European Security Strategy, through its external action the European Union takes on a responsibility for contributing to global security and building a safer world. Acting through and in conjunction with the United Nations and other international or regional organisations, the EU will work to build the international consensus and promote international standards for countering terrorism. The EU will promote efforts in the UN to develop a global strategy for

combating terrorism. Continuing to make counter-terrorism a high priority in dialogue with key partner countries, including the USA, will also be a core part of the European approach.

5. Given that the current international terrorist threat affects and has roots in many parts of the world beyond the EU, co-operation with and the provision of assistance to priority third countries—including in North Africa, the Middle East and South East Asia—will be vital. Finally, working to resolve conflicts and promote good governance and democracy will be essential elements of the Strategy, as part of the dialogue and alliance between cultures, faiths and civilisations, in order to address the motivational and structural factors underpinning radicalisation.

Prevent

6. In order to prevent people from turning to terrorism and to stop the next generation of terrorists from emerging, the EU has agreed a comprehensive strategy and action plan for combating radicalisation and recruitment into terrorism. This strategy focuses on countering radicalisation and recruitment to terrorist groups such as Al Qaeda and the groups it inspires, given that this type of terrorism currently represents the main threat to the Union as a whole.

7. Terrorism can never be justified. There can be no excuse or impunity for terrorist acts. The vast majority of Europeans, irrespective of belief, do not accept extremist ideologies. Even amongst the small number that do, only a few turn to terrorism. The decision to become involved in terrorism varies from one individual to another, even though the motives behind such a decision are often similar. We must identify and counter the methods, propaganda and conditions through which people are drawn into terrorism.

8. The challenge of combating radicalisation and terrorist recruitment lies primarily with the Member States, at a national, regional and local level. However, EU work in this field, including the contribution of the European Commission, can provide an important framework to help co-ordinate national policies; share information and determine good practice. But addressing this challenge is beyond the power of governments alone and will require the full engagement of all populations in Europe and beyond.

9. There are practical steps an individual must take to become involved in terrorism. The ability to put ideas into action has been greatly enhanced by globalisation: ease of travel, transfer of money and communication—including through the internet—mean easier access to radical ideas and training. We need to spot such behaviour for example through community policing and monitoring travel to conflict zones. We also need to disrupt such behaviour by: limiting the activities of those playing a role in radicalisation; preventing access to terrorist training; establishing a strong legal

framework to prevent incitement and recruitment; and examining ways to impede terrorist recruitment through the internet.

10. The propagation of a particular extremist worldview brings individuals to consider and justify violence. In the context of the most recent wave of terrorism, for example, the core of the issue is propaganda which distorts conflicts around the world as a supposed proof of a clash between the West and Islam. To address these issues, we need to ensure that voices of mainstream opinion prevail over those of extremism by engaging with civil society and faith groups that reject the ideas put forward by terrorists and extremists that incite violence. And we need to get our own message across more effectively, to change the perception of national and European policies. We must also ensure that our own policies do not exacerbate division. Developing a non-emotive lexicon for discussing the issues will support this.

11. There is a range of conditions in society which may create an environment in which individuals can become more easily radicalised. These conditions include poor or autocratic governance; rapid but unmanaged modernisation; lack of political or economic prospects and of educational opportunities. Within the Union these factors are not generally present but in individual segments of the population they may be. To counter this, outside the Union we must promote even more vigorously good governance, human rights, democracy as well as education and economic prosperity, and engage in conflict resolution. We must also target inequalities and discrimination where they exist and promote inter-cultural dialogue and long-term integration where appropriate.

12. Radicalisation and recruitment is an international phenomenon. There is much we can do with our partners overseas to assist them in combating radicalisation, including through co-operation and assistance programmes with third countries and work through international organisations.

13. Key priorities for 'Prevent' are to:

- Develop common approaches to spot and tackle problem behaviour, in particular the misuse of the internet;
- Address incitement and recruitment in particular in key environments, for example prisons, places of religious training or worship, notably by implementing legislation making these behaviours offences;
- Develop a media and communication strategy to explain better EU policies;
- Promote good governance, democracy, education and economic prosperity through Community and Member State assistance programmes;
- Develop inter-cultural dialogue within and outside the Union;

- Develop a non-emotive lexicon for discussing the issues;
- Continue research, share analysis and experiences in order to further our understanding of the issues and develop policy responses.

Protect

14. Protection is a key part of our Counter Terrorism Strategy. We must strengthen the defences of key targets, by reducing their vulnerability to attack, and also by reducing the resulting impact of an attack.

15. While Member States have the primary responsibility for improving the protection of key targets, the interdependency of border security, transport and other cross-border infrastructures require effective EU collective action. In areas where EU-level security regimes exist, such as border and transport security, the EU and European Commission in particular have played an important role in raising standards. Further work between Member States, with the support of the European institutions, will provide an important framework in which Member States are able to co-ordinate their policies, share information about responses developed at national level, determine good practice, and work together to develop new ideas.

16. We need to enhance protection of our external borders to make it harder for known or suspected terrorists to enter or operate within the EU. Improvements in technology for both the capture and exchange of passenger data, and the inclusion of biometric information in identity and travel documents, will increase the effectiveness of our border controls and provide greater assurance to our citizens. The European Borders Agency (Frontex) will have a role in providing risk assessment as part of the effort to strengthen controls and surveillance at the EU's external border. The establishment of the Visa Information System and second generation Schengen Information System will ensure that our authorities can share and access information and if necessary deny access to the Schengen area.

17. We also must work collectively to raise standards in transport security. We must enhance the protection of airports, seaports, and aircraft security arrangements in order to deter terrorist attacks and address the vulnerabilities in domestic and overseas transport operations. These measures will be developed by a combination of specific assessments of threat and vulnerability, the implementation of agreed EU legislation on aviation and maritime security, and the agreement of revised EU legislation on aviation security. There is also scope for working together to increase road and rail security. To support work in all of these fields, EU research and development policy including the European Commission's R&D programmes should continue to include security related research in the context of terrorism.

18. Reducing the vulnerability across Europe of critical infrastructure to physical and electronic attack is essential. To further enhance our protection, we agreed to establish a Programme of work aimed at improving the protection of critical infrastructure across Europe. We will continue work to this end, developing an all hazard approach which recognises the threat from terrorism as a priority.

19. We must also ensure that our collective work, and particularly EU research efforts, contribute to developing methodologies for protecting crowded places and other soft targets from attacks.

20. Internationally, we must work with partners and international organisations on transport security, and non-proliferation of CBRN materials and small arms/light weapons, as well as provide technical assistance on protective security to priority third countries as a component of our wider technical assistance programmes.

21. Key priorities for 'Protect' are to:

- Deliver improvements to the security of EU passports through the introduction of biometrics;
- Establish the Visa Information System (VIS) and the second generation Schengen Information System (SISII);
- Develop through Frontex effective risk analysis of the EU's external border;
- Implement agreed common standards on civil aviation, port and maritime security;
- Agree a European programme for critical infrastructure protection;
- Make best use of EU and Community level research activity.

Pursue

22. We will further strengthen and implement our commitments to disrupt terrorist activity and pursue terrorists across borders. Our objectives are to impede terrorists' planning, disrupt their networks and the activities of recruiters to terrorism, cut off terrorists' funding and access to attack materials, and bring them to justice, while continuing to respect human rights and international law.

23. As agreed in the Hague Programme, when preserving national security, Member States will also focus on the security of the Union as a whole. The Union will support the efforts of Member States to disrupt terrorists by encouraging the exchange of information and intelligence between them, providing common analyses of the threat, and strengthening operational co-operation in law enforcement.

24. At national level the competent authorities need to have the necessary tools to collect and analyse intelligence and to pursue and investigate terrorists, requiring Member States to update their policy response and legislative provisions where necessary. In this respect our common aim is to follow up and take full account of the recommendations identified during the EU's peer evaluation process. Member States will report back on how they have improved their national capabilities and machinery in light of these recommendations.

25. Developing a common understanding of the threat is fundamental to developing common policies to respond to it. The Joint Situation Centre's assessments, based on the contributions of national security and intelligence agencies and Europol, should continue to inform decisions across the range of the EU's policies.

26. Instruments such as the European Arrest Warrant are proving to be important tools in pursuing and investigating terrorists across borders. Priority should now be given to other practical measures in order to put into practice the principle of mutual recognition of judicial decisions. A key measure is the European Evidence Warrant, which will enable Member States to obtain evidence from elsewhere in the EU to help convict terrorists. Member States should also improve further the practical co-operation and information exchange between police and judicial authorities, in particular through Europol and Eurojust. In addition, Joint Investigation Teams should be established where necessary for cross-border investigations. Evaluation of the implementation of legislative measures will be important and will inform further work, and Member States should ensure that they implement agreed European measures as well as ratify relevant international Treaties and Conventions, to ensure an appropriate legislative response to the threat.

27. To move from ad hoc to systematic police co-operation, one important step will be developing and putting into practice the principle of availability of law enforcement information. In addition, the development of new IT systems such as the Visa Information System and the next generation Schengen Information System, while safeguarding data protection, should provide improved access to those authorities responsible for internal security thereby widening the base of information at their disposal. Consideration should also be given to developing common approaches to the sharing of information on potential terrorists and on individuals deported for terrorism-related offences.

28. Terrorists must also be deprived of the means by which they mount attacks—whether directly (eg weapons and explosives) or indirectly (eg false documentation to enable undetected travel and residence). Their ability to communicate and plan undetected should be impeded by measures

such as the retention of telecommunications data. They must also be deprived as far as possible of the opportunities offered by the Internet to communicate and spread technical expertise related to terrorism.

29. Creating a hostile operating environment for terrorists also means tackling terrorist financing. The EU has already put in place provisions for freezing terrorist assets. The next stage is to implement the EU-wide legislation concerning money laundering and cash transfers, and to agree steps to impede money (wire) transfers by terrorists. In addition, tackling the misuse of the non-profit sector remains a priority. We must also ensure that financial investigation is an integral part of all terrorism investigations. These measures and others which build on the Financial Action Task Force's recommendations, form part of the EU's comprehensive strategy for combating terrorist financing. A review of the EU's performance against terrorist financing is currently being conducted to ensure our approach is kept up to date.

30. Much of the terrorist threat to Europe originates outside the EU. 'Pursue' must therefore also have a global dimension. The EU will work to reinforce the international consensus through the United Nations and other international bodies and through dialogue and agreements (which include counter-terrorism clauses) with key partners, and will work for agreement of a UN Comprehensive Convention against Terrorism. Assistance will be provided to priority countries to help them introduce and implement the necessary mechanisms to disrupt terrorism, in coordination with the work of other donors.

31. Key priorities on 'Pursue' are to:

- Strengthen national capabilities to combat terrorism, in light of the recommendations of the peer evaluation of national anti-terrorism arrangements;
- Make full use of Europol and Eurojust to facilitate police and judicial cooperation, and continue to integrate the Joint Situation Centre's threat assessments into CT policy making;
- Further develop mutual recognition of judicial decisions, including by adopting the European Evidence Warrant;
- Ensure full implementation and evaluation of existing legislation as well as the ratification of relevant international Treaties and Conventions;
- Develop the principle of availability of law enforcement information;
- Tackle terrorist access to weapons and explosives, ranging from components for homemade explosive to CBRN material;

- Tackle terrorist financing, including by implementing agreed legislation, working to prevent the abuse of the non-profit sector, and reviewing the EUs overall performance in this area;
- Deliver technical assistance to enhance the capability of priority third countries.

Respond

32. We cannot reduce the risk of terrorist attacks to zero. We have to be able to deal with attacks when they occur, recognising that attacks can have effects across EU borders. The response to an incident will often be similar whether that event is natural, technological or man-made, hence the response systems in place to manage the consequences of natural disasters may also be used to alleviate the effects on citizens in the aftermath of a terrorist attack. Our response to any such events should make full use of the existing structures, including the Civil Protection Mechanism, which the EU has developed to respond to other major European and international crises, and be co-ordinated with the action of other international organisations involved.

33. In the event of an incident with cross border effects there will be a need for rapid sharing of operational and policy information, media co-ordination and mutual operational support, drawing on all available means, including military resources. The ability of the EU to take consistent or collective action will also be essential to an effective and efficient response. The development of EU crisis co-ordination arrangements, supported by the necessary operational procedures, will help ensure the coherence of the EU response to terrorist attacks.

34. Member States have the lead role in providing the emergency response to a terrorist incident on their territory. Nevertheless, there remains a need to ensure that the EU collectively, supported by the European Institutions including the Commission, has the capability to respond in solidarity to an extreme emergency which might overwhelm the resources of a single Member State, and could constitute a serious risk to the Union as a whole. Reviewing and revising the current framework for mutual support—the Community Mechanism for civil protection—is important in ensuring this safeguard.

35. Developing a risk based approach to capability assessment—focusing on preparing for those events which are judged most likely to occur, and which would have the greatest impact—will enable Member States to develop their capabilities to respond in the event of an emergency. The shared EU database listing the resources and assets which Member States might be able to contribute to dealing with such events in other Member States or overseas complements this work.

36. The solidarity, assistance and compensation of the victims of terrorism and their families constitutes an integral part of the response to terrorism at national and European level. Member States should ensure that appropriate compensation is available to victims. Through sharing of best practice on national arrangements, and the development of contact between national victims' associations, the European Commission will enable the EU to take steps to enhance the support offered to those who most suffer from terrorist attacks.

37. Internationally, there is a need to provide assistance to EU citizens in third countries and to protect and assist our military and civilian assets on EU crisis management operations. We should also ensure that our work on disaster response is closely co-ordinated with related work in international organisations and in particular the United Nations. Finally, the technical assistance provided by the EU to priority third countries will need to factor in assistance on managing the consequences of terrorist attacks.

38. Key priorities on 'Respond' are to:

- Agree EU Crisis Co-ordination Arrangements and the supporting operational procedures for them;
- Revise the legislation on the Community Mechanism for civil protection;
- Develop risk assessment as a tool to inform the building of capabilities to respond to an attack;
- Improve co-ordination with international organisations on managing the response to terrorist attacks and other disasters;
- Share best practice and develop approaches for the provision of assistance to victims of terrorism and their families.

Democratic Accountability

39. The European Council will review progress on the Strategy once every six months.

40. Once per Presidency, and ahead of the European Council's review of progress, a High Level Political Dialogue on Counter-Terrorism, bringing together the Council, European Commission, and European Parliament, will meet to allow the three Institutions to consider progress together and promote transparency and balance in the EU's approach.

41. This Strategy will be complemented by a detailed Action Plan listing all the relevant measures under the four strands of this strategy. This will allow for detailed progress to be monitored on a regular basis by the Committee of Permanent Representatives, with regular follow-up and updates from the Counter-Terrorism Co-ordinator and the European Commission.

DOCUMENT NO. 9

FINANCING A PILOT PROJECT CONTAINING A SET OF PREPARATORY ACTIONS WITH A VIEW TO STRENGTHEN THE FIGHT AGAINST TERRORISM

Draft Commission Decision
The Commission of the European Community

Brussels, 15 September 2005

THE COMMISSION OF THE EUROPEAN COMMUNITIES,

Having regard to the Treaty establishing the European Community,

Having regard to Council Regulation (EC, Euratom) N° 1605/2002 of 25 June 2002 on the Financial Regulation applicable to the general budget of the European Communities,[1] hereafter referred to as the Financial Regulation and, in particular, article 110 thereof,

Having regard to Commission Regulation (EC, Euratom) N° 2342/2002 of 23 December 2002,[2] laying down detailed rules for the implementation of Council Regulation (EC, Euratom) n° 1605/2002 on the Financial Regulation applicable to the general budget of the European Communities in particular, article 166 thereof

Whereas:

(1) Article 18 05 06 of the 2005 general budget of the European Union for the financial year 2005 has established a pilot project for the fight against terrorism, to further improve the security of citizens, in particular by filling the gaps between existing activities;

(2) On 25 March of 2004 the European Council adopted a Declaration on the Fight against terrorism setting strategic objectives for the Union's fight against terrorism and at that and subsequent meetings has set priorities for the Union's action in this important field;

[1] OJ L 248–16.9.2002, p. 1.
[2] OJ L 357–31.12.2002, p. 1.

(3) The European Revised Action Plan on Fighting Terrorism of June 2004 identifies numerous measures required in this area and the Commission responsibility for proposing and/or undertaking many of those;

(4) On 20 October 2004 the Commission has adopted a set of four Communications on the Prevention, Preparedness and response to terrorist attacks, including the protection of critical infrastructure. These contain a number of important proposals including on the establishment of new capabilities such as the rapid alert systems on critical infrastructures (CIWIN) and the law enforcement network (LEN). These Communications were positively received by the Council and the European Council in respective conclusions of 13 and 17 December 2004;

(5) Activities foreseen by Council Decision 1999/847 of 9 December 1999 and Council Decision 2001/792 of 23 October 2001 are excluded from the scope of the present Decision

(6) The Secretary General/High Representative and the Commission presented to the European Council of December 2004 a report outlining an EU strategy for the fight against terrorist financing. The paper includes a series of recommendations for further action by the Member States, the Commission and other stakeholders.

(7) At the invitation of the Council and European Council, in conformity with the revised action plan on fighting terrorism and the Hague programme, the Commission has adopted on 19 July 2005 a Communication on the subject of explosives and firearms and is currently finalising one additional Communication on violent radicalisation and the recruitment of terrorists;

(8) Grants are subject to an annual programme, published at the start of the financial year, in conformity with Article 110 of the Financial Regulation and Article 166 of its implementing rules.

(9) Under Article 15 of the internal rules on the implementation of the 2005 budget, the appropriations which may be implemented without basic act, in conformity with Article 49, paragraph 2 of the Financial Regulation, must however be subject to a framework equivalent to a financing decision adopted by the Commission.

(10) Under Article 166 of the implementing rules of the Financial Regulation, the annual work programme for grants is adopted by the Commission. It specifies the basic act, the objectives and the schedule of calls for proposals with the indicative amount and the results expected.

HAS ADOPTED THIS DECISION:

Article 1

The actions and activities which jointly constitute this Pilot Project aim to tap into the full potential of the fight against terrorism and to speed up the Community's activities to further improve the security of citizens and to combat terrorism, in particular by filling the gaps between the various existing Community activities.

Article 2

The Pilot Project is hereby adopted. The budget lines and actions covered by this decision are described in the annex. They will focus in particular on:

- Mobilising, preparing and informing the public on terrorism;
- Supporting a civic and democratic debate on "fighting terrorism, securing freedom";
- Improving the understanding and monitoring of violent radicalisation and terrorism and supporting positive preventive measures involving civil society actors, e.g. in the social, religious, education and communication fields;
- Capacity building and technological enhancement of public stakeholders
- Linking up the law enforcement community to a facility for information and crisis management to be established in Directorate General Justice Freedom and Security, notably by means of the Law Enforcement Network (LEN) and, as appropriate, the Critical Infrastructure Warning and Information Network (CIWIN);
- Supporting the forthcoming European Programme for critical Infrastructure Protection
- Supporting a Public-Private Security Dialogue on measures required in the prevention, preparedness and response to terrorisms which require active participation from the Private sector, including in the protection of critical infrastructure;
- Creating and developing exchange of experiences and best practices in the field of resilience enhancement activities and crisis management related to terrorist attacks;
- Enhancing understanding of the effectiveness of current and envisaged activities in the fight against the financing of terrorism.
- Studies on violent radicalisation and terrorism in Europe;
- Supporting cooperation with international partners

Done at Brussels,

For the Commission

Member of the Commission

Work Programme 2005

1. Introduction

The actions and activities undertaken by the Commission in the course of 2005 respond in particular to the strategic objectives set in the European Council declaration on terrorism of 25 March 2004 and the need to implement the relevant actions contained in the EU revised Action Plan on Fighting terrorism adopted in June 2004. Most of the specific activities to be financed under the current financing decision aim to prepare actions proposed or announced by the Commission in the four October 2004 Communications on the "Prevention, preparedness and response to terrorist attacks" and which were endorsed by the Council and by the European Council in their respective conclusions of December 2004.

1.1. General Objectives

The General objective of this Decision, as defined in the budgetary description of the article, is to tap the full potential of the fight against terrorism and to speed up the Community's activities to further improve the security of citizens and to combat terrorism, in particular by filling the gaps between the various existing Community activities.

1.2. Specific Objectives

More specifically, the objectives for the fight against terrorism are:

(a) Preparing and Informing the Public

Objective: to raise public awareness and involvement on the importance of countering terrorism by defending the principles of democracy, peace, tolerance, diversity, respect for human rights, and the rule of law as well as conducting information campaigns on consequence management in the event of a terrorist attack of any kind. Importance in this regard will be given to the role played by the media.

(b) Linking Up the Law Enforcement Community

Objective: to improve communications between law enforcement authorities and between them and the capacity for information and crisis management to be established in the Directorate General for Justice, Freedom and Security in order to allow them to exchange information that is vital for the effective prevention, preparedness and response to a terrorist attack, particularly for attacks having cross-border effects and—in the event of a crisis—to contribute to and draw on the information and analysis available.

(c) Capacity Building and Technological Enhancement of Public Stakeholders

Objective: to identify technical solutions to enable effective exchange of information between the different Crisis Management facilities in the Commission and establish a law enforcement related information and crisis management capacity in DG JLS, enhance protection of critical infrastructure and conduct studies to support EU policy initiatives as well as the integration of open source information both in rapid alert and crisis management.

(d) Public-Private Security Dialogue

Objective: to engage the private sector as a valuable potential player for the EU in the prevention of, and in the preparedness and response to, terrorism, including the protection of critical infrastructure.

(e) Strengthening the Fight against the Financing of Terrorism

Objective: to evaluate the current and planned initiatives in the fight against the financing of terrorism as set out in the joint strategy paper presented to the December 2004 European Council in the context also of international standards of the Financial Action Task Force.

Account will be taken of the Regulation adopted by the Council on 12 July 2005 aimed at strengthening directive 91/308/EEC on the prevention of the use of the financial system for money laundering, in order to better combat terrorist financing by providing a common system for the controls of cash entering or leaving the Community.

(f) Supporting Studies in Social Sciences

Objective: supporting and ensuring an integrated approach to studies in social sciences in Europe, notably in the areas of violent radicalisation and terrorism

(g) International cooperation

Objective: to share expertise and practices with third countries and organisations.

Under several of the above areas, the Commission will endeavour to address some factors that could act as catalysts for the emergence of terrorism, such as poverty and social exclusion, to promote good governance and transparency in the financial, fiscal and judicial areas, and to improve the security of citizens including ensuring their security of life, property, political, economic and social rights

(h) Supporting the European Programme for Critical Infrastructure Protection

Objective: supporting the identification and development of measures to protect critical infrastructure; including the development and refinement of methodologies

1.3. Actions and Priorities for 2005

General details as to how the following actions will be implemented (e.g. through tendering etc) can be found further below

- **Linking up the law enforcement community**
  - Conduct feasibility studies on **a European law enforcement network (LEN)** linked to the Commission's Crisis management systems (see below), to serve the law enforcement community in the EU.
- **Capacity building and technological enhancement of public actors**
  - **Interconnecting the Commission's Crisis Rooms, rapid alert and response systems** with a view to emergencies requiring action at European level. This will respect the specific characteristics, competence and expertise of the individual and specialised systems already managed by the Commission which will continue to carry out their current functions;
  - **Establishment of a capacity for information and crisis management of the DG Justice, Freedom and Security (JLS).** The above will not affect the competencies on the internal measures concerning the security of the Commission's personnel, buildings and infrastructures.
  - Preparation of an **EU Critical infrastructure Warning Information Network (CIWIN)** to be established by the Commission to assist Member States, and owners and operators of critical infrastructure to exchange information on shared threats, vulnerabilities and appropriate measures and strategies to mitigate risk in support of critical infrastructure protection, particularly infrastructure whose disruption or destruction could cause cross-border effects. This network will complement existing ones and due care will be taken to avoid duplication.
  - Launching of pilot **networks of scientific and technological experts** from both public and private sector institutions with a view notably to support development of EU policy initiatives and rapid response advice on security concerns, such as a Network of experts on Violent Radicalisation and Terrorism or a Network of institutes and research centres on the economics of security;

- Engagement of experts and academics from various fields in order to support and complement the Commission's analysis of the factors contributing to violent **radicalisation and recruitment to terrorism** that will result in a Commission contribution to the Council.
- Engagement of experts and academics in assessing the effectiveness of the **fight against the financing of terrorism** as set out in the joint strategy paper presented to the December 2004 European Council in the context also of international standards of the Financial Action Task Force, including the identification of new initiatives which may be necessary such as in view of the implementation of the new Regulation on controls of cash entering or leaving the Community and the prioritisation of areas indicated in the joint strategy paper.

- **Public-Private Security Dialogue**
  - Setting up specific Joint Public-Private Task Forces to work on issues such as the security enhancement of explosives and detonators from design to end use and on a European modular detection portal concept.
- **Involving, preparing and informing the citizens**
  - Development of an internet Forum on "Fighting Terrorism; Securing Freedom" and related initiatives through other media aiming at greater civic awareness, involvement and informed debate of citizens and civil society on counter-terrorism policy in democratic, open and free societies.
  - Development of relevant information material destined for the general public and particular groups, notably youth.
  - Examining, in cooperation with private sector operators, ways and means including technologies/techniques for real time information of the public in incident management (e.g. cell phone broadcasts).
- **International cooperation**
  - Pilot programme on sharing expertise and practices with experts of third country which are not eligible for financing under the Stability Instrument, e.g. on scientific police, forensic and cyber security techniques and risk-selection criteria. This will be conducted in cooperation with CEPOL, Europol or Eurojust.

1.4. Target Groups

The Commission will be in charge of respective capacity building and technological enhancement. Member States will manage pilot projects on critical infrastructure protection.

Representatives of private sector federations, sectors and operators will participate in different initiatives.

Scientific and academic experts, researchers and other relevant professional categories—e.g. media professionals, internet service providers, banking community, etc) will play important roles in various initiatives.

Citizens in general and organised civil society will be the target for several awareness raising, information and involvement activities, for example in topics relating to victims and youth.

1.5. Monitoring and Evaluation

The preparatory work for the inter-connexion and creation of networks (including LEN and CIWIN) will be monitored by the Commission to ensure that the goals for which the networks will be created are reached: involvement of law enforcement authorities via LEN and interconnection between critical structure warning information systems of the Member States via CIWIN. Use of resources allocated to Member States' institutions will be monitored by the Commission.

The overall results of the pilot project will be subject to a final evaluation to be conducted jointly with Member States experts on the different areas of prevention, preparedness and response to terrorist attacks.

2. Annual Work Programme 2005

2.1. Grants

Amount allocated for grants: 3.350.000€

EPCIP (European Program for Critical Infrastructure Protection)

Amount allocated on the basis of calls for proposals: 3.000.000€

Grants will be notably given to Member States' authorities responsible for the protection of critical infrastructures, relevant national and EU research institutions and the operators of such infrastructures for the purpose of funding pilot projects that have a potential for transferability at EU level in the field of security oriented critical infrastructure protection. Themes will include:

- Enhancement of protection measures for critical infrastructure
- Vulnerabilities and resilience of critical infrastructure, including developing methodologies
- Risk mitigation strategies and threat assessments for critical infrastructure
- Development of contingency plans
- Development of common security standards and innovative technologies for protection of critical infrastructure

- Trans-national projects, which must involve partners in at least two Member States, or at least one Member State and an applicant country

This EU contribution to the cost of the activities concerned will be limited to 85% of all eligible costs.

Emergency Actions

Amount allocated for grants: 350.000€

Grants will be given, without a call for proposals and in the terms of article 168 of the Implementing Rules, to activities related to the study and preparation of urgent measures by the Union in the event of a significant terrorist threat or attack.

The EU contribution to the cost of the activities concerned may cover the totality of eligible costs.

2.2. Open Calls for Tenders

Amount Allocated to Open Calls for Tenders

The amount allocated to these calls call for tenders will be € 2.100.000

Type and Object of Call for Tenders (e.g. Studies, Technical Assistance)

2.2.1. Interconnection of Commission Crisis Rooms and existing rapid alert and response systems and establishment of LEN and CIWIN

A call for tender (800.000€) will be made for a service contract to:

(1) Study the technical specifications of the existing rapid alert and response systems in order to develop a solution for the interconnection of Commission Crisis Rooms and existing rapid alert and response systems allowing a possible future interface with the national crisis management systems of the Member States and of other EU institutions. It will specifically include[3]

(a) Interconnection of Commission Crisis Rooms and existing rapid alert and response systems

- The definition of the technical specifications of the required hardware and software;
- Analysis, development and/or adaptation of software;

(2) Study the technical aspects required to develop an IT solution for the LEN and for connecting each as appropriate with existing systems. It will specifically include:

[3] The detailed terms of reference for the technical studies will be submitted to and agreed by services concerned.

- The identification of the appropriate location for hosting LEN, more particularly whether to host it in Europol, JLS or another location based on existing systems in the Member States
- The identification of the hardware and software necessary to install and run the system
- The possible development of a prototype software IT solution for the logistical interface of LEN
- The identification of the security specifications required for an electronically and physically protected space to host LEN

(3) study the technical aspects required to develop an IT solution for the logistical interface of CIWDST and for connecting it with existing systems. It will specifically include:

- The identification of the hardware and software necessary to install and run the system
- The development and testing of a functional prototype of the CIWIN system
- The identification of the security specifications required for an electronically and physically protected space to host CIWIN

2.2.2. Studies on "Violent Radicatisation and Terrorism" and on "financing of terrorism"

A call for tenders, will be launched (500.000€) for:

(1) Studies (450.000€) on "violent radicalisation and terrorism" on themes that will include *inter alia:*[4]

- Motivation and desisting factors for violent radicalisation
- Socio-economic factors contributing to violent radicalisation

(2) A study (50.000€) to evaluate the effectiveness of the fight against the financing of terrorism as set out in the joint strategy paper presented to the December 2004 European Council and in the context also of international standards of the Financial Action Task Force. The study will also address the possible identification of new initiatives which may be necessary in the fight against the financing of terrorism and the prioritisation of areas indicated in the joint strategy paper.

[4] The detailed definition of the areas to be covered will be finalised in accordance with the Commission Communication on Violet radicalisation and the recruitment of terrorist and subsequent inter-institutional work on the subject.

2.2.3. Meetings and Conferences

A call for tenders (800.000€) will be made for the organisation of conferences, meetings and workshops:

1. *General subjects (400.000€). i.a:*

Explosives: to engage the private sector with a view to a possible public-private plan on the security enhancement of explosives, detonators and related technologies, following the related Commission Communication.

Detection technologies: to explore the need for an EU initiative. Other conferences or seminars of this type may be organised depending on the remaining budget allocated.

Radicalisation: on aspects of violent radicalisation and recruitment to terrorism, possibly drawing on topics identified by the network of European experts be established through other funds, e.g. with media.

Communication with the public during emergency or crisis situations: to gather officials in the field of public safety and emergency communications services to facilitate a more permanent dialogue between emergency service operators and authorities on:

- interoperable systems for emergency handling; and
- innovative concepts for public warning systems and procedures

2. *Cooperation with international partners (400.000€)*

The above contract will also enable the Commission to support the organisation of workshops (which could, in substance, significantly draw upon the expertise and actively involve respectively CEPOL, Eurojust or Europol) aimed at exchanging practices and experiences between EU and member states authorities and practitioners and counterparts from third countries, regions or organisation on topics related to combating terrorism, which may include one or more of the following themes:

- Law enforcement cooperation, including police, customs and judicial cooperation to combat terrorism and enhanced cooperation between judges and prosecutors
- Development of inter-agency coordination at strategic and operational level in police, security and intelligence services
- Improving exchange of information and intelligence between law enforcement authorities to ensure that all relevant criminal intelligence related to terrorism is addressed as soon as it is available
- Maximise capacity to detect, investigate and prosecute terrorists and prevent terrorist attacks
- Role of border management and data protection in the fight against terrorism

- Incorporation of biometric features into passports and visas
- Cooperation in the fight against financing of terrorism, including money laundering, freezing of assets and implementation of the special recommendations of the Financial Action Task Force (FATF)
- Adequate protection of witnesses in terrorist cases
- Fighting the use of internet by terrorists for terrorist purposes
- Shared development of intelligence gathering and threat analysis techniques
- Shared development of special investigation techniques (communication interception, technical and human surveillance etc)
- Issues of common interest for EU and US in the fight against terrorism
- "Root causes"

2.3. Framework Contracts, Restricted Tenders and Direct Procurement

The amount allocated to these type of expenditure will be € 1.550.000

Type and Object of Expenditures (Studies, Technical Assistance, . . .)

2.3.1. Establishment of an internet based Forum on Securing Freedom (including a youth forum)[5]

Funds will be used by JLS (200.000€) to:

- Develop the design, architecture, and content of the referred multi language Forum (including a specific youth section and possibly an area specifically consecrated to the victims' representatives) including integrated data bases for contributions. The Internet site concerned will be developed on the basis of a user oriented methodology involving user test groups;
- Producing content and information material for the general forum as well as specific information material for the youth forum,
- Awareness raising and information costs in other media,

The above costs will be met through existing framework contracts.

2.3.2. Establishment of a capacity for information and crisis management of the DG Justice, Freedom and Security (JLS).

Funds will be used by JLS (1.000.000€) to:

- Establish a law enforcement related facility enabling JLS to provide the appropriate policy response as well as effective interfacing with Europol and law enforcement authorities in the member states;

[5] Detailed terms of reference are currently being elaborated and will be submitted to the Interservice group on terrorism prior to the conclusion of the relevant contract

- Acquire the means of physical access control and of sound and electromagnetic protection to ensure the required level of security;
- acquire the necessary platforms and other equipment to operate the referred facility and to operate within a secure environment
- Gather, appraising and adapting for the purpose monitoring and analysing relevant open source information related to terrorism and counter terrorism, open source collection and analysis and data mining tools that have already been developed by or for the Commission,
- Acquire the knowledge for crisis management, information response system and resilience enhancement activities;
- acquire specialised equipment to allow close and secure cooperation with analogous facilities and possibly in the future in other EU and Member State institutions, as well as—in the event of crisis—contributing with own and seconded capacity towards, monitoring and interpreting relevant information.
- Meet related telecommunications costs;
- Access content subscription services;
- Translation/interpretation costs;
- Acquire dedicated software and related training;
- Establish a service framework contract with specialised private contractors for the elaboration, over 2005 and 2006, of a number of open source based, focused and quick information surveys on terrorism and counter terrorism related subjects.
- Develop, as necessary, new tools, aiming notably to integrate the resulting products into the crisis management capacity of the Commission

850.000€ will be mobilised through different relevant framework contracts and through restricted tendering.

However, given the proprietary nature of some of the referred software and content which entails a *de facto* monopoly, the need to ensure interoperability with existing capacity elsewhere in the Commission and, in some cases, for security reasons—e.g. encryption—the Commission will in this regard and up to a maximum amount of 150.000€ use a negotiated procedure without prior publication of a contract notice.

2.3.3. Networks of experts on terrorism

Funds will be made available (350.000€) to create and support security networks on, inter alia:

- European experts and researchers in the field of Violent radicalisation and Terrorism who will advise the Commission and the Union on related policy,

- Specialised institutes and centres working on the economics of security

These funds will cover organisation of meetings, travel and related costs of participating experts, publication, establishment of secure sites for exchange of confidential material and access to open source information and tools to support security activities. These different costs will be met mainly through a number of existing framework contracts.

Budget Allocation (Summary)

Technical studies on crisis systems:	€ 800.000
EPCIP:	€ 3 Mio
Networks of experts on terrorism:	€ 350 000
JLS capacity:	€ 1 Mio€
Studies:	
i) Violent radicalisation and terrorism	€ 450.000
ii) Financing of terrorism	€ 50 000
Forum on Securing Freedom	€ 200 000
Meetings, Conferences and workshops:	
i) General	€ 400.000
ii) International Cooperation	€400.000
Emergency Actions:	€ 350 000

Timetable

– **Publication of apportionment of grants for preparatory studies for EPCIP in the second half of 2005 (1.500.000€)**

– **Publication of apportionment of grants for studies under initial phase of EPCIP in the first half of 2006 (1.500.000€)**

– **Publication of a calls for tender in the third quarter of 2005 for:**

- Technical studies on crisis systems
- Organisation of meetings and conferences, including External Relations workshops
- Studies on Violent Radicalisation and Terrorism and on the Financing of Terrorism

DOCUMENT NO. 10

THE HAGUE PROGRAMME: TEN PRIORITIES FOR THE NEXT FIVE YEARS

Commission of the European Communities
COM(2005) 184

Brussels, 10 October 2005

1. Introduction

The European Council of 4–5 November 2004 endorsed the Hague Multiannual Programme for strengthening the area of freedom, security and justice.

The Hague Programme is the successor to the Tampere Programme, which was endorsed by the European Council on 15–16 October 1999. This was the first multiannual programme to fix priorities for an area of freedom, security and justice. The Commission evaluated the results of the last five years in its Communication of 2 June 2004[1].

The Hague Programme marks the end of a cycle and the beginning of a new one. It is no surprise, therefore, that this second multiannual programme builds upon the positive experience of the past five years. In order to carry out the Hague Programme, the European Council invited the Commission to present an Action Plan to the Council in which the aims and priorities of the Programme are to be translated into concrete actions, including a timetable for the adoption and implementation of all actions.

This Action Plan is therefore composed of two parts. The first part (chapter 2) gives an overview of the issues at stake, and of some of the most important aspects of the Programme. It also identifies, from among the orientations of the Programme, ten specific priorities upon which the Commission believes efforts for the next five years should be concentrated. The second part (chapter 3) consists of an annex listing the concrete measures and actions to be taken

[1] "Area of Freedom, Security and Justice: Assessment of the Tampere Programme and future orientations"—COM(2004) 401, 2.6.2004.

over the next five years. This list closely adheres to the structure of the Hague Programme.

It is also important to note that this Action Plan needs to be read in conjunction with other Plans and Strategy papers regarding specific policy issues in the area of freedom, security and justice: it will be the Commission's task to ensure the general coherence of these exercises. Some of these documents have been presented by the Commission very recently or are about to be presented (the EU Action Plan on Drugs of 14 February 2005,[2] following the new European Strategy on Drugs 2005–2012; the Communication on Perspectives for the development of mutual recognition of decisions in criminal matters and of mutual confidence and the Communication "Developing a Strategic Concept on Tackling Organised Crime".

The Hague Programme calls for a mid-term review of the Action Plan by 1 November 2006. To that end, the Commission will timely present a report on the progress made and on the possible adjustments needed to the Programme.

2. The Action Plan Implementing the Hague Programme: Translating Political Priorities and Monitoring Implementation

2.1. The Political Mandate of the Hague Programme

The Hague Programme reaffirms the importance that the European Union attaches to the area of freedom, security and justice, placing it as a high priority on the Union's agenda—not only because it figures among the fundamental objectives of the Union, but in particular because it is at the heart of citizens' interests.

The Programme sets out the framework and main objectives for the next five years. It seeks to respond to the expectations of our citizens and deals with all aspects of policies relating to the area of freedom, security and justice and it addresses both general orientations (fundamental rights, implementation and evaluation) and specific orientations, focusing on (1) strengthening freedom[3] (2) strengthening security (3) strengthening justice and (4) external relations. The European Strategy on Drugs 2005–2012 endorsed by the European Council in December 2004 is an integral part of the Hague programme.

The Programme calls for a Strategy covering the external dimension of Union policy on freedom, security and justice, and asks the Commission to present it in close collaboration with the Council Secretary-General/ High Representative. It should reflect the Union's special relations with

[2] COM(2005) 45, 14.2.2005.

third countries and regions and focus on the specific needs for JHA cooperation with them. As a first step, the Commission will present a Communication to prepare the Strategy which complements this Action Plan.

The European Council "noted that due account should be taken of the financial implications for the multiannual agenda in the area of freedom, security and justice." It is clear that one of the essential pre-conditions for achieving the policy objectives which have been fixed is to match these objectives with adequate financial resources. The Commission has presented on 6 April 2005 three Framework Programmes on (1) Solidarity and Management of Migration Flows, (2) Security and Safeguarding Liberties and (3) Fundamental Rights and Justice[4]. The three proposals are fully in line with the strategic priorities set by the Hague Programme.

The Commission's evaluation of the Tampere Programme of 2 June 2004[5] and the Recommendation adopted by the European Parliament on 14 October 2004[6] have been taken into account in the Hague Programme, in particular in connection with the introduction of the procedure under Article 251 TEC (co-decision procedure) for areas of Title IV TEC. Given the political impetus from the European Council, on 22 December 2004 the Council was able to adopt a decision applying co-decision and qualified majority voting to all Title IV measures with the exception of legal immigration, as of 1 January 2005[7]. This is the first success of the Hague Programme. Not only is the enhanced role of the European Parliament an improvement in democratic legitimacy, but the rate of completion of the work is likely to increase with the abolition of unanimous voting.

However, the Council Decision of 22 December 2004 did not include, as foreseen by Article 67 of the Treaty, any provision adapting the powers of the Court. The Commission continues to believe that in this area, which so closely touches the right of individuals, an increased access to the Court of Justice is essential. The matter of increased access to the Court of Justice for preliminary rulings is an issue which must call for consideration particularly—as is recognised by the fourth paragraph of Article III-369 of the

[3] It is worth noting that the notion of freedom covers all parts of this Action Plan. For the purposes of this document, however, freedom reflects the specific meaning contained in the Hague Programme.

[4] COM(2005) 122, 123 and 124, 6.4.2005.

[5] "Area of Freedom, Security and Justice: Assessment of the Tampere Programme and future orientations"—COM(2004) 401, 2.6.2004.

[6] "European Parliament recommendation to the Council and to the European Council on the future of the area of freedom, security and justice as well as on the measures required to enhance the legitimacy and effectiveness thereof"—P6_TA(2004)0022, 14.10.2004.

[7] Council Decision 2004/927/EC of 22 December 2004 providing for certain areas covered by Title IV of Part Three of the Treaty establishing the European Community to be governed by the procedure laid down in Article 251 of that Treaty (OJ L 396, 31.12.2004, p. 45).

Constitution and referred to in the Hague Programme—given the need to ensure speedy treatment of such cases.

2.2. The Hague Programme and the Constitution

The Hague Programme reflects the ambitions expressed in the Constitution which, subject to national ratification procedures, should enter into force on 1 November 2006, bringing about a significant revision of the existing provisions governing the area of freedom, security and justice and the integration of the Charter of Fundamental Rights. The innovations arising from the Constitution could not be applied before the end of the ratification period. Coherently, the Commission is committed to undertake the necessary preparatory work so that measures could be taken immediately after the entry into force of the Constitution.

2.3. Ten Priorities for the Next Five Years: A Partnership for European Renewal

In preparing the Action Plan implementing the Hague Programme, the Commission has provided a list of the actions which the Programme calls for. The achievement of the ambitious objectives of the Hague Programme should be ensured through a collective effort of the Council, the European Parliament and the Commission within the framework of a strong and effective partnership.

Within the strategic objectives already agreed upon by the European Council in the Hague Programme in view of the strengthening of the area of Freedom, Security and Justice, and which are translated into concrete measures in chapter 3 (annex) following the order of the Hague Programme itself, the Commission has identified ten priorities on which it believes the collective efforts must be particularly concentrated in the next five years. The ten priorities are equally important and cover the whole spectrum of the Hague objectives. This exercise will avoid a dispersal of efforts and ensure that the Programme's aims are achieved. The Commission also believes that it is crucial to identify the added value at European level of any legislative and non-legislative initiative to be taken in the area of Freedom, Security and Justice, by fully applying the principle of subsidiarity and exploiting the better regulation mechanisms as well as by conducting impact assessment on the main proposals to be presented.

The Strategic Objectives 2005–2009[8] refers specifically to the development of a partnership in view of the strengthening of an area of Freedom, Security and Justice. Within the objectives of (a) strengthening freedom (b) strengthening security (c) strengthening justice, the main ten priorities identified by the Commission can be summarised as follows:

Fundamental rights and citizenship: creating fully-fledged policies Ensure the full development of policies monitoring and promoting respect for fundamental rights for all people and of policies enhancing citizenship. The fight against terrorism: working toward a global response Focus on different aspects of prevention, preparedness and response in order to further enhance, and where necessary complement, Member States capabilities to fight terrorism, in relevant areas such as recruitment, financing, risk analysis, protection of critical infrastructures and consequence management. A common asylum area: establish an effective harmonized procedure in accordance with the Union' values and humanitarian tradition Work towards the establishment of a common asylum area taking into account the humanitarian tradition and respect of international obligations of the Union and the effectiveness of a harmonised procedure. Migration management; defining a balanced approach Define a balanced approach to migration management by developing a common immigration policy which addresses legal migration at Union level, while further strengthening the fight against illegal migration, smuggling and trafficking in human beings, in particular women and children. Integration: maximising the positive impact of migration on our society and economy Develop supportive measures to help Member States and deliver better policies on integration so as to maximise the positive impact of migration on our society and economy and to prevent isolation and social exclusion of immigrant communities. This will contribute to understanding and dialogue between religions and cultures, based on the fundamental values of the Union. Internal borders, external borders and visas: developing an integrated management of external borders for a safer Union Further develop an integrated management of external borders and a common visa policy, while ensuring the free movement of persons (people-to-people). Privacy and security in sharing information: striking the right balance Strike the right balance between privacy and security in the sharing of information among law enforcement and judicial authorities, by supporting and encouraging a constructive dialogue between all parties concerned to identify balanced solutions, while fully respecting fundamental rights of privacy and data protection, as well as the principle of availability of information as laid down in the Hague Programme. Organised crime: developing a strategic concept Develop and implement a strategic concept on tackling organised crime at EU level. Make full use of and further develop Europol and Eurojust. Civil and criminal justice: guaranteeing an effective European area of justice for all Guarantee an European area of justice by ensuring an effective access to justice for all and the enforcement of judgments. Approximation will be pursued, in particular through the adoption of rules ensuring a high degree of protection of persons, with a view to

[8] "Strategic objectives 2005-2009, Europe 2010: a partnership for European renewal"—COM(2005) 12, 26.1.2005.

building mutual trust and strengthening mutual recognition, which remains the cornerstone of judicial cooperation. Improve the EU substantive contract law. Freedom, Security and Justice: sharing responsibility and solidarity Give practical meaning to notions of shared responsibility and solidarity between Member States by providing adequate financial resources that can meet the objectives of Freedom, Security and Justice in the most efficient way.

10. (1) Fundamental Rights and Citizenship: Creating Fully-Fledged Policies

Fundamental rights are at the core of the Union's values. Full development of policies monitoring and promoting respect for fundamental rights for all people and of policies enhancing citizenship must be ensured.

The Constitution places the individual at the heart of the European project by integrating the Charter of Fundamental Rights and by providing for accession to the European Convention for the Protection of Human Rights and Fundamental Freedoms.

Furthermore, it is important to provide decision-makers with accurate and reliable data on the respect for fundamental rights in the Union. The conversion of the European Monitoring Centre for Racism and Xenophobia toward the establishment of a fully-fledged Fundamental Rights Agency will be another important element in the promotion and protection of fundamental rights.

Among those rights, the Commission will devote special attention to the rights of the child, in view of their protection, since children are among the most vulnerable in the population. The Constitution explicitly includes "the promotion and the protection of the rights of the child" among the objectives of the Union.

Furthermore, the Commission will, in collaboration with member States, pursue its efforts to combat violence against women and provide support to victims.

The Commission will pursue its action to combat discrimination in all its forms. This will include ensuring effective implementation and enforcement of EU anti-discrimination legislation.

Particular attention must be dedicated to the protection of personal data, which has been recognised by the Charter of Fundamental Rights and by the Constitution as a fundamental right of its own, distinct from the right to privacy.

Citizenship of the Union entails a number of crucial rights such as free movement within the EU, diplomatic and consular protection or voting rights in European Parliament and local elections. Measures are envisaged in all of these areas in order to improve the exercise of citizenship rights of EU citizens.

(2) The Fight Against Terrorism: Working Toward a Global Response

A global response is required to address terrorism. The expectations that citizens have of the Union cannot be ignored, and nor can the Union fail to respond to them.

Attention must focus on different aspects of prevention, preparedness and response to further enhance, and where necessary complement, Member States' capabilities to fight terrorism, concentrating particularly on recruitment, financing, risk analysis, protection of critical infrastructures and consequence management.

The fight against terrorism calls for an integrated and coherent approach, covering a wide range of issues which the Hague Programme has identified. A crucial area that demands the Union's attention is cooperation between the different competent authorities of Member States, most notably in exchanging information relevant for the investigation of terrorist activities.

It is also of the utmost importance to understand the complex phenomenon that is terrorism in Europe: the processes of indoctrination and recruitment and the type of environment that allows terrorist ideas and movements to take root. Efforts in the fight against the financing of terrorism should be further pursued.

The efforts of Member States and the EU must be complemented by external cooperation, working with third countries to fight terrorism, notably assisting them in funding counter-terrorism and capacity-building projects, as well as tackling the roots of terrorism.

(3) A Common Asylum Area: Establish an Effective Harmonized Procedure in Accordance with the Union's Values and Humanitarian Tradition

The establishment of a Common European Asylum System is another priority. In the next few years, the work will focus on concluding the evaluation of the first phase instruments by 2007, and to submit the second phase instruments and measures in developing a common asylum policy, which will seek to establish a common procedure and uniform status for persons benefiting from asylum or subsidiary protection before the end of 2010.

Administrative cooperation between the national services of Member States must be reinforced, and funds earmarked to assist Member States in processing the applications and the reception of third country nationals. The Hague Programme has also indicated the need to study the possibility of joint processing of asylum applications.

The development of EU-Regional Protection Programmes and Resettlement Schemes is being launched by the Commission.

(4) Migration Management: Defining a Balanced Approach

A new balanced approach to migration management, dealing both with legal and illegal migration, needs to be defined and a common immigration policy addressing the situation of legal migrants at Union level needs to be developed, while further strengthening the fight against illegal migration, migrant smuggling and trafficking in human beings, notably women and children.

While the decision as to how many migrants coming from third countries can be admitted to each Member State to seek work in an employed or self-employed capacity remains a national decision, an area of free movement demands a common immigration policy, covering admission procedures and criteria and delivering a secure legal status and a guaranteed set of rights to assist the integration of those who are admitted. Furthermore, immigration plays a fundamental role in the economies and societies of Member States as well as of countries of origin and transit, which also justifies the need for a common approach based on a rational use of an immigrant workforce.

The human, social and economic costs of illegal migration—not only in host countries but also in countries of origin and transit—are extremely high, calling for rules on return procedures, the speeding up of the conclusion of readmission agreements, and further coordination to combat smuggling and trafficking in human beings. However, the respect for the rights and dignity of third country nationals, including in an irregular situation in the Union must always remain a guiding principle in EU policy. In particular, the treatment of persons trafficked into or within the EU must respect their specific situation and human rights standards.

A common immigration policy cannot confine itself to admission and return policies: successful management of migrations flows must become an integral element and comprise a serious investment in relations with third countries, both of origin and of transit, notably through assistance and cooperation, in the mutual interest of third-countries and of the Union.

(5) Integration: Maximising the Positive Impact of Migration on our Society and Economy

In order to maximise the positive impact of immigration on our society and economy and, as a matter of outmost importance, to prevent isolation and social exclusion of immigrant communities, it is necessary to support and encourage Member States to deliver better policies on integration. A successful integration policy must contribute to understanding and dialogue between religions and cultures.

The integration of third-country nationals requires mobilising a range of mainstream policies, also including employment and education.

Greater contact between national authorities is needed in order to exchange experiences and information on integration.

It is therefore necessary to establish a European Framework on Integration based upon the common principles endorsed by the European Council ensuring respect for EU values and upholding non-discrimination.

(6) Internal Borders, External Borders and Visas: Developing an Integrated Management of External Borders for a Safer Union

An area where the free movement of persons is fully ensured demands further efforts leading to integrated control of the access to the territory of the Union, based on an integrated management of external borders, a common visa policy and with the support of new technologies, including the use of biometric identifiers.

Following the Union's latest enlargement, it will be a priority to achieve internal free movement, and to be able to fully abolish controls of persons at internal border. In this sense, the establishment of SIS II and the smooth running of evaluations, foreseen by the Accession treaties, are fundamental in order to pave the way for the new Member States.

An important step in the management of external borders is the creation of the Border Management Agency, which will be responsible for coordinating and assisting Member States' action in surveillance and controlling of external borders.

The development of an effective visa policy will be facilitated through the availability of the Visa Information System. This will call for the reinforcement of the cooperation between Member States to create common application centres for visas, which could be a first step towards a future European common consular service.

Another important element is the inclusion of biometric identifiers in travel and identification documents, enhancing document security while maintaining full respect for fundamental rights. Furthermore, possible synergies between EU and national information systems, based on interoperability, should be fully exploited.

(7) Privacy and Security in Sharing of Information: Striking the Right Balance

Effective maintenance of law and order and the investigation of cross-border criminality in an area of free movement cannot be allowed to be impeded by cumbersome procedures for the exchange of information.

The Union should support and encourage a constructive dialogue between all parties concerned to identify balanced solutions, fully respecting fundamental rights to privacy and data protection, as well as the principle of availability of information.

The principle of availability, as laid out in the Hague Programme, states that information for law enforcement purposes needed by the authorities of one Member State will be made available by the authorities of another Member State, subject to certain conditions. The Commission will present proposals to this end, including the possibility of mutual consultation of databases of Member States.

In this area, the right balance between privacy and security should be found in sharing information among law enforcement and judicial authorities.

The balance between privacy and security should also be carefully considered in the area of the exchange of airlines passenger data for aviation security and anti-terrorism purposes.

(8) Organised Crime: Developing a Strategic Concept

A strategic concept on tackling organised crime at EU level will be developed and implemented. To this end, the Commission will shortly present a Communication "Developing a Strategic Concept on Tackling Organised Crime". This includes measures designed for improving knowledge of the phenomenon and for strengthening prevention, investigation and cooperation on organised crime within the EU. The strategy must also contemplate intensifying cooperation with third countries and international organisations on this issue as one of its priorities.

Fighting organised crime requires improving cooperation between law enforcement services (police, justice, customs) as well as making full use of and further developing Europol and Eurojust. Working towards a European criminal intelligence model is one of the more important tasks ahead in this field and will require the shared efforts of Member States, EU institutions and bodies.

(9) Civil and Criminal Justice: Guaranteeing an Effective European Area of Justice for All

A European area of justice is more than an area where judgements obtained in one Member State are recognised and enforced in other Member States, but rather an area where effective access to justice is guaranteed in order to obtain and enforce judicial decisions. To this end, the Union must envisage not only rules on jurisdiction, recognition and conflict of laws, but also measures which build confidence and mutual trust among Member States, creating minimum procedural standards and ensuring high standards of quality of justice systems, in particular as regards fairness and respect for the rights of defence. Mutual understanding can be further pursued through the progressive creation of a "European judicial culture" that the Hague Programme calls for, based on training and networking. A coherent strategy in the EU's relations with third countries and international organisations is also needed.

In the field of civil justice, completion of the Programme on mutual recognition of decisions in civil and commercial matters is of the utmost importance. It will involve the adoption of legislative proposals already presented by the Commission, or in the process of being put forward, and launching consultations in order to prepare new legislation not yet subject to mutual recognition (such as family property issues, successions and wills). Another fundamental aspect to be addressed is the enforcement of judicial decisions and mutual recognition of public and private documents. Regarding the EU substantive contract law, a Common Frame of Reference (CFR), to be used as a toolbox to improve coherence and quality of EU legislation, will be adopted in 2009 at the latest.

Regarding criminal justice, approximation and the establishment of minimum standards of several aspects of procedural law (such as ne bis in idem, handling evidence or judgements in absentia) are instrumental in building mutual confidence and pursuing mutual recognition. Concerning the latter, several actions must be carried forward in order to ensure efficient and timely action by law enforcement authorities (such as mutual recognition of non-custodial pre-trial supervision measures, or recognition and execution of prison sentences) and, more generally, to replace traditional mutual assistance with new instruments based on mutual recognition. Eurojust should be considered as the key actor for developing European judicial cooperation in criminal matters. Its role should be supported and its potentialities fully exploited in the light of the experience acquired and in view of future developments. In this context, the Commission will also follow up its previous work and the possibilities afforded by the Constitution, as regards improving the protection of the Union's financial interests.

(10) Sharing Responsibility and Solidarity

No policy objective can be reached without adequate financial resources and the Hague Programme established a clear connection between those two elements. To this end, in April 2005 the Commission presented three Framework Programmes, which seek to give practical meaning to the concepts of shared responsibility and solidarity between Member States by reviewing the type of policy and financial instruments that can meet the objectives of freedom, security and justice in the most efficient way.

2.4. Implementation, Evaluation and Flexibility

The Commission fully shares the importance the Hague Programme recognised to the implementation dimension and to the need of establishing mechanisms which can adequately evaluate and assess the implementation by Member States of measures in the area of freedom, security and justice.

The Constitution provides in Article III-260 for the adoption of measures enabling the Commission and Member States to evaluate impartially and objectively implementation of Union policies in this area. The Commission will present a Communication in early 2006 outlining the main objectives of the future mechanism and it intends to present proposals following the entry into force of the Constitution.

In the meantime, however, the European Council has invited the Commission to present an annual report on implementation of EU measures (a "scoreboard") and to inform the European Parliament and national parliaments.

This will allow having a more complete overview of the state of play of policy regarding the area of freedom, security and justice and of the effective implementation of adopted measures by the Member States. The first Scoreboard will be presented in December 2005, and it will require the active participation of Member States, who will be invited to regularly notify their progress in implementing the adopted measures.

In addition, the European Council urged the Council to develop practical methods to facilitate timely implementation in all policy areas: requiring that proper plans for implementation are developed at national level, ensuring that the length of the implementation period is adequate, and examining regular progress reports from the Commission.

Given the general political environment in the area of freedom, security and justice, new political priorities are likely to emerge as a result of unexpected events, often of an international nature and dimension. The Action Plan has to be flexible and adaptable, particularly in the longer term, in order to allow for new priorities which may emerge in the coming years. The Constitution will permit a significant rationalisation of the legal and institutional framework. Here too, the European Council considered it important to allow for some flexibility, imposing a review of the Hague Programme.

3. Identifying Concrete Actions

The Hague Programme requires that the Commission should translate the Hague objectives into concrete measures. To this end, the annex to this

Communication consists of an Action Plan listing the main actions and measures to be taken over the next five years, including a specific set of deadlines for their presentation to the Council and the European Parliament.

Following the endorsement of the Tampere conclusions in 1999 and of the Hague Programme in 2004, the European Council should preserve its guiding role in the definition of strategic guidelines and the planning of future action in an area of freedom, security and justice. The Commission invites the Council to discuss this Communication and its accompanying Action Plan with a view to an endorsement by the June 2005 European Council.

Annex

The Hague Programme: Ten Priorities for the Next Five Years
List of Measures and Timetable for Adoption

1. General Orientations

- Setting up of a system for objective and impartial evaluation of the implementation of EU measures in the field of Freedom, Security and Justice
- Communication on and Proposal for the creation of an evaluation mechanism, as envisaged by Article III-260 of the Constitutional Treaty (2006)

1.1. Respect and Active Promotion of Fundamental Rights

- Framework Programme "Fundamental Rights and Justice" under the new Financial Perspectives (2005)
- Specific Programme on Citizenship and Fundamental Rights (2007)
- Specific Programme on Fight against violence (Daphne) and drugs prevention and information (2007)
- Accession of the European Union to the European Convention for the protection of human rights and fundamental freedoms (informal discussions to be started in 2005)
- Proposal extending the mandate of the European Monitoring Centre on Racism and Xenophobia towards a Fundamental Rights Agency (proposal in 2005)
- Daphne II programme: 2006 work programme (2005)
- Study on prevention measures to combat violence against women (2006)
- Communication on the protection of the rights of the child (2005)

1.2. European Strategy on Drugs

- EU Action Plans on drugs 2005–2008 (2005) and 2009–2012 (2009)
- Continuous evaluation of the EU Action Plan on Drugs 2005–2008 (annual)
- Green Paper on the role of civil society in formulating policies in the drugs field (2006)
- Report on the implementation and functioning of the Framework Decision on drugs trafficking (2007)
- Progress report on and impact assessment of the EU Action Plan on drugs 2005–2008 (2008)

- Communication on an EU Action Plan on drugs 2009–2012 (2009)

2. Strengthening Freedom

2.1. Citizenship of the Union

- Reports on the application of Directives 90/364, 90/365 and 93/96 on the right of residence of pensioners, students and inactive persons and of
- Directive 93/109/EC on the right to vote in the EP elections, including in the new Member States and, if appropriate, proposals for the amendment of the latter Directive (2005/2006)
- Proposal to facilitate diplomatic and consular protection (2006)
- Proposal on provisions and conditions required for a European citizens' initiative (2007)
- Examination of possible measures to strengthen and to add to the rights laid down under the citizenship provisions of the Treaties (Article 22 TEC) (2008)
- Allowing EU citizens and members of their family to move within the European Union on similar terms to nationals of a Member State moving around or changing their place of residence in their own country
- Control of transposition, compliance and correct application of Directive 2004/38/EC on free movement and residence (2006)
- Report on application of Directives 90/364/EEC, 90/365/EEC and 93/96/EEC on free movement and residence (2006)
- Report on application of Directive 2004/38/EC on free movement and residence and, if appropriate, proposals for the amendment of the Directive (2008)

2.2. Asylum, Migration and Border Policy

- Framework Programme "Solidarity and Management of Migration Flows" under the new Financial Perspectives (2005)
- Establishment of an External Borders Fund (2007)
- Establishment of an Integration Fund (2007)[9]
- Establishment of a Return Fund (2007)
- Adaptation of the European Refugee Fund (2007)

[9] This Fund will be complementary to the European Social Fund.

- Common analysis of migratory phenomena in all their aspects (Reinforcing the collection, provision, exchange and efficient use of up-to-date information and data)
- Annual reports on migration and asylum statistics (on-going)
- Adoption of an EU Framework Regulation on the collection of migration and asylum statistics (2005)
- Green Paper on the future of the European Migration Network (2005)
- Proposal establishing a European Migration Monitoring Centre (2006)

2.3. Common European Asylum System

- Adoption of the Asylum Procedures Directive (2005)
- Evaluation of the first phase legal instruments
- Monitoring the transposition and implementation of first phase instruments (2005–2007)
- Second phase of development of a common policy on asylum, establishment of a common asylum procedure and a uniform status for those who are granted asylum or subsidiary protection
- Proposal on long-term resident status for refugees (2005)
- Second-phase instruments and measures to be presented to the Council and the European Parliament (adoption before the end of 2010)
- Establishment of structures involving the national asylum services of the Member States for promoting cooperation (Communication—2005)
- Studies on the implications of joint processing of asylum applications
- Study on the joint processing of asylum applications within the Union (2006)
- Study, to be conducted in close consultation with the United Nations High Commissioner for Refugees (UNHCR), on joint processing of asylum applications outside EU territory, (2006)
- Establishing a European support office for all forms of cooperation between Member States relating to the Common European Asylum System (after the establishment of a common asylum procedure and on the basis of an evaluation)
- Establishment of the European Refugee Fund (ERF) 2005–2013 to assist Member States in the processing of asylum applications and in the reception of certain categories of third-country nationals
- Final Report on the European Refugee Fund (2005)

- Proposal for amending European Refugee Fund decision to assist Member States in the reception of certain categories of third-country nationals (2005)
- Approvals of European Refugee Fund national multiannual programming (2005, 2008 and 2011)
- Adaptation of the European Refugee Fund (2007)

2.3.1. Legal Migration Including Admission Procedures

- Developing policy on legal migration
- Assessment and monitoring of the transposition and implementation of first phase directives on legal migration (2005–2011)
- Debate on Green Paper on economic migration (2005)
- On the basis of the outcome of the public consultation on the Green Paper on economic migration, presentation of a Policy Plan on legal migration, including admission procedures (2005)

2.3.2. Integration of Third-Country Nationals

- Establishment of a coherent European framework for integration
- Communication on a European framework for integration (2005)
- Promotion of the structural exchange of experience and information on integration[10]
- Management of INTI preparatory actions (2005–2006)
- Annual reports on immigration and integration (2005 on-going)
- Handbook on integration (second edition 2006, on-going)
- Development of a website on the Internet (2006)
- Establishment of an Integration Fund (2007)

2.3.3. Fight Against Illegal Immigration

- Contribution to management of immigration liaison networks in relevant third countries (2005 on-going)
- Annual report on the common policy on illegal migration (2005 on-going)
- Adoption of a Commission Decision establishing a secure web-based information network for Member States migration services (ICONET) (2005)

---

[10] In addition, complementary activities are undertaken in the framework of the European Employment Strategy and the Social Inclusion Process.

- Proposal for the conclusion and signature of the Council of Europe Convention on action against trafficking in human beings (CAHTEH) (2005)
- Establishment of an effective removal and repatriation policy based on common standards and a closer cooperation and mutual technical assistance
- Proposal on return procedures (2005)
- Launching of the preparatory actions for financial support to Return Management (2005)
- Appointment of a Commission Special Representative for a common readmission policy (2005)
- Conclusion of Community readmission agreements and management of existing agreements (timely)
- Establishment of a Return Fund (2007)

2.3.4. External Dimension of Asylum and Migration

- Cooperation with third countries in managing migration and asylum
- Communication on migration and development (2005)
- Revised version for 2006 of the reference document of the AENEAS Programme, 2004–2006 (2005)
- Completing the integration of migration into the Country and Regional Strategy Papers for all relevant third countries (2005)
- Development of EU-Regional Protection Programmes
- Plan of action for EU Regional Protection Programme, including EU resettlement scheme (2005)
- Launching pilot protection programmes (2005)
- Intensified cooperation with countries of transit to enable these countries better to manage migration and to provide adequate protection for refugees
- Report on progress and achievements in asylum and migration, within the context of the European Neighbourhood Policy (2005)

2.3.5. Border Management, Biometrics, Information Systems and Visa Policy

- Abolition of controls of persons at the internal borders
- Proposal on SIS II legal instruments (2005)
- Start of evaluation of the implementation of the non-SIS II related acquis in the new Member States (2006)

- Evaluation of SIS II related acquis in the new Member States (after SIS II operational–2007)
- Adoption of the Council Decision on the lifting of controls at the borders with and between the new Member States (2007)
- Proposal for supplementing existing Schengen evaluation mechanism with a supervisory mechanism (as soon as the abolition of controls of persons at internal borders in the new Member States has been completed) (2007–2008)
- Establishment of an integrated management system for external borders
- Proposal on teams of national experts to support Member States in the control and surveillance of external borders within the framework of the Border Management Agency (2005)
- "Handbook for Border Guards" (after adoption of the Community Code on the rules governing the movement of persons across borders)
- Proposal on the executive powers conferred to Member States' officials operating at the external borders of another Member State (2006)
- Evaluation report on the External Border Agency, including a review of the tasks of the Agency and an assessment of whether it should concern itself with other aspects of border management (including the evaluation of the functioning of the teams of national experts and the feasibility of a system of European border guards) (2007)
- Establishment of an External Borders Fund (2007)
- Partial application of the Schengen acquis
- Adoption of the Council Decision on the partial implementation of the Schengen acquis by Ireland (2005)
- Adoption of the Council Decision on the partial implementation of the Schengen acquis (SIS) by the United Kingdom (2005)
- Coherent approach and harmonised solutions in the EU on biometric identifiers and data
- Proposal modifying the Common Consular Instructions concerning standards and procedures for taking biometric data, including the obligation to provide such data and specifying the exceptions to this obligation (2005)
- Preparation for the development of minimum standards for national ID-cards (from 2005 onwards)
- Preparation for the development of minimum standards for sectors' specific ID-cards, if appropriate (from 2005 onwards)
- Integration of biometric identifiers in travel documents, visa, residence permits, EU citizens' passports and information systems (2006)

- Communication on enhanced synergies between SIS II, VIS and Eurodac (2006)
- Visa policy, including the development of the Visa Information System (VIS)
- Meetings with third countries of the positive visa list in order to ensure visa-free travel for citizens of the Member States to all those third countries (ongoing, to be combined with the review of the visa list)
- Proposals relating to the necessary amendments to further enhance visa policies and the establishment of common application centres for visas (2005)
- Regular review of the visa list (Regulation 539/2001) (regularly)
- Proposal on visa facilitation procedures for members of the Olympic Family—Turin 2006 (2005)
- Report on the implementation of Regulation 1295/2003 "Visa facilitation procedures for members of the Olympic Family—Athens 2004" (2005)
- Proposal amending the Common Consular Instructions on visa fees (2005)
- ARGO Work Programme (2005 and 2006)
- Proposals on transit: unilateral recognition of Schengen documents by the new Member States/recognition of Swiss residence permits by the Member States (2005)
- Recommendation for negotiation directives for visa waiver agreements between the EC and the third countries on the conditions to move freely within the Union for a period between three and six months (2005)
- Adoption of a proposal establishing a regime on local border traffic (2005)
- Report on the operation of the Kaliningrad transit scheme (2005)
- Kaliningrad facility[11] (2005–2006)
- Schengen Facility for seven Member States (2005 and 2006)
- Specific recommendations for negotiating directives on visa facilitation with third countries in the context of the EC readmission policy, where possible and on the basis of reciprocity, in view of developing a real partnership on migration management issues (2005–2009)
- Proposal modifying the Common Consular Instructions on local consular cooperation (2006)

[11] The Kaliningrad Facility will be replaced by specific provisions within the proposed External Border Fund for the period 2007–2013 as part of the framework programme "Solidarity and the Management of migration flows".

- Proposal on the review of Common Consular Instructions (2006)
- Technical implementation of the VIS, starting with the functionalities for processing alphanumeric data and photographs (2006) and adding the functionalities for biometric data (2006)
- Proposal on the creation of common consular offices (2007)

3. Strengthening Security

- Framework Programme "Security and Safeguarding Liberties" under the new Financial Perspectives (2005)
- Specific Programme on "Prevention of and fight against crime" (2007)
- Specific Programme on "Prevention, Preparedness and Consequence Management of Terrorism" (2007)

3.1. Sharing of Information Among Law Enforcement and Judicial Authorities While Striking the Right Balance Between Privacy and Security

- Proposal on the retention of data processed in connection with the provision of public electronic communication services for the detection, investigation and prosecution of criminal offences (2005)
- Identification of adequate safeguards and effective legal remedies for the transfer of personal data in the context of police and judicial co-operation in criminal matters
- Implementation of the principle of availability for the exchange of law enforcement information
- Proposal on the establishment of a principle of availability of law enforcement relevant information (2005)
- Proposal on adequate safeguards for the transfer of personal data for the purpose of police and judicial co-operation in criminal matters (2005)
- Proposal concerning a common EU approach to the use of passengers data for border and aviation security and other law enforcement purposes (2005)
- Proposal on access by law enforcement to the VIS (2005)
- Development of links between the SIS II and the Europol information system (2007)
- Joint review on the Air Passengers Data (PNR) agreement with the USA (2005)
- Completion of negotiations of PNR agreements with Canada and Australia (2005), and with other countries if necessary

- Definition of international guidelines ensuring a high degree of protection of privacy for the access to PNR data in the framework of International Civil Aviation Organisation (ICAO)
- Proposal on mutual consultation of DNA Databases (2005)
- Proposal on mutual consultation of fingerprint databases (2007)
- Proposal for a general Community architecture on forensic/police databases (2008)

3.2. Terrorism

- Establishment of a coherent overall approach to combat terrorism
- Follow-up to the pilot project in favour of victims of terrorism (2006)
- Reinforcement of cooperation between law enforcement authorities to combat terrorism through the designation of a specialised contact point in each Member State, which will have access to all relevant information and intelligence with respect to terrorist activities involving persons, groups or entities listed in the annex to common position 2001/931/CFSP (2005)
- Creation of a European Law Enforcement Network (LEN) for the fight against terrorism (2005)
- Communication on greater security of explosives, bomb-making equipment (2005)
- Second terrorism report (2005)
- Communication on violent radicalisation (2005) and follow-up actions if needed (2007)
- Proposal for preventing misuse of charitable organisations for the financing of terrorism (2006)
- Communication on results of the peer evaluation mechanism on terrorism in the 25 Member States (2006/2007)
- Definition of need and scope for legal instruments to ensure that all Member States can freeze assets of designated persons on a preventive basis in accordance with Special Recommendations of the Financial Action Task Force (2007)
- Contribution to the on-going work on thwarting the production and spread of chemical, nuclear and biological arms (2007)
- Establishment of a specific Programme on "Prevention, Preparedness and Consequence management of Terrorism" (2007)
- Review and adaptation of Community legislation in parallel with measures to be adopted in order to combat terrorism

- Second report based on Article 11 of the Council Framework Decision of 13.6.2002 on combating terrorism (2005)

3.3. Prevention of and Fight Against Organised Crime

- Communication on developing a strategic concept on tackling organised crime (2005)
- Establishment of a specific Programme on "Prevention of and fight against crime" (2007)
- Improve the knowledge of organised crime and strengthen the gathering and analysis of information
- Communication on an action plan—EU Crime statistics (2005)
- Commission staff working paper on criminal intelligence-led law enforcement (2005)
- Recommendations for a standard methodology for vulnerability in crime proofing (2007)
- Presentation of a European Crime report (2007)
- Strengthen prevention of organised crime
- Crime-proofing of legislation and the design of crime preventive measures into products and services (2005)
- Report on the results of a study further to the Council resolution of 2001 on the contribution of civil society in finding missing or sexually exploited children (2005)
- Action Plan on private/public partnerships to protect public organisations and private companies from organised crime (2006)
- Improving European coordination and cooperation between high-tech crime units in Member States, and with the private sector (Cyber crime Intelligence Network) including the development of a European Cyber crime manual (2006)
- Communication on cyber crime and cyber security policy (2006)
- Anti-corruption measures:
- Development of codes of conduct on ethics and integrity for public officials (2007)
- Proposal introducing certain obligations on officials with regard to reporting bribery as well as the disclosure of assets and business interests (2008)
- Strengthen tools to address financial aspects of organised crime

- Initiatives to promote use of financial investigation as a law enforcement technique and to establish common minimum training standards (2005–2007):
- Common set of training standards in financial investigation skills (2005)
- Recommendation for a Memorandum of Understanding regarding feedback from financial intelligence units to reporting bodies on suspicious transaction reports (2006)
- Recommendation and/or proposal to enhance transparency of legal entities to reduce vulnerability to infiltration by organised crime (2006)
- Promotion of the establishment of criminal asset intelligence units in EU Member States (continuous)
- Examination of standards for the return of confiscated or forfeited assets as compensation or restitution to identifiable victims of crime or charitable organisations (2008)
- Improve legislation and review existing legal instruments where needed
- Legislative package on the fight against counterfeiting (2005)
- Communication on trafficking in human beings (2005)
- Review and, where appropriate, further development of the present legislation on trafficking in human beings, for example in order to facilitate public-private cooperation, EU wide coordination and the involvement of Europol (2006)
- Review and, where appropriate, further development of the legal framework preventing and combating trafficking in human organs, tissues and cells (2006)
- Review and, where appropriate, strengthening of the present legislation on confiscation of criminal assets, whether or not requiring criminal conviction (2007)
- Comparative study to evaluate the need for instruments to combat activities of Organised Crime related to Fiscal Fraud within EU Member States and acceding and candidate countries' (2005)
- Proposal for the approximation of legislation in criminal matters, in particular regarding the constituent elements of an penalties in the field of tax fraud or on standards and best practices for the purpose of improving law enforcement cooperation in the fight against organised tax fraud(2007)
- Proposal on identity theft and identity management measures including a database of identity documents (2007)
- Study and research towards further approximation of legislation, e.g. in the fields of illicit arms trafficking, racketeering and extortion (2008)

- Improve monitoring and evaluation
- Second report based on Article 6 of the Council Framework Decision of 26 June 2001 on money laundering, the identification, tracing, freezing, seizing and confiscation of instrumentalities and the proceeds of crime (2005)
- Second report based on Article 14 of the Council Framework Decision of 28 May 2001 combating fraud and counterfeiting of non-cash means of payment (2005)
- Implementation report Framework Decision "Private sector corruption" (2005)
- Report on the implementation of the Framework Decision of 27 January 2003 on Protection of the environment through criminal law (2005)
- Report on the implementation of the Framework Decision on Confiscation of Crime-Related Proceeds, Instrumentalities and Properties (2007)
- Evaluation regarding Member States' implementation of customs cooperation (Naples II Convention) (2008)
- Evaluation regarding Member States' anti-corruption policies (2009)
- Evaluation regarding measures to combat financial crime (2010)

3.4. Police and Customs Cooperation

- Implementation of the work programme concerning customs cooperation approved by the JAI Council on 30.3.2004 following the Council Resolution of 2.10.2003 on a strategy for customs cooperation (2004–2006)
- Communication on the fight against the illicit cross-border trafficking in restricted or prohibited goods (2007)
- Proposal on Europol, including the role of the European Parliament and national parliaments in the scrutiny of Europol's activities (no later than 1 January 2008)
- Definition of a policy on the relationship between Europol and Eurojust (no later than 2008)
- Definition of the role of the security committee (COSI) (no later than 1 January 2008)
- Improvement of law enforcement co-operation and
- Development of the Schengen acquis in respect of cross-border operational police cooperation
- Proposal on improvement of law-enforcement co-operation in particular at the internal borders between Member States (2005)

- Communication and proposal for a Directive on improved transport safety and increased security through the creation of an area of police and judicial cooperation on the Trans European transport Networks (2005)
- Updating of the SIRENE manual (2005)
- Proposal on access by law enforcement to the VIS (2005)
- Development of links between the SIS II and the Europol information system (2007)
- Common quality standard rules (police ethics, monitoring programmes) regarding police (2008)
- Harmonisation of the quality standards of forensic laboratories (2008)
- Systematic exchange programmes for law enforcement officers' authorities
- Adoption of the proposal aimed at establishing CEPOL (European Police College) as a body of the Union (2005)
- Improvement of operational cooperation between law enforcement authorities of one Member State with the other Member States
- Set up short-duration joint customs and police operations and/or multidisciplinary joint teams (continuous)
- Elaboration of minimum standards for the cross-jurisdictional use of investigation techniques (2006)
- Best practice guide for the promotion and expansion of the use of special forms of cooperation for customs administrations as provided by the Naples II Convention (2007)
- Improvement of the European cooperation between anti-corruption bodies by setting-up a network between anti-corruption authorities (including police, judicial, prosecutorial and customs) at EU and transnational level (2008)

3.5. Management of Crisis Within the European Union

- Commission Decision creating a secure general rapid alert system (ARGUS) and a Commission Crisis Centre to coordinate existing alert systems (2005)
- Proposal creating a Critical Infrastructure Warning Information Network (CIWIN) (2005)
- Plan on the protection of critical infrastructures (2005)
- Integrated EU crisis management arrangements (to be implemented by 1 July 2006)

3.6. General Crime Prevention

- Developing the European Crime Prevention Network (2005)

4. Strengthening Justice

- See also Framework Programme "Fundamental Rights and Justice" under the new Financial Perspectives (2005)
- Specific Programme on Judicial Cooperation in Civil and Commercial Matters (2007)
- Specific Programme on Judicial Cooperation in Criminal Matters (2007)

4.1. Confidence Building and Mutual Trust

- Enhancing cooperation
- Support by the Union to networks of judicial organisations and institutions (continuous)
- Continuation of the development of the web site of the European Judicial Network and of the databases on the European instruments case law (continuous)
- Constant updating and improvement of the European Judicial Atlas (continuous)
- Annual celebration of the European Day of Civil Justice (continuous)
- Creating a "European Judicial culture"
- Evaluation of quality of justice (Communication—2006)
- Communication from the Commission on judicial training in EU (2005), continuation of the pilot project for exchange of magistrates (2005) and Preparatory action (2006)
- Creation, from the existing structures, of an effective European training network for judicial authorities for both civil and criminal matters (2007)
- Developing networking of judicial organisations and institutions
- Report on the functioning of the European Judicial Network in civil and commercial matters (2005) and proposal for amendment, as appropriate (2006)
- EU workshops to promote cooperation between members of the legal professions with a view to establishing best practices (2006)
- Coherence and better quality of EU legislation
- Proposal for the amendment of Regulation 1348/2000 on the service in the Member States of judicial and extrajudicial documents in civil or commercial matters (2005)

- Report on the functioning of the Regulation n° 1206/2001 on the taking of evidence and proposal for amendment, as appropriate (2007)
- Report on the functioning of "Brussels I" Regulation (2007) and proposal for amendment, as appropriate (2009)
- Final research report including a draft Common Frame of Reference (2007)
- Adoption of Common Frame of Reference (CFR) in EU contract law (2009 at the latest)

4.2. Judicial Cooperation in Criminal Matters

- Establishment of a specific Programme on Judicial Cooperation in Criminal Matters (2007)
- Pursuing the implementation of the mutual recognition principle:
- Communication on mutual recognition of decisions in criminal matters and reinforcement of mutual trust between Member States (2005)
- White Paper on the exchanges of information on convictions and the effect of such convictions in the EU (2005)
- Proposal on taking into account of convictions in the Member States of the European Union in the course of new criminal proceedings (2005)
- Proposal on the transmission to, and keeping by, the Member State of nationality of information on criminal convictions (2005)
- Communication on the creation of an index of non EU nationals convicted in a EU Member State (2005)
- Initiative on the European Enforcement Order and the transfer of sentenced persons between Member States of the EU (2005)
- Proposal on mutual recognition of non-custodial pre-trial supervision measures (2005)
- Communication on disqualification (2005)
- Report on the implementation of the Framework Decision on the European arrest warrant and the surrender procedures between Member States (2005)
- Initiative on the recognition and enforcement in the European Union of prohibitions arising from convictions for sexual offences committed against children (2005)
- Proposal on driving disqualifications (reformatting 1998 Convention) (2006)
- Report on the implementation of the Framework Decision of 22.7.2003 on the execution in the EU of orders freezing property or evidence (2006)

- Report on the implementation of the Framework Decision on the application of the principle of mutual recognition to financial penalties (2006)
- Proposal on recognition and execution of alternative sanctions and on suspended sentence (2007)
- Proposal completing the European Evidence Warrant (2008)
- Approximation
- Green Paper on Conflicts of Jurisdiction and Double Jeopardy (ne bis in idem) (2005)
- Green Paper on presumption of innocence (2005)
- Second report on the implementation of the Framework Decision of 15.3.2001 on the standing of victims in criminal proceedings (2005)
- Third report on the Framework Decision of 15.3.2001 on the standing of victims in criminal proceedings (2006)
- Proposal on conflicts of jurisdiction and the ne bis in idem principle (2006)
- Green Paper on handling of evidence (2006)
- Green Paper on default (in absentia) judgements (2006)
- Proposal on minimum standards relating to the taking of evidence (2007)
- Proposal on default judgements (in absentia) (2007)
- Proposal on the approximation of sectoral criminal sanctions (no later than 2007)
- Others instruments in the field of judicial cooperation in criminal matters:
- Recommendation on minimum standards for capturing and exchanging electronic evidence (2006)
- Proposal on the wilful destruction of documentary evidence (2007)
- Proposal on the protection of witnesses and collaborators of justice (2007)
- Study on the cross-border use of intelligence as evidence (2008)
- Evaluation of the efficiency of specialised judicial bodies for dealing with the investigation of cases linked to organised crime (2009)
- Eurojust
- 2nd report on the legal transposition of the Council Decision of 28.2.2002 setting up Eurojust (2005)
- Proposal on Eurojust (no later than 1 January 2008)
- White Paper on enhancing the protection of the Union's financial interests (by 2009)

4.3. Strengthening Efficiency of Justice and Improving Mutual Recognition and Effective Access to Justice in Civil Matters

- Green Paper on successions (2005)
- Green Paper on conflict of laws and jurisdiction on divorce matters (Rome III) (2005)
- Proposal on conflicts of laws regarding contractual obligations (Rome I) (2005)
- Proposal on small claims (2005)
- Proposal on maintenance obligations (2005)
- Adoption of the "Rome II" proposal on conflicts of laws regarding non-contractual obligations (2006)
- Adoption of the Payment Order Regulation (2006)
- Adoption of a Directive on Alternative Dispute Resolution (ADR)—mediation (2006)
- Green Paper on property consequences of matrimonial relations and partnerships (2006)
- Green Paper(s) on the effective enforcement of judicial decisions (2006–2007)
- Green Paper on the abolition/reduction of legislation and administrative measures for the free circulation of documents (2007)
- Green Paper on mutual recognition in matters related to Civil Status (2008)
- Green Paper on minimum standards for some aspects of procedural law (2008)
- Evaluation of the possibility of the suppression of exequatur and legislative proposals, as appropriate (2008–2010)
- Establishment of a specific Programme on Judicial Cooperation in Civil and Commercial Matters (2007)

4.4. International Legal Order

- Conclusion of negotiations relating to the convention on the choice of forum (2005)
- Proposal for the conclusion of the so-called "parallel agreements" with Denmark on "Brussels I" and service of documents (2005)
- Negotiation of the Convention on Terrorism in the Council of Europe (2005)

- Active involvement of the activities of the Council of Europe and other international organisations and fora (G8, UN, OECD, OSCE, FATF) in criminal matters (2005–2009)
- Examination of the case for bilateral agreements between the EU with third countries on extradition (2005–2009)
- Examination of the case for bilateral agreements between the EU with third countries on mutual legal assistance (2005–2009)
- Proposal on the conclusion and on the signature of the Council of Europe Convention against money laundering and terrorist financing on behalf of EC (2005/2006)
- Accession of the Community to the Hague Conference on private international law (2006)
- Proposal for the conclusion of a new Lugano Convention (2006)
- Inclusion of provisions on counter-terrorist assistance in proposed revision of existing instruments governing external assistance (2006)
- Proposal on conclusion of the United Nations Convention against Corruption on behalf of the EC (2006)
- Conclusion of negotiations relating to the convention on maintenance obligations (2007)
- Proposal on conclusion of the United Nations Protocol against the illicit manufacturing of and trafficking in firearms, their parts and components, and ammunition on behalf of the EC (2007)

5. External Relations

- Strategy on all the external aspects of the Union policy on freedom, security and justice, based on the measures developed in the Hague programme (2005)
- Communication on all the external aspects of the Union policy on freedom, security and justice (mid-2005—contribution to the Strategy).

DOCUMENT NO. 11

TERRORISM IN EUROPE: HOW DOES THE UNION OF 25 RESPOND TO THIS PHENOMENON?

Remarks by Dr. Javier Solana
EU High Representative for the Common Foreign and Security Policy
S0266/04

Berlin, 7 October 2004

Ladies and Gentlemen,

It is a great pleasure for me to be in Berlin and share some thoughts with you on the issue of terrorism.

The form of terrorism we have been facing, since the atrocious attacks against New York and Washington on 9/11, is new. It is more fanatical, more lethal, more global than anything we have known so far.

Terrorism is a global scourge that requires a global response. In our European Security Strategy, we have identified terrorism as one of the key strategic threats facing Europe.

I would like to structure my remarks around four themes. First, our strategic vision. Second, intelligence. Third, international cooperation. Fourth, policies.

I would like to stress from the outset, that all our efforts in the field of the fight against terrorism relate to the bigger vision. This is the vision we have set out in the European Security Strategy: to make the world a better place, to make the world more secure. We have identified the existential threats of the 21st century. Terrorism is one of them. The EU has understood the challenge. We are developing a comprehensive response. We are making use of all instruments at our disposal. To this end, we are promoting all our effective mechanisms for a multilateral approach.

At the same time, we will continue to address the underlying causes of terrorism, however difficult this might be. We need to address poverty, alienation, radicalisation. We need to prevent weak states from collapsing. We need to reinforce our dialogue with other cultures.

While fully committed to the fight against terrorism, it is our duty to protect human rights. This is a very deep conviction of ours. It is a matter of preserving our basic values. I keep saying that there is absolutely no trade-off between security and human rights protection and the rule of law. The violation of human rights in the fight against terrorism is not only morally undesirable, but also ineffective in the long run.

As one would expect at a meeting such as this, one cannot neglect the role that intelligence can play in the struggle against terrorism.

The first objective of intelligence is to fight terrorists, prevent them from acting, thwart their design, track them after an attack. This is the kind of operational intelligence that is best done at the national level.

Many arrests, or disruptions or operations in Europe are the result of cooperation and sharing between services. I was particularly struck that the day I briefed Justice and Interior Ministers on ideas for improving the sharing of strategic intelligence, I had to take questions from the press as whether this was sufficient and whether there should be European mechanisms for the sharing of operational intelligence. Yet, that very day there were simultaneous arrests in five European countries in a joint operation. This can only have been the product of close operational cooperation between services.

Still, I am not complacent. For that reason it is good that Europe's security services are working closely together within the Counter-Terrorist Group to exchange experience and to build stronger operational connection. The reestablishment of Europol's Counter-Terrorist Task Force is also to be welcomed, as are moves to strengthen the links between Chiefs of Police.

Member States also need intelligence derived from ongoing case work. But this is needed not for policy work, at least not directly, but for preventative work: to disrupt and dismantle networks and prevent attacks. This information is in many ways more sensitive, and widespread sharing is not needed or appropriate. Services share on a task basis: not at 25 for the sake of it.

Beyond that, I see another main role for intelligence: to inform our political action. To educate us on the process of terrorism, explaining the origins of the alienation that underpins terrorism, how radicalisation and recruitment happens, highlighting the goals and methods and the targeting strategies. Only when we understand this, can we develop the most appropriate and concrete policies. We need to take away the foundation for terrorism, and establish barriers to its activities and its spread.

For this we need good strategic assessed intelligence. The Member States have structures to provide this, and with their support and inputs we are building structures at a European level, in the Council's Joint Situation Centre, to bring this information to European policy makers. Europol is performing a similar function with material derived from police work and we are working to ensure a synergy between these two efforts. This is a different level of intelligence, more analytical, where there is real added value to European Union's action.

International cooperation is fundamental in the fight against terrorism. At the aftermath of the Madrid bombings, the EU has been focusing on some more internal aspects of the fight against terrorism. However, this does not mean that the EU plans to become an introverted power, or a 'closed system' in today's world. This is just not possible-and not effective altogether.

The United Nations and its agencies play a key role in the global fight against terrorism. We must build on it and strengthen the work of the United Nations. We support the Counter Terrorism Committee, including on the monitoring of implementation. We are strengthening the work of other multilateral organisations as well.

We are working closely with many partners in this global fight. Our transatlantic relationship is extremely important in this respect. There has been a sea change in our cooperation. Last year we concluded two Europol agreements, as well as an Extradition and Mutual Legal Assistance Agreement. We have intelligence cooperation. We have set up a high-level group on border and transport security. We are carrying forward work on terrorist financing. Both the EU and the US will share their data on lost and stolen passports with Interpol. Deeds matter more than words, and deeds on the transatlantic level have been swift and decisive, even when we had strong divergences over Iraq.

Generally, counter-terrorism is very high on our international agenda and is becoming better integrated into our political dialogue with third countries. We are better targeting our external assistance and capacity building programmes. We are negotiating counter-terrorism clauses. We have realised that we should be ready to use our trade and economic muscle, when necessary. Overall, we should not take care only of the willing, but unable countries. We also need to address those who are able but unwilling.

Our policies are wide-ranging. They cut across all areas of EU's counter-terrorism action. To facilitate this task of following through this complex policy-making, we now have a Plan of Action, approved by the European Council, which sets out with clarity who does what, in what deadline. This also helps national Parliaments to have a clear idea of EU's objectives, and to facilitate their own legislative planning.

With a view to assisting me in this important and challenging coordination task, I have recently appointed a counter-terrorism coordinator.

In the area of Justice and Home Affairs, we have a considerable number of agreed new instruments. The decisions which the Council has adopted provide real added value in the fight against terrorism. The European Arrest Warrant is already producing concrete results. We have been developing the 'free movement of judicial decisions' in the EU, through the mutual recognition of judicial decisions, such as arrest and surrender of suspects, confiscation, freezing of assets, etc. There are new priorities: Enhanced cooperation on information exchange. Closer cooperation between Member States and European bodies, such as Europol and Eurojust. Inclusion of biometrics into travel documents. Work is ongoing on data retention, for internet service providers to preserve the records of communications. Furthermore, the Regulation setting up the European Border Agency will be adopted by the Council on 25 October. This means that the new Agency will be operational in 2005.

The prevention of the financing of terrorism is of great importance. We have done a lot; more needs to be done. As requested by the European Council, I am developing, in cooperation with the Commission, a strategy against the financing of terrorism. Even on this front, our success will rely, to a considerable degree, on securing the appropriate interaction, and right flow of intelligence, between the relevant services and the financial and banking communities.

In the fight against terrorism, the role of Member States remains key. Therefore, we should see to it that we create a coordinated and harmonised approach among Member States. Allow me to say, on this point, that the draft Constitutional Treaty, once adopted, will offer a stronger impetus to our efforts to streamline our strengthened cooperation.

I firmly believe that the military option alone cannot offer a solution. What I have mentioned above, i.e. judicial, police cooperation, intelligence-sharing, should be the center of gravity of our action. This does not mean that we are not working on how European Security and Defense Policy (ESDP) can offer a meaningful contribution. Quite the contrary; work is ongoing in the field, e.g. of consequence management. But, I repeat, ESDP is not at the core of our efforts.

Another issue I would like to touch upon briefly is the field of critical infrastructure. The European Council asked that existing cooperation on civil protection be enhanced, and work is currently underway in this field. Furthermore, the European Council has invited us to assess the capabilities of Member States in preventing and coping with the consequences of any type of terrorist attack, to identify best practices and propose necessary measures. The Council, in close coordination with the Commission, will prepare an overall strategy to enhance the protection of critical infrastructures.

Terrorism, as well as proliferation, have been identified in the European Security Strategy as two of the most serious threats facing our continent and the world. The ultimate catastrophic scenario is the acquisition by terrorists of WMD.

To address this threat, we have developed a non-proliferation strategy at the EU level, based on our effective multilateralism approach. All EU Member States have adhered to the additional protocol to the Non-Proliferation Treaty and support its universal application. We are enhancing our cooperation with the International Atomic Energy Agency (IAEA), and the Organisation for the Prohibition of Chemical Weapons. We are working to improve export controls, to prevent proliferation of NBC material and conventional weapons. We support the creation of a multilateral binding instrument for the identification and tracing of illicit small arms and light weapons.

I wish to conclude by saying that the European Union is developing an entire set of policies aimed at tackling the issue of terrorism head-on. But, at the same time, as I pointed out at the beginning of my remarks, we are working to 'take away the oxygen' from the terrorists. This will involve addressing the factors which contribute to support for, and recruitment into, terrorism. Regional conflicts cause anger and feed the terrorist propaganda. The unresolved Arab-Israeli problem leads to the rise of radicalism and extremism.

We will be tough on terrorism and tough on the causes of terrorism. These are not two fights. It is one fight. And we are determined to meet the challenge.

It is our objective to fight against terrorism and to make this world a better place for everybody

DOCUMENT NO. 12

EUROPEAN UNION DECLARATION ON COMBATING TERRORISM

European Council

1 May 2004

1. Introduction

The European Council, deeply shocked by the terrorist attacks in Madrid, expresses its sympathy and solidarity to the victims, their families and to the Spanish people.

The callous and cowardly attacks served as a terrible reminder of the threat posed by terrorism to our society. Acts of terrorism are attacks against the values on which the Union is founded.

The Union and its Member States pledge to do everything within their power to combat all forms of terrorism in accordance with the fundamental principles of the Union, the provisions of the Charter of the United Nations and the obligations set out under United Nations Security Council Resolution 1373 (2001).

The threat of terrorism affects us all. A terrorist act against one country concerns the international community as a whole. There will be neither weakness nor compromise of any kind when dealing with terrorists. No country in the world can consider itself immune. Terrorism will only be defeated by solidarity and collective action.

The European Council endorses the proposal of the European Parliament to declare 11 March a European day commemorating the victims of terrorism.

2. Solidarity Clause

The European Council welcomes the political commitment of the Member States and of the acceding States, taken as of now, to act jointly against terrorist acts, in the spirit of the Solidarity Clause contained in Article 42 of the draft Constitution for Europe.

A separate Declaration is attached.

3. Security Strategy

The European Security Strategy, adopted by the European Council last December, identified terrorism as one of the key threats to EU interests and requested the Presidency and Secretary-General/High Representative Solana, in coordination with the Commission, to present concrete proposals for implementing the Strategy, including recommendations for combating the threat posed by terrorism and dealing with its root causes.

In light of the events in Madrid, the European Council believes that full implementation of measures to combat terrorism is a matter of urgency.

The European Council calls for the development of an EU long-term strategy to address all the factors which contribute to terrorism. As we stated in the Conclusions of our meeting on 21 September 2001, the Union must increase its involvement in the efforts of the international community to prevent and stabilise regional conflicts and promote good governance and the rule of law.

In addition, the European Council calls for work to be rapidly pursued to develop the contribution of ESDP to the fight against terrorism, on the basis of actions taken since the Seville European Council.

The European Union will seek ways to improve the security of its citizens who are resident, or travelling, in third countries and exposed to a terrorist threat.

4. Assistance to Victims

The European Council calls for the adoption, before 1st May 2004, of the Council Directive on compensation to crime victims.

The European Council invites the Commission to ensure the allocation, as a matter of urgency, of the funds available in the 2004 budget for supporting victims of terrorism.

5. Building on Existing Cooperation

At its meeting on 21 September 2001, the European Council adopted a Plan of Action to Combat Terrorism which has since been supplemented by many important initiatives. The effective combating of terrorism requires that measures adopted by the Council be effectively and comprehensively implemented by Member States.

(a) Legislative Measures

The European Council acknowledges that the legislative framework created by the Union for the purpose of combating terrorism and improving judicial cooperation has a decisive role to play in combating terrorist activities.

It urges all Member States to take any measures that remain necessary to implement fully and without delay the following legislative measures:

- Framework Decision on the European Arrest Warrant
- Framework Decision on Joint Investigation Teams
- Framework Decision on Combating Terrorism
- Framework Decision on money laundering, the identification, tracing, freezing and confiscation of instrumentalities and the proceeds of crime;
- Decision establishing Eurojust;
- Decision on the implementation of specific measures for police and judicial cooperation to combat terrorism;

Any such measures should be in place no later than June 2004.

The European Council calls on Member States to implement the Framework Decision on the execution of orders freezing property or evidence and to ratify the Convention on the Mutual Assistance in Criminal Matters, its Protocol and the three Protocols to the Europol Convention by December 2004.

In addition, the Framework Decision on the Confiscation of Crime Related Proceeds, Instrumentalities and Property and the Framework Decision on Attacks against Information Systems should be finalised by June 2004. Work on the Framework Decision on the Mutual Recognition of Confiscation Orders should also be concluded by June 2004 and work on the Framework Decision on a European Evidence Warrant taken forward.

The European Council, with a view to the further development of the legislative framework set out above, instructs the Council to examine measures in the following areas:

- proposals for establishing rules on the retention of communications traffic data by service providers;
- exchanges of information on convictions for terrorist offences;
- cross-border hot pursuit;
- a European register on convictions and disqualifications;
- a data base on forensic material; and
- simplifying the exchange of information and intelligence between law enforcement authorities of the Member States.

Priority should be given to the proposals under the retention of communication traffic data and exchange of information on convictions with a view to adoption by June 2005.

Member States reaffirm their commitment to reinforce judicial cooperation. They are invited to ensure the execution of any request for mutual legal assistance related to terrorist offences and to provide each other with the fullest cooperation.

The Commission is invited to bring forward a proposal aimed at the creation of a European Programme for the protection of witnesses in terrorist cases.

(b) Reinforcing Operational Cooperation

The European Council calls on Member States to ensure that law enforcement agencies (security services, police, customs etc.) cooperate with each other and exchange all information relevant to combating terrorism as extensively as possible.

The European Council calls on Member States to ensure that the optimum and most effective use is made of existing EU bodies, in particular Europol and Eurojust, to promote cooperation in the fight against terrorism. It calls on Member States, to ensure that:

- Eurojust national correspondents for terrorist matters are designated by all Member States and Eurojust is used to the maximum extent for the purpose of cooperation in cross-border terrorism cases;
- Europol and Eurojust representatives are associated with the work of Joint Investigation Teams as far as possible;
- The Europol/Eurojust agreement is adopted by May 2004.

The European Council also calls on Member States to reinforce the role of Europol in the fight against terrorism by:

- reinforcing its counter-terrorism capacities and reactivating the Counter-Terrorist Task Force; and
- ensuring that Europol is provided by Member States law enforcement authorities with all relevant criminal intelligence related to terrorism as soon as it is available.

The European Council calls on Europol to proceed with implementation of the Europol Information System as quickly as possible.

In addition, the European Council underlines the role of the Police Chiefs' Task Force in coordinating operational measures in response to, and prevention of, terrorist acts. The European Council calls on the Task Force to review how its operational capacity can be reinforced and to focus on proactive intelligence. The Task Force is invited to draw up, with the assistance of experts from intelligence services and from Europol, a report on the terrorist attacks in Madrid.

The European Council calls on the Council to examine an interim report on the outcome of the process of peer evaluation of national arrangements in the fight against terrorism by September 2004 and a final report covering the Accession States by September 2005.

The European Council, with a view to building on this cooperation, also instructs the Council to put in place new committee structures capable of ensuring greater operational cooperation on security and terrorism within the Union.

The European Council recognises that there is a need to ensure terrorist organisations and groups are starved of the components of their trade. In particular there is a need to ensure greater security of firearms, explosives, bomb-making equipment, and the technologies that contribute to the perpetration of terrorist outrages. It instructs the Council to examine the scope for measures in this area.

(c) Maximising the Effectiveness of Information Systems.

The European Council calls on the Council to adopt the necessary measures to enable the Draft Council Regulation and Draft Decision on the introduction of new functions for the Schengen Information System (SIS), to come into force by June 2004.

Decisions should be taken on the location, management and financing of SIS II by May 2004 in order to allow the Commission to take forward its full development. The Commission and the Council are urged to take forward work on the Visa Information System (VIS) in line with the conclusions adopted in February 2004. The European Council calls on the Commission to submit proposals for enhanced interoperability between European databases and to explore the creation of synergies between existing and future information systems (SIS II, VIS and EURODAC) in order to exploit their added value within their respective legal and technical frameworks in the prevention and fight against terrorism.

The European Council invites the Commission to bring forward proposals to the June European Council in relation to exchange of personal information (DNA, fingerprints and visa data) for the purpose of combating terrorism. The Commission proposals should also include provisions to enable national law enforcement agencies to have access to the EU systems.

The Council is also invited to consider the criteria that should be applied for the purposes of Article 96 of the Schengen Convention in relation to certain persons reported for the purpose of being refused entry.

6. Strengthening Border Controls and Document Security

Improved border controls and document security play an important role in combating terrorism. The European Council therefore emphasises that work on measures in this area needs to be expedited. In particular, work will be taken forward on:

- the proposal for a Regulation establishing a European Borders Agency with a view to adoption by May 2004 and the Agency made operational by 1 January 2005;
- the proposed Council Directive on the obligation of carriers to communicate passenger data with view to an early conclusion on this measure; and
- the adoption of the Draft Strategy for Customs Cooperation and a related work plan by May 2004, and the subsequent implementation of measures to combat terrorism as a matter of urgency.

The European Council also instructs the Council to adopt by the end of 2004 the Commission's proposals for the incorporation of biometric features into passports and visas, with a view to the finalisation of the technical specification to be adopted by the Commission by the same deadline.

The European Council, with a view to further developments of these measures instructs the Council to take forward, on the basis of a proposal from the Commission, work on the creation by end 2005 of an integrated system for the exchange of information on stolen and lost passports having recourse to the SIS and the Interpol database.

It also invites the Commission to bring forward a proposal no later than June 2004 for a common EU approach to the use of passengers data for border and aviation security and other law enforcement purposes.

7. EU Guidelines for a Common Approach to Combating Terrorism

The European Council welcomes the EU Guidelines for a Common Approach to Combating Terrorism which demonstrate the commitment of the Union to prevent and suppress terrorism in a visible and coherent manner.

8. Strategic Objectives for a Revised EU Plan of Action to Combat Terrorism

Building on existing cooperation, the European Council agreed updated Strategic Objectives to enhance the EU Plan of Action to Combat Terrorism (contained in Annex I).

The following high level Strategic Objectives will be implemented:

- Deepen the international consensus and enhance international efforts to combat terrorism
- Reduce the access of terrorists to financial and other economic resources.

- Maximise capacity within EU bodies and Member States to detect, investigate and prosecute terrorists and prevent terrorist attacks
- Protect the security of international transport and ensure effective systems of border control
- Enhance the capability of Member States to deal with the consequences of a terrorist attack
- Address the factors which contribute to support for, and recruitment into, terrorism
- Target actions under EU external relations towards priority Third Countries where counter-terrorist capacity or commitment to combating terrorism needs to be enhanced

The European Council requests the Council to complete the adoption of the revised Plan of Action and to report back to the June European Council.

9. Sharing of Intelligence

Underlining the importance of more efficient intelligence cooperation and improved threat assessment, the European Council calls upon Member States to improve mechanisms for cooperation and the promotion of effective systematic collaboration between police, security and intelligence services.

The flow of intelligence in relation to all aspects of terrorism to Europol should be improved. The further development of the relationship between Europol and intelligence services will also be taken forward.

The European Council endorses the efforts of Secretary-General/High Representative Solana to integrate, within the Council Secretariat, an intelligence capacity on all aspects of the terrorist threat with a view to informing EU policy and invites him to make proposals in advance of the June European Council.

10. Preventing the Financing of Terrorism

The European Council believes that strong preventive action must continue to be taken on the sources of financing of terrorist organisations and to swiftly disrupt the flow of financial resources to terrorist groups and related entities and individuals, while respecting the rule of law. In this regard, it invites the Council to identify measures to improve the effectiveness and efficiency of the mechanism set up to freeze the assets of terrorists and terrorist organisations and to identify the holders and true beneficiaries of bank accounts, irrespective of their place of residence.

The European Council calls on all Member States to ratify and fully implement the 1999 UN Convention for the Suppression of the Financing of

Terrorism and to give effect to the provisions of UNSCR 1373 directed to the freezing of assets.

Member States are invited to increase cooperation between national competent authorities, Financial Intelligence Units and private financial institutions to facilitate improved exchange of information on terrorist financing.

The Commission will consider improvements on regulation and transparency of legal entities, including charities and alternative remittance systems, which may be used by terrorists to acquire funding for their activities.

The EU will pursue dialogue with third countries on this crucial issue in order to step up the fight against the financing of terrorism.

11. Measures to Protect Transport and Population

The European Council calls for the strengthening of the security of all forms of transport systems, including through the enhancement of the legal framework and the improvement of prevention mechanisms. The Commission is, in particular, invited to bring forward a proposal for enhancing the security measures in harbours and ships.

Further action is needed to strengthen capacity within Member States to alleviate the consequences of attacks on the civilian population, including in the areas of health security and civil protection, building on existing EU Health Security and CBRN programmes.

The Commission, the Council and the Member States, as appropriate, should develop policies to strengthen the protection of citizens, essential services (such as water supplies, energy and communications) and production systems (agro-food and process industries), as well as to establish mechanisms (surveillance, early warning, alert and response systems and procedures) to deal with the consequences of any terrorist attacks.

12. International Cooperation

Supporting the key role of the United Nations, the European Council will continue to work to ensure universal adherence to, and full implementation of, all UN Security Council Resolutions, UN Conventions on Terrorism and related Protocols.

The European Union will work with and within international, regional and sub-regional organisations to strengthen international solidarity in countering terrorism.

The European Union will ensure effective and practical cooperation with Third countries in combating terrorism, in particular through the following measures:

- Development of technical assistance strategies, to facilitate vulnerable Third countries in enhancing their counter-terrorism capability, and by addressing counter-terrorism concerns into all relevant external assistance programmes to promote good governance and the rule of law

- ensure that counter-terrorism is a key element of political dialogue at all levels with Third Countries, in particular those which represent a potential terrorist threat to international peace and security.
- The European Union will analyse and evaluate the commitment of countries to combat terrorism on an ongoing basis. This will be an influencing factor in EU relations with them.

The European Council calls for the optimum use of all EU police resources deployed in Third countries, also in the context of EU crisis management.

13. Cooperation with US and Partners

Building on the solidarity and cooperation enshrined in the 2001 Plan of Action to Combat Terrorism, the European Council will seek to further strengthen cooperation with the US and other partners in countering the threat posed by terrorism.

14. Establishment of the Position of a Counter-Terrorism Coordinator

The European Council emphasises that a comprehensive and strongly coordinated approach is required in response to the threat posed by terrorism.

The European Council accordingly agrees to the establishment of the position of a Counter-Terrorism Co-ordinator.

The Co-ordinator, who will work within the Council Secretariat, will co-ordinate the work of the Council in combating terrorism and, with due regard to the responsibilities of the Commission, maintain an overview of all the instruments at the Union's disposal with a view to regular reporting to the Council and effective follow-up of Council decisions.

The European Council welcomes the decision of Secretary General/High Representative Solana to appoint Mr. Gijs de Vries to the position of Counter-Terrorism Coordinator.

15. The Way Forward

The European Council invites the Council, in cooperation with Secretary-General/High Representative Solana and the Commission, to report in detail to the June European Council on the state of implementation of these measures.

Annex I

***European Union Strategic Objectives to Combat Terrorism* (Revised Plan of Action)**

Objective 1: To deepen the international consensus and enhance international efforts to combat terrorism

- Support the key role of the United Nations in sustaining the international consensus and mobilizing the international community as a whole, in particular the General Assembly and the work of the Security Council, inter alia, through its Counter Terrorism Committee and the Taliban/Al Quaeda Sanctions Committee, as well as the Terrorism Prevention Branch of the UN Office of Drugs and Crime
- Work to ensure universal adherence to, and full implementation of, the United Nations Conventions on Terrorism, and to agree a Comprehensive UN Convention against Terrorism and agree a comprehensive UN Convention on the Suppression of Acts of Nuclear Terrorism
- Work with and within regional and international organizations to ensure their effective contribution to combating terrorism in accordance with UN obligations
- Include effective counter-terrorism clauses in all agreements with third countries

Objective 2: To reduce the access of terrorists to financial and other economic resources

- Ensure the effectiveness of EU asset freezing procedures, including the non-financial economic resources, in accordance with UN obligations and the need to respect due process and the Rule of Law
- Establish operational links and improve cooperation between relevant bodies to facilitate enhanced exchange of information on terrorist financing
- Develop and implement an EU strategy on the suppression of terrorist financing, including the regulation of charitable organisations and alternative remittance systems
- Cooperate closely with the Financial Action Task Force (FATF) on all issues regarding the financing of terrorism and ensure that the EU legal framework is adapted to the eight special recommendations on terrorist financing
- Pursue political and technical dialogue with Third Countries, in order to step up the fight against the financing of terrorism

Objective 3: To maximise capacity within EU bodies and Member States to detect, investigate and prosecute terrorists and prevent terrorist attacks

- Ensure optimum and effective use of existing EU bodies such as Europol, Eurojust and the Police Chiefs Task Force
- Improve mechanisms for cooperation for the sharing of expertise on protective, investigative and preventive security policies between police and security services
- Promote effective, systematic collaboration in intelligence exchange between Member States
- Enhance the capacity of appropriate EU bodies in the preparation of intelligence assessments of all aspects of the terrorist threat, with a closer linkage to EU policymaking
- Work to identify, disrupt and dismantle arrangements for supply of weapons to terrorists

Objective 4: To protect the security of international transport and ensure effective systems of border control

- Ensure the integration of counter-terrorist considerations into the work of relevant EU bodies (transport, border controls, identity documentation etc)
- Work to develop further EU transport security standards, in coordination with relevant international organisations and third countries
- Develop and implement a common EU approach to the exchange and analysis of passenger information
- Encourage and support non-EU states to comply fully with ICAO and IMO standards
- Enhance capacities for the identification of terrorists and the detection of terrorist devices, materials or funds at ports, airports and land borders
- Reinforce the protection of European citizens in third countries

Objective 5: To enhance the capability of the European Union and of Member States to deal with the consequences of a terrorist attack

- Identify areas for closer cooperation in consequence management with other international organisations within their respective competences, including NATO
- Ensure full implementation of the EU Health Security and CBRN programmes

- Develop strategies to improve the capacity of Member States to communicate with citizens in the event of a major terrorist attack
- Ensure that support and assistance is provided to the victims of terrorist crimes, and protect minority communities who may be at risk of a backlash in the event of a major attack

Objective 6: To address the factors which contribute to support for, and recruitment into, terrorism

- Identify factors which contribute to recruitment to terrorism, both within the EU and internationally, and develop a long-term strategy to address these
- Continue to investigate the links between extreme religious or political beliefs, as well as socio-economic and other factors, and support for terrorism, building on work already undertaken in this area, and identify appropriate response measures
- Make more efficient use of external assistance programmes to address factors which can contribute to the support for terrorism, including in particular support for good governance and the rule of law
- Develop and implement a strategy to promote cross-cultural and inter-religious understanding between Europe and the Islamic World

Objective 7: To target actions under EU external relations towards priority Third Countries where counter-terrorist capacity or commitment to combating terrorism needs to be enhanced

- Expand the role of the SitCen in the carrying out of threat assessments to enable working groups to focus on the development of policy
- Develop capacities to analyse and evaluate third country activities in counter-terrorism
- Develop technical assistance strategies to enhance the counter-terrorist capacity of priority countries, in coordination with other international organisations and Donor states
- Ensure that specific counter-terrorism issues, including effective counter-terrorism clauses in all agreements reflecting the priorities of the revised Plan of Action are a key element of EU relations at all levels with priority countries
- Mainstream counter-terrorist objectives into the work of the geographical working groups and external assistance programmes

Draft Declaration on Solidarity Against Terrorism

We, the Heads of State or Government of the Member States of the European Union, and of the States acceding to the Union on 1 May, have declared our firm intention as follows:

In the spirit of the solidarity clause laid down in Article 42 of the draft Treaty establishing a Constitution for Europe, the Member States and the acceding States shall accordingly act jointly in a spirit of solidarity if one of them is the victim of a terrorist attack. They shall mobilise all the instruments at their disposal, including military resources to:

- prevent the terrorist threat in the territory of one of them;
- protect democratic institutions and the civilian population from any terrorist attack;
- assist a Member State or an acceding State in its territory at the request of its political authorities in the event of a terrorist attack.

It shall be for each Member State or acceding State to the Union to choose the most appropriate means to comply with this solidarity commitment towards the affected State.

DOCUMENT NO. 13

EUROPEAN SECURITY STRATEGY, A SECURE EUROPE IN A BETTER WORLD

European Union Council

Brussels, 12 December 2003

Synopsis:

In this document, the European Union clarifies its security strategy, which is aimed at achieving a secure Europe in a better world, identifying the threats facing the Union, defining its strategic objectives and setting out the political implications for Europe.

Summary

The European security strategy was drawn up under the authority of the EU's High Representative for the Common Foreign and Security Policy, Javier Solana, and adopted by the Brussels European Council of 12 and 13 December 2003. It identifies the global challenges and key threats to the security of the Union and clarifies its strategic objectives in dealing with them, such as building security in the EU's neighbourhood and promoting an international order based on effective multilateralism. It also assesses the policy implications that these objectives have for Europe.

The Security Environment: Global Challenges and Key Threats

In the context of ever-increasing globalisation, the internal and external aspects of security are inextricably linked. Flows of trade and investment, the development of technology and the spread of democracy have brought prosperity and freedom to many people, while others have perceived globalisation as a cause of frustration and injustice. In much of the developing world, poverty and diseases such as AIDS give rise to security concerns, and in many cases economic failure is linked to political problems and violent conflict. Security is a precondition for development. Competition for natural resources is likely to create further turbulence. Energy dependence is a special concern for Europe.

The security strategy identifies three key threats facing Europe:

- **Terrorism.** Concerted European action against terrorism is indispensable. Terrorism puts lives at risk and seeks to undermine the openness and tolerance of our societies. It arises out of complex causes, including the pressures of modernisation, cultural, social and political crises, and the alienation of young people living in foreign societies.
- **Proliferation of weapons of mass destruction (WMD).** This is potentially the greatest threat to our security. International treaty régimes and export control arrangements have slowed the spread of WMD, but we are entering a new and dangerous period. Advances in the biological sciences may increase the potency of biological weapons. The most frightening scenario is one in which terrorist groups acquire weapons of mass destruction. In this event, a small group would be able to inflict damage on a scale previously possible only for States and armies.
- **Regional conflicts.** These can have a direct or indirect impact on European interests, regardless of their geographical location. They pose a threat to minorities, fundamental freedoms and human rights. They can lead to extremism and terrorism and provoke state failure.
- **State failure.** Civil conflict and bad governance—corruption, abuse of power, weak institutions and lack of accountability—corrode States from within. This can lead to a collapse of state institutions. Afghanistan under the Taliban is a well-known example. State failure is an alarming phenomenon that undermines global governance and adds to regional instability.
- **Organised crime.** Europe is a prime target for organised crime, which has an important external dimension, namely trafficking in drugs, women, children and arms, which does not stop at the Union's borders. Such criminal activity is often associated with weak or failing states. For example, revenues from drugs have helped to undermine state structures in several drug-producing countries. Organised crime can have links with terrorism. In extreme cases, it can come to dominate the State.

The European Union's Strategic Objectives

To defend its security and promote its values, the European Union pursues three strategic objectives:

- **Addressing the threats.** The Union continues to take steps to tackle the key threats. It responded after 11 September with measures that included the adoption of the European Arrest Warrant and steps against terrorist financing. The Union continues to pursue its policies against arms proliferation, in part by strengthening international treaties and their verification provisions. It has intervened to help deal with regional conflicts and to put failed States back on their feet. Restoring good government promotes democracy and is a way of tackling organised crime. Until the end of the Cold War, our traditional concept of self-defence was based on the threat of invasion. With the new threats, however, the first line of defence will often be abroad. We should be ready to act before a crisis occurs. Today, each threat requires a combination of responses, which the Union is particularly well equipped to provide.

- **Building security in its neighbourhood.** It is in the Union's interest that countries on our borders are well governed. Our task is to promote a ring of well-governed countries to the east of the European Union and on the shores of the Mediterranean with whom we can enjoy close and cooperative relations. Resolution of the Arab-Israeli conflict is a strategic priority. Without this, there will be little chance of dealing with other problems in the Middle East.
- **Developing an international order based on effective multilateralism.** Our security and prosperity increasingly depend on an effective multilateral system. The Union aims to develop a stronger international society, well-functioning international institutions—such as the United Nations, whose Charter constitutes the fundamental framework for international relations—and a rule-based international order. The best protection for our security is a world of well-governed democratic States. EU policies are aimed at bringing this about.

Policy Implications for Europe

The European Union has made progress towards a coherent foreign policy and effective crisis management. However, according to the security strategy, the Union must:

- **be more active in pursuing its strategic objectives.** Active policies are needed to counter the new threats. The Union needs to develop a strategic culture that fosters early, rapid and, when necessary, robust intervention. A more active EU taking on greater responsibilities will also carry greater political weight.
- **increase its capabilities.** Steps such as the creation of a European defence agency take us in the direction of a more capable Europe. The armies of the Union's Member States must be transformed into more flexible and more mobile forces to enable them to address the new threats. The Union also needs more capacity to bring all necessary civilian resources to bear in crises and post-crisis situations. In addition,

the Union must go further in combining the diplomatic capabilities of its Member States with those of the EU.

- **pursue coherent policies.** The challenge is to bring together the different tools and capabilities of EU policy, such as European assistance programmes, the European Development Fund and the Member States' military and civilian capabilities. The Union must pursue coherent policies. Diplomatic efforts and development, trade and environmental policies should follow the same agenda.
- **work with its partners.** As things stand now, neither the Union nor any Member State is alone capable of addressing the threats we are faced with. Multilateral cooperation and bilateral partnerships with key actors are a priority and a necessity. The transatlantic relationship is irreplaceable. However, the EU must also work for closer relations with partners such as Russia, Japan, China, Canada and India.

The European Union: A Global Player

The violence of the two world wars that marked the first half of the twentieth century has given way to a period of peace, stability and prosperity unprecedented in European history. The creation of the European Union has been central to this development. European countries are now committed to dealing peacefully with disputes and to cooperating through common institutions.

The United States has played a critical role in European integration and European security, especially through NATO. Now that the Cold War is over, it has become the single dominant military power. However, no country is able to tackle today's complex problems on its own. As a union of 25 states with a total population of over 450 million, the EU has inevitably become a global player. It should therefore be ready to share in the responsibility for creating global security and building a better world.

B. TERROR FUNDING AND FINANCIAL RECORDS

DOCUMENT NO. 14

PEOPLE'S MOJAHEDIN ORGANIZATION OF IRAN
v.
COUNCIL OF THE EUROPEAN UNION
EUROPEAN COURT OF JUSTICE (CT. FIRST INSTANCE)
14 February 2008*

Case T-256/07

An act of terrorism—Lack of Interest 321

People's Mojahedin Organization of Iran, established in Auvers-sur-Oise (France), represented by J.-P. Spitzer, lawyer, and D. Vaughan, QC, applicant,

v

Council of the European Union, represented by M. Bishop and E. Finnegan, acting as Agents, defendant,

supported by

United Kingdom of Great Britain and Northern Ireland, represented by V. Jackson and T. Harris, acting as Agents, assisted by S. Lee, Barrister,

by

Commission of the European Communities, represented initially by S. Boelaert and J. Aquilina, then by S. Boelaert and P. Aalto, acting as Agents,

and by

Kingdom of the Netherlands, represented by M. de Grave and Y. de Vries, acting as Agents, interveners,

ACTION for partial annulment of Council decision 2007/445/EC of 28 June 2007 implementing Article 2(3) of Regulation (EC) No 2580/2001 on specific restrictive measures directed against certain persons and entities with a view to combating terrorism and repealing Decisions 2006/379/EC and 2006/1008/EC (OJ 2007 L 169, p. 58),

*Language of the case: English

THE PRESIDENT OF THE SEVENTH CHAMBER OF THE COURT OF FIRST INSTANCE makes the following

Order

Procedure

1 By application lodged at the Registry of the Court of First Instance on 16 July 2007, the People's Mojahedin Organization of Iran ('the applicant') brought an action under the fourth paragraph of Article 230 EC, by which it seeks partial annulment of Council decision 2007/445/EC of 28 June 2007 implementing Article 2(3) of Regulation (EC) No 2580/2001 on specific restrictive measures directed against certain persons and entities with a view to combating terrorism and repealing Decisions 2006/379/EC and 2006/1008/EC (OJ 2007 L 169, p. 58).

2 By order of 20 November 2007, after the parties had been heard, the President of the Seventh Chamber of the Court of First Instance granted the United Kingdom of Great Britain and Northern Ireland, the Commission of the European Communities and the Kingdom of the Netherlands leave to intervene in the proceedings in support of the form of order sought by the Council.

3 By document lodged at the Registry of the Court of First Instance on 6 December 2007, Farideh Khezadeh, Ebtesam Jalizavi, Mohammed Jalizavi, Elham Jalizavi, Abdolnabi Beit-Salem and Massoumeh Youssofi-Nissi ('the applicants for leave') applied for leave to intervene in the proceedings in support of the form of order sought by the Council.

4 The application for leave to intervene was served on the parties in accordance with Article 116 (1) of the Rules of Procedure of the Court of First Instance. The applicant and the Commission objected to its admissibility. The Council and the United Kingdom deferred to the wisdom of the Court.

Law

5 Under the second paragraph of Article 40 of the Statute of the Court of Justice, which applies to proceedings before the Court of First Instance by virtue of the first paragraph of Article 53 of that Statute, any person establishing an interest in the result of a case, save in cases between Member States, between institutions of the Community or between Member States and institutions of the Community, has the right to intervene in the proceedings.

6 It has consistently been held that the concept of an interest in the result of the case, within the meaning of that provision, must be defined in the light of the precise subject-matter of the dispute and be understood as meaning a direct, existing interest in the ruling on the forms of order sought and not as

an interest in relation to the pleas in law or arguments put forward. The expression 'result' is to be understood as meaning the operative part of the final judgment which the parties ask the Court to deliver. It is necessary, in particular, to ascertain whether the prospective intervener is directly affected by the contested act and whether its interest in the result of the case is established. It is also settled case-law that it is necessary to distinguish between prospective interveners establishing a direct interest in the ruling on the specific act annulment of which is sought and those who can establish only an indirect interest in the result of the case by reason of similarities between their situation and that of one of the parties (order of the President of the Court of Justice in Case C-464/07 P(I) *Provincia di Ascoli Piceno and Comune di Monte Urano* v *Apache Footwear and Others* [not yet reported], paragraph 5; and Order of the Court of First Instance in Case T-410/03 *Hoechst* v *Commission* [2004] ECR II-4451, paragraph 14 and the case-law cited).

7 The interest of the applicants for leave in the result of the present case must be assessed in the light of that case-law.

8 In this case, the applicants for leave justify their application to intervene by the assertion that on 25 November 1999, the applicant carried out an attack in Iran, in the course of which members of their families were killed or injured. This attack is said to be related to a case of criminal association with a terrorist organisation and of financing of a terrorist organisation, in relation to which a preliminary investigation was initiated in France in April 2001. On 10 May 2004, the applicants for leave filed a civil suit, by way of intervention, before the examining magistrate in charge of that preliminary investigation. By order of 6 December 2005, the examining magistrate ruled that the said civil suit was inadmissible, essentially on the ground that there was no established connection between the facts which he was investigating and the attack referred to by the applicants for leave. The appeal filed by the applicants for leave against the said order was rejected as lacking legal basis by judgment of the Court of Appeal of Paris (France) on 22 December 2006. On 26 December 2006, the applicants for leave filed an appeal to the French Cour de cassation.

9 It is under those circumstances that the applicants for leave wish to intervene in the present case. They contend, in particular, that as a collective group of victims of attacks committed by the applicant, they have an obvious interest in the result of the case and in the maintenance of the applicant on the list of persons, groups and entities affected by a freezing of funds at EC level. More specifically, they intend to allege, on the one hand, that the Council was not bound to remove the applicant from the said list in the light of the judgment of the Court of First Instance in Case T-228/02 *Organisation des Modjahedines du peuple d'Iran* v *Council* [2006] ECR II-4665, and, on the other hand, that the rights of defence should be strictly limited for terrorist organisations.

10 By so doing, the applicants for leave have not referred to any special circumstances capable of establishing the existence of a personal interest in the dismissal of the application in the main proceedings and have not demonstrated in any way that their position could be affected in a sufficiently specific manner by the outcome of the dispute before this Court. Whatever such outcome, it has no possible incidence on the outcome of the judicial proceedings currently under way in France, since this Court is not called upon to determine the question of the involvement of the applicant in the attack of 25 November 1999 in Iran referred to by the applicants for leave, nor the question of the connection made by the latter between that attack and the facts covered by the preliminary investigation referred to at paragraph 8 above.

11 For the rest, it follows from the case-law cited at paragraph 6 above that the interests of the applicants for leave in relation to the pleas in law that they intend to put forward in the oral proceedings does not confer on them, as such, an interest in the result of the case, within the meaning of Article 40 of the Statute of the Court of Justice.

12 In those circumstances, the applicants for leave have not established an interest in intervening in the present proceedings, and their application for leave to intervene must therefore be dismissed.

Costs

13 Under Article 87 (2) of the Rules of Procedure of the Court of First Instance, the unsuccessful party is to be ordered to pay the costs if they have been applied for in the successful party's pleadings. Under Article 87 (4) of the Rules of Procedure, the Member States and institutions which have intervened in the proceedings are to bear their own costs.

14 In the present case, the applicant has applied for its costs to be paid by the applicants for leave. The Council has made no application for costs. Accordingly, the applicants for leave must be ordered to bear their own costs and to pay those incurred by the applicant in connection with the application to intervene.

On those grounds,

THE PRESIDENT OF THE SEVENTH CHAMBER OF THE COURT OF FIRST INSTANCE hereby orders:

1. The application for leave to intervene lodged by Farideh Khezadeh, Ebtesam Jalizavi, Mohammed Jalizavi, Elham Jalizavi, Abdolnabi Beit-Salem and Massoumeh Youssofi-Nissi is dismissed.
2. Farideh Khezadeh, Ebtesam Jalizavi, Mohammed Jalizavi, Elham Jalizavi, Abdolnabi Beit-Salem and Massoumeh Youssofi-Nissi shall

bear their own costs and pay those incurred by the applicant in connection with the application to intervene.

3. The Council, the United Kingdom of Great Britain and Northern Ireland, the Commission and the Kingdom of the Netherlands shall bear their own costs in connection with the application to intervene.

Luxembourg, 14 February 2008.

DOCUMENT NO. 15

Al BARAKAAT INTERNATIONAL FOUNDATION
v.
COUNCIL OF THE EUROPEAN UNION AND COMMISSION OF THE EUROPEAN COMMUNITIES

EUROPEAN COURT OF JUSTICE

23 January 2008[1]

Case C-415/05 P

Opinion of Advocate General Poiares Maduro

1. The appellant in the present proceedings has been designated by the Sanctions Committee of the United Nations Security Council as an entity suspected of supporting terrorism, of which the funds and other financial resources are to be frozen. Before the Court of First Instance, the appellant challenged the lawfulness of the regulation by which the Council has implemented the freezing order in the Community. The appellant argued—unsuccessfully—that the Community lacked competence to adopt that regulation, that the regulation was adopted in contravention of Article 249 EC, and, moreover, that the regulation breached the appellant's fundamental rights. On what are essentially the same grounds, the appellant now asks the Court of Justice to set aside the judgment of the Court of First Instance. The Council and the Commission disagree with the appellant on all three counts. Most importantly, however, they contend that the regulation is necessary for the implementation of binding Security Council resolutions, and, accordingly, that the Community Courts should not assess its conformity with fundamental rights. Essentially they argue that, when the Security Council has spoken, the Court must remain silent.

---

[1] Original language: English.

I–Background to the Appeal

2. Al Barakaat International Foundation ('the appellant') is established at Spånga (Sweden). On 12 November 2001, the appellant was included in the list in Annex I to Regulation No 467/2001 as an entity suspected of supporting terrorism.[2] As a consequence, the appellant's funds and other financial resources in the Community were to be frozen. On 27 May 2002, that regulation was repealed and replaced by Council Regulation (EC) No 881/2002 ('the contested regulation').[3] However, the appellant continued to be listed—in Annex I to the contested regulation—as an entity suspected of supporting [32703mterrorism whose funds were to be frozen.

3. The contested regulation was adopted on the basis of Articles 60 EC, 301 EC and 308 EC in order to give effect, within the Community, to Council Common Position 2002/402/CFSP.[4] That Common Position, in turn, reflected Resolutions 1267(1999),[5] 1333(2000)[6] and 1390(2002)[7] of the United Nations Security Council. Considering that the suppression of international terrorism is essential for the maintenance of international peace and security, the Security Council adopted those resolutions under Chapter VII of the UN Charter.

4. The resolutions provide, inter alia, that all States are to take measures to freeze the funds and other financial assets of individuals and entities associated with Usama bin Laden, the Al-Qaida network and the Taliban, as designated by a committee of the Security Council composed of all its members ('the Sanctions Committee'). On 8 March 2001, the Sanctions Committee published a first consolidated list of the persons and entities that were to be subjected to the freezing of funds. That list has since been amended and supplemented several times. The name of the appellant was added to the list by the Sanctions Committee on 9 November 2001.

5. On 20 December 2002, the Security Council adopted Resolution 1452(2002), intended to facilitate the implementation of counter-terrorism measures. That resolution provides for a number of exceptions to the freezing

---

[2] Council Regulation (EC) No 467/2001 prohibiting the export of certain goods and services to Afghanistan, strengthening the flight ban and extending the freeze of funds and other financial resources in respect of the Taliban of Afghanistan, and repealing Regulation (EC) No 337/2000 (OJ 2001 L 67, p. 1). The appellant's name was added by Commission Regulation (EC) No 2062/2001 of 19 October 2001, amending, for the third time, Regulation (EC) No 467/2001 (OJ 2001 L 277, p. 25).

[3] Imposing certain specific restrictive measures directed against certain persons and entities associated with Usama bin Laden, the Al-Qaida network and the Taliban, and repealing Council Regulation (EC) No 467/2001 (OJ 2002 L 139, p. 9).

[4] Concerning restrictive measures against Usama bin Laden, members of the Al-Qaida organisation and the Taliban and other individuals, groups, undertakings and entities associated with them and repealing Common Positions 96/746/CFSP, 1999/727/CFSP, 2001/154/CFSP and 2001/771/CFSP (OJ 2002 L 139, p. 4). See, in particular, Article 3 and the ninth recital in the Preamble.

[5] S/RES/1267(1999) of 15 October 1999.

[6] S/RES/1333(2000) of 19 December 2000.

[7] S/RES/1390(2002) of 16 January 2002.

of funds imposed by Resolutions 1267(1999), 1333(2000) and 1390(2002) that may be granted by the States on humanitarian grounds, on condition that the Sanctions Committee has been notified and has not objected or, in some cases, has given its consent. In addition, on 17 January 2003, the Security Council adopted Resolution 1455(2003), intended to improve the implementation of the measures for the freezing of funds.

6. In the light of those resolutions, the Council adopted Common Position 2003/140/CFSP[8] in order to provide for the exceptions permitted by the Security Council. In addition, on 27 March 2003, the Council amended the contested regulation as regards exceptions to the freezing of funds and economic resources.[9]

7. The contested regulation, as amended, provides in Article 2 that 'all funds and other financial resources belonging to, or owned or held by, a natural or legal person, group or entity designated by the Sanctions Committee and listed in Annex I shall be frozen'. Article 2a provides for certain exceptions, for instance as regards reasonable legal fees, on condition that the Sanctions Committee has been notified and has not objected.

8. By application lodged on 10 December 2001, the appellant, together with Messrs Abdirisak Aden, Abdulaziz Ali and Ahmed Yusuf, brought an action before the Court of First Instance against the Council and the Commission, claiming inter alia that that Court should annul Regulations Nos 2062/2001 and 467/2001. The United Kingdom was given leave to intervene in support of the defendants. Following the repeal of Regulation No 467/2001, the Court of First Instance decided to treat the case as an action for annulment of the contested regulation directed against the Council alone, supported by the Commission and the United Kingdom. While the proceedings before the Court of First Instance were still pending, the Sanctions Committee decided to remove the persons known as 'Abdi Abdulaziz Ali' and 'Abdirisak Aden' from the list of persons to whom and groups and entities to which the freezing of funds and other economic resources must apply. These names were subsequently removed from Annex I to the contested regulation. Messrs Abdirisak Aden and Adbulaziz Ali informed the Court of First Instance that they wished to discontinue their action. The names of those two applicants were accordingly removed from the register.

9. Before the Court of First Instance, Al Barakaat International Foundation and Mr Yusuf put forward three grounds of annulment: the first alleged that the Council was incompetent to adopt the contested regulation, the

[8] Concerning exceptions to the restrictive measures imposed by Common Position 2002/402/CFSP (OJ 2003 L 53, p. 62).

[9] Council Regulation (EC) No 561/2003 amending, as regards exceptions to the freezing of funds and economic resources, Regulation (EC) No 881/2002 (OJ 2003 L 82, p. 1).

second alleged infringement of Article 249 EC and the third alleged breach of their fundamental rights. By judgment of 21 September 2005 in Case T-306/01 *Yusuf and Al Barakaat International Foundation* v *Council and Commission* ('the judgment under appeal'),[10] the Court of First Instance upheld the contested regulation. On 21 November 2005, the appellant and Mr Yusuf brought the present appeal against the judgment of the Court of First Instance. While the appeal proceedings before this Court were still pending, the Sanctions Committee decided to remove Mr Yusuf from the list of persons to whom and groups and entities to which the freezing of funds and other economic resources must apply. His name was subsequently removed from Annex I to the contested regulation. Mr Yusuf informed this Court that he wished to discontinue his action and his name was accordingly removed from the register. Apart from Al Barakaat International Foundation, the parties to the present appeal proceedings are the Council, the Commission and the United Kingdom, as well as Spain, France and the Netherlands, as interveners in the appeal. For the sake of brevity I shall refer, on occasion, to the Council, the Commission and the United Kingdom as 'the respondents'.

10. The appellant raises three pleas in law in support of its application to have the judgment under appeal set aside. Those pleas relate, firstly, to the legal basis of the contested regulation. The second plea is based on Article 249 EC and relates to the choice of an act in the form of a regulation, rather than a decision, as the legal instrument for the purpose of freezing the appellant's assets. The third plea concerns the fundamental rights of the appellant. I shall turn, first, to the question of the legal basis.

II–The Legal Basis of the Contested Regulation

11. The appellant's first plea relates to the legal basis of the contested regulation. The judgment under appeal devotes considerable attention to this issue. Upon consideration of various alternatives, the Court of First Instance concluded that the combined effect of Articles 60 EC, 301 EC and 308 EC gave the Community power to adopt the contested regulation.[11] The appellant argues that this finding is mistaken in law and maintains that the Community lacked competence altogether to adopt the contested regulation. Though relying on slightly different justifications, both the Council and the United Kingdom agree with the Court of First Instance that the contested regulation finds its legal basis in Articles 60 EC, 301 EC and 308 EC. The Commission, however, takes a different view and concludes that Articles 60 EC and 301 EC alone would have provided a sufficient legal basis.

[10] [2005] ECR II-3533.
[11] Paragraphs 107 to 171 of the judgment under appeal.

12. I agree with that argument. The Court of First Instance considered that the powers to impose economic and financial sanctions provided for by Articles 60 EC and 301 EC, namely, the interruption or reduction of economic relations with one or more third countries, do not cover the interruption or reduction of economic relations with individuals within those countries, but only with their governing regimes. That view is difficult to reconcile with the wording and the purpose of those provisions. Article 301 EC authorises the Council to 'interrupt or to reduce . . . economic relations with one or more third countries' through unspecified 'urgent measures' that are necessary to carry out the Union's Common Foreign and Security Policy ('CFSP'). As such, Article 301 EC is fundamentally concerned with the objectives of these measures, namely the objectives of the CFSP, to be achieved by affecting the Community's economic relations with third countries. Article 60(1) EC authorises the Council to take such measures with respect to the 'movement of capital and on payments as regards the third countries concerned'. It therefore indicates the means for carrying out the objectives stated earlier; those means involve restricting the flow of funds into and out of the Community. Beyond these two provisions, the EC Treaty does not regulate what shape the measures should take, or who should be the target or bear the burden of the measures. Rather, the only requirement is that the measures 'interrupt or reduce' economic relations with third countries, in the area of movement of capital or payments.

13. The financial sanctions in the contested regulation meet that requirement: they are targeted predominantly at individuals and groups within third countries. By affecting economic relations with entities within a given country, the sanctions necessarily affect the overall state of economic relations between the Community and that country. Economic relations with individuals and groups from within a third country are part of economic relations with that country; targeting the former necessarily affects the latter. To exclude economic relations with individuals or groups from the ambit of 'economic relations with . . . third countries' would be to ignore a basic reality of international economic life: that the governments of most countries do not function as gatekeepers for the economic relations and activities of each specific entity within their borders.

14. Moreover, the Court of First Instance's restrictive reading of Article 301 EC deprives this provision of much of its practical use. Within the framework of the CFSP, the Union may decide, for reasons relating to the maintenance of international peace and security, to impose economic and financial sanctions against non-State actors who are situated in third countries. I fail to see why Article 301 EC should be interpreted more narrowly. As the Court of First Instance itself recognised, 'the Union and its Community pillar are not to be prevented from adapting to [threats to international peace

and security] by imposing economic and financial sanctions not only on third countries, but also on associated persons, groups, undertakings or entities developing international terrorist activity or in any other way striking a blow at international peace and security'.[12]

15. The Court of First Instance found that Article 308 EC had to be brought into play in order to impose financial sanctions on individuals who do not exercise government control. However, the reliance on the notion of government control as a distinguishing factor highlights an underlying tension in the reasoning of the Court of First Instance. The Court of First Instance construed Article 308 EC as a 'bridge' between the CFSP and the Community pillar. However, while Article 301 EC might be seen as a cross-pillar bridge, Article 308 EC surely cannot fulfil that function. Article 308 EC, like Article 60(1) EC, is strictly an enabling provision: it provides the means, but not the objective. Even though it refers to 'objectives of the Community', these objectives are exogenous to Article 308 EC; they cannot be introduced by Article 308 EC itself. Hence, if one excludes the interruption of economic relations with non-State actors from the realm of acceptable means to achieve the objectives permitted by Article 301 EC, one cannot use Article 308 EC to bring those means back in. Either a measure directed against non-State actors fits the objectives of the CFSP which the Community can pursue by virtue of Article 301 EC, or, if it does not, then Article 308 EC is of no help.

16. My conclusion, therefore, is that the judgment of the Court of First Instance is vitiated by an error in law. If the Court were to follow my analysis concerning the legal basis it would have enough ground to set aside the judgment under appeal. It is for that reason that I shall not address the appellant's second plea in law. However, I believe that, where pleas are raised concerning alleged breaches of fundamental rights, it is preferable for the Court to make use of the possibility of reviewing those pleas as well, both for reasons of legal certainty and in order to prevent a possible breach of fundamental rights from subsisting in the Community legal order, albeit by virtue of a measure that merely has a different form or legal basis. I shall accordingly proceed to assess the appellant's third plea in law.

III–The jurisdiction of the Community Courts to determine whether the contested regulation breaches fundamental rights

17. In the proceedings before the Court of First Instance, the appellant claimed that the contested regulation breached the right to a fair hearing, the right to respect for property, and the right to effective judicial review.[13]

[12] Paragraph 169 of the judgment under appeal.
[13] Paragraph 190 et seq. of the judgment under appeal.

However, before assessing the substance of these claims, the Court of First Instance examined the scope of its own jurisdiction to assess the conformity of the contested regulation with fundamental rights.[14] In order to ascertain the appropriate scope of judicial review, the Court of First Instance considered the relationship between the Community legal order and the legal order established under the UN Charter. The reasoning of the Court of First Instance is extensive and sophisticated, but may be summarised as follows.

18. First, the Court of First Instance identified what essentially amounts to a rule of primacy, flowing from the EC Treaty, according to which Security Council resolutions adopted under Chapter VII of the UN Charter prevail over rules of Community law. The Court of First Instance essentially found that Community law recognises and accepts that, in keeping with Article 103 of the UN Charter, Security Council resolutions take precedence over the Treaty.[15] Secondly, the Court of First Instance held that, in consequence, it had no authority to review, even indirectly, Security Council resolutions in order to assess their conformity with fundamental rights as protected by the Community legal order. It observed that the Security Council resolutions at issue left no margin of discretion and, therefore, that it could not assess the contested regulation without engaging in such indirect review. None the less, the Court of First Instance considered, thirdly, that it was empowered to review the Security Council resolutions at issue in order to assess their conformity with the protection of fundamental rights, in so far as those rights formed part of the principle of *jus cogens*.

19. By its third plea, the appellant argues that the Court of First Instance applied the wrong standard of review when assessing the alleged breaches of fundamental rights. The appellant maintains that the application of the appropriate standard of review would have resulted, in particular, in a finding of a breach of the right to a fair hearing and of the right to effective judicial review. The appellant points out that the Court of First Instance did not take any view as to the conformity of the contested regulation with fundamental rights as they result from the general principles of Community law. Instead, the Court of First Instance confined its analysis to the question whether the Security Council resolutions which the contested regulation seeks to implement were in conformity with principles of *jus cogens*.[16]

[14] In paragraphs 226 to 283 of the judgment under appeal.

[15] Article 103 of the UN Charter provides: 'In the event of a conflict between the obligations of the Members of the United Nations under the present Charter and their obligations under any other international agreement, their obligations under the present Charter shall prevail.' It is generally recognised that this obligation extends to binding Security Council decisions. See the Order of 14 April 1992 of the International Court of Justice in *Questions of Interpretation and Application of the 1971 Montreal Convention arising from the Aerial Incident at Lockerbie (Libyan Arab Jamahiriya v. United Kingdom), Provisional Measures, Order of 14 April 1992, I.C.J. Reports 1992*, p. 3, at paragraph 39.

[16] See paragraphs 286 to 346 of the judgment under appeal.

According to the appellant, there is no basis in Community law for restricting judicial control in respect of the contested regulation in this way.

20. Essentially, the argument raised by the appellant is that the Court of First Instance embraced a mistaken view of its own judicial powers, because it mischaracterised the relationship between the international legal order and the Community legal order. This brings us to the question of how the relationship between the international legal order and the Community legal order must be described.

21. The logical starting point of our discussion should, of course, be the landmark ruling in *Van Gend en Loos*, in which the Court affirmed the autonomy of the Community legal order.[17] The Court held that the Treaty is not merely an agreement between States, but an agreement between the *peoples* of Europe. It considered that the Treaty had established a 'new legal order', beholden to, but distinct from the existing legal order of public international law. In other words, the Treaty has created a municipal legal order of trans-national dimensions, of which it forms the 'basic constitutional charter'.[18]

22. This does not mean, however, that the Community's municipal legal order and the international legal order pass by each other like ships in the night. On the contrary, the Community has traditionally played an active and constructive part on the international stage. The application and interpretation of Community law is accordingly guided by the presumption that the Community wants to honour its international commitments.[19] The Community Courts therefore carefully examine the obligations by which the Community is bound on the international stage and take judicial notice of those obligations.[20]

23. Yet, in the final analysis, the Community Courts determine the effect of international obligations within the Community legal order by reference to conditions set by Community law. The case-law provides a number of examples. There are cases in which the Court has barred an international agreement from having effect within the Community legal order on the ground that the agreement was concluded on the wrong legal basis. The Court did so, recently, in *Parliament* v *Council and Commission*.[21] The Court's approach is easy to understand once one realises that it would have

[17] Case 26/62 *Van Gend en Loos* [1963] ECR 1, at p. 12.

[18] Case 294/83 *Les Verts* [1986] ECR 1339, paragraph 23.

[19] See, for instance, Case 41/74 *Van Duyn* [1974] ECR 1337, paragraph 22, and Case C-286/90 *Poulsen and Diva Navigation* [1992] ECR I-6019, paragraphs 9 to 11.

[20] See, for instance, Case C-431/05 *Merck Genéricos-Produtos Farmacêuticos* [2007] ECR I-0000; Case C-300/98 *Dior and Others* [2000] ECR I-11307, paragraph 33; Case C-162/96 *Racke* [1998] I-3655; Joined Cases 21/72 to 24/72 *International Fruit Company and Others* [1972] ECR 1219; and *Poulsen and Diva Navigation*, cited in footnote 19.

[21] Joined Cases C-317/04 and C-318/04 [2006] ECR I-4721. See also Case C-327/91 *France* v *Commission* [1994] ECR-3641.

'fundamental institutional implications for the Community and for the Member States'[22] if an agreement that was adopted without a proper legal basis—or according to the wrong decision-making procedure—were to produce effects within the Community legal order. A similar concern underpins cases in which the Court has held that, when entering into commitments on the international stage, Member States and Community institutions are under a duty of loyal cooperation.[23] If an international agreement is concluded in breach of that duty, it can be denied effect in the Community legal order. Even more apposite, in the context of the present case, is the fact that the Court has verified, on occasion, whether acts adopted by the Community for the purpose of giving municipal effect to international commitments were in compliance with general principles of Community law. For instance, in *Germany* v *Council* the Court annulled the Council decision concerning the conclusion of the WTO Agreement to the extent that it approved the Framework Agreement on Bananas.[24] The Court considered that provisions of that Framework Agreement infringed a general principle of Community law: the principle of non-discrimination.

24. All these cases have in common that, although the Court takes great care to respect the obligations that are incumbent on the Community by virtue of international law, it seeks, first and foremost, to preserve the constitutional framework created by the Treaty.[25] Thus, it would be wrong to conclude that, once the Community is bound by a rule of international law, the Community Courts must bow to that rule with complete acquiescence and apply it unconditionally in the Community legal order. The relationship between international law and the Community legal order is governed by the Community legal order itself, and international law can permeate that legal order only under the conditions set by the constitutional principles of the Community.

25. It follows that the present appeal turns fundamentally on the following question: is there any basis in the Treaty for holding that the contested regulation is exempt from the constitutional constraints normally imposed by Community law, since it implements a sanctions regime imposed by Security Council resolutions? Or, to put it differently: does the Community legal order accord supra-constitutional status to measures that are necessary for the implementation of resolutions adopted by the Security Council?

---

[22] Opinion 2/94 [1996] ECR I-1759, paragraph 35.

[23] See, for instance, Ruling 1/78 of 14 November 1978 [1978] ECR 2151, paragraph 33; Opinion 2/91 [1993] ECR I-1061, paragraphs 36 to 38; and Case C-25/94 *Commission* v *Council* [1996] ECR I-1469, paragraphs 40 to 51.

[24] Case C-122/95 [1998] ECR I-973.

[25] See, for instance, Opinion 2/94, cited in footnote 22, paragraphs 30, 34 and 35.

26. In this regard, the ruling of this Court in *Bosphorus*[26] immediately comes to mind. In that ruling, the Court assessed whether a regulation that was adopted to implement a Security Council resolution which imposed a trade embargo on the Federal Republic of Yugoslavia infringed fundamental rights and the principle of proportionality. The Court held that the interest of 'putting an end to the state of war in the region and to the massive violations of human rights and humanitarian law in the Republic of Bosnia-Herzegovina' outweighed the interest of a wholly innocent party to be able to pursue its economic activities using assets it had leased from a company based in the Federal Republic of Yugoslavia.[27] The Court made no suggestion whatsoever that it might not have powers of review because the regulation was necessary in order to implement a sanctions regime that was drawn up by the Security Council.[28]

27. Nevertheless, the Council, the Commission and the United Kingdom claim that the judgment in *Bosphorus* is silent on the matter of the scope of the Court's jurisdiction, because, at any rate, the regulation did not infringe fundamental rights. I do not consider this argument very persuasive. True, while the Advocate General dismissed the idea in passing, the Court did not explicitly address whether the fact that the regulation implemented a Security Council resolution could preclude it from exercising judicial review. None the less, I would suppose that, instead of deliberately leaving the matter undecided, the Court accepted as self-evident what the Advocate General had felt useful to spell out, namely that 'respect for fundamental rights is . . . a condition of the lawfulness of Community acts'.[29]

28. In any event, even if one were to accept the suggestion that the Court sidestepped the problem of its jurisdiction in *Bosphorus*, the fact remains that the Council, the Commission and the United Kingdom fail to identify any basis in the Treaty from which it could logically follow that measures taken for the implementation of Security Council resolutions have supra-constitutional status and are hence accorded immunity from judicial review.

29. The United Kingdom suggests that such immunity from review can be derived from Article 307 EC. The first paragraph of that article provides: 'The rights and obligations arising from agreements concluded before 1 January 1958 or, for acceding States, before the date of their accession, between one or more Member States on the one hand, and one or more

[26] Case C-84/95 [1996] ECR I-3953.

[27] *Bosphorus*, cited in footnote 26, paragraph 26.

[28] The impounding of the aircraft of Bosphorus Airways took place in accordance with Security Council Resolution 820(1993). The UN Sanctions Committee had decided that a failure on the part of the authorities to impound the aircraft would amount to a breach of the resolution.

[29] Opinion of Advocate General Jacobs in *Bosphorus*, cited in footnote 26, paragraph 53. See also paragraph 34 of Opinion 2/94, cited in footnote 22.

third countries on the other, shall not be affected by the provisions of this Treaty.' In the view of the United Kingdom, that provision, read in conjunction with Article 10 EC, would impose on the Community an obligation not to impair Member State compliance with Security Council resolutions. In consequence, the Court should abstain from judicial review of the contested regulation. I shall state at the outset that I am not convinced by that argument, but it is nevertheless worth looking into the matter in some detail, particularly since Article 307 EC figured prominently in the reasoning of the Court of First Instance.[30]

30. At first sight, it may not be entirely clear how Member States would be prevented from fulfilling their obligations under the United Nations Charter if the Court were to annul the contested regulation. Indeed, in the absence of a Community measure, it would in principle be open to the Member States to take their own implementing measures, since they are allowed, under the Treaty, to adopt measures which, though affecting the functioning of the common market, may be necessary for the maintenance of international peace and security.[31] None the less, the powers retained by the Member States in the field of security policy must be exercised in a manner consistent with Community law.[32] In the light of the Court's ruling in *ERT*,[33] it may be assumed that, to the extent that their actions come within the scope of Community law, Member States are subject to the same Community rules for the protection of fundamental rights as the Community institutions themselves. On that assumption, if the Court were to annul the contested regulation on the ground that it infringed Community rules for the protection of fundamental rights, then, by implication, Member States could not possibly adopt the same measures without—in so far as those measures came within the scope of Community law—acting in breach of fundamental rights as protected by the Court. Thus, the argument based on Article 307 EC is of indirect relevance only.

31. The crucial problem with the argument raised by the United Kingdom, however, is that it presents Article 307 EC as the source of a possible derogation from Article 6(1) EU, according to which 'the Union is founded on the principles of liberty, democracy, respect for human rights and fundamental freedoms, and the rule of law'. I see no basis for such an interpretation of Article 307 EC. Moreover, it would be irreconcilable with Article 49 EU, which renders accession to the Union conditional on respect for the principles set out in Article 6(1) EU. Furthermore, it would potentially

---

30 Paragraphs 235 to 241 of the judgment under appeal.

31 Articles 297 EC and 60(2) EC. See also: Case C-70/94 *Werner* [1995] ECR I-3189; Case C-83/94 *Leifer and Others* [1995] ECR I-3231; and the Opinion of Advocate General Jacobs in Case C-120/94 *Commission* v *Greece* [1996] ECR I-1513.

32 Case C-124/95 *Centro-Com* [1997] ECR I-81, paragraph 25.

33 Case C-260/89 [1991] ECR I-2925. See also Case C-368/95 *Familiapress* [1997] ECR I-3689 and Case C-60/00 *Carpenter* [2002] ECR I-6279.

enable national authorities to use the Community to circumvent fundamental rights which are guaranteed in their national legal orders even in respect of acts implementing international obligations.[34] This would plainly run counter to firmly established case-law of this Court, according to which the Community guarantees a complete system of judicial protection in which fundamental rights are safeguarded in consonance with the constitutional traditions of the Member States. As the Court stated in *Les Verts*, 'the European Community is a community based on the rule of law inasmuch as neither its Member States nor its institutions can avoid a review of the question whether the measures adopted by them are in conformity with the basic constitutional charter, the Treaty'.[35] More straightforwardly, in *Schmidberger*, the Court reaffirmed that 'measures which are incompatible with the observance of human rights . . . are not acceptable in the Community'.[36] In short, the United Kingdom's reading of Article 307 EC would break away from the very principles on which the Union is founded, while there is nothing in the Treaty to suggest that Article 307 EC has a special status—let alone a special status of that magnitude—in the constitutional framework of the Community.

32. Besides, the obligations under Article 307 EC and the related duty of loyal cooperation flow in both directions: they apply to the Community as well as to the Member States.[37] The second paragraph of Article 307 EC provides that 'the Member State or States concerned shall take all appropriate steps to eliminate . . . incompatibilities' between their prior treaty obligations and their obligations under Community law. To this end, Member States shall 'assist each other . . . and shall, where appropriate adopt a common attitude'. That duty requires Member States to exercise their powers and responsibilities in an international organisation such as the United Nations in a manner that is compatible with the conditions set by the primary rules and the general principles of Community law.[38]

[34] In certain legal systems, it seems very unlikely that national measures for the implementation of Security Council resolutions would enjoy immunity from judicial review (which incidentally shows that a decision by this Court to exclude measures such as the contested regulation from judicial review might create difficulties for the reception of Community law in some national legal orders). See, for instance, the following sources. Germany: Bundesverfassungsgericht, Order of 14 October 2004 (Görgülü) 2 BvR 1481/04, reported in NJW 2004, p. 3407-3412. The Czech Republic: Ústavní soud, 15 April 2003 (I. ÚS 752/02); Ústavní soud, 21 February 2007 (I. ÚS 604/04). Italy: Corte Costituzionale, 19 March 2001, No 73. Hungary: 4/1997 (I. 22.) AB határezat. Poland: Orzecznictwo Trybunału Konstytucyjnego (zbiór urzędowy), 27 April 2005, P 1/05, pkt 5.5, Seria A, 2005 Nr 4, poz. 42; and Orzecznictwo Trybunału Konstytucyjnego (zbiór urzędowy), 2 July 2007, K 41/05, Seria A, 2007 Nr 7, poz. 72.

[35] *Les Verts*, cited in footnote 18, paragraph 23.

[36] Case C-112/00 *Schmidberger* [2003] ECR I-5659, paragraph 73.

[37] For a recent example of a case concerning the obligations of Member States under Article 307 EC, see Case C-203/03 *Commission* v *Austria* [2005] ECR I-935, paragraph 59.

[38] See, in a similar vein, on the requirement of unity in the international representation of the Community, Opinion 1/94 [1994] ECR I-5267, paragraphs 106 to 109, and *Commission* v *Council*, cited in footnote 23, paragraphs 40 to 51.

As Members of the United Nations, the Member States, and particularly—in the context of the present case—those belonging to the Security Council, have to act in such a way as to prevent, as far as possible, the adoption of decisions by organs of the United Nations that are liable to enter into conflict with the core principles of the Community legal order. The Member States themselves, therefore, carry a responsibility to minimise the risk of conflicts between the Community legal order and international law.

33. If Article 307 EC cannot render the contested regulation exempt from judicial review, are there perhaps any other rules of Community law that can? The Council, the Commission and the United Kingdom argue that, as a matter of general principle, it is not for the Court to cast doubt on Community measures that implement resolutions which the Security Council has considered necessary for the maintenance of international peace and security. In this connection, the Commission evokes the notion of 'political questions'.[39] In brief, one could say that the Commission, the Council and the United Kingdom contend that the specific subject-matter at issue in the present case does not lend itself to judicial review. They claim that the European Court of Human Rights takes a similar position.

34. The implication that the present case concerns a 'political question', in respect of which even the most humble degree of judicial interference would be inappropriate, is, in my view, untenable. The claim that a measure is necessary for the maintenance of international peace and security cannot operate so as to silence the general principles of Community law and deprive individuals of their fundamental rights. This does not detract from the importance of the interest in maintaining international peace and security; it simply means that it remains the duty of the courts to assess the lawfulness of measures that may conflict with other interests that are equally of great importance and with the protection of which the courts are entrusted. As Justice Murphy rightly stated in his dissenting opinion in the *Korematsu* case of the United States Supreme Court:

> 'Like other claims conflicting with the asserted constitutional rights of the individual, [that] claim must subject itself to the judicial process of having its reasonableness determined and its conflicts with other interests reconciled. What are the allowable limits of [discretion], and whether or not they have been overstepped in a particular case, are judicial questions.'[40]

[39] The term 'political question' was coined by United States Supreme Court Chief Justice Taney in *Luther* v. *Borden*, 48 U.S. 1 (1849), 46–47. The precise meaning of this notion within the Community context is far from clear. The Commission did not dwell upon the argument, which it raised at the hearing, but the suggestion appears to be that the Court should abstain from exercising judicial review, since there are no judicial criteria by which the matters presently under consideration may be measured.

[40] United States Supreme Court, *Korematsu* v. *United States*, 323 U.S. 214, 233–234 (1944) (Murphy, J., dissenting) (internal quotation marks omitted).

35. Certainly, extraordinary circumstances may justify restrictions on individual freedom that would be unacceptable under normal conditions. However, that should not induce us to say that 'there are cases in which a veil should be drawn for a while over liberty, as it was customary to cover the statues of the gods'.[41] Nor does it mean, as the United Kingdom submits, that judicial review in those cases should be only 'of the most marginal kind'. On the contrary, when the risks to public security are believed to be extraordinarily high, the pressure is particularly strong to take measures that disregard individual rights, especially in respect of individuals who have little or no access to the political process. Therefore, in those instances, the courts should fulfil their duty to uphold the rule of law with increased vigilance. Thus, the same circumstances that may justify exceptional restrictions on fundamental rights also require the courts to ascertain carefully whether those restrictions go beyond what is necessary. As I shall discuss below, the Court must verify whether the claim that extraordinarily high security risks exist is substantiated and it must ensure that the measures adopted strike a proper balance between the nature of the security risk and the extent to which these measures encroach upon the fundamental rights of individuals.

36. According to the Council, the Commission and the United Kingdom, the European Court of Human Rights relinquishes its powers of review when a contested measure is necessary in order to implement a Security Council resolution. Yet, I seriously doubt that the European Court of Human Rights limits its own jurisdiction in that way.[42] Moreover, even if it were to do so, I do not think that that would be of consequence in the present case.

---

[41] Montesquieu, *De l'Esprit des Lois*, Book XII ('Il y a des cas où il faut mettre, pour un moment, un voile sur la liberté, comme l'on cache les statues des dieux').

[42] The European Court of Human Rights has held that 'the Contracting States may not, in the name of the struggle against . . . terrorism, adopt whatever measures they deem appropriate' (Klass and Others, judgment of 6 September 1978, Series A no. 28, § 49). Moreover, in its judgment in *Bosphorus Airways*, the same Court discussed the issue of its jurisdiction at length, without even hinting at the possibility that it might not be able to exercise review because the impugned measures implemented a resolution of the Security Council (Bosphorus Hava Yollari Turizm ve Ticaret Anonim Şirketi (Bosphorus Airways) v. Ireland [GC], no. 45036/98). Therefore, the judgment in *Bosphorus Airways* seems to bolster the argument in favour of judicial review. Still, according to the Council, the Commission and the United Kingdom, it would follow from the admissibility decision in *Behrami* that measures that are necessary for the implementation of Security Council resolutions automatically fall outside the ambit of the Convention (Behrami and Behrami v. France and Saramati v. France, Germany and Norway (dec.) [GC], nos. 71412/01 and 78166/01 ECtHR, 2 May 2007); see also the admissibility decisions of 5 July 2007 in Kasumaj v. Greece (dec.), no. 6974/05, and of 28 August 2007 in Gajic v. Germany (dec.), no. 31446/02). However, that seems to be an overly expansive reading of the Court's decision. The *Behrami* case concerned an alleged infringement of fundamental rights by a security force deployed in Kosovo which operated under the auspices of the United Nations. The respondent States had contributed troops to this security force. Yet, the European Court of Human Rights declined jurisdiction *ratione personae* mainly because the ultimate authority and control over the security mission remained with the Security Council and, therefore, the impugned actions and inactions were attributable to the United Nations and not to the respondent States (see §§121 and 133 to 135 of the decision). Indeed, in this respect the Court carefully distinguished the case from *Bosphorus Airways* (see, in particular, §151 of the decision). Thus, the position of the European Court of Human Rights seems to be that, where, pursuant to the rules of public international

37. It is certainly correct to say that, in ensuring the observance of fundamental rights within the Community, the Court of Justice draws inspiration from the case-law of the European Court of Human Rights.[43] None the less, there remain important differences between the two courts. The task of the European Court of Human Rights is to ensure the observance of the commitments entered into by the Contracting States under the Convention. Although the purpose of the Convention is the maintenance and further realisation of human rights and fundamental freedoms of the individual, it is designed to operate primarily as an interstate agreement which creates obligations between the Contracting Parties at the international level.[44] This is illustrated by the Convention's intergovernmental enforcement mechanism.[45] The EC Treaty, by contrast, has founded an autonomous legal order, within which States as well as individuals have immediate rights and obligations. The duty of the Court of Justice is to act as the constitutional court of the municipal legal order that is the Community. The European Court of Human Rights and the Court of Justice are therefore unique as regards their jurisdiction *ratione personae* and as regards the relationship of their legal system with public international law. Thus, the Council, the Commission and the United Kingdom attempt to draw a parallel precisely where the analogy between the two Courts ends.

38. The Council asserted at the hearing that, by exercising its judicial task in respect of acts of Community institutions which have their source in Security Council resolutions, the Court would exceed its proper function and 'speak on behalf of the international community'. However, that assertion clearly goes too far. Of course, if the Court were to find that the contested resolution cannot be applied in the Community legal order, this is likely to have certain repercussions on the international stage. It should be noted, however, that these repercussions need not necessarily be negative. They are the immediate consequence of the fact that, as the system governing the functioning of the United Nations now stands, the only option available to individuals who wish to have access to an independent tribunal in order to obtain adequate protection of their fundamental rights is to challenge domestic implementing measures before a domestic court.[46]

law, the impugned acts are attributable to the United Nations, the court has no jurisdiction *ratione personae*, since the United Nations are not a contracting party to the Convention. By contrast, when the authorities of a contracting State have taken procedural steps to implement a Security Council resolution in the domestic legal order, the measures thus taken are attributable to that State and therefore amenable to judicial review under the Convention (see also §§ 27 to 29 of the admissibility decision of 16 October 2007 in Beric and Others v. Bosnia and Herzegovina).

[43] See, for instance, Case C-36/02 *Omega Spielhallen* [2004] ECR I-9609, paragraph 33.

[44] See the Preamble to the European Convention on Human Rights and Fundamental Freedoms, as well as Article 19 ECHR and Article 46(1) ECHR.

[45] See Article 46(2) ECHR.

[46] See paragraph 39 of the Report of 16 August 2006 of the UN Special Rapporteur on the promotion and protection of human rights and fundamental freedoms while countering terrorism (A/61/267): 'Given that the effect of inclusion [on the list] is the freezing of assets, the right to contest inclusion is

Indeed, the possibility of a successful challenge cannot be entirely unexpected on the Security Council's part, given that it was expressly contemplated by the Analytical Support and Sanctions Monitoring Team of the Sanctions Committee.[47]

39. Moreover, the legal effects of a ruling by this Court remain confined to the municipal legal order of the Community. To the extent that such a ruling would prevent the Community and its Member States from implementing Security Council resolutions, the legal consequences within the international legal order remain to be determined by the rules of public international law. While it is true that the restrictions which the general principles of Community law impose on the actions of the institutions may inconvenience the Community and its Member States in their dealings on the international stage, the application of these principles by the Court of Justice is without prejudice to the application of international rules on State responsibility or to the rule enunciated in Article 103 of the UN Charter. The Council's contention that, by reviewing the contested regulation, the Court would assume jurisdiction beyond the perimeters of the Community legal order is therefore misconceived.

40. I accordingly conclude that the Court of First Instance erred in law in holding that it had no jurisdiction to review the contested regulation in the light of fundamental rights that are part of the general principles of Community law. In consequence, the Court should consider the appellant's third plea well founded and set aside the judgment under appeal.

IV–The Alleged Breaches of Fundamental Rights

41. Instead of referring the matter back to the Court of First Instance, I suggest that the Court make use of the possibility of giving final judgment in this case.[48] For reasons of expediency, I think it would be appropriate, in this regard, to concentrate on the principal aspect of the case, namely the issue whether the contested regulation infringes the appellant's fundamental rights.

---

a necessity. At the international level, these procedures do not at present exist. They are present, in some instances, at the national level. The Special Rapporteur is of the view that if there is no proper or adequate international review available, national review procedures—even for international lists—are necessary. These should be available in the States that apply the sanctions'.

[47] See, in particular, the Second Report of the Analytical Support and Sanctions Monitoring Team (S/2005/83), in which it is noted, in paragraph 54, that 'the way entities or individuals are added to the terrorist list maintained by the Council and the absence of review or appeal for those listed raise serious accountability issues and possibly violate fundamental rights norms and conventions' and, in paragraph 58, that 'revisions to the process could help to reduce the possibility of one or more potentially negative court decisions'. In that connection, the Report specifically mentions the European Court of Justice. See also Annex I to the Sixth Report of the Analytical Support and Sanctions Monitoring Team (S/2007/132) for an overview of legal challenges to aspects of the sanctions programme.

[48] In accordance with Article 61 of the Statute of the Court.

42. The appellant alleges that the contested regulation infringes a number of its fundamental rights and, on those grounds, seeks the annulment of that regulation. The respondents—in particular the Commission and the United Kingdom—argue that, to the extent that the contested regulation may interfere with the appellant's fundamental rights, this is justified for reasons relating to the suppression of international terrorism. In this connection, they also argue that the Court should not apply normal standards of review, but instead should—in the light of the international security interests at stake—apply less stringent criteria for the protection of fundamental rights.

43. I disagree with the respondents. They advocate a type of judicial review that at heart is very similar to the approach taken by the Court of First Instance under the heading of *jus cogens*. In a sense, their argument is yet another expression of the belief that the present case concerns a 'political question' and that the Court, unlike the political institutions, is not in a position to deal adequately with such questions. The reason would be that the matters at issue are of international significance and any intervention of the Court might upset globally-coordinated efforts to combat terrorism. The argument is also closely connected with the view that courts are ill equipped to determine which measures are appropriate to prevent international terrorism. The Security Council, in contrast, presumably has the expertise to make that determination. For these reasons, the respondents conclude that the Court should treat assessments made by the Security Council with the utmost deference and, if it does anything at all, should exercise a minimal review in respect of Community acts based on those assessments.

44. It is true that courts ought not to be institutionally blind. Thus, the Court should be mindful of the international context in which it operates and conscious of its limitations. It should be aware of the impact its rulings may have outside the confines of the Community. In an increasingly interdependent world, different legal orders will have to endeavour to accommodate each other's jurisdictional claims. As a result, the Court cannot always assert a monopoly on determining how certain fundamental interests ought to be reconciled. It must, where possible, recognise the authority of institutions, such as the Security Council, that are established under a different legal order than its own and that are sometimes better placed to weigh those fundamental interests. However, the Court cannot, in deference to the views of those institutions, turn its back on the fundamental values that lie at the basis of the Community legal order and which it has the duty to protect. Respect for other institutions is meaningful only if it can be built on a shared understanding of these values and on a mutual commitment to protect them. Consequently, in situations where the Community's fundamental values are in the balance, the Court

may be required to reassess, and possibly annul, measures adopted by the Community institutions, even when those measures reflect the wishes of the Security Council.

45. The fact that the measures at issue are intended to suppress international terrorism should not inhibit the Court from fulfilling its duty to preserve the rule of law. In doing so, rather than trespassing into the domain of politics, the Court is reaffirming the limits that the law imposes on certain political decisions. This is never an easy task, and, indeed, it is a great challenge for a court to apply wisdom in matters relating to the threat of terrorism. Yet, the same holds true for the political institutions. Especially in matters of public security, the political process is liable to become overly responsive to immediate popular concerns, leading the authorities to allay the anxieties of the many at the expense of the rights of a few. This is precisely when courts ought to get involved, in order to ensure that the political necessities of today do not become the legal realities of tomorrow. Their responsibility is to guarantee that what may be politically expedient at a particular moment also complies with the rule of law without which, in the long run, no democratic society can truly prosper. In the words of Aharon Barak, the former President on the Supreme Court of Israel:

> 'It is when the cannons roar that we especially need the laws . . . Every struggle of the state—against terrorism or any other enemy—is conducted according to rules and law. There is always law which the state must comply with. There are no "black holes". . . . The reason at the foundation of this approach is not only the pragmatic consequence of the political and normative reality. Its roots lie much deeper. It is an expression of the difference between a democratic state fighting for its life and the fighting of terrorists rising up against it. The state fights in the name of the law and in the name of upholding the law. The terrorists fight against the law, while violating it. The war against terrorism is also law's war against those who rise up against it.'[49]

46. There is no reason, therefore, for the Court to depart, in the present case, from its usual interpretation of the fundamental rights that have been invoked by the appellant. The only novel question is whether the concrete needs raised by the prevention of international terrorism justify restrictions on the fundamental rights of the appellant that would otherwise not be acceptable. This does not entail a different conception of those fundamental rights and the applicable standard of review. It simply means that the weight to be given to the different interests which are always to be balanced in the application of the fundamental rights at issue may be different as a consequence of the specific needs arising from the prevention of international terrorism. But this is to be assessed in a normal exercise of judicial review by

[49] Supreme Court of Israel, HCJ 769/02 [2006] *The Public Committee Against Torture in Israel et. al. v. The Government of Israel et. al.*, paragraphs 61 and 62 (internal quotation marks omitted).

this Court. The present circumstances may result in a different balance being struck among the values involved in the protection of fundamental rights but the standard of protection afforded by them ought not to change.

47. The problem facing the appellant is that its financial interests within the Community have been frozen for several years, without limit of time and in conditions where there appear to be no adequate means for the appellant to challenge the assertion that it is involved in supporting terrorism. The appellant has invoked the right to property, the right to be heard, and the right to effective judicial review. In the context of this case, these rights are closely connected. Clearly, the indefinite freezing of someone's assets constitutes a far-reaching interference with the peaceful enjoyment of property. The consequences for the person or entity concerned are potentially devastating, even where arrangements are made for basic expenses. Of course, this explains why the measure has such a strong coercive effect and why 'smart sanctions' of this type might be considered a suitable or even necessary means to prevent terrorist acts. However, it also underscores the need for procedural safeguards which require the authorities to justify such measures and demonstrate their proportionality, not merely in the abstract, but in the concrete circumstances of the given case. The Commission rightly points out that the prevention of international terrorism may justify restrictions on the right to property. However, that does not *ipso facto* relieve the authorities of the requirement to demonstrate that those restrictions are justified in respect of the person or entity concerned. Procedural safeguards are necessary precisely to ensure that that is indeed the case. In the absence of those safeguards, the freezing of assets for an indefinite period of time infringes the right to property.

48. The appellant contends that, regarding the sanctions at issue, no such safeguards are in place. In this context, the appellant seeks to rely on the right to be heard by the administrative authorities, as well as on the right to effective judicial review by an independent tribunal.

49. Both the right to be heard and the right to effective judicial review constitute fundamental rights that form part of the general principles of Community law. According to settled case-law, 'observance of the right to be heard is, in all proceedings initiated against a person which are liable to culminate in a measure adversely affecting that person, a fundamental principle of Community law which must be guaranteed even in the absence of any rules governing the proceedings in question . . . That principle requires that the addressees of decisions which significantly affect their interests should be placed in a position in which they may effectively make known their views'.[50] As to the right to effective judicial review, the Court has held: 'The European

[50] Case C-32/95 P *Lisrestal and Others* [1996] ECR I-5373, paragraph 21. See also Article 41(2) of the Charter on Fundamental Rights of the European Union.

Community is . . . a community based on the rule of law in which its institutions are subject to judicial review of the compatibility of their acts with the Treaty and with the general principles of law which include fundamental rights. . . . Individuals are therefore entitled to effective judicial protection of the rights they derive from the Community legal order, and the right to such protection is one of the general principles of law stemming from the constitutional traditions common to the Member States'.[51] Moreover, it follows from the same case-law that both natural persons and legal persons enjoy the right to be heard and the right to effective judicial review.

50. The respondents argue, however, that in so far as there have been restrictions on the right to be heard and the right to effective judicial review, these restrictions are justified. They maintain that any effort on the part of the Community or its Member States to provide administrative or judicial procedures for challenging the lawfulness of the sanctions imposed by the contested regulation would contravene the underlying Security Council resolutions and therefore jeopardise the fight against international terrorism. In consonance with that view, they have not made any submissions that would enable this Court to exercise review in respect of the specific situation of the appellant.

51. I shall not dwell too much upon the alleged breach of the right to be heard. Suffice it to say that, although certain restrictions on that right may be envisaged for public security reasons, in the present case the Community institutions have not afforded any opportunity to the appellant to make known its views on whether the sanctions against it are justified and whether they should be kept in force. The existence of a de-listing procedure at the level of the United Nations offers no consolation in that regard. That procedure allows petitioners to submit a request to the Sanctions Committee or to their government for removal from the list.[52] Yet, the processing of that request is purely a matter of intergovernmental consultation. There is no obligation on the Sanctions Committee actually to take the views of the petitioner into account. Moreover, the de-listing procedure does not provide even minimal access to the information on which the decision was based to include the petitioner in the list. In fact, access to such information is denied regardless of any substantiated claim as to the need to protect its confidentiality. One of the crucial reasons for which the

---

[51] Case C-50/00 P *Unión de Pequeños Agricultores* v *Council* [2002] ECR I-6677, paragraphs 38 and 39. See also Article 47 of the Charter on Fundamental Rights and Articles 6 and 13 ECHR.

[52] The de-listing procedure has undergone several changes since the original adoption of the measures against the appellant. Under the initial regime, the person concerned could only submit requests for de-listing to their State of citizenship or of residence. Under the current procedure, petitioners seeking to submit a request for de-listing can do so either through a United Nations 'focal point' or through their State of residence or citizenship. However, the fundamentally intergovernmental nature of the de-listing process has not changed. See Security Council Resolution 1730(2006) of 19 December 2006 and the Sanction Committee's Guidelines for the Conduct of its Work, available at http://www.un.org/sc/committees/1267/index.shtml.

right to be heard must be respected is to enable the parties concerned to defend their rights effectively, particularly in legal proceedings which might be brought after the administrative control procedure has come to a close. In that sense, respect for the right to be heard is directly relevant to ensuring the right to effective judicial review. Procedural safeguards at the administrative level can never remove the need for subsequent judicial review. Yet, the absence of such administrative safeguards has significant adverse affects on the appellant's right to effective judicial protection.

52. The right to effective judicial protection holds a prominent place in the firmament of fundamental rights. While certain limitations on that right might be permitted if there are other compelling interests, it is unacceptable in a democratic society to impair the very essence of that right. As the European Court of Human Right held in *Klass and Others*, 'the rule of law implies, inter alia, that an interference by the executive authorities with an individual's rights should be subject to an effective control which should normally be assured by the judiciary, at least in the last resort, judicial control offering the best guarantees of independence, impartiality and a proper procedure'.[53]

53. The appellant has been listed for several years in Annex I to the contested regulation and still the Community institutions refuse to grant the appellant an opportunity to dispute the grounds for its continued inclusion on the list. They have, in effect, levelled extremely serious allegations against the appellant and have, on that basis, subjected the appellant to severe sanctions. Yet, they entirely reject the notion of an independent tribunal assessing the fairness of these allegations and the reasonableness of these sanctions. As a result of this denial, there is a real possibility that the sanctions taken against the appellant within the Community may be disproportionate or even misdirected, and might nevertheless remain in place indefinitely. The Court has no way of knowing whether that is the case in reality, but the mere existence of that possibility is anathema in a society that respects the rule of law.

54. Had there been a genuine and effective mechanism of judicial control by an independent tribunal at the level of the United Nations, then this might have released the Community from the obligation to provide for judicial control of implementing measures that apply within the Community legal order. However, no such mechanism currently exists. As the Commission and the Council themselves have stressed in their pleadings, the decision whether or not to remove a person from the United Nations sanctions list remains within the full discretion of the Sanctions Committee—a diplomatic organ. In those circumstances, it must be held that the right to

[53] ECtHR, Klass and Others, cited in footnote 42, § 55.

judicial review by an independent tribunal has not been secured at the level of the United Nations. As a consequence, the Community institutions cannot dispense with proper judicial review proceedings when implementing the Security Council resolutions in question within the Community legal order.

55. It follows that the appellant's claim that the contested regulation infringes the right to be heard, the right to judicial review, and the right to property is well founded. The Court should annul the contested regulation in so far as it concerns the appellant.

V–Conclusion

56. I propose that the Court should:

1) set aside the judgment of the Court of First Instance of 21 September 2005 in Case T-306/01 *Yusuf and Al Barakaat International Foundation* v *Council and Commission;*

2) annul, in so far as it concerns the appellant, Council Regulation (EC) No 881/2002 of 27 May 2002 imposing certain specific restrictive measures directed against certain persons and entities associated with Usama bin Laden, the Al-Qaida network and the Taliban, and repealing Council Regulation (EC) No 467/2001 prohibiting the export of certain goods and services to Afghanistan, strengthening the flight ban and extending the freeze of funds and other financial resources in respect of the Taliban of Afghanistan.

DOCUMENT NO. 16

EUROPEAN PARLIAMENT LEGISLATIVE RESOLUTION OF 14 NOVEMBER 2007 ON THE PREVENTION OF THE USE OF THE FINANCIAL SYSTEM FOR THE PURPOSE OF MONEY LAUNDERING AND TERRORIST FINANCING

The European Parliament,

- having regard to the Commission proposal to the European Parliament and the Council (COM(2006)0906),
- having regard to Article 251(2) and Article 47(2), first and third sentences, and Article 95 of the EC Treaty, pursuant to which the Commission submitted the proposal to Parliament (C6-0022/2007),
- having regard to Rule 51 of its Rules of Procedure,
- having regard to the report of the Committee on Civil Liberties, Justice and Home Affairs (A6-0225/2007),

1. Approves the Commission proposal as amended;

2. Calls on the Commission to refer the matter to Parliament again if it intends to amend the proposal substantially or replace it with another text;

3. Instructs its President to forward its position to the Council and the Commission.

Position of the European Parliament adopted at first reading on *14 November 2007* with a view to the adoption of Directive *2007/. . . /EC* of the European Parliament and of the Council amending Directive 2005/60/ EC on the prevention of the use of the financial system for the purpose of money laundering and terrorist financing, as regards the implementing powers conferred on the Commission

THE EUROPEAN PARLIAMENT AND THE COUNCIL OF THE EUROPEAN UNION,

Having regard to the Treaty establishing the European Community, and in particular Article 47(2), first and third sentences, and Article 95 thereof,

Having regard to the proposal from the Commission,

Having regard to the opinion of the European Economic and Social Committee,[1]

Having regard to the opinion of the European Central Bank[2],

Acting in accordance with the procedure laid down in Article 251 of the Treaty,[3]

Whereas:

(1) Directive 2005/60/EC of the European Parliament and of the Council[4] provides that certain measures are to be adopted in accordance with Council Decision 1999/468/EC of 28 June 1999 laying down the procedures for the exercise of implementing powers conferred on the Commission.[5]

(2) Decision 1999/468/EC *was* amended by Decision 2006/512/EC, which introduced a regulatory procedure with scrutiny for measures of general scope designed to amend non-essential elements of a basic instrument adopted in accordance with the procedure referred to in Article 251 of the Treaty, *inter alia* by deleting some of those elements or by supplementing the instrument *with* new non-essential elements.

(3) In accordance with the statement *by* the European Parliament, the Council and the Commission *concerning* Decision 2006/512/EC,[6] *for this new procedure to be applicable to* instruments already in force *adopted in accordance with the procedure referred to in Article 251 of the Treaty, they* must be adjusted in accordance with the applicable procedures. That statement indicates a list of instruments which should be adjusted as a matter of urgency, including Directive 2005/60/EC.

(4) In particular the Commission *should be empowered* to adopt the measures necessary for the implementation of Directive 2005/60/EC in order to take account of technical developments in the fight against money laundering or terrorist financing and to ensure uniform application of that Directive. More particularly, those measures are designed to clarify the technical aspects of some of the definitions provided *for* under Directive 2005/60/EC, to establish technical criteria for assessing whether situations present a low risk—or on the contrary, a high risk—of money laundering or terrorist financing, whether it is justified or not to apply that Directive to persons carrying out a financial activity on an occasional or very limited basis, and to adapt

---

[1] OJ C [...], [...], p. [...].

[2] *OJ C 39, 23.2.2007, p. 1.*

[3] *Position of the European Parliament of 14 November 2007.*

[4] OJ L 309, 25.11.2005, p. 15. Directive as amended by Commission Directive 2006/70/EC (OJ L 214, 4.8.2006, p. 29).

[5] OJ L 184, 17.7.1999, p. 23. Decision as amended by Decision 2006/512/EC (OJ L 200, 22.7.2006, p.11).

[6] OJ C 255, 21.10.2006, p. 1.

the amounts *provided for* in that Directive, taking account of economic developments and changes in international standards. Since those measures are of general scope and are designed to amend *non-essential elements of* Directive 2005/60/EC, *inter alia by supplementing it with* new non-essential elements, they *must* be adopted in accordance with the regulatory procedure with scrutiny provided for in Article 5a of Decision 1999/468/EC.

(5) Directive 2005/60/EC *provides* for a time restriction concerning the implementing powers conferred *on* the Commission. In their statement on Decision 2006/512/EC, the European Parliament, the Council and the Commission have stated that Decision 2006/512/EC provides a horizontal and satisfactory solution to the European Parliament's wish to scrutinise the implementation of instruments adopted under the co-decision procedure and that, accordingly, implementing powers should be conferred on the Commission without time-limit. The European Parliament and Council *have* also *stated* that they would make sure that the proposals aimed at repealing the provisions in the instruments that provide for a time-limit on the delegation of implementing powers to the Commission are adopted as rapidly as possible. Following the introduction of the regulatory procedure with scrutiny, the provision establishing that time restriction in Directive 2005/60/EC should be deleted.

(6) ***The Commission should, at regular intervals, evaluate the functioning of the provisions concerning the implementing powers conferred on it in order to allow the European Parliament and the Council to determine whether the extent of those powers and the procedural requirements imposed on the Commission are appropriate and ensure both efficiency and democratic accountability.***

(7) Directive 2005/60/EC should therefore be amended accordingly.

(8) Since the amendments to be made to Directive 2005/60/EC by this Directive are adjustments of a technical nature which only concern the committee procedures, they do not need to be transposed by the Member States. It is therefore not necessary to lay down provisions to that effect,

HAVE ADOPTED THIS DIRECTIVE:

Article 1

Directive 2005/60/EC is amended as follows:

(1) Article 40(1) is amended as follows:

(a) The terms "in accordance with the procedure referred to in Article 41(2)" are deleted.

(b) The following subparagraph is added:

"The measures referred to in the first subparagraph, designed to amend non-essential elements of this Directive, *inter alia* by supplementing it, shall be adopted in accordance with the regulatory procedure with scrutiny referred to in Article 41(2a)."

(2) Article 40(3) is amended as follows:

(a) The terms "in accordance with the procedure referred to in article 41(2)" are deleted.

(b) The following subparagraph is added:

The measures referred to in the first subparagraph, designed to amend non-essential elements of this Directive, shall be adopted in accordance with the regulatory procedure with scrutiny referred to in Article 41(2a)

(3) Article 41 is amended as follows:

(a) The following paragraph 2a is inserted:

"Where reference is made to this paragraph, Article 5a(1) to (4) and Article 7 of Decision 1999/468/EC shall apply, having regard to the provisions of Article 8 thereof."

(b) Paragraphs 3 and 4 are replaced by the following paragraph:

"3. By 31 December 2010, and thereafter at least every 3 years, the Commission shall review the provisions concerning its implementing powers and present a report to the European Parliament and to the Council on the functioning of those powers. The report shall examine, in particular, the need for the Commission to propose amendments to this Directive in order to ensure the appropriate scope of the implementing powers conferred on the Commission. The conclusion as to whether an amendment is necessary or not shall be accompanied by a detailed statement of reasons. If necessary, the report shall be accompanied by a legislative proposal to modify the provisions conferring implementing powers on the Commission."

Article 2

This Directive shall enter into force on the [. . .] day following that of its publication in the Official Journal of the European Union.

Article 3

This Directive is addressed to the Member States.

Done at,

For the European Parliament For the Council

The President The President

DOCUMENT NO. 17

MÖLLENDORF CASE

EUROPEAN COURT OF JUSTICE (CT FIRST INSTANCE)

11 October 2007*

Case C 117/06

REFERENCE for a preliminary ruling under Article 234 EC made by the Kammergericht Berlin (Germany) by decision of 21 February 2006, received at the Court on 1 March 2006, in the proceedings brought by

Gerda Möllendorf,

Christiane Möllendorf-Niehuus,

THE COURT (Second Chamber),

composed of C.W.A. Timmermans (Rapporteur), President of Chamber, L. Bay Larsen, K. Schiemann, P. Kūris and J.-C. Bonichot, Judges,

Advocate General: P. Mengozzi,

Registrar: J. Swedenborg, Administrator,

having regard to the written procedure and further to the hearing on 8 March 2007,

after considering the observations submitted on behalf of:

- Ms Möllendorf and Ms Möllendorf-Niehuus, by K. Alich, Notar,
- the German Government, by C. Schulze-Bahr and by M. Lumma and A. Dittrich, acting as Agents,
- the Italian Government, by I.M. Braguglia, acting as Agent, assisted by G. Aiello, avvocato dello Stato,
- the Commission of the European Communities, by F. Hoffmeister and A. Manville, acting as Agents,

after hearing the Opinion of the Advocate General at the sitting on 8 May 2007,

gives the following

---

* Language of the case: German

Judgment

1. The reference for a preliminary ruling relates to the interpretation of Articles 2(3) and 4(1) of Council Regulation (EC) No 881/2002 of 27 May 2002 imposing certain specific restrictive measures directed against certain persons and entities associated with Usama bin Laden, the Al-Qaida network and the Taliban, and repealing Council Regulation (EC) No 467/2001 prohibiting the export of certain goods and services to Afghanistan, strengthening the flight ban and extending the freeze of funds and other financial resources in respect of the Taliban of Afghanistan (OJ 2002 L 139, p. 9), as amended by Council Regulation (EC) No 561/2003 of 27 March 2003 (OJ 2003 L 82, p. 1) ('Regulation No 881/2002').

2. This reference has been made in the course of proceedings brought by Gerda Möllendorf and Christiane Möllendorf-Niehuus ('the sellers') against a decision of the Grundbuchamt (the Land Registry) rejecting their application for registration in the Grundbuch ('the Land Register') of the transfer of the ownership of some immovable property, in implementation of a notarially recorded instrument of sale.

Legal context

The United Nations Security Council Resolutions

3. On 16 January 2002, the United Nations Security Council ('the Security Council') adopted Resolution 1390 (2002), laying down the measures that States must take with respect to Usama bin Laden, members of the Al-Qaida organisation and the Taliban and other individuals, groups, undertakings and entities associated with them, as referred to in the list created pursuant to Security Council Resolutions 1267 (1999) and 1333 (2000).

4. Paragraph 2(a) of Resolution 1390 (2002) states:

> '[The Security Council] *[d]ecides* that all States shall take the following measures with respect to Usama bin Laden, members of the Al-Qaida organisation and the Taliban and other individuals, groups, undertakings and entities associated with them, as referred to in the list created pursuant to resolutions 1267 (1999) and 1333 (2000) to be updated regularly by the Committee established pursuant to resolution 1267 (1999) hereinafter referred to as "the Committee" [the Sanctions Committee]:
>
> (a) Freeze without delay the funds and other financial assets or economic resources of these individuals, groups, undertakings and entities, including funds derived from property owned or controlled, directly or indirectly, by them or by persons acting on their behalf or at their direction, and ensure that neither these nor any other funds, financial assets or economic resources are made available, directly or indirectly, for such persons' benefit, by their nationals or by any persons within their territory'.

5. On 20 December 2002, the Security Council adopted Resolution 1452 (2002), designed to facilitate the implementation of counter-terrorism obligations.

In relation to the freezing of funds and economic resources imposed by Resolutions 1267 (1999), 1333 (2000) and 1390 (2002), paragraph 1 of Resolution 1452 (2002) provides for a certain number of derogations and exceptions which States may apply on humanitarian grounds, subject to the approval of the Sanctions Committee.

6. Paragraph 2 of Resolution 1452 (2002) provides:

> '[The Security Council] [*d*]*ecides* that all States may allow for the addition to accounts subject to the provisions of paragraph 4(b) of resolution 1267 (1999) and paragraphs 1 and 2(a) of resolution 1390 (2002) of:
>
> (a) interest or other earnings due on those accounts, or
>
> (b) payments due under contracts, agreements or obligations that arose prior to the date on which those accounts became subject to the provisions of resolutions 1267 (1999), 1333 (2000), or 1390 (2002),
>
> provided that any such interest, other earnings and payments continue to be subject to those provisions. '

7. On 6 July 2004, the Sanctions Committee added the name 'Aqeel Abdulaziz Al-Aqil' to the consolidated list of natural persons and entities to be made subject to the freezing of funds pursuant to resolutions 1267 (1999) and 1333 (2000).

Legislation of the European Union and the European Community

8. On 27 May 2002, in order to give effect to Resolution 1390 (2002), the Council of the European Union adopted Common Position 2002/402/CFSP concerning restrictive measures against Usama bin Laden, members of the Al-Qaida organisation and the Taliban and other individuals groups, undertakings and entities associated with them and repealing Common Positions 96/746/CFSP, 1999/727/CFSP, 2001/154/CFSP and 2001/771/CFSP (OJ 2002 L 139, p. 4).

9. As is clear in particular from Recital 4 in the preamble thereto, Regulation No 881/2002 was adopted in order to implement, inter alia, Resolution 1390 (2002).

10. Article 1 of Regulation No 881/2002 provides:

> 'For the purpose of this Regulation, the following definitions shall apply:
>
> ...
>
> 2. "economic resources" means assets of every kind, whether tangible or intangible, movable or immovable, which are not funds but can be used to obtain funds, goods or services;
>
> ...
>
> 4. "freezing of economic resources" means preventing their use to obtain funds, goods or services in any way, including, but not limited to, by selling, hiring or mortgaging them.'

11. Article 2 of Regulation No 881/2002 states:

> '1. All funds and economic resources belonging to, or owned or held by, a natural or legal person, group or entity designated by the Sanctions Committee and listed in Annex I shall be frozen.
>
> 2. No funds shall be made available, directly or indirectly, to, or for the benefit of, a natural or legal person, group or entity designated by the Sanctions Committee and listed in Annex I.
>
> 3. No economic resources shall be made available, directly or indirectly, to, or for the benefit of, a natural or legal person, group or entity designated by the Sanctions Committee and listed in Annex I, so as to enable that person, group or entity to obtain funds, goods or services.'

12. Under Article 4(1) of Regulation No 881/2002:

> 'The participation, knowingly and intentionally, in activities, the object or effect of which is, directly or indirectly, to circumvent Article 2 or to promote the transactions referred to in Article 3, shall be prohibited.'

13. Article 7(1) of Regulation No 881/2002 empowers the Commission of the European Communities, inter alia, to 'amend or supplement Annex I on the basis of determinations made by either the . . . Security Council or the Sanctions Committee'.

14. Article 9 of Regulation No 881/2002 is worded as follows:

> 'This Regulation shall apply notwithstanding any rights conferred or obligations imposed by any international agreement signed or any contract entered into or any licence or permit granted before the entry into force of this Regulation.'

15. Annex I to Regulation No 881/2002 contains the '(l)ist of persons, groups and entities referred to in Article 2' thereof.

16. On 27 February 2003, on the view that Community action was necessary to give effect to Resolution 1452 (2002), the Council adopted Common Position 2003/140/CFSP concerning exceptions to the restrictive measures imposed by Common Position 2002/402 (OJ 2003 L 53, p. 62).

17. Recital 4 in the preamble to Regulation No 561/2003 states that, in view of Resolution 1452 (2002), it is necessary to adjust the measures imposed by the Community.

18. Paragraph 4 of Article 2a of Regulation No 881/2002—an article inserted in that regulation by Regulation No 561/2003—provides:

> 'Article 2(2) [of Regulation No 881/2002] shall not apply to the addition to frozen accounts of:
>
> (a) interest or other earnings due on those accounts; or

(b) payments due under contracts, agreements or obligations that arose prior to the date on which those accounts became subject to the provisions of . . . Security Council resolutions implemented successively through Regulation (EC) No 337/2000 . . . , Regulation (EC) No 467/2001 . . . or this Regulation.

In the same manner as the account to which they are added, such interest, other earnings and payments shall also be frozen.'

19. On 12 July 2004, the Commission adopted Regulation (EC) No 1277/2004 amending for the 37th time Regulation No 881/2002 (OJ 2004 L 241, p. 12).

20. Pursuant to Article 1 of Regulation No 1277/2004 and paragraph 2 of the Annex thereto, Annex I to Regulation No 881/2002 was amended so as to include the entry 'Aqeel Abulaziz Al-Aqil. Date of birth: 29 April 1949' under the heading 'Natural persons'.

21. In accordance with Article 2 thereof, Regulation No 1277/2004 entered into force on the day of its publication in the *Official Journal of the European Union*, that is to say, on 13 July 2004.

The Main Proceedings and the Questions Referred for a Preliminary Ruling

22. By notarially recorded instrument of 19 December 2000, a contract of sale was concluded between the sellers, as members of a partnership constituted under civil law, and Salem-Abdul Ghani El-Rafei, Kamal Rafehi and Ageel A. Al-Ageel ('the buyers'), also acting as members of such a partnership.

23. By that contract, the sellers agreed to sell land and buildings belonging to them in Berlin to the buyers in exchange for payment by the latter of a sale price of DEM 2 375 000.

24. Under the contract of sale, the parties agree that ownership of the immovable property is to be transferred to the buyers and the transfer of ownership registered in the Land Register.

25. Under the same contract, the sale price had to be deposited in a trust account of the attesting notary ('the notary'), and then paid to the sellers when the property transfer was provisionally registered in the Land Register, pending final registration.

26. On 8 March 2001, the transfer of ownership to the buyers was provisionally registered in the Land Register.

27. By decision of 29 October 2003, the Grundbuchamt attached to the Amtsgericht (Local Court) Lichtenberg rejected the application made by the notary on 22 January 2003 for final registration in the Land Register of the transfer of ownership, on the ground that certain documents, production of

which had been requested by letter of 28 March 2003, had not been provided in the time allowed.

28. On 9 December 2004, the notary submitted a new application for final registration in the Land Register of the transfer of ownership to the buyers on the basis of the notarially recorded instrument of 19 December 2000.

29. By decision of 21 April 2005, the Grundbuchamt—having ascertained that the name of one of the buyers appeared in the list in Annex I to Regulation No 881/2002—refused to accept the application for final registration, relying on Articles 2(3) and 4(1) of that regulation.

30. On 3 May 2005, the notary submitted a complaint against that decision to the Grundbuchamt. Acting on its own initiative, the Grundbuchamt referred the complaint, by decision of 11 May 2005, to the Landgericht (Regional Court) Berlin, which dismissed it by order of 27 September 2005.

31. On 7 October 2005, the notary brought an appeal against that decision before the Kammergericht (Higher Regional Court) Berlin.

32. According to the order for reference, the sellers submit before that court, first, that Articles 2(3) and 4(1) of Regulation No 881/2002—and, in particular, the phrases 'made . . . available to' and 'made available for the benefit of' in Article 2(3)—should be interpreted as referring only to transactions in which there is an economic imbalance between the consideration given and the consideration received. As it is, in the present case, the sale price agreed by the parties for the immovable property was a substantial sum and, what is more, it had already been paid to the sellers.

33. The second submission of the sellers before the Kammergericht Berlin is that, if the contract of sale were to be annulled, the buyers would have a right, enforceable against the sellers, to repayment of the purchase price for the immovable property: in other words, a sum of money equivalent to the purchase price would be made available to the buyers. That, however, would be contrary to Recital 7 in the preamble to Regulation No 881/2002 and to Article 2(1) thereof.

34. The referring court explains that, under German law, ownership of immovable property cannot be acquired directly as a result of a notarially recorded contract of sale between seller and buyer. If title to the property is effectively to pass to the buyer, it is also necessary for the two parties to conclude, in accordance with Article 925 of the Civil Code (Bürgerliches Gesetzbuch, 'the BGB'), an agreement that ownership is to be transferred and for that transfer to be registered in the Land Register, in accordance with Article 873 of the BGB.

35. The order for reference adds that, under German law, if there is any restriction on the right to dispose of property—as in the case before the referring

court because of the supervening obligation to freeze the funds of one of the buyers—and if that restriction comes into being after conclusion of both the notarially recorded contract of sale and the agreement to transfer ownership, but before the application for registration of the transfer in the Land Register, the Grundbuchamt must, as a general rule, take account of that restriction.

36. The Kammergericht Berlin adds that the legal impediment to registration of the transfer of ownership in the Land Register precludes completion of the contract of sale, with the consequence that the sellers are required, under Articles 275 and 323 of the BGB, to repay the sale price to the buyers.

37. The question arises, however, whether such a repayment is compatible with the prohibition laid down in Article 2(2) of Regulation No 881/2002.

38. In a supplementary order of 23 February 2006, the referring court observes that it cannot be inferred from Articles 2(1) to (3) and 4(l) of Regulation No 881/2002 that the seller may be ordered to deposit a sum of money corresponding to the sale price of the property concerned if, at the time when the sale contract was concluded or the sale price was received, the seller had no knowledge of the sanctions affecting the buyer.

39. In the same order, the referring court states that it is also unclear whether, in cases where there is more than one buyer or, as in the main proceedings, where a number of buyers are members of a partnership, the right to repayment of the sale price must be suspended in its entirety or only in proportion to the entitlement of the buyer affected by the restrictive measures.

40. In those circumstances, on the view that the outcome of the proceedings before it is dependent on the interpretation of Regulation No 881/2002, the Kammergericht Berlin decided to stay proceedings and to refer the following questions to the Court of Justice for a preliminary ruling:

'(1) Do the provisions of Articles 2(3) and 4(1) of Council Regulation (EC) No 881/2002 . . . prohibit property from being conveyed in performance of a sale and purchase agreement to a natural person listed in Annex I to that regulation?

(2) If Question 1 is to be answered in the affirmative: does Regulation . . . No 881/2002 prohibit the entry in the land register necessary for transferring ownership in the property even when the underlying sale and purchase agreement has been concluded, and the conveyance declared binding, before publication of the restriction on disposal in the *Official Journal of the European Communities*, and the contractual purchase price to be paid by the natural person listed in Annex I to the regulation, as buyer, has already been

(a) deposited in the notarial trust account, or

(b) paid to the seller?'

The Questions Referred for a Preliminary Ruling

41. By the two questions, which it is appropriate to examine together, the referring court asks in essence whether, in a situation where both the contract for the sale of immovable property and the agreement on transfer of ownership of that property have been concluded before the date on which the buyer is included in the list in Annex I to Regulation No 881/2002 and where the sale price has also been paid before that date, Articles 2(3) and 4(1) of that regulation must be interpreted as prohibiting the final registration, in performance of that contract, of the transfer of ownership in the Land Register subsequent to that date.

42. By way of preliminary, it should be pointed out that those questions must be examined solely in the light of Article 2(3) of Regulation No 881/2002.

43. As the Advocate General stated in point 62 of his Opinion, there is nothing in the order for reference to explain why Article 4(1) of Regulation No 881/2002, which concerns the possible circumvention of Article 2 thereof, could be relevant in a situation such as that at issue in the main proceedings.

44. As the Commission has stated without being contradicted, the fact that the buyers have concluded the contract of sale in question as members of a partnership does not entail any risk of circumvention since, if final registration of the transfer of ownership in the Land Register were to be accepted, the names of all of the members—including the name of the person listed in Annex I to Regulation No 881/2002—would have to be entered in the Register.

45. In the present case, the essential question is whether, in circumstances such as those of the case before the referring court, final registration of transfer of ownership in the Land Register implies that an economic resource is made available, directly or indirectly, to natural or legal persons, groups or entities designated by the Sanctions Committee and listed in Annex I to Regulation No 881/2002 so as to enable them to obtain funds, goods or services within the meaning of Article 2(3) of that regulation.

46. In that regard, it is important to note, first, that the asset in question in the main proceedings, namely immovable property consisting in buildings and land, is an economic resource for the purposes of Article 2(3) of Regulation No 881/2002 and, accordingly, such an asset is clearly covered by the definition of 'economic resources' in Article 1(2) of that regulation, since it is tangible immoveable property which does not consist of funds, but can be used to obtain funds, goods or services.

47. Next, it is clear from the order for reference that one of the three buyers is a natural person who is included both in the list drawn up by the Sanctions Committee and in the list in Annex I to Regulation No 881/2002.

48. Consequently, there remains only the question whether final registration in the Land Register of the transfer of ownership of the property concerned is an act which must be categorised, for the purposes of Article 2(3) of Regulation No

881/2002, as '[making an economic resource] available, directly or indirectly' to the natural person included in those lists, 'so as to enable [that person] to obtain funds, goods or services'.

49. There is nothing in the wording of Article 2(3) of Regulation No 881/2002 to support the inference, argued for by the sellers, that that provision does not cover the obtaining of economic resources in the particular context of the case before the referring court, namely a transaction in which there is an economic balance between the consideration given and the consideration received.

50. On the contrary, the prohibition laid down in Article 2(3) of Regulation No 881/2002 is framed in particularly broad terms, as evidenced by the use of the words 'directly or indirectly'.

51. In addition, the expression 'made available' has a wide meaning: rather than denoting a specific legal category of act, it encompasses all the acts necessary under the applicable national law if a person is effectively to obtain full power of disposal in relation to the property concerned.

52. The inescapable conclusion is that final registration in the Land Register of the transfer of ownership of property constitutes such an act, since it is common ground that, under German law, it is only after final registration that the buyer has the power not only to mortgage the immovable property, ownership of which has thus been transferred to him, but also and above all to transfer title to that property.

53. Moreover, it is precisely acts of that kind that Article 2(3) of Regulation No 881/2002 seeks to prohibit, since they enable a person on the list in Annex I to that regulation to obtain funds, goods or services.

54. It is relevant to add that, for the purposes of interpreting Regulation No 881/2002, account must also be taken of the wording and purpose of Resolution 1390 (2002) which, according to Recital 4 in the preamble to Regulation No 881/2002, that regulation is designed to implement (see, to that effect, Case C-84/95 *Bosphorus* [1996] ECR I-3953, paragraphs 13 and 14, and Case C-371/03 *Aulinger* [2006] ECR I-2207, paragraph 30).

55. Under paragraph 2(a) of Resolution 1390 (2002), States must 'ensure that neither these nor any other funds [belonging to individuals, groups, undertakings or entities associated with them, as referred to in the list created pursuant to resolutions 1267 (1999) and 1333 (2000)], financial assets or economic resources are made available, directly or indirectly, for such persons' benefit, by their nationals or by any persons within their territory'.

56. The broad and unambiguous terms of that provision confirm that Article 2(3) of Regulation No 881/2002 applies to any mode of making available an economic resource and therefore also to any act, such as that at issue in the main proceedings, which flows from the execution of a contract imposing

mutual obligations and which has been agreed in exchange for payment of pecuniary consideration.

57. Lastly, it cannot be disputed that application, in the case before the referring court, of the prohibition laid down in Article 2(3) of Regulation No 881/2002, in so far as it affects a person considered to be associated with Usama Bin Laden, the Al-Qaida network or with the Taliban, who participates in the financing of acts of terrorism—that is to say, who may even organise such acts, facilitate them, prepare them, carry them out or support them—falls within the objectives of the sanctions provided for by Resolution 1390 (2002), as is apparent in particular from the third and ninth recitals in the preamble to that resolution and from paragraph 4 thereof, those objectives being to combat and root out international terrorism, inter alia by cutting off international terrorism networks from their financial sources.

58. Moreover, as the German Government rightly states, if the argument put forward by the sellers were to be accepted, it would be necessary to determine on the facts of each case whether there is a true economic balance between the consideration given under a contract and the consideration received, with the attendant risk that the prohibition might be circumvented, and presenting the Member States with difficult problems of implementation.

59. As the German Government further submits, even if there were such an economic balance in the case before the referring court, the possibility remains that the asset obtained by the person on the list in Annex I to Regulation No 881/2002 may offer better prospects for value enhancement: that asset may, for example, be easier to convert, or it may even be possible, as observed by the Advocate General in point 72 of his Opinion, by a subsequent act of disposal of the property, to obtain sums of money greater than those expended for its acquisition.

60. The conclusion from the foregoing must be that a transaction such as final registration of transfer of ownership of immovable property in the Land Register is prohibited under Article 2(3) of Regulation No 881/2002 if, in consequence of that transaction, were it to be allowed, an economic resource is made available to a person listed in Annex I to that regulation, which would enable the latter to obtain funds, goods or services.

61. That conclusion cannot be affected, first, by the fact that, in the case before the referring court, a number of steps in the property transaction which are necessary, under the relevant German law, to transfer the ownership of immovable property—in particular, conclusion both of the contract of sale and of the agreement on transfer of ownership, and in addition payment of the sale price—had already been accomplished before that prohibition became applicable to one of the buyers following his inclusion on the list.

62. Article 9 of Regulation No 881/2002 must be understood as meaning that the measures laid down in that regulation, including the freezing of economic resources, preclude also the completion of acts which implement contracts concluded before the entry into force of that regulation, such as final registration of transfer of ownership in the Land Register.

63. As the Advocate General stated in point 78 of his Opinion, the application in that way of those measures, with immediate effect, is moreover consistent with the objective pursued by Regulation No 881/2002—namely, immediately to prevent persons associated with Usama bin Laden, the Al-Qaida network or the Taliban from having at their disposal any financial or economic resources, in order to impede the financing of terrorist activities—which could not be achieved as effectively if those persons were allowed to complete transactions concluded before their inclusion in the list in Annex I to that regulation.

64. Further confirmation that the provisions of Regulation No 881/2002 are to apply immediately is to be found in the fact that the Community legislation allows no exception under which it would be possible, after the date on which the regulation entered into force, to carry out an act in implementation of a contract concluded before that date, such as (as in the case before the referring court) final registration of the transfer of ownership in the Land Register, an act which, as has already been stated, entails making available the property concerned within the meaning of Article 2(3) of the regulation.

65. In that connection, it should be noted that Article 2a(4)(b) of Regulation No 881/2002, which reproduces verbatim the content of paragraph 2 of Resolution 1452 (2002), provides for an exception to the prohibition laid down in Article 2(2) of that regulation, as regards the addition to frozen accounts of payments due under contracts, agreements or obligations that arose prior to the date on which those accounts became subject to the provisions of the Security Council resolutions implemented, inter alia, by Regulation No 881/2002, requiring such payments also to be frozen, in the same manner as the account to which they are added.

66. However, no such exception is provided for in the Community legislation as regards the prohibition laid down in Article 2(3) of Regulation No 881/2002 concerning the making available of economic resources such as those at issue in the main proceedings. Nor is any such exception to be found in the relevant Security Council Resolutions.

67. Next, the conclusion reached as to the applicability of the prohibition laid down in Article 2(3) of Regulation No 881/2002 in circumstances such as those of the case before the referring court cannot be called in question, either, by the difficulties which would be caused, according to the referring court, by the fact that it would not be possible to proceed with final registration of the

transfer of ownership of the immovable property concerned in the Land Register.

68. As the referring court stated, it follows from the relevant national law that, since the lack of such registration precludes completion of the contract of sale, the sellers are under an obligation to repay to the buyers the sale price paid by the latter for the immovable property. There then arises the question whether such repayment is compatible with the prohibition provided for in Article 2(2) of Regulation No 881/2002.

69. In that regard, it must be stated that, even if such a difficulty were to arise as a result of the implications under national law of the application of Article 2(3) of Regulation No 881/2002, it cannot on any view have any effect on the answer to be given to the question whether, under Community law, the prohibition laid down in that provision applies in a case such as that before the referring court.

70. In any event, the repayment of the sale price, as provided for under national law, certainly seems to be permitted under Article 2a(4)(b) of Regulation No 881/2002. That provision in fact provides for an exception to the prohibition laid down in Article 2(2) of that regulation, provided that the conditions for the application of that exception are met, one such condition being the freezing of the funds repaid.

71. Furthermore, as regards the question whether, in cases where there is more than one buyer and, in particular, where the buyers are all members of a partnership, repayment of the sale price for the property concerned must be suspended in its entirety or only in proportion to the entitlement of the buyer affected by the restrictive measures, it must be held that this also is a question which relates to the implementation, in the light of the national law, of the prohibition laid down in Article 2(3) of Regulation No 881/2002.

72. However, as has already been stated in paragraph 69 of this judgment, such a question, which concerns the implications of rules of national law relating to the consequences entailed by application of the prohibition, cannot affect the interpretation which must be given by the Court to Article 2(3) of Regulation No 881/2002.

73. On that point, it is appropriate to point out that, in accordance with Article 8 of Regulation No 881/2002, the Commission and the Member States are to inform each other, inter alia, of any problems relating to the implementation of the regulation.

74. Lastly, the sellers and the notary submitted at the hearing that the application, in the proceedings before the referring court, of the prohibition laid down in Article 2(3) of Regulation No 881/2002 is incompatible with the fundamental right of disposal enjoyed by the owners of property.

75. In that regard, it should be stated that there is no question in this case of an alleged disproportionate infringement of the right to property of a person listed in Annex I to Regulation No 881/2002 as a result of the restrictive measures provided for in that regulation in respect of such a person.

76. The alleged infringement of the right to property concerns indirect effects, on the property rights of persons other than those so listed, brought about by the obligation to repay which may arise, in accordance with the applicable national law, as a result of the fact that, pursuant to Article 2(3) of Regulation No 881/2002 it is not possible to proceed with final registration of the transfer of ownership of the immovable property in the Land Register.

77. Consequently, the question whether, in view of the special features of the case before the referring court, such an obligation to make repayment is a disproportionate infringement of the right to property cannot have any effect on the question whether Article 2(3) of Regulation No 881/2002 applies to a situation such as that in the case before the referring court. That question is therefore a matter of national law and cannot be examined in the context of the present reference for a preliminary ruling.

78. However, as regards the application of Regulation No 881/2002, it should also be pointed out that, in accordance with settled case-law, the requirements flowing from the protection of fundamental rights within the Community legal order are also binding on Member States when they implement Community rules, and that consequently they are bound, as far as possible, to apply the rules in accordance with those requirements (see, inter alia, Joined Cases C-20/00 and C-64/00, *Booker Aquaculture and Hydro Seafood* [2003] ECR I-7411, paragraph 88 and case-law cited there).

79. Accordingly, it is for the referring court to determine whether, in view of the special features of the case before it, repayment of the sums received by the sellers would constitute a disproportionate infringement of their right to property and, if that is the case, to apply the national legislation in question, so far as is possible, in such a way that the requirements flowing from Community law are not infringed.

80. In the light of the foregoing, the answer to the questions referred must be that in a situation where both the contract for the sale of immovable property and the agreement on transfer of ownership of that property have been concluded before the date on which the buyer is included in the list in Annex I to Regulation No 881/2002 and where the sale price has also been paid before that date, Article 2(3) of that regulation must be interpreted as prohibiting the final registration, in performance of that contract, of the transfer of ownership in the Land Register subsequent to that date.

Costs

81. Since these proceedings are, for the parties to the main proceedings, a step in the action pending before the national court, the decision on costs is a matter for that court. Costs incurred in submitting observations to the Court, other than the costs of those parties, are not recoverable.

On those grounds, the Court (Second Chamber) hereby rules:

In a situation where both the contract for the sale of immovable property and the agreement on transfer of ownership of that property have been concluded before the date on which the buyer is included in the list in Annex I to Council Regulation (EC) No 881/2002 of 27 May 2002 imposing certain specific restrictive measures directed against certain persons and entities associated with Usama bin Laden, the Al-Qaida network and the Taliban, and repealing Council Regulation (EC) No 467/2001 prohibiting the export of certain goods and services to Afghanistan, strengthening the flight ban and extending the freeze of funds and other financial resources in respect of the Taliban of Afghanistan, as amended by Council Regulation (EC) No 561/2003 of 27 March 2003, and where the sale price has also been paid before that date, Article 2(3) of that regulation, as amended by Regulation No 561/2003, must be interpreted as prohibiting the final registration, in performance of that contract, of the transfer of ownership in the Land Register subsequent to that date.

[Signatures]

DOCUMENT NO. 18

AL-AQSA
v.
COUNCIL OF THE EUROPEAN UNION

EUROPEAN COURT OF JUSTICE (CT. FIRST INSTANCE, SECOND CHAMBER)

11 July 2007*

European Court of Justice

Judgment of the Court of First Instance (Second Chamber)

Stichting Al-Aqsa, established in Heerlen (Netherlands), represented by V. Koppe and L. Janssen, lawyers, applicant,

v

Council of the European Union, represented by M. Bishop and S. Marquardt, acting as Agents, defendant,

supported by

Kingdom of the Netherlands, represented by S. Terstal and C. Wissels, acting as Agents, intervener,

APPLICATION, originally, for annulment in part of Council Decision 2003/480/EC of 27 June 2003 implementing Article 2(3) of Regulation (EC) No 2580/2001 on specific restrictive measures directed against certain persons and entities with a view to combating terrorism and repealing Decision 2002/974/EC (OJ 2003 L 160, p. 81) and, subsequently, of Council Decision 2003/646/EC of 12 September 2003 implementing Article 2(3) of Regulation (EC) No 2580/2001 and repealing Decision 2003/480 (OJ 2003 L 229, p. 22),

THE COURT OF FIRST INSTANCE OF THE EUROPEAN COMMUNITIES (Second Chamber),

composed of J. Pirrung, President, N.J. Forwood and S. Papasavvas, Judges,

* Language of the case: English.

Registrar: C. Kristensen, Administrator,

having regard to the written procedure and further to the hearing on 16 January 2007,

gives the following

Judgment

Legal Framework and Background to the Dispute

1. On 28 September 2001 the Security Council of the United Nations ('the Security Council') adopted Resolution 1373 (2001) laying down strategies to combat terrorism by all means, in particular the financing thereof. Paragraph 1(c) of that resolution provides, inter alia, that all States must freeze without delay funds and other financial assets or economic resources of persons who commit, or attempt to commit, terrorist acts or participate in or facilitate the commission of terrorist acts; of entities owned or controlled by such persons; and of persons and entities acting on behalf of, or at the direction of, such persons and entities.

2. Taking the view that action by the Community was necessary in order to implement, in accordance with its Member States' obligations under the Charter of the United Nations, Security Council Resolution 1373 (2001), on 27 December 2001 the Council of the European Union adopted, under Articles 15 EU and 34 EU, Common Position 2001/930/CFSP on combating terrorism (OJ 2001 L 344, p, 90) and Common Position 2001/931/CFSP on the application of specific measures to combat terrorism (OJ 2001 L 344, p. 93).

3. Article 1(1) of Common Position 2001/931 provides that it applies 'to persons, groups and entities involved in terrorist acts and listed in the Annex'. The applicant's name is not included in the list in the Annex

4. Article 1(2) and (3) of Common Position 2001/931 defines 'persons, groups and entities involved in terrorist acts' and 'terrorist act', respectively.

5. Article 1(4) of Common Position 2001/931 provides that the list in the Annex is to be drawn up on the basis of precise information or material in the relevant file which indicates that a decision has been taken by a competent authority in respect of the persons, groups and entities concerned, irrespective of whether it concerns the instigation of investigations or prosecution for a terrorist act, an attempt to perpetrate, participate in or facilitate such an act based on serious and credible evidence or clues, or condemnation [sic] for such deeds. 'Competent authority' means a judicial authority, or, where judicial authorities have no competence in the area covered, an equivalent competent authority in that area.

6. Article 1(6) of Common Position 2001/931 provides that the names of persons and entities on the list in the Annex are to be reviewed at regular intervals and at least once every six months to ensure that there are grounds for keeping them on the list.

7. Articles 2 and 3 of Common Position 2001/931 provide that the European Community, acting within the limits of the powers conferred on it by the EC Treaty, is to order the freezing of the funds and other financial assets or economic resources of persons, groups and entities listed in the Annex, and is to ensure that funds, financial assets or economic resources or financial or other related services are not made available, directly or indirectly, for the benefit of those persons.

8. Taking the view that a regulation was required in order to implement the measures set out in Common Position 2001/931 at Community level, on 27 December 2001 the Council adopted, on the basis of Articles 60 EC, 301 EC and 308 EC, Regulation (EC) No 2580/2001 on specific restrictive measures directed against certain persons and entities with a view to combating terrorism (OJ 2001 L 344, p. 70) ('the contested regulation'). Under that regulation, except as permitted thereby, all funds belonging to a natural or legal person, group, or entity included in the list referred to in Article 2(3) must be frozen. In the same way, it is prohibited to make funds or financial services available to those persons, groups or entities. The Council, acting unanimously, is to establish, review and amend the list of persons, groups and entities to which the Regulation applies, in accordance with the provisions of Article 1(4), (5) and (6) of Common Position 2001/931.

9. The original list of the persons, groups and entities to which the contested regulation applies was set out in Council Decision 2001/927/EC of 27 December 2001 establishing the list provided for in Article 2(3) of Regulation No 2580/2001 (OJ 2001 L 344, p. 83). The applicant's name is not included in it.

10. On 27 June 2003, the Council adopted, under Articles 15 EU and 34 EU, Common Position 2003/482/CFSP updating Common Position 2001/931 and repealing Common Position 2003/402/CFSP (OJ 2003 L 160, p. 100). The Annex thereto updates the list of persons, groups and entities to whom and to which Common Position 2001/931 is applicable. Part 2 of that Annex, headed 'Groups and entities', includes in particular the name of the applicant, described as follows:

> '32. Stichting Al-Aqsa (a.k.a. Stichting Al-Aqsa Nederland, a.k.a. Al-Aqsa Nederland).'

11. By Decision 2003/480/EC of 27 June 2003 implementing Article 2(3) of the contested regulation and repealing Decision 2002/974/EC (OJ 2003 L 160, p. 81), the Council adopted an updated list of the persons, groups and

entities to which the contested regulation applies. The applicant's name is repeated in that list under the heading 'Groups and entities', in the same terms as those used in the Annex to Common Position 2003/482.

12. On 12 September 2003 the Council adopted, under Articles 15 EU and 34 EU, Common Position 2003/651/CFSP updating Common Position 2001/931 and repealing Common Position 2003/482 (OJ 2003 L 229 p. 42). The applicant's name is repeated in the list set out in the Annex to that common position, in the same terms as those used in the Annex to Common Position 2003/482.

13. By Decision 2003/646/EC of 12 September 2003 implementing Article 2(3) of the contested regulation and repealing Decision 2003/480 (OJ 2003 L 229, p. 22), the Council adopted an updated list of the persons, groups and entities to whom and to which the contested regulation is applicable. The applicant's name is repeated in that list, in the same terms as those used in the Annexes to Common Positions 2003/482 and 2003/651 and in the Annex to Decision 2003/480.

14. Since then, the Council has adopted several common positions and decisions updating the lists provided for under Common Position 2001/931 and the contested regulation (as regards the common positions see, most recently, Council Common Position 2006/380/CFSP of 29 May 2006 updating Common Position 2001/931 and repealing Common Position 2006/231/CFSP (OJ 2006 L 144, p. 25); as regards the decisions, see, in particular, Council Decision 2003/902/EC of 22 December 2003 implementing Article 2(3) of the contested regulation No 2580/2001 and repealing Decision 2003/646 (OJ 2003 L 340, p. 63) and, most recently, Council Decision 2006/379/EC of 29 May 2006 implementing Article 2(3) of Regulation No 2580/2001 and repealing Decision 2005/930/EC (OJ 2006 L 144, p. 21)). The applicant's name has continued to appear in the list at issue as updated by the abovementioned measures.

Facts

15. The file shows that the applicant is a foundation governed by Netherlands law, constituted in 1993. It describes itself as an Islamic social welfare institution. It states that, according to its constitution, its objects include the social welfare and improvement of the living conditions of Palestinians living in the Netherlands and also the provision of assistance to Palestinians living in the territories occupied by Israel. One of its main objectives as a charitable institution is to help to alleviate the humanitarian emergencies in the West Bank and the Gaza Strip. To that end, it cooperates with several organisations in Israel and in the occupied territories, to which it gives financial support in order to carry out humanitarian projects. It also provides emergency cash assistance, food and medical care and educational

and psychological services. Its most substantial projects involve orphans. The applicant states that it is politically unaffiliated and claims to have collected almost EUR 1 million by way of donations in the Netherlands in the financial year 2001–02.

16. On 3 April 2003 the Minister for Foreign Affairs of the Netherlands adopted, on the basis of Security Council Resolution 1373 (2001) and of the Sanctiewet 1977 (Netherlands Law on sanctions of 1977), as amended by a law of 16 May 2002, the Sanctieregeling Terrorisme 2003 (Regulation on sanctions for the suppression of terrorism 2003, *Staatscourant* of 7 April 2003, No 68, p. 11, 'the Sanctieregeling'), which ordered, inter alia, the freezing of all the applicant's funds and financial assets.

17. It is clear from the statement of reasons in the Sanctieregeling that, pending the adoption of a Community decision directed at the applicant on the basis of the contested regulation, the Sanctieregeling was adopted on the ground that there was evidence that the applicant had made transfers of funds to organisations supporting terrorism in the Middle East. The statement of reasons for the Sanctieregeling makes it clear that the latter will be repealed as soon as such a Community decision enters into force.

18. The applicant brought proceedings against the Netherlands State before the Rechtbank te 's-Gravenhage, sector civiel recht, voorzieningenrechter (District Court of The Hague, civil law section, court hearing applications for interim measures ('the court hearing the application for interim measures') seeking, in particular, suspension of the application of the measures laid down by the Sanctieregeling.

19. By a first interim order of 13 May 2003, the court hearing the application for interim measures held that the Sanctieregeling was based primarily on an official memorandum sent by the director of the Algemene Inlichtingen- en Veiligheidsdienst (General Intelligence and Security Service) ('the AIVD') to the Director General of Political Affairs of the Netherlands Ministry of Foreign Affairs of 9 April 2003 (point 1.11). The court hearing the application for interim measures held that that memorandum contained only general assertions and that factual information to substantiate those assertions was lacking, with the result that neither it nor the applicant could assess the veracity of that memorandum (point 3.8). It therefore considered that, in the circumstances of the case and in the light of the issues raised by the applicant, reference to that memorandum alone could not suffice to justify the position of the defendant State (point 3.9). The court hearing the application for interim measures next stated that the Netherlands Government had proposed that the court alone should inspect the information from the AIVD on the basis of which the memorandum had been drawn up, that the applicant had not disputed the Government's interest in keeping that information secret and that it had in addition

agreed that matters should proceed in that way (point 3.10). In that regard, the court hearing the application for interim measures observed that confidential inspection of the relevant documents by the court appeared to be at odds with the fundamental principle that all parties should be heard, but that it was nevertheless possible for an exception to be made to that principle on grounds of public order (point 3.11). It took the view that that was the case in the circumstances, holding that it was important that the parties had agreed that such an exception should be made and, having regard to the administrative law aspects of the case, that confidential inspection by the judge is not unusual in that area of the law (ibid.). The court hearing the application for interim measures accordingly ordered the Netherlands Government to put it in a position in which it could carry out a confidential inspection of the AIVD's file of confidential information on which the memorandum was based. The Netherlands Government complied with that order and on 21 May 2003 the court hearing the application for interim measures inspected the file in question in the offices of the AIVD.

20. By a second interim order of 3 June 2003 ('the order of the court hearing the application for interim measures'), the court hearing the application for interim measures dismissed the proceedings brought by the applicant. In point 3.2 of that second order, the court hearing the application for interim measures held, on the basis of its investigations, that the findings of the AIVD provided adequate grounds to support the latter's conclusion that the funds collected by the applicant in the Netherlands had been used for the benefit of organisations linked to the Palestinian Islamist movement Hamas, and also the conclusion that several of those organisations linked to Hamas provided funds enabling the perpetration or facilitation of terrorist acts by Hamas. In point 3.3 of that order, the court hearing the application for interim measures added that it had uncovered no fact or circumstance that might show that the AIVD had performed improperly the task entrusted to it under the Wet op de inlichtingen- en veiligheidsdiensten (Law on the intelligence and security services).

21. The Sanctieregeling was repealed on 3 August 2003 (Stcrt. 2003, No 146).

Procedure and Forms of Order Sought by the Parties

22. By application lodged at the Registry of the Court of First Instance on 19 September 2003, the applicant brought this action against the Council and the Commission pursuant to the fourth paragraph of Article 230 EC, in which it claims that the Court should:

- annul Decision 2003/480 'and/or' Decision 2003/646 in so far as those acts concern the applicant;

– declare the contested regulation to be unlawful pursuant to Article 241 EC;

– order the Council and the Commission to pay the costs.

23. By separate document lodged at the Registry of the Court of First Instance on 12 December 2003, the Commission raised an objection of inadmissibility under Article 114 of the Rules of Procedure of the Court of First Instance against the action in so far as it was directed against that institution.

24. In its defence, the Council contends that the Court should:

– dismiss the action in its entirety;

– order the applicant to pay the costs.

25. By document lodged at the Registry of the Court of First Instance on 12 January 2004, the Kingdom of the Netherlands sought leave to intervene in the present proceedings in support of the Council's first head of claim. By order of 11 February 2004 the President of the Second Chamber of the Court granted leave to intervene.

26. In its reply lodged at the Registry of the Court of First Instance on 12 March 2004, the applicant stated that it amended its heads of claim, pleas in law and arguments so as to refer to Decision 2003/902 and any subsequent decision of the Council which might retain its name in the list at issue. To refuse to allow the applicant to proceed in that way would, in its view, enable the Council de facto to evade review by the courts by constantly adopting new decisions.

27. The Council has stated that it has no objection to those amendments to the applicant's heads of claim, pleas in law and arguments. The Kingdom of the Netherlands considers that the action must be directed against the most recent of the decisions retaining the applicant's name in the list at issue, the previous decisions having been repealed.

28. By order of the Second Chamber of the Court of First Instance of 3 May 2004, the action was dismissed as inadmissible in so far as it was directed against the Commission.

29. Upon hearing the report of the Judge-Rapporteur, the Court of First Instance (Second Chamber) decided to open the oral procedure.

30. The parties presented oral argument and replied to the questions put by the Court at the hearing on 16 January 2007.

31. In answer to a question put by the Court, the applicant stated that its claims, pleas in law and arguments were to be regarded as seeking annulment both of Decision 2006/379, in force at the date of the hearing, and of any other subsequent decision of the Council that might continue to include

it in the list at issue, in so far as those acts concern the applicant, of which formal note was taken in the minutes of the hearing.

The Procedural Consequences of Repealing and Replacing Decisions 2003/480 and 2003/646

32. As is clear from paragraph 14 above, the acts originally challenged by this action, namely, Decisions 2003/480 ('the decision originally challenged') and Decision 2003/646 (taken together, 'the decisions originally challenged'), have been repealed and replaced on a number of occasions, since the application was lodged, by acts which have always continued to include the applicant in the list at issue. On the date on which the oral procedure was closed, the measure in question was Decision 2006/379.

33. It is to be observed that where a decision is, during the proceedings, replaced by another decision with the same subject-matter, this is to be considered a new factor allowing the applicant to adapt its claims and pleas in law. It would be contrary to the principle of the sound administration of justice and to the requirements of procedural economy to oblige the applicant to make a fresh application to the Court (Case 14/81 *Alpha Steel* v *Commission* [1982] ECR 749, paragraph 8; Joined Cases 351/85 and 360/85 *Fabrique de Fer de Charleroi and Dillinger Hüttenwerke* v *Commission* [1987] ECR 3639, paragraph 11; Case 103/85 *Stahlwerke Peine-Salzgitter* v *Commission* [1988] ECR 4131, paragraphs 11 and 12; and Joined Cases T-46/98 and T-151/98 *CCRE* v *Commission* [2000] ECR II-167, paragraph 33).

34. In its judgments in Case T-306/01 *Yusuf and Al Barakaat International Foundation* v *Council and Commission* [2005] ECR II-3533 (now under appeal, '*Yusuf*'), paragraph 73, and Case T-315/01 *Kadi* v *Council and Commission* [2005] ECR II-3649 (now under appeal, '*Kadi*'), paragraph 54, the Court applied that case-law to the situation in which a regulation of direct and individual concern to an individual is replaced, during the proceedings, by a regulation having the same subject-matter.

35. In accordance with that case-law, it is therefore appropriate in the present case to allow in part the applicant's requests, mentioned in paragraphs 26 and 31 above, to consider that his action, on the date of closure of the oral procedure, seeks annulment of Decision 2006/379, in so far as the latter concerns it, and to allow the parties to reformulate their claims, pleas and arguments in the light of those new factors, which implies, for those parties, the right to submit additional claims, pleas and arguments.

36. In addition, the Court considers that only actions for annulment of an act in existence adversely affecting the applicant may be brought before it. Therefore, even if, as held in the previous paragraph, the applicant may be

permitted to reformulate its claims so as to seek annulment of acts which have, during the proceedings, replaced the decisions originally challenged, that solution cannot authorise the speculative review of the lawfulness of hypothetical acts which have not yet been adopted (Case T-228/02 *Organisation des Modjahedines du peuple d'Iran* v *Council* [2006] ECR II-0000, 'the *OMPI* judgment', paragraph 32, and case-law cited).

37. It follows that there are no grounds for allowing the applicant to reformulate its claims so that they are directed not only against Decision 2006/379 but also, as the case may be, against any other subsequent decision of the Council capable of including it in the list at issue, in so far as those acts concern the applicant.

38. For the purposes of the present action, the Court's review will therefore concern only that act already adopted and still in force and challenged on the date of closure of the oral procedure, that is to say, Decision 2006/379 ('the contested decision'), even if that decision has in turn been repealed and replaced by other decisions before the date of delivery of the present judgment.

39. In such circumstances, first, the applicant still has in fact an interest in obtaining annulment of the contested decision, in that the repeal of an act of an institution does not constitute recognition of the unlawfulness of that act and has effect ex nunc, unlike a judgment annulling an act, by which the act is removed retroactively from the legal order and deemed never to have existed. Moreover, if the contested decision were to be annulled, the Council would be obliged to take the measures necessary to comply with that judgment, pursuant to Article 233 EC, which might involve its amending or withdrawing, as the case may be, any acts which had repealed and replaced the acts contested after the closure of the oral procedure (the *OMPI* judgment, paragraph 35, and case-law cited).

The Claim for Annulment in Part of the Contested Decision

40. In support of its heads of claim, the applicant relies on a series of pleas in law alleging infringement of essential procedural requirements and of Article 253 EC, infringement of the contested regulation and infringement of the general principles of Community law. It also pleads that the contested regulation is unlawful because it infringes the same procedural requirements and general principles of Community law, in particular the obligation to state reasons, the right to a fair hearing and the principle of proportionality.

41. It is appropriate to examine first the plea alleging infringement of Article 253 EC.

Arguments of the Parties

42. The applicant maintains that the contested decision fails to satisfy the requirement to state reasons laid down by Article 253 EC.

43. In particular, the contested decision does no more than refer to the criteria set out in general terms in the contested regulation and in Common Position 2001/931, without specifying the particular facts on which it is based and without providing any explanation of the reasons for, and the detailed rules for implementing, those criteria in the present case. The applicant is accordingly not in a position either to know the reasons for the measure adopted or to defend its rights, and the Court is not in a position to exercise its power of review.

44. According to the applicant, the gravity of the sanctions imposed on it for an undefined period and the interests involved required, on the contrary, a high degree of precision in the reasons for the decision to include it in the list at issue. In view of the applicant's material interest in knowing the reasons for that measure, the Council was not entitled simply to refer to generalities such as the fight against terrorism or its funding.

45. In so far as the Council is of the view that it is also appropriate to take account of a decision taken by a competent national authority in order to assess whether the contested decision is adequately reasoned, the applicant adds that the Council is itself responsible for ensuring that persons concerned are informed of the reasons for their inclusion in the list at issue. To allow the Council to hide behind the Member States would make the requirement to state reasons meaningless.

46. The applicant observes that its request for access to the documents on the basis of which the Council adopted the decision originally challenged, made under Regulation (EC) No 1049/2001 of the European Parliament and of the Council of 30 May 2001 regarding public access to European Parliament, Council and Commission documents (OJ 2001 L 145, p. 43), was rejected on the basis of the first and third indents of Article 4(1)(a) of that regulation, on the ground that the only document concerned, namely document '11 311/03 EXT 1 CRS/CRP', is classified as 'CONFIDENTIAL EU' and that its disclosure would undermine the protection of the public interest as regards public security and international relations. The applicant's request that the Council should reconsider its position was rejected for the same reason and, in addition, on the basis of the second indent of Article 4(2) of Regulation No 1049/2001, on the ground that to disclose the document in question would also undermine the protection of judicial proceedings. The applicant claims in that regard that there has been an infringement of the principle of transparency laid down in Article 255(2) EC and in Regulation No 1049/2001, which aggravates the infringement of Article 253 EC alleged in this action.

47. In its reply, the applicant states that there is, moreover, a contradiction between those grounds for the decisions to refuse access to the document in question and the explanations given by the Council in its defence, stating that the only evidence supporting the inclusion of the applicant in the list at issue is a public document, namely, the order of the court hearing applications for interim measures of 3 June 2003 (paragraph 20 above). The grounds relied on by the Council are therefore confused and incoherent.

48. In their written pleadings, the Council and the Kingdom of the Netherlands accept that the contested decision, which consists merely of an updated list of persons and entities covered by the contested regulation, does not itself contain a detailed statement of reasons. It is none the less clear, in their view, from the legal base cited and the recitals in the preamble that that implementing decision is based on that regulation, Article 2(3) of which sets out the criteria governing the inclusion of persons in the list at issue and Article 1(4) of which defines a terrorist act by reference to Article 1(3) of Common Position 2001/931. Furthermore, the objective of Regulation No 2580/2001, namely, to combat any form of financing of terrorist activities, is made clear in the second recital. It also makes reference to Security Council Resolution 1373 (2001) which itself sets out the grounds for the measures imposed on the Member States of the United Nations. The contested regulation must also be read together with Common Position 2001/931, which contains further relevant material.

49. The contested acts, taken together, thus satisfy the obligation to state reasons set out in Article 253 EC, as interpreted in the case-law. In that regard, the Council and the Kingdom of the Netherlands emphasise that it is not necessary for details of all relevant factual and legal aspects to be given and that regard should be had to the context and to all the legal rules governing the matter in question. The degree of precision of the statement of reasons for a decision must also be weighed against practical realities and the time and technical facilities available for making the decision (Case 16/65 *Schwarze* [1965] ECR 877, 888, and Case C-350/88 *Delacre and Others* v *Commission* [1990] ECR I-395, paragraphs 15 and 16). Now, according to the Council, it would not have been possible to provide, in respect of each person, group or entity to be included in the list at issue, the specific factual elements on which the Council based its decision.

50. The Kingdom of the Netherlands adds that in Case T-199/99 *Sgaravatti Mediterranea* v *Commission* [2002] ECR II-3731, paragraph 45, the Court of First Instance ruled that the Commission could legitimately rely on the detailed findings of fact made by the national authorities and was not obliged to conduct a fresh investigation. The same principle ought, in the view of that Member State, also to apply to the Council in the circumstances of the present case.

51. With respect to the applicant's argument summarised at paragraph 45 above, the Council considers that it proceeds from confusion of the question of the reasons given for the contested decision with the question of observance of the rights of the defence. The Council submits in that regard that the obligation to state reasons, which serves the purpose of enabling the Court to exercise proper judicial review and the person concerned to defend his rights, must be distinguished from the question whether the applicant had a right to be heard before the contested decision was adopted.

52. With respect to the applicant's arguments summarised at paragraphs 46 and 47 above, the Council contends that a clear distinction falls to be drawn between the rules governing access by the public to documents held by the institutions and the principles relating to observance of the rights of the defence. In its view, the purpose of those rules is not to ensure that persons are given a 'fair hearing' when a decision implementing a legislative instrument such as the contested regulation is adopted.

Findings of the Court

53. In the *OMPI* judgment (paragraph 109), the Court held that, as a rule, the safeguard relating to the obligation to state reasons provided for by Article 253 EC is fully applicable in the context of the adoption of a decision to freeze funds under the contested regulation. That principle has not been called in question by any of the parties.

54. Again in the *OMPI* judgment (paragraph 151 and, by reference, paragraphs 116, 125 and 126), the Court has inferred from that principle, interpreted in the light of the case-law, that the statement of reasons for an initial decision to freeze funds as referred to in Article 1(4) of Common Position 2001/931 must at least make actual and specific reference to the reasons why the Council considers, having regard to the precise information or material in the relevant file available to it, that a decision satisfying the definition given in Article 1(4) has been taken by a competent authority of a Member State in respect of the person concerned, unless overriding considerations concerning the security of the Community and its Member States, or the conduct of their international relations, militate against it, and subject also to the possibility of publishing a non-confidential version of that decision in the *Official Journal*, in accordance with what was held in paragraph 147 of that judgment. The statement of the reasons for such a decision must, furthermore, indicate why the Council takes the view, in the exercise of its discretion, that the person concerned must be the subject of such a measure. Moreover, the statement of reasons for a subsequent decision to freeze funds as referred to in Article 1(6) of Common Position 2001/931 must, subject to the same reservations, indicate the actual and specific reasons why the Council considers, following re-examination, that

there are still grounds for the freezing of the funds of the party concerned, where appropriate on the basis of fresh information or evidence. On this head it may be added, in answer to an argument put forward by the Council at the hearing, that when the grounds of such a subsequent decision are in essence the same as those already relied on when a previous decision was adopted, a mere statement to that effect may suffice, particularly when the person concerned is a group or entity.

55. In the circumstances of the present case, neither the decisions originally challenged nor the contested decision satisfy the requirement of a statement of reasons as set out above, for they do no more than state, in the second recital in the preambles thereto, that it is 'desirable' or that it has been 'decided' to adopt an up-to-date list of the persons, groups and entities to which the contested regulation applies.

56. That finding is not shaken by the argument, adduced at the hearing by the Council and the intervening Government, that actual and specific reasoning was not required in this case since the applicant was, in their view, quite well aware that the contested decision had been adopted on 27 June 2003, following and in light of only the order of 3 June 2003 made by the court hearing the application for interim measures. According to the Council and the Kingdom of the Netherlands, that situation distinguishes the facts of the present case from those at issue in the case giving rise to the *OMPI* judgment.

57. That argument is based not only on mere speculation as to what the applicant might have been aware of, but also on the mistaken premiss that there was a clear and unambiguous link between the order made by the court hearing the application for interim measures and the adoption of the decision originally challenged.

58. Here it is to be borne in mind that, according to settled case-law, the statement of reasons required by Article 253 EC must disclose in a clear and unequivocal fashion the reasoning followed by the institution which adopted the measure in question in such a way as to enable the persons concerned to ascertain the reasons for the measure and to enable the competent court to exercise its power of review of the lawfulness thereof. It is not necessary for the statement of reasons to specify all the relevant matters of fact and law, since the question whether the statement of reasons meets the requirements of Article 253 EC must be assessed with regard not only to its wording but also to its context and to all the legal rules governing the matter in question. In particular, the reasons given for an act adversely affecting a party are sufficient if it was adopted in circumstances known to the party concerned which enable him to understand the scope of the measure concerning him (the *OMPI* judgment, paragraph 141, and the case-law cited).

59. In the circumstances, as has been stated in paragraph 17 above, it was stated in the reasons given for the Sanctieregeling that that measure was

adopted, pending the adoption of a Community decision directed at the applicant, on the ground that there was evidence that the applicant had made transfers of funds to organisations supporting terrorism in the Middle East, and that it would be repealed as soon as such a decision entered into force. It would thus seem that the Netherlands Minister for Foreign Affairs considered that the Sanctieregeling, at the time of its adoption, constituted in itself a decision of a competent national authority within the meaning of Article 1(4) of Common Position 2001/931, so permitting the Council to adopt the decision originally challenged.

60. In those circumstances, and having regard to the case-law cited in paragraph 58 above, the mere fact that the applicant knew of the order made by the court hearing the application for interim measures does not suffice to mitigate the lack of reasons for the decision originally challenged. In particular, taking account of the words used by the Netherlands Minister for Foreign Affairs in the Sanctieregeling, and in the absence of any reasoning expressly appearing in the decision originally challenged, the applicant has not been put in a position in which it is able to understand, clearly and unequivocally, the reasoning following which the Council took the view that the conditions laid down in Article 1(4) of Common Position 2001/931 and in Article 2(3) of the contested regulation had been satisfied in the circumstances of the case. In particular, it had not been able to understand whether the Council meant to take as the basis the Sanctieregeling itself, or the order made by the court hearing the application for interim measures or some other decision of which it had no knowledge.

61. The state of uncertainty in which, on the contrary, the applicant has been left, regarding the actual and specific reasons for its inclusion in the list at issue, has been exacerbated by the reply given, even before this action was brought, to its request for access to all the documents made use of by the Council before adopting the decision originally challenged. That request, made pursuant to Regulation No 1049/2001 and lodged as early as 26 August 2003, was rejected by decision of the Secretary General of the Council of 5 September 2003, notified to the applicant that same day, on the ground that the only document concerned, namely document '11 311/03 EXT 1 CRS/CRP', was classified as 'CONFIDENTIAL EU' and that its disclosure would undermine the protection of the public interest as regards public security and international relations.

62. While there is indeed reason, as the Council emphasises, to distinguish clearly the rules governing access by the public to documents held by the institutions from the principles relating to observance of the rights of the defence or the obligation to state reasons, the fact nevertheless remains that, in this case, the grounds of the decision to refuse access to the Council's documents may have led the applicant to regard, in all good faith, as impossible the notion that the decision originally challenged, the basis of which,

according to those grounds, is a document classified as 'CONFIDENTIAL EU', had been adopted having regard only to the order of the court hearing the application for interim measures, an official act which is, as a rule, publicly accessible. At the very least, it cannot be inferred from that context that the applicant 'must necessarily know' that the decision originally challenged had been adopted in light of that order alone.

63. It is also clear from the application that the applicant has established no clear and unambiguous link between the order made by the court hearing the application for interim measures and the decision originally challenged. So, in its second plea, the applicant has maintained, first, that in contravention of Article 2(3) of the contested regulation and of Article 1(4) of Common Position 2001/931, that when the decision originally challenged was adopted there was no precise information or material in the file to show that a decision concerning it had been taken by a competent authority, judicial or equivalent thereto. The applicant has moreover asserted that it had been included in the list at issue on the basis of material in the confidential files of security services supplied by the Netherlands Government, when those matters have not been checked by a competent authority and when it has never been charged with the commission of a criminal offence and when no investigations relating to the commission of, or an attempt to commit, or participation in or facilitation of the commission of, acts of terrorism, have been conducted. The applicant has also mentioned, in its application, that the decision originally challenged might have been adopted by the Council on the basis of information other than that, examined by the court hearing the application for interim measures, on the basis on which the Sanctieregeling was adopted.

64. In the absence of any indication, in the contested decision, of the actual and specific reasons justifying it, the applicant has not been placed in a position to avail itself of its right of action before the Court, given the connection between the safeguarding of the obligation to state reasons and the safeguarding of the right to an effective legal remedy (the *OMPI* judgment, paragraph 89). In particular, the applicant has been unable to make an effective challenge, from the moment this action was brought, to the Council's opinion that the order made by the court hearing the application for interim measures satisfied the definition given by Article 1(4) of Common Position 2001/931, a challenge that it was unable to make except purely hypothetically in its application and that it really developed with full knowledge of the facts only at the stage of its reply, in connection with the plea alleging infringement of the contested regulation and of Common Position 2001/931.

65. On this head, it is to be borne in mind that, according to the case-law, failure to state reasons cannot be remedied by the fact that the person concerned learns the reasons for the act during the proceedings before the

Community judicature (*OMPI*, paragraph 139, and the case-law cited). In fact, the possibility of remedying the total absence of a statement of reasons after an action has been brought would prejudice the rights of the defence because the applicant would have only the reply in which to set out his pleas contesting the reasons which he would not know until after he had lodged his application. The principle of equality of the parties before the Community judicature would accordingly be adversely affected (the *OMPI* judgment, paragraphs 139 and 165, and the case-law cited).

66. The foregoing considerations cannot but lead to the annulment of the contested decision, in so far as it concerns the applicant, and there is no need to give a ruling on the other pleas in law and arguments in the action.

67. That being so, there is no need to rule on the claim for a declaration, pursuant to Article 241 EC, that the contested decision is unlawful.

Costs

68. Under Article 87(2) of the Rules of Procedure, the unsuccessful party is to be ordered to pay the costs if they have been applied for in the successful party's pleadings. Since the defendant has been unsuccessful, it must be ordered to pay the costs, as applied for by the applicant.

69. Under the first subparagraph of Article 87(4) of the Rules of Procedure, the Member States which have intervened in the proceedings are to bear their own costs.

On those grounds,

THE COURT OF FIRST INSTANCE (Second Chamber)

hereby:

1. **Annuls Council Decision 2006/379/EC of 29 May 2006 implementing Article 2(3) of Regulation (EC) No 2580/2001 on specific restrictive measures directed against certain persons and entities with a view to combating terrorism and repealing Decision 2005/930 in so far as it concerns Stichting Al-Aqsa;**
2. **Declares that there is no need to rule on the claim for a declaration, pursuant to Article 241 EC, that Council Regulation No 2580/2001 of 27 December 2001 is unlawful;**
3. **Orders the Council to bear, in addition to its own costs, the costs of Stichting Al-Aqsa:**
4. **Orders the Kingdom of the Netherlands to pay its own costs.**

Delivered in open court in Luxembourg on 11 July 2007.

DOCUMENT NO. 19

SISON
v.
COUNCIL OF THE EUROPEAN UNION

EUROPEAN COURT OF JUSTICE (CT FIRST INSTANCE, SECOND CHAMBER)

11 July 2007*

Case T-47/03

Jose Maria Sison, residing in Utrecht (Netherlands), represented by J. Fermon, A. Comte, H. Schultz, D. Gurses and T. Olsson, lawyers, applicant,

supported by

Negotiating Panel of the National Democratic Front of the Philippines, established in Utrecht,

Luis G. Jalandoni, residing in Utrecht,

Fidel V. Agcaoili, residing in Utrecht,

Maria Consuelo K. Ledesma, residing in Utrecht,

represented by B. Tomlow, lawyer, interveners,

v

Council of the European Union, represented by M. Vitsentzatos and M. Bishop, acting as Agents, defendant,

supported by

Kingdom of the Netherlands, represented by H. Sevenster, acting as Agent,

and by

United Kingdom of Great Britain and Northern Ireland, represented initially by R. Caudwell and subsequently by C. Gibbs, acting as Agents, and by S. Moore, Barrister, interveners,

* Language of the case: English.

APPLICATION for, first, partial annulment of Council Decision 2002/974/EC of 12 December 2002 implementing Article 2(3) of Regulation (EC) No 2580/2001 on specific restrictive measures directed against certain persons and entities with a view to combating terrorism and repealing Decision 2002/848/EC (OJ 2002 L 337, p. 85) and, secondly, compensation,

THE COURT OF FIRST INSTANCE OF THE EUROPEAN COMMUNITIES (Second Chamber),

composed of J. Pirrung, President, N. J. Forwood and S. Papasavvas, Judges,

Registrar: K. Pocheć, Administrator,

having regard to the written procedure and further to the hearing on 30 May 2006,

gives the following

Judgment

Legal Framework and Background to the Dispute

1. Article 301 EC states:

> 'Where it is provided, in a common position or in a joint action adopted according to the provisions of the Treaty on European Union relating to the common foreign and security policy, for an action by the Community to interrupt or to reduce, in part or completely, economic relations with one or more third countries, the Council shall take the necessary urgent measures.'

2. Article 60(1) EC provides:

> 'If, in the cases envisaged in Article 301, action by the Community is deemed necessary, the Council may, in accordance with the procedure provided for in Article 301, take the necessary urgent measures on the movement of capital and on payments as regards the third countries concerned.'

3. Article 308 EC provides:

> 'If action by the Community should prove necessary to attain, in the course of the operation of the common market, one of the objectives of the Community, and this Treaty has not provided the necessary powers, the Council shall, acting unanimously on a proposal from the Commission and after consulting the European Parliament, take the appropriate measures.'

4. On 28 September 2001 the United Nations Security Council ('the Security Council') adopted Resolution 1373 (2001) laying down strategies to combat terrorism, in particular the financing of terrorism, by all possible means.

Paragraph 1(c) of that resolution provides, in particular, that all States must freeze without delay funds and other financial assets or economic resources of persons who commit, or attempt to commit, terrorist acts or participate in or facilitate the commission of terrorist acts; of entities owned or controlled by such persons, and of persons and entities acting on behalf of, or at the direction of, such persons and entities.

5. On 27 December 2001, taking the view that action by the Community was needed in order to implement Security Council Resolution 1373 (2001), the Council adopted Common Position 2001/930/CFSP on combating terrorism (OJ 2001 L 344, p. 90) and Common Position 2001/931/CFSP on the application of specific measures to combat terrorism (OJ 2001 L 344, p. 93).

6. Article 1(1) of Common Position 2001/931 provides that the latter applies 'to persons, groups and entities involved in terrorist acts and listed in the Annex'. The applicant's name does not appear in that list.

7. Article 1(2) and (3) of Common Position 2001/931 defines what is to be understood by 'persons, groups and entities involved in terrorist acts' and by 'terrorist act', respectively.

8. The first subparagraph of Article 1(4) of Common Position 2001/931 states that 'the list in the Annex shall be drawn up on the basis of precise information or material in the relevant file which indicates that a decision has been taken by a competent authority in respect of the persons, groups and entities concerned, irrespective of whether it concerns the instigation of investigations or prosecution for a terrorist act, an attempt to perpetrate, participate in or facilitate such an act based on serious and credible evidence or clues, or condemnation for such deeds'. The second subparagraph of Article 1(4) of Common Position 2001/931 states: '"competent authority" shall mean a judicial authority, or, where judicial authorities have no competence in the area covered by this paragraph, an equivalent competent authority in that area'.

9. Article 1(5) of Common Position 2001/931 provides that 'the Council shall work to ensure that names of natural or legal persons, groups or entities listed in the Annex have sufficient particulars appended to permit effective identification of specific human beings, legal persons, entities or bodies, thus facilitating the exculpation of those bearing the same or similar names'.

10. Article 1(6) of Common Position 2001/931 states that 'the names of persons and entities in the list in the Annex shall be reviewed at regular intervals and at least once every six months to ensure that there are grounds for keeping them in the list.'

11. Articles 2 and 3 of Common Position 2001/931 provide that the European Community, acting within the limits of the powers conferred on it by the EC

Treaty, is to order the freezing of the funds and other financial assets or economic resources of persons, groups and entities listed in the Annex and is to ensure that funds, financial assets or economic resources or financial or other related services are not made available, directly or indirectly, for their benefit.

12. Taking the view that a regulation was required in order to implement the measures set out in Common Position 2001/931 at Community level, the Council adopted on 27 December 2001, on the basis of Articles 60 EC, 301 EC and 308 EC, Regulation (EC) No 2580/2001 on specific restrictive measures directed against certain persons and entities with a view to combating terrorism (OJ 2001 L 344, p. 70). That regulation provides that, except as permitted thereunder, all funds belonging to a natural or legal person, group or entity included in the list referred to in Article 2(3) thereof are to be frozen. Likewise, it is prohibited to make funds available or provide financial services to those persons, groups or entities. The Council, acting unanimously, is to establish, review and amend the list of persons, groups and entities to which the regulation applies, in accordance with the provisions laid down in Article 1(4), (5) and (6) of Common Position 2001/931.

13. The original list of persons, groups and entities to whom and to which Regulation No 2580/2001 applied was established by Council Decision 2001/927/EC of 27 December 2001 establishing the list provided for in Article 2(3) of Council Regulation (EC) No 2580/2001 (OJ 2001 L 344, p. 83). The applicant's name is not included in that list.

14. On 28 October 2002 the Council adopted, under Articles 15 EU and 34 EU, Common Position 2002/847/CFSP updating Common Position 2001/931/CFSP and repealing Common Position 2002/462/CFSP (OJ 2002 L 295, p. 1). The Annex thereto updates the list of persons, groups and entities to which Common Position 2001/931 applies.

15. Part 1 of that Annex, headed 'Persons', includes inter alia the name of the applicant, who is described as follows:

> '32. SISON Jose Maria (aka Armando Liwanag, aka Joma, in charge of NPA), born 8.2.1939 in Cabugao, Philippines.'

16. Part 2 of that Annex, headed 'Groups and Entities', includes the name of the New People's Army ('the NPA'), which is described as follows:

> '17. New People's Army (NPA), Philippines, linked to Sison Jose Maria C. (aka Armando Liwanag, aka Joma, in charge of NPA).'

17. By Decision 2002/848/EC of 28 October 2002 implementing Article 2(3) of Regulation (EC) No 2580/2001 and repealing Decision 2002/460/EC (OJ 2002 L 295, p. 12), the Council adopted an updated list of the persons, groups and entities to whom and which that regulation applied. The names of the applicant and of the NPA are repeated in that list, in the same terms as those used in the Annex to Common Position 2002/847.

18. By Decision 2002/974/EC of 12 December 2002 implementing Article 2(3) of Regulation (EC) No 2580/2001 and repealing Decision 2002/848/EC (OJ 2002 L 337, p. 85), the Council adopted a fresh updated list of the persons, groups and entities to which that regulation applied. The names of the applicant and the NPA are repeated in that list, in the same terms as those used in the Annex to Common Position 2002/847 and the Annex to Decision 2002/848.

19. Since then, the Council has adopted several common positions and decisions updating the lists provided for under Common Position 2001/931 and Regulation No 2580/2001, respectively ('the lists at issue') (see, most recently, Council Common Position 2005/936/CFSP of 21 December 2005 updating Common Position 2001/931 and repealing Common Position 2005/847/CFSP (OJ 2005 L 340, p. 80); see also, in order of adoption, Council Decision 2003/480/EC of 27 June 2003 implementing Article 2(3) of Regulation No 2580/2001 and repealing Decision 2002/974 (OJ 2003 L 160, p. 81), Council Decision 2003/646/EC of 12 September 2003 implementing Article 2(3) of Regulation No 2580/2001 and repealing Decision 2003/480 (OJ 2003 L 229, p. 22), Council Decision 2003/902/EC of 22 December 2003 implementing Article 2(3) of Regulation No 2580/2001 and repealing Decision 2003/646 (OJ 2003 L 340, p. 63), Council Decision 2004/306/EC of 2 April 2004 implementing Article 2(3) of Regulation No 2580/2001 and repealing Decision 2003/902 (OJ 2004 L 99, p. 28), Council Decision 2005/221/CFSP of 14 March 2005 implementing Article 2(3) of Regulation (EC) No 2580/2001 and repealing Decision 2004/306/EC (OJ 2005 L 69, p. 64), Council Decision 2005/428/CFSP of 6 June 2005 implementing Article 2(3) of Regulation (EC) No 2580/2001 and repealing Decision 2005/221/CFSP (OJ 2005 L 144, p. 59), Council Decision 2005/722/EC of 17 October 2005 implementing Article 2(3) of Regulation (EC) No 2580/2001 and repealing Decision 2005/428/CFSP (OJ 2005 L 272, p. 15), Council Decision 2005/848/EC of 29 November 2005 implementing Article 2(3) of Regulation (EC) No 2580/2001 and repealing Decision 2005/722/EC (OJ 2005 L 314, p. 46), Council Decision 2005/930/EC of 21 December 2005 implementing Article 2(3) of Regulation (EC) No 2580/2001 and repealing Decision 2005/848/EC (OJ 2005 L 340, p. 64), and Council Decision 2006/379/EC of 29 May 2006 implementing Article 2(3) of Regulation (EC) No 2580/2001 and repealing Decision 2005/930 (OJ 2006 L 144, p. 21)). The acts thus adopted continued to include the applicant's name in the lists at issue, both in the list of persons and, associated with the name of the NPA, in the list of groups and entities.

Procedure

20. By application lodged at the Registry of the Court of First Instance on 6 February 2003, the applicant brought an action against the Council

and the Commission for partial annulment of Decision 2002/974 and for compensation.

21. By separate document lodged at the Registry of the Court of First Instance on 28 February 2003, the applicant brought an application for interim measures against the same institutions, seeking, first, suspension of the operation of Article 1, point 1.25 and point 2.14, of Decision 2002/974 in so far as it mentions his name; secondly, that the Council and the Commission be prohibited from mentioning his name in any fresh decision implementing Article 2(3) of Regulation No 2580/2001 and, thirdly, an order requiring the Council and the Commission to inform all the Member States that the restrictive measures taken in his regard are without any legal basis.

22. By separate document lodged at the Registry of the Court of First Instance on 12 March 2003, the Commission raised, under Article 114 of the Rules of Procedure of the Court of First Instance, an objection of inadmissibility against the action in so far as it was directed against that institution.

23. By order of the President of the Court of First Instance of 7 May 2003, the application for interim measures against the Commission was removed from the register.

24. By order of 15 May 2003, the President of the Court of First Instance dismissed the application for interim measures against the Council on the ground that the requirement of urgency was not satisfied, reserving costs.

25. By documents lodged at the Registry of the Court of First Instance on 27 May 2003 and 11 June 2003 respectively, the Kingdom of the Netherlands and the United Kingdom of Great Britain and Northern Ireland sought leave to intervene in these proceedings in support of the forms of order sought by the Council and the Commission. By document lodged at the Registry of the Court of First Instance on 10 June 2003, the Negotiating Panel of the National Democratic Front of the Philippines, together with Messrs Jalandoni and Agcaoili and Ms Ledesma ('the Negotiating Panel and its members'), sought leave to intervene in these proceedings in support of the forms of order sought by the applicant. By orders of 16 July 2003 and 22 October 2003, the President of the Second Chamber of the Court of First Instance granted leave to intervene. The interveners lodged their statements and the other parties were able to lodge their observations on them within the prescribed periods.

26. By a document lodged at the Registry of the Court of First Instance on 11 July 2003, the applicant stated that he was abandoning his application in so far as it was directed against the Commission.

27. By order of the President of the Second Chamber of the Court of First Instance of 22 September 2003, Case T-47/03 was removed from the register in so far as it was directed against the Commission.

28. In his reply, lodged at the Registry of the Court of First Instance on 15 July 2003 and thereafter by docum ent lodged at the Registry of the Court of First Instance on 29 September 2003, in his observations on the statements in intervention of the United Kingdom and of the Netherlands, lodged at the Registry of the Court of First Instance on 5 February 2004, by a document lodged at the Registry of the Court of First Instance on 7 May 2004, by a document lodged at the Registry of the Court of First Instance on 4 May 2005, by a document lodged at the Registry of the Court of First Instance on 7 July 2005, by a document lodged at the Registry of the Court of First Instance on 17 December 2005, and lastly by a document lodged at the Registry of the Court of First Instance on 16 February 2006, the applicant amended in turn the forms of order sought by him, his pleas in law and his arguments so as to refer in turn to Decision 2003/480 repealing Decision 2002/974, Decision 2003/646 repealing Decision 2003/480, Decision 2003/902 repealing Decision 2003/646, Decision 2004/306 repealing Decision 2003/902, Decision 2005/221 repealing Decision 2004/306, Decision 2005/428 repealing Decision 2005/221, Decision 2005/722 repealing Decision 2005/428, Decision 2005/848 repealing Decision 2005/722, and lastly Decision 2005/930 repealing Decision 2005/848. He relied, to that end, on the case-law which states that where a Community measure is replaced during the course of proceedings by another measure having the same object, the latter measure must be regarded as a new factor, enabling the applicant to adapt his claims and pleas in law. The applicant added that his application should be regarded as challenging the lawfulness of all decisions including him in the lists at issue.

29. The Council has stated that it has no objection to those amendments to the forms of order sought by the applicant and his pleas in law and arguments. In its written observations lodged at the Registry of the Court of First Instance on 22 March 2006, that institution took the view that this action must be regarded as directed against Decision 2005/930 or against any other decision having the same content and the same object, in so far as it concerns the applicant, that was in force on the date of the closure of the oral procedure.

30. By a letter lodged at the Registry of the Court of First Instance on 22 October 2003, the applicant asked to be allowed to lodge his observations on the rejoinder. That request was rejected both on the ground that the Rules of Procedure do not allow for such a possibility and on the ground that the applicant could submit his observations at the hearing.

31. In the document lodged at the Registry of the Court of First Instance on 17 December 2005 and referred to in paragraph 28 above, the applicant

made certain remarks on the relevance, for the purposes of this case, of the judgment of the Court of First Instance of 21 December 2005 in Case T-306/01 *Yusuf and Al Barakaat International Foundation* v *Council and Commission* [2005] ECR II-3533 (now under appeal, '*Yusuf*'). Those remarks and the written observations made in response by the other parties were placed in the file.

32. Upon hearing the report of the Judge-Rapporteur, the Court of First Instance (Second Chamber) decided to open the oral procedure and, by way of measures of organisation of procedure as laid down in Article 64 of the Rules of Procedure of the Court of First Instance, to put written questions to the Netherlands and the Council, inviting them to reply at the hearing.

33. The parties, other than the United Kingdom, which offered apologies for its absence, presented oral argument and their answers to the Court's written and oral questions at the hearing on 30 May 2006.

34. By document lodged at the Registry of the Court of First Instance on 5 June 2006, the applicant sought leave to amend the forms of order sought, his pleas in law and arguments so that they were directed against Decision 2006/379. This document was interpreted by the Court of First Instance as involving a request for the oral procedure to be reopened, with a view to the adoption of a measure of organisation of procedure enabling the applicant to amend his claims, pleas in law and arguments in the light of the adoption of that decision. That document was added to the file and notified to the other parties, the Court of First Instance's decision on the applications they contain being reserved to a later stage of the proceedings.

35. By order of 24 May 2007, the Court of First Instance (Second Chamber) decided to order the reopening of the oral procedure, in accordance with Article 62 of the Rules of Procedure. By letter of the Registrar of 30 May 2007, the other parties were requested to express their views on the application for the adoption of measures of organisation of procedure contained in the document referred to in paragraph 34 above. Those parties having been heard, the Court of First Instance's decision on that application was reserved and the oral procedure was again closed by decision of 12 June 2007.

Concerning the procedural consequences of the repeal and replacement of the decision originally challenged

36. As is apparent from paragraphs 18 and 19 above, the act originally challenged in this action, namely, Decision 2002/974 ('the decision originally challenged'), has been repealed and replaced on various occasions since the application was lodged by acts which have always kept the applicant in the list at issue. These are Decision 2005/930, at the date on which the

oral procedure was closed and Decision 2006/379, at the date of delivery of this judgment.

37. It is to be observed that where a decision is, during the proceedings, replaced by another decision with the same subject-matter, this is to be considered a new factor allowing the applicant to adapt its claims and pleas in law. It would be contrary to the principle of the sound administration of justice and to the requirements of procedural economy to oblige the applicant to make a fresh application to the Court (Case 14/81 *Alpha Steel* v *Commission* [1982] ECR 749, paragraph 8; Joined Cases 351/85 and 360/85 *Fabrique de Fer de Charleroi and Dillinger Hüttenwerke* v *Commission* [1987] ECR 3639, paragraph 11; Case 103/85 *Stahlwerke Peine-Salzgitter* v *Commission* [1988] ECR 4131, paragraphs 11 and 12; and Joined Cases T-46/98 and T-151/98 *CCRE* v *Commission* [2000] ECR II-167, paragraph 33).

38. In its judgments in *Yusuf*, paragraph 73, and Case T-315/01 *Kadi* v *Council and Commission* [2005] ECR II-3649 (now under appeal, '*Kadi*'), paragraph 54, the Court applied that case-law to the situation in which a regulation of direct and individual concern to an individual is replaced, during the proceedings, by a regulation having the same subject-matter.

39. In accordance with that case-law, it is therefore appropriate in the present case to allow the applicant's various requests, mentioned in paragraphs 28 and 34 above, and to consider that his action, on the date on which this judgment is delivered, seeks annulment of Decision 2006/379 ('the contested decision'), in so far as the latter concerns him, after allowing the parties to reformulate their claims, pleas and arguments in the light of those new factors.

40. In addition, the Court considers that only actions for annulment of an act in existence adversely affecting the applicant may be brought before it. Therefore, even if, as held in paragraph 39 above, the applicant may be permitted to reformulate his claims so as to seek annulment of acts which have, during the proceedings, replaced the decision originally challenged, that solution cannot authorise the speculative review of the lawfulness of hypothetical acts which have not yet been adopted (see order in Case T-22/96 *Langdon* v *Commission* [1996] ECR II-1009, paragraph 16, and case-law cited).

41. It follows that there are no grounds for allowing the applicant to reformulate his claims so that they are directed not only against the contested decision but also, as the case may be, against any other decisions capable of including him, in future, in the list at issue (see paragraph 28 above).

Forms of order sought by the parties

42. The applicant claims that the Court should:

- on the basis of Article 230 EC, annul Article 1 of Decision 2006/379 in so far as it mentions his name;

– declare Regulation No 2580/2001 to be unlawful on the basis of Article 241 EC;

– order the Community and the Council to compensate the applicant, on the basis of Article 235 EC and the second paragraph of Article 288 EC, in an amount to be fixed *ex aequo et bono* of not less than EUR 100 000;

– order the Council to pay the costs.

43. The Negotiating Panel and its members support the first two forms of order sought by the applicant and claim in addition that the Council should be ordered to pay the costs of their intervention.

44. The Council contends that the Court should:

– dismiss the action in its entirety;

– order the applicant to pay the costs;

– order the Negotitating Panel and its members to pay the costs arising as a result of their intervention.

45. The Kingdom of the Netherlands and the United Kingdom support the first form of order sought by the Council.

Facts

Administrative and Judicial Proceedings Relating to the Applicant in the Netherlands

46. The papers before the Court indicate that the applicant, who has Filipino nationality, has resided in the Netherlands since 1987. In September 1988, after the Philippine Government withdrew his passport, he applied for refugee status and a residence permit in the Netherlands on humanitarian grounds. That application was refused by decision of the State Secretary for Justice ('the State Secretary') of 13 July 1990, on the basis of Article 1F of the Geneva Convention of 28 July 1951 on the status of refugees, amended by the New York Protocol of 31 January 1967 ('the Geneva Convention'), which states that the provisions of that Convention are not to apply to any person with respect to whom there are serious reasons for considering that:

> '(a) he has committed a crime against peace, a war crime, or a crime against humanity, as defined in the international instruments drawn up to make provision in respect of such crimes;
>
> (b) he has committed a serious non-political crime outside the country of refuge prior to his admission to that country as a refugee;
>
> (c) he has been guilty of acts contrary to the purposes and principles of the United Nations.'

47. His request for a review of that decision having been impliedly rejected by the State Secretary, the applicant brought an action before the Raad

van State (Netherlands Council of State) against that implied decision to reject.

48. By judgment of 17 December 1992 ('the judgment of the Raad van State of 1992'), the Raad van State annulled the implied decision to reject. It held essentially that the State Secretary had not demonstrated to the requisite legal standard which of the acts allegedly committed by the applicant had led him to conclude that the applicant fell within the scope of Article 1F of the Geneva Convention. The Raad van State stated in that regard that the documents supplied to it on a confidential basis by the State Secretary were not sufficiently clear on the point. Since the confidential nature of the documents in question meant that that lack of clarity could not be remedied by an inter partes hearing, the Raad van State held that the information contained in those documents, in so far as it was unclear, could not be construed in a manner which was unfavourable to the applicant.

49. By decision of 26 March 1993, the State Secretary again rejected the applicant's request for a review of his decision of 13 July 1990. That decision to reject was taken primarily on the basis of Article 1F of the Geneva Convention and in the alternative on the basis of the second paragraph of Article 15 of the Vreemdelingenwet (Netherlands Law on Aliens), by reason of the overriding interests of the Netherlands State, that is to say the integrity and credibility of the Netherlands as a sovereign State, particularly with regard to its responsibilities towards other States.

50. In an action to challenge that brought by the applicant, the Raad van State annulled the State Secretary's decision of 26 March 1993 by judgment of 21 February 1995 ('the judgment of the Raad van State of 1995').

51. In that judgment, the Raad van State held that the State Secretary had reached his decision on the basis of the following factors:

- a letter from the Binnenlandse Veiligheidsdienst (Netherlands internal security service, 'the BVD') of 3 March 1993, which stated, first, that the applicant held the post of chairman and was the head of the Communist Party of the Philippines ('the CPP') and, second, that the military wing of the CPP, the NPA, was under the Central Committee of the CPP and, accordingly, the applicant;
- the findings of the BVD, first, that the applicant was, in fact, the head of the NPA and, second, that the NPA—and thus the applicant—was responsible for a large number of terrorist acts in the Philippines.

52. The Raad van State noted the following examples of such terrorist acts, given by the State Secretary in his decision of 26 March 1993:

- the murder of 40 inhabitants (mostly defenceless women and children) of the village of Digos, on the Island of Mindanao (Philippines) on 25 June 1989;

- the shooting of 14 people, including six children, in the village of Dipalog (Philippines) in August 1989;
- the execution of four inhabitants of the village of Del Monte (Philippines) on 16 October 1991.

53. The Raad van State also noted that the State Secretary had mentioned the purges carried out in 1985 in the CPP and the NPA, in the course of which it was estimated that 800 of their members were assassinated without any form of trial taking place.

54. Lastly, the Raad van State noted that, according to the State Secretary, the BVD had also determined that the CPP and the NPA maintained contacts with terrorist organisations throughout the world and that personal contacts between the applicant and representatives of those organisations had also been observed.

55. The Raad van State next examined by special procedure certain confidential evidence in the State Secretary's file together with the 'operational material' on which the letter sent to him by the BVD on 3 March 1993 (paragraph 51 above) was based.

56. Taking the above matters into account, the Raad van State went on to rule as follows:

> 'In the light of the above evidence, the [Raad van State] holds there to be sufficient indication that the [applicant] was, at the time the decision [of 26 March 1993] was taken, the chairman and the head of the CPP. In addition, the evidence supports the conclusion that the NPA is subject to the Central Committee of the CPP and the conclusion that, at the time the decision [of 26 March 1993] was taken, the [applicant] had at least attempted to effectively direct the NPA from the Netherlands. The [Raad van State] also holds there to be sufficient indication based on public sources alone, such as reports by Amnesty International, that the NPA is responsible for a large number of terrorist acts in the Philippines. The evidence also provides support for the conclusion that the [applicant] has at least attempted to direct the abovementioned activities carried out under the control of the NPA in the Philippines. The evidence supplied also provides support for the [State Secretary's] contention that the CPP/NPA maintain contacts with terrorist organisations throughout the world and that there have been personal contacts between the [applicant] and representatives of such organisations. However, the evidence does not provide support for the conclusion that the [applicant] directed the operations in question and is responsible for them to such an extent that it may be held that there are serious reasons to suppose that the [applicant] has actually committed the serious crimes referred to in [Article 1F of the Geneva Convention]. In that regard, the [Raad van State] has expressly taken into account the fact that, as it has already held in its judgment of 17 December 1992, Article 1F of the Geneva Convention must be narrowly construed.

> The [Raad van State] considers accordingly that the [State Secretary] was not entitled to conclude, on the basis of the abovementioned evidence, that the [applicant] should be denied the protection afforded by the [Geneva] Convention.'

57. The Raad van State also held that the applicant had sound reasons to fear that he would be persecuted if he was sent back to the Philippines and that he should accordingly be treated as a refugee for the purposes of Article 1(A)(2) of the Geneva Convention.

58. The Raad van State then considered the merits of the State Secretary's alternative reason for refusing the applicant admission to the Netherlands on grounds of public interest, on the basis of the second paragraph of Article 15 of the Netherlands Law on Aliens.

59. In that regard, the Raad van State held in particular as follows:

> 'While the [Raad van State] acknowledges the importance of the [State Secretary's] concern, particularly in view of the indications he has recorded of personal contacts between the [applicant] and representatives of terrorist organisations, that cannot justify recourse to the second paragraph of Article 15 of the Law on Aliens if there is no guarantee that the [applicant] will be permitted to enter a country other than the Philippines. It is precluded by the fact that such a refusal to admit the [applicant] must be regarded as being contrary to Article 3 of the European Convention for the Protection of Human Rights and Fundamental Freedoms.'

60. Following that judgment, the State Secretary, by decision of 4 June 1996, again rejected the applicant's request for review of his decision of 13 July 1990. He ordered the applicant to leave the Netherlands, but decided at the same time that the applicant should not be deported to the Philippines for so long as he had a well-founded fear of being persecuted within the meaning of the Geneva Convention or of treatment contrary to Article 3 of the European Convention for the Protection of Human Rights and Fundamental Freedoms ('the ECHR').

61. By decision of 11 September 1997 ('the decision of the Rechtbank'), the Arrondissementsrechtbank te's-Gravenhage, Sector Bestuursrecht, Rechtseenheidskamer Vreemdelingenzaken (the Hague District Court, Administrative law section, Chamber responsible for the uniform application of the law, cases involving aliens, 'the Rechtbank') dismissed the action brought by the applicant against the State Secretary's decision of 4 June 1996 on the basis that it was unfounded.

62. In the course of the proceedings before the Rechtbank, all the documents relating to the investigation carried out by the BVD into the applicant's activities in the Netherlands, and in particular the letter from that organisation to the State Secretary of 3 March 1993 (paragraph 51 above),

as well as the operational material on which that letter is based, were produced in confidence to the Rechtbank. The President of the Rechtbank examined them under a special procedure. On the basis of the report prepared by its President, the Rechtbank decided that the restriction on making those documents available to the applicant was justified. As the latter had given the consent to that effect required by the legislation, the Rechtbank none the less took account of the content of those documents in order to decide the case.

63. The Rechtbank then considered whether the decision contested before it could be upheld, in so far as it refused the applicant admission as a refugee and the granting to him of a residence permit.

64. With regard to the facts on which the decision was based, the Rechtbank referred back to the judgment of the Raad van State of 1995.

65. On the basis of that judgment, the Rechtbank considered that it must be regarded as settled in law that Article 1F of the Geneva Convention could not be invoked against the applicant, that the latter had a well-founded fear of being persecuted within the meaning of Article 1A of that Convention and of Article 15 of the Netherlands Law on Aliens and that Article 3 of the ECHR prevented the applicant from being deported, directly or indirectly, to his country of origin.

66. The Rechtbank next considered the question whether the judgment of the Raad van State of 1995 entitled the State Secretary to refuse the applicant admission as a refugee, pursuant to the second paragraph of Article 15 of the Netherlands Law on Aliens, which provides that 'admission can be refused only on important grounds of public interest if that refusal would compel the alien to go immediately to a country referred to in the first paragraph', when the State Secretary had failed to guarantee the applicant admission to a country other than the Philippines.

67. In that regard the Rechtbank quoted in full the paragraph of the judgment of the Raad van State of 1995 set out in paragraph 59 above.

68. The Rechtbank then ruled on the question whether the State Secretary had properly exercised his power to derogate from the rule that an alien is normally to be admitted to the Netherlands as a refugee where he can establish a well-founded fear of being persecuted within the meaning of Article 1A of the Geneva Convention and no other country will admit him as an asylum seeker, as, in the Rechtbank's opinion, was the position in that case. In that regard, the Rechtbank held as follows:

> 'In the opinion of the Rechtbank, it cannot be argued that the [State Secretary] has not used this power reasonably in respect of the [applicant], taking into account the "essential interests of the Netherlands State, namely the integrity and credibility of the Netherlands as a sovereign State, particularly with

regard to its responsibilities towards other States", also recognised by the [Raad van State]. The facts on which the [Raad van State] based that assessment are also of overriding importance as far as the Rechtbank is concerned. It has not been shown that a different significance should have been attributed to those facts by the [State Secretary] at the time the decision [at issue in the case] was taken. The [applicant's] observations on the changed political situation in the Philippines and on his role in the negotiations between the Philippine authorities and the [CPP] do not affect that, since the important reasons—as is clear from the judgment of the [Raad van State]—are based on other facts'.

69. The Rechtbank accordingly dismissed as unfounded the applicant's appeal against the refusal to admit him to the Netherlands as a refugee.

70. The Rechtbank also dismissed as unfounded the applicant's challenge to the refusal to grant him a residence permit. Ruling more particularly on the question whether the State Secretary had taken his decision after a reasonable weighing up of interests, the Rechtbank referred to its findings quoted in paragraph 68 above and added that the State Secretary had acted reasonably in attaching less weight to the interests invoked by the applicant in that regard.

Other Factual Allegations Made by the Parties

71. The applicant states that he is a Filipino intellectual and patriot, who has held various academic positions and received several literary awards. From the 1960s until the 1980s, he was, with President Ferdinand E. Marcos and Senator Benigno 'Ninoy' Aquino Jr., one of the three key personalities on the political scene in the Philippines.

72. He admits that he was chairman of the Central Committee of the CPP from 26 December 1968 until 10 November 1977, on which date he was replaced in that post by Rodolfo Salas, following his arrest and imprisonment by the Marcos regime, which lasted until 5 March 1986. After his release, he taught briefly at the University of the Philippines, under constant surveillance by the military authorities and without any opportunity of being involved in any underground activity. On 31 August 1986, he left the Philippines to start a lecture tour in universities, first in the Asia-Pacific region and then, from 23 January 1987, in Europe. Since then, he has lived in exile, carrying out research, writing and participating in various peaceful activities in the Filipino community. The applicant contends that at no point in his stay abroad from 1986 to the present has it been possible for him to assume the position of chairman of the Central Committee of the CPP, as the CPP Constitution requires that that person be present in the Philippines on a daily basis.

73. Following civil proceedings brought before the United States courts in 1986 with the assistance of the American Civil Liberties Union (ACLU), the estate of Ferdinand E. Marcos agreed in 1997 to a 'stipulated judgment' awarding the applicant USD 750 000 by way of damages. That sum has never been paid to the applicant.

74. The applicant states that he is not the subject of 'any valid criminal charge' anywhere in the world and that, historically, neither the Philippine Government nor the international community has ever regarded him as a terrorist or a common criminal. He adds, however, that recently the administration of Philippine President Mrs Gloria Macapagal-Arroyo has brought criminal charges against him. He maintains that those charges are baseless and form part of a campaign to persecute him.

75. With more particular regard to the Philippines, the applicant refers to two certificates confirming the absence of any criminal charges against him, issued to him on 2 March 1994 by the Office of the public prosecutor of the City of Manila (Philippines) and on 20 April 1998 by the Secretary of Justice of the Philippine Government. The latter document refers inter alia to a decision of a Philippine court of 22 September 1992 dismissing the charges brought against the applicant in October 1998 for subversive activities, following the repeal of the anti-subversion law in 1992. It also refers to a decision of 2 March 1994 dismissing for 'lack of sufficient evidence' the charges brought against the applicant in 1991 by the Office of the public prosecutor of the City of Manila. According to the applicant, those charges involved an accusation of multiple murders in connection with a bombing in 1971.

76. With more particular regard to the Netherlands, the applicant refers to a statement by the Minister of Foreign Affairs, Mr J. De Hoop Scheffer, who confirmed, in reply to a parliamentary question put on 16 August 2002, that the public prosecutor's office was of the view there was no basis for instigating a criminal investigation against the applicant.

77. The applicant, supported by the Negotiating Panel and its members, states that he has been the chief political consultant of the National Democratic Front of the Philippines ('the NDFP') since 1990 and that in that capacity he plays an important role in the negotiations between the NDFP and the Philippine Government, seeking to find a peaceful solution to the continuing armed conflict in the Philippines. In resolutions adopted in 1997 and 1999, the European Parliament gave its support to those negotiations. They were also supported by the whole of the Filipino people and the international community, in particular the Netherlands, Belgian and Norwegian Governments.

78. The applicant concludes from the above that for over 25 years he has been prevented, both physically and for organisational reasons, from play-

ing a leading role, or even participating, in the continuing civil war in the Philippines.

79. The applicant states, however, that on 9 August 2002 the United States Secretary of State designated the CPP and the NPA as 'foreign terrorist organisations' and that on 12 August 2002 the Office of Foreign Assets Control (OFAC) of the United States Treasury Department included the CPP and the NPA and the applicant in the list of individual and terrorist groups covered by Executive Order No 13224, signed by President George W. Bush on 23 September 2001, and ordered the freezing of their assets.

80. The applicant goes on to state that on 13 August 2002, the Netherlands Minister of Foreign Affairs adopted a regulation on the fight against terrorism (Sanctieregeling Terrorisme 2002 III, Staatscourant No 153) which places the CPP and the NPA and the applicant on a list of individuals and groups subject to economic sanctions. On the same day, the Netherlands Minister of Finance ordered, and subsequently put into effect, the freezing of the postal bank account held by the applicant jointly with his wife, and the cancellation of the social security benefits which he received as a refugee in the Netherlands. Those benefits were partially restored on 9 October 2002 on humanitarian grounds, and then suspended again on 13 December 2002.

81. Lastly, the applicant claims that in late January 2003 the Minister for Foreign Affairs of the Philippines made the following statement:

> 'Once there is a peace agreement, I will request the European Union, the United States and other countries to delist [the rebels] as terrorists. If they sign, they will no longer be terrorists.'

82. Messrs Jalandoni and Agcaoili and Ms Ledesma state that they are members of the Negotiating Panel of the NDFP. In that capacity, they have participated in peace negotiations between the NDFP and the Philippine Government. In the course of those negotiations, they have concluded, on behalf of the NDFP, various agreements with that Government.

83. At the hearing, the Council indicated, in answer to a written question asked by the Court, that it had taken no account at all of any criminal investigations or proceedings brought in the Philippines against the applicant, according to the latter (see paragraph 74 above), when adopting any of the acts that have successively updated the lists at issue.

84. At the hearing the Netherlands Government stated, moreover, in answer to a written question put by the Court, that no decision to open investigations, to prosecute or convict in respect of a terrorist act, for the purposes of Article 1(4) of Common Position 2001/931 and Article 2(3) of Regulation No 2580/2001, had been taken by any competent authority of the Netherlands vis-à-vis the applicant between the date on which the Rechtbank delivered its decision and the date of the hearing in this case.

85. Finally, the Netherlands Government stated at the hearing that the applicant had received no more social security benefits in the Netherlands since he had been included in the lists at issue. The requests for derogation from the freezing of funds, made pursuant to Articles 5 and 6 of Regulation No 2580/2001, were rejected by decisions of the Minister for Finance of 7 March and 16 May 2003, subsequently confirmed by a judgment of the Raad van State of 28 September 2005. It states that the applicant's very existence is not in danger, for he is lodged and maintained by his wife, who is herself the holder of a residence permit and the recipient of social security benefits in the Netherlands.

The Application for Annulment

Preliminary Observations

86. In support of his claim for annulment of the contested decision, the applicant puts forward eleven pleas in law. The first alleges infringement of Article 253 EC. The second is based on a manifest error of assessment and infringement of Article 2(3) of Regulation No 2580/2001. The third is based on breach of the principle of proportionality and the right to life. The fourth is based on infringement of Article 56 EC. The fifth alleges infringements of the right to a fair trial, the rights of the defence and of the presumption of innocence. The sixth alleges breach of the principle that every punishment must have a lawful basis. The seventh alleges infringement of the right to freedom of expression and of association. The eighth alleges infringement of the right to property. The ninth is a plea by way of objection based on the Council's lack of competence to adopt Regulation No 2580/2001. The tenth is a plea by way of objection based on breach of the principle of proportionality and of the principle of legal certainty. Finally, the eleventh is a plea by way of objection based on misuse of power. The Negotiating Panel and its members put forward arguments which, while seeking to establish their own interest in having the contested decision annulled, essentially aim to support the applicant's plea of misuse of powers.

87. Priority must be given to the examination of the heads of claims based on the Community's lack of competence to adopt the acts under challenge and, then, together to the heads of claim alleging breaches of the duty to provide reasons, of the rights of the defence and of the right to a fair trial.

The Heads of Claim Based on the Community's Lack of Competence to Adopt the Acts Under Challenge

88. These heads of claim are formulated in connection with the ninth plea in law alleging, by way of objection, that the Council was not competent to adopt Regulation No 2580/2001.

Arguments of the Parties

89. The applicant argues that the Council was not competent to adopt the contested regulation on the legal basis of Articles 60 EC, 301 EC and 308 EC.

90. First, Articles 60 EC and 301 EC authorise only the adoption of measures against third countries and not, as in the present case, against individuals and organisations within the Community.

91. Secondly, Article 308 EC does not authorise the Council, under the pretext of ensuring the effectiveness of Community action, to exercise powers inconsistent with its fundamental nature, which is that of an executive body. In that regard, the applicant states that Article 2(3) of Regulation No 2580/2001 confers on the Council the power to establish, unilaterally and without reference to any objective criteria, the list of individuals and groups allegedly linked to terrorism and to whom and to which sanctions of a penal nature are to apply. In so doing, Regulation No 2580/2001 confers on the Council, an institution already equipped with broad executive powers, a judicial role which is not provided for in the Treaty, resulting in an unprecedented concentration of powers.

92. In support of his arguments, the applicant refers to the Resolution of the European Parliament o f 24 October 2002 on assessment of and prospects for the European Union strategy on terrorism one year after 11 September 2001. In that resolution, the Parliament expressed 'doubts that effective coordination of a European anti-terrorism policy is possible under the present structure of the Union' and urged the Convention on the Future of Europe to create 'the necessary legal basis to allow the European Union to freeze assets and cut off funds of persons, groups and entities of the European Union involved in terrorist acts and included in the European Union list'.

93. In his reply, the applicant adds that it is clear from Opinion 2/94 of the Court of Justice of 28 March 1996 ([1996] ECR I-1759, paragraphs 29 and 30) that Article 308 EC cannot be regarded as a sufficient legal basis for the adoption of the contested measures.

94. The Council and the intervening Governments recognise that Regulation No 2580/2001 refers inter alia to entities and individuals, such as the applicant, who are not necessarily linked to the government of or the regime controlling a third country. It is precisely for that reason that the legal basis of Articles 60 EC and 301 EC was supplemented by that of Article 308 EC. The Council and the intervening Governments maintain that, by proceeding in that way, the Community has been able to keep pace with the development of international practice, which has been to adopt 'smart sanctions' aimed at individuals and entities who pose a threat to international security, having regard in particular to the altered political circumstances

after 11 September 2001. In that respect, Regulation No 2580/2001 is in line with Security Council Resolution 1373 (2001).

95. The Council adds that the use of Articles 60 EC and 301 EC to give effect to a common position adopted as part of the common foreign and security policy (CFSP) is in accordance with the requirement to ensure consistency in the activities of the Union laid down by Article 3 EU. Furthermore, one of the primary objectives of the CFSP is to preserve peace and strengthen international security, in accordance with the principles of the Charter of the United Nations (Article 11 EU). In addition, the EC Treaty itself includes a reference in the preamble to the Charter of the United Nations and expresses the resolve of the High Contracting Parties to preserve and strengthen peace and liberty. The Council deduces from that that the promotion of international peace and security is a principle of the Charter of the United Nations which is reflected in the general framework of the EC Treaty, and more specifically in Articles 60 EC and 301 EC. However, inasmuch as neither of those articles, nor any other specific Treaty provision, covers the situation of persons such as the applicant, the use of Article 308 EC is shown to be necessary and justified.

96. The United Kingdom submits that measures aimed at freezing the funds of individuals with a view to interrupting economic relations with international terrorist organisations, rather than with third countries, cannot be regarded as widening 'the scope of Community powers beyond the general framework created by the provisions of the Treaty as a whole', as stated in Opinion 2/94, cited in paragraph 93 above. Under the general framework of the Treaty the Community has competence to take action to regulate capital movements and, moreover, to do this by taking action against individuals.

97. The Netherlands claim that the areas of competence of the Community have frequently been supplemented on the occasion of Treaty amendments, with Article 308 EC having been used as a legal basis before those changes were adopted. According to that Government, when Article 301 EC was adopted, it was not possible to foresee that sanctions might have to be imposed on persons, groups and entities. As that necessity has subsequently become clear, recourse to Article 308 EC is justified pending amendment of the Treaty in the future. In that regard, the Netherlands point out that the draft constitutional treaty resulting from the preparatory work of the Convention on the Future of Europe (Doc. CONV 850/03) states at Article III-282(2) that the Council may adopt restrictive measures against natural or legal persons and non-State groups or bodies

Findings of the Court

98. Like Council Regulation (EC) No 881/2002 of 27 May 2002 imposing certain specific restrictive measures directed against certain persons and

entities associated with Usama bin Laden, the Al-Qaeda network and the Taliban, and repealing Council Regulation (EC) No 467/2001 (OJ 2001 L 139, p. 9), which was at issue in the cases giving rise to the judgments in *Yusuf* and *Kadi*, Regulation No 2580/2001 was adopted on the basis of Articles 60 EC, 301 EC and 308 EC. As is made clear in the fifth recital in the preamble thereto, that regulation is designed to implement in the Community the CFSP aspects of Common Position 2001/931, itself adopted in order to give effect at Union level to Security Council Resolution 1373 (2001). Just like those provided for by Regulation No 881/2002, those measures consist in substance of the adoption of economic and financial sanctions (freezing of funds) directed at private parties (persons and entities) in connection with the combating of terrorism. The 14th recital in the preamble to Regulation No 2580/2001 expressly recognises that the measures in question may include persons and entities in no way linked or related to third countries.

99. The question whether the Community is competent to adopt such measures directed against private parties, without establishing any connection whatsoever between them and one or more third countries, was examined by the Court of First Instance in *Yusuf* (paragraphs 107 to 170) and *Kadi* (paragraphs 87 to 134). At the end of that examination, the Court concluded that 'the institutions and the United Kingdom [were] therefore right to maintain that the Council was competent to adopt [Regulation No 881/2002] which sets in motion the economic and financial sanctions provided for by Common Position 2002/402, on the joint basis of Articles 60 EC, 301 EC and 308 EC' (*Yusuf*, paragraph 170, and *Kadi*, paragraph 135).

100. On that occasion the Court provided exhaustive answers to arguments in substance the same as those put forward by the parties in relation to that question in this action (see, in respect of the similar arguments put forward by the parties in the cases giving rise to *Yusuf* and *Kadi*, paragraphs 80 to 106 of *Yusuf* and paragraphs 64 to 86 of *Kadi*).

101. The allegation that the Council has arrogated to itself a judicial role and powers in criminal matters not envisaged by the Treaty, which is the only allegation that can distinguish this case from those giving rise to *Yusuf* and *Kadi*, must be rejected without any other form of examination since it would appear to be a mere corollary of the applicant's other arguments relating to competence. It is after all based on the mistaken premiss that the restrictive measures at issue in this case are of a criminal nature. The assets of the persons concerned not having been confiscated as the proceeds of crime but rather frozen as a precautionary measure, those measures do not constitute criminal sanctions and do not, moreover, imply any accusation of a criminal nature (see, to that effect and by analogy, *Yusuf*, paragraph 299, and *Kadi*, paragraph 248).

102. The applicant's complaints alleging that the Community lacked competence to adopt Regulation No 2580/2001, set out in connection with the ninth plea, are accordingly to be rejected (with regard to the Community judicature's power to give reasons for its judgment by reference to an earlier judgment ruling on largely identical questions, see Case C-229/04 *Crailsheimer Volksbank* [2005] ECR I-9273, paragraphs 47 to 49, and Case T-253/02 *Ayadi* v *Council* [2006] ECR II-2139, under appeal, paragraph 90; see also the order of the Court of Justice of 5 June 2002 in Case C-204/00 P *Aalborg Portland* v *Commission*, not published in the ECR, paragraph 29).

The Heads of Claim Alleging Breaches of the Duty to State Reasons, the Rights of the Defence and Right to a Fair Trial

103. These heads of claim are put forward in the first plea in law, on the one hand, as regards the alleged infringement of Article 253 EC, and in the fifth plea in law, on the other, as regards the breach of the right to a fair trial, the rights of the defence and the presumption of innocence.

Arguments of the Parties

– Allegation of infringement of the duty to state reasons

104. The applicant maintains that the contested decision fails to satisfy the requirement to state reasons laid down by Article 253 EC, as the second recital merely states that it has been 'decided to adopt an updated list of the persons, groups and entities to which Regulation (EC) No 2580/2001 applies', without actually stating the reasons which led the Council to draw up that list in the form in which it is presented. In particular, the Council provides no links between the general criteria set out in Regulation No 2580/2001 and the personal situation of the person concerned and does not even mention the 'precise information' or the 'material in the relevant file' to indicate that a decision justifying his inclusion in the lists at issue has been taken in his respect by a competent authority. It is thus impossible for the applicant to know the justification for the serious sanctions imposed on him, in order that he may defend his rights, and the Community judicature cannot exercise its power of review of the lawfulness of the contested decision (Joined Cases 67/85, 68/85 and 70/85 *Van der Kooy and Others* v *Commission* [1988] ECR 219, Case C-350/88 *Delacre* v *Commission* [1990] ECR I-395, paragraph 15, and Case T-105/95 *WWF UK* v *Commission* [1997] ECR II-313, paragraph 66).

105. According to the applicant, the requirement to state adequate reasons applies with particular force in the present case since the Council has a broad discretion and the effects of the discretionary measure are severe (see Joined Cases 36, 37 and 38/59 and 40/59 *Geitling* v *High Authority* [1960] ECR 423; Case C-367/95 P *Commission* v *Sytraval and Brink's France*

[1998] ECR I-1719; and Joined Cases T-44/01, T-119/01 and T 126/01 *Vieira and Vieira Argentina* v *Commission* [2003] ECR II-1209). In this connection, the applicant also points out, in his observations on *Yusuf*, that, unlike what was held in that case with regard to Usama bin Laden and the persons associated with him, the applicant has never been listed by the UN Security Council. The decision to freeze his funds was therefore taken on the initiative of the Council in the exercise of a discretionary power of assessment. Paragraph 225 of the judgment in *Yusuf* makes it clear that in such cases the Council itself acknowledges that judicial review must extend to examination of the evidence relied on against the persons on whom the sanctions are imposed. The attitude of the Council in the present case is in total contradiction with that statement, however. The Council has never presented the slightest evidence to enable the applicant to defend itself and the Court to exercise a full review.

106. The applicant adds that his various requests for access to the documents on the basis of which the Council adopted the contested decision, made under Regulation (EC) No 1049/2001 of the European Parliament and of the Council of 30 May 2001 regarding public access to European Parliament, Council and Commission documents (OJ 2001 L 145, p. 43), were systematically refused on the ground that those documents are classified as 'CONFIDENTIAL EU' and that their disclosure would undermine the protection of the public interest as regards security and international relations. In his reply, the applicant states that there is a clear contradiction between those reasons for the decisions to refuse access to the documents in question and the explanations given by the Council in its defence, from which it appears that the only basis for justifying the applicant's inclusion in the lists at issue is a public document, namely the decision of the Rechtbank. That contradiction affects the validity of the contested decision.

107. The Council and the Netherlands accept that the contested decision, which consists merely of an updated list of persons covered by Regulation No 2580/2001, does not itself contain a detailed statement of reasons. It is none the less clear, in their view, from the legal base cited and the recitals in the preamble that that implementing decision is based on that regulation, Article 2(3) of which sets out the criteria governing the inclusion of persons in the lists at issue and Article 1(4) of which defines a terrorist act by reference to Article 1(3) of Common Position 2001/931. Furthermore, the objective of Regulation No 2580/2001, namely, to combat any form of financing of terrorist activities, is made clear in the second recital.

108. The contested acts, taken together, satisfy the obligation to state reasons set out in Article 253 EC, as interpreted in the case-law. In that regard, the Council and the Netherlands point out that it is not necessary for details of all relevant factual and legal aspects to be given and that regard should be had to the context and to all the legal rules governing the

matter in question. The degree of precision of the statement of reasons for a decision must also be weighed against practical realities and the time and technical facilities available for making the decision (*Delacre*, cited in paragraph 104 above, paragraphs 15 and 16).

109. In its rejoinder, the Council adds that it was not under any obligation to disclose the specific factual elements which led it to conclude that the applicant was involved in terrorist activities, since the applicable procedure involved the use of sensitive material which could not be made publicly available without seriously compromising public security.

110. In its observations on *Yusuf*, the Council acknowledges that it has a wider margin of discretion in this case than it had in the case giving rise to *Yusuf*. It also accepts that the scope for judicial review of the contested decision may be greater than it was in the circumstances of *Yusuf*. However, that does not mean that there are grounds for disclosing and reviewing, in these proceedings, all the evidence concerning the applicant. That applies particularly as regards the documents examined by the Raad van State and the Rechtbank, the confidential nature of which was accepted by those courts.

– Alleged infringements of the rights of the defence and of the right to a fair trial

111. In the first of these heads of claim, the applicant maintains that the contested decision was taken in breach of his rights of defence. In effect, the sanctions in question have been imposed on the applicant in the present case, and he has been accused of the crime of terrorism, without his previously having been heard or having had the opportunity of defending himself, without his having had any access to the confidential documents and information on the basis of which those measures were taken and without those measures having been subjected to the slightest judicial review. An irregularity of that kind cannot be remedied at the stage of proceedings before the Court of First Instance (Joined Cases T-305/94 to T-307/94, T-313/94 to T-316/94, T–318/94, T-325/94, T-328/94, T-329/94 and T-335/94 *LVM* v *Commission* [1999] ECR II-931, paragraph 1022).

112. In reply to the Council's argument that the legislation at issue in the present case does not provide for the right to be heard before a decision is taken, the applicant states that the right to be heard represents an application of the general principle that a person whose interests are perceptibly affected by a decision taken by a public authority must be given the opportunity to make his point of view known. He adds that observance of the rights of the defence in all proceedings which may result in sanctions being imposed is a fundamental principle of Community law which must be respected in all circumstances, even in the absence of any provision to that effect (*LVM*, cited in paragraph 111 above, at paragraph 1011).

113. The Council's argument based on the precedent of the sanctions taken against the former Federal Republic of Yugoslavia (paragraph 128 below) is equally irrelevant because in that precedent, by contrast to the present case, the companies included in the 'black list' had had prior contacts with the German authorities, which had alerted them to their imminent inclusion in that list. They were thus in a position to submit their detailed observations to the German authorities and to the Commission. It was precisely for that reason that the Court of First Instance refused to declare that their rights of defence had been infringed (order of the President of the Second Chamber of the Court of First Instance in Case T-189/00 R *Invest Import und Export and Invest Commerce* v *Commission* [2000] ECR II-2993, paragraph 41).

114. In his observations on the judgment in *Yusuf*, the applicant acknowledges that in paragraph 308 of that judgment the Court found that it was unarguable that to have heard the persons concerned before their funds were frozen would have been liable to jeopardise the effectiveness of the sanctions and would thus have been incompatible with the public-interest objective pursued. The applicant considers, however, that the necessity of taking advantage of the effect of surprise must not lead to the removal of all guarantees. The effectiveness of the measure could thus be preserved by a hearing after the event. The applicant refers in this regard to the legal guarantees provided for by criminal procedural law in the Member States where prosecuting authorities or investigating magistrates decide to freeze funds.

115. In the second of those heads of claim, the applicant maintains that the contested decision infringes the right to a fair trial before an impartial court, guaranteed by Article 6(1) of the ECHR and recognised in the case-law of the Court of Justice.

116. He argues in that regard that his inclusion in the lists at issue is tantamount to being 'charged with a criminal offence' for the purposes of those provisions, as interpreted in a 'material' and not a 'formal' manner by the European Court of Human Rights (*Deweer*, ECHR judgment of 27 February 1980, Series A no 35, § 44). In that context, the applicant argues that the European Court of Human Rights considers that three criteria determine whether such a charge exists, namely, the legal classification of the infringement in national law, the nature of the charge, and the nature and degree of severity of the sanctions imposed. In the present case, those three criteria are satisfied. First, the contested decision is concerned with the fight against terrorism, which forms an integral part of Community criminal law, as is confirmed by the adoption of the Council Framework Decision of 13 June 2002 on combating terrorism (OJ 2002 L 164, p. 3). Secondly, the nature of the charge leaves no room for doubt, since the contested regulation refers to persons who 'commit, or attempt to commit, terrorist acts or who participate in or facilitate the commission of any such acts'. Thirdly, the freezing

of funds is comparable to a total deprivation, for an unspecified duration, of the right of ownership of the frozen assets.

117. By the contested decision, the Council imposes, moreover, a criminal penalty on the applicant, without any judicial decision's having been taken upon the conclusion of a fair trial.

118. In reply to the Council's argument that the applicant's right to a fair trial was guaranteed in the present case under the national procedures leading to his inclusion in the lists at issue, the applicant submits that the proceedings before the Raad van State and the Rechtbank were wholly irrelevant in that regard, because they did not concern his involvement in terrorist acts, but only the recognition of his refugee status and the issuing of a residence permit. There was thus no national procedure guaranteeing the right to a fair trial.

119. In reply to the Council's argument that the right to a fair trial is also guaranteed in the present proceedings, the applicant states that they fail to provide such a guarantee, by reason of the nature and the limits of the Court's jurisdiction in actions for annulment.

120. The Council argues that the procedure leading to the inclusion of the applicant in the lists at issue is such that his rights of defence are guaranteed at both national and Community level.

121. First, the Council notes that Article 1(4) of Common Position 2001/931 provides that a person may be included in the lists at issue only where it is established that a decision has been taken in his respect by a competent national authority, that is to say, by a court or its equivalent (see paragraph 8 above). The Council states that that authority will naturally have had to respect the rights of defence of the person concerned. The Netherlands Government confirms that such a decision must be subject to all the guarantees required by the national legal order.

122. In the present case, the applicant was the subject of several sets of administrative and judicial proceedings in the Netherlands to determine his administrative status (see paragraphs 46 to 70 above) and he had ample opportunity to state his position effectively in the course of those proceedings, subject to the rules applied by the courts and tribunals concerned to safeguard the confidentiality of sensitive information.

123. In reply to the applicant's argument that those proceedings should not be taken into account because they concerned the issuing of a resident's permit and not his involvement in terrorist activities, the Council states that that involvement played a fundamental part in the decision of the State Secretary, confirmed by the decision of the Rechtbank, to refuse to issue such a permit to him. Far from being regarded as peripheral, the facts show that that involvement was held by the Rechtbank to be 'of overriding importance' (see paragraph 68 above).

124. Secondly, the Council points out that the applicant has had the opportunity of bringing the present action for annulment and compensation before the Court of First Instance. In a decision of 23 May 2002 in *Segi and Others and Gestoras pro Amnistía* v *The 15 Member States of the European Union* (Nos 6422/02 and 9916/02, *Reports of Judgments and Decisions*, 2002-V), the European Court of Human Rights dismissed the claim of certain entities included in the lists at issue for the very reason, inter alia, that the contested regulation is subject to review by the Community judicature.

125. On the other hand, the Council denies that the applicant should have been heard in person before the contested decision was adopted.

126. In that regard, the Council notes, first, that the case-law on which the applicant relies concerns the right to a hearing in regulated administrative procedures relating to competition and anti-dumping. Referring to paragraphs 326 and 327 of *Yusuf*, the Council adds that it did not have, in this case, 'extensive powers of investigation and inquiry' to determine whether the applicant's funds should be frozen. The Community institutions have neither the powers nor the resources to conduct the kind of investigation and inquiry which would be necessary to establish whether a person such as the applicant is involved in terrorist activities. For those matters they are therefore bound to rely on the assessment made by the national authorities. Consequently, it is also before those national authorities that the rights of defence of those concerned fall to be exercised.

127. Secondly, the Council and the United Kingdom contend that it would not have been possible in any event to provide for a procedure involving the prior consultation of the persons concerned where funds were to be frozen, as that would have rendered the measure wholly ineffective. The United Kingdom adds that there are likely to be compelling reasons of national security for not disclosing the information and evidence upon which a competent authority may take a decision finding that a person is involved in terrorism.

128. Thirdly, the Council submits that, according to the case-law of the Court of First Instance, there is no requirement for a hearing of the parties concerned by the Community institutions when the latter draw up, on the basis of names put forward by the national authorities, a 'blacklist' of persons subject to sanctions, such as the list drawn up under Council Regulation (EC) No 1294/99 of 15 June 1999 concerning a freeze of funds and a ban on investment in relation to the Federal Republic of Yugoslavia (FRY) and repealing Regulations (EC) No 1295/98 and (EC) No 1607/98 (OJ 1999 L 153, p. 63). Such a list is drawn up in a two-stage administrative procedure in which the national authorities play a considerable part and the right of parties concerned to be heard must actually be secured in the first place in their relations with the national administrative authority (order in *Invest Import und Export and Invest Commerce* v *Commission*, cited in paragraph 113

above, paragraph 40; see also *Yusuf*, paragraphs 315 and 316). In this case the applicant would have had ample opportunity to present his point of view before the Raad van State and the Rechtbank.

129. Fourthly, there is nothing in the case-law of the European Court of Human Rights to suggest that the guarantees laid down in Article 6 of the ECHR should have been made applicable to the procedure leading to the adoption of the contested decision. The Council notes, in particular, that the freezing of the applicant's funds is not a criminal conviction for the purposes of that case-law, since there has not been any classification as a criminal offence, since the measure in question concerns only a specific group of persons and since the severity of the measure is not sufficient for such purpose (see *Engel*, cited in paragraph 157 above, *Öztürk*, ECHR judgment of 21 February 1984, Series A no. 73, and *Campbell and Fell*, ECHR judgment of 28 June 1984, Series A no. 80).

130. The *United Kingdom* also denies that Article 6(1) of the European Convention on Human Rights concerns the adoption of legislative measures. It applies only to disputes regarding civil rights and obligations or criminal charges, and the guarantees laid down under it in the former case are applicable only to the extent that there is a dispute requiring a determination. Accordingly, it does not confer on an individual the right to be heard before the adoption of legislation which affects his rights to property. In such a case, an individual is entitled to challenge the lawfulness of that legislation or its application to the circumstances at issue only after the measure has been adopted (see *Lithgow and Others*, ECHR judgment of 8 July 1986, Series A no. 102, § 192, and *James and Others*, ECHR judgment of 21 February 1986, Series A no. 98, § 81. The distinction between administrative and legislative acts for the purposes of the application of the right to be heard was recognised by the Court of First Instance in Case T-521/93 *Atlanta and Others* v *European Community* [1996] ECR II-1707, paragraphs 70 to 74).

131. In the present case, the United Kingdom maintains that neither the inclusion of the applicant in the lists at issue nor, accordingly, the freezing of his assets was covered by Article 6(1) of the ECHR. Those measures did not involve a determination of the applicant's civil rights or a criminal charge against him but the adoption of legislation by the Community institutions. The question of 'rights of the defence' therefore simply does not arise. However, the applicant's rights under Article 6(1) of the ECHR are protected by having access to a court or tribunal which can determine whether the legislation in question has been lawfully enacted and/or whether the applicant properly falls within its scope. Furthermore, the applicant has availed himself of those rights in bringing the present action before the Court of First Instance.

132. In its observations on *Yusuf*, the United Kingdom adds that the issue is whether the applicant's right of access to a court has been infringed by reason of the fact that he cannot challenge, before a court, the merits of the decision to list him. The United Kingdom considers that this does not amount to a violation of the applicant's fundamental rights.

133. First, the applicant is able to challenge the lawfulness of the decisions ordering the freezing of his funds, relying on the grounds set out in the second paragraph of Article 230 EC (see, to that effect, *Kadi*, paragraphs 278 and 279).

134. Secondly, although it is impossible for the applicant to challenge the merits of the policy decision to add his name to the list in question, the United Kingdom argues that, according to the case-law of the European Court of Human Rights, the fundamental right of access to a court or tribunal is an implied right which is subject to inherent limitations (see also, to that effect, *Kadi*, paragraph 287). According to that case-law, the right of access to the courts to contest the merits of a decision or piece of legislation is often restricted, and in those circumstances it is necessary to weigh up the interests of the individual and those of society as a whole in order to evaluate the lawfulness of such restrictions (see *Ashingdane*, ECHR judgment of 28 May 1985, Series A no. 93, and *Alatulkkila and Others* v *Finland*, ECHR judgment of 28 July 2005, no. 33538/96, not published in the Reports of Judgments and Decisions).

135. In the circumstances of this case, the limitation of the applicant's right of access to the courts is justified both by the nature of the decisions that the Council has been required to take in order to give effect to UN Security Council Resolution 1373 (2001) and by the legitimate objective pursued by those measures (see, to this effect, *Kadi*, paragraphs 284 and 289). The applicant's interest in having a court hear his case on its merits is not enough to outweigh the greater interest in the maintenance of international peace and security in the face of a threat identified by the security forces of the Member States. That is a sphere in which policy choices and political judgment clearly obtain and in which the competent authorities must enjoy the broadest discretion.

136. The United Kingdom stresses, however, that in this context the applicant is not deprived of all protection or of all means of redress. First, there are mechanisms to ensure that the list at issue is drawn up on the basis of precise and detailed information or material (see Article 1(4) and (5) of Common Position 2001/931). Secondly, the relevant measures provide for regular review of that list (see Article 1(6) of Common Position 2001/931). On that occasion, the Member States are able to raise the question of continuing to include one or more persons in that list if they believe that there are grounds for considering removal. It is thus open to the applicant to attempt to persuade the competent national authorities to

reverse their decision and, if they refuse to do so, to bring an action for judicial review in accordance with domestic law (see, to that effect, *Kadi*, paragraph 270).

Findings of the Court

137. It is appropriate to begin by examining, together, the pleas alleging infringement of the rights of the defence, infringement of the obligation to state reasons and infringement of the right to effective judicial protection, for they are closely linked. First, the safeguarding of the rights of the defence helps to ensure the proper exercise of the right to effective judicial protection. Second, there is a close link between the right to an effective judicial remedy and the obligation to state reasons. As held in settled case-law, the Community institutions' obligation under Article 253 EC to state the reasons on which a decision is based is intended to enable the Community judicature to exercise its power to review the lawfulness of the decision and the persons concerned to know the reasons for the measure adopted so that they can defend their rights and ascertain whether or not the decision is well founded (Case 24/62 *Germany* v *Commission* [1963] ECR 63, 69; Case C-400/99 *Italy* v *Commission* [2005] ECR I-3657, paragraph 22; Joined Cases T-346/02 and T-347/02 *Cableuropa and Others* v *Commission* [2003] ECR II-4251, paragraph 225). Thus, the parties concerned can make genuine use of their right to a judicial remedy only if they have precise knowledge of the content of and the reasons for the act in question (see, to that effect, Case C-309/95 *Commission* v *Council* [1998] ECR I-655, paragraph 18, and Case T-89/96 *British Steel* v *Commission* [1999] ECR II-2089, paragraph 33).

138. In the light of the principal arguments put forward by the Council and the intervening Governments, the Court will begin by considering whether the rights and safeguards alleged by the applicant to have been infringed may, in principle, apply in the context of the adoption of a decision to freeze funds on the basis of Regulation No 2580/2001. The Court will then determine the purpose of, and identify the restrictions on, those rights and safeguards in such a context. Lastly, the Court will rule on the alleged infringement of the rights and safeguards in question, in the specific circumstances of the present case.

Applicability of the safeguards relating to observance of the rights of the defence, the obligation to state reasons and the right to effective judicial protection in the context of the adoption of a decision to freeze funds on the basis of Regulation No 2580/2001

– Rights of the defence

139. According to settled case-law, observance of the rights of the defence is, in all proceedings initiated against a person which are liable to culminate in

a measure adversely affecting that person, a fundamental principle of Community law which must be guaranteed even in the absence of any rules governing the procedure in question. That principle requires that any person on whom a penalty may be imposed must be placed in a position in which he can effectively make known his view of the evidence adduced against him on which the penalty is based (Case C-135/92 *Fiskano* v *Commission* [1994] ECR I-2885, paragraphs 39 and 40, and the case-law cited).

140. In the present case, the contested decision, by which an individual economic and financial sanction (freezing of funds) has been imposed on the applicant undeniably affects him adversely (see also paragraph 146 below). That case-law is, therefore, relevant to the present case.

141. It follows from that case-law that, subject to exceptions (see paragraph 174 et seq. below), the safeguarding of the rights of the defence comprises, in principle, two main parts. First, the party concerned must be informed of the evidence adduced against it to justify the proposed administrative sanction ('notification of the evidence adduced'). Second, he must be afforded the opportunity effectively to make known his view on that evidence ('hearing').

142. Understood in that way, the safeguarding of the rights of the defence in the context of the administrative procedure itself is to be distinguished from the safeguarding of the right to an effective judicial remedy against the act having adverse effects which may be adopted at the end of that procedure (see, to that effect, Case T-372/00 *Campolargo* v *Commission* [2002] ECR-SC I-A-49 and II-223, paragraph 36). The arguments of the Council and the United Kingdom relating to Article 6 of the ECHR (see paragraphs 77 to 79 above) are thus irrelevant to this head of claim.

143. Moreover, the safeguard relating to observance of the rights of the defence proper, in the context of the adoption of a decision to freeze funds on the basis of Regulation No 2580/2001, cannot be denied to the parties concerned solely on the ground, relied on by the Council and the United Kingdom (see paragraphs 78 and 79 above), that neither the ECHR nor the general principles of Community law confer on individuals any right whatsoever to be heard before the adoption of an act of a legislative nature (see, to that effect and by analogy, *Yusuf*, paragraph 322).

144. It is true that the case-law relating to the right to be heard cannot be extended to the context of a Community legislative process culminating in the enactment of legislation involving a choice of economic policy and applying to the generality of the traders concerned (*Atlanta and Others* v *European Community*, paragraph 130 above, paragraph 70, upheld on appeal in Case C-104/97 P *Atlanta* v *European Community* [1999] ECR I-6983, paragraphs 34 to 38).

145. It is also true that the contested decision, which maintains the applicant in the list at issue, after he had been included by the decision originally challenged, is of the same general application as Regulation No 2580/2001 and, like that regulation, is directly applicable in all Member States. Therefore, despite its title, it shares that act's legislative nature for the purposes of Article 249 EC (see, by analogy, order in Case T-45/02 *DOW AgroSciences* v *Parliament and Council* [2003] ECR II-1973, paragraphs 31 to 33, and case-law cited, and *Yusuf*, paragraphs 184 to 188).

146. However, that decision is not of an exclusively legislative nature. While being of general application, it is of direct and individual concern to the applicant, to whom moreover it refers by name as having to be included in the list of persons, groups and entities whose funds are to be frozen pursuant to Regulation No 2580/2001. Since it is an act which imposes an individual economic and financial sanction (see paragraph 140 above), the case-law cited in paragraph 144 above is therefore irrelevant (see, by analogy, *Yusuf*, paragraph 324).

147. It is, moreover, appropriate to mention the aspects which distinguish the present case from the cases which gave rise to the judgments in *Yusuf* and *Kadi*, in which it was held that the Community institutions were not required to hear the parties concerned in the context of the adoption and implementation of a similar measure freezing the funds of persons and entities linked to Usama bin Laden, Al-Qaeda and the Taliban.

148. That solution was justified in those cases by the fact that the Community institutions had merely transposed into the Community legal order, as they were bound to do, resolutions of the Security Council and decisions of its Sanctions Committee that imposed the freezing of the funds of the parties concerned, designated by name, without in any way authorising those institutions, at the time of actual implementation, to provide for any Community mechanism whatsoever for the examination or re-examination of individual situations. The Court inferred therefrom that the principle of Community law relating to the right to be heard could not apply in such circumstances, where to hear the person concerned could not in any case lead the institutions to review their position (*Yusuf*, paragraph 328, and *Kadi*, paragraph 258).

149. In the present case, by contrast, although Security Council Resolution 1373 (2001) provides inter alia in Paragraph 1(c) that all States must freeze without delay funds and other financial assets or economic resources of persons who commit, or attempt to commit, terrorist acts or participate in or facilitate the commission of terrorist acts, of entities owned or controlled directly or indirectly by such persons, and of persons and entities acting on behalf of, or at the direction of, such persons and entities, it does not specify individually the persons, groups and entities who or which are to be

subject to those measures. Nor did the Security Council establish specific legal rules concerning the procedure for freezing funds, or the safeguards or judicial remedies ensuring that the persons or entities affected by such a procedure would have a genuine opportunity to challenge the measures adopted by the States in respect of them.

150. Thus, in the context of Resolution 1373 (2001), it is for the Member States of the United Nations (UN)—and, in this case, the Community, through which its Member States have decided to act—to identify specifically the persons, groups and entities whose funds are to be frozen pursuant to that resolution, in accordance with the rules in their own legal order.

151. In that connection, the Council and the United Kingdom have acknowledged, in substance, in their written observations on *Yusuf*, that, in the implementation of Security Council Resolution 1373 (2001), the measures adopted by the Council under circumscribed powers and thereby benefiting from the principle of primacy arising under Articles 25 and 103 of the Charter of the United Nations are essentially those provided for by the relevant provisions of Regulation No 2580/2001, which determine the content of the restrictive measures to be adopted in relation to the persons referred to in Paragraph 1(c) of that resolution. However, unlike the acts at issue in the case which gave rise to the judgment in *Yusuf*, the acts which specifically apply those restrictive measures to a given person or entity, such as the contested decision, do not fall within the exercise of circumscribed powers and accordingly do not benefit from the 'primacy' effect in question (see also paragraph 110 above). The Council submits that the adoption of those acts falls instead within the ambit of the exercise of the broad discretion it enjoys in the area of the CFSP.

152. Those considerations may, in substance, be approved by the Court, subject to the possible difficulties in applying Paragraph 1(c) of Resolution 1373 (2001) which may be caused by the absence, to date, of a universally accepted definition of the concepts of 'terrorism' and 'terrorist act' in international law (see, on this point, Final Document (A/60/L1) adopted by the UN General Assembly on 15 September 2005, on the occasion of the world summit celebrating the 60th anniversary of the UN).

153. Last, it is to be noted that the Community does not act under powers circumscribed by the will of the Union or by that of its Member States as it may be expressed in a common position adopted in the sphere of the CFSP when, as in the present case, the Council adopts economic sanctions measures on the basis of Articles 60 EC, 301 EC and 308 EC. That point of view is, moreover, the only one compatible with the actual wording of Article 301 EC, according to which the Council is to decide on the matter 'by a qualified majority on a proposal from the Commission', and that of Article 60(1)

EC, according to which the Council 'may take', following the same procedure, the urgent measures necessary for an act under the CFSP.

154. Since the identification of the persons, groups and entities contemplated in Security Council Resolution 1373 (2001), and the adoption of the ensuing measure to freeze funds, involve the exercise of the Community's own powers, entailing a discretionary assessment by the Community, the Community institutions concerned, in this case the Council, are as a rule bound to observe the rights of the defence of the parties concerned when they act with a view to giving effect to that resolution.

155. It follows that the safeguarding of the rights of the defence is, in principle, fully applicable in the context of the adoption of a decision to freeze funds under Regulation No 2580/2001.

– Obligation to state reasons

156. As a rule, the safeguard relating to the obligation to state reasons provided for by Article 253 EC is also fully applicable in the context of the adoption of a decision to freeze funds under Regulation No 2580/2001, which has not, moreover, been questioned by any of the parties.

– The right to effective judicial protection

157. As to the safeguard relating to the right to effective judicial protection, it should be borne in mind that, according to settled case-law, individuals must be able to avail themselves of effective judicial protection of the rights they have under the Community legal order, the right to such protection forming part of the general legal principles deriving from the constitutional traditions common to the Member States and being enshrined in Articles 6 and 13 of the ECHR (see Case T-279/02 *Degussa* v *Commission* [2006] ECR II-897, paragraph 421, and case-law cited).

158. That applies in particular to measures to freeze the funds of persons or organisations suspected of terrorist activities (see, to that effect, Article XIV of the Guidelines on Human Rights and the Fight against Terrorism, adopted by the Committee of Ministers of the Council of Europe on 11 July 2002).

159. In the present case, the only reservation expressed by the Council, in relation to the applicability of the principle of that safeguard, is that in its view the Court has no jurisdiction to review the internal lawfulness of the substantive provisions of Regulation No 2580/2001, because they were adopted by virtue of powers circumscribed by Security Council Resolution 1373 (2001) and therefore benefit from the principle of primacy referred to in paragraph 151 above.

160. It is not, however, necessary for the Court to rule on the merits of that reservation because the present dispute can be resolved, as will be explained below, solely on the basis of judicial review of the lawfulness of the con-

tested decision, and none of the parties denies that that indeed comes within the Court's jurisdiction.

Purpose and limitations of the safeguards relating to observance of the rights of the defence, the obligation to state reasons and the right to effective judicial protection in relation to the adoption of a decision to freeze funds pursuant to Regulation No 2580/2001

– Rights of the defence

161. It is appropriate first, to define the purpose of the safeguarding of the rights of the defence in relation to the adoption of a decision to freeze funds under Article 2(3) of Regulation No 2580/2001, distinguishing between an initial decision to freeze funds referred to in Article 1(4) of Common Position 2001/931 ('the initial decision to freeze funds') and any one of the subsequent decisions to maintain a freeze of funds, following a periodic review, as referred to in Article 1(6) of that common position ('subsequent decisions to freeze funds').

162. In this context, it is first of all to be stressed that the rights of the defence fall to be exercised with regard only to the elements of fact and law which are capable of determining the application of the measure in question to the person concerned, in accordance with the relevant legislation.

163. In the instant case, the relevant rules are laid down in Article 2(3) of Regulation No 2580/2001, under which the Council, acting unanimously, is to establish, review and amend the list of persons, groups and entities to which that regulation applies, in accordance with the provisions laid down in Article 1(4) to (6) of Common Position 2001/931. The list in question must therefore be drawn up, in accordance with Article 1(4) of Common Position 2001/931, on the basis of precise information or material in the relevant file which indicates that a decision has been taken by a competent authority in respect of the persons, groups or entities concerned, irrespective of whether it concerns the instigation of investigations or prosecution for a terrorist act, an attempt to perpetrate, participate in or facilitate such an act based on serious and credible evidence or clues, or conviction for such actions. 'Competent authority' means a judicial authority or, where judicial authorities have no jurisdiction in the relevant area, an equivalent competent authority in that area. Moreover, the names of persons and entities in the list are to be reviewed at regular intervals and at least once every six months to ensure that there are still grounds for continuing to include them in the list, in accordance with Article 1(6) of Common Position 2001/931.

164. As rightly pointed out by the Council and the Member States which have intervened, the procedure which may culminate in a measure to freeze funds under the relevant rules takes place therefore at two levels,

one national, the other Community. Initially, a competent national authority, generally judicial, must take in respect of the party concerned a decision complying with the definition in Article 1(4) of Common Position 2001/931. If that is a decision to instigate investigations or prosecution, it must be based on serious and credible evidence or clues. Secondly, the Council, acting unanimously, must decide whether to include the person concerned in the list at issue, on the basis of precise information or material in the relevant file which indicates that such a decision has been taken. Subsequently, the Council must, at regular intervals, and at least once every six months, ensure that there are still grounds for continuing to include the person concerned in the list. Verification that there exists a decision of a national authority meeting that definition appears to be an essential precondition for the adoption, by the Council, of an initial decision to freeze funds, whereas verification of the consequences of that decision at national level appears necessary in relation to the adoption of a subsequent decision to freeze funds.

165. Accordingly, the issue of observance of the rights of the defence in relation to the adoption of a decision to freeze funds may also arise at those two levels (see, to that effect and by analogy, *'Invest' Import und Export and Invest Commerce* v *Commission*, paragraph 113 above, paragraph 40).

166. The rights of the defence of the party concerned must first of all be effectively safeguarded in the national procedure which led to the adoption, by the competent national authority, of the decision referred to in Article 1(4) of Common Position 2001/931. It is essentially in that national context that the person concerned must be placed in a position in which he can effectively make known his view of the matters on which the decision is based, subject to possible restrictions on the rights of the defence which are legally justified in national law, particularly on grounds of public policy, public security or the maintenance of international relations (see, to that effect, ECHR judgment of 10 July 1998, *Tinnelly & Sons and Others and McElduff and Others* v *United Kingdom, Reports of Judgments and Decisions,* 1998-IV, §78.

167. Next, the rights of the defence of the person concerned must be effectively safeguarded in the Community procedure culminating in the adoption, by the Council, of the decision to include or maintain him in the disputed list, in accordance with Article 2(3) of Regulation No 2580/2001. As a rule, in that area, the party concerned need be afforded only the opportunity effectively to make known his views on the legal conditions of application of the Community measure in question, namely, where it is an initial decision to freeze funds, whether there exists specific information or material in the file which shows that a decision meeting the definition laid down in Article 1(4) of Common Position 2001/931 was taken in respect of him by a competent national authority or, where it is a subsequent decision to

freeze funds, whether there are reasons for continuing to include him in the list at issue.

168. However, in so far as the decision in question was adopted by a competent authority of a Member State, observance of the rights of the defence at Community level does not usually at that stage require the party concerned again to be afforded the opportunity to express his views on the appropriateness and validity of that decision, for those questions may not be raised except at national level, before the authority in question or, where the party concerned brings an action, before the competent national court. Likewise, as a rule, it is not for the Council to decide whether the proceedings instigated against the party concerned and resulting in that decision, as provided for by the national law of the relevant Member State, were correctly conducted, or whether the fundamental rights of the party concerned were respected by the national authorities. That power belongs exclusively to the competent national courts or, as the case may be, to the European Court of Human Rights (see, by analogy, Case T-353/00 *Le Pen* v *Parliament* [2003] ECR II-1729, paragraph 91, upheld on appeal in Case C-208/03 P *Le Pen* v *Parliament* [2005] ECR I-6051).

169. Nor, if the Community measure to freeze funds is adopted on the basis of a decision by a national authority of a Member State concerning investigations or prosecutions (rather than on the basis of conviction and sentence), does the observance of the rights of the defence require, as a rule, that the person concerned should be afforded the opportunity effectively to make known his views on whether that decision is 'based on serious and credible evidence or clues', as required by Article 1(4) of Common Position 2001/931. Although that factor is one of the legal conditions of application of the measure in question, the Court finds that it would be inappropriate, having regard to the duty to cooperate in good faith referred to in Article 10 EC, to make it subject to the exercise of the rights of the defence at Community level.

170. The Court notes that, under Article 10 EC, relations between the Member States and the Community institutions are governed by reciprocal duties to cooperate in good faith (see Case C-339/00 *Ireland* v *Commission* [2003] ECR I-11757, paragraphs 71 and 72, and case-law cited). That principle is of general application and is especially binding in the area of police and judicial cooperation in criminal matters (commonly known as 'Justice and Home Affairs') (JHA) governed by Title VI of the EU Treaty, which is moreover entirely based on cooperation between the Member States and the institutions (Case C-105/03 *Pupino* [2005] ECR I-5285, paragraph 42).

171. In a case of application of Article 1(4) of Common Position 2001/931 and Article 2(3) of Regulation No 2580/2001, provisions which introduce a specific form of cooperation between the Council and the Member States in

the context of combating terrorism, the Court finds that that principle entails, for the Council, the obligation to defer as far as possible to the assessment conducted by the competent national authority, at least where it is a judicial authority, both in respect of the issue of whether there are 'serious and credible evidence or clues' on which its decision is based and also in respect of recognition of potential restrictions on access to that evidence or those clues, legally justified under national law for overriding reasons of public policy, public security or the maintenance of international relations (see, by analogy, Case T-353/94 *Postbank* v *Commission* [1996] ECR II-921, paragraph 69, and case-law cited).

172. It must, however, be added that these considerations are valid only in so far as the evidence or clues in question have in fact been assessed by the competent national authority referred to in the preceding paragraph. If, on the other hand, in the course of the procedure before it, the Council bases its initial decision or a subsequent decision to freeze funds on information or evidence communicated to it by representatives of the Member States without having been assessed by the competent national authority, that information must be considered to be fresh incriminating evidence which must, as a rule, be the subject of notification and of a hearing at Community level, by reason of its not having already been so at national level.

173. It follows from the foregoing that, in the context of relations between the Community and its Member States, observance of the rights of the defence has a relatively limited purpose at the level of the Community procedure for freezing funds. In the case of an initial decision to freeze funds, it requires as a rule, first, that the party concerned should be informed by the Council of the specific information or material in the file which indicates that a decision meeting the definition given in Article 1(4) of Common Position 2001/931 has been taken in respect of it by a competent authority of a Member State, and also, where applicable, any new material as referred to in paragraph 172 above and, second, that that party should be placed in a position in which it can effectively make known its view on the information or material in the file. In the case of a subsequent decision to freeze funds, observance of the rights of the defence similarly requires, first, that the party concerned should be informed of the information or material in the file which, in the view of the Council, justifies continuing to include it in the lists at issue and also, where applicable, of any new material as referred to in paragraph 172 above and, second, that it should be afforded the opportunity effectively to make known its view on the matter.

174. At the same time, certain restrictions on the rights of the defence, so defined in terms of their purpose, may nevertheless legitimately be envisaged and imposed on the parties concerned, in circumstances such as those of the present case, where specific restrictive measures are at issue that

consist of a freeze of the funds and financial assets of the persons, groups and entities identified by the Council as being involved in terrorist acts.

175. Thus the Court finds, as was held in *Yusuf* and as submitted in the present case by the Council and the United Kingdom, that notification of the evidence adduced and a hearing of the parties concerned, before the initial decision to freeze funds was adopted, would be liable to jeopardise the effectiveness of the sanctions and would thus be incompatible with the public-interest objective pursued by the Community in accordance with Security Council Resolution 1373 (2001). An initial measure freezing funds must, by its very nature, be able to benefit from a surprise effect and to be applied with immediate effect. Such a measure cannot, therefore, be the subject-matter of a prior notification before it is implemented (*Yusuf*, paragraph 308; see also, to that effect and by analogy, the Opinion of Advocate General Warner in Case 136/79 *National Panasonic* v *Commission* [1980] ECR 2033, 2061, 2068, 2069).

176. However, if the parties concerned are to be able to defend their rights effectively, particularly in legal proceedings which might be brought before the Court of First Instance, it is also necessary that they should be notified of the evidence adduced against them, in so far as reasonably possible, either concomitantly with or as soon as possible after the adoption of the initial decision to freeze funds (see also paragraph 186 below).

177. In that context, the parties concerned must also have the opportunity to request an immediate re-examination of the initial measure freezing their funds (see, to that effect, in the case-law of the Community civil service, Case T-211/98 *F* v *Commission* [2000] ECR-SC I-A-107 and II-471, paragraph 34; Case T-333/99 *X* v *ECB* [2001] ECR-SC II-3021, paragraph 183, and *Campolargo* v *Commission*, paragraph 142 above, paragraph 32). The Court recognises, however, that such a hearing after the event is not automatically required in the context of an initial decision to freeze funds, in the light of the possibility that the parties concerned also have immediately to bring an action before the Court of First Instance, which ensures that a balance is also struck between observance of the fundamental rights of the persons included in the list at issue and the need to take preventive measures to combat international terrorism (see, to that effect and by analogy, the Opinion of Advocate General Warner in *National Panasonic* v *Commission*, paragraph 175 above, [1980] ECR 2069).

178. It must be emphasised, however, that the considerations just mentioned are not relevant to subsequent decisions to freeze funds adopted by the Council in connection with the re-examination, at regular intervals, at least every six months, of the justification for continuing to include the parties concerned in the list at issue, provided for by Article 1(6) of Common Position 2001/931. At that stage, the funds are already frozen and it is

accordingly no longer necessary to ensure a surprise effect in order to guarantee the effectiveness of the sanctions. Any subsequent decision to freeze funds must accordingly be preceded by the possibility of a further hearing and, where appropriate, notification of any new incriminating evidence.

179. The Court cannot accept the argument that the Council need not hear the parties concerned, in the context of the adoption of a subsequent decision to freeze funds, unless they have previously made an express request to that effect. Under Article 1(6) of Common Position 2001/931, the Council may adopt such a decision only after ascertaining that continuing to include the parties concerned in the list at issue remains justified, which implies that it must first give them the opportunity effectively to make known their views on the matter.

180. Next, the Court recognises that, in circumstances such as those of this case, where what is at issue is a protective measure restricting the availability of the property of certain persons, groups and entities in connection with combating terrorism, overriding considerations concerning the security of the Community and its Member States, or the conduct of their international relations, may preclude the communication to the parties concerned of certain evidence adduced against them and, in consequence, the hearing of those parties with regard to such evidence, during the administrative procedure (see, by analogy, *Yusuf*, paragraph 320).

181. Such restrictions are consistent with the constitutional traditions common to the Member States. Thus, exceptions to the general right to be heard in the course of an administrative procedure are permitted in many Member States on grounds of public interest, public policy or the maintenance of international relations, or when the purpose of the decision to be taken would or could be jeopardised if that right were observed.

182. They are, moreover, consistent with the case-law of the European Court of Human Rights which, even in the more stringent context of adversarial criminal proceedings subject to the requirements of Article 6 of the ECHR, acknowledges that, in cases concerning national security and, more specifically, terrorism, certain restrictions on the right to a fair hearing may be envisaged, especially concerning disclosure of evidence adduced or terms of access to the file (see, for example, *Chahal* v *United Kingdom*, judgment of 15 November 1996, Report 1996-V, § 131, and *Jasper* v *United Kingdom*, judgment of 16 February 2000, No 27052/95, not published in Reports of Judgments and Decisions, §§ 51 to 53, and case-law cited; see also Article IX.3 of the Guidelines adopted by the Committee of Ministers of the Council of Europe, referred to in paragraph 158 above).

183. In the circumstances of this case, those considerations apply above all to the 'serious and credible evidence or clues' on which the national decision to instigate an investigation or prosecution is based, in so far as

they may have been brought to the attention of the Council, but it is also conceivable that restrictions on access may concern the specific content of or the particular reasoning of that decision, or even the identity of the authority that took it. It is even possible that, in certain, very specific circumstances, the identification of the Member State or third country in which a competent authority has taken a decision in respect of a person may be liable to jeopardise public security, by providing the party concerned with sensitive information which it could misuse.

184. It follows from all of the foregoing that the general principle of observance of the rights of the defence requires, unless this is precluded by overriding considerations concerning the security of the Community or its Member States, or the conduct of their international relations, that the evidence adduced against the party concerned, as identified in paragraph 173 above, should be notified to it, in so far as possible, either concomitantly with or as soon as possible after the adoption of an initial decision to freeze funds. Subject to the same reservations, any subsequent decision to freeze funds must, as a rule, be preceded by notification of any new incriminating evidence and a hearing. However, observance of the rights of the defence does not require either that the evidence adduced against the party concerned should be notified to it prior to the adoption of an initial measure to freeze funds, or that that party should automatically be heard after the event in such a context.

– Obligation to state reasons

185. According to settled case-law, the purpose of the obligation to state the reasons for an act adversely affecting a person is, first, to provide the person concerned with sufficient information to make it possible for him to determine whether the act is well founded or whether it is vitiated by an error which may permit its validity to be contested before the Community judicature and, second, to enable the latter to review the lawfulness of that act (Case C-199/99 P *Corus UK* v *Commission* [2003] ECR I-11177, paragraph 145, and Joined Cases C-189/02 P, C-202/02 P, C-205/02 P to C-208/02 P and C-213/02 P *Dansk Rørindustri and Others* v *Commission* [2005] ECR I-5425, paragraph 462). The obligation to state reasons thus set down constitutes an essential principle of Community law from which derogation is possible only on compelling grounds (see Case T-218/02 *Napoli Buzzanca* v *Commission* [2005] ECR-SC I-A-267 and II-1221, paragraph 57, and case-law cited).

186. The statement of reasons must therefore as a rule be notified to the person concerned at the same time as the act adversely affecting him. Failure to state reasons cannot be remedied by the fact that the person concerned learns the reasons for the act during the proceedings before the Community judicature (Case 195/80 *Michel* v *Parliament* [1981] ECR 2861,

paragraph 22, and *Dansk Rørindustri and Others* v *Commission*, paragraph 185 above, paragraph 463). In fact, the possibility of remedying the total absence of a statement of reasons after an action has been brought would prejudice the rights of the defence because the applicant would have only the reply in which to set out his pleas contesting the reasons which he would not know until after he had lodged his application. The principle of equality of the parties before the Community judicature would accordingly be adversely affected (Case T-132/03 *Casini* v *Commission* [2005] ECR-SC I-A-253 and II-1169, paragraph 33, and *Napoli Buzzanca* v *Commission*, paragraph 185 above, paragraph 62).

187. If the party concerned is not afforded the opportunity to be heard before the adoption of an initial decision to freeze funds, compliance with the obligation to state reasons is all the more important because it constitutes the sole safeguard enabling the party concerned, at least once that decision has been adopted, to make effective use of the legal remedies available to it to challenge the lawfulness of that decision (Case T-237/00 *Reynolds* v *Parliament* [2005] ECR SC I-A-385 and II-1731, paragraph 95; see also, to that effect, Joined Cases T-371/94 and T-394/04 *British Airways and British Midland Airways* v *Commission* [1998] ECR II-2405, paragraph 64).

188. The Court has consistently held that the statement of reasons required by Article 253 EC must be appropriate to the measure at issue and to the context in which it was adopted. It must disclose in a clear and unequivocal fashion the reasoning followed by the institution which adopted the measure in question in such a way as to enable the persons concerned to ascertain the reasons for the measure and to enable the competent court to exercise its power of review of the lawfulness thereof. The requirements to be satisfied by the statement of reasons depend on the circumstances of each case, in particular the content of the measure in question, the nature of the reasons given and the interest which the addressees of the measure, or other parties to whom it is of direct and individual concern, may have in obtaining explanations. It is not necessary for the statement of reasons to specify all the relevant matters of fact and law, since the question whether the statement of reasons meets the requirements of Article 253 EC must be assessed with regard not only to its wording but also to its context and to all the legal rules governing the matter in question. In particular, the reasons given for an act adversely affecting a party are sufficient if it was adopted in circumstances known to the party concerned which enable him to understand the scope of the measure concerning him (Case 125/80 *Arning* v *Commission* [1981] ECR 2539, paragraph 13; Case C-367/95 P *Commission* v *Sytraval and Brink's France* [1998] ECR I-1719, paragraph 63; Case C-301/96 *Germany* v *Commission* [2003] ECR I-9919, paragraph 87; Case C-42/01 *Portugal* v *Commission* [2004] ECR I-6079, paragraph 66; and Joined Cases T-228/99 and T-233/99 *Westdeutsche Landesbank*

Girozentrale and Land Nordrhein-Westfalen v *Commission* [2003] ECR II-435, paragraphs 278 to 280). Moreover, the degree of precision of the statement of the reasons for a decision must be weighed against practical realities and the time and technical facilities available for making the decision (see *Delacre and Others* v *Commission*, paragraph 104 above, paragraph 16, and case-law cited).

189. In the context of the adoption of a decision to freeze funds under Regulation No 2580/2001, the grounds for that decision must be assessed primarily in the light of the legal conditions of application of that regulation to particular circumstances, as set out in Article 2(3) thereof and, by reference, in Article 1(4) or Article 1(6) of Common Position 2001/931, depending on whether it is an initial decision or a subsequent decision to freeze funds.

190. The Court cannot accept that, as the Council and the Netherlands maintain, the statement of reasons may consist of no more than general and formulaic wording, modelled on the drafting of Article 2(3) of Regulation No 2580/2001 and Article 1(4) or (6) of Common Position 2001/931. In accordance with the principles referred to above, the Council is bound to state the matters of fact and law on which the legal reasoning of its decision depends and the considerations which led it to adopt that decision. The grounds for such a measure must therefore indicate the actual and specific reasons why the Council considers that the relevant rules are applicable to the party concerned (see, to that effect, Case T-117/01 *Roman Parra* v *Commission* [2002] ECR-SC I-A-27 and II-121, paragraph 31, and *Napoli Buzzanca* v *Commission*, paragraph 185 above, paragraph 74).

191. That means, as a rule, that the statement of reasons for an initial decision to freeze funds must at least refer to each of the aspects referred to in paragraph 163 above and also, where applicable, the aspects referred to in paragraphs 172 and 173 above, whereas the statement of reasons for a subsequent decision to freeze funds must indicate the actual and specific reasons why the Council considers, following re-examination, that there are still grounds for the freezing of the funds of the party concerned.

192. Moreover, when unanimously adopting a measure to freeze funds under Regulation No 2580/2001, the Council does not act under circumscribed powers. Article 2(3) of Regulation No 2580/2001, read together with Article 1(4) of Common Position 2001/931, is not to be construed as meaning that the Council is obliged to include in the list at issue any person in respect of whom a decision has been taken by a competent authority within the meaning of those provisions. This interpretation is confirmed by Article 1(6) of Common Position 2001/931, to which Article 2(3) of Regulation No 2580/2001 also refers, and according to which the Council is to conduct a 'review' at regular intervals, at least once every

six months, to ensure that 'there are grounds' for keeping the parties concerned in the disputed list.

193. It follows that, as a rule, the statement of reasons for a measure to freeze funds under Regulation No 2580/2001 must refer not only to the legal conditions of application of that regulation, but also to the reasons why the Council considers, in the exercise of its discretion, that such a measure must be adopted in respect of the party concerned.

194. The considerations set out in paragraphs 190 to 193 above must nevertheless take account of the fact that a decision to freeze funds under Regulation No 2580/2001, whilst imposing an individual economic and financial sanction, is, like that act, also legislative in nature, as explained in paragraphs 145 and 146 above. Moreover, a detailed publication of the charges levelled at the parties concerned might not only conflict with the overriding considerations of public interest which will be discussed in paragraph 195 below, but also jeopardise the legitimate interests of the persons and entities in question, in that it would be capable of causing serious damage to their reputations. Accordingly, the Court finds, exceptionally, that only the operative part of the decision and a general statement of reasons, of the type referred to in paragraph 190 above, need appear in the version of the decision to freeze funds published in the Official Journal, it being understood that the actual, specific statements of reasons for that decision must be formalised and brought to the knowledge of the parties concerned by any other appropriate means.

195. Moreover, in circumstances such as those of this case, it must be recognised that the overriding considerations concerning the security of the Community and its Member States, or the conduct of their international relations, may preclude disclosure to the parties concerned of the specific and complete reasons for the initial or subsequent decision to freeze their funds, just as they may preclude the evidence adduced against those parties from being communicated to them during the administrative procedure. In that connection the Court refers to the considerations set out above, in particular in paragraphs 180 to 184 above, regarding the restrictions on the general principle of observance of the rights of the defence which may be permitted in such a context. Those considerations are valid, mutatis mutandis, in respect of the restrictions which may be imposed on the obligation to state reasons.

196. Although it is not applicable to the circumstances of the present case, the Court also considers that inspiration may be drawn from the provisions of Directive 2004/38/EC of the European Parliament and of the Council of 29 April 2004 on the right of citizens of the Union and their family members to move and reside freely within the territory of the Member States amending Regulation (EEC) No 1612/68 and repealing Directives 64/221/EEC, 68/360/EEC, 72/194/EEC, 73/148/EEC, 75/34/EEC,

75/35/EEC, 90/364/EEC, 90/365/EEC and 93/96/EEC (OJ 2004 L 158, p. 77, corrigendum OJ 2004 L 229, p. 35, corrigendum to the corrigendum OJ 2005 L 197, p. 34). Article 30(2) of that directive provides that 'the persons concerned shall be informed, precisely and in full, of the public policy, public security or public health grounds on which the decision [restricting the freedom of movement and residence of a citizen of the Union or a member of his family] taken in their case is based, unless this is contrary to the interests of State security'.

197. In accordance with the case-law of the Court of Justice (Case 36/75 *Rutili* [1975] ECR 1219, and Case 131/79 *Santillo* [1980] ECR 1585) concerning Council Directive 64/221/EEC of 25 February 1964 on the coordination of special measures concerning the movement and residence of foreign nationals which are justified on grounds of public policy, public security or public health (OJ, English Special Edition 1963-1964, p. 117), repealed by Directive 2004/38, Article 6 of which was essentially identical to Article 30(2) of the latter, any person enjoying the protection of the provisions cited must be entitled to a twofold safeguard, consisting of notification to him of the grounds on which any restrictive measure has been adopted in his case, unless grounds related to the security of the State militate against it, and the availability of a right of appeal. Subject to the same reservation, this requirement means in particular that the State concerned must, when notifying an individual of a restrictive measure adopted in his case, give him a precise and comprehensive statement of the grounds for the decision, to enable him to take effective steps to prepare his defence.

198. It follows from all of the foregoing that, unless overriding considerations concerning the security of the Community and its Member States, or the conduct of their international relations, militate against it, and subject also to what has been set out in paragraph 194 above, the statement of reasons for an initial decision to freeze funds must at least make actual and specific reference to each of the aspects referred to in paragraph 163 above and also, where applicable, to the aspects referred to in paragraphs 172 and 173 above, and state the reasons why the Council considers, in the exercise of its discretion, that such a measure must be taken in respect of the party concerned. Moreover, the statement of reasons for a subsequent decision to freeze funds must, subject to the same reservations, state the actual and specific reasons why the Council considers, following re-examination, that the freezing of the funds of the party concerned remains justified.

– Right to effective judicial protection

199. Last, with respect to the safeguard relating to the right to effective judicial protection, this is effectively ensured by the right the parties concerned have to bring an action before the Court of First Instance against a decision to freeze their funds, pursuant to the fourth paragraph of Article 230 EC

(see, to that effect, European Court of Human Rights, *Bosphorus* v *Ireland*, judgment of 30 June 2005, No 45036/98, not yet published in the Reports of Judgments and Decisions, § 165, and the decision in *Segi and Others and Gestoras pro Amnistía* v *The 15 Member States of the European Union*, paragraph 124 above.

200. In that context, the judicial review of the lawfulness of a decision to freeze funds taken pursuant to Article 2(3) of Regulation No 2580/2001 is that provided for in the second paragraph of Article 230 EC, under which the Community judicature has jurisdiction in actions brought on grounds of lack of competence, infringement of an essential procedural requirement, infringement of the EC Treaty or of any rule of law relating to its application, or misuse of powers.

201. As part of that review, and having regard to the grounds for annulment put forward by the party concerned or raised by the court of its own motion, it is for the Court to ensure, inter alia, that the legal conditions for applying Regulation No 2580/2001 to particular circumstances, as laid down in Article 2(3) of that regulation and, by reference, in either Article 1(4) or Article 1(6) of Common Position 2001/931, depending on whether it is an initial decision or a subsequent decision to freeze funds, have been fulfilled. That implies that judicial review of the lawfulness of the decision in question extends to the assessment of the facts and circumstances relied on as justifying that decision, and to the evidence and information on which that assessment is based, as the Council expressly recognised in its written pleadings in the case giving rise to the judgment in *Yusuf*, (paragraph 225). The Court must also be satisfied that the rights of the defence have been observed and that the requirement of a statement of reasons has been complied with and also, where applicable, that the overriding considerations relied on exceptionally by the Council, in order to escape those obligations, are justified.

202. In the present case, that review is all the more imperative because it constitutes the only procedural safeguard capable of ensuring that a fair balance is struck between the need to combat international terrorism and the protection of fundamental rights. Since the restrictions imposed by the Council on the rights of the defence of the parties concerned must be offset by a strict judicial review which is independent and impartial (see, to that effect, Case C-341/04 *Eurofood* [2006] ECR I-3813, paragraph 66), the Community judicature must be able to review the lawfulness and merits of the measures to freeze funds without its being possible to raise objections that the evidence and information used by the Council is secret or confidential.

203. It must be emphasised that, although the European Court of Human Rights recognises that the use of confidential information may be necessary

when national security is at stake, that does not mean, in its view, that national authorities are free from any review by the national courts simply because they state that the case concerns national security and terrorism (see Eur. Court H.R., *Chahal* v *United Kingdom*, paragraph 182 above, § 131, and case-law cited, and *Öcalan* v *Turkey*, judgment of 12 March 2003, No 46221/99, not published in the Reports of Judgments and Decisions, § 106, and case-law cited).

204. The Court finds that, here also, inspiration may be drawn from the provisions of Directive 2004/38. In accordance with the case-law referred to in paragraph 197 above, Article 31(1) of that directive provides that the persons concerned are to have access to judicial and, where appropriate, administrative means of redress in the host Member State to appeal against or seek review of any decision taken against them on the grounds of public policy, public security or public health. Moreover, Article 31(3) of that directive provides that the means of redress are to allow for an examination of the lawfulness of the decision, as well as of the facts and circumstances on which the proposed measure is based.

205. The question whether the applicant and/or his lawyers may be provided with the evidence and information alleged to be confidential, or whether they may be provided only to the Court, in accordance with a specific procedure which remains to be defined so as to safeguard the public interest at issue whilst affording the party concerned a sufficient degree of judicial protection, is a separate issue on which it is not necessary for the Court to rule in the present action (see nevertheless Eur. Court H.R., *Chahal* v *United Kingdom*, paragraph 182 above, §§ 131 and 144; *Tinnelly & Sons and Others and McElduff and Others* v *United Kingdom*, paragraph 166 above, §§ 49, 51, 52 and 78; *Jasper* v *United Kingdom*, paragraph 182 above, §§ 51 to 53; and *Al-Nashif* v *Bulgaria*, judgment of 20 June 2002, No 50963/99, not published in the Reports of Judgments and Decisions, §§ 95 to 97, and also Article IX.4 of the Guidelines adopted by the Committee of Ministers of the Council of Europe, cited in paragraph 158 above).

206. Lastly, it is to be recognised that the Council enjoys broad discretion in its assessment of the matters to be taken into consideration for the purpose of adopting economic and financial sanctions on the basis of Articles 60 EC, 301 EC and 308 EC, consistent with a common position adopted on the basis of the CFSP. Because the Community judicature may not, in particular, substitute its assessment of the evidence, facts and circumstances justifying the adoption of such measures for that of the Council, the review carried out by the Court of First Instance of the lawfulness of decisions to freeze funds must be restricted to checking that the rules governing procedure and the statement of reasons have been complied with, that the facts are materially accurate, and that there has been no manifest error of assessment of the facts or misuse of power. That limited review applies,

especially, to the assessment of the considerations of appropriateness on which such decisions are based (see paragraph 193 above and, to that effect, Eur. Court H.R., *Leander* v *Sweden*, judgment of 26 March 1987, Series A No 116, § 59, and *Al-Nashif* v *Bulgaria*, paragraph 205 above, §§ 123 and 124).

Application to the Circumstances of the Case

207. The Court notes, first, that the relevant legislation, namely Regulation No 2580/2001 and Common Position 2001/931 to which it refers, does not explicitly provide for any procedure for notification of the evidence adduced or for a hearing of the parties concerned, either before or concomitantly with the adoption of an initial decision to freeze their funds or, in the context of the adoption of subsequent decisions, with a view to having them removed from the list at issue. At the very most, Article 1(6) of Common Position 2001/931 states that '[t]he names of persons and entities in the list in the Annex shall be reviewed at regular intervals and at least once every six months to ensure that there are grounds for keeping them on the list', and Article 2(3) of Regulation No 2580/2001 provides that 'the Council . . . shall . . . review and amend the list . . ., in accordance with the provisions laid down in Article 1 . . . (6) of Common Position 2001/931'.

208. Next, the Court finds that at no time before this action was brought was the evidence adduced against the applicant notified to him. The applicant rightly points out that neither the initial decision to freeze his funds nor the subsequent decisions, up to and including the contested decision, even mention the 'specific information' or 'material in the file' showing that a decision justifying his inclusion in the disputed list was taken in respect of him by a competent national authority.

209. Both before this action was introduced and again later, during the proceedings, the applicant has attempted in vain to remedy that situation by making various requests to the Council under Regulation No 1049/2001 for access to the documents on the basis of which the Council adopted the decisions concerning him. The Council has consistently refused to allow his requests for access to those documents, including the decision of the national authority referred to in Article 1(4) of Common Position 2001/931, on the ground that they are classified 'CONFIDENTIAL EU' and that to disclose them would prejudice the protection of the public interest with regard to security and international relations. The Council has even gone so far as to refuse to inform the applicant of the identity of the Member State which was the author of that decision, on the ground that that State opposed such disclosure (see, on those matters, Joined Cases T-110/03, T-150/03 and T-405/03 *Sison* v *Council* [2005] ECR II-1429).

210. While the Court in that judgment did dismiss the actions for annulment brought by the applicant against the refusals in question, that was only under the provisions of Regulation No 1049/2001 governing the

public's general right of access to documents held by the institutions, and not without ruling in paragraph 55 of that judgment that the issue whether the documents requested were necessary to the defence of the applicant's position in that case was a separate matter falling within the scope of the examination of that question.

211. As a result of that examination, which it is now appropriate to undertake, the Court of First Instance finds that, according to explanations offered by the Council and the Netherlands in their written pleadings, both the decision originally challenged and the contested decision are based first and foremost on the decision of the Rechtbank of 1997 and, indirectly, on the judgments of the Raad van State of 1992 and 1995, and also on the BVD's confidential file which was produced—but not communicated to the applicant—in the course of the proceedings before those courts. Thus the Council maintained in its rejoinder that it had taken due account 'not only [of] the abovementioned judgments of the Dutch courts, but also further . . . evidence as referred to therein', namely, information supplied by the BVD after investigating 'the applicant's participation in terrorist activities'. In paragraphs 21 to 24 of their statement in intervention, the Netherlands confirmed that the national decision on the basis of which the decision originally challenged was adopted was the decision of the Rechtbank of 1997, taken as a consequence of the judgment of the Raad van State of 1995 and on the basis of the BVD's file. The Netherlands have furthermore declared, in their statement in intervention, that 'other matters on file played a role in the decision taken by the Council'. According to the Netherlands, '[t]hese matters are confidential, the information has not been made public and was not kept by the Council'.

212. In accordance with the principles set out in paragraphs 161 to 183 above and summarised in paragraph 184 above, the Court finds that, in so far as the Council intended to base the measure freezing the applicant's funds on those matters, it was incumbent on the Council at the very least to make the applicant aware, either simultaneously with the decision originally challenged or as soon as possible after it was adopted, that the judgments of the Raad van State of 1992 and 1995, and the decision of the Rechtbank of 1997 had been used against him as incriminating evidence. Since those were official acts adopted at the end of public judicial proceedings to which the applicant had been a party, it is plain that their communication to the applicant was not prevented by any requirement of confidentiality.

213. In accordance with those same principles, the Court considers furthermore that the subsequent decisions adopted with regard to the applicant, up to and including the contested decision, ought to have been preceded by communication of any new evidence adduced against him, subject to its being of a confidential nature, and also by a hearing.

214. Clearly that was not the case, in breach of the applicant's rights of the defence.

215. The foregoing considerations, ascertaining whether the rights of the defence have been observed, are also applicable, mutatis mutandis, to ascertaining whether the obligation to state reasons has been fulfilled.

216. In the circumstances of the present case, neither the contested decision nor any one of the subsequent decisions, up to and including the contested decision, satisfies the requirement of a statement of reasons as set out above, for they do no more than state, in the second recital in the preambles thereto, that it is 'desirable' or that it has been 'decided' to adopt an up-to-date list of the persons, groups and entities to which Regulation (EC) No 2580/2001 applies. Such general and formulaic wording is tantamount to a total failure to state reasons.

217. In accordance with the principles set out in paragraphs 185 to 197 above, and summarised in paragraph 198 above, the Court holds that, inasmuch as the Council intended to base the decision originally challenged on the factors referred to in paragraph 211 above, the statement of reasons given for that decision ought to have mentioned, at the very least, the judgments of the Raad van State of 1992 and 1995 and the decision of the Rechtbank of 1997 and, subject to their possibly being of a confidential nature, to have indicated the main reasons why the Council took the view, in the exercise of its discretion, that the applicant was to be the subject of such a decision on the basis of those judgments and that decision. Moreover, in stating the reasons for the subsequent decisions to freeze funds, the Council ought, subject to the same reservations, to have indicated the main reasons why, after re-examination, it considered that there were still grounds for the freezing of the applicant's funds.

218. Clearly that was not the case, in breach of Article 253 EC.

219. The applicant has not only been unable effectively to make his views known to the Council but also, given the lack of any statement, in the decision originally challenged or in the contested decision, of the actual and specific grounds justifying those decisions, has not been placed in a position to make good use of his right of action before the Court, given the aforementioned links between the guarantees of the rights of the defence, of the obligation to state reasons and of the right to an effective legal remedy. It is to be borne in mind that the possibility of regularising the total lack of a statement of reasons after an action has been brought is now considered in the case-law to be prejudicial to the rights of the defence and is therefore prohibited (see paragraph 186 above).

220. More specifically, the applicant has been unable to challenge, from the moment these proceedings were initiated, the Council's opinion that the

judgments of the Raad van State of 1992 and 1995 and the decision of the Rechtbank satisfy the definition given in Article 1(4) of Common Position 2001/931, a challenge that he was not able to formulate, and that he indeed did not formulate, until the stage of the reply.

221. In this respect, the Court points out that, while the applicant himself made mention of the judgments of the Raad van State of 1992 and 1995 in his application, he seems not to have been aware that those two judgments were regarded by the Council as justification for his inclusion in the lists at issue. Quite the contrary: the applicant referred to those two judgments, in his application, in so far as the supreme administrative court of the Netherlands held therein, in opposition to the opinion of the State Secretary, that the applicant must be given refugee status in the Netherlands. Furthermore, it was only at the stage of the defence that the decision of the Rechtbank of 1997 was pleaded and produced by the Council.

222. The fact remains, moreover, that the parties' written pleadings and the documents in the case produced before the Court do not make it possible to determine with any certainty whether the decision originally challenged was actually adopted having regard only to the matters contained in the judgments of the Raad van State of 1992 and 1995, the decision of the Rechtbank of 1997 and the BVD file to which those courts had access, as maintained by the Council in the course of the written procedure. Although the Council's pleadings do not imply any such thing, legitimate doubt arises in that regard on reading the Netherlands' statement in intervention, which declares that 'other matters on file played a role in the decision taken by the Council' and states that '[t]hese matters are confidential, the information has not been made public and was not kept by the Council' (see paragraph 211 above).

223. For want of any other information on that head supplied by the Council or the intervening Governments at the hearing, the Court is not in a position either to exclude the possibility that those 'other matters on file' exist and in fact 'played a role' in the Council's assessment, or to determine whether the applicant ought to have been informed of those matters, if they exist, or whether communication of them could legitimately be refused by reason of their confidential nature.

224. Lastly, the fact remains that at the hearing the Council maintained, in answer to the Court's questions, that the competent national authority in this case, for the purposes of Article 2(3) of Regulation No 2580/2001 and of Article 1(4) of Common Position 2001/931, was the State Secretary. It is hard to reconcile that argument with that proposed by the Council in its written pleadings, namely that the decision originally challenged was based, first and foremost, on the decision of the Rechtbank of 1997 (see paragraph 211 above). In contrast, the Kingdom of the Netherlands defended the argument that the competent national authority in the case in

point was the Rechtbank. Even though the Council subsequently stated that the decision of the State Secretary was not to be considered in isolation, but together with the decision of the Rechtbank, the wavering of the defendant institution on that score makes impossible, even at this stage of the proceedings, judicial review of the actual grounds on which the contested decision is based.

225. In those circumstances, the Court considers that it is not in a position to carry out adequately its review of the lawfulness of the decision originally challenged or, in consequence, that of the contested decision, in light of the other pleas in law, grounds of challenge and substantive arguments invoked in support of the application for annulment.

226. In conclusion, the Court finds that no statement of reasons has been given for the contested decision and that the latter was adopted in the course of a procedure during which the applicant's rights of the defence were not observed. What is more, the Court is not, even at this stage of the procedure, in a position to undertake the judicial review of the lawfulness of that decision in light of the other pleas in law, grounds of challenge and substantive arguments invoked in support of the application for annulment.

227. Those considerations cannot but lead to the annulment of the contested decision, in so far as it concerns the applicant.

The Application for Compensation

Arguments of the Parties

228. The applicant relies on the second paragraph of Article 288 EC and describes as follows the damage he has sustained by reason of the contested acts:

(a) the freezing of his financial assets, in particular of his bank account;

(b) the prohibition on any financial institution or insurance agency's providing him with services;

(c) the suspension of payment of his social security benefits and the refusal of the Netherlands Government to grant him a residence permit;

(d) the obstacle raised to payments due to the applicant on various scores, in particular as a creditor of the estate of Ferdinand E. Marcos (see paragraph 73 above), as author of books and articles, teacher, lecturer and heir to property left by members of his family;

(e) unwarranted restrictions on his freedom of movement, increased surveillance of his person and orders given to border police and customs authorities to hinder his passage;

(f) material and non-material damage caused by libel, slander and the applicant's being branded a 'terrorist' in official instruments, in the press and in public opinion;

(g) the endangering of his personal safety and physical integrity by the risks and threats arising from his being branded a 'terrorist';

(h) the prejudice to the applicant's role as chief political consultant to the NDFP in peace negotiations, and the resulting threats to the peace process as a whole.

229. In his reply, the applicant states that the wrongful conduct relied on in the present case consists in the manifest error of assessment committed by the Council in his regard by including him in the lists at issue and categorising him as a terrorist, without affording him any procedural guarantee and without providing any valid statement of reasons.

230. The Council submits that the Community can incur liability only where a sufficiently serious breach has occurred of a superior rule of law for the protection of individuals (Joined Cases C-104/89 and C-37/90 *Mulder and Others* v *Council and Commission* [1992] ECR I-3061, paragraph 12).

231. In the circumstances of this case the contested measures, in its view, offend against no rule of law.

Findings of the Court

232. It is settled case-law that, in order for the Community to incur non-contractual liability under the second paragraph of Article 288 EC for the unlawful conduct of its institutions, a number of conditions must be satisfied: the institutions' conduct must be unlawful, actual damage must have been sustained and there must be a causal link between the conduct and the damage pleaded (Case T-69/00 *FIAMM and FIAMM Technologies* v *Council and Commission* [2005] ECR II-5393, paragraph 85, and the case-law cited).

233. Since those three conditions for the incurring of liability are cumulative, failure to meet one of them is sufficient for an action for damages to be dismissed, without it being therefore necessary to examine the other conditions (see Case T-226/01 *CAS Succhi di Frutta* v *Commission* [2006] ECR II-0000, paragraph 27, and the case-law cited).

234. The unlawful conduct alleged against a Community institution must consist of a sufficiently serious breach of a rule of law intended to confer rights on individuals (Case C-352/98 P *Bergaderm and Goupil* v *Commission* [2000] ECR I-5291, paragraphs 40 to 42, and *FIAMM and FIAMM Technologies* v *Council and Commission*, paragraph 232 above, paragraph 86). Contrary to the Council's submission on the basis of the case-law as it stood before *Bergaderm and Goupil* v *Commission*, there are no longer grounds for drawing a distinction between a 'rule of law' and a 'superior rule of law'.

235. The decisive test for finding that that requirement is fulfilled is whether the Community institution concerned manifestly and gravely disregarded the limits set on its discretion. Where an institution has only a considerably reduced, or even no, discretion, the mere infringement of Community law may be sufficient to establish the existence of a sufficiently serious breach (*FIAMM and FIAMM Technologies* v *Council and Commission*, paragraph 232 above, paragraphs 88 and 89, and the case-law cited).

236. It is in the light of those observations that the applicant's claim for compensation falls to be examined.

237. In the instant case, the Court has already held, in connection with the application for annulment, that no adequate statement of reasons was given for the contested decision and that the latter was adopted in the course of proceedings in which the applicant's rights of the defence were not observed.

238. With regard to the first of those defects, the Court remarks that, in accordance with settled case-law, failure to fulfil the obligation to state reasons is not, in itself, such as to cause the Community to incur liability (Case 106/81 *Kind* v *EEC* [1982] ECR 2885, paragraph 14; Case C-119/88 *AERPO and Others* v *Commission* [1990] ECR I-2189; Case C-76/01 *Eurocoton and Others* v *Council* [2003] ECR I-10091, paragraph 98; Case T-164/94 *Nölle* v *Council and Commission* [1995] ECR II-2589, paragraph 57; Joined Cases T-481/93 and T-484/93 *Exporteurs in Levende Varkens and Others* v *Commission* [ECR] II-2941, paragraph 104, and Case T-18/99 *Cordis* v *Commission* [2001] ECR II-913, paragraph 79).

239. With regard to the second of those defects, however, it is to be borne in mind that the fundamental principle of observance of the rights of the defence is a rule of law the purpose of which is to confer rights on individuals (see, to that effect, *Fiskano* v *Commission*, paragraph 139 above, paragraphs 39 and 40, and *Exporteurs in Levende Varkens and Others* v *Commission*, paragraph 238 above, paragraph 102).

240. In the circumstances of this case, the Court considers that the breach of the applicant's rights of the defence is sufficiently serious for the Community to incur liability.

241. Nevertheless, the fundamental principle that the rights of the defence must be observed being essentially a procedural guarantee (Case C-344/05 P *Commission* v *De Bry* [2006] ECR I-10915, paragraph 39), the Court considers that, in the circumstances, annulment of the contested act will constitute adequate compensation for the damage caused by that breach (see, to that effect, Joined Cases T-120/01 and T-300/01 *De Nicola* v *BEI* [2004] ECR-SC I-A-365 and II-1671, paragraphs 140 to 142, and the case-law cited).

242. For the rest, the Court has already held, in connection with the application for annulment, that it was not, at this stage of the procedure, in a

position to undertake the judicial review of the lawfulness of the contested decision in light of the other pleas in law, grounds of challenge and substantive arguments invoked by the applicant. Nor, as a result, is it in a position in connection with the application for compensation to ascertain, even now, in the light of those same pleas in law, grounds of challenge and substantive arguments whether the condition relating to the unlawfulness of the conduct in question, as defined by the case-law, has in this instance been satisfied. In particular, it is unable to determine even now whether the Council committed a manifest error of assessment in deciding to freeze the applicant's funds on the basis of the information available to it or whether it manifestly and gravely disregarded the limits set on its discretion under Article 2(3) of Regulation No 2580/2001. That is precisely one of the reasons why the contested decision must be annulled.

243. However, the claim for compensation must, in any event, be dismissed, for neither the fact and extent of the damage alleged, as set out in paragraph 228 above, nor the existence of a causal link between that damage and the instances of material unlawfulness pleaded in support of that claim has been proved to the requisite legal standard.

244. The Court of First Instance recalls that, in an action based on Article 235 EC in conjunction with the second paragraph of Article 288 EC, the applicant has to prove not only the unlawfulness of the conduct of which the institution concerned is accused and the fact of the damage but also the existence of a causal link between that conduct and the damage pleaded (see Joined Cases 197/80 to 200/80, 243/80, 245/80 and 247/80 *Ludwigshafener Walzmühle and Others* v *Council and Commission* [1981] ECR 3211, paragraph 18; Case C-257/90 *Italsolar* v *Commission* [1993] ECR I-9, paragraph 33; Case T-175/94 *International Procurement Services* v *Commission* [1996] ECR II-729, paragraph 44, and Case T-72/99 *Meyer* v *Commission* [2000] ECR II-2521, paragraph 49). As for the latter condition, it is settled case-law that the damage must be a sufficiently direct consequence of the conduct complained of (Joined Cases 64/76, 113/76, 167/78, 239/78, 27/79, 28/79 and 45/79 *Dumortier Frères and Others* v *Council* [1979] ECR 3091, paragraph 21). A causal link for the purposes of the second paragraph of Article 288 EC is thus recognised where there is a direct link of cause and effect between the fault committed by the institution concerned and the damage pleaded (*CAS Succhi di Frutta* v *Commission*, paragraph 233 above, paragraph 37, and the case-law cited).

245. In the present case, with more particular regard to the damage referred to in (a), (b) and (d) of paragraph 228 above, it is appropriate to note that the freezing of the applicant's funds, financial assets and other economic resources is a temporary precautionary measure which, unlike confiscation, does not affect the very substance of the right of the person concerned to property in the assets in question but only the use (*Yusuf*, paragraph 299)

and therefore the availability of those assets. The same is true so far as concerns interest and other income produced by those assets.

246. As regards the damage caused by the unavailability of those funds, financial assets or other economic resources, consisting of the loss of enjoyment, the fact remains that it doe not arise from the adoption of the Community measures at issue in these proceedings but from the adoption, first, of the Office of Foreign Assets Control's decision of 12 August 2002 ordering the freezing of the applicant's assets in the United States and, second, of the decision of the Netherlands Minister of Finance of 13 August 2002 ordering the freezing of the applicant's assets in the Netherlands. The applicant having neither proved, nor even argued, that those two decisions have been repealed or withdrawn since the Community measures at issue in this instance were adopted, it must be concluded that there is no proof of any direct causal link between those measures and the various losses alleged.

247. The same finding must be made with regard to the material and non-material damage referred to in (f) of paragraph 228 above. In fact, that damage too originates in, first, the adoption of the national decisions mentioned in the previous paragraph and, second, the adoption of Common Position 2001/931, which falls outside the jurisdiction of the Court of First Instance in these proceedings (see, to that effect, the order in Case T-338/02 *Segi and Others* v *Council* [2004] ECR II-1647, paragraph 40, upheld on appeal by judgment in Case C-355/04 P *Segi and Others* v *Council* [2007] ECR I-0000). What is more, no evidence has been adduced of the existence of any additional damage directly and specifically attributable to the adoption of the Community measures at issue in this case.

248. With more particular regard to the damage referred to in (c) of paragraph 228 above, it may in addition be emphasised that the application of the derogations from the freezing of funds authorised under Articles 5 and 6 of Regulation No 2580/2001, which include social security benefits and extend to the grant of a work permit (*Ayadi*, paragraph 102 above, paragraphs 127 to 132), falls within the competence and, therefore, the responsibility of the Member States. Any difficulties encountered on that head by the applicant in his relations with the Netherlands authorities cannot, therefore, of themselves cause the Community to incur liability.

249. With more particular regard to the damage referred to in (d), (e), (g) and (h) of paragraph 228 above, in addition to there being no evidence of a causal link with the Community measures at issue here, which must be found to be the case for the reasons set out in paragraph 246 above, the inevitable conclusion is that their actual existence is itself not supported by any evidence. On the contrary, with more particular regard to the damage in (e) and (h), the Netherlands Government asserted at the hearing, without being effectively contradicted by the applicant, that the latter was

regularly given laissez-passer so that he could participate in peace negotiations. Furthermore, with more particular regard to the damage in (h), even if that were proved, it would have been suffered by the NDFP and not by the applicant personally.

250. Finally, it is to be stressed that the applicant has not sought to evaluate, even approximately, the amount of those various heads of damage, in respect of which he does no more than claim compensation 'in an amount to be fixed *ex aequo et bono* of not less than EUR 100 000'. Now, every claim for compensation for damage, whether the damage is material or non-material, and whether the indemnity is symbolic or actual, must give particulars of the nature of the damage alleged in connection with the conduct at issue and must quantify the whole of that damage, even if approximately (see Case T-277/97 *Ismeri Europa* v *Court of Auditors* [1999] ECR II-1825, paragraph 81, and case-law cited).

251. In those circumstances, and subject to the considerations set out in paragraphs 240 and 241 above, the application for compensation must be rejected.

Costs

252. Under Article 87(2) of the Rules of Procedure, the unsuccessful party is to be ordered to pay the costs if they have been applied for in the successful party's pleadings. Pursuant to Article 87(3) of the Rules of Procedure, the Court of First Instance may order that the costs be shared or that each party bear its own costs where each party succeeds on some and fails on other heads. In the circumstances of this case, the Council having been unsuccessful in its main submissions, it must be decided that the Council is to bear, in addition to its own costs, all the applicant's costs, including those incurred in the proceedings for interim measures, and all the costs of the Negotiating Panel and its members.

253. Under the first subparagraph of Article 87(4) of the Rules of Procedure, Member States which intervene in the proceedings are to bear their own costs.

On those grounds,

THE COURT OF FIRST INSTANCE (Second Chamber)

hereby:

1. **Annuls Council Decision 2006/379/EC of 29 May 2006 implementing Article 2(3) of Regulation (EC) No 2580/2001 on specific restrictive measures directed against certain persons and entities with a view to combating terrorism and repealing Decision 2005/930/EC in so far as it concerns the applicant;**

2. Rejects the application for compensation;

3. Orders the Council to bear, in addition to its own costs, the applicant's costs, including those incurred in the proceedings for interim measures, and also the costs of the Negotiating Panel of the National Democratic Front of the Philippines, Luis G. Jalandoni, Fidel V. Agcaoili and Maria Consuelo K. Ledesma;

4. Orders the Kingdom of the Netherlands and the United Kingdom of Great Britain and Northern Ireland to bear their own costs.

Delivered in open court in Luxembourg on 11 July 2007.

DOCUMENT NO. 20

PROCESSING AND PROTECTION OF PERSONAL DATA SUBPOENAED BY THE TREASURY DEPARTMENT FROM THE US-BASED OPERATION CENTRE OF THE SOCIETY FOR WORLDWIDE INTERBANK FINANCIAL TELECOMMUNICATION (SWIFT)

Report 11291/2/07 REV 2
Council of the European Union

Luxembourg, 28 June 2007

The Council took note of a letter of the United States Secretary for the Treasury presenting Representations regarding the processing and protection of personal data subpoenaed by the Treasury Department from the US based operation centre of the Society for Worldwide Interbank Financial Telecommunication (SWIFT) in the United States under the Terrorist Finance Tracking Programme (TFTP).

These unilateral Representations describe the controls and safeguards governing the handling, use and dissemination of data by the US authorities under the Treasury Department's TFTP.

The TFTP contains layers of governmental and independent controls to ensure that the data, which are limited in nature, are used strictly for counterterrorism purposes, that data are retained only for as long as necessary for counterterrorism purposes and that all data are maintained in a secure environment and properly handled.

Once SWIFT, as a Belgian-based company, and the financial institutions (banks) within the Community making use of its services have completed the necessary arrangements to respect EC law, in particular though the provision of information to their clients that personal data will be transferred for commercial purposes to the United States and, as regard SWIFT, the respect of the "Safe Harbour" principles,[1] subject to lawful access by the US Treasury Department, the Council is confident that SWIFT and the said financial institutions will be in compliance with their respective legal responsibilities under European data protection law.

To ensure effective oversight of the Representations, the Commission, in consultation with US Treasury and after having consulted the President of the Permanent Representatives Committee (COREPER) and the President of the Committee of Civil Liberties, Justice and Home Affairs (LIBE) of the European Parliament, will appoint an "eminent European" to serve as an independent authority who will monitor compliance with the Representations and will report to the Commission which in turn shall report to the European Parliament and the Council. The task of this person will be to confirm that the program is implemented consistently with the Representations for the purpose of verifying the protection of EU-originating personal data. The process of identifying appropriate candidates will now begin so that this work can begin in the first semester of 2008.

The Council authorized the Presidency to sign, together with a Representative of the Commission, a reply to the US letter.

Background

Following press reports in June 2006, it was revealed that the US Treasury's Office of Foreign Assets Control ("OFAC") operating on the basis of powers under the TFTP has served administrative subpoenas on the Society for Worldwide Interbank Financial Telecommunication ("SWIFT").[2] These subpoenas require SWIFT in the US to transfer personal data held on its United States[3] server to OFAC where they are used for counter terrorism purposes regarding suspected individuals or entities.

According to the US Treasury, the use of SWIFT data has enhanced the United States' and third countries' ability to identify financiers of terrorism, to map terrorist networks and to disrupt the activities of terrorists and their supporters.

Immediately after these facts were unveiled by the press, the Belgian Data Protection Authority issued its opinion of 27 July 2006 stating that SWIFT

---

1 The Safe Harbour principles, which are designed to protect personal data transferred from the Community to the US, provide for limitations to the protection by those principles "to extent necessary to meet national security, public interest or law enforcement requirements" (ANNEX 1 to Commission Decision of 26th July 2000 on safe harbour privacy principles).

2 SWIFT is a Belgium-based company with offices in the United States and which operates a worldwide messaging system used to transmit, inter alia, bank transaction information. It has been estimated that SWIFT handles 80% of the worldwide traffic for electronic value transfers.

3 For security of data reasons SWIFT operates two identical "mirror" servers, one located in the European Union and the other in the United States. All financial messaging data are held on each server for a period of 124 days.

processing activities for the execution of interbank payments were in breach of Belgian Data Protection Law, which implements Directive 95/46/EC on the protection of personal data ("the Data Protection Directive").[4] In its opinion the Belgian Data Protection Authority found several breaches to the fundamental data protection principles, including relating to transfers of personal data to third countries. SWIFT is now in discussions with the Belgian Data Protection Authority, in order to comply with Belgian data protection law.

In late November 2006 the Article 29 Working Party (the independent advisory body to the European Commission on data protection and privacy) issued an opinion on the processing of personal data by SWIFT. The opinion concluded that SWIFT and its instructing financial institutions had breached Community data protection law as set out in Directive 95/46/EC, including as regards the transfer of personal data to the United States without ensuring adequate protection and failure to inform data subjects about the way in which their personal data were being processed. The Article 29 Working Party continues to follow the issues and coordinates the actions by the Data Protection Supervisory Authorities at national level.

The current EC data protection legal framework provides for a specific instrument for personal data transfers to the US: pursuant to Article 25 (6) of the Data Protection Directive 95/46/EC, the Commission adopted a Decision of 26th July 2000 on the adequacy of protection provided by the Safe Harbour principles. In this Decision the Commission declares that Safe Harbour Principles provide an adequate level of protection for the transfers of data from the Community to the United States. This is an Adequacy Finding which only applies to companies which certify that they will respect the data protection principles set forth therein.

SWIFT is in the final stages of discussions with competent US authorities regarding entry into the Safe Harbour which would allow the transfer of SWIFT data for commercial purposes to the US. It is understood that SWIFT may be in a position to join the Safe Harbour by early July 2007. In addition SWIFT and its customers (banks) are assessing the appropriate measures to be taken to ensure that bank and other financial institution customers are properly informed about the processing of SWIFT data, including transfers to the United States for commercial purpose and the possible processing of those data by the US Treasury for counter terrorism purposes.

The Safe Harbour principles, which are designed to protect personal data, recognize limitations to those principles "to the extent necessary to meet national security, public interest or law enforcement requirements". It is nec-

[4] Directive 95/46/EC of the European Parliament and of the Council of 24 October 1995 on the protection of individuals with regard to the processing of personal data and on the free movement of such data; OJ L 281, 23.11.1995, p. 31–50.

essary therefore to ascertain whether US national security or law enforcement limitations to the Safe Harbour principles are necessary and proportionate. To that end representatives of the Commission, and of the Council Presidency,[5] have had the opportunity to discuss with the US Treasury a set of "Representations" (see annex) drafted by US Treasury under which it unilaterally commits itself to process personal data originating from EU Member States in compliance with specific data protection principles. The Parliament (LIBE Committee) and Council (COREPER) have been kept regularly informed of these discussions, as well as the Article 29 Working Party.

The Representations provide safeguards on the processing of personal data originating from EU Member States which are subpoenaed from SWIFT in the US by US Treasury. These include, for example, commitments by US Treasury to use any data received from SWIFT exclusively for counter terrorism investigations and not to search the data for any other purpose. The Representations provide significant assurances about the security of the SWIFT data maintained by US Treasury, about the restricted access to SWIFT data and about the circumstances in which SWIFT-derived information can be shared with other US agencies and the use which those agencies can make of those data. The Representations also contain commitments by the US Treasury to analyse on an on-going basis the data it holds to identify and delete any data which are not necessary for purposes of the TFTP and to retain data no longer than for specified periods.[6]

---

[5] The judgment of the Court of Justice in Joined Cases C-317/04 and 318/04 ("PNR judgement") of 30 May 2006 held that direct access to personal data by law enforcement services cannot be regulated on a Community basis. The SWIFT situation is distinguishable from that prevailing in the PNR judgement. This is because in the SWIFT situation the transfer of personal data to the United States is for commercial purposes (any access by the US authorities to that data takes place subsequently, in the United States) whereas in the PNR scenario, the transfer directly to the United States authorities was regarded by the Court as exclusively for law enforcement purposes.

[6] The Representations envisage publication both in the US Federal Register and in the Official Journal. Data which are received by US Treasury after the date of publication will be retained for no longer than five years from the date of receipt. Data which US Treasury received before the date of publication will be retained for no more than five years from the publication date.

Annex

Terrorist Finance Tracking Program Representations of the United States Department of the Treasury

These representations describe the US Department of the Treasury's Terrorist Financing Tracking Program (TFTP) and, in particular, the rigorous controls and safeguards governing the handling, use, and dissemination of data received from SWIFT under compulsion of administrative subpoenas. These controls and safeguards apply to all persons having access to the SWIFT data, unless otherwise noted in specific examples such as those describing the sharing of lead information derived from the SWIFT data with foreign governments.

The TFTP is grounded in law, carefully targeted, powerful and successful, and bounded by privacy safeguards. It represents exactly what citizens expect and hope their governments are doing to protect them from terrorist threats.

The Treasury Department's Terrorist Finance Tracking Program

Shortly after the September 11, 2001 attacks, as part of an effort to employ all available means to track terrorists and their networks, the Treasury Department initiated the TFTP. Under the TFTP, the Treasury Department has issued administrative subpoenas for terrorist-related data to the US operations center of the Society for Worldwide Interbank Financial Telecommunication (SWIFT), a Belgium-based cooperative that operates a worldwide messaging system used to transmit financial transaction information. These subpoenas require SWIFT to provide the Treasury Department with certain financial transaction records—which are maintained by SWIFT's US operations center in the ordinary course of its business—to be used exclusively for counterterrorism purposes as specified in the following sections.

Fundamental Principles Underlying the TFTP

From its inception, the TFTP has been designed and implemented to meet applicable US legal requirements, to contribute meaningfully to combating global terrorism, and to respect and protect the potential commercial sensitivity of and privacy interests in the SWIFT data held in the United States. The TFTP takes into consideration the potential commercial sensitivity and individual privacy interests in the information it encompasses, and the safeguards detailed in these representations apply irrespective of the nationality or place of residence of the individuals involved. The program contains multiple, overlapping layers of governmental and independent controls to ensure that the data, which are limited in nature, are searched only for counterterrorism purposes and that all data are maintained in a secure environment and properly handled.

All actions by the Treasury Department to obtain specified information from SWIFT's US operations center and to use that information exclusively for investigating, detecting, preventing, and/or prosecuting terrorism or its financing or related follow-on investigations and prosecutions are in accordance with US law. Moreover, the data submitted by SWIFT are not searched to collect evidence or detect activity that is not related to terrorism or its financing, even though such activity in itself may be unlawful. The Treasury Department does not perform searches on SWIFT data, nor can the information be used, in connection with general investigations of tax evasion, money laundering, economic espionage, narcotics trafficking or other criminal activity, unless in a particular instance such activity has been connected to terrorism or its financing.

The data received from SWIFT under compulsion of subpoenas consist of copies of completed financial transaction messages, *i.e*, electronic copies of business records maintained at SWIFT's US operations center in the ordinary course of business. Though this data may undergo some processing in the sense of the very restricted counterterrorism search-and-retrieval capacity described herein, there is no alteration, manipulation, addition or deletion of data within individual transaction messages within the searchable database.

The TFTP has proven to be a powerful investigative tool that has contributed significantly to protecting US citizens and other persons around the world and to safeguarding America's and other countries' national security. The program has been instrumental in identifying and capturing terrorists and their financiers, and it has generated many leads that have been disseminated to counterterrorism experts in intelligence and law enforcement agencies around the world.

Concerns Raised within the European Union

After the public media disclosure of the TFTP in June 2006, concerns were raised in the EU about the TFTP program and, in particular, the possibility that the Treasury Department might have access to personal data relating to an identified or identifiable natural person contained in financial transactions processed by SWIFT. In particular, questions were raised on the TFTP's consistency with obligations under the Data Protection Directive (Directive 95/46/EC of the European Parliament and of the Council of 24 October 1995 on the protection of individuals with regard to the processing of personal data and on the free movement of such data), as well as Member State laws implementing that Directive.

Nature of SWIFT Data

The financial transaction records provided by SWIFT under compulsion of subpoena may include identifying information about the originator and/or recipient of the transaction, including name, account number, address, national identification number, and other personal data. It would be highly unusual for SWIFT financial records to include "sensitive" data as referred to in Article 8 of Directive 95/46/EC (*i.e.*, personal data revealing racial or ethnic origin, political opinions, religious or philosophical beliefs, trade union membership, and data concerning the health or sex life of the individual).

International Counterterrorist Financing Principles

The SWIFT financial data used in the TFTP is extraordinarily valuable in combating global terrorism and its financing, and in carrying out the government's responsibility to defend the public and safeguard national security and to detect, prevent, investigate and prosecute terrorist crimes.

The international community and national authorities recognize that money is the lifeblood of terrorism. This is reflected in the 1999 United Nations International Convention for the Suppression of the Financing of Terrorism and numerous United Nations resolutions relating to the prevention and suppression of the financing of terrorists acts, particularly United Nations Security Council Resolution 1373. In the United States, the Treasury Department and the Congress established the Office of Terrorism and Financial Intelligence in 2004 to marshal the Department's enforcement and intelligence functions with the twin aims of safeguarding the financial system against illicit use and combating, among others, terrorists and other national security threats. The office's various components gather and analyze information from the law enforcement, intelligence, and financial communities as to how terrorists (and other criminals) earn, move, and store money. These activities enable the office to freeze terrorists' assets, to combat terrorism generally, and to develop and promote counterterrorist financing standards in the United States and abroad.

These and other initiatives reflect the everyday reality that terrorists depend on a regular cash flow to pay operatives, arrange for travel, train new members, forge documents, pay bribes, acquire weapons, and stage attacks. In order to send money through the banking system, they often provide information that yields the kinds of concrete leads that can advance a terrorism investigation. This is why counterterrorism officials place a high premium on financial intelligence, including that derived from programs such as the TFTP, which has proved to be of inestimable value in combating global terrorism.

This is also why the financial industry is subject to extensive recordkeeping and reporting requirements that are designed to support governmental counterterrorism efforts. Countries throughout the world have mandated this by law, consistent with the recommendations of the Financial Action Task Force. For example, in the United States, the primary statutory authority is the Bank Secrecy Act. In Europe, similar provisions have been implemented into national law consistent with the Third Money Laundering Directive and, most recently, Regulation (EC) No 1781/2006 of the European Parliament and of the Council of 15 November 2006 on information on the payer accompanying transfers of funds.

Legal Authority to Obtain and Use SWIFT Data

The subpoenas served on SWIFT are based on longstanding statutory authorities and a related Executive order for combating terrorism and its financing. The International Emergency Economic Powers Act of 1977 (IEEPA) authorizes the President of the United States, during a declared national emergency, to investigate bank transfers and other transactions in which a foreign person has any interest. Similarly, the United Nations Participation Act of 1945 (UNPA) authorizes the President, when implementing United Nations Security Council Resolutions, to investigate economic relations or means of communication between any foreign person and the United States.

On September 23, 2001, the President, relying in part on IEEPA and UNPA and citing United Nations Security Council Resolutions targeting the Taliban and Al Qaida, issued Executive Order 13224. In that Order, the President declared a national emergency to deal with the 9/11 terrorist attacks and the continuing and immediate threat of further attacks, and blocked the property of, and prohibited transactions with, persons who commit, threaten to commit, or support terrorism.

For the purposes of Executive Order 13224, section 3 contains the following definition:

the term "terrorism" means an activity that—

(i) involves a violent act or an act dangerous to human life, property, or infrastructure; and

(ii) appears to be intended—

(A) to intimidate or coerce a civilian population;

(B) to influence the policy of a government by intimidation or coercion; or

(C) to affect the conduct of a government by mass destruction, assassination, kidnapping, or hostage-taking.

In section 7 of the Order, the President authorized the Secretary of the Treasury Department to employ all powers granted to the President by IEEPA and UNPA as may be necessary to carry out the purposes of the Order. He also authorized the Secretary of the Treasury to redelegate any of these functions to other officers and agencies of the US Government, and directed all agencies of the US Government to take all appropriate measures within their authority to carry out the provisions of the Order. IEEPA and the Order, as implemented through the Global Terrorism Sanctions Regulations, authorize the Director of the Treasury Department's Office of Foreign Assets Control (OFAC) to require any person to furnish financial transaction or other data in connection with an economic sanctions-related investigation. These are the legal authorities under which OFAC issues subpoenas to SWIFT for financial data that are related to terrorism investigations.

Access Control and Computer System Security

The data obtained from SWIFT, consistent with US Government procedures for the handling of information related to the investigation of terrorism and its financing more generally, are subject to strict technical and organizational measures to protect the information against accidental or unlawful destruction, loss, alteration or access. All of the following security measures are subject to independent audit.

The SWIFT data are maintained in a secure physical environment, stored separately from any other data, and the computer systems have high-level intrusion controls and other protections to limit access to the data solely as described herein. No copies of SWIFT data are made, other than for disaster recovery backup purposes. Access to the data and the computer equipment are limited to persons with appropriate security clearances. Even among such persons, access to the SWIFT data is on a read-only basis and is limited through the TFTP on a strict need-to-know basis to analysts dedicated to the investigation of terrorism and to persons involved in the technical support, management, and oversight of the TFTP.

Extraction and Usage Limited to the Investigation of Terrorism

The TFTP does not involve data mining or any other type of algorithmic or automated profiling or computer-filtering. Multiple layers of strict controls have been built into the TFTP to limit the information collected, to ensure that information is extracted and used only for counterterrorism purposes, and to protect the privacy interests of individuals not connected with terrorism or its financing. These overlapping safeguards continuously narrow and significantly restrict access to and use of the financial data handled by SWIFT in its day-to-day operations

As a threshold matter, the subpoenas served upon SWIFT are carefully and narrowly tailored to limit the amount of data furnished to the Treasury Department. SWIFT is required to provide only data the Treasury Department believes will be necessary in combating terrorist financing, on the basis of past analyses focusing on message types and geography, as well as perceived threats and vulnerabilities. Additionally, searches are narrowly tailored to minimize the extraction of messages that are not relevant to a terrorism investigation. The data provided by SWIFT are searched to extract only information that is related to an identified, preexisting terrorism investigation. This means that every search that is conducted must specifically cite to and record documented evidence supporting the belief that the target is connected with terrorism or its financing. Each and every search of the SWIFT data under the TFTP is also logged contemporaneously, including such affirmative terrorism nexus required to initiate the search.

As a result of the foregoing safeguards, only a minute fraction *(i.e.,* substantially less than one percent) of the subset of the SWIFT messages furnished to the Treasury Department has been actually accessed, and only because those messages have been directly responsive to a targeted, terrorism-related search.

Independent Oversight

In addition to the Treasury Department's ongoing exercise of the controls described herein, the TFTP includes multiple complementary layers of independent oversight: by representatives of SWIFT itself, an independent auditing firm, and other independent US government authorities, including the US Congress.

SWIFT and outside auditors it has retained exercise their independent oversight of the TFTP in several mutually complementary ways. First, certain SWIFT representatives have been granted appropriate security clearances to have 24-hour access to the equipment and data and the ability to monitor, in real time and retrospectively, the use of the data to ensure that they are accessed only for counterterrorism purposes. Additionally, these SWIFT representatives may stop any specific search immediately, and even have the ability to shut down the entire system, if they have any concerns.

With respect to the independent, outside auditors, the maintenance, access to, and use of the SWIFT data are subject to continued, periodic independent audit pursuant to carefully delineated protocols consistent with international auditing standards. These audits cover the access control and computer system security safeguards, as well as the limitation of data usage for the investigation of terrorism, as described above. The independent auditors report their conclusions to the audit and finance committee of SWIFT's Board of Directors.

In addition, consistent with US law, various congressional committees have been repeatedly briefed on the TFTP and its operation, and they continue to be briefed on a regular basis. The TFTP has also been the subject of congressional hearings.

Finally, the Privacy and Civil Liberties Oversight Board, which was established pursuant to the Intelligence Reform and Terrorism Prevention Act of 2004, exercises oversight of the TFTP. The Board's mission is to ensure that concerns with respect to privacy and civil liberties are appropriately considered in the implementation of all US laws, regulations, and executive branch policies related to efforts to protect the United States against terrorism. The Board also is responsible for reviewing the terrorism information-sharing practices of executive branch departments and agencies to determine whether guidelines designed to appropriately protect privacy and civil liberties are being followed.

As described below, this extensive, independent oversight works in tandem with restrictive dissemination controls that operate to further restrict access to information derived from the SWIFT financial records and to further protect privacy interests.

Dissemination and Information Sharing

The international community has recognized the critical importance of sharing terrorism information. For example, UNSCR 1373 calls upon all States to find ways to intensify and accelerate the exchange of operational terrorism information and to exchange information to prevent the commission of terrorist acts. Similarly, section 6 of Executive Order 13224 requires the Secretary of the Treasury (and other officials) to make all relevant efforts to cooperate and coordinate with other countries to achieve the objectives of the Order, including preventing and suppressing acts of terrorism, denying financing and financial services to terrorists, and sharing intelligence about funding activities in support of terrorism. It is against this backdrop that information derived from the SWIFT data is appropriately shared with domestic and international partners. As is true with all other facets of the TFTP, this information-sharing is in accordance with US law and subject to a series of safeguards that are designed to protect the SWIFT data and the privacy interests of the persons to whom it may pertain.

The counterterrorism analysts conducting TFTP searches verify the relevance of any information produced in response to a search before that information is prepared for dissemination through secure channels. The Treasury Department also exercises originator control on any subsequent dissemination of the information, meaning that no recipient is permitted to further disseminate the information without the Treasury Department's express approval. In that regard, as with any unauthorized access to the SWIFT data, any unauthorized disclosure of TFTP-derived information may result in strict disciplinary action or the imposition of civil or criminal penalties.

Information derived from the SWIFT data is shared under strict controls with other US agencies in the intelligence and law enforcement communities to be used exclusively for the purpose of investigating, detecting, preventing, and/or prosecuting terrorism or its financing or related follow-on investigations and prosecutions. This sharing is mandated by the National Security Act, the Intelligence Reform and Terrorism Prevention Act of 2004, and a series of Memoranda of Understanding and related Executive orders. The recipient agencies have the same obligations under US law as the Treasury Department to protect TFTP-derived information. It is also important to note that TFTP-derived information is shared with other US agencies for lead purposes only, which limits its use as affirmative evidence in legal proceedings. Recipient agencies use their own, existing legal authorities to pursue their investigations, including to obtain documentation from other sources that could later be used as evidence in legal proceedings.

These other government agencies also share lead information derived from the SWIFT data with their foreign counterparts for the same purposes, with case-by-case approval from the Treasury Department when justified by national security and law enforcement interests. Many TFTP-derived leads have been shared with foreign authorities, as a general matter without revealing the TFTP as the source.

As for possible public dissemination of SWIFT data, the Treasury Department treats the data as classified, law enforcement sensitive, business confidential information. Accordingly, the Treasury Department does not and would not make the data publicly available unless required to do so by law. In that regard, the Treasury Department will take the position in connection with any administrative or judicial proceeding arising out of a Freedom of Information Act (FOIA) request from third parties for TFTP data, that such records are exempt from disclosure under FOIA.

Redress

The confined nature of the data in an individual SWIFT transaction message, the restricted manner in which certain SWIFT data can be accessed through the TFTP as part of a preexisting investigation of terrorism, and the limits on dissemination as lead information significantly reduce the pertinence of a redress mechanism as part of the TFTP itself. That notwithstanding, appropriate redress for possible misuse by governmental authorities is available under US law.

With regard to an interest of a specific natural person about the use of data and the ability to seek redress for possible misuse, a distinction must be made between the searchable data submitted by SWIFT and messages extracted as part of a targeted terrorism investigation that may serve as the basis for an administrative decision or other governmental action. The data received from SWIFT under compulsion of OFAC subpoenas consist of copies of completed financial transaction messages, *i.e.*, electronic copies of business records maintained at SWIFT's US facility in the ordinary course of business. Though this data may undergo some processing in the sense of the very restricted counterterrorism search-and-retrieval capacity described herein, there is no alteration, manipulation, addition or deletion of data within individual transaction messages within the searchable database.

Additionally, it is again important to emphasize that the vast majority of the transaction messages provided by SWIFT will never be viewed even by counterterrorism analysts, and thus are not known. Consequently, responding to a privacy-related inquiry from a natural person as to whether information about that individual is included in the database would require, in almost all instances, accessing data that would never be accessed in the normal operation of the TFTP. Such access would be inconsistent with the TFTP requirement that every search have a preexisting nexus to terrorism. Finally, because there is no alteration, manipulation, deletion or addition of the data within the searchable database, there exists no basis to "rectify" any information. Moreover, this would serve to alter the completed business records sought by the OFAC subpoena.

Further processing of the data in an individual transaction message will only occur with respect to the relatively few individual transaction messages directly responsive to a targeted terrorism search that are extracted from the search database. Once extracted and subject to the multiple controls limiting dissemination for counterterrorism purposes, redress for alleged misuse could properly be sought following the appropriate administrative and judicial procedures with respect to the government's acting upon that disseminated information.

The opportunity for redress can be illustrated as follows with respect to an administrative action taken by OFAC to block property under the Global Terrorism Sanctions Regulations that implement Executive Order 13224. A person may seek administrative reconsideration by OFAC of his or her designation as a specially designated global terrorist, whereby that person is given the opportunity to demonstrate that "the circumstances resulting in the designation no longer apply" and to "submit arguments or evidence that the person believes establishes that an insufficient basis exists for the designation." A specially designated global terrorist also may seek judicial review of an agency's decision under relevant provisions of the Administrative Procedure Act. These administrative and judicial avenues to seek redress would apply to any person that is the object of the government decision, regardless of nationality.

Retention Period

The period of time for retention of counterterrorism (and any other) information is a function of numerous, well-established factors, including investigative requirements, applicable statutes of limitation, and regulatory limits for claims or prosecution. The applicability and operation of these and other factors vary from agency to agency, depending on the nature of the agency's specific duties and missions. Accordingly, the retention periods for certain types of terrorism-related information compiled by various agencies depend on the nature of the information and the investigation to which it relates.

Within the US Government, retention and disposition schedules for agency records are approved by the National Archives and Records Administration (NARA) pursuant to various statutes and regulations. All records not deemed to have permanent value must be scheduled for destruction after a specified period of time based on explained administrative, fiscal, and legal values. Factors considered by NARA in approving an agency's record retention periods include applicable statutes of limitation; regulatory limits for claims or prosecution; the potential for fraud; litigation risks and substantive rights; and statutes or regulations granting or limiting a specific legal right.

With regard to a period of time for retention of TFTP-related information, a distinction again must be made between the data subpoenaed from SWIFT and the extracted data that serve as the basis for an administrative decision or other governmental action.

The Treasury Department will endeavour on an ongoing and at least annual basis to identify and delete all non-extracted data that are not necessary for the execution of purposes referred to in these Representations. Subject to the results of the above-mentioned necessity-based analysis, all non-extracted data received by the Treasury Department from SWIFT after the date of publication of these Representations will be deleted by the Treasury Department not later than five years after receipt by the Treasury Department. Subject to the results of the above-mentioned necessity-based analysis, all other non-extracted data will be deleted not later than five years after the date of publication of these Representations.

Extracted data directly responsive to a targeted terrorism search that have been subjected to the multiple dissemination controls described above for counterterrorism purposes, shall be subject to the retention period applicable to the particular government authority with respect to its particular investigative records.

For example, SWIFT data extracted through the TFTP could be used in the investigation of an individual for possible designation under OFAC's Global Terrorism Sanctions Regulations. Under OFAC's NARA-approved record retention schedule, if a final administrative decision is made to designate an individual (which decision would be made public), the information on which the decision was made will be retained permanently as a written record of the evidence supporting the agency's action. The evidentiary file is retained for possible administrative or judicial review in the event a designation is challenged, and also to support further terrorism investigations. Alternatively, if an investigation is closed without a designation, the investigatory files are subject to on-site destruction no later than one year after the investigation is completed.

Finally, consistent with the above-described US legal framework, the retention period for lead information derived from the TFTP that has been disseminated is governed by the regulations and schedules of the recipient agency or government. For example, any derived information that is used in a Justice Department prosecution will be subject to applicable Justice Department retention periods.

Ongoing Counterterrorism Cooperation

The TFTP has been of great value in fighting terrorism globally, including in Europe. The US Government will continue to judiciously assess whether any information obtained through the TFTP may contribute to the investigation, prevention, combating or prosecution of terrorism or its financing in one or more European Union Member States and, in all appropriate cases, will make that information available to the proper authorities in the most expedient manner.

As a sign of our commitment and partnership in combating global terrorism, an eminent European person will be appointed to confirm that the program is implemented consistent with these Representations for the purpose of verifying the protection of EU-originating personal data. In particular, the eminent person will monitor that processes for deletion of non-extracted data have been carried out.

The eminent person will have appropriate experience and security clearances, and will be appointed for a renewable period of two years by the European Commission in consultation with the Treasury Department. The eminent person shall act in complete independence in the performance of his or her duties. The eminent person shall, in the performance of his or her duties, neither seek nor take instructions from anybody. The eminent person shall refrain from any action incompatible with his or her duties under this appointment.

The eminent person will report his or her findings and conclusions annually in writing to the Commission. The Commission in turn will report to the European Parliament and the Council as appropriate.

The Treasury Department will give the eminent person access, information and data necessary for the discharge of his or her duties. The eminent person will at all times act in compliance with secrecy and confidentiality requirements imposed by law. Practical details will be agreed with the Treasury Department.

The Treasury Department also will advise the European Union of any material changes to the safeguards set forth in these representations and of the passage of any US legislation that materially affects the statements made in the Representations.

The Treasury Department will endeavor to have these Representations published in the Federal Register and consents to their publication in the Official Journal of the European Union.

DOCUMENT NO. 21

EC REGULATION 1889/2005 OF 26 OCTOBER 2005 ON CONTROLS OF CASH ENTERING OR LEAVING THE COMMUNITY

THE EUROPEAN PARLIAMENT AND THE COUNCIL OF THE EUROPEAN UNION,

Having regard to the Treaty establishing the European Community, and in particular Articles 95 and 135 thereof,

Having regard to the proposal from the Commission,[1]

[1] OJ C 227 E, 24.9.2002, p. 574.

After consulting the European Economic and Social Committee,

Acting in accordance with the procedure referred to in Article 251 of the Treaty,[2]

[2] Opinion of the European Parliament of 15 May 2003 (OJ C 67 E, 17.3.2004, p. 259), Council Common Position of 17 February 2005 (OJ C 144 E, 14.6.2005, p. 1) and Position of the European Parliament of 8 June 2005. Council Decision of 12 July 2005.

Whereas:

(1) One of the Community's tasks is to promote harmonious, balanced and sustainable development of economic activities throughout the Community by establishing a common market and an economic and monetary union. To that end the internal market comprises an area without internal frontiers in which the free movement of goods, persons, services and capital is ensured.

(2) The introduction of the proceeds of illegal activities into the financial system and their investment after laundering are detrimental to sound and sustainable economic development. Accordingly, Council Directive 91/308/EEC of 10 June 1991 on prevention of the use of the financial system for the purpose of money laundering[1] introduced a

[1] OJ L 166, 28.6.1991, p. 77. Directive as amended by Directive 2001/97/EC of the European Parliament and of the Council (OJ L 344, 28.12.2001, p. 76).

Community mechanism to prevent money laundering by monitoring transactions through credit and financial institutions and certain types of professions. As there is a risk that the application of that mechanism will lead to an increase in cash movements for illicit purposes, Directive 91/308/EEC should be supplemented by a control system on cash entering or leaving the Community.

(3) At present such control systems are applied by only a few Member States, acting under national legislation. The disparities in legislation are detrimental to the proper functioning of the internal market. The basic elements should therefore be harmonised at Community level to ensure an equivalent level of control on movements of cash crossing the borders of the Community. Such harmonisation should not, however, affect the possibility for Member States to apply, in accordance with the existing provisions of the Treaty, national controls on movements of cash within the Community.

(4) Account should also be taken of complementary activities carried out in other international fora, in particular those of the Financial Action Task Force on Money Laundering (FATF), which was established by the G-7 Summit held in Paris in 1989. Special Recommendation IX of 22 October 2004 of the FATF calls on governments to take measures to detect physical cash movements, including a declaration system or other disclosure obligation.

(5) Accordingly, cash carried by any natural person entering or leaving the Community should be subject to the principle of obligatory declaration. This principle would enable the customs authorities to gather information on such cash movements and, where appropriate, transmit that information to other authorities. Customs authorities are present at the borders of the Community, where controls are most effective, and some have already built up practical experience in the matter. Use should be made of Council Regulation (EC) No 515/97 of 13 March 1997 on mutual assistance between the administrative authorities of the Member States and cooperation between the latter and the Commission to ensure the correct application of the law on customs and agricultural matters.[1] This mutual assistance should ensure both the correct application of cash controls and the transmission of information that might help to achieve the objectives of Directive 91/308/EEC.

[1] OJ L 82, 22.3.1997, p. 1. Regulation as amended by Regulation (EC) No 807/2003 (OJ L 122, 16.5.2003, p. 36).

(6) In view of its preventive purpose and deterrent character, the obligation to declare should be fulfilled upon entering or leaving the Community. However, in order to focus the authorities' action on significant movements of cash, only those movements of EUR

10 000 or more should be subject to such an obligation. Also, it should be specified that the obligation to declare applies to the natural person carrying the cash, regardless of whether that person is the owner.

(7) Use should be made of a common standard for the information to be provided. This will enable competent authorities to exchange information more easily.

(8) It is desirable to establish the definitions needed for a uniform interpretation of this Regulation.

(9) Information gathered under this Regulation by the competent authorities should be passed on to the authorities referred to in Article 6(1) of Directive 91/308/EEC.

(10) Directive 95/46/EC of the European Parliament and of the Council of 24 October 1995 on the protection of individuals with regard to the processing of personal data and on the free movement of such data[1] and Regulation (EC) No 45/2001 of the European Parliament and of the Council of 18 December 2000 on the protection of individuals with regard to the processing of personal data by the Community institutions and bodies and on the free movement of such data[2] apply to the processing of personal data by the competent authorities of the Member States pursuant to this Regulation.

[1] OJ L 281, 23.11.1995, p. 31. Directive as amended by Regulation (EC) No 1882/2003 (OJ L284, 31.10.2003, p. 1).
[2] OJ L 8, 12.1.2001, p. 1.

(11) Where there are indications that the sums of cash are related to any illegal activity, associated with the movement of cash, as referred to in Directive 91/308/EEC, information gathered under this Regulation by the competent authorities may be passed on to competent authorities in other Member States and/or to the Commission. Similarly, provision should be made for certain information to be transmitted whenever there are indications of cash movements involving sums lower than the threshold laid down in this Regulation.

(12) Competent authorities should be vested with the powers needed to exercise effective control on movements of cash.

(13) The powers of the competent authorities should be supplemented by an obligation on the Member States to lay down penalties. However, penalties should be imposed only for failure to make a declaration in accordance with this Regulation.

(14) Since the objective of this Regulation cannot be sufficiently achieved by the Member States and can therefore, by reason of the transnational

scale of money laundering in the internal market, be better achieved at Community level, the Community may adopt measures, in accordance with the principle of subsidiarity as set out in Article 5 of the Treaty. In accordance with the principle of proportionality, as set out in that Article, this Regulation does not go beyond what is necessary in order to achieve that objective.

(15) This Regulation respects the fundamental rights and observes the principles recognised in Article 6(2) of the Treaty on European Union and reflected in the Charter of Fundamental Rights of the European Union, in particular in Article 8 thereof,

HAVE ADOPTED THIS REGULATION:

Article 1
Objective

1. This Regulation complements the provisions of Directive 91/308/EEC concerning transactions through financial and credit institutions and certain professions by laying down harmonised rules for the control, by the competent authorities, of cash entering or leaving the Community.

2. This Regulation shall be without prejudice to national measures to control cash movements within the Community, where such measures are taken in accordance with Article 58 of the Treaty.

Article 2
Definitions

For the purposes of this Regulation:

1) "competent authorities" means the customs authorities of the Member States or any other authorities empowered by Member States to apply this Regulation;

2) "cash" means:

(a) bearer negotiable instruments including monetary instruments in bearer form such as travellers cheques, negotiable instruments (including cheques, promissory notes and money orders) that are either in bearer form, endorsed without restriction, made out to a fictitious payee, or otherwise in such form that title thereto passes upon delivery and incomplete instruments (including cheques, promissory notes and money orders) signed, but with the payee's name omitted;

(b) currency (banknotes and coins that are in circulation as a medium of exchange).

Article 3
Obligation to Declare

1. Any natural person entering or leaving the Community and carrying cash of a value of EUR 10 000 or more shall declare that sum to the competent authorities of the Member State through which he is entering or leaving the Community in accordance with this Regulation. The obligation to declare shall not have been fulfilled if the information provided is incorrect or incomplete.
2. The declaration referred to in paragraph 1 shall contain details of:
   (a) the declarant, including full name, date and place of birth and nationality;
   (b) the owner of the cash;
   (c) the intended recipient of the cash;
   (d) the amount and nature of the cash;
   (e) the provenance and intended use of the cash;
   (f) the transport route;
   (g) the means of transport.
3. Information shall be provided in writing, orally or electronically, to be determined by the Member State referred to in paragraph 1. However, where the declarant so requests, he shall be entitled to provide the information in writing. Where a written declaration has been lodged, an endorsed copy shall be delivered to the declarant upon request.

Article 4
Powers of the Competent Authorities

1. In order to check compliance with the obligation to declare laid down in Article 3, officials of the competent authorities shall be empowered, in accordance with the conditions laid down under national legislation, to carry out controls on natural persons, their baggage and their means of transport.
2. In the event of failure to comply with the obligation to declare laid down in Article 3, cash may be detained by administrative decision in accordance with the conditions laid down under national legislation.

Article 5
Recording and Processing of Information

1. The information obtained under Article 3 and/or Article 4 shall be recorded and processed by the competent authorities of the Member State referred to in Article 3(1) and shall be made available to the authorities referred to in Article 6(1) of Directive 91/308/EEC of that Member State.

2. Where it appears from the controls provided for in Article 4 that a natural person is entering or leaving the Community with sums of cash lower than the threshold fixed in Article 3 and where there are indications of illegal activities associated with the movement of cash, as referred to in Directive 91/308/EEC, that information, the full name, date and place of birth and nationality of that person and details of the means of transport used may also be recorded and processed by the competent authorities of the Member State referred to in Article 3(1) and be made available to the authorities referred to in Article 6(1) of Directive 91/308/EEC of that Member State.

Article 6
Exchange of Information

1. Where there are indications that the sums of cash are related to any illegal activity associated with the movement of cash, as referred to in Directive 91/308/EEC, the information obtained through the declaration provided for in Article 3 or the controls provided for in Article 4 may be transmitted to competent authorities in other Member States.

   Regulation (EC) No 515/97 shall apply mutatis mutandis.

2. Where there are indications that the sums of cash involve the proceeds of fraud or any other illegal activity adversely affecting the financial interests of the Community, the information shall also be transmitted to the Commission.

Article 7
Exchange of Information with Third Countries

In the framework of mutual administrative assistance, the information obtained under this Regulation may be communicated by Member States or by the Commission to a third country, subject to the consent of the competent authorities which obtained the information pursuant to Article 3 and/or Article 4 and to compliance with the relevant national and Community provisions on the transfer of personal data to third countries. Member States shall notify the Commission of such exchanges of information where particularly relevant for the implementation of this Regulation.

Article 8
Duty of Professional Secrecy

All information which is by nature confidential or which is provided on a confidential basis shall be covered by the duty of professional secrecy. It shall not be disclosed by the competent authorities without the express permission of the person or authority providing it. The communication of information shall, however, be permitted where the competent authorities are obliged to do so pursuant to the provisions in force, particularly in connection with legal proceedings. Any disclosure or communication of information shall fully comply with prevailing data protection provisions, in particular Directive 95/46/EC and Regulation (EC) No 45/2001.

Article 9
Penalties

1. Each Member State shall introduce penalties to apply in the event of failure to comply with the obligation to declare laid down in Article 3. Such penalties shall be effective, proportionate and dissuasive.
2. By . . .,* Member States shall notify the Commission of the penalties applicable in the event of failure to comply with the obligation to declare laid down in Article 3.

* 18 months after the date of entry into force of this Regulation.

Article 10
Evaluation

The Commission shall submit to the European Parliament and the Council a report on the application of this Regulation four years after its entry into force.

Article 11
Entry into Force

This Regulation shall enter into force on the twentieth day following that of its publication in the Official Journal of the European Union.

It shall apply from . . . .*

* 18 months after the date of entry into force of this Regulation.

This Regulation shall be binding in its entirety and directly applicable in all Member States.

Done at Strasbourg,

For the European Parliament	*For the Council*
The President	*The President*

DOCUMENT NO. 22

EC DIRECTIVE 2005/60 OF 26 OCTOBER 2005 ON THE PREVENTION OF THE USE OF THE FINANCIAL SYSTEM FOR THE PURPOSE OF MONEY LAUNDERING AND TERRORIST FINANCING

THE EUROPEAN PARLIAMENT AND THE COUNCIL OF THE EUROPEAN UNION,

Having regard to the Treaty establishing the European Community, and in particular Article 47(2), first and third sentences, and Article 95 thereof,

Having regard to the proposal from the Commission,

Having regard to the Opinion of the European Economic and Social Committee,[1]

[1] Opinion delivered on 11 May 2005 (not yet published in the Official Journal).

Having regard to the Opinion of the European Central Bank,[2]

[2] OJ C 40, 17.2.2005, p. 9.

Acting in accordance with the procedure laid down in Article 251 of the Treaty,[3]

[3] Opinion of the European Parliament of 26 May 2005 (not yet published in the Official Journal) and Council Decision of 19 September 2005.

Whereas:

(1) Massive flows of dirty money can damage the stability and reputation of the financial sector and threaten the single market, and terrorism shakes the very foundations of our society. In addition to the criminal law approach, a preventive effort via the financial system can produce results.

(2) The soundness, integrity and stability of credit and financial institutions and confidence in the financial system as a whole could be seriously jeopardised by the efforts of criminals and their associates either to disguise the origin of criminal proceeds or to channel lawful or unlawful money for terrorist purposes. In order to avoid Member States' adopting measures to protect their financial systems which could be inconsistent with the functioning of the internal market and with the prescriptions of the rule of law and Community public policy, Community action in this area is necessary.

(3) In order to facilitate their criminal activities, money launderers and terrorist financers could try to take advantage of the freedom of capital movements and the freedom to supply financial services which the integrated financial area entails, if certain coordinating measures are not adopted at Community level.

(4) In order to respond to these concerns in the field of money laundering, Council Directive 91/308/EEC of 10 June 1991 on prevention of the use of the financial system for the purpose of money laundering[1] was adopted. It required Member States to prohibit money laundering and to oblige the financial sector, comprising credit institutions and a wide range of other financial institutions, to identify their customers, keep appropriate records, establish internal procedures to train staff and guard against money laundering and to report any indications of money laundering to the competent authorities.

[1] OJ L 166, 28.6.1991, p. 77. Directive as amended by Directive 2001/97/EC of the European Parliament and of the Council (OJ L 344, 28.12.2001, p. 76).

(5) Money laundering and terrorist financing are frequently carried out in an international context. Measures adopted solely at national or even Community level, without taking account of international coordination and cooperation, would have very limited effects. The measures adopted by the Community in this field should therefore be consistent with other action undertaken in other international fora. The Community action should continue to take particular account of the Recommendations of the Financial Action Task Force (hereinafter referred to as the "FATF"), which constitutes the foremost international body active in the fight against money laundering and terrorist financing. Since the FATF Recommendations were substantially revised and expanded in 2003, this Directive should be in line with that new international standard.

(6) The General Agreement on Trade in Services (GATS) allows Members to adopt measures necessary to protect public morals and prevent fraud and adopt measures for prudential reasons, including for ensuring the stability and integrity of the financial system.

(7) Although initially limited to drugs offences, there has been a trend in recent years towards a much wider definition of money laundering based on a broader range of predicate offences. A wider range of predicate offences facilitates the reporting of suspicious transactions and international cooperation in this area. Therefore, the definition of serious crime should be brought into line with the definition of serious crime in Council Framework Decision 2001/500/JHA of 26 June 2001 on money laundering, the identification, tracing, freezing, seizing and confiscation of instrumentalities and the proceeds of crime.[1]

[1] OJ L 182, 5.7.2001, p. 1.

(8) Furthermore, the misuse of the financial system to channel criminal or even clean money to terrorist purposes poses a clear risk to the integrity, proper functioning, reputation and stability of the financial system. Accordingly, the preventive measures of this Directive should cover not only the manipulation of money derived from crime but also the collection of money or property for terrorist purposes.

(9) Directive 91/308/EEC, though imposing a customer identification obligation, contained relatively little detail on the relevant procedures. In view of the crucial importance of this aspect of the prevention of money laundering and terrorist financing, it is appropriate, in accordance with the new international standards, to introduce more specific and detailed provisions relating to the identification of the customer and of any beneficial owner and the verification of their identity. To that end a precise definition of "beneficial owner" is essential. Where the individual beneficiaries of a legal entity or arrangement such as a foundation or trust are yet to be determined, and it is therefore impossible to identify an individual as the beneficial owner, it would suffice to identify the class of persons intended to be the beneficiaries of the foundation or trust. This requirement should not include the identification of the individuals within that class of persons.

(10) The institutions and persons covered by this Directive should, in conformity with this Directive, identify and verify the identity of the beneficial owner. To fulfil this requirement, it should be left to those institutions and persons whether they make use of public records of beneficial owners, ask their clients for relevant data or obtain the information otherwise, taking into account the fact that the extent of such customer due diligence measures relates to the risk of money laundering and terrorist financing, which depends on the type of customer, business relationship, product or transaction.

(11) Credit agreements in which the credit account serves exclusively to settle the loan and the repayment of the loan is effected from an account which was opened in the name of the customer with a credit institution covered by this Directive pursuant to Article 8(1)(a) to (c) should generally be considered as an example of types of less risky transactions.

(12) To the extent that the providers of the property of a legal entity or arrangement have significant control over the use of the property they should be identified as a beneficial owner.

(13) Trust relationships are widely used in commercial products as an internationally recognised feature of the comprehensively supervised wholesale financial markets. An obligation to identify the beneficial owner does not arise from the fact alone that there is a trust relationship in this particular case.

(14) This Directive should also apply to those activities of the institutions and persons covered hereunder which are performed on the Internet.

(15) As the tightening of controls in the financial sector has prompted money launderers and terrorist financers to seek alternative methods for concealing the origin of the proceeds of crime and as such channels can be used for terrorist financing, the anti-money laundering and anti-terrorist financing obligations should cover life insurance intermediaries and trust and company service providers.

(16) Entities already falling under the legal responsibility of an insurance undertaking, and therefore falling within the scope of this Directive, should not be included within the category of insurance intermediary.

(17) Acting as a company director or secretary does not of itself make someone a trust and company service provider. For that reason, the definition covers only those persons that act as a company director or secretary for a third party and by way of business.

(18) The use of large cash payments has repeatedly proven to be very vulnerable to money laundering and terrorist financing. Therefore, in those Member States that allow cash payments above the established threshold, all natural or legal persons trading in goods by way of business should be covered by this Directive when accepting such cash payments. Dealers in high-value goods, such as precious stones or metals, or works of art, and auctioneers are in any event covered by this Directive to the extent that payments to them are made in cash in an amount of EUR 15 000 or more. To ensure effective monitoring of compliance with this Directive by that potentially wide group of institutions and persons, Member States may focus

their monitoring activities in particular on those natural and legal persons trading in goods that are exposed to a relatively high risk of money laundering or terrorist financing, in accordance with the principle of risk-based supervision. In view of the different situations in the various Member States, Member States may decide to adopt stricter provisions, in order to properly address the risk involved with large cash payments.

(19) Directive 91/308/EEC brought notaries and other independent legal professionals within the scope of the Community anti-money laundering regime; this coverage should be maintained unchanged in this Directive; these legal professionals, as defined by the Member States, are subject to the provisions of this Directive when participating in financial or corporate transactions, including providing tax advice, where there is the greatest risk of the services of those legal professionals being misused for the purpose of laundering the proceeds of criminal activity or for the purpose of terrorist financing.

(20) Where independent members of professions providing legal advice which are legally recognised and controlled, such as lawyers, are ascertaining the legal position of a client or representing a client in legal proceedings, it would not be appropriate under this Directive to put those legal professionals in respect of these activities under an obligation to report suspicions of money laundering or terrorist financing. There must be exemptions from any obligation to report information obtained either before, during or after judicial proceedings, or in the course of ascertaining the legal position for a client. Thus, legal advice shall remain subject to the obligation of professional secrecy unless the legal counsellor is taking part in money laundering or terrorist financing, the legal advice is provided for money laundering or terrorist financing purposes or the lawyer knows that the client is seeking legal advice for money laundering or terrorist financing purposes.

(21) Directly comparable services need to be treated in the same manner when provided by any of the professionals covered by this Directive. In order to ensure the respect of the rights laid down in the European Convention for the Protection of Human Rights and Fundamental Freedoms and the Treaty on European Union, in the case of auditors, external accountants and tax advisors, who, in some Member States, may defend or represent a client in the context of judicial proceedings or ascertain a client's legal position, the information they obtain in the performance of those tasks should not be subject to the reporting obligations in accordance with this Directive.

(22) It should be recognised that the risk of money laundering and terrorist financing is not the same in every case. In line with a risk-based approach, the principle should be introduced into Community legislation that simplified customer due diligence is allowed in appropriate cases.

(23) The derogation concerning the identification of beneficial owners of pooled accounts held by notaries or other independent legal professionals should be without prejudice to the obligations that those notaries or other independent legal professionals have pursuant to this Directive. Those obligations include the need for such notaries or other independent legal professionals themselves to identify the beneficial owners of the pooled accounts held by them.

(24) Equally, Community legislation should recognise that certain situations present a greater risk of money laundering or terrorist financing. Although the identity and business profile of all customers should be established, there are cases where particularly rigorous customer identification and verification procedures are required.

(25) This is particularly true of business relationships with individuals holding, or having held, important public positions, particularly those from countries where corruption is widespread. Such relationships may expose the financial sector in particular to significant reputational and/or legal risks. The international effort to combat corruption also justifies the need to pay special attention to such cases and to apply the complete normal customer due diligence measures in respect of domestic politically exposed persons or enhanced customer due diligence measures in respect of politically exposed persons residing in another Member State or in a third country.

(26) Obtaining approval from senior management for establishing business relationships should not imply obtaining approval from the board of directors but from the immediate higher level of the hierarchy of the person seeking such approval.

(27) In order to avoid repeated customer identification procedures, leading to delays and inefficiency in business, it is appropriate, subject to suitable safeguards, to allow customers to be introduced whose identification has been carried out elsewhere. Where an institution or person covered by this Directive relies on a third party, the ultimate responsibility for the customer due diligence procedure remains with the institution or person to whom the customer is introduced. The third party, or introducer, also retains his own responsibility for all the requirements in this Directive, including the requirement to report suspicious transactions and maintain

records, to the extent that he has a relationship with the customer that is covered by this Directive.

(28) In the case of agency or outsourcing relationships on a contractual basis between institutions or persons covered by this Directive and external natural or legal persons not covered hereby, any anti-money laundering and anti-terrorist financing obligations for those agents or outsourcing service providers as part of the institutions or persons covered by this Directive, may only arise from contract and not from this Directive. The responsibility for complying with this Directive should remain with the institution or person covered hereby.

(29) Suspicious transactions should be reported to the financial intelligence unit (FIU), which serves as a national centre for receiving, analysing and disseminating to the competent authorities suspicious transaction reports and other information regarding potential money laundering or terrorist financing. This should not compel Member States to change their existing reporting systems where the reporting is done through a public prosecutor or other law enforcement authorities, as long as the information is forwarded promptly and unfiltered to FIUs, allowing them to conduct their business properly, including international cooperation with other FIUs.

(30) By way of derogation from the general prohibition on executing suspicious transactions, the institutions and persons covered by this Directive may execute suspicious transactions before informing the competent authorities, where refraining from the execution thereof is impossible or likely to frustrate efforts to pursue the beneficiaries of a suspected money laundering or terrorist financing operation. This, however, should be without prejudice to the international obligations accepted by the Member States to freeze without delay funds or other assets of terrorists, terrorist organisations or those who finance terrorism, in accordance with the relevant United Nations Security Council resolutions.

(31) Where a Member State decides to make use of the exemptions provided for in Article 23(2), it may allow or require the self-regulatory body representing the persons referred to therein not to transmit to the FIU any information obtained from those persons in the circumstances referred to in that Article.

(32) There has been a number of cases of employees who report their suspicions of money laundering being subjected to threats or hostile action. Although this Directive cannot interfere with Member States' judicial procedures, this is a crucial issue for the effectiveness of the anti-money laundering and anti-terrorist financing system.

Member States should be aware of this problem and should do whatever they can to protect employees from such threats or hostile action.

(33) Disclosure of information as referred to in Article 28 should be in accordance with the rules on transfer of personal data to third countries as laid down in Directive 95/46/EC of the European Parliament and of the Council of 24 October 1995 on the protection of individuals with regard to the processing of personal data and on the free movement of such data.[1] Moreover, Article 28 cannot interfere with national data protection and professional secrecy legislation.

[1] OJ L 281, 23.11.1995, p. 31. Directive as amended by Regulation (EC) No 1882/2003 (OJ L 284, 31.10.2003, p. 1).

(34) Persons who merely convert paper documents into electronic data and are acting under a contract with a credit institution or a financial institution do not fall within the scope of this Directive, nor does any natural or legal person that provides credit or financial institutions solely with a message or other support systems for transmitting funds or with clearing and settlement systems.

(35) Money laundering and terrorist financing are international problems and the effort to combat them should be global. Where Community credit and financial institutions have branches and subsidiaries located in third countries where the legislation in this area is deficient, they should, in order to avoid the application of very different standards within an institution or group of institutions, apply the Community standard or notify the competent authorities of the home Member State if this application is impossible.

(36) It is important that credit and financial institutions should be able to respond rapidly to requests for information on whether they maintain business relationships with named persons. For the purpose of identifying such business relationships in order to be able to provide that information quickly, credit and financial institutions should have effective systems in place which are commensurate with the size and nature of their business. In particular it would be appropriate for credit institutions and larger financial institutions to have electronic systems at their disposal. This provision is of particular importance in the context of procedures leading to measures such as the freezing or seizing of assets (including terrorist assets), pursuant to applicable national or Community legislation with a view to combating terrorism.

(37) This Directive establishes detailed rules for customer due diligence, including enhanced customer due diligence for high-risk customers or

business relationships, such as appropriate procedures to determine whether a person is a politically exposed person, and certain additional, more detailed requirements, such as the existence of compliance management procedures and policies. All these requirements are to be met by each of the institutions and persons covered by this Directive, while Member States are expected to tailor the detailed implementation of those provisions to the particularities of the various professions and to the differences in scale and size of the institutions and persons covered by this Directive.

(38) In order to ensure that the institutions and others subject to Community legislation in this field remain committed, feedback should, where practicable, be made available to them on the usefulness and follow-up of the reports they present. To make this possible, and to be able to review the effectiveness of their systems to combat money laundering and terrorist financing Member States should keep and improve the relevant statistics.

(39) When registering or licensing a currency exchange office, a trust and company service provider or a casino nationally, competent authorities should ensure that the persons who effectively direct or will direct the business of such entities and the beneficial owners of such entities are fit and proper persons. The criteria for determining whether or not a person is fit and proper should be established in conformity with national law. As a minimum, such criteria should reflect the need to protect such entities from being misused by their managers or beneficial owners for criminal purposes.

(40) Taking into account the international character of money laundering and terrorist financing, coordination and cooperation between FIUs as referred to in Council Decision 2000/642/JHA of 17 October 2000 concerning arrangements for cooperation between financial intelligence units of the Member States in respect of exchanging information,[1] including the establishment of an EU FIU-net, should be encouraged to the greatest possible extent. To that end, the Commission should lend such assistance as may be needed to facilitate such coordination, including financial assistance.

[1] OJ L 271, 24.10.2000, p. 4.

(41) The importance of combating money laundering and terrorist financing should lead Member States to lay down effective, proportionate and dissuasive penalties in national law for failure to respect the national provisions adopted pursuant to this Directive. Provision should be made for penalties in respect of natural and legal persons. Since legal persons are often involved in complex money laundering

or terrorist financing operations, sanctions should also be adjusted in line with the activity carried on by legal persons.

(42) Natural persons exercising any of the activities referred to in Article 2(1)(3)(a) and (b) within the structure of a legal person, but on an independent basis, should be independently responsible for compliance with the provisions of this Directive, with the exception of Article 35.

(43) Clarification of the technical aspects of the rules laid down in this Directive may be necessary to ensure an effective and sufficiently consistent implementation of this Directive, taking into account the different financial instruments, professions and risks in the different Member States and the technical developments in the fight against money laundering and terrorist financing. The Commission should accordingly be empowered to adopt implementing measures, such as certain criteria for identifying low and high risk situations in which simplified due diligence could suffice or enhanced due diligence would be appropriate, provided that they do not modify the essential elements of this Directive and provided that the Commission acts in accordance with the principles set out herein, after consulting the Committee on the Prevention of Money Laundering and Terrorist Financing.

(44) The measures necessary for the implementation of this Directive should be adopted in accordance with Council Decision 1999/468/EC of 28 June 1999 laying down the procedures for the exercise of implementing powers conferred on the Commission.[1] To that end a new Committee on the Prevention of Money Laundering and Terrorist Financing, replacing the Money Laundering Contact Committee set up by Directive 91/308/EEC, should be established.

[1] OJ L 184, 17.7.1999, p. 23.

(45) In view of the very substantial amendments that would need to be made to Directive 91/308/EEC, it should be repealed for reasons of clarity.

(46) Since the objective of this Directive, namely the prevention of the use of the financial system for the purpose of money laundering and terrorist financing, cannot be sufficiently achieved by the Member States and can therefore, by reason of the scale and effects of the action, be better achieved at Community level, the Community may adopt measures, in accordance with the principle of subsidiarity as set out in Article 5 of the Treaty. In accordance with the principle of proportionality, as set out in that Article, this Directive does not go beyond what is necessary in order to achieve that objective.

(47) In exercising its implementing powers in accordance with this Directive, the Commission should respect the following principles: the need for high levels of transparency and consultation with institutions and persons covered by this Directive and with the European Parliament and the Council; the need to ensure that competent authorities will be able to ensure compliance with the rules consistently; the balance of costs and benefits to institutions and persons covered by this Directive on a long-term basis in any implementing measures; the need to respect the necessary flexibility in the application of the implementing measures in accordance with a risk-sensitive approach; the need to ensure coherence with other Community legislation in this area; the need to protect the Community, its Member States and their citizens from the consequences of money laundering and terrorist financing.

(48) This Directive respects the fundamental rights and observes the principles recognised in particular by the Charter of Fundamental Rights of the European Union. Nothing in this Directive should be interpreted or implemented in a manner that is inconsistent with the European Convention on Human Rights,

HAVE ADOPTED THIS DIRECTIVE:

Chapter I
Subject-matter, Scope and Definitions

Article 1

1. Member States shall ensure that money laundering and terrorist financing are prohibited.
2. For the purposes of this Directive, the following conduct, when committed intentionally, shall be regarded as money laundering:
   (a) the conversion or transfer of property, knowing that such property is derived from criminal activity or from an act of participation in such activity, for the purpose of concealing or disguising the illicit origin of the property or of assisting any person who is involved in the commission of such activity to evade the legal consequences of his action;
   (b) the concealment or disguise of the true nature, source, location, disposition, movement, rights with respect to, or ownership of property, knowing that such property is derived from criminal activity or from an act of participation in such activity;
   (c) the acquisition, possession or use of property, knowing, at the time of receipt, that such property was derived from criminal activity or from an act of participation in such activity;
   (d) participation in, association to commit, attempts to commit and aiding, abetting, facilitating and counselling the commission of any of the actions mentioned in the foregoing points.
3. Money laundering shall be regarded as such even where the activities which generated the property to be laundered were carried out in the territory of another Member State or in that of a third country.
4. For the purposes of this Directive, "terrorist financing" means the provision or collection of funds, by any means, directly or indirectly, with the intention that they should be used or in the knowledge that they are to be used, in full or in part, in order to carry out any of the offences within the meaning of Articles 1 to 4 of Council Framework Decision 2002/475/JHA of 13 June 2002 on combating terrorism.[1]

[1] OJ L 164, 22.6.2002, p. 3.

5. Knowledge, intent or purpose required as an element of the activities mentioned in paragraphs 2 and 4 may be inferred from objective factual circumstances.

Article 2

1. This Directive shall apply to:

   (1) credit institutions;

   (2) financial institutions;

   (3) the following legal or natural persons acting in the exercise of their professional activities:

      (a) auditors, external accountants and tax advisors;

      (b) notaries and other independent legal professionals, when they participate, whether by acting on behalf of and for their client in any financial or real estate transaction, or by assisting in the planning or execution of transactions for their client concerning the:

         (i) buying and selling of real property or business entities;

         (ii) managing of client money, securities or other assets;

         (iii) opening or management of bank, savings or securities accounts;

         (iv) organisation of contributions necessary for the creation, operation or management of companies;

         (v) creation, operation or management of trusts, companies or similar structures;

      (c) trust or company service providers not already covered under points (a) or (b);

      (d) real estate agents;

      (e) other natural or legal persons trading in goods, only to the extent that payments are made in cash in an amount of EUR 15 000 or more, whether the transaction is executed in a single operation or in several operations which appear to be linked;

      (f) casinos.

2. Member States may decide that legal and natural persons who engage in a financial activity on an occasional or very limited basis and where there is little risk of money laundering or terrorist financing occurring do not fall within the scope of Article 3(1) or (2).

Article 3

For the purposes of this Directive the following definitions shall apply:

(1) "credit institution" means a credit institution, as defined in the first subparagraph of Article 1(1) of Directive 2000/12/EC of the European Parliament and of the Council of 20 March 2000 relating to the taking up

and pursuit of the business of credit institutions,[1] including branches within the meaning of Article 1(3) of that Directive located in the Community of credit institutions having their head offices inside or outside the Community;

[1] OJ L 126, 26.5.2000, p. 1. Directive as last amended by Directive 2005/1/EC (OJ L 79, 24.3.2005, p. 9).

(2) "financial institution" means:

(a) an undertaking other than a credit institution which carries out one or more of the operations included in points 2 to 12 and point 14 of Annex I to Directive 2000/12/EC, including the activities of currency exchange offices (bureaux de change) and of money transmission or remittance offices;

(b) an insurance company duly authorised in accordance with Directive 2002/83/EC of the European Parliament and of the Council of 5 November 2002 concerning life assurance,[1] insofar as it carries out activities covered by that Directive;

[1] OJ L 345, 19.12.2002, p. 1. Directive as last amended by Directive 2005/1/EC.

(c) an investment firm as defined in Article 4(1) of Directive 2004/3 9/EC of the European Parliament and of the Council of 21 April 2004 on markets in financial instruments;[2]

[2] OJ L 145, 30.4.2004, p. 1.

(d) a collective investment undertaking marketing its units or shares;

(e) an insurance intermediary as defined in Article 2(5) of Directive 2002/92/EC of the European Parliament and of the Council of 9 December 2002 on insurance mediation,[3] with the exception of intermediaries as mentioned in Article 2(7) of that Directive, when they act in respect of life insurance and other investment related services;

[3] OJL 9, 15.1.2003, p. 3.

(f) branches, when located in the Community, of financial institutions as referred to in points (a) to (e), whose head offices are inside or outside the Community;

(3) "property" means assets of every kind, whether corporeal or incorporeal, movable or immovable, tangible or intangible, and legal documents or instruments in any form including electronic or digital, evidencing title to or an interest in such assets.

(4) "criminal activity" means any kind of criminal involvement in the commission of a serious crime.

(5) "serious crimes" means, at least:

(a) acts as defined in Articles 1 to 4 of Framework Decision 2002/475/JHA;

(b) any of the offences defined in Article 3(1)(a) of the 1988 United Nations Convention against Illicit Traffic in Narcotic Drugs and Psychotropic Substances;

(c) the activities of criminal organisations as defined in Article 1 of Council Joint Action 98/733/JHA of 21 December 1998 on making it a criminal offence to participate in a criminal organisation in the Member States of the European Union;[1]

[1] OJL 351, 29.12.1998, p. 1.

(d) fraud, at least serious, as defined in Article 1(1) and Article 2 of the Convention on the Protection of the European Communities' Financial Interests;[1]

[1] OJC 316, 27.11.1995, p. 49.

(e) corruption;

(f) all offences which are punishable by deprivation of liberty or a detention order for a maximum of more than one year or, as regards those States which have a minimum threshold for offences in their legal system, all offences punishable by deprivation of liberty or a detention order for a minimum of more than six months,

(6) "beneficial owner" means the natural person(s) who ultimately owns or controls the customer and/or the natural person on whose behalf a transaction or activity is being conducted. The beneficial owner shall at least include:

(a) in the case of corporate entities:

(i) the natural person(s) who ultimately owns or controls a legal entity through direct or indirect ownership or control over a sufficient percentage of the shares or voting rights in that legal entity, including through bearer share holdings, other than a company listed on a regulated market that is subject to disclosure requirements consistent with Community legislation or subject to equivalent international standards; a percentage of 25% plus one share shall be deemed sufficient to meet this criterion;

(ii) the natural person(s) who otherwise exercises control over the management of a legal entity;

(b) in the case of legal entities, such as foundations, and legal arrangements, such as trusts, which administer and distribute funds:

(i) where the future beneficiaries have already been determined, the natural person(s) who is the beneficiary of 25% or more of the property of a legal arrangement or entity;

(ii) where the individuals that benefit from the legal arrangement or entity have yet to be determined, the class of persons in whose main interest the legal arrangement or entity is set up or operates;

(iii) the natural person(s) who exercises control over 25% or more of the property of a legal arrangement or entity;

(7) "trust and company service providers" means any natural or legal person which by way of business provides any of the following services to third parties:

(a) forming companies or other legal persons;

(b) acting as or arranging for another person to act as a director or secretary of a company, a partner of a partnership, or a similar position in relation to other legal persons;

(c) providing a registered office, business address, correspondence or administrative address and other related services for a company, a partnership or any other legal person or arrangement;

(d) acting as or arranging for another person to act as a trustee of an express trust or a similar legal arrangement;

(e) acting as or arranging for another person to act as a nominee shareholder for another person other than a company listed on a regulated market that is subject to disclosure requirements in conformity with

Community legislation or subject to equivalent international standards;

(8) "politically exposed persons" means natural persons who are or have been entrusted with prominent public functions and immediate family members, or persons known to be close associates, of such persons;

(9) "business relationship" means a business, professional or commercial relationship which is connected with the professional activities of the institutions and persons covered by this Directive and which is expected, at the time when the contact is established, to have an element of duration;

(10) "shell bank" means a credit institution, or an institution engaged in equivalent activities, incorporated in a jurisdiction in which it has no physical presence, involving meaningful mind and management, and which is unaffiliated with a regulated financial group.

Article 4

1. Member States shall ensure that the provisions of this Directive are extended in whole or in part to professions and to categories of undertakings, other than the institutions and persons referred to in Article 2(1), which engage in activities which are particularly likely to be used for money laundering or terrorist financing purposes.
2. Where a Member State decides to extend the provisions of this Directive to professions and to categories of undertakings other than those referred to in Article 2(1), it shall inform the Commission thereof.

Article 5

The Member States may adopt or retain in force stricter provisions in the field covered by this Directive to prevent money laundering and terrorist financing.

Chapter II
Customer Due Diligence

Section 1
General Provisions

Article 6

Member States shall prohibit their credit and financial institutions from keeping anonymous accounts or anonymous passbooks. By way of derogation from Article 9(6), Member States shall in all cases require that the owners and beneficiaries of existing anonymous accounts or anonymous passbooks be made the subject of customer due diligence measures as soon as possible and in any event before such accounts or passbooks are used in any way.

Article 7

The institutions and persons covered by this Directive shall apply customer due diligence measures in the following cases:

(a) when establishing a business relationship;

(b) when carrying out occasional transactions amounting to EUR 15 000 or more, whether the transaction is carried out in a single operation or in several operations which appear to be linked;

(c) when there is a suspicion of money laundering or terrorist financing, regardless of any derogation, exemption or threshold;

(d) when there are doubts about the veracity or adequacy of previously obtained customer identification data.

Article 8

1. Customer due diligence measures shall comprise:

(a) identifying the customer and verifying the customer's identity on the basis of documents, data or information obtained from a reliable and independent source;

(b) identifying, where applicable, the beneficial owner and taking risk-based and adequate measures to verify his identity so that the institution or person covered by this Directive is satisfied that it knows who the beneficial owner is, including, as regards legal persons, trusts and similar legal arrangements, taking risk-based and adequate measures to understand the ownership and control structure of the customer;

(c) obtaining information on the purpose and intended nature of the business relationship;

(d) conducting ongoing monitoring of the business relationship including scrutiny of transactions undertaken throughout the course of that relationship to ensure that the transactions being conducted are consistent with the institution's or person's knowledge of the customer, the business and risk profile, including, where necessary, the source of funds and ensuring that the documents, data or information held are kept up-to-date.

2. The institutions and persons covered by this Directive shall apply each of the customer due diligence requirements set out in paragraph 1, but may determine the extent of such measures on a risk-sensitive basis depending on the type of customer, business relationship, product or transaction. The institutions and persons covered by this Directive shall be able to demonstrate to the competent authorities mentioned in Article 37, including self-regulatory bodies, that the extent of the measures is appropriate in view of the risks of money laundering and terrorist financing.

Article 9

1. Member States shall require that the verification of the identity of the customer and the beneficial owner takes place before the establishment of a business relationship or the carrying out of the transaction.

2. By way of derogation from paragraph 1, Member States may allow the verification of the identity of the customer and the beneficial owner to be completed during the establishment of a business relationship if this is necessary not to interrupt the normal conduct of business and where there is little risk of money laundering or terrorist financing occurring. In such situations these procedures shall be completed as soon as practicable after the initial contact.

3. By way of derogation from paragraphs 1 and 2, Member States may, in relation to life insurance business, allow the verification of the identity of the beneficiary under the policy to take place after the business relationship has been established. In that case, verification shall take place at or before the time of payout or at or before the time the beneficiary intends to exercise rights vested under the policy.

4. By way of derogation from paragraphs 1 and 2, Member States may allow the opening of a bank account provided that there are adequate safeguards in place to ensure that transactions are not carried out by the customer or on its behalf until full compliance with the aforementioned provisions is obtained.

5. Member States shall require that, where the institution or person concerned is unable to comply with points (a), (b) and (c) of Article 8(1), it may not carry out a transaction through a bank account, establish a business relationship or carry out the transaction, or shall terminate the business relationship, and shall consider making a report to the financial intelligence unit (FIU) in accordance with Article 22 in relation to the customer.

Member States shall not be obliged to apply the previous subparagraph in situations when notaries, independent legal professionals, auditors, external accountants and tax advisors are in the course of ascertaining the legal position for their client or performing their task of defending or representing that client in, or concerning judicial proceedings, including advice on instituting or avoiding proceedings.

6. Member States shall require that institutions and persons covered by this Directive apply the customer due diligence procedures not only to all new customers but also at appropriate times to existing customers on a risk-sensitive basis.

Article 10

1. Member States shall require that all casino customers be identified and their identity verified if they purchase or exchange gambling chips with a value of EUR 2 000 or more.
2. Casinos subject to State supervision shall be deemed in any event to have satisfied the customer due diligence requirements if they register, identify and verify the identity of their customers immediately on or before entry, regardless of the amount of gambling chips purchased.

Section 2
Simplified Customer Due Diligence

Article 11

1. By way of derogation from Articles 7(a), (b) and (d), 8 and 9(1), the institutions and persons covered by this Directive shall not be subject to the requirements provided for in those Articles where the customer is a credit or financial institution covered by this Directive, or a credit or financial institution situated in a third country which imposes requirements equivalent to those laid down in this Directive and supervised for compliance with those requirements.

2. By way of derogation from Articles 7(a), (b) and (d), 8 and 9(1) Member States may allow the institutions and persons covered by this Directive not to apply customer due diligence in respect of:

   (a) listed companies whose securities are admitted to trading on a regulated market within the meaning of Directive 2004/3 9/EC in one or more Member States and listed companies from third countries which are subject to disclosure requirements consistent with Community legislation;

   (b) beneficial owners of pooled accounts held by notaries and other independent legal professionals from the Member States, or from third countries provided that they are subject to requirements to combat money laundering or terrorist financing consistent with international standards and are supervised for compliance with those requirements and provided that the information on the identity of the beneficial owner is available, on request, to the institutions that act as depository institutions for the pooled accounts;

   (c) domestic public authorities,

   or in respect of any other customer representing a low risk of money laundering or terrorist financing which meets the technical criteria established in accordance with Article 40(1)(b).

3. In the cases mentioned in paragraphs 1 and 2, institutions and persons covered by this Directive shall in any case gather sufficient information to establish if the customer qualifies for an exemption as mentioned in these paragraphs.

4. The Member States shall inform each other and the Commission of cases where they consider that a third country meets the conditions laid down in paragraphs 1 or 2 or in other situations which meet the technical criteria established in accordance with Article 40(1)(b).

5. By way of derogation from Articles 7(a), (b) and (d), 8 and 9(1), Member States may allow the institutions and persons covered by this Directive not to apply customer due diligence in respect of:

   (a) life insurance policies where the annual premium is no more than EUR 1 000 or the single premium is no more than EUR 2 500;

   (b) insurance policies for pension schemes if there is no surrender clause and the policy cannot be used as collateral;

   (c) a pension, superannuation or similar scheme that provides retirement benefits to employees, where contributions are made by way of deduction from wages and the scheme rules do not permit the assignment of a member's interest under the scheme;

(d) electronic money, as defined in Article 1(3)(b) of Directive 2000/46/EC of the European Parliament and of the Council of 18 September 2000 on the taking up, pursuit of and prudential supervision of the business of electronic money institutions,[1] where, if the device cannot be recharged, the maximum amount stored in the device is no more than EUR 150, or where, if the device can be recharged, a limit of EUR 2 500 is imposed on the total amount transacted in a calendar year, except when an amount of EUR 1 000 or more is redeemed in that same calendar year by the bearer as referred to in Article 3 of Directive 2000/46/EC,

[1] OJ L 275, 27.10.2000, p. 39.

or in respect of any other product or transaction representing a low risk of money laundering or terrorist financing which meets the technical criteria established in accordance with Article 40(1)(b).

Article 12

Where the Commission adopts a decision pursuant to Article 40(4), the Member States shall prohibit the institutions and persons covered by this Directive from applying simplified due diligence to credit and financial institutions or listed companies from the third country concerned or other entities following from situations which meet the technical criteria established in accordance with Article 40(1)(b).

Section 3
Enhanced Customer Due Diligence

Article 13

1. Member States shall require the institutions and persons covered by this Directive to apply, on a risk-sensitive basis, enhanced customer due diligence measures, in addition to the measures referred to in Articles 7, 8 and 9(6), in situations which by their nature can present a higher risk of money laundering or terrorist financing, and at least in the situations set out in paragraphs 2, 3, 4 and in other situations representing a high risk of money laundering or terrorist financing which meet the technical criteria established in accordance with Article 40(1)(c).
2. Where the customer has not been physically present for identification purposes, Member States shall require those institutions and persons to take specific and adequate measures to compensate for the higher risk,

for example by applying one or more of the following measures:

(a) ensuring that the customer's identity is established by additional documents, data or information;

(b) supplementary measures to verify or certify the documents supplied, or requiring confirmatory certification by a credit or financial institution covered by this Directive;

(c) ensuring that the first payment of the operations is carried out through an account opened in the customer's name with a credit institution.

3. In respect of cross-frontier correspondent banking relationships with respondent institutions from third countries, Member States shall require their credit institutions to:

(a) gather sufficient information about a respondent institution to understand fully the nature of the respondent's business and to determine from publicly available information the reputation of the institution and the quality of supervision;

(b) assess the respondent institution's anti-money laundering and anti-terrorist financing controls;

(c) obtain approval from senior management before establishing new correspondent banking relationships;

(d) document the respective responsibilities of each institution;

(e) with respect to payable-through accounts, be satisfied that the respondent credit institution has verified the identity of and performed ongoing due diligence on the customers having direct access to accounts of the correspondent and that it is able to provide relevant customer due diligence data to the correspondent institution, upon request.

4. In respect of transactions or business relationships with politically exposed persons residing in another Member State or in a third country, Member States shall require those institutions and persons covered by this Directive to:

(a) have appropriate risk-based procedures to determine whether the customer is a politically exposed person;

(b) have senior management approval for establishing business relationships with such customers;

(c) take adequate measures to establish the source of wealth and source of funds that are involved in the business relationship or transaction;

(d) conduct enhanced ongoing monitoring of the business relationship.

5. Member States shall prohibit credit institutions from entering into or continuing a correspondent banking relationship with a shell bank and shall

require that credit institutions take appropriate measures to ensure that they do not engage in or continue correspondent banking relationships with a bank that is known to permit its accounts to be used by a shell bank.

6. Member States shall ensure that the institutions and persons covered by this Directive pay special attention to any money laundering or terrorist financing threat that may arise from products or transactions that might favour anonymity, and take measures, if needed, to prevent their use for money laundering or terrorist financing purposes.

Section 4
Performance by Third Parties

Article 14

Member States may permit the institutions and persons covered by this Directive to rely on third parties to meet the requirements laid down in Article 8(1)(a) to (c). However, the ultimate responsibility for meeting those requirements shall remain with the institution or person covered by this Directive which relies on the third party.

Article 15

1. Where a Member State permits credit and financial institutions referred to in Article 2(1)(1) or (2) situated in its territory to be relied on as a third party domestically, that Member State shall in any case permit institutions and persons referred to in Article 2(1) situated in its territory to recognise and accept, in accordance with the provisions laid down in Article 14, the outcome of the customer due diligence requirements laid down in Article 8(1)(a) to (c), carried out in accordance with this Directive by an institution referred to in Article 2(1)(1) or (2) in another Member State, with the exception of currency exchange offices and money transmission or remittance offices, and meeting the requirements laid down in Articles 16 and 18, even if the documents or data on which these requirements have been based are different to those required in the Member State to which the customer is being referred.

2. Where a Member State permits currency exchange offices and money transmission or remittance offices referred to in Article 3(2)(a) situated in its territory to be relied on as a third party domestically, that Member State shall in any case permit them to recognise and accept, in accordance with Article 14, the outcome of the customer due diligence requirements laid down in Article 8(1)(a) to (c), carried out in accordance with this Directive by the same category of institution in another Member State and meeting the requirements laid down in Articles 16 and 18, even if the documents or data on which these requirements have been based

are different to those required in the Member State to which the customer is being referred.

3. Where a Member State permits persons referred to in Article 2(1)(3)(a) to (c) situated in its territory to be relied on as a third party domestically, that Member State shall in any case permit them to recognise and accept, in accordance with Article 14, the outcome of the customer due diligence requirements laid down in Article 8(1)(a) to (c), carried out in accordance with this Directive by a person referred to in Article 2(1)(3)(a) to (c) in another Member State and meeting the requirements laid down in Articles 16 and 18, even if the documents or data on which these requirements have been based are different to those required in the Member State to which the customer is being referred.

Article 16

1. For the purposes of this Section, "third parties" shall mean institutions and persons who are listed in Article 2, or equivalent institutions and persons situated in a third country, who meet the following requirements:
   (a) they are subject to mandatory professional registration, recognised by law;
   (b) they apply customer due diligence requirements and record keeping requirements as laid down or equivalent to those laid down in this Directive and their compliance with the requirements of this Directive is supervised in accordance with Section 2 of Chapter V, or they are situated in a third country which imposes equivalent requirements to those laid down in this Directive.
2. Member States shall inform each other and the Commission of cases where they consider that a third country meets the conditions laid down in paragraph 1(b).

Article 17

Where the Commission adopts a decision pursuant to Article 40(4), Member States shall prohibit the institutions and persons covered by this Directive from relying on third parties from the third country concerned to meet the requirements laid down in Article 8(1)(a) to (c).

Article 18

1. Third parties shall make information requested in accordance with the requirements laid down in Article 8(1)(a) to (c) immediately available to

the institution or person covered by this Directive to which the customer is being referred.

2. Relevant copies of identification and verification data and other relevant documentation on the identity of the customer or the beneficial owner shall immediately be forwarded, on request, by the third party to the institution or person covered by this Directive to which the customer is being referred.

Article 19

This Section shall not apply to outsourcing or agency relationships where, on the basis of a contractual arrangement, the outsourcing service provider or agent is to be regarded as part of the institution or person covered by this Directive.

Chapter III
Reporting Obligations

Section 1
General Provisions

Article 20

Member States shall require that the institutions and persons covered by this Directive pay special attention to any activity which they regard as particularly likely, by its nature, to be related to money laundering or terrorist financing and in particular complex or unusually large transactions and all unusual patterns of transactions which have no apparent economic or visible lawful purpose.

Article 21

1. Each Member State shall establish a FIU in order effectively to combat money laundering and terrorist financing.
2. That FIU shall be established as a central national unit. It shall be responsible for receiving (and to the extent permitted, requesting), analysing and disseminating to the competent authorities, disclosures of information which concern potential money laundering, potential terrorist financing or are required by national legislation or regulation. It shall be provided with adequate resources in order to fulfil its tasks.
3. Member States shall ensure that the FIU has access, directly or indirectly, on a timely basis, to the financial, administrative and law enforcement information that it requires to properly fulfil its tasks.

Article 22

1. Member States shall require the institutions and persons covered by this Directive, and where applicable their directors and employees, to cooperate fully:
   (a) by promptly informing the FIU, on their own initiative, where the institution or person covered by this Directive knows, suspects or has reasonable grounds to suspect that money laundering or terrorist financing is being or has been committed or attempted;
   (b) by promptly furnishing the FIU, at its request, with all necessary information, in accordance with the procedures established by the applicable legislation.

2. The information referred to in paragraph 1 shall be forwarded to the FIU of the Member State in whose territory the institution or person forwarding the information is situated. The person or persons designated in accordance with the procedures provided for in Article 34 shall normally forward the information.

Article 23

1. By way of derogation from Article 22(1), Member States may, in the case of the persons referred to in Article 2(1)(3)(a) and (b), designate an appropriate self-regulatory body of the profession concerned as the authority to be informed in the first instance in place of the FIU. Without prejudice to paragraph 2, the designated self-regulatory body shall in such cases forward the information to the FIU promptly and unfiltered.
2. Member States shall not be obliged to apply the obligations laid down in Article 22(1) to notaries, independent legal professionals, auditors, external accountants and tax advisors with regard to information they receive from or obtain on one of their clients, in the course of ascertaining the legal position for their client or performing their task of defending or representing that client in, or concerning judicial proceedings, including advice on instituting or avoiding proceedings, whether such information is received or obtained before, during or after such proceedings.

Article 24

1. Member States shall require the institutions and persons covered by this Directive to refrain from carrying out transactions which they know or suspect to be related to money laundering or terrorist financing until they have completed the necessary action in accordance with Article 22(1)(a). In conformity with the legislation of the Member States, instructions may be given not to carry out the transaction.
2. Where such a transaction is suspected of giving rise to money laundering or terrorist financing and where to refrain in such manner is impossible or is likely to frustrate efforts to pursue the beneficiaries of a suspected money laundering or terrorist financing operation, the institutions and persons concerned shall inform the FIU immediately afterwards.

Article 25

1. Member States shall ensure that if, in the course of inspections carried out in the institutions and persons covered by this Directive by the competent authorities referred to in Article 37, or in any other way, those

authorities discover facts that could be related to money laundering or terrorist financing, they shall promptly inform the FIU.

2. Member States shall ensure that supervisory bodies empowered by law or regulation to oversee the stock, foreign exchange and financial derivatives markets inform the FIU if they discover facts that could be related to money laundering or terrorist financing.

Article 26

The disclosure in good faith as foreseen in Articles 22(1) and 23 by an institution or person covered by this Directive or by an employee or director of such an institution or person of the information referred to in Articles 22 and 23 shall not constitute a breach of any restriction on disclosure of information imposed by contract or by any legislative, regulatory or administrative provision, and shall not involve the institution or person or its directors or employees in liability of any kind.

Article 27

Member States shall take all appropriate measures in order to protect employees of the institutions or persons covered by this Directive who report suspicions of money laundering or terrorist financing either internally or to the FIU from being exposed to threats or hostile action.

Section 2
Prohibition of Disclosure

Article 28

1. The institutions and persons covered by this Directive and their directors and employees shall not disclose to the customer concerned or to other third persons the fact that information has been transmitted in accordance with Articles 22 and 23 or that a money laundering or terrorist financing investigation is being or may be carried out.

2. The prohibition laid down in paragraph 1 shall not include disclosure to the competent authorities referred to in Article 37, including the self-regulatory bodies, or disclosure for law enforcement purposes.

3. The prohibition laid down in paragraph 1 shall not prevent disclosure between institutions from Member States, or from third countries provided that they meet the conditions laid down in Article 11(1), belonging to the same group as defined by Article 2(12) of Directive 2002/87/EC of the European Parliament and of the Council of 16 December 2002

on the supplementary supervision of credit institutions, insurance undertakings and investment firms in a financial conglomerate.[1]

[1] OJ L 35, 11.2.2003, p. 1.

4. The prohibition laid down in paragraph 1 shall not prevent disclosure between persons referred to in Article 2(1)(3)(a) and (b) from Member States, or from third countries which impose requirements equivalent to those laid down in this Directive, who perform their professional activities, whether as employees or not, within the same legal person or a network. For the purposes of this Article, a "network" means the larger structure to which the person belongs and which shares common ownership, management or compliance control.
5. For institutions or persons referred to in Article 2(1)(1), (2) and (3)(a) and (b) in cases related to the same customer and the same transaction involving two or more institutions or persons, the prohibition laid down in paragraph 1 shall not prevent disclosure between the relevant institutions or persons provided that they are situated in a Member State, or in a third country which imposes requirements equivalent to those laid down in this Directive, and that they are from the same professional category and are subject to equivalent obligations as regards professional secrecy and personal data protection. The information exchanged shall be used exclusively for the purposes of the prevention of money laundering and terrorist financing.
6. Where the persons referred to in Article 2(1)(3)(a) and (b) seek to dissuade a client from engaging in illegal activity, this shall not constitute a disclosure within the meaning of the paragraph 1.
7. The Member States shall inform each other and the Commission of cases where they consider that a third country meets the conditions laid down in paragraphs 3, 4 or 5.

Article 29

Where the Commission adopts a decision pursuant to Article 40(4), the Member States shall prohibit the disclosure between institutions and persons covered by this Directive and institutions and persons from the third country concerned.

Chapter IV
Record Keeping and Statistical Data

Article 30

Member States shall require the institutions and persons covered by this Directive to keep the following documents and information for use in any investigation into, or analysis of, possible money laundering or terrorist financing by the FIU or by other competent authorities in accordance with national law:

(a) in the case of the customer due diligence, a copy or the references of the evidence required, for a period of at least five years after the business relationship with their customer has ended;

(b) in the case of business relationships and transactions, the supporting evidence and records, consisting of the original documents or copies admissible in court proceedings under the applicable national legislation for a period of at least five years following the carrying-out of the transactions or the end of the business relationship.

Article 31

1. Member States shall require the credit and financial institutions covered by this Directive to apply, where applicable, in their branches and majority-owned subsidiaries located in third countries measures at least equivalent to those laid down in this Directive with regard to customer due diligence and record keeping.

   Where the legislation of the third country does not permit application of such equivalent measures, the Member States shall require the credit and financial institutions concerned to inform the competent authorities of the relevant home Member State accordingly.

2. Member States and the Commission shall inform each other of cases where the legislation of the third country does not permit application of the measures required under the first subparagraph of paragraph 1 and coordinated action could be taken to pursue a solution.

3. Member States shall require that, where the legislation of the third country does not permit application of the measures required under the first subparagraph of paragraph 1, credit or financial institutions take additional measures to effectively handle the risk of money laundering or terrorist financing.

Article 32

Member States shall require that their credit and financial institutions have systems in place that enable them to respond fully and rapidly to enquiries from the FIU, or from other authorities, in accordance with their national law, as to whether they maintain or have maintained during the previous five years a business relationship with specified natural or legal persons and on the nature of that relationship.

Article 33

1. Member States shall ensure that they are able to review the effectiveness of their systems to combat money laundering or terrorist financing by maintaining comprehensive statistics on matters relevant to the effectiveness of such systems.
2. Such statistics shall as a minimum cover the number of suspicious transaction reports made to the FIU, the follow-up given to these reports and indicate on an annual basis the number of cases investigated, the number of persons prosecuted, the number of persons convicted for money laundering or terrorist financing offences and how much property has been frozen, seized or confiscated.
3. Member States shall ensure that a consolidated review of these statistical reports is published.

Chapter V
Enforcement Measures

Section 1
Internal Procedures, Training and Feedback

Article 34

1. Member States shall require that the institutions and persons covered by this Directive establish adequate and appropriate policies and procedures of customer due diligence, reporting, record keeping, internal control, risk assessment, risk management, compliance management and communication in order to forestall and prevent operations related to money laundering or terrorist financing.
2. Member States shall require that credit and financial institutions covered by this Directive communicate relevant policies and procedures where applicable to branches and majority-owned subsidiaries in third countries.

Article 35

1. Member States shall require that the institutions and persons covered by this Directive take appropriate measures so that their relevant employees are aware of the provisions in force on the basis of this Directive.

   These measures shall include participation of their relevant employees in special ongoing training programmes to help them recognise operations which may be related to money laundering or terrorist financing and to instruct them as to how to proceed in such cases.

   Where a natural person falling within any of the categories listed in Article 2(1)(3) performs his professional activities as an employee of a legal person, the obligations in this Section shall apply to that legal person rather than to the natural person.
2. Member States shall ensure that the institutions and persons covered by this Directive have access to up-to-date information on the practices of money launderers and terrorist financers and on indications leading to the recognition of suspicious transactions.
3. Member States shall ensure that, wherever practicable, timely feedback on the effectiveness of and follow-up to reports of suspected money laundering or terrorist financing is provided.

Section 2
Supervision

Article 36

1. Member States shall provide that currency exchange offices and trust and company service providers shall be licensed or registered and casinos be licensed in order to operate their business legally. Without prejudice to future Community legislation, Member States shall provide that money transmission or remittance offices shall be licensed or registered in order to operate their business legally.
2. Member States shall require competent authorities to refuse licensing or registration of the entities referred to in paragraph 1 if they are not satisfied that the persons who effectively direct or will direct the business of such entities or the beneficial owners of such entities are fit and proper persons.

Article 37

1. Member States shall require the competent authorities at least to effectively monitor and to take the necessary measures with a view to ensuring compliance with the requirements of this Directive by all the institutions and persons covered by this Directive.
2. Member States shall ensure that the competent authorities have adequate powers, including the power to compel the production of any information that is relevant to monitoring compliance and perform checks, and have adequate resources to perform their functions.
3. In the case of credit and financial institutions and casinos, competent authorities shall have enhanced supervisory powers, notably the possibility to conduct on-site inspections.
4. In the case of the natural and legal persons referred to in Article 2(1)(3)(a) to (e), Member States may allow the functions referred to in paragraph 1 to be performed on a risk-sensitive basis.
5. In the case of the persons referred to in Article 2(1)(3)(a) and (b), Member States may allow the functions referred to in paragraph 1 to be performed by self-regulatory bodies, provided that they comply with paragraph 2.

Section 3
Cooperation

Article 38

The Commission shall lend such assistance as may be needed to facilitate coordination, including the exchange of information between FIUs within the Community.

Section 4
Penalties

Article 39

1. Member States shall ensure that natural and legal persons covered by this Directive can be held liable for infringements of the national provisions adopted pursuant to this Directive. The penalties must be effective, proportionate and dissuasive.
2. Without prejudice to the right of Member States to impose criminal penalties, Member States shall ensure, in conformity with their national law, that the appropriate administrative measures can be taken or administrative sanctions can be imposed against credit and financial institutions for infringements of the national provisions adopted pursuant to this Directive. Member States shall ensure that these measures or sanctions are effective, proportionate and dissuasive.
3. In the case of legal persons, Member States shall ensure that at least they can be held liable for infringements referred to in paragraph 1 which are committed for their benefit by any person, acting either individually or as part of an organ of the legal person, who has a leading position within the legal person, based on:

   (a) a power of representation of the legal person,

   (b) an authority to take decisions on behalf of the legal person, or

   (c) an authority to exercise control within the legal person.
4. In addition to the cases already provided for in paragraph 3, Member States shall ensure that legal persons can be held liable where the lack of supervision or control by a person referred to in paragraph 3 has made possible the commission of the infringements referred to in paragraph 1 for the benefit of a legal person by a person under its authority.

Chapter VI
Implementing Measures

Article 40

1. In order to take account of technical developments in the fight against money laundering or terrorist financing and to ensure uniform implementation of this Directive, the Commission may, in accordance with the procedure referred to in Article 41(2), adopt the following implementing measures:

   (a) clarification of the technical aspects of the definitions in Article 3(2)(a) and (d), (6), (7), (8), (9) and (10);

   (b) establishment of technical criteria for assessing whether situations represent a low risk of money laundering or terrorist financing as referred to in Article 11(2) and (5);

   (c) establishment of technical criteria for assessing whether situations represent a high risk of money laundering or terrorist financing as referred to in Article 13;

   (d) establishment of technical criteria for assessing whether, in accordance with Article 2(2), it is justified not to apply this Directive to certain legal or natural persons carrying out a financial activity on an occasional or very limited basis.

2. In any event, the Commission shall adopt the first implementing measures to give effect to paragraphs 1(b) and 1(d) by . . .*.

* 6 months following the date of entry into force of this Directive.

3. The Commission shall, in accordance with the procedure referred to in Article 41(2), adapt the amounts referred to in Articles 2(1)(3)(e), 7(b), 10(1) and 1 1(5)(a) and (d) taking into account Community legislation, economic developments and changes in international standards. 6 months following the date of entry into force of this Directive.

4. Where the Commission finds that a third country does not meet the conditions laid down in Article 11(1) or (2), Article 28(3), (4) or (5), or in the measures established in accordance with paragraph 1(b) of this Article or in Article 16(1)(b), or that the legislation of that third country does not permit application of the measures required under the first subparagraph of Article 31(1), it shall adopt a decision so stating in accordance with the procedure referred to in Article 41(2).

Article 41

1. The Commission shall be assisted by a Committee on the Prevention of Money Laundering and Terrorist Financing, hereinafter "the Committee".
2. Where reference is made to this paragraph, Articles 5 and 7 of Decision 1999/468/EC shall apply, having regard to the provisions of Article 8 thereof and provided that the implementing measures adopted in accordance with this procedure do not modify the essential provisions of this Directive.

   The period laid down in Article 5(6) of Decision 1999/468/EC shall be set at three months.
3. The Committee shall adopt its Rules of Procedure.
4. Without prejudice to the implementing measures already adopted, the implementation of the provisions of this Directive concerning the adoption of technical rules and decisions in accordance with the procedure referred to in paragraph 2 shall be suspended four years after the entry into force of this Directive. On a proposal from the Commission, the European Parliament and the Council may renew the provisions concerned in accordance with the procedure laid down in Article 251 of the Treaty and, to that end, shall review them prior to the expiry of the four-year period.

Chapter VII
Final Provisions

Article 42

By . . .,* and at least at three-yearly intervals thereafter, the Commission shall draw up a report on the implementation of this Directive and submit it to the European Parliament and the Council. For the first such report, the Commission shall include a specific examination of the treatment of lawyers and other independent legal professionals.

* Four years following the date of entry into force of this Directive.

Article 43

By . . .,* the Commission shall present a report to the European Parliament and to the Council on the threshold percentages in Article 3(6), paying particular attention to the possible expediency and consequences of a reduction of the percentage in points (a)(i), (b)(i) and (b)(iii) of Article 3(6) from 25% to 20%. On the basis of the report the Commission may submit a proposal for amendments to this Directive.

* Five years following the date of entry into force of this Directive.

Article 44

Directive 91/308/EEC is hereby repealed.

References made to the repealed Directive shall be construed as being made to this Directive and should be read in accordance with the correlation table set out in the Annex.

Article 45

1. Member States shall bring into force the laws, regulations and administrative provisions necessary to comply with this Directive by . . . .** They shall forthwith communicate to the Commission the text of those provisions together with a table showing how the provisions of this Directive correspond to the national provisions adopted.

** Two years after the date of entry into force of this Directive.

When Member States adopt those measures, they shall contain a reference to this Directive or be accompanied by such a reference on the occasion of their official publication. The methods of making such reference shall be laid down by Member States.

2. Member States shall communicate to the Commission the text of the main provisions of national law which they adopt in the field covered by this Directive.

Article 46

This Directive shall enter into force on the twentieth day after its publication in the *Official Journal of the European Union*.

Article 47

This Directive is addressed to the Member States.

Done at Strasbourg,

For the European Parliment	*For the Council*
The President	*The President*

Annex

Correlation Table

This Directive	Directive 91/308/EEC
Article 1(1)	Article 2
Article 1(2)	Article 1(C)
Article 1(2)(a)	Article 1(C) 1st point
Article 1(2)(b)	Article 1(C) 2nd point
Article 1(2)(c)	Article 1(C) 3rd point
Article 1(2)(d)	Article 1(C) 4th point
Article 1(3)	Article 1(C), 3rd paragraph
Article 1(4)	
Article 1(5)	Article 1(C), 2nd paragraph
Article 2(1)(1)	Article 2a(1)
Article 2(1)(2)	Article 2a(2)
Article 2(1)(3)(a), (b) and (d) to (f)	Article 2a(3) to (7)
Article 2(1)(3)(c)	
Article 2(2)	
Article 3(1)	Article 1(A)
Article 3(2)(a)	Article 1(B)(1)
Article 3(2)(b)	Article 1(B)(2)
Article 3(2)(c)	Article 1(B)(3)
Article 3(2)(d)	Article 1(B)(4)
Article 3(2)(e)	
Article 3(2)(f)	Article 1(B), 2nd paragraph
Article 3(3)	Article 1(D)
Article 3(4)	Article 1(E), 1st paragraph
Article 3(5)	Article 1(E), 2nd paragraph
Article 3(5)(a)	
Article 3(5)(b)	Article 1(E), 1st indent
Article 3(5)(c)	Article 1(E), 2nd indent
Article 3(5)(d)	Article 1(E), 3rd indent
Article 3(5)(e)	Article 1(E), 4th indent
Article 3(5)(f)	Article 1(E), 5th indent, and 3rd paragraph

This Directive	Directive 91/308/EEC
Article 3(6)	
Article 3(7)	
Article 3(8)	
Article 3(9)	
Article 3(10)	
Article 4	Article 12
Article 5	Article 15
Article 6	
Article 7(a)	Article 3(1)
Article 7(b)	Article 3(2)
Article 7(c)	Article 3(8)
Article 7(d)	Article 3(7)
Article 8(1)(a)	Article 3(1)
Article 8(1)(b) to (d)	
Article 8(2)	
Article 9(1)	Article 3(1)
Article 9(2) to (6)	
Article 10	Article 3(5) and (6)
Article 11(1)	Article 3(9)
Article 11(2)	
Article 11(3) and (4)	
Article 11 (5)(a)	Article 3(3)
Article 11 (5)(b)	Article 3(4)
Article 11 (5)(c)	Article 3(4)
Article 11 (5)(d)	
Article 12	
Article 13(1) and (2)	Article 3(10) and (11)
Article 13(3) to (5)	
Article 13(6)	Article 5
Article 14	
Article 15	
Article 16	
Article 17	

This Directive	Directive 91/308/EEC
Article 18	
Article 19	
Article 20	Article 5
Article 21	
Article 22	Article 6(1) and (2)
Article 23	Article 6(3)
Article 24	Article 7
Article 25	Article 10
Article 26	Article 9
Article 27	
Article 28(1)	Article 28(1)
Article 28(2) to (7)	
Article 29	
Article 30(a)	Article 4, 1st indent
Article 30(b)	Article 4, 2nd indent
Article 31	
Article 32	
Article 33	
Article 34(1)	Article 11(1) (a)
Article 34(2)	
Article 35(1), 1st paragraph	Article 11(1)(b), first sentence
Article 35(1), 2nd paragraph	Article 11(1)(b) second sentence
Article 35(1), 3rd paragraph	Article 11(1), second paragraph
Article 35(2)	Article 11(2)
Article 35(3)	
Article 36	
Article 37	
Article 38	
Article 39(1)	Article 14
Article 39(2) to (4)	
Article 40	
Article 41	

This Directive	Directive 91/308/EEC
Article 42	Article 17
Article 43	
Article 44	
Article 45	Article 16
Article 46	Article 16

C. MULTI-STATE COOPERATION AND INFORMATION-SHARING

DOCUMENT NO. 23

COUNCIL RECOMMENDATION 2007/562/EC OF 12 JUNE 2007 CONCERNING SHARING OF INFORMATION ON TERRORIST KIDNAPPINGS

THE COUNCIL OF THE EUROPEAN UNION,

Whereas:

(1) Kidnappings by groups/individuals that can be placed within the spectrum of international terrorism pose a huge challenge to Member States.

(2) To successfully resolve such situations, Member States must gather background information, establish contacts and initiate discussions in a confidential setting.

(3) The capacities of the Member State concerned would be significantly strengthened if it were able to resort to experience which other Member States have gained in comparable situations.

(4) To this end, each Member State should submit a data sheet containing key information on past kidnappings to the other Member States giving only unclassified information after the incident has been resolved and restricted to incidents related to international terrorism,

HEREBY RECOMMENDS,

1. Member States:

(a) to submit, after a kidnapping incident has been resolved, the following data:[1]

— country and region in which the kidnapping took place,

— number and nationality of the hostage(s),

— time and date of the kidnapping,

[1] In case of a kidnapping this information could help to quickly identify whether another Member State already has experience with kidnappings of EU citizens in the same region, by the same terrorist group or under comparable circumstances. The Member State concerned can then contact the specified contact person. Further information and experience should be shared bilaterally in accordance with national law.

— time and date of the end of the incident,

— perpetrators/responsible terrorist group,

— *modus operandi* of the kidnapping,

— motivation for the kidnapping,

— involvement of a mediator yes/no,

— contact person in the Member State concerned.

This information should be submitted in accordance with the format set out in Annex 1.

(b) to also submit the following additional information if appropriate:

— hostages' reason for being in the country, language skills, gender of the hostage,

— ideology, nationality, language skills of the perpetrators,

— means used by the perpetrators to address the public,

— details on the perpetrators' *modus operandi*.

This optional information should be submitted in accordance with the format set out in Annex 2.

2. If personal data are to be included, such data are to be submitted in accordance with national law.

3. Member States to compile information on all incidents which have occurred since 1 January 2002 and submit this summary to the other Member States.

4. Member States to share information on the basis of the abovementioned principles through the BdL network for EU-wide information sharing on terrorist incidents.

5. Member States to share, as far as possible, the information also with Europol and on the basis of the amount and type of shared data, after one year, to examine whether it would be advisable to set up a database at Europol.

6. Member States to draw up a list of contact details and exchange this list in order to facilitate direct communication between contact points.

Annex 1

Notification of Terrorist Kidnap (or Suspected Terrorist Kidnap)

Please complete all fields in this box

National single point of contact/competent authority:	
Name:	**Reporting Member State:**
Rank/position:	**Dept/section:**
Telephone:	**Fax:**
Mobile:	**E-mail:**
Motivation for the kidnap:	
Time/date of kidnap/hostage taking:	End of incident time/date:
Number/nationality of hostage(s):	
Country/Region of the crime:	
Perpetrators/responsible group:	
Summary of *modus operandi* **(more detail can be provided on the next page):**	
Involvement of interpreters/mediators:	

Annex 2

Completion of the following information is optional in accordance with national law

Hostage #1 (optional)		
Name:	**Date of birth:**	**Gender:**
Reason for being in country?	**First language:**	**Second language:**
Telephone:	**Nationality:**	
Hostage #2 (optional)		
Name:	**Date of birth:**	**Gender:**
Reason for being in country?	**First language:**	**Second language:**
Telephone:	**Nationality:**	

Hostage #3 (optional)		
Name:	**Date of birth:**	**Gender:**
Reason for being in country?	**First language:**	**Second language:**
Telephone:	**Nationality:**	

Perpetrators/responsible group #1 (if details known)		
Name:	**Ideology:**	**Nationality:**
Is English spoken?	**First language:**	**Second language:**
Use of publicity:	**Means of publicity:**	
Perpetrators/responsible group #2 (if details known)		
Name:	**Ideology:**	**Nationality:**
Is English spoken?	**First language:**	**Second language:**
Use of publicity:	**Means of publicity:**	

Modus operandi ***Summary of the circumstances of the kidnap. You should consider the following:*** *The nature of the hostage taking, i.e. environment* *The nature of the demand, i.e. monetary gain, political aim or concession* *To whom the demand was made, including how the demand was made*	

Language/interpreter *Hostage profile (victimological aspects, e.g. residence permit status, professional background)* *Negotiation strategy* *Delaying tactics* *Telephone tactics* *Technical issues* *Violence used* *The outcome of the incident, including details of resolution, was the hostage released, was the hostage rescued, were suspects detained/ killed?* *Any other issues of note* *Are there any issues that you feel should be considered as 'good practice'?*	

DOCUMENT NO. 24

PRÜM TREATY: CROSS-BORDER COOPERATION IN COMBATING TERRORISM AND CROSS-BORDER CRIME

European Parliament Legislative Resolution

7 June 2007

[*European Parliament Legislative Resolution of 7 June 2007 on the initiative by the Kingdom of Belgium, the Republic of Bulgaria, the Federal Republic of Germany, the Kingdom of Spain, the French Republic, the Grand Duchy of Luxembourg, the Kingdom of the Netherlands, the Republic of Austria, the Republic of Slovenia, the Slovak Republic, the Italian Republic, the Republic of Finland, the Portuguese Republic, Romania and the Kingdom of Sweden on the stepping up of cross-border cooperation, particularly in combating terrorism and cross-border crime (6566/2007—C6-0079/2007 2007/0804(CNS))*]

(Consultation procedure)

The European Parliament,

- having regard to the initiative by the Kingdom of Belgium, the Republic of Bulgaria, the Federal Republic of Germany, the Kingdom of Spain, the French Republic, the Grand Duchy of Luxembourg, the Kingdom of the Netherlands, the Republic of Austria, the Republic of Slovenia, the Slovak Republic, the Italian Republic, the Republic of Finland, the Portuguese Republic, Romania and the Kingdom of Sweden (6566/2007),
- having regard to the Council's drafting amendments (7273/1/2007 of 17 April 2007),
- having regard to Article 34(2)(c) of the EU Treaty,
- having regard to Article 39(1) of the EU Treaty, pursuant to which the Council consulted Parliament (C6-0079/2007),
- having regard to the opinion of the Committee on Legal Affairs on the proposed legal basis,

– having regard to Rules 93, 51 and 35 of its Rules of Procedure,

– having regard to the report of the Committee on Civil Liberties, Justice and Home Affairs (A6-0207/2007),

1. Approves the initiative by the Kingdom of Belgium, the Republic of Bulgaria, the Federal Republic of Germany, the Kingdom of Spain, the French Republic, the Grand Duchy of Luxembourg, the Kingdom of the Netherlands, the Republic of Austria, the Republic of Slovenia, the Slovak Republic, the Italian Republic, the Republic of Finland, the Portuguese Republic, Romania and the Kingdom of Sweden as amended;

2. Calls on the Council to amend the text accordingly;

3. Calls on the Council to notify Parliament if it intends to depart from the text approved by Parliament;

4. Calls on the Council to consult Parliament if it intends to amend the initiative by the Kingdom of Belgium, the Republic of Bulgaria, the Federal Republic of Germany, the Kingdom of Spain, the French Republic, the Grand Duchy of Luxembourg, the Kingdom of the Netherlands, the Republic of Austria, the Republic of Slovenia, the Slovak Republic, the Italian Republic, the Republic of Finland, the Portuguese Republic, Romania and the Kingdom of Sweden substantially;

5. Regrets the obligation imposed on Parliament by the Council to express its opinion as a matter of urgency, without adequate and appropriate time for Parliamentary review and the absence both of a comprehensive impact assessment and an evaluation of the application of the Prüm Treaty to date, and of an adequate framework decision for the protection of personal data in police and judicial cooperation, which it considers necessary before any legislation is adopted under the third pillar;

6. Instructs its President to forward its position to the Council and the Commission, and the governments of the Kingdom of Belgium, the Republic of Bulgaria, the Federal Republic of Germany, the Kingdom of Spain, the French Republic, the Grand Duchy of Luxembourg, the Kingdom of the Netherlands, the Republic of Austria, the Republic of Slovenia, the Slovak Republic, the Italian Republic, the Republic of Finland, the Portuguese Republic, Romania and the Kingdom of Sweden.

Text proposed by the Kingdom of Belgium, the Republic of Bulgaria, the Federal Republic of Germany, the Kingdom of Spain, the French Republic, the Grand Duchy of Luxembourg, the Kingdom of the Netherlands, the Republic of Austria, the Republic of Slovenia, the Slovak Republic, the Italian Republic, the Republic of Finland, the Portuguese Republic, Romania and the Kingdom of Sweden	Amendments by Parliament

Amendment 1

Title

COUNCIL DECISION 2007/. . ./ JHA of . . . on the stepping up of cross-border cooperation, particularly in combating terrorism and cross-border crime	COUNCIL ***FRAMEWORK*** DECISION 2007/. . ./JHA of... on the stepping up of cross-border cooperation, particularly in combating terrorism and cross-border crime *(This amendment applies throughout the text.)*

Amendment 2

Citation 1

Having regard to the Treaty on European Union, and in particular Article 30(1)(a) and (b), Article 31(1)(a), Article 32 and ***Article 34(2)(c)*** thereof,	Having regard to the Treaty on European Union, and in particular Article 30(1)(a) and (b), Article 31(1)(a), Article 32 and ***Article 34(2)(b)*** thereof,

Amendment 3

Citation 2 a (new)

	Having regard to the opinion of the European Data Protection Supervisor of 4 April 2007,

Amendment 4

Recital 1

(1) The Council of the European Union attaches fundamental importance to the ***establishment of an*** area of freedom, security and justice, which is ***a*** fundamental ***concern of*** the people of the ***States brought together in the*** Union.	(1) The Council of the European Union attaches fundamental importance to the area of freedom, security and justice, which is fundamental ***to*** the people of the ***European*** Union.

Amendment 5

Recital 10

(10) These requirements are satisfied by the Prüm Treaty of 27 May 2005 between the Kingdom of Belgium, the Federal Republic of Germany, the Kingdom of Spain, the French Republic, the Grand Duchy of Luxembourg, the Kingdom of the Netherlands and the Republic of Austria on the stepping up of cross-border cooperation, particularly in combating terrorism, cross-border crime and illegal migration. In order ***that*** the substantive requirements of the Hague Programme ***can be fulfilled*** for all Member States ***and that its targets in terms of time-scale can be achieved***, the ***essential parts of*** the Prüm Treaty ***need*** to be made applicable to all Member States. This Council Decision ***should*** therefore ***be based on*** the main provisions of the Prüm Treaty.	(10) These requirements are satisfied by the Prüm Treaty of 27 May 2005 between the Kingdom of Belgium, the Federal Republic of Germany, the Kingdom of Spain, the French Republic, the Grand Duchy of Luxembourg, the Kingdom of the Netherlands and the Republic of Austria on the stepping up of cross-border cooperation, particularly in combating terrorism, cross-border crime and illegal migration. In order ***to fulfil*** the substantive requirements of the Hague Programme for all Member States, the Prüm Treaty ***need***s to be made applicable to all Member States. This Council ***Framework*** Decision therefore ***includes some of*** the main provisions of the Prüm Treaty, ***namely those related to police and judicial cooperation in the European Union***.

Amendment 6

Recital 11 a (new)

(11a) These improvements in the exchange of data constitute a step forward in making the information available between law enforcement officers in the Member States. It is appropriate to ensure that there are reasons for automated searches in national DNA and fingerprint databases whenever personal data are concerned.

Amendment 7

Recital 15

(15) Subject to certain conditions, Member States should be able to supply personal and non-personal data in order to improve the exchange of information in connection with major events with a cross-border dimension.

(15) Subject to certain conditions, Member States should be able to supply personal and non-personal data in order to improve the exchange of information in connection with major events with a cross-border dimension *and the purpose of which is to prevent terrorist offences. The supplying of the data should be necessary and proportionate and based on particular circumstances that give reason to believe that criminal offences will be committed.*

Amendment 8

Recital 15 a (new)

(15a) Within the framework of its mandate, Europol should also be granted access to national databases.

Amendment 9

Recital 16

(16) As international cooperation, particularly in combating cross-border crime, is to be further improved, this Decision, in addition to improving the exchange of information, should allow, amongst other things, closer cooperation between police authorities, for example by means of joint security operations (e.g. joint patrols) ***and cross-border intervention in the event of immediate danger to life or limb.***	(16) As international cooperation, particularly in combating cross-border crime, is to be further improved, this ***Framework*** Decision, in addition to improving the exchange of information, should allow, amongst other things, closer cooperation between police authorities, for example by means of joint security operations (e.g. joint patrols).

Amendment 10

Recital 18

(18) ***Aware of the importance which this Decision has for protecting the rights of individuals, and aware*** that the supply of personal data to another Member State requires ***a sufficient standard*** of data protection on the part of the receiving Member State, ***Member States should provide for efficient implementation of all data protection rules contained in the Decision.***	(18) ***The hit/no hit system provides a structure for comparing anonymous profiles, where additional personal data are exchanged only after a hit, and guarantees an adequate system of data protection, it being understood*** that the supply of personal data to another Member State requires ***an adequate level*** of data protection on the part of the receiving Member State.

Amendment 11

Recital 18 a (new)

	(18a) Special categories of data concerning racial or ethnic origin, political opinions, religious or philosophical beliefs, party or trade union membership, sexual orientation or health should

be processed only if absolutely necessary and proportionate for the purpose of a specific case and in compliance with specific safeguards.

Amendment 12

Recital 18 b (new)

(18b) These specific rules on data protection are created in absence of an adequate third pillar legal instrument on data protection. When approved, that general legal instrument should be applied to the entire area of police and judicial cooperation in criminal matters provided always that its level of data protection is adequate and not lower than the protection laid down in the Council of Europe Convention for the Protection of Individuals with regard to automatic Processing of Personal Data of 28 January 1981 and its additional Protocol of 8 November 2001 and takes account of Recommendation No R (87) 15 of 17 September 1987 of the Committee of Ministers to Member States regulating the use of personal data in the police sector, also where data are not processed automatically.

Amendment 13

Recital 18 c (new)

(18c) The European Parliament should be consulted on any measure implementing this Framework Decision.

Amendment 14

Recital 18 d (new)

(18d) It is necessary for the Council to adopt the Framework Decision on Procedural Rights as soon as possible in order to lay down certain minimum rules on the availability of legal assistance to individuals in the Member States.

Amendment 15

Recital 18 e (new)

(18e) With regard to the supply of information and assistance in connection with major events and mass gatherings, the overall framework must be reconciled with Joint Action 97/339/JHA of 26 May 1997 with regard to cooperation on law and order and security[3] *and the Council Resolution of 29 April 2004 on security at the European Council meetings and other comparable events*[4] *and the Initiative of the Kingdom of the Netherlands with a view to the adoption of a Council Decision on strengthening cross-border police cooperation with regard to meetings attended by large numbers of people from more than one Member State, at which policing is primarily aimed at maintaining law and order and security and preventing and combating criminal offences.*[5]

---

[3] *OJ L1 147, 5.6.1997, p. 1.*

[4] *OJ C 116, 30.4.2004, p. 18.*

[5] *OJ C 101, 27.4.2005, p. 36.*

Amendment 16

Recital 20

(20) This Decision respects the fundamental rights and observes the principles *set out* in particular *in the* Charter of Fundamental Rights of the European Union,	(20) This *Framework* Decision respects the fundamental rights and observes the principles *recognised,* in particular, *by the* Charter of Fundamental Rights of the European Union. *In particular, this Framework Decision seeks to ensure full compliance with citizens' fundamental rights to respect for their private life and communications and to the protection of their personal data as enshrined in Articles 7 and 8 of the Charter.*

Amendment 17

Recital 20 a (new)

	(20a) The full review and evaluation of the functioning of the Prüm Treaty to date and the establishment of a third pillar data protection framework decision are prerequisites for the effectiveness and correct implementation of this Framework Decision.

Amendment 19

Article 1, point 4

4) Provisions on the conditions and procedure for stepping up border police cooperation through various measures (Chapter 5).	4) Provisions on the conditions and procedure for stepping up border police cooperation through various *defined* measures (Chapter 5);

Amendment 20

Article 1, point 4 a (new)

4a) Provisions on data protection (Chapter 6, Article 14(2) and Article 16(2) and (4)).

Amendment 21

Article 1 a (new)

Article 1a

For the purposes of this Framework Decision:

1) "criminal offences" shall mean the offences listed in Article 2 of Council Framework Decision 2002/584/JHA;

2) "terrorist offences" shall mean the criminal offences listed in Articles 1 to 4 of Council Framework Decision 2002/475/JHA;

3) "personal data" shall mean any information relating to an identified or identifiable natural person ('data subject'); an "identifiable person" means a person who can be identified, directly or indirectly, in particular by reference to an identification number or to one or more factors specific to his physical or physiological identity;

4) "processing of personal data" shall mean any operation or set of operations which is performed upon personal data, whether or not by automated means, such as collection, recording, organisation, storage, adaptation or alteration, sorting, retrieval, consultation, use, disclosure by supply, dissemination or otherwise making available, alignment, combination, blocking, erasure or destruction of data; processing within the meaning of this Framework Decision shall also include notification of whether or not a hit exists;

5) "automated search procedure" shall mean direct access to the automated files of another body where the response to the search procedure does not require human intervention;

6) "referencing of data" shall mean the marking of stored personal data without the aim of limiting their processing in future;

7) "blocking of data" shall mean the marking of stored personal data with the aim of limiting their processing in future;

8) "non-coding part of DNA" shall mean chromosome zones containing no genetic expression, i.e. not known to provide information about specific hereditary characteristics; notwithstanding any scientific progress, no more information shall be revealed from the non-coding part of DNA either now nor in future.

Amendment 22

Article 1 b (new)

Article 1b

Member States shall provide for a clear distinction to be made between the personal data of

	– a person who is suspected of having committed or having taken part in a criminal offence,
	– a person who has been convicted of a criminal offence,
	– a person with regard to whom there are serious grounds for believing that he or she will commit a criminal offence,
	– a person who might be called on to testify in investigations in connection with criminal offences or subsequent criminal proceedings,
	– a person who has been the victim of a criminal offence or with regard to whom certain facts give reasons for believing that he or she could be the victim of a criminal offence,
	– a person who can provide information about criminal offences,
	– a contact or associate of one of the persons listed above, and
	– a person who does not fall within any of the categories referred to above.

Amendment 23

Article 2, paragraph 1

1. Member States shall open and keep national DNA analysis files for the investigation of criminal offences. Processing of data ***kept*** in those files, under this Decision, shall be carried out in accordance with ***this Decision***, in compliance with the national law applicable to the processing.	1. Member States shall open and keep national DNA analysis files for the investigation of criminal offences. Processing of ***personal*** data in those files, under this ***Framework*** Decision, shall be carried out in accordance with ***the rules on data protection laid down in Chapter 6***, in compliance with the national law applicable to the processing.

Amendment 24

Article 2, paragraph 2

2. For the purpose of implementing this Decision, the Member States shall ensure ***the availability of*** reference data from their national DNA analysis files ***as referred to in the first sentence of paragraph 1***. Reference data shall only include DNA profiles established from the non-coding part of DNA and a reference number. Reference data shall not contain any data from which the data subject can be directly identified. Reference data which is not attributed to any individual ("unidentified DNA-profiles") shall be recognisable as such.	2. For the purpose of implementing this ***Framework*** Decision, the Member States shall ensure ***access to*** reference data from their national DNA analysis files ***opened for the investigation of criminal offences***. Reference data shall only include DNA profiles established from the non-coding part of DNA and a reference number. Reference data shall not contain any data from which the data subject can be directly identified. Reference data which is not attributed to any individual ("unidentified DNA-profiles") shall be recognisable as such.

Amendment 25

Article 3, paragraph 1

1. For the investigation of criminal offences, Member States shall allow other Member States' national contact points ***as referred to in Article 6***, access to the reference data in their DNA analysis files, with the power to conduct automated searches by comparing DNA profiles. Searches may be conducted only in individual cases and in compliance with the requesting Member State's national law.	1. For the investigation of criminal offences, Member States shall allow other Member States' national contact points, access to the reference data in their DNA analysis files, with the power to conduct automated searches by comparing DNA profiles. Searches may be conducted only in individual cases and in compliance with ***the rules on data protection laid down in Chapter 6 and*** the requesting Member State's national law.

Amendment 26

Article 5

Should the procedures referred to in Articles 3 and 4 show a match between DNA profiles, the supply of ***any available*** further personal data and other information relating to the reference data shall be governed by the national law, including the legal assistance rules, of the requested Member State.	Should the procedures referred to in Articles 3 and 4 show a match between DNA profiles, the supply of further personal data and other information relating to the reference data shall be governed by the national law, including the legal assistance rules, of the requested Member State ***and the rules on data protection laid down in Chapter 6.***

Amendment 27

Article 6

Article 6 *National contact point and implementing measures* ***1. For the purposes of the supply of data as referred to in Articles 3 and 4, each Member State shall designate a national contact point. The powers of the national contact points shall be governed by the applicable national law.*** ***2. Details of technical arrangements for the procedures set out in Articles 3 and 4 shall be laid down in the implementing measures as referred to in Article 34.***	*deleted*

Amendment 28

Article 7, paragraph 1, introductory wording

Where, in ongoing investigations or criminal proceedings, there is no DNA profile available for a particular individual present within a requested Member State's territory, the requested Member State shall provide legal assistance by collecting and examining cellular material from that individual and by supplying the DNA profile obtained, if:	*1.* Where, in ongoing investigations or criminal proceedings ***relating to the commission of criminal offences***, there is no DNA profile available for a particular individual ***who is suspected of having committed such a criminal offence and who is*** present within a requested Member State's territory, the requested Member State shall provide legal assistance by collecting and examining cellular material from that individual and by supplying the DNA profile obtained, if:

Amendment 29

Article 7, paragraph 1 a (new)

	1a. The collection of cellular material shall take place only on the basis of national law and only for a specific purpose and shall meet the requirements of necessity and proportionality.

Amendment 30

Article 8

For the purpose of implementing this Decision, Member States shall ensure ***the availability of*** reference data from the file for the national automated fingerprint identification systems established for the prevention and investigation	For the purpose of implementing this ***Framework*** Decision, Member States shall ensure ***access to*** reference data from the file for the national automated fingerprint identification systems established for the prevention and investigation

of criminal offences. Reference data shall only include dactyloscopic data and a reference number. Reference data shall not contain any data from which the data subject can be directly identified. Reference data which is not attributed to any individual ("unidentified dactyloscopic data") must be recognisable as such.

of criminal offences. Reference data shall only include dactyloscopic data and a reference number. Reference data shall not contain any data from which the data subject can be directly identified. Reference data which is not attributed to any individual ("unidentified dactyloscopic data") must be recognisable as such.

Amendment 31

Article 9, paragraph 1

1. For the prevention and investigation of criminal offences, Member States shall allow other Member States' national contact points, as referred to in Article 11, access to the reference data in the automated fingerprint identification systems which they have established for that purpose, with the power to conduct automated searches by comparing dactyloscopic data. Searches may be conducted only in individual cases and in compliance with the requesting Member State's national law.

1. For the prevention and investigation of criminal offences, Member States shall allow other Member States' national contact points, as referred to in Article 11, access to the reference data in the automated fingerprint identification systems which they have established for that purpose, with the power to conduct automated searches by comparing dactyloscopic data. Searches may be conducted only in individual cases and in compliance with ***the rules on data protection laid down in Chapter 6 and*** the requesting Member State's national law.

Amendment 32

Article 10

Should the procedure referred to in Article 9 show a match between dactyloscopic data, the supply of ***any available*** further personal data and other information relating to the reference data shall be governed by the national law, including the legal assistance rules, of the requested Member State.	Should the procedure referred to in Article 9 show a match between dactyloscopic data, the supply of further personal data and other information relating to the reference data shall be governed by the national law, including the legal assistance rules, of the requested Member State ***and the rules on data protection laid down in Chapter 6.***

Amendment 33

Article 11

Article 11 *National contact point and implementing measures* ***1. For the purposes of the supply of data as referred to in Article 9, each Member State shall designate a national contact point. The powers of the national contact points shall be governed by the applicable national law.*** ***2. Details of technical arrangements for the procedure set out in Article 9 shall be laid down in the implementing measures as referred to in Article 34.***	*deleted*

Amendment 34

Article 12, paragraph 1

1. For the prevention and investigation of criminal offences and in dealing with other offences coming within the jurisdiction of the courts or the public prosecution service in the searching Member State, ***as well as in maintaining public order and security***, Member States shall allow other Member States' national contact points, as referred to in paragraph 2, access to the following national vehicle registration data, with the power to conduct automated searches in individual cases:	1. For the prevention and investigation of criminal offences and in dealing with other offences coming within the jurisdiction of the courts or the public prosecution service in the searching Member State, Member States shall allow other Member States' national contact points, as referred to in paragraph 2, access to the following national vehicle registration data, with the power to conduct automated searches in individual cases:
1) data relating to owners or operators, and	1) data relating to owners or operators, and
2) data relating to vehicles.	2) data relating to vehicles.
Searches may be conducted only with a full chassis number or a full registration number. Searches may be conducted only in compliance with the searching Member State's national law.	Searches may be conducted only with a full chassis number or a full registration number. Searches may be conducted only in compliance with ***the rules on data protection laid down in Chapter 6 and*** the searching Member State's national law.

Amendment 35

Article 12, paragraph 2

2. For the purposes of the supply of data as referred to in paragraph 1, each Member State shall designate a national contact point for incoming requests. The powers of the national contact points shall be governed by the applicable national law. Details of technical arrangements for the procedure	*deleted*

shall be laid down in the implementing measures as referred to in Article 34.

Amendment 36

Article 14, paragraph 1

1. For the prevention of criminal offences and in maintaining public order and security for major events with a cross-border dimension, in particular for sporting events or European Council meetings, Member States shall, both upon request and of their own accord, supply one another with personal data if any final convictions or other circumstances give reason to believe that the data subjects will commit criminal offences at the event or pose a threat to public order and security, in so far as the supply of such data is permitted under the supplying Member State's national law.

1. For the prevention of criminal offences and in maintaining public order and security for major events with a cross-border dimension, in particular for sporting events or European Council meetings, Member States shall, both upon request and of their own accord, supply one another with personal data if any final convictions or other circumstances give reason to believe that the data subjects will commit criminal offences at the event or pose a threat to public order and security, in so far as the supply of such data is permitted under the supplying Member State's national law ***and when necessary and proportionate in a democratic society, for a specific purpose and on a case-by-case basis.***

Amendment 37

Article 15

Article 15

National contact point

For the purposes of the supply of data as referred to in Articles 13 and 14, each Member State shall designate a national contact point. The powers of the national contact points shall be governed by the applicable national law.

deleted

Amendment 38

Article 16, paragraph 1

1. For the prevention of terrorist offences, Member States may, in compliance with national law, in individual cases, even without being requested to do so, supply other Member States' national contact points, ***as referred to in paragraph 3***, with the personal data and information specified in paragraph 2, in so far as is necessary because particular circumstances give reason to believe that the data subjects will commit ***criminal*** offences ***as referred to in Articles 1 to 3 of EU Council Framework Decision 2002/475/JHA of 13 June 2002 on combating terrorism..***	1. For the prevention of terrorist offences, Member States may, in compliance with national law, ***basic principles of law and fundamental rights***, in individual cases, even without being requested to do so, supply other Member States' national contact points with the personal data and information specified in paragraph 2, in so far as is necessary because particular circumstances give reason to believe that the data subjects will commit ***terrorist*** offences.

Amendment 39

Article 16, paragraph 2

2. The data to be supplied shall comprise ***surname, first names, date and place of birth and*** a description of the circumstances giving rise to the belief referred to in paragraph 1.	2. The data to be supplied shall comprise ***only personal data and*** a description of the circumstances giving rise to the belief referred to in paragraph 1.

Amendment 40

Article 16, paragraph 3

3. Each Member State shall designate a national contact point for exchange of information with other Member States' national contact points. The powers of the national contact points shall be governed by the applicable national law.	***deleted***

Amendment 41

Article 16, paragraph 4 a (new)

	4a. Regardless of those conditions, personal data may be processed only for the purposes specified in paragraph 1. The data supplied shall be deleted without delay once the purposes specified in paragraph 1 have been achieved or can no longer be achieved, and in any event after no more than two years from the date of supply.

Amendment 42

Article 17, paragraph 2

2. Each Member State may, as a host Member State, in compliance with its own national law, and with the seconding Member State's consent, confer executive powers on the seconding Member States' officers involved in joint operations *or, in so far as the host Member State's law permits, allow the seconding Member States' officers to exercise their executive powers in accordance with the seconding Member State's law*. Such executive powers may be exercised only under *the guidance* and, as a rule, in the presence of officers from the host Member State. *The seconding Member States' officers shall be subject to the host Member State's national law. The host Member State shall assume responsibility for their actions.*	2. *The seconding Member States' officers shall be subject to the host Member State's national law.* Each Member State may, as a host Member State, in compliance with its own national law, and with the seconding Member State's consent, confer executive powers on the seconding Member States' officers involved in joint operations. Such executive powers may be exercised only under *instructions from* and, as a *general* rule, in the presence of officers from the host Member State.

Amendment 43

Article 17 a (new)

Article 17a

Measures in the event of imminent danger

1. In urgent situations, officers from one Member State may, without the prior consent of another Member State ("the host Member State", cross the border between the two States so that, within an area of the host Member State's territory close to the border and in compliance with the host Member State's national law, they may take any provisional measures necessary to avert an imminent danger to the physical integrity of individuals.

2. An urgent situation as referred to in paragraph 1 shall be deemed to arise if there is a risk that the danger will materialise in the event of there being any delay before the host Member State's officers take responsibility as stipulated in Article 17(2).

3. The officers crossing the border shall immediately notify the host Member State of their presence. The host Member State shall confirm receipt of such notification and take the necessary measures without delay to avert the danger and take charge of the operations. The officers crossing the border may operate in the host Member State only until the host Member State has taken the necessary protective measures. The officers crossing the border shall be required to follow the host Member State's instructions.

4. The Member States shall specify in a separate agreement the authorities to be notified without delay, as stipulated in paragraph 3. The officers crossing the border shall be required to comply with the provisions of this Article and with the law of the host Member State.

5. The host Member State shall assume responsibility for the measures taken by the officers crossing the border.

Amendment 44

Article 18 a (new)

Article 18a

Cooperation upon request

1. The competent authorities of the Member States shall provide one another with assistance, upon request, within the scope of their powers and in compliance with their own national law.

2. Those competent authorities shall provide one another with assistance, in accordance with the first sentence of Article 39(1) of the Convention of 19 June 1990 implementing the Schengen Agreement of 14 June 1985 on the gradual abolition of checks at common borders, in particular by:

(1) identifying owners and operators of vehicles and providing information on drivers, masters and captains of vehicles, vessels and aircraft, in so far as not already provided for in Article 12;

(2) supplying information on driving licences, navigation licences and similar permits;

(3) ascertaining the whereabouts and place of residence of individuals;

(4) checking residence permits;

(5) ascertaining the identity of telephone subscribers and subscribers to other telecommunications services, where publicly accessible;

(6) establishing the identity of individuals;

(7) investigating the origin of items such as arms, motor vehicles and vessels (enquiries via trade channels);

(8) supplying data from police databases and police records and supplying information from official records accessible to the public;

(9) issuing urgent alerts concerning arms and explosives and alerts concerning currency counterfeiting and securities fraud;

(10) supplying information on practical implementation of cross-border surveillance, cross-border hot pursuit and controlled deliveries, and

(11) ascertaining an individual's willingness to make a statement.

3. If the authority to which the request is made does not have the power to deal with the request, it shall pass it on to an authority with the power to do so. The requested authority shall notify

the requesting authority of the passing on of the request and of the authority empowered to deal with it. The latter authority shall deal with the request and send the requesting authority the result.

Amendment 45

Article 19, paragraph 1

1. Officers from a seconding Member State *who are involved in a joint operation within another Member State's territory may wear their own national uniforms there. They* may carry *such arms,* ammunition and equipment as they are allowed to under the seconding Member State's national law. The host Member State may prohibit the carrying of *particular arms,* ammunition or equipment by a seconding Member State's officers.

1. Officers from a seconding Member State may carry *such service weapons,* ammunition and equipment as they are allowed to under the seconding Member State's national law. The host Member State may prohibit the carrying of *certain service weapons,* ammunition or equipment by a seconding Member State's officers *provided its own legislation applies the same prohibition to its own officers.*

Amendment 46

Article 19, paragraph 2 a (new)

2a. Officers from a seconding Member State who are involved in a joint operation in another Member State's territory shall wear their own national uniforms. A common distinctive sign must be carried by all members of the joint operation. The host Member State must deliver an accreditation document to the seconding Member States' officers, including the name, rank and a digitised photograph of the officer.

Amendment 47

Article 24, paragraph 1

1. For the purposes of this Chapter: 1) "processing of personal data" shall mean any operation or set of operations which is performed upon personal data, whether or not by automatic means, such as collection, recording, organisation, storage, adaptation or alteration, sorting, retrieval, consultation, use, disclosure by supply, dissemination or otherwise making available, alignment, combination, blocking, erasure or destruction of data. Processing within the meaning of this Decision shall also include notification of whether or not a hit exists; *2) "automated search procedure" shall mean direct access to the automated files of another body where the response to the search procedure is fully automated;* *3) "referencing" shall mean the marking of stored personal data without the aim of limiting their processing in future;* *4) "blocking" shall mean the marking of stored personal data with the aim of limiting their processing in future.*	*deleted*

Amendment 48

Article 24, paragraph 2

2. The following provisions shall apply to data which are or have been supplied pursuant to this Decision, save as otherwise provided in the preceding Chapters.	*2. The following provisions shall apply to the collection and processing of DNA material and fingerprints in a Member State and to the supply of further personal data within the scope of this Framework Decision.* *The following provisions shall also apply to data which are or have been supplied pursuant to this Framework Decision.*

Amendment 49

Article 25, paragraph 1 a (new)

	1a. Member States shall take into account the various categories of personal data and the various purposes for which they are collected with a view to laying down time limits for their storage and appropriate conditions for their collection, further processing and transfer. Personal data relating to persons who are not suspected of having committed or taken part in a criminal offence may be processed only for the purpose for which they were collected and for a limited period. Member States shall lay down appropriate limitations on access to and transmission of such data.

Amendment 50

Article 25, paragraph 3

3. Paragraph 2 shall not apply to those Member States where the supply of personal data as provided for in this Decision has already started pursuant to the Treaty of 27 May 2005 between the Kingdom of Belgium, the Federal Republic of Germany, the Kingdom of Spain, the French Republic, the Grand Duchy of Luxembourg, the Kingdom of the Netherlands and the Republic of Austria on the stepping up of cross-border cooperation, in particular in combating terrorism, cross-border crime and illegal migration ("Prüm Treaty").	*deleted*

Amendment 51

Article 25, paragraph 3 a (new)

	3a. Data processed under this **Framework** *Decision shall not be transferred or made available to a third country or to any international organisation.*

Amendment 52

Article 26, paragraph 1

1. Processing of personal data by the receiving Member State shall be permitted solely for the purposes for which the data have been supplied in accordance with this Decision. Processing for other purposes shall be permitted solely with the prior authorisation of the Member State administering the file	1. Processing of personal data by the receiving Member State shall be permitted solely for the purposes for which the data have been supplied in accordance with this *Framework* Decision. Processing for other purposes shall be permitted solely with the prior authorisation of the Member State administering the

and subject only to the national law of the receiving Member State. Such authorisation may be granted provided that processing for such other purposes is permitted under the national law of the Member State administering the file.	file and subject only to the national law of the receiving Member State. Such authorisation may be granted provided that processing for such other purposes is permitted under the national law of the Member State administering the file ***and on a case-by-case basis***.

Amendment 53

Article 27

Personal data supplied may be processed only by the authorities, bodies and courts with responsibility for a task in furtherance of the aims mentioned in Article 26. In particular, data may be supplied to other entities only with the prior authorisation of the supplying Member State and in compliance with the law of the receiving Member State.	Personal data supplied may be processed only by the authorities, bodies and courts with responsibility for a task in furtherance of the aims mentioned in Article 26. In particular, data may be supplied to other entities only with the prior authorisation of the supplying Member State ***on a case-by-case basis*** and in compliance with the law of the receiving Member State.

Amendment 54

Article 28, paragraph 2 a (new)

	2a. Special categories of data concerning racial or ethnic origin, political opinions, religious or philosophical beliefs, party or trade union membership, sexual orientation or health shall be processed only if absolutely necessary and proportionate for the purpose of a specific case and in compliance with specific safeguards.

Amendment 55

Article 28, paragraph 3, point (2)

2) following the expiry of the maximum period *for keeping data laid down in the national law of the supplying Member State where the supplying body informed the receiving body of those maximum periods at the time of supplying the data.*	2) following the expiry of the maximum period *of two years, except in the cases laid down in Articles 14 and 16.*

Amendment 56

Article 29, paragraph 2, point (1)

1) *state-of-the-art* technical measures are taken to ensure data protection and data security, in particular data confidentiality and integrity;	1) *the best available* technical measures are taken to ensure data protection and data security, in particular data confidentiality and integrity;

Amendment 57

Article 30, paragraph 2, introductory wording

2. *The following shall apply to automated searches for data based on Articles 3, 9, 12 and automated comparison pursuant to Article 4:*	*deleted*

Amendment 58

Article 30, paragraph 4

4. The recorded data shall be protected with suitable measures against inappropriate use and other forms of improper use and shall be kept for *two* years. After the conservation period the recorded data shall be deleted immediately.	4. The recorded data shall be protected with suitable measures against inappropriate use and other forms of improper use and shall be kept for *three* years. After the conservation period the recorded data shall be deleted immediately.

Amendment 59

Article 31, paragraph 1

1. *At the request of the data subject under national law, information* shall be *supplied* in compliance with national law *to the data subject upon production of proof of his identity,* without unreasonable expense, in general comprehensible terms and without unacceptable delays, *on the data processed in respect of his person, the origin of the data, the recipient or groups of recipients, the intended purpose of the processing and the legal basis for the processing.* Moreover, the data subject shall be entitled to have inaccurate data corrected and unlawfully processed data deleted. *The* Member States shall also ensure that, in the event of violation of his rights in relation to data protection, the data subject shall be able to lodge an effective complaint to an independent court or a tribunal within the meaning of Article 6(1) of the European Convention on Human Rights or an independent supervisory authority within the meaning of Article 28 of Directive 95/46/EC of the European Parliament and of the Council of 24 October 1995 on the protection of individuals with regard to the processing of personal data and on the free movement of such data and that he is given the possibility to claim for damages or to seek another form of legal compensation. The detailed rules for the procedure to assert these rights and the reasons for limiting the right of access shall be governed by the relevant	1. *Information about data collected, data supplied to other Member States and authorisations concerning those data* shall be *dealt with* in compliance with national law without unreasonable expense, in general comprehensible terms and without unacceptable delays. Moreover, the data subject shall be entitled to have inaccurate data corrected and unlawfully processed data deleted, *of which the data subject shall also be informed.* Member States shall also ensure that, in the event of violation of his rights in relation to data protection, the data subject shall be able to lodge an effective complaint to an independent court or a tribunal within the meaning of Article 6(1) of the European Convention on Human Rights or an independent supervisory authority within the meaning of Article 28 of Directive 95/46/EC of the European Parliament and of the Council of 24 October 1995 on the protection of individuals with regard to the processing of personal data and on the free movement of such data and that he is given the possibility to claim for damages or to seek another form of legal compensation. The detailed rules for the procedure to assert these rights and the reasons for limiting the right of access shall be governed by the relevant national legal provisions of the Member State where the data subject asserts his rights.

national legal provisions of the Member Steate where the data subject assrts his rights.

Amendment 60

Article 32 a (new)

Article 32a

Member States shall adopt suitable measures to ensure the full implementation of the provisions of this Chapter and shall lay down effective, proportionate and dissuasive sanctions to be imposed in the event of infringement thereof, notably those provisions aimed at ensuring the confidentiality and security of personal data processing.

Amendment 61

Article 32 b (new)

Article 32b

1. For the purpose of the supply of data as referred to in Articles 3, 4, 9, 12, 14 and 16, each Member State shall designate one or several national contact points.

2. The powers of the national contact points shall be governed by the applicable national law. National contact points shall be available at all times.

3. The list of all national contact points shall be sent by each Member State to the other Member States and shall be published in the Official Journal of the European Union.

Amendment 62

Article 33, paragraph 2

2. Declarations submitted in accordance with paragraph 1 may be amended at any time by means of a declaration submitted to the General Secretariat of the Council. The General Secretariat of the Council shall forward any declarations received to the Member States and the Commission.	2. Declarations submitted in accordance with paragraph 1 may be amended at any time by means of a declaration submitted to the General Secretariat of the Council. The General Secretariat of the Council shall forward any declarations received to the Member States, ***the European Parliament*** and the Commission.

Amendment 63

Article 33, paragraph 2 a (new)

	2a. Declarations, except for those referred to in Article 19(4), shall be published in the Official Journal of the European Union.

Amendment 64

Article 34

The Council shall adopt measures ***necessary to implement this Decision at the level of the Union in accordance with the procedure laid down in the second sentence of Article 34(2)(c) of the EU Treaty.***	1. The Council shall adopt ***implementing measures only after consulting the European Parliament.***
	2. The implementing measures shall also be communicated to the European Data Protection Supervisor, who may give his or her opinion thereon.

Amendment 65

Article 35

Each Member State shall bear the operational costs incurred by its own authorities in connection with the implementation of this Decision. ***In special cases, the Member States concerned may agree on different arrangements.***	Each Member State shall bear the operational costs incurred by its own authorities in connection with the implementation of this *Framework* Decision. ***However, the general budget of the European Union shall bear the costs relating to the functioning of TESTA II (Trans European Services for Telematics between Administrations) or any other network used to exchange the data referred to in Chapter 2 of this Framework Decision.***

Amendment 66

Article 36, paragraph 2

2. Member States may conclude or bring into force bilateral or multilateral agreements or arrangements which concern the scope of this Decision after it has entered into force in so far as such agreements or arrangements provide for the objectives of this Decision to be extended or enlarged.	2. Member States may conclude or bring into force bilateral or multilateral agreements or arrangements which concern the scope of this *Framework* Decision after it has entered into force in so far as such agreements or arrangements provide for the objectives of this *Framework* Decision to be extended or enlarged, ***including the data protection objectives of this Framework Decision.***

Amendment 67

Article 36, paragraph 4

4. Member States shall inform the Council and the Commission within [. . . years] of entry into force of this Decision of existing agreements or arrangements within the meaning of the first paragraph which they wish to continue to apply.	4. Member States shall inform ***the European Parliament,*** the Council and the Commission within [. . . years] of entry into force of this *Framework* Decision of existing agreements or arrangements within the meaning of the first paragraph which they wish to continue to apply.

Amendment 68

Article 36, paragraph 5

5. Member States shall also inform the Council and the Commission of all new agreements or arrangements within the meaning of paragraph 2 within 3 months of their signing or, in the case of instruments which were signed before adoption of this Decision, within three months of their entry into force.	5. Member States shall also inform ***the European Parliament,*** the Council and the Commission of all new agreements or arrangements within the meaning of paragraph 2 within 3 months of their signing or, in the case of instruments which were signed before adoption of this *Framework* Decision, within three months of their entry into force.

Amendment 69

Article 37, paragraph 2

2. Member States shall transmit to the General Secretariat of the Council ***and the Commission*** the text of the provisions transposing into their national law the obligations imposed on them under this Decision. When doing so, each Member State may indicate that it will apply immediately this Decision in its relations with those	2. Member States shall transmit to the General Secretariat of the Council the text of the provisions transposing into their national law the obligations imposed on them under this *Framework* Decision. When doing so, each Member State may indicate that it will apply immediately this *Framework* Decision in its relations with those

Member States which have given the same notification.

Member States which have given the same notification. ***The General Secretariat of the Council shall forward the notifications received to the Member States, the European Parliament and the Commission.***

Amendment 70

Article 37 a (new)

Article 37a

1. The Council shall carry out an evaluation of the administrative, technical and financial application and implementation of this Framework Decision every two years.

2. The modalities of the automated searching and comparison of DNA and dactyloscopic data shall be evaluated six months after the date on which this Framework Decision takes effect. For vehicle registration data, this first evaluation shall take place three months after that date.

3. Evaluation reports shall be transmitted to the European Parliament and the Commission.

DOCUMENT NO. 25

AGREEMENT WITH THE USA ON THE USE OF PASSENGER NAME RECORD DATA

European Parliament Recommendation P6_TA(2006)0354

Strassbourg, 7 September 2006

[*European Parliament Recommendation to the Council on the Negotiations for an Agreement with the United States of America on the use of Passenger Name Records (PNR) data to Prevent and Combat Terrorism and Transnational Crime, Including Organised Crime (2006/2193(INI))*]

The European Parliament,

– having regard to the proposal for a recommendation to the Council by Sophia in't Veld on behalf of the ALDE Group on the content of the Agreement with the United States of America on the use of Passenger Name Records (PNR) data to prevent and combat terrorism and transnational crime, including organised crime (B6–0382/2006),

– having regard to Rule 114(3) and Rule 94 of its Rules of Procedure,

– having regard to the report of the Committee on Civil Liberties, Justice and Home Affairs (A6–0252/2006),

A. recalling its previous resolutions on the PNR issue,[1] in which Parliament expressed from the outset:

[1] Parliament resolutions of 13 March 2003 on transfer of personal data by airlines in the case of transatlantic flights (OJ C 61 E, 10.3.2004, p. 381), of 9 October 2003 on transfer of personal data by airlines in the case of transatlantic flights: state of negotiations with the USA (OJ C 81 E, 31.3.2004, p. 105) and of 31 March 2004 on the draft Commission decision noting the adequate level of protection provided for personal data contained in the Passenger Name Records (PNRs) transferred to the US Bureau of Customs and Border Protection (OJ C 103 E, 29.4.2004, p. 665).

– its readiness to authorise access by public authorities to passengers' personal data for security purposes when necessary for the purposes of identifying them and cross-checking them against a "watch list" of dangerous persons or known criminals and terrorists (as is done in the EU in connection with Schengen Implementing Convention or under Directive 2004/82/EC,[2] which give access to identification data managed by airlines through the Advanced Passenger Information System (APIS), and

[2] Council Directive 2004/82/EC of 29 April 2004 on the obligation of carriers to communicate passenger data (OJ L 261, 6.8.2004, p. 24).

– its deep concerns about the systematic access by the public authorities to data, such as the credit card number, the e-mail address, any affiliation to a particular group, frequent-flyer information, linked to the behaviour of ordinary passengers (i.e. people not recorded in the receiving country as dangerous or criminal) in order to check only against a theoretical pattern whether such a passenger might constitute a potential threat to the flight, his or her country of destination or a country through which he or she will transit;

B. being aware that systematic access to "behaviour" data, even if not acceptable in the EU, is currently required by countries including the USA, Canada and Australia for the protection of their internal security, but pointing out that:

– in the case of Canada and Australia, domestic legislation provides for access to data which is limited in scope and time and as regards the amount of data covered and is under the control of a judicial authority, on account of which those systems have been considered adequate by Parliament and by the national data protection authorities in the EU,

– in the case of the US, even after long negotiations with the Commission and some goodwill stated in the "undertakings", there is still no legal US data protection in the field of air transport; therefore, all PNR data can be accessed, with the sole exception of "sensitive" data, and the data can be retained for years after the security check has been carried out; furthermore, there is no judicial protection for non-US citizens,

C. considering that since the atrocities of 11 September 2001, a host of single security measures has been introduced worldwide, which often involve the systematic collection and monitoring of personal data of all citizens, notably data on money transfers and telecommunications and passenger data; considering that, in the absence of a coherent EU security policy, the position of the individual citizen *vis à vis* the state risks being undermined;

D. recalling that Parliament brought proceedings before the Court of Justice of the European Communities seeking the annulment of Council

Decision 2004/496/EC[1] on the conclusion of an agreement with the USA, negotiated on the basis of Commission Decision 2004/535/EC,[2] on the grounds that the decision lacked both a legal basis and legal clarity and because the collection of personal data authorised under the agreement was excessive when weighed against the need to combat organised crime and terrorism,

[1] Council Decision 2004/496/ECof 17 May 2004 on the conclusion of an Agreement between the European Community and the United States of America on the processing and transfer of PNR data by Air Carriers to the United States Department of Homeland Security, Bureau of Customs and Border Protection (OJ L 183, 20.5.2004, p. 83).

[2] Commission Decision 2004/535/EC of 14 May 2004 on the adequate protection of personal data contained in the Passenger Name Record of air passengers transferred to the United States' Bureau of Customs and Border Protection (OJ L 235, 6.7.2004, p. 11).

E. welcoming the annulment by the Court of Justice of Council Decision 2004/496/EC and Commission Decision 2004/535/EC,[3]

[3] Judgment of 30 May 2006 in Joined Cases C-317/04 and C-318/04.

F. regretting that the Court of Justice did not respond to Parliament's concerns about the legal structure of the agreement and the congruency of its content with the data protection principles laid down in Article 8 of the European Convention for the Protection of Human Rights and Fundamental Freedoms (ECHR);

G. taking into account the fact that the Court of Justice held that Council Decision 2004/496/EC could not be adopted validly on the basis of Article 95 of the EC Treaty in conjunction with Directive 95/46/EC[1], because the transfer to and the use of PNR data by the US Bureau of Customs and Border Protection (CBP) relates to data processing operations concerning public security and state activities in areas of criminal law, which fall outside the scope of Directive 95/46/EC and the first pillar;

[1] Directive 95/46/EC of the European Parliament and of the Council of 24 October 1995 on the protection of individuals with regard to the processing of personal data and on the free movement of such data (OJ L 281, 23.11.1995, p. 31).

H. taking into account the expressed willingness of the Commission and the Council to cooperate closely with the Parliament in order to ensure full compliance with the Court's judgment; however, regretting that the Council has failed to involve the Parliament in the ongoing negotiations;

I. sharing the opinion adopted on 14 June 2006 by the Article 29 Working Party on the necessary follow-up to the Court's judgment,[2]

[2] Opinion 5/2006 on the ruling by the European Court of Justice of 30 May 2006 in Joined Cases C-317/04 and C-318/04 on the transmission of Passenger Name Records to the United States (see: http://ec.europa.eu/justice_home/fsj/privacy/workinggroup/wpdocs/2006_en.htm)

J. considering the importance of the issue to be such that the EU should, in any event, come to an arrangement with the USA on a proper international agreement which, with due respect for fundamental rights, would lay down:

(a) which data are necessary for identification purposes and should be transferred systematically in an automated way (APIS) and which data relating to passenger "behaviour" could be transferred on a case-by-case basis in respect of people recorded on public security "watch lists" as "dangerous" on account of criminal or terrorist activity,

(b) the list of serious crimes in respect of which any additional request could be made,

(c) the list of authorities and agencies that could share the data and the data-protection conditions to be respected,

(d) the data-retention period for the two kinds of data, it being clear that data relating to the prevention of serious crimes must be exchanged in accordance with the EU-US agreement on mutual legal assistance[3] and extradition,[4]

[3] OJ L 181, 19.7.2003, p. 34.

[4] OJ L 181, 19.7.2003, p. 27.

(e) the role to be played by airlines, the Computerized Reservation Systems or private organisations (such as the SITA and AMADEUS) in transferring passengers' data and the means envisaged (APIS, PNR, etc.) for public-security purposes,

(f) the guarantees to be afforded to passengers in order to enable them to correct the data relating to them or to provide an explanation in the event of a discrepancy between the data relating to a travel contract and the data shown in identity documents, visas, passports and other official documents,

(g) the airlines' responsibilities as regards passengers and public authorities in the event of transcription or encoding errors and as regards protection of the data processed,

(h) the right to appeal to an independent authority and redress mechanisms in the event of infringements of passengers' rights;

(i) the need to strictly comply with Article 6(d) of Regulation (EEC) No 2299/89 of 24 July 1989 on a code of conduct for computerized reservation systems,[1] which requires the previous consent of the passenger for any transfer of personal information;

[1] OJ L 220, 29.7.1989, p. 1.

1. Addresses the following recommendations to the Council:

General Principles

(a) to avoid a legal lacuna at European level from 1 October 2006 for the transfer of passenger data and to ensure that the rights and freedoms of passengers are protected to an even greater extent than they are at present under the unilateral undertakings submitted by the US administration;

(b) to base any new agreements in this field on the EC principles on data protection as drawn from Article 8 ECHR;

As Regards the Negotiation Procedure:

(c) to negotiate, subject to calendar constraints,

- a new short-term international agreement to cover the period between 1 October 2006 and November 2007 (the period originally covered by the US/EC agreement that was the subject of the Court's judgment),
- for the medium to long term, a more coherent approach at International Civil Aviation Organisation (ICAO) level towards the exchange of passenger data in order to ensure both air-traffic security and respect of human rights at global level;

(d) to mandate the Presidency, assisted by the Commission, to inform Parliament of the negotiations on the agreement and to involve representatives of the relevant committee as observers in the dialogue with the US administration;

As Regards the Content of the Short-Term Agreement

(e) to overcome, in the first instance, the shortcomings outlined in the first joint EU/US review of the agreement[2] and to take into account the recommendations of the European Data Protection Supervisor and the Article 29 Working Party;[3]

[2] Joint Review of the implementation by the US Bureau of Customs and Border Protection of the Undertakings set out in Commission Decision 2004/535/EC of 14 May 2004 (Redacted version of 12.12.2005).

[3] (see: http://ec.europa.eu/justice_home/fsj/privacy/workinggroup/wpdocs/2006_en.htm)

(f) to include the content of the undertakings in the body of the agreement so that they may become legally binding, thereby making it necessary for the two parties to establish or modify any existing legislation and for the judiciary to protect persons covered by the agreement;

(g) to incorporate immediately, as proof of good faith on the part of the US administration, into the new agreement the commitments, which are still not fully implemented over two years after the entry into force of the agreement, as follows:

- the strict purpose limitation, as formerly provided for in Undertaking 3, so that behaviour data may not be used for checking financial crimes or to prevent avian flu; such a limitation should also be laid down for the onward transfer of such data;
- the shift to a PUSH system (as provided for in Undertaking 13), as in the case of EC agreements with Canada and Australia, since all the technical requirements are in place and this is already done, for instance by SITA;
- provision of information to passengers on the PNR rules, and the introduction of proper judicial complaint procedures, as provided for in Undertakings 36–42 and by the PNR agreements with Canada and Australia;
- the need to ensure adequate instructions and training of the staff who handle the data, and the need to secure the IT systems;
- the annual joint review, as provided for in Undertaking 43, which should indeed take place annually, be conducted in cooperation with the national data protection authorities and be published in full and must assess not only the implementation of the undertakings but also the results of the agreement in terms of eliminating terrorism and crime;

As Regards the Content of the Medium-Term Agreement

(h) to provide the EU with a clear legal framework, namely by adopting, as a matter of urgency, the Draft Data Protection Framework Decision;

(i) to avoid an artificial division between the "pillars" by creating a consistent cross-pillar data protection framework in the Union by activating the *passarelle* clause under Article 42 of the Treaty on European Union in order to ensure that the new agreement is concluded in association with Parliament and is subject to the scrutiny of the Court of Justice;

(j) to limit the amount of data that may be requested and to filter at source sensitive data as required by Article 8 of Directive 95/46/EC; notes that carriers are required to submit only the data available to them, so that, in practice, the CBP rarely receives all 34 categories of data requested; concludes that for the purposes of the agreement, namely to prevent and combat terrorism and transnational crime, including organised crime, even APIS data would be sufficient; calls on the Council Presidency and the Commission to raise this matter in the negotiations;

2. Reiterates its previous demand that the new agreement should grant to European passengers the same level of data protection as is enjoyed by US citizens;

3. Stresses its previous position that the EU should avoid the indirect creation of a European PNR system through the transfer of the relevant data by the CBP to police and judicial authorities in the Member States; considers that the systematic collection of the data of ordinary citizens outside the framework of a judicial procedure or police investigation should remain forbidden in the EU and that data should be exchanged where necessary in accordance with the existing EU/US agreement on mutual legal assistance and extradition;

4. Proposes that a dialogue in which parliamentary representatives would take part be launched before the end of 2006 between the EU, the US, Canada and Australia with a view to preparing jointly the 2007 review and establishing a global standard for the transmission of PNR, if that is deemed necessary;

5. Strongly recommends that Parliament organise a joint session in this respect with the US Congress, being the democratically representative institutions of the citizens concerned, so as to start a dialogue on the fight against terrorism and its consequences for civil liberties and human rights;

6. Instructs its President to forward this resolution to the Council and, for information, to the Commission.

DOCUMENT NO. 26

TOWARDS ENHANCING ACCESS TO INFORMATION BY LAW ENFORCEMENT AGENCIES

Communication from the Commission of the European Communities to the European Parliament and the Council

16 June 2004

Exchange of Information Between the Law Enforcement Authorities of the Member States:

In order to step up the fight against terrorism and organised crime, the European Commission wishes to enhance the exchange of information between the law enforcement authorities of the Member States. It proposes introducing a European information policy for these authorities aimed at better exchange of information, at intelligence-led law enforcement and at building trust on the basis of respect for fundamental rights.

Summary

In this communication, the Commission proposes an approach aimed at improving free circulation of information between the law enforcement authorities of the Member States and the authority in charge of crime prevention. These authorities include the police forces, customs authorities, financial intelligence units, the judicial authorities and all the public bodies involved in the detection of security threats, conviction and punishment. The Commission's proposals come in the wake of the declaration on combating terrorism of the European Council of 25 March 2004 and encompass legal, technical and organisational measures for combating terrorist threats and organised crime.

The Commission points out that there are two main obstacles to this free circulation of information. The first is that the information tends to be compartmentalised at both organisational and legal levels. For example, it is divided between different ministries and services and is intended for use in different procedures, thereby affecting the nature and sensitivity of the information that can be handled by the services. The second obstacle is the lack of a clear policy on information channels, resulting in disagreement on the choice of channel and on how to handle sensitive and confidential information.

The three main objectives proposed by the Commission are therefore the following:

- to take stock and analyse the conditions needed to improve access to, and the use and exchange of, relevant information on law enforcement and crime prevention;
- to introduce an EU intelligence-led police and judicial policy;
- to maintain a strict balance between effective respect for citizens' rights and an increase in state powers of obtaining and using information in order to ensure that the security level demanded by these citizens is maintained by democratic processes.

In order to achieve these objectives, the Commission points out that the policy on exchange of information between the law enforcement agencies must take into account several factors. Firstly, there must be common and concerted action by the national, European and international agencies. As well as security, respect for individual rights, human rights and fundamental freedoms must be ensured. Compatible information exchange systems protected against unlawful access are also needed, as are common standards for information storage, analysis and exchange between the relevant services.

The Commission calls on the Member States to implement an information policy aimed at:

- making accessible necessary and relevant data for the law enforcement authorities and those responsible for preventing crime and terrorism;
- promoting the production and use of EU criminal intelligence that is of high-quality in both strategic and operational terms;
- building trust between the relevant services, in particular through personal data protection.

Access to Data and Information

The main aim of the information policy is to make the information needed for combating terrorism and organised crime accessible to all the EU law enforcement authorities who need this information in order to carry out their statutory tasks. To this end, the Commission proposes launching initiatives associated with conditions for access to information and with data collection and exchange.

The main obstacles to data sharing identified by the Commission are created by the lack of:

- common standards for data processing and access;
- compatible crime definitions and statistics;
- culture of cooperation between the relevant authorities and between public—and private-sector players;
- awareness of data protection rules.

The Commission proposes laying down transparent and straightforward conditions for access to data. Member States will be responsible for the implementation of these conditions. The Commission intends to launch studies on:

- needs and restrictions in this area;
- conditions of access;
- data protection and security procedures.

The information policy introduces the principle of right of equivalent access to data. Once established, this principle would allow mutual exchange of data between the authorities and agencies in the Member States based on the standards and conditions applicable in the Member State in which the data are to be accessed.

This principle of equivalent access is underpinned by the following basic considerations:

- the security of the Union and its citizens is a joint responsibility;
- Member States depend on each other to enforce laws in order to combat terrorism and organised crime;
- the law enforcement authorities in the various Member States fulfil similar tasks;
- the law enforcement authorities act lawfully when accessing data.

In order to develop further the principle of equivalent access, the Commission proposes introducing minimum standards for the collection of data. It also plans to create a network of databases or a central database.

Lastly, the Commission wishes to promote research on security co-financed by the *AGIS* programme. In addition, a preparatory security research action for 2004-06 is aimed at launching a comprehensive European security research programme from 2007.

Enforcement of EU Intelligence-Led Law

The second objective of the information policy is to establish measures aimed at developing intelligence-led law enforcement in the EU. The police and judicial authorities are to be encouraged to enhance cooperation through intelligence-led actions. The Commission intends to make the necessary information available to a criminal intelligence network and to format this information so that it can be used throughout the EU. The aim is to improve the security of the EU and its citizens while respecting individuals' fundamental rights and the rule of law.

The Commission envisages a two-phased approach. In the first phase, it proposes that the Member States' criminal intelligence services should meet on a monthly basis, under the aegis of *Europol*, to exchange intelligence and discuss their strategic assessments. In the second phase, these services could produce criminal intelligence using standardised analytical tools.

To this end, the Commission would like to involve Europol more closely and increase its importance. It also plans to call on the Chiefs of Police Task Force (CPTF) to set up a common curriculum for training intelligence officials of the *European Police College* (CEPOL).

Building of Trust

The third objective of the information policy is to contribute to the building of trust between the authorities, officials and partners responsible for law enforcement in Europe by establishing a joint platform of shared values, standards and policies. Another aim of the information policy is to develop working relations between the Member States. The Commission plans to present more proposals in this area by the end of 2005.

Related Acts

Draft Framework Decision of 28 April 2004 on the retention of data processed and stored in connection with the provision of publicly available electronic communications services or data on public communications networks for the purpose of prevention, investigation, detection and prosecution of crime and criminal offences, including terrorism [JAI(2004) 8—Not published in the Official Journal].

This draft framework decision is an initiative of France, Ireland, Sweden and the United Kingdom. It proposes retaining data processed or transmitted on public communications networks in order to prevent, detect and prosecute crimes and criminal offences, including organised crime and terrorism.

Communication from the Commission to the Council and the European Parliament of 16 December 2003: Transfer of Air Passenger Name Record

(PNR) Data: A Global EU Approach [*COM(2003) 826* final—Not published in the Official Journal].

This communication proposes better standards of protection for personal data transferred from the EU in the context of reinforced aviation and border security as part of the fight against terrorism.

Directive *2002/58/EC* of the European Parliament and of the Council of 12 July 2002 concerning the processing of personal data and the protection of privacy in the electronic communications sector (*Directive on privacy and electronic communications*) [Official Journal L 201 of 31 July 2002].

D. DEFINING AND CATEGORIZING TERRORIST ORGANIZATIONS

DOCUMENT NO. 27

GESTORAS PRO AMNISTÍA

EUROPEAN COURT OF JUSTICE

27 February 2007*

Case C-354/04 P

Judgment of the Court (Grand Chamber)

APPEAL under Article 56 of the Statute of the Court of Justice lodged at the Court on 17 August 2004,

Gestoras Pro Amnistía, established at Hernani (Spain),

Juan Mari Olano Olano, residing in Madrid (Spain),

Julen Zelarain Errasti, residing in Madrid (Spain),

represented by D. Rouget, avocat, appellants,

the other parties to the proceedings being:

Council of the European Union, represented by E. Finnegan and M. Bauer, acting as Agents, defendant at first instance,

Kingdom of Spain, represented by the Abogacía del Estado,

United Kingdom of Great Britain and Northern Ireland, interveners at first instance,

THE COURT (Grand Chamber),

composed of V. Skouris, President, P. Jann, C.W.A. Timmermans, A. Rosas, K. Lenaerts and R. Schintgen, Presidents of Chambers, A. Tizzano, J.N. Cunha Rodrigues, R. Silva de Lapuerta, L. Bay Larsen, P. Lindh, J.-C. Bonichot (Rapporteur) and T. von Danwitz, Judges,

Advocate General: P. Mengozzi,

Registrar: R. Grass,

* Language of the case: French.

having regard to the written procedure,

after hearing the Opinion of the Advocate General at the sitting on 26 October 2006

gives the following

Judgment

1. By their appeal Gestoras Pro Amnistía, Mr Olano Olano and Mr Zelarain Errasti request the Court to set aside the order of the Court of First Instance of the European Communities of 7 June 2004 in Case T-333/02 *Gestoras Pro Amnistía and Others* v *Council* (not published in the European Court Reports, 'the order under appeal'), by which the Court of First Instance dismissed their action for damages for the harm allegedly sustained by the applicants at first instance due to the inclusion of Gestoras Pro Amnistía in the list of persons, groups or entities referred to in Article 1 of Council Common Position 2001/931/CFSP of 27 December 2001 on the application of specific measures to combat terrorism (OJ 2001 L 344, p. 93), in Article 1 of Council Common Position 2002/340/CFSP of 2 May 2002 updating Common Position 2001/931 (OJ 2002 L 116, p. 75), and in Article 1 of Council Common Position 2002/462/CFSP of 17 June 2002 updating Common Position 2001/931 and repealing Common Position 2002/340 (OJ 2002 L 160, p. 32).

Background to the Dispute

2. The background to the dispute was set out as follows in paragraphs 1 to 11 of the order under appeal:

> '1. It is apparent from the documents before the Court that Gestoras Pro Amnistía is an organisation whose object is the protection of human rights in the Basque country and, in particular, the protection of the rights of political prisoners and exiles. According to the applicants, this organisation was created in 1976 and is established in Hernani (Spain). It has appointed Mr J.M. Olano Olano and Mr J. Zelarain Errasti its spokespersons. No official documentation has been provided in this respect.
>
> 2. On 28 September 2001, the United Nations Security Council adopted Resolution 1373 (2001), by which, in particular, it decided that all States should afford one another the greatest measure of assistance in connection with criminal investigations or criminal proceedings relating to the financing or support of terrorist acts, including assistance in obtaining evidence in their possession necessary for the proceedings.
>
> 3. By orders of 2 and 19 November 2001 the central investigating judge No 5 at the Audiencia Nacional (National High Court), Madrid (Spain), ordered the imprisonment of the alleged leaders of Gestoras Pro Amnistía, including its two spokespersons, and declared its activities illegal, on the ground that that organisation was an integral part of the Basque separatist organisation ETA. Gestoras Pro Amnistía appealed against that decision.

4. On 27 December 2001, considering that action by the Community [and the Member States] was necessary in order to implement Resolution 1373 (2001) of the United Nations Security Council, the Council [of the European Union] adopted Common Position 2001/931 . . . . That common position was adopted on the basis of Article 15 EU, which comes under Title V of the EU Treaty entitled "Provisions on a common foreign and security policy" (CFSP), and Article 34 EU, which comes under Title VI of the EU Treaty entitled "Provisions on police and judicial cooperation in criminal matters".

. . .

5. Articles 1 and 4 of Common Position 2001/931 provide:

> "Article 1
>
> 1. This Common Position applies in accordance with the provisions of the following Articles to persons, groups and entities involved in terrorist acts and listed in the Annex.
>
> . . .
>
> 6. The names of persons and entities on the list in the Annex shall be reviewed at regular intervals and at least once every six months to ensure that there are grounds for keeping them on the list."
>
> "Article 4
>
> Member States shall, through police and judicial cooperation in criminal matters within the framework of Title VI of the [EU] Treaty, afford each other the widest possible assistance in preventing and combating terrorist acts. To that end they shall, with respect to enquiries and proceedings conducted by their authorities in respect of any of the persons, groups and entities listed in the Annex, fully exploit, upon request, their existing powers in accordance with acts of the European Union and other international agreements, arrangements and conventions which are binding upon Member States."

6. The annex to Common Position 2001/931 indicates in point 2 entitled "Groups and entities":

> "*—Euskadi Ta Askatasuna/Tierra Vasca y Libertad/Basque Fatherland and Liberty (E.T.A.)"
>
> (The following organisations are part of the terrorist group E.T.A.: K.a.s., Xaki, Ekin, Jarrai-Haika-Segi, Gestoras pro amnistía.)".

7. The note at the bottom of this annex states that "[p]ersons marked with an * shall be the subject of Article 4 only".

8. On 27 December 2001, the Council also adopted Common Position 2001/930/CFSP on combating terrorism (OJ 2001 L 344, p. 90), Regulation (EC) No 2580/2001 on specific restrictive measures directed against certain persons and entities with a view to combating terrorism (OJ 2001 L 344, p. 70) and Decision 2001/927/EC establishing the list provided for in Article 2(3) of Regulation (EC) No 2580/2001 (OJ 2001 L 344, p. 83). None of those texts mentions the applicants.

9. According to the Council declaration [of 18 December 2001] annexed to the minutes at the time of the adoption of Common Position 2001/931 and Regulation No 2580/2001 ("the Council declaration concerning the right to compensation"):

"The Council recalls regarding Article 1(6) of Common Position [2001/931] that in the event of any error in respect of the persons, groups or entities referred to, the injured party shall have the right to seek judicial redress."

10. By decision of 23 May 2002, the European Court of Human Rights dismissed as inadmissible the action brought by the applicants against the 15 Member States, concerning Common Position 2001/931, on the ground that the situation complained of did not entitle them to be regarded as victims of an infringement of the European Convention on Human Rights and Fundamental Freedoms [signed at Rome on 4 November 1950, "ECHR"] [*Reports of Judgments and Decisions* 2002-V].

11. On 2 May and 17 June 2002, the Council adopted, on the basis of Articles 15 EU and 34 EU, Common Positions 2002/340/CFSP and 2002/462/CFSP updating Common Position 2001/931 (OJ 2002 L 116, p. 75, and OJ 2002 L 160, p. 32). The annexes to these two common positions contain the name "Gestoras Pro Amnistía", which appears in the same way as it does in Common Position 2001/931.'

3. In addition to that account of the background to the dispute, it is to be noted that, as provided in the first subparagraph of Article 1(4) of Common Position 2001/931:

'The list in the Annex [of persons, groups and entities involved in terrorist acts] is to be drawn up on the basis of precise information or material in the relevant file which indicates that a decision has been taken by a competent authority in respect of [those] persons, groups and entities . . ., irrespective of whether it concerns the instigation of investigations or prosecution for a terrorist act, an attempt to perpetrate, participate in or facilitate such an act based on serious and credible evidence or clues, or condemnation [sic] for such deeds . . .'

4. Gestoras Pro Amnistía applied to the Council for access to the documents on which the Council relied in entering it in the list annexed to Common Position 2001/931. By letter of 27 March 2002 the Secretary-General of the Council communicated to Gestoras Pro Amnistía a series of documents relating to that Common Position. Taking the view that those documents did not concern it specifically or personally, the association addressed a fresh request to the Council which the latter rejected by letter of 21 May 2002, on the ground that the information necessary for the drawing up of that list had been returned to the national delegations concerned after it had been examined and the decision adopted.

The Action Before the Court of First Instance and the Order Under Appeal

5. By application lodged at the Registry of the Court of First Instance on 31 October 2002 the appellants claimed that the Court should:

- order the Council to pay the sum of EUR 1 000 000 to Gestoras Pro Amnistía and the sum of EUR 100 000 each to Mr Olano Olano and Mr Zelarain Errasti, as compensation for the damage allegedly suffered as a result of the inclusion of Gestoras Pro Amnistía in the list of persons, groups and entities referred to in Article 1 of Common Positions 2001/931, 2002/340 and 2002/462 respectively;
- order that those sums should bear default interest at the rate of 4.5% per annum from the date of the decision of the Court of First Instance until actual payment should have been effected; and
- order the Council to pay the costs.

6. By separate document lodged at the Registry of the Court of First Instance on 12 February 2003, the Council raised an objection of inadmissibility pursuant to Article 114 of the Rules of Procedure of the Court of First Instance, arguing that the action should be declared manifestly inadmissible and that 'the applicant' should be ordered to pay the costs.

7. By order of 5 June 2003 the President of the Second Chamber of the Court of First Instance granted the requests of the Kingdom of Spain and the United Kingdom of Great Britain and Northern Ireland for leave to intervene in support of the forms of order sought by the Council. Only the Kingdom of Spain submitted its observations on the objection of inadmissibility.

8. In their observations on the plea of inadmissibility, the appellants claimed that the Court of First Instance should:

- declare the action for damages admissible;
- alternatively, find that the Council had infringed general principles of Community law;
- in any event, order the Council to pay the costs.

9. By the order under appeal, made pursuant to Article 111 of its Rules of Procedure, the Court of First Instance dismissed the action without opening the oral procedure.

10. First, it held that it clearly had no jurisdiction, in the legal system of the European Union, to hear and determine the appellants' claim for damages.

11. In reaching that conclusion the Court of First Instance noted that the appellants were affected only by Article 4 of Common Position 2001/931, by virtue of which the Member States are to afford one another the widest

possible assistance through the police and judicial cooperation in criminal matters provided for by Title VI of the EU Treaty and, accordingly, that the measures which, it was claimed, gave rise to the alleged damage had as their sole relevant legal basis Article 34 EU. It found that the only legal remedies provided by Article 35(1), (6) and (7) EU, referred to by Article 46 EU, were the reference for a preliminary ruling, the action for annulment and the procedure for settling disputes between Member States. In consequence, it found that no judicial remedy allowing for an order for damages was available under Title VI of the EU Treaty.

12. Second, the Court of First Instance held that it did, nevertheless, have jurisdiction to rule on the action, but only in so far as the latter was based on infringement of the powers of the Community.

13. The Court of First Instance noted that the Community judicature did have jurisdiction to consider whether an act adopted under the EU Treaty does not affect the powers of the Community. So it investigated, in paragraphs 41 to 47 of the order under appeal, whether in adopting the contested measures the Council had not unlawfully encroached upon the powers of the Community.

14. That court considered, however, that the appellants had failed to cite any legal basis in the EC Treaty that had been disregarded. It held that the Council was fully entitled to rely on Title VI of the EU Treaty in order to adopt the acts at issue and that, therefore, in so far as the action was based on a failure to observe the powers of the Community, it had to be dismissed as manifestly unfounded.

Forms of Order Sought by the Parties Before the Court of Justice

15. The appellants claim that the Court should:

- set aside the order under appeal;
- itself give a ruling on the action and grant the forms of order requested before the Court of First Instance by the appellants, and
- order the Council to pay the costs.

16. The Council contends that the Court should:

- dismiss the appeal as clearly inadmissible;
- in the alternative, dismiss it as unfounded;
- if necessary, refer the case back to the Court of First Instance, and
- order the appellants to pay the costs.

17. The Kingdom of Spain seeks forms of order identical to those of the Council.

Concerning the Appeal

Admissibility of the Appeal

Arguments of the Parties

18. The Council and the Kingdom of Spain maintain that the arguments put forward by the appellants are in substance identical to those set out at first instance, and do not make specific reference to the error of law which they claim vitiates the order under appeal. The appeal should therefore be dismissed as clearly inadmissible.

Findings of the Court

– With regard to the part of the appeal challenging the order in so far as the latter rejects the plea alleging that the Council encroached upon the powers conferred on the Community

19. Before the Court of First Instance the appellants argued that the Council, in adopting Common Position 2001/931, confirmed by Common Positions 2002/340 and 2002/462, deliberately encroached on the powers conferred on the Community for the purpose of depriving the persons referred to in that common position of the right to an effective remedy

20. In the order under appeal, the Court of First Instance held that it had jurisdiction to take cognisance of the action brought by the appellants only in so far as it was based on failure to have regard to the powers of the Community, referring in particular to Case C-170/96 *Commission* v *Council* [1998] ECR I-2763, paragraph 17. In paragraphs 45 and 46 of the order under appeal, the Court held that Article 34 EU was the relevant legal basis for the adoption of Article 4 of Common Position 2001/931 and that the appellants had failed to cite a legal basis in the EC Treaty that had been disregarded.

21. In their appeal before the Court of Justice, the appellants do no more than reaffirm that the Council adopted those common positions on the legal basis of Article 34 EU for the sole purpose of depriving them of the right to a remedy. They do not, however, put forward any argument in support of that claim.

22. It is clear from Article 225 EC, from the first paragraph of Article 58 of the Statute of the Court of Justice and from Article 112(1)(c) of its Rules of Procedure that an appeal must indicate precisely the contested elements of the judgment or order which the appellant seeks to have set aside, and also the legal arguments specifically advanced in support of the appeal (see, in particular, Case C 352/98 P *Bergaderm and Goupil* v *Commission* [2000] ECR I-5291, paragraph 34; Case C 248/99 P *France* v *Monsanto and Commission* [2002] ECR I-1, paragraph 68; and the order in Case C-488/01 P *Martínez* v *Parliament* [2003] ECR I-13355, paragraph 40).

23. In the present case, as the Council and the Kingdom of Spain maintain, the appeal does not state why the legal ground relied on by the Court of First Instance in paragraphs 45 and 46 of the order under appeal is incorrect. The appeal is therefore and to that extent inadmissible.

– With regard to the part of the appeal challenging the order in so far as the latter finds that the Court of First Instance has no jurisdiction to hear and determine the action for damages

24. As stated above, it is clear from Article 225 EC, from the first paragraph of Article 58 of the Statute of the Court of Justice and from Article 112(1)(c) of its Rules of Procedure that an appeal must indicate precisely the contested elements of the judgment or order which the appellant seeks to have set aside, and also the legal arguments specifically advanced in support of the appeal.

25. In this case, and contrary to the submissions of the Council and the Kingdom of Spain, the appeal, in so far as it concerns the refusal of the Court of First Instance to hold that it had jurisdiction to entertain the action for damages, is not confined to a reproduction of the pleas in law and arguments raised before the Court of First Instance, but does indicate the contested elements of the order under appeal and the legal arguments specifically advanced in support of the appeal.

26. It follows that the appeal is admissible in so far as it challenges that part of the order under appeal in which the Court of First Instance held that it had no jurisdiction to entertain the action for damages.

The Admissibility of Certain Grounds of Challenge Put Forward in Support of the Appeal

Arguments of the Parties

27. With regard to the admissibility of certain grounds of appeal, the Council and the Kingdom of Spain maintain, moreover, that the ground relating to the examination of the two successive versions of the footnote in the Annex to Common Position 2001/931, which marks with an * the classes that are to be 'the subject of Article 4 only', was put forward for the first time in the reply and is therefore inadmissible. According to the appellants, that examination demonstrated that, before being amended by the Council's Common Position 2003/482/CFSP of 27 June 2003 (OJ 2003 L 160, p. 100), that footnote covered only 'persons', that is to say, natural persons to the exclusion of 'groups and entities' and that, in those circumstances, on 31 October 2002, the date on which it brought its action before the Court of First Instance, Gestoras Pro Amnistía did not belong to the class of 'persons [who are to] be the subject of Article 4 only' but to that of groups and entities subject to the actions of the Community mentioned in Articles 2 and 3 of Common Position 2001/931.

28. In addition, the Council maintains that two grounds of appeal raised by the appellants were not put before the Court of First Instance and are therefore inadmissible. The first is the plea claiming that the Member States are bound to perform their obligations under earlier agreements, in accordance with Article 30 of the Vienna Convention on the Law of Treaties of 23 May 1969 on the application of successive treaties relating to the same subject-matter and with Article 307 of the EC Treaty. Those obligations under earlier agreements guarantee effective observance of human rights and fundamental freedoms. The second ground which the Council regards as inadmissible is the claim that there exists in the Court's case-law a principle of interpretation called 'wider jurisdiction', by virtue of which the Court has already accepted jurisdiction outside the bounds of the Treaty.

Findings of the Court

29. Under Article 48(2) of the Rules of Procedure of the Court of First Instance, no new plea in law may be introduced in the course of proceedings unless it is based on matters of law or of fact which have come to light in the course of the procedure.

30. To allow a party to put forward for the first time before the Court of Justice a plea in law which it has not raised before the Court of First Instance would be to allow it to bring before the Court, whose jurisdiction in appeals is limited, a case of wider ambit than that which came before the Court of First Instance. In an appeal the Court's jurisdiction is confined to review of the findings of law on the pleas argued before the Court of First Instance (see Case C-136/92 P *Commission* v *Brazzelli Lualdi and Others* [1994] ECR I-1981, paragraphs 58 and 59).

31. In the present case, the grounds of appeal relating to the altered wording of the footnote in the Annex to Common Position 2001/931, to the performance by the Member States of their obligations under earlier agreements or treaties and to the principle of general interpretation relating to a 'wider jurisdiction' of the Court were not raised by the appellants before the Court of First Instance.

32. Those grounds of appeal are, consequently, inadmissible.

Substance

Arguments of the Parties

33. The appellants maintain that the Court of First Instance erred in declining jurisdiction to consider their action for damages.

34. The Union is a community governed by the rule of law, guaranteeing by virtue of Article 6(2) EU the right to an effective remedy laid down in

Article 13 of the ECHR and the right to a tribunal provided by Article 6 of that convention.

35. Furthermore, by its declaration concerning the right to redress, the Council has, in the appellants' view, accepted that any error in drawing up the list annexed to Common Position 2001/931 amounts to fault on its part, which gives entitlement to redress. In that declaration, the Council stated that that right must be afforded to persons, groups and entities referred to, like the appellants, in Article 4 of Common Position 2001/931, on the same conditions as it is to the persons, groups and entities entered in the list annexed to Regulation No 2580/2001 or covered by Article 3 of that Common Position, who may apply to the Court of First Instance if they are mentioned in acts adopted under the EC Treaty. In this connection the appellants refer to the order of the President of the Court of First Instance of 15 May 2003 in Case T-47/03 R *Sison* v *Council* [2003] ECR II-2047).

36. Since the act giving rise to the alleged damage is an act of the Council, adopted jointly by all the Member States, an action for damages cannot be brought before the national courts, which would lack jurisdiction to entertain it, the liability of the Member States not being severable.

37. It is also pointed out that in the eighth recital in the preamble to Council Decision 2003/48/JHA of 19 December 2002 on the implementation of specific measures for police and judicial cooperation to combat terrorism in accordance with Article 4 of Common Position 2001/931 (OJ 2003 L 16, p. 68) it is stated that '[t]his Decision respects the fundamental rights and observes the principles recognised by Article 6 of the Treaty on European Union. Nothing in this Decision may be interpreted as allowing infringement of the legal protection afforded under national law to the persons, groups and entities listed in the Annex to Common Position 2001/931/CFSP'.

38. The Council declaration concerning the right to redress, clarified by the eighth recital in the preamble to Decision 2003/48, constitutes, together with Article 6(2) EU, a firm legal base for the assertion of the jurisdiction of the Community judicature. It is argued that the Court of First Instance therefore vitiated the order under appeal by an error of law in declaring that it had no jurisdiction to rule on the appellants' claims for damages.

39. In addition, the appellants claim that, with a view to combating terrorism, the Council adopted a number of measures on various legal bases for the purpose of depriving certain classes of persons, groups and entities of the right to an effective remedy.

40. The Council maintains that the appeal is unfounded. The Court of First Instance correctly considered that no claim for damages is provided for under Title VI of the EU Treaty. Since what was at issue was not an act

adopted in the context of the European Community but an act adopted under the provisions governing the Union, an action for damages may not be brought on the basis of Article 288 EC. In support of its view the Council relies on the judgment in Case 99/74 *Grands moulins des Antilles* v *Commission* [1975] ECR 1531, paragraph 17.

41. The eighth recital in the preamble to Decision 2003/48 mentions only the legal protection afforded 'under national law', not under Community law. Neither that document nor the Council's declaration concerning the right to redress is such as to enable the Community judicature to give a ruling on the appellants' claim for damages, which is not provided for by the EU Treaty.

42. The Kingdom of Spain states that Gestoras Pro Amnistía's activities were declared illegal by order of 19 December 2001 of central investigating judge No 5 of the Audiencia Nacional de Madrid. The same central investigating judge issued an international warrant for the arrest of Mr Olano Olano, who had several times been sentenced by Spanish courts for, inter alia, possession of arms, munitions or explosives. He was arrested by the French police on 3 December 2001, handed over to the Spanish authorities and then imprisoned in Madrid. Mr Zelarain Errasti was arrested on 31 October 2001 by reason of his responsibility within Gestoras Pro Amnistía and prosecuted before the Spanish courts in the proceedings brought against that association and in other proceedings on the ground that he belonged to a terrorist organisation.

43. On the merits, the Kingdom of Spain supports the Council's views. There is nothing in the appeal capable of calling into question the legality of the order under appeal.

Findings of the Court

– The ground of appeal alleging disregard for the provisions of Title VI of the EU Treaty

44. It follows from Article 46 EU that the provisions of the EC and EAEC Treaties concerning the powers of the Court of Justice are applicable to Title VI of the EU Treaty only 'under the conditions provided for by Article 35 EU'.

45. That article provides that the Court of Justice has jurisdiction in three situations. First, by virtue of Article 35(1) EU, it has jurisdiction to give preliminary rulings on the validity and interpretation of framework decisions and decisions, on the interpretation of conventions established under Title VI of the EU Treaty and on the validity and interpretation of the measures implementing them. Second, Article 35(6) EU provides also for the Court of Justice to have jurisdiction to review the legality of framework decisions and decisions in actions brought by a Member State or the Commission of the European Communities on grounds of lack of

competence, infringement of an essential procedural requirement, infringement of the EU Treaty or of any rule of law relating to its application, or misuse of powers. Last, Article 35(7) EU provides for the Court of Justice to have jurisdiction to rule on any dispute between Member States regarding the interpretation or the application of acts adopted under Article 34(2) EU whenever such dispute cannot be settled by the Council within six months of its being referred to the latter by one of its members.

46. In contrast, Article 35 EU confers no jurisdiction on the Court of Justice to entertain any action for damages whatsoever.

47. In addition, Article 41(1) EU does not include, among the articles of the Treaty establishing the European Community applicable to the areas referred to in Title VI of the Treaty on European Union, the second paragraph of Article 288 EC, according to which the Community must, in accordance with the general principles common to the laws of the Member States, make good any damage caused by its institutions or by its servants in the performance of their duties, or Article 235 EC, under which the Court has jurisdiction in disputes relating to compensation for damage provided for in the second paragraph of Article 288 EC (see, by analogy, Case C-160/03 *Spain* v *Eurojust* [2005] ECR I-2077, paragraph 38).

48. It follows from the foregoing that the Court of First Instance did not vitiate its order by any error of law in finding that no action for damages is provided for under Title VI of the EU Treaty. The ground of appeal must therefore be rejected.

– The ground of appeal alleging disregard for the right to effective judicial protection

49. The appellants also invoked before the Court of First Instance the observance of fundamental rights, in particular the right to effective judicial protection under Article 6(2) EU. In essence they argue that they have no means of challenging Gestoras Pro Amnistía's inclusion in the list annexed to Common Position 2001/931 and that the order under appeal prejudices their right to effective judicial protection.

50. It is true that, as regards the Union, the treaties have established a system of legal remedies in which, by virtue of Article 35 EU, the jurisdiction of the Court is less extensive under Title VI of the Treaty on European Union than it is under the EC Treaty (see, to this effect, Case C-105/03 *Pupino* [2005] ECR I-5285, paragraph 35). It is even less extensive under Title V. While a system of legal remedies, in particular a body of rules governing non-contractual liability, other than that established by the treaties can indeed be envisaged, it is for the Member States, should the case arise, to reform the system currently in force in accordance with Article 48 EU.

51. Nevertheless, the appellants cannot validly argue that they are deprived of all judicial protection. As is clear from Article 6 EU, the Union is founded on the principle of the rule of law and it respects fundamental rights as general principles of Community law. It follows that the institutions are subject to review of the conformity of their acts with the treaties and the general principles of law, just like the Member States when they implement the law of the Union.

52. Here it is to be noted that Article 34 EU provides that the Council may adopt acts varying in nature and scope. Under Article 34(2)(a) EU the Council may 'adopt common positions defining the approach of the Union to a particular matter'. A common position requires the compliance of the Member States by virtue of the principle of the duty to cooperate in good faith, which means in particular that Member States are to take all appropriate measures, whether general or particular, to ensure fulfilment of their obligations under European Union law (see *Pupino*, paragraph 42). Article 37 EU thus provides that the Member States are to defend the common positions '[w]ithin international organisations and at international conferences in which they take part'. However, a common position is not supposed to produce of itself legal effects in relation to third parties. That is why, in the system established by Title VI of the EU Treaty, only framework decisions and decisions may be the subject of an action for annulment before the Court of Justice. The Court's jurisdiction, as defined by Article 35(1) EU, to give preliminary rulings also does not extend to common positions but is limited to rulings on the validity and interpretation of framework decisions and decisions, on the interpretation of conventions established under Title VI and on the validity and interpretation of the measures implementing them.

53. Article 35(1) EU, in that it does not enable national courts to refer a question to the Court for a preliminary ruling on a common position but only a question concerning the acts listed in that provision, treats as acts capable of being the subject of such a reference for a preliminary ruling all measures adopted by the Council and intended to produce legal effects in relation to third parties. Given that the procedure enabling the Court to give preliminary rulings is designed to guarantee observance of the law in the interpretation and application of the Treaty, it would run counter to that objective to interpret Article 35(1) EU narrowly. The right to make a reference to the Court for a preliminary ruling must therefore exist in respect of all measures adopted by the Council, whatever their nature or form, which are intended to have legal effects in relation to third parties (see, by analogy, Case 22/70 *Commission* v *Council (ERTA)* [1971] ECR 263, paragraphs 38 to 42, and Case C-57/95 *France* v *Commission* [1997] ECR I-1627, paragraph 7 et seq.).

54. As a result, it has to be possible to make subject to review by the Court a common position which, because of its content, has a scope going beyond that assigned by the EU Treaty to that kind of act. Therefore, a national court hearing a dispute which indirectly raises the issue of the validity or interpretation of a common position adopted on the basis of Article 34 EU, as is the case in this instance for part of Common Position 2001/931 and in any event for Article 4 thereof and the Annex thereto, and which has serious doubts whether that common position is really intended to produce legal effects in relation to third parties, would be able, subject to the conditions fixed by Article 35 EU, to ask the Court to give a preliminary ruling. It would then fall to the Court to find, where appropriate, that the common position is intended to produce legal effects in relation to third parties, to accord it its true classification and to give a preliminary ruling.

55. The Court would also have jurisdiction to review the lawfulness of such acts when an action has been brought by a Member State or the Commission on the conditions fixed by Article 35(6) EU.

56. Finally, it is to be borne in mind that it is for the Member States and, in particular, their courts and tribunals, to interpret and apply national procedural rules governing the exercise of rights of action in a way that enables natural and legal persons to challenge before the courts the lawfulness of any decision or other national measure relating to the drawing up of an act of the European Union or to its application to them and to seek compensation for any loss suffered.

57. It follows that the appellants are incorrect in maintaining that the contested common position leaves them without a remedy, contrary to the requirement of effective judicial protection, and that the order under appeal prejudices their right to such protection. That ground of appeal must, in consequence, be rejected.

– The ground of appeal alleging disregard for the declaration made by the Council in its decision 15453/01 of 18 December 2001

58. Before the Court of First Instance the appellants invoked the declaration made by the Council in its decision 15453/01 of 18 December 2001 according to which: 'The Council recalls regarding Article 1(6) of the Common Position on the application of specific measures to combat terrorism, and Article 2(3) of the regulation on specific restrictive measures directed against certain persons and entities with a view to combating terrorism that in the event of any error in respect of the persons, groups or entities referred to, the injured party shall have the right to seek judicial redress'.

59. According to the appellants, that declaration must be interpreted in the light of the eighth recital in the preamble to Council Decision 2003/48/JHA

of 19 December 2002 on the implementation of specific measures for police and judicial cooperation to combat terrorism, which states that '[t]his Decision respects the fundamental rights and observes the principles recognised by Article 6 of the Treaty on European Union. Nothing in this Decision may be interpreted as allowing infringement of the legal protection afforded under national law to the persons, groups and entities listed in the Annex to Common Position 2001/931/CFSP'.

60. It is, however, clear from the Court's settled case-law that such a declaration is insufficient to create a legal remedy not provided for by the applicable texts and that it cannot therefore be given any legal significance or be used in the interpretation of law emanating from the EU Treaty where, as in this case, no reference is made to the content of the declaration in the wording of the provision in question (see, to this effect, Case C-292/89 *Antonissen* [1991] ECR I-745, paragraph 18; Case C-329/95 *VAG Sverige* [1997] ECR I-2675, paragraph 23; and Case C-49/02 *Heidelberger Bauchemie* [2004] ECR I-6129, paragraph 17).

61. There was, therefore, no error of law in the Court of First Instance's finding in the order under appeal that the declaration made by the Council in its decision 15453/01 of 18 December 2001 could not suffice to confer jurisdiction on the Court to hear and determine an action for damages under Title VI of the EU Treaty.

62. It follows from all the foregoing that it was without vitiating its order by any error of law that the Court of First Instance declared that it manifestly had no jurisdiction to entertain the action for damages seeking compensation for any damage that might have been caused to the appellants by the inclusion of Gestoras Pro Amnistía in the list annexed to Common Position 2001/931, as updated by Common Positions 2002/340 and 2002/462.

63. None of the grounds of appeal being well founded, the appeal must be dismissed.

Costs

64. Under Article 69(2) of the Rules of Procedure, which is applicable to the procedure on appeal pursuant to Article 118 of those Rules, the unsuccessful party is to be ordered to pay the costs if they have been applied for in the successful party's pleadings. Since the Council has applied for costs against the appellants and the latter have been unsuccessful, they must be ordered to pay the costs.

65. Pursuant to the first subparagraph of Article 69(4) of the Rules of Procedure, which also applies to appeals by virtue of Article 118 thereof, the Member States which have intervened in the proceedings are to bear

their own costs. In accordance with that provision, it must therefore be ordered that the Kingdom of Spain is to bear its own costs.

On those grounds, the Court (Grand Chamber) hereby:

1. Dismisses the appeal;
2. Orders Gestoras Pro Amnistía, Mr J.M. Olano Olano and Mr J. Zelarain Errasti to pay the costs;
3. Orders the Kingdom of Spain to bear its own costs.

[Signatures]

DOCUMENT NO. 28

KURDISTAN WORKERS' PARTY (PKK)

EUROPEAN COURT OF JUSTICE

18 January 2007*

Case C-229/05P

Judgment of the Court (First Chamber)

APPEAL under Article 56 of the Statute of the Court of Justice, brought on 9 May 2005,

Osman Ocalan, on behalf of the Kurdistan Workers' Party (PKK),

Serif Vanly, on behalf of the Kurdistan National Congress (KNK),

represented by M. Muller QC, E. Grieves and P. Moser, Barristers, and J.G. Peirce, Solicitor, appellants,

the other parties to the proceedings being:\

Council of the European Union, represented by E. Finnegan and M. Bishop, acting as Agents, defendant at first instance,

United Kingdom of Great Britain and Northern Ireland, represented by R. Caudwell, acting as Agent, with an address for service in Luxembourg,

Commission of the European Communities,

interveners at first instance,

THE COURT (First Chamber),

composed of P. Jann, President of the Chamber, K. Lenaerts, E. Juhász, J.N. Cunha Rodrigues (Rapporteur) and M. Ilešič, Judges,

Advocate General: J. Kokott,

Registrar: J. Swedenborg, Administrator,

* Language of the case: English.

having regard to the written procedure and further to the hearing on 14 September 2006,

after hearing the Opinion of the Advocate General at the sitting on 27 September 2006, gives the following

Judgment

1. By their appeal, Osman Ocalan, on behalf of the Kurdistan Workers' Party (PKK), and Serif Vanly, on behalf of the Kurdistan National Congress (KNK), request the Court to set aside the order of the Court of First Instance of the European Communities of 15 February 2005 in Case T-229/02 *PKK and KNK* v *Council* [2005] ECR II-539 ('the contested order'), by which the Court of First Instance dismissed as inadmissible their action for annulment of Council Decision 2002/334/EC of 2 May 2002 implementing Article 2(3) of Regulation (EC) No 2580/2001 on specific restrictive measures directed against certain persons and entities with a view to combating terrorism and repealing Decision 2001/927/EC (OJ 2002 L 116, p. 33) and of Council Decision 2002/460/EC of 17 June 2002 implementing Article 2(3) of Regulation (EC) No 2580/2001 on specific restrictive measures directed against certain persons and entities with a view to combating terrorism and repealing Decision 2002/334/EC (OJ 2002 L 160, p. 26).

Legal Context

The European Convention for the Protection of Human Rights and Fundamental Freedoms

2. The European Convention for the Protection of Human Rights and Fundamental Freedoms, signed at Rome on 4 November 1950 ('the ECHR'), provides in Article 6, which is headed 'Right to a fair trial', as follows:

> '1. In the determination of his civil rights and obligations or of any criminal charge against him, everyone is entitled to a fair and public hearing within a reasonable time by an independent and impartial tribunal established by law. Judgment shall be pronounced publicly but the press and public may be excluded from all or part of the trial in the interests of morals, public order or national security in a democratic society, where the interests of juveniles or the protection of the private life of the parties so require, or to the extent strictly necessary in the opinion of the court in special circumstances where publicity would prejudice the interests of justice.

. . .'

3. Article 13 of the ECHR, headed 'Right to an effective remedy', states:

> 'Everyone whose rights and freedoms as set forth in this Convention are violated shall have an effective remedy before a national authority

notwithstanding that the violation has been committed by persons acting in an official capacity.'

4. Article 34 of the ECHR, headed 'Individual applications', provides:

'The [European] Court [of Human Rights] may receive applications from any person, non-governmental organisation or group of individuals claiming to be the victim of a violation by one of the High Contracting Parties of the rights set forth in the Convention or the protocols thereto. The High Contracting Parties undertake not to hinder in any way the effective exercise of this right.'

Community Law

5. Taking the view that action by the European Community was needed in order to implement Resolution 1373 (2001) of the United Nations Security Council, on 27 December 2001 the Council of the European Union adopted Common Position 2001/930/CFSP on combating terrorism (OJ 2001 L 344, p. 90) and Common Position 2001/931/CFSP on the application of specific measures to combat terrorism (OJ 2001 L 344, p. 93).

6. Article 1 of Common Position 2001/931 provides:

'1. This Common Position applies in accordance with the provisions of the following Articles to persons, groups and entities involved in terrorist acts and listed in the Annex.

...

4. The list in the Annex shall be drawn up on the basis of precise information or material in the relevant file which indicates that a decision has been taken by a competent authority in respect of the persons, groups and entities concerned, irrespective of whether it concerns the instigation of investigations or prosecution for a terrorist act, an attempt to perpetrate, participate in or facilitate such an act based on serious and credible evidence or clues, or condemnation for such deeds. Persons, groups and entities identified by the Security Council of the United Nations as being related to terrorism and against whom it has ordered sanctions may be included in the list.

For the purposes of this paragraph "competent authority" shall mean a judicial authority, or, where judicial authorities have no competence in the area covered by this paragraph, an equivalent competent authority in that area.

5. The Council shall work to ensure that names of natural or legal persons, groups or entities listed in the Annex have sufficient particulars appended to permit effective identification of specific human beings, legal persons, entities or bodies, thus facilitating the exculpation of those bearing the same or similar names.

6. The names of persons and entities on the list in the Annex shall be reviewed at regular intervals and at least once every six months to ensure that there are grounds for keeping them on the list.'

7. Article 2 of Common Position 2001/931 states:

> 'The European Community, acting within the limits of the powers conferred on it by the Treaty establishing the European Community, shall order the freezing of the funds and other financial assets or economic resources of persons, groups and entities listed in the Annex.'

8. On 27 December 2001, the Council adopted Regulation (EC) No 2580/2001 on specific restrictive measures directed against certain persons and entities with a view to combating terrorism (OJ 2001 L 344, p. 70).

9. Article 2 of that regulation provides:

'1. Except as permitted under Articles 5 and 6:

(a) all funds, other financial assets and economic resources belonging to, or owned or held by, a natural or legal person, group or entity included in the list referred to in paragraph 3 shall be frozen;

(b) no funds, other financial assets and economic resources shall be made available, directly or indirectly, to, or for the benefit of, a natural or legal person, group or entity included in the list referred to in paragraph 3.

2. Except as permitted under Articles 5 and 6, it shall be prohibited to provide financial services to, or for the benefit of, a natural or legal person, group or entity included in the list referred to in paragraph 3.

3. The Council, acting by unanimity, shall establish, review and amend the list of persons, groups and entities to which this Regulation applies, in accordance with the provisions laid down in Article 1(4), (5) and (6) of Common Position 2001/931/CFSP; such list shall consist of:

(i) natural persons committing, or attempting to commit, participating in or facilitating the commission of any act of terrorism;

(ii) legal persons, groups or entities committing, or attempting to commit, participating in or facilitating the commission of any act of terrorism;

(iii) legal persons, groups or entities owned or controlled by one or more natural or legal persons, groups or entities referred to in points (i) and (ii); or

(iv) natural legal persons, groups or entities acting on behalf of or at the direction of one or more natural or legal persons, groups or entities referred to in points (i) and (ii).'

Background

10. The contested order states as follows:

'1. It is apparent from the documents before the Court that the [PKK] emerged in 1978 and engaged in an armed struggle against the Turkish Government to obtain recognition of the Kurds' right to self-determination.

According to Mr [Osman] Ocalan's written evidence, the PKK declared a unilateral ceasefire, whilst reserving the right to self-defence, in July 1999. According to that evidence, in April 2002, in order to reflect that reorientation, the Congress of the PKK decided that "all activities under the name of 'PKK' would cease as of 4 April 2002 and that any activities taken under the name of the PKK would be deemed illegitimate" (annex 2 to the application, paragraph 16). A new group, the Kongreya AzadÓ š Demokrasiya Kurdistan (Kurdistan Freedom and Democracy Congress—KADEK), was founded in order to attain political objectives democratically on behalf of the Kurdish minority. Mr [Abdullah] Ocalan was appointed president of KADEK.

2. The [KNK] is an umbrella organisation comprising approximately 30 individual entities. The KNK's purpose is "to strengthen the unity and cooperation of the Kurds in all parts of Kurdistan and [to] support their struggle based on the best interests of the Kurdish nation" (Article 7A of the KNK's Charter). According to the written evidence of Mr [Serif] Vanly, President of the KNK, the leader of the PKK was among those who spearheaded the creation of the KNK. The PKK was a member of the KNK and the individual members of the PKK partly financed the KNK.'

11. On 2 May 2002 the Council adopted Decision 2002/334. This decision added the PKK to the list envisaged in Article 2(3) of Regulation No 2580/2001 ('the disputed list').

12. By application registered under number T-206/02, the KNK brought an action for annulment of Decision 2002/334. The Court of First Instance dismissed this action as inadmissible by order of 15 February 2005. No appeal was brought against this order.

13. On 17 June 2002 the Council adopted Decision 2002/460. This decision kept the PKK on the disputed list. The list was then regularly updated by various Council decisions.

Procedure Before the Court of First Instance

14. By application lodged at the Registry of the Court of First Instance on 31 July 2002, the PKK, represented by Osman Ocalan, and the KNK, represented by Serif Vanly, brought an action for annulment of Decisions 2002/334 and 2002/460. The action was registered as Case T-229/02.

15. The application was accompanied by a power of attorney on behalf of the PKK, which reads as follows:

'I, Osman Ocalan, a former member, and on behalf of the organisation formerly known as the PKK hereby authorise

Mark Muller, a barrister at 10-11 [Gray's] Inn Square

Edward Grieves, a barrister at 10-11 [Gray's] Inn Square

Gareth Peirce, a partner at Birnberg Peirce solicitors

to commence and pursue proceedings in the Court of First Instance of the European Communities for the annulment of Decision 2002/334/EC and Regulation No 2580/2001 and take any other step, including the delegation of any matter to another person, applying for interim relief and any necessary appeal to the Court of Justice of the European Communities, to that end.'

16. By document lodged on 27 November 2002, the Council raised an objection of inadmissibility pursuant to Article 114(1) of the Rules of Procedure of the Court of First Instance. The United Kingdom of Great Britain and Northern Ireland and the Commission of the European Communities were granted leave to intervene in support of the Council. The Commission lodged observations on the objection of inadmissibility. The United Kingdom waived its right to do so.

17. In the contested order the Court of First Instance, ruling on the objection of inadmissibility, dismissed the action as inadmissible.

The Contested Order

18. The Court of First Instance concluded that the application of Osman Ocalan on behalf of the PKK was inadmissible on the following grounds:

'27. It must be held, first of all, that the PKK is to be regarded as being directly and individually concerned by [Decisions 2002/334 and 20002/460], since it is named therein.

28. It is appropriate, next, to make clear that the rules governing the admissibility of an action for annulment as regards a person mentioned in the disputed list—namely the list of persons, groups and entities to which specific restrictive measures for combating terrorism apply—must be construed according to the circumstances of the case. As regards, in particular, those groups or entities it may be that they do not exist legally, or that they were not in a position to comply with the legal rules which usually apply to legal persons. Therefore, excessive formalism would amount to the denial, in certain cases, of any possibility of applying for annulment, even though those groups and entities were the object of restrictive Community measures.

. . .

32. In accordance with the principles identified in paragraph 28 above, Mr [Osman] Ocalan, a natural person, is entitled to demonstrate, by any available evidence, that he is acting validly on behalf of the legal person, the PKK, whose representative he claims to be. However, such evidence must, at least, show that the PKK did indeed wish to bring this action and that it was not used as an instrument by a third party, albeit, as the case may be, one of its members.

33. It is appropriate, also, to make clear that it is not for the Court, when examining the admissibility of the action, to rule on the reality of the PKK's existence. The question raised in the course of that examination is strictly limited to whether Mr [Osman] Ocalan has the capacity to bring an action on behalf of the PKK.

34. First, it must be noted that the action is formally brought by Mr [Osman] Ocalan, "on behalf of" the PKK.

35. Secondly, the fact remains that the applicants firmly declare that the PKK was dissolved in April 2002. What is more, according to Mr [Osman] Ocalan's evidence annexed to the application, the PKK's Congress, having pronounced its dissolution, adopted, at the same time, the declaration that "all activities under the name of 'PKK' would [henceforth] be deemed illegitimate".

36. Thirdly, it must be pointed out that nowhere in the applicants' pleadings is Mr [Osman] Ocalan mentioned otherwise than as the PKK's representative. In particular, it is never claimed that he could have any individual interest in the annulment of [Decisions 2002/334 and 2002/460].

37. Far from demonstrating Mr [Osman] Ocalan's legal capacity to represent the PKK, the applicants state, on the contrary, that the PKK no longer exists. It cannot be accepted that a legal person which has ceased to exist, assuming that is so, may validly appoint a representative.

38. The impossibility of accepting that Mr [Osman] Ocalan validly represents the PKK is further strengthened by his own evidence that any activity under the name of the "PKK" is illegitimate after April 2002. According to that evidence, the action which Mr [Osman] Ocalan claims to bring on behalf of the PKK has been declared illegitimate by his principal itself.

39. Therefore, the applicants confront the Court with the paradoxical situation in which the natural person deemed to represent a legal person is not only unable to demonstrate that he represents it validly, but, further, explains why he is unable to represent it.

40. As to the applicants' argument that there are no other remedies available, that cannot lead to the admission of actions of any person who wishes to defend a third party's interests.

41. The Court is therefore bound to hold that Mr [Osman] Ocalan has, on his own authority, brought an action on behalf of the PKK. Therefore, the action brought by Mr [Osman] Ocalan on behalf of the PKK is inadmissible.'

19. The Court of First Instance held that the application of Serif Vanly on behalf of the KNK was inadmissible on the following grounds:

43. . . . the KNK has already challenged Decision 2002/334 in its action in Case T-206/02. Therefore, because of the identity of the subject-matter,

cause of action and parties, this action, in so far as it is brought by the KNK against Decision 2002/334, is inadmissible by virtue of *lis pendens.*

. . .

45. As regards the action brought against Decision 2002/460 by the KNK, it follows from settled case-law that an association formed for the protection of the collective interests of a category of persons cannot be considered to be individually concerned, for the purposes of the fourth paragraph of Article 230 EC, by a measure affecting the general interests of that category, and is therefore not entitled to bring an action for annulment if its members cannot do so individually (Joined Cases 19/62 to 22/62 *Fédération nationale de la boucherie en gros et du commerce en gros des viandes and Others* v *Council* [1962] ECR 491, [at p. 499,] and Case T-69/96 *Hamburger Hafen—und Lagerhaus and Others* v *Commission* [2001] ECR II-1037, paragraph 49).

46. In this case, it must be noted that, under Article 7A of its Charter, the KNK aims to strengthen the unity and cooperation of the Kurds in all parts of Kurdistan and to support their struggle, based on the best interests of the Kurdish nation. The KNK must therefore be considered to be an association formed for the protection of the collective interests of a category of persons.

47. That conclusion is also supported by the applicants' argument that the PKK's listing has a "profoundly chilling effect" on the KNK's ability to pursue those aims and objectives. By virtue of the above-cited case-law, it cannot be concerned individually in that respect.

48. It must next be established whether the KNK can avail itself of the fact that one or more of its members would be entitled to bring an action for annulment of [Decision 2002/460].

49. As regards the PKK, it must be held that the applicants, by claiming that it no longer exists, acknowledge, at the very least, that the PKK is no longer a member of the KNK. In that regard, it cannot be accepted that a person's past membership of an association enables that association to avail itself of that person's possible right of action. To accept such reasoning would be tantamount to conferring on an association some sort of perpetual right to bring proceedings, despite the fact that that association can no longer claim to represent the interests of its former member.

50. As regards KADEK, the applicants rely on the fact, in essence, that that body, a potential member of the KNK, is affected by Decision 2002/460 to the point of not being able to join the KNK. Even if KADEK might have been entitled to challenge Decision 2002/460 at the date this action was brought, which seems possible, particularly if it could be regarded as the successor in law and/or in fact to the PKK, the KNK cannot avail itself of KADEK's membership of its organisation, since it is not a member.

51. The applicants allege, finally, that the KNK and its members in general are individually concerned on the ground that their activities are curtailed by the fear of having their assets frozen if they cooperate with an entity named on the disputed list. It must be recalled, in that regard, that the prohibition by [Decision 2002/460] on making funds available to the PKK is of general application, because it is addressed to all persons who are subject to Community law. [Decision 2002/460] thus applies to objectively determined situations and entails legal effects for categories of persons regarded generally and in the abstract (see, to that effect, Case 307/81 *Alusuisse Italia* v *Council and Commission* [1982] ECR 3463, paragraph 9).

52. It must be recalled that natural or legal persons can claim to be concerned individually by a measure of general application only if they are affected by reason of certain attributes which are peculiar to them or by reason of circumstances in which they are differentiated from any other person (Case 25/62 *Plaumann* v *Commission* [1963] ECR 95, at p. 107, and Case T-12/93 *CCE de Vittel and Others* v *Commission* [1995] ECR II-1247, paragraph 36). The KNK and its members are bound to comply with the prohibition laid down by [Decision 2002/460] concerning the PKK, like all other persons in the Community. The fact that, because of their political opinions, the KNK and its members are more likely than others to suffer the effects of that prohibition is not such as to differentiate them from all other persons within the Community. The fact that a measure of general application may have specific effects which differ according to the various persons to whom it applies is not such as to differentiate them in relation to all the other persons concerned, where that measure is applied on the basis of an objectively determined situation (see Case T-138/98 *ACAV and Others* v *Council* [2000] ECR II-341, paragraph 66, and the case-law there cited).

. . .

56. Since the KNK cannot avail itself of the fact that one of its members is entitled to bring an action for annulment of [Decision 2002/460], it must be held that it is not individually concerned by that decision.

57. Accordingly, the action, in so far as it is brought by the KNK against Decision 2002/460, is inadmissible.'

Procedure Before the Court of Justice and forms of Order Sought

20. By application lodged at the Registry of the Court of Justice on 9 May 2005, Osman Ocalan, on behalf of the PKK, and Serif Vanly, on behalf of the KNK, brought an appeal against the contested order. They claim that the Court of Justice should set the order aside, declare the action brought by Osman Ocalan on behalf of the PKK and by Serif Vanly on behalf of the KNK to be admissible, and order the Council to pay the costs relating to the proceedings on admissibility.

21. The appellants adduce as an annex to their appeal a statement made on 9 May 2005 by Mark Muller, one of the lawyers representing them in the present proceedings, which reads as follows:

> '1. I MARK MULLER, hereby confirm that I represent Abdullah Ocalan in proceedings before the European Court of Human Rights.
>
> 2. Throughout the course of those proceedings I have regularly visited Mr [Abdullah] Ocalan in prison on Imrali Island . . . in Turkey. I can confirm that prior to the submission of the current application before the Court of First Instance Mr [Abdullah] Ocalan gave me instructions to challenge the proscription of the PKK in Europe. In addition I have also had cause to meet with other high ranking representatives of the PKK and its alleged successor organisation KADEK in Europe. Once again, I received instructions to pursue the present proceedings.
>
> 3. In order to comply with the rules of procedure of the Court [of First Instance] I requested that a power of attorney be obtained from Mr Osman Ocalan who was at that time a high ranking representative of both the organisation formerly known as the PKK and KADEK.
>
> 4. Had the Court [of First Instance] sought clarification about this matter I would have immediately instituted steps to obtain all requisite evidence to confirm the aforesaid representations. I did not believe that this was necessary as the Court [of First Instance] had accepted the power of attorney submitted and had communicated the application to the Defendant.'

22. The Council contends that the Court should dismiss the appeal by both appellants as inadmissible, or in the alternative as unfounded, if necessary refer the case back to the Court of First Instance, and order the appellants to pay the costs of these proceedings.

23. The Commission and the United Kingdom, which intervened at first instance, have not submitted any written observations.

Consideration of the Appeal

Admissibility of the Application of Osman Ocalan on Behalf of the PKK

24. Osman Ocalan on behalf of the PKK ('the first appellant') sets out seven grounds of appeal. It is appropriate to begin by examining the fourth of those grounds.

The Fourth Ground of Appeal

– Arguments of the parties

25. In his fourth ground, the first appellant contends that the Court of First Instance distorted the clear sense of the evidence which he submitted so far as concerns the dissolution of the PKK. A close reading of the statement by Osman Ocalan submitted to the Court of First Instance does not show that

the PKK has been dissolved in all regards, including for the purposes of challenging its proscription. On the contrary, Osman Ocalan consistently refers in the statement to the continued existence of the PKK and its creation of an allied organisation, KADEK. Accordingly, the Court of First Instance misread the evidence regarding the PKK's dissolution and existence.

26. The Council's primary submission is that the fourth ground of appeal is inadmissible because it consists of a repetition of the pleadings at first instance and because it relates to a finding of fact made by the Court of First Instance, namely that the PKK could not have validly appointed Osman Ocalan as its representative for the purposes of the proceedings at first instance.

27. In the alternative, the Council submits that this ground of appeal is clearly unfounded.

28. First of all, the Court of First Instance specifically stated, in paragraph 33 of the contested order, that it was not for it to rule on the reality of the PKK's existence. The question which the Court of First Instance answered in the negative was simply whether Osman Ocalan had the capacity to bring an action on behalf of the PKK.

29. It was the appellants themselves who indicated that the PKK had officially dissolved. Paragraph 16 of Osman Ocalan's statement annexed to the application at first instance clearly indicates that any activities taken under the name of the PKK would be deemed illegitimate as of 4 April 2002.

30. Next, the submissions of the first appellant are confused in several respects. For example, paragraph 25 of the appeal states that Osman Ocalan is bringing the action on behalf of a subsisting organisation hitherto entitled the PKK. This statement implies that the action is in fact brought on behalf of another unnamed organisation which is no longer the PKK itself. However, the application does not explain what other organisation this might be.

31. Finally, the Court of First Instance made a careful examination of the applicants' pleadings. The Council considers that the Court's conclusion in paragraphs 37 to 41 of the contested order that the PKK could not validly appoint a representative was justified on the evidence before it, and submits that the first appellant has not adduced any new arguments in this appeal which cast doubt on that conclusion.

– Findings of the Court

32. In accordance with the Court's case-law, an appeal is inadmissible if, without even including an argument specifically identifying the error of law allegedly vitiating the decision under appeal, it merely repeats or

reproduces verbatim the pleas in law and arguments previously submitted to the Court of First Instance. By contrast, provided that the appellant challenges the interpretation or application of Community law by the Court of First Instance, the points of law examined at first instance may be discussed again in the course of an appeal. Indeed, if an appellant could not thus base his appeal on pleas in law and arguments already relied on before the Court of First Instance, an appeal would be deprived of part of its purpose (see, to this effect, Case C-25/05 P *Storck* v *OHIM* [2006] ECR I-0000, paragraphs 47 and 48, and the case-law cited).

33. The fourth ground of appeal alleges that the Court of First Instance erred in finding that Osman Ocalan had asserted that the PKK lacked capacity to bring an action. This ground contains detailed criticism of the contested order. Furthermore, it relates to a finding made by the Court of First Instance in the contested order, so it could not have been put forward at first instance.

34. Accordingly, the Council's argument seeking the rejection of the fourth ground of appeal inasmuch as it repeats submissions made at first instance is unfounded and must therefore be rejected.

35. As to the Council's argument that the fourth ground of appeal is inadmissible because it relates to a finding of fact made by the Court of First Instance, it must be pointed out that, in accordance with the case-law of the Court of Justice, complaints based on findings of fact and on the assessment of those facts in the contested decision are admissible on appeal where the appellant contends that the Court of First Instance has made findings which the documents in the file show to be substantially incorrect or that it has distorted the clear sense of the evidence before it (see, to this effect, Case C-82/01 P *Aéroports de Paris* v *Commission* [2002] ECR I-9297, paragraph 56). That is indeed the case here.

36. Consequently, the ground of appeal is admissible.

37. With regard to the ground's merits, it must be examined whether the Court of First Instance distorted the clear sense of the evidence. As the Advocate General has indicated in point 42 of her Opinion, there is such distortion where, without recourse to new evidence, the assessment of the existing evidence appears to be clearly incorrect (see, to this effect, Case C-551/03 P *General Motors* v *Commission* [2006] ECR I-3173, paragraph 54).

38. In light of this test, it is to be noted that the evidence adduced before the Court of First Instance concerning the PKK's existence comprises the statement by Osman Ocalan annexed to the application, the power of attorney which he gave to the lawyers to represent the first appellant, the positions adopted by the Council, and Serif Vanly's statement, which is also annexed to the application.

39. As regards, first, Osman Ocalan's statement, he indicates in paragraph 1 thereof that the PKK 'was, and remains, a political organisation of central importance to the Kurdish people'.

40. In paragraph 11, Osman Ocalan states:

> 'In July 1999 the PKK declared a unilateral ceasefire. The aim was to work towards a peaceful and democratic solution to the question of Kurdish rights. The PKK declared that all guerrilla activities would halt until further orders were received.'

41. Paragraphs 15 to 19 of the statement are worded as follows:

> '15. [The 8th Congress of the PKK, which took place between 4 and 10 April 2002,] described the PKK as the symbolic name of the "Apoist" movement ["Apo" being a term used for Abdullah Ocalan] in the period of Kurdish national awareness and resistance. It also declared that the PKK symbolised the Kurdish national spirit, conscience and identity.
>
> 16. It was decided by the Congress that in order to mirror the major transformations undergone by the PKK, all activities under the name of "PKK" would cease as of 4 April 2002 and that any activities taken under the name of the PKK would be deemed illegitimate.
>
> 17. The Congress resolved to carry forward the developments that had been carried out in a planned manner since the [1999] ceasefire and following the event of 7th Congress ["The Peace Project" incorporating the PKK position as evaluated at the 7th Congress on 10 January 2000 is exhibited to this statement].
>
> 18. A new constitution was adopted which altered the structure and organisation of the PKK and set out the strategy of the Apoist Movement. A coordinating organisation would accommodate the various different organisations to be created within parts of Kurdistan and the attendant countries. It was therefore decided to found [KADEK].
>
> 19. A new Management Committee was elected and Abdullah Ocalan was elected as the President of KADEK.'

42. Rather than proclaiming the PKK's dissolution, this document appears to state that the PKK progressively abandoned violent means of action in favour of other means of action. Osman Ocalan explains in particular that the PKK declared a unilateral ceasefire in July 1999, participated in a 'Peace Project' at its 7th Congress, held on 10 January 2000, and decided at its 8th Congress, which took place from 4 to 10 April 2002, to cease 'all activities' from 4 April 2002. Read in their context, the words 'all activities' could simply refer to the abandonment by the PKK of all its violent activities.

43. Furthermore, it appears from paragraphs 18 and 19 of Osman Ocalan's statement that the structure and organisation of the PKK were simply altered and that the PKK continued to exist under the name KADEK, Abdullah Ocalan remaining its president.

44. Likewise, the verb 'remains' used in paragraph 1 of the statement indicates that the PKK continues to exist.

45. In any event, Osman Ocalan does not expressly state anywhere in his statement that the 8th Congress of the PKK pronounced the PKK's dissolution.

46. Accordingly, when this statement is read as a whole it cannot properly be interpreted as affirming that the PKK was entirely dissolved.

47. As regards, second, the power of attorney given to the lawyers to represent the first appellant, Osman Ocalan specifies therein that he is acting 'on behalf of the organisation formerly known as the PKK'. These words indicate only a change of name and not the PKK's dissolution.

48. As regards, third, the positions adopted by the Council, it is apparent that, from 2 April 2004, the decisions which in succession replaced Decisions 2002/334 and 2002/460 refer to the PKK as the 'Kurdistan Workers' Party (PKK) (a.k.a. KADEK, a.k.a. KONGRA-GEL' (see, in particular, Council Decision 2004/306/EC of 2 April 2004 implementing Article 2(3) of Regulation (EC) No 2580/2001 on specific restrictive measures directed against certain persons and entities with a view to combating terrorism and repealing Decision 2003/902/EC (OJ 2004 L 99, p. 28)). This shows that the Council regards the PKK as continuing to exist, but under other names.

49. As regards, finally, the statement by Serif Vanly, President of the KNK, which is annexed to the application at first instance, while it is true that he refers therein to the dissolution of the PKK, that is, however, in the context of the following passage:

> 'Since the KNK's inception the [PKK] has been a member organisation of the KNK. The PKK spearheaded the creation of the KNK and it has since been a central driving force within the KNK, its aims and objectives being aligned with that of the KNK. The PKK is no longer an official member of the KNK after its dissolution in April 2002. However, the organisation born from the PKK, KADEK, seeks to join the KNK. The Honorary President of the KNK remains Abdullah Ocalan.'

50. This passage does not dictate the conclusion that the PKK ceased entirely to exist in April 2002. Read in its entirety, it suggests rather that the PKK retained a certain existence after this time in a reorganised form and under another name. Serif Vanly's statement therefore does not contradict the other evidence which has just been examined.

51. It follows that the finding in paragraph 35 of the contested order that, 'according to Mr [Osman] Ocalan's evidence annexed to the application, the PKK's Congress . . . pronounced [the PKK's] dissolution' is incorrect and contrary to the wording of his statement to which the finding refers.

52. Likewise, the statement in paragraph 37 of the contested order that, 'far from demonstrating Mr [Osman] Ocalan's legal capacity to represent the PKK, the applicants state, on the contrary, that the PKK no longer exists' is not consistent with the evidence available to the Court of First Instance.

53. The findings of fact in paragraphs 35 and 37 of the contested order are therefore incorrect and distort the clear sense of the evidence available to the Court of First Instance. It follows that the fourth ground of appeal is well founded.

54. Accordingly, the contested order must be set aside in so far as it declares the first appellant's application to be inadmissible, and there is no need to consider the other grounds of appeal relied upon by him.

Admissibility of the Application of Serif Vanly on Behalf of the KNK

55. Serif Vanly on behalf of the KNK ('the second appellant') sets out two grounds of appeal (the eighth and ninth grounds of appeal).

The Eighth Ground of Appeal

– Arguments of the parties

56. In the eighth ground of appeal, the second appellant observes that in the contested order the Court of First Instance held that the action was inadmissible in so far as it was brought by the KNK on the ground that it was not individually concerned, for the purposes of the fourth paragraph of Article 230 EC, by Decision 2002/460. The second appellant submits that that test is too restrictive when dealing with fundamental rights guaranteed under the ECHR. The test for admissibility in such circumstances should be applied more broadly, in line with the admissibility criteria of the European Court of Human Rights, in order not to bar the way to an effective judicial remedy.

57. The second appellant contends that if the Court of Justice were to rule that the KNK's application is inadmissible in the current proceedings, when, in the same circumstances, the European Court of Human Rights would hold an action brought before it to be admissible, the second appellant would be denied access to the effective remedy to which he is entitled, that is to say, an application seeking examination of whether Regulation No 2580/2001 and Decision 2002/460 infringe his fundamental rights as set out in the ECHR. To refuse such an examination when there is an arguable and admissible case under the ECHR would be in contravention of Article 13 of that Convention in that the second appellant would be purely and simply denied the remedy to which he is entitled.

58. The Council observes that the second appellant does not seek to prove that the Court of First Instance applied incorrectly the provisions of the

EC Treaty, as interpreted in Community case-law, when it held that the KNK was not individually concerned by Decision 2002/460. In reality, the second appellant is requesting the Court to disregard the fourth paragraph of Article 230 EC, as interpreted in Community case-law, and to adopt instead the rules on standing provided for by the ECHR.

59. In so far as this ground of appeal concerns the Court of First Instance's conclusion that the second appellant was not individually concerned, for the purposes of the fourth paragraph of Article 230 EC, by Decision 2002/460, the Council submits that the second appellant has failed to make any new arguments in the appeal and that, consequently, this part of the appeal is inadmissible. In the alternative, the Council pleads that this part of the appeal is unfounded since the Court of First Instance correctly applied settled case-law.

60. In so far as this ground of appeal develops an argument derived from the ECHR, the Council submits that this argument is inadmissible at the appeal stage, as it was not debated between the parties at first instance and the Court of First Instance did not make any finding in relation to it. In the alternative, the argument is unfounded because the European Union and the Community protect fundamental rights in a manner equivalent to that for which the ECHR provides.

– Findings of the Court

61. Regarding the admissibility of this ground of appeal, it is to be remembered that, under Article 118 of the Rules of Procedure of the Court of Justice, Article 42(2) of those rules, which prohibits generally the introduction of new pleas in law in the course of the procedure, applies to the procedure before the Court of Justice on appeal from a decision of the Court of First Instance. In an appeal the Court's jurisdiction is thus confined to review of the assessment by the Court of First Instance of the pleas argued before it (see Joined Cases C-199/01 P and C-200/01 P *IPK-München* v *Commission* [2004] ECR I-4627, paragraph 52).

62. At first instance the Council put forward in its objection of inadmissibility a plea alleging that the second appellant did not meet the conditions laid down in the fourth paragraph of Article 230 EC. In his observations on the objection of inadmissibility, the second appellant responded that that provision had to be interpreted in such a way that he was considered to meet those conditions. In this context, the second appellant submitted inter alia that there must be an effective remedy in the case of an act of the Community institutions which infringes fundamental rights and Community law. In the contested order, the Court of First Instance rejected the second appellant's submissions, but without expressing a view on the consideration that the action brought before it was designed to defend the second appellant's fundamental rights.

63. It is clear that the interpretation of the fourth paragraph of Article 230 EC and its application to the second appellant's circumstances were discussed in the proceedings before the Court of First Instance. The present ground of appeal seeks to contest in a detailed manner the Court of First Instance's interpretation and application of that provision in relation to the second appellant. It follows that the present ground of appeal is not a new plea whose introduction at the appeal stage would be prohibited by Articles 42(2) and 118 of the Rules of Procedure.

64. Where a ground of appeal is admissible, it is in principle for the appellant to set out arguments in support of it as he sees fit, whether by relying on arguments already used before the Court of First Instance or by developing new arguments, in particular in relation to the positions adopted by that Court. If it were otherwise, an appeal would be deprived of part of its purpose (see, to this effect, *Storck*, paragraph 48, and the case-law cited).

65. It follows that the second appellant is not required to support the present ground of appeal exclusively with new arguments relating to the interpretation of the fourth paragraph of Article 230 EC in Community case-law. The Council's argument to that effect is unfounded and must be rejected.

66. As regards the admissibility of the arguments derived from the ECHR, it follows from Article 58 of the Statute of the Court of Justice, in conjunction with Article 113(2) of the Rules of Procedure of the Court of Justice, that, on appeal, an appellant may put forward any relevant argument, provided only that the subject-matter of the proceedings before the Court of First Instance is not changed in the appeal. Contrary to the Council's assertions, there is no requirement that each argument put forward on appeal must previously have been discussed at first instance. A restriction to this effect cannot be accepted because an appeal would thereby be deprived of a significant part of its purpose.

67. Since it is evident that the present ground of appeal does not change the subject-matter of the proceedings before the Court of First Instance, the Council's argument concerning the ground's inadmissibility in so far as it refers to the ECHR is unfounded and must be rejected.

68. It follows that the present ground of appeal is admissible in its entirety.

69. As to the merits of the ground of appeal, the second appellant submits that Decisions 2002/334 and 2002/460 are of concern to him since, in particular, the KNK provides a representative platform for the PKK and for any deemed successor organisation of the PKK.

70. It is settled case-law that a link of that kind is not sufficient to establish that an entity is individually concerned for the purposes of the fourth

paragraph of Article 230 EC. An association which represents a category of natural or legal persons cannot be considered to be individually concerned, for the purposes of that provision, by a measure affecting the general interests of that category (see, to this effect, *Fédération nationale de la boucherie en gros et du commerce en gros des viandes and Others* v *Council*, at p. 499, and the order in Case 117/86 *UFADE* v *Council and Commission* [1986] ECR 3255, paragraph 12).

71. The second appellant further submits that the KNK would be in danger of having its own funds frozen, pursuant to Decisions 2002/334 and 2002/460, if it dealt with the PKK.

72. In accordance with settled case-law, natural or legal persons can claim to be concerned individually by a measure of general application only if they are affected by reason of certain attributes which are peculiar to them or by reason of circumstances in which they are differentiated from any other person (see, to this effect, *Plaumann* v *Commission*, at p. 107, and Case C-50/00 P *Unión dePequeños Agricultores* v *Council* [2002] ECR I-6677, paragraph 36).

73. If the KNK runs the risk of having its funds frozen, that is by virtue of an objectively defined prohibition which applies in the same way to all persons subject to Community law. In those circumstances, the KNK cannot claim to be individually concerned, for the purposes of the fourth paragraph of Article 230 EC, by Decisions 2002/334 and 2002/460.

74. In concluding, in particular in paragraphs 45, 46, 51 and 52 of the contested order, that the KNK was not individually concerned for the purposes of the fourth paragraph of Article 230 EC, the Court of First Instance correctly applied that provision as interpreted by the case-law.

75. The second appellant contends, however, that when the fourth paragraph of Article 230 EC is interpreted in that way it lays down a condition of admissibility so restrictive that the provision conflicts with the ECHR.

76. Fundamental rights form an integral part of the general principles of law the observance of which the Court ensures. For that purpose, the Court draws inspiration from the constitutional traditions common to the Member States and from the guidelines supplied by international instruments for the protection of human rights on which the Member States have collaborated or to which they are signatories. The ECHR has special significance in that respect (see, inter alia, Case C-112/00 *Schmidberger* [2003] ECR I-5659, paragraph 71, and Case C-540/03 *European Parliament* v *Council* [2006] ECR I-0000, paragraph 35).

77. In addition, Article 6(2) EU provides:

> 'The Union shall respect fundamental rights, as guaranteed by the [ECHR] and as they result from the constitutional traditions common to the Member States, as general principles of Community law.'

78. It is within that framework that the present argument must be considered.

79. As provided in Article 34 of the ECHR, the European Court of Human Rights may receive applications from any person, non-governmental organisation or group of individuals claiming to be the victim of a violation by one of the High Contracting Parties of the rights set forth in the ECHR.

80. According to the case-law of the European Court of Human Rights, Article 34 of the ECHR requires as a general rule that, in order to be considered a victim within the meaning of that article, an applicant must claim to have been affected by a violation of the ECHR that has already taken place (see Eur. Court H.R., *Klass and Others v. Germany*, judgment of 6 September 1978, Series A no. 28, § 33). It is only in highly exceptional circumstances that an applicant may nevertheless claim to be a victim of a violation of the ECHR owing to the risk of a future violation (see Eur. Commission H.R., *Tauira and Others v. France*, no. 28204/95, decision of 4 December 1995, Decisions and Reports 83-B, p. 112, at p. 130). It is apparent, however, from the case-law of the European Court of Human Rights that persons who claim to be linked to an entity included in the list annexed to Common Position 2001/931, but who are not included in it themselves, do not have the status of victims of a violation of the ECHR within the meaning of Article 34 thereof and that, consequently, their applications are inadmissible (see Eur. Court H.R., *Segi and Gestoras Pro-Amnistia and Others v. 15 States of the European Union* (dec.), nos. 6422/02 and 9916/02, ECHR 2002-V).

81. The KNK's situation is comparable to that of the persons linked to the abovementioned entities Segi and Gestoras Pro-Amnistia. The KNK is not included in the disputed list and is therefore not subject to the restrictive measures envisaged by Regulation No 2580/2001.

82. In those circumstances, the case-law of the European Court of Human Rights, as it currently stands, appears to indicate that the KNK would not be able to establish that it has the status of a victim within the meaning of Article 34 of the ECHR and therefore would not be able to bring an action before that court.

83. Consequently, in the circumstances of the present case no conflict between the ECHR and the fourth paragraph of Article 230 EC has been established.

84. The present ground of appeal must accordingly be rejected as unfounded.

The Ninth Ground of Appeal

– Arguments of the parties

85. The second appellant contends that paragraph 49 of the contested order is marred by an error since it is founded on the assumption that the PKK no longer existed, thus prejudging a matter of substance in order to reject an argument concerning the admissibility of the action.

86. The Council states that the Court of First Instance did not rule on the existence or otherwise of the PKK. For the purposes of assessing whether the KNK could rely on the fact that one or more of its members would be entitled to bring an action for annulment of the contested decision, it simply held that by claiming that the PKK no longer existed the second appellant had at the very least acknowledged that the PKK was no longer a member of the KNK.

– Findings of the Court

87. It is apparent from paragraphs 69 to 82 of the present judgment that the KNK is neither individually concerned, for the purposes of the fourth paragraph of Article 230 EC, by Decisions 2002/334 and 2002/460 nor a victim of those decisions within the meaning of Article 34 of the ECHR, irrespective of whether the PKK exists or not. In those circumstances, an erroneous finding by the Court of First Instance that the PKK did not exist could not in any event result in the contested order being set aside as regards the second appellant.

88. The present ground of appeal is thus immaterial.

89. It follows that the appeal brought by the second appellant is unfounded and must be dismissed.

90. Since the second appellant has been unsuccessful, he must be ordered to pay the costs of the appeal which he brought, pursuant to Articles 69(2) and 122 of the Rules of Procedure of the Court of Justice.

Consideration of the Action Before the Court of First Instance

91. In accordance with the second sentence of the first paragraph of Article 61 of the Statute of the Court of Justice, if the decision of the Court of First Instance is set aside the Court of Justice may give final judgment in the matter where the state of the proceedings so permits. That is so in the case of the dispute between the first appellant and the Council so far as concerns the admissibility of the application.

92. The Council puts forward two pleas in support of its request that the first appellant's application be declared inadmissible. First, in so far as it relates to Decision 2002/334, the application was lodged out of time. Second, the PKK lacks the capacity to be a party to judicial proceedings because it no longer exists.

The First Plea

Arguments of the Parties

93. According to the Council, the deadline for bringing an action challenging Decision 2002/334 was 29 July 2002. The original of the application was lodged at the Registry of the Court of First Instance on 31 July 2002. Consequently, the application was lodged out of time in so far as it relates to that decision.

94. The Commission, as an intervener at first instance, supported this reasoning and added that the inadmissibility of the application challenging Decision 2002/334 means that the application challenging Decision 2002/460 is inadmissible, since the latter is merely a decision confirming the former.

95. The first appellant responds that his representatives are convinced that they lodged the original of the application, along with five copies, at the Registry of the Court of First Instance on 24 July 2002, even though they lodged a replacement original on 31 July 2002. In those circumstances, and since fundamental rights are at stake, to prevent the first appellant from seeking the annulment of Decision 2002/334 would be unduly formalistic.

96. In any event, in the first appellant's submission, Decision 2002/460 is an independent decision which was certainly contested within the time-limit.

Findings of the Court

97. Decision 2002/334 was adopted on 2 May 2002 and published in the *Official Journal of the European Communities* on 3 May 2002. In addition to the period of two months for bringing an action for annulment which is laid down in the fifth paragraph of Article 230 EC, it is necessary to include in the calculation a period of 14 days from the date of publication of the contested measure, pursuant to Article 102(1) of the Rules of Procedure of the Court of First Instance, and of a single period of 10 days on account of distance, pursuant to Article 102(2) of those rules. The final day of the period determined in accordance with these provisions was 27 July 2002. Since that was a Saturday, the period for bringing an action was extended until the end of Monday, 29 July 2002, pursuant to the first subparagraph of Article 101(2) of the Rules of Procedure.

98. Article 43(1) of the Rules of Procedure of the Court of First Instance requires the original of every pleading to be lodged.

99. It appears from the documents before the Court of First Instance that only copies, without an original, were lodged at the Registry of the Court of First Instance on 24 July 2002. Even though the first appellant asserts that his representatives lodged the original of the application together with the copies lodged on that date, he does not adduce any evidence of this.

Furthermore, the text of the original lodged on 31 July 2002 displays some differences compared with the copies lodged on 24 July 2002. It must therefore be found that the original of the application was not lodged at the Registry of the Court of First Instance until 31 July 2002, as the Registry's stamp on it attests.

100. Since the original of the application was not lodged at the Registry of the Court of First Instance within the period required, the first appellant's application is inadmissible in so far as it challenges Decision 2002/334.

101. This conclusion is not affected by the circumstance, pleaded by the first appellant, that fundamental rights are at stake. Rules concerning time-limits for bringing proceedings are mandatory and must be applied by the court in question in such a way as to safeguard legal certainty and equality of persons before the law.

102. On the other hand, it is common ground that the first appellant challenged Decision 2002/460 within the time-limit laid down.

103. As the Court of First Instance correctly held in paragraph 44 of the contested order, that decision is a new decision in relation to Decision 2002/334. As provided in Article 2(3) of Regulation No 2580/2001 and Article 1(6) of Common Position 2001/931, each decision revising the disputed list results from a review by the Council of the situation of the persons, groups and entities covered.

104. It follows that Decision 2002/460 does not merely confirm Decision 2002/334 and that the inadmissibility of the application in so far as it challenges Decision 2002/334 does not prevent the first appellant from contesting Decision 2002/460.

The Second Plea

Arguments of the Parties

105. The Council submits that the PKK does not have the capacity to bring an action for annulment because, according to the first appellant's own statements, it has been dissolved. Its non-existence is illustrated by the fact that it does not have headed notepaper. The power of attorney given to the lawyers to represent it is simply set out on a blank sheet of paper bearing Osman Ocalan's signature.

106. The first appellant contends, first, that he has not stated that the PKK was dissolved and, second, that the PKK retains at least a residual capacity sufficient to contest its inclusion in the disputed list.

Findings of the Court

107. As has been found in paragraphs 38 to 52 of the present judgment, the available evidence tends to indicate that the PKK was not dissolved at its

Congress from 4 to 10 April 2002. It appears in fact, on examining that evidence, that the PKK continued to operate after the Congress, probably in a reorganised form and under other names.

108. Even though the field of the PKK's activities after 4 April 2002 cannot be defined absolutely precisely in the light of that evidence, it is in any event certain that it retains an existence sufficient to contest its inclusion in the disputed list.

109. The European Community is a community based on the rule of law in which its institutions are subject to judicial review of the compatibility of their acts with the EC Treaty and with the general principles of law which include fundamental rights. Individuals are therefore entitled to effective judicial protection of the rights they derive from the Community legal order, and the right to such protection is one of the general principles of law stemming from the constitutional traditions common to the Member States. That right has also been enshrined in Articles 6 and 13 of the ECHR (see *Unión de Pequeños Agricultores* v *Council*, paragraphs 38 and 39).

110. It is particularly important for that judicial protection to be effective because the restrictive measures laid down by Regulation No 2580/2001 have serious consequences. Not only are all financial transactions and financial services thereby prevented in the case of a person, group or entity covered by the regulation, but also their reputation and political activity are damaged by the fact that they are classified as terrorists.

111. Under Article 2(3) of Regulation No 2580/2001, read in conjunction with Article 1(4) to (6) of Common Position 2001/931, a person, group or entity can be included in the disputed list only if there is certain reliable information, and the persons, groups or entities covered must be precisely identified. In addition, it is made clear that the name of persons, groups or entities can be kept on the list only if the Council reviews their situation periodically. All these matters must be open to judicial review.

112. It follows that since, by Decision 2002/460, the Community legislature took the view that the PKK retains an existence sufficient for it to be subject to the restrictive measures laid down by Regulation No 2580/2001, it must be accepted, on grounds of consistency and justice, that that entity continues to have an existence sufficient to contest this measure. The effect of any other conclusion would be that an organisation could be included in the disputed list without being able to bring an action challenging its inclusion.

113. In order to be permitted to bring an action on behalf of such an organisation, it is necessary to show that the organisation concerned does indeed wish to bring the action and that the lawyers who claim to represent it have in fact been instructed for that purpose.

114. The Statute of the Court of Justice, in particular Article 21, the Rules of Procedure of the Court of Justice, in particular Article 38, and the Rules of Procedure of the Court of First Instance, in particular Article 44, were not devised with a view to the commencement of actions by organisations lacking legal personality, such as the PKK. In this exceptional situation, the procedural rules governing the admissibility of an action for annulment must be applied by adapting them, to the extent necessary, to the circumstances of the case. As the Court of First Instance rightly stated in paragraph 28 of the contested order, it is a question of avoiding excessive formalism which would amount to the denial of any possibility of applying for annulment even though the entity in question has been the object of restrictive Community measures.

115. It follows that Osman Ocalan is entitled to demonstrate, by any available evidence, that he is acting validly on behalf of the PKK whose representative he claims to be.

116. Regarding the validity of the representation of the PKK by Osman Ocalan, a doubt arises from the fact that he presents himself in the power of attorney as a former member of the PKK, without his entitlement to represent it being justified on any other basis.

117. However, in the appeal the first appellant has submitted to the Court a statement by Mark Muller, a lawyer, which tends to justify that power of attorney. As confirmed by the judgment of the European Court of Human Rights of 12 May 2005 in *Abdullah Ocalan v. Turkey*, no. 46221/99, not yet published, Mark Muller represents before that court Abdullah Ocalan who was the leader of the PKK and has been imprisoned in Turkey since 1999. Mark Muller states that, on a visit by him to Abdullah Ocalan in prison, the latter gave him instructions to challenge the proscription of the PKK in Europe. Mark Muller further states that several other high-ranking representatives of the PKK and its successor, KADEK, instructed him to pursue the proceedings brought by the application made to the Court of First Instance.

118. Moreover, Mark Muller states that, when Osman Ocalan signed the power of attorney given to the lawyers to make the application, he was a high-ranking representative of both the PKK and KADEK.

119. These statements, made by a member of the bar of one of the Member States, who is subject as such to a code of professional conduct, are sufficient, in the particular circumstances of the case, to establish that Osman Ocalan is qualified to represent the PKK and in particular to instruct lawyers to act on its behalf.

120. This finding is not affected by the Council's argument relating to the absence of headed notepaper.

121. It is true that in the case of a legal person governed by private law it is customary for the power of attorney given to its lawyers to be set out on headed notepaper, although that is not required by the provisions relating to the procedure before the Court of Justice or the Court of First Instance. However, in the case of an organisation which is not established in accordance with the legal rules that usually apply to legal persons, this factor has little evidential value.

122. In those circumstances, it must be held that Osman Ocalan is authorised to represent the PKK and to instruct lawyers for that purpose.

123. It follows that the first appellant's application is admissible in so far as it challenges Decision 2002/460. The case must accordingly be referred back to the Court of First Instance for judgment on the substance.

124. Since the case is being referred back to the Court of First Instance for continuation of the proceedings in so far as they concern the first appellant, costs should be reserved in his regard.

On those grounds, the Court (First Chamber) hereby:

1. **Sets aside the order of the Court of First Instance of the European Communities of 15 February 2005 in Case T-229/02 *PKK and KNK* v *Council* in so far as it dismisses the application of Osman Ocalan on behalf of the Kurdistan Workers' Party (PKK);**

2. **Dismisses the appeal as to the remainder;**

3. **Orders Serif Vanly on behalf of the Kurdistan National Congress (KNK) to pay the costs of the appeal brought by him;**

4. **Dismisses the application of Osman Ocalan on behalf of the PKK as inadmissible in so far as it challenges Council Decision 2002/334/EC of 2 May 2002 implementing Article 2(3) of Regulation (EC) No 2580/2001 on specific restrictive measures directed against certain persons and entities with a view to combating terrorism and repealing Decision 2001/927/EC;**

5. **Declares that the application of Osman Ocalan on behalf of the PKK is admissible in so far as it challenges Council Decision 2002/460/EC of 17 June 2002 implementing Article 2(3) of Regulation (EC) No 2580/2001 on specific restrictive measures directed against certain persons and entities with a view to combating terrorism and repealing Decision 2002/334/EC, and refers the case back to the Court of First Instance of the European Communities for judgment on the substance;**

6. **Reserves the costs of Osman Ocalan on behalf of the PKK.**

[Signatures]

E. RELIGIOUS EXTREMISM

DOCUMENT NO. 29

EUROPEAN PARLIAMENT RESOLUTION OF 13 DECEMBER 2007 ON COMBATING THE RISE OF EXTREMISM IN EUROPE

The European Parliament,

- having regard to its previous resolutions on racism, xenophobia and extremism, particularly that of 20 February 1997 on racism, xenophobia and the extreme right,[1] that of 15 June 2006 on the increase in racist and homophobic violence in Europe[2] and its position of 29 November 2007 on the proposal for a Council Framework Decision on combating certain forms and expressions of racism and xenophobia by means of criminal law,[3]
- having regard to its resolution of 27 January 2005 on the Holocaust, anti-Semitism and racism,[4]
- having regard to Articles 6, 7 and 29 of the EU Treaty and Article 13 of the EC Treaty, which commit the EU and its Member States to upholding human rights and fundamental freedoms and which provide it with the means to fight racism, xenophobia and discrimination, to the Charter of Fundamental Rights of the European Union (the Charter of Fundamental Rights) and to the Council Regulation (EC) No 168/2007 of 15 February 2007 establishing the European Union Fundamental Rights Agency[5] (the Fundamental Rights Agency),
- having regard to the international human rights instruments which prohibit discrimination based on racial and ethnic origin, notably the International Convention on the Elimination of All Forms of Racial Discrimination and the European Convention for the Protection of Human Rights and Fundamental Freedoms (ECHR), both signed by all the Member States and a large number of other States,

---

1 OJ C 85,17.3.1997, p. 150.
2 OJ C 300 E, 9.12.2006, p. 491.
3 Texts adopted, **P6_TA(2007)0552.**
4 OJ C 253 E, 13.10.2005, p. 37.
5 OJ L 53, 22.2.2007, p. 1.

- having regard to European Union activities to fight racism, xenophobia, anti-Semitism and homophobia, in particular the two anti-discrimination directives (Directive 2000/43/EC implementing the principle of equal treatment of persons irrespective of racial or ethnic origin[6] and Directive 2000/78/EC establishing a general framework for equal treatment in employment and occupation,[7] as well as to the above-mentioned Framework Decision on combating racism and xenophobia,
- having regard to Resolution 1344 of 29 September 2003 of the Parliamentary Assembly of the Council of Europe on the threat posed to democracy by extremist parties and movements in Europe,
- having regard to the Report on Racism and Xenophobia in the Member States of the EU published in 2007 by the Fundamental Rights Agency,
- having regard to the report by the Organization for Security and Co-operation in Europe (OSCE) entitled 'Challenges and Responses to Hate-Motivated Incidents in the OSCE Region' of October 2006,
- having regard to Rule 103(4) of its Rules of Procedure,

A. seriously concerned at the resurgence in Europe of extremist movements and paramilitary groups and parties, some of which even have governmental responsibilities, which base their ideology, political discourse, practices and conduct on discrimination, including racism, intolerance, incitement to religious hatred, exclusion, xenophobia, anti-Semitism, anti-Gypsyism, homophobia, misogyny and ultra-nationalism, and whereas several European countries have recently experienced hatred, violent events and killings,

B. seriously alarmed at the Islamic fundamentalist recruitment and violent propaganda campaign with terrorist attacks within the European Union, based on the hatred of European values and anti-semitism,

C. whereas these extremist ideologies are incompatible with the principles of liberty, democracy, respect for human rights and fundamental freedoms and the rule of law as set out in Article 6 of the EU Treaty, which reflect the values of diversity and equality on which the European Union is based,

D. whereas no Member State is immune from the intrinsic threats that extremism poses to democracy and, therefore combating the spread of xenophobic attitudes and extremist political movements is a European challenge that requires a joint and coordinated approach,

E. whereas some political parties and movements, including those currently in power in a number of countries or represented at local, national or European level, have deliberately placed intolerance and/or violence based

6 OJ L 180, 19.7.2000, p. 22.
7 OJ L 303, 2.12.2000, p. 16.

on race, ethnic origin, nationality, religion and sexual orientation at the heart of their agenda,

F. whereas neo-Nazi, paramilitary and other extremisms are directing their violent attacks against a wide variety of vulnerable population groups, including migrants, the Roma, homosexuals, anti-racist activists and the homeless,

G. whereas the existence of public and easily accessible websites which incite to hatred raises serious concerns as to how to counteract the problem without violating freedom of expression,

1. Strongly condemns all racist and hate attacks, and calls on all authorities to do everything in their power to punish those responsible; expresses its solidarity with all victims of such attacks and their families;

2. Points out that fighting extremism must not have any negative effects on the permanent obligation to respect fundamental rights and fundamental legal principles, including freedom of expression and association, as enshrined in Article 6 of the EU Treaty;

3. Deplores the fact that some mainstream parties have seen fit to give credibility and acceptance to extremist parties by entering into coalition agreements, thereby sacrificing their moral integrity for the sake of short-term political gain and expediency;

4. Notes that the increasing number of extremist organisations, which often contain neo-fascist elements, can exacerbate fears in society that can lead to manifestations of racism in a broad range of areas, including employment, housing, education, health, policing, access to goods and services and the media;

5. Urges the Commission and Council to lead the search for appropriate political and legal responses, especially at the preventive stage with reference to young people's education and public information, teaching against totalitarianism and disseminating the principles of human rights and fundamental freedoms in order to keep alive the memory of European history; calls upon the Member States to develop policies of education for democratic citizenship based on citizens' rights and responsibilities;

6. Urges the Commission to monitor the full application of the existing legislation designed to prohibit incitement to political and religious violence, racism and xenophobia; calls on Member States to monitor the strict implementation and constant improvement of anti-racist laws, information and awareness-raising campaigns in the media and educational establishments;

7. Urges all democratic political forces, regardless of ideology, to avoid any support for extremist parties of a racist or xenophobic character, whether

explicit or implicit, and hence also any alliance whatsoever with their elected representatives;

8. Warns, looking ahead to the 2009 European elections, of the possibility that extremist parties may secure representation in the European Parliament and calls on the political groups to take the appropriate measures in order to ensure that a democratic institution is not used as a platform for financing and echoing anti-democratic messages;

9. Calls on the EU institutions to give a clear mandate to the Fundamental Rights Agency to investigate the structures of extremist groups in order to assess whether some of them coordinate their work within their groups across the European Union or at regional level;

10. Reiterates its belief that public personalities should refrain from statements that encourage or incite to hatred or stigmatisation of groups of people on the basis of their race, ethnic origin, religion, disability, sexual orientation or nationality; believes that if public personalities incite to hatred, the fact that they have a high public profile should be considered an aggravating circumstance; condemns, in particular, the worrying prevalence of anti-semitism;

11. Calls on the media to inform the public about the dangers of hate speech and to help promote the principles and values of democracy, equality and tolerance;

12. Requests all Member States to at least provide for the possibility - after a court ruling—of withdrawing public funding from political parties that do not condemn violence and terrorism and do not respect human rights and fundamental freedoms, democracy and the rule of law as set out in the ECHR and the Charter of Fundamental Rights; and calls on those that already have this possibility to do so without delay; also calls on the Commission to ensure that no EU funding is available to media which are used as a platform to widely promote racist, xenophobic and homophobic ideas;

13. Calls on the Commission to support NGOs and civil society organisations devoted to promoting democratic values, human dignity, solidarity, social inclusion, inter-cultural dialogue and social awareness of the dangers of radicalisation and violent extremism, and which are devoted to fighting all forms of discrimination;

14. Instructs its President to forward this resolution to the Council, the Commission, the governments of the Member States and the Council of Europe.

DOCUMENT NO. 30

THE EU STRATEGY FOR COMBATING RADICALISATION AND RECRUITMENT

Report 15443/07
Council of the European Union

Brussels, 23 November 2007

from:	Counter-terrorism Coordinator
to:	Coreper/Council
Subject:	The EU Strategy for Combating Radicalisation and Recruitment – Implementation report

1. In December 2005, the Council adopted the European Union Strategy for Combating Radicalisation and Recruitment to Terrorism.[1] The Strategy sets out three general strands for EU action: to disrupt the activities of networks and individuals who draw people into terrorism, to ensure that voices of mainstream opinion prevail over those of extremism and to promote—yet more vigorously—security, justice, democracy and opportunity for all. The Strategy and the accompanying classified Action Plan (updated under the German Presidency) contain both joint standards and new measures. While recognising the primacy of the Member States in the field of radicalisation and recruitment, the Strategy proposes a set of specific measures for implementation at European level. These measures cover all three pillars and require close cooperation between the Council and the Commission.

[1] 14781/1/05

2. The Coordinator has been tasked with drawing up an annual review of implementation of the Strategy. The first annual review was sent to the Council in November 2006. This document contains the second annual review of the implementation of the Strategy for Combating Radicalisation and Recruitment.

3. This report mainly covers the implementation of the EU Strategy for Combating Radicalisation and Recruitment by the EU institutions. Where this is particularly relevant, reference is made to activities undertaken by Member States as reported by them in response to the recent Commission survey on policies to address violent radicalisation.

4. Over the last twelve months, the Council and the Commission have made some progress in the implementation of the Strategy. Overall, however, implementation has been uneven. While in some areas new initiatives were launched, in others (such as EU cooperation with regard to the prevention of radicalisation at educational institutions, training for religious leaders, and community policing) cooperation remained limited to exchange of information on a limited scale.

5. An impetus for new work in the field of justice and home affairs came from the Commission, which developed a number of initiatives to carry out the recommendations of the Strategy. In the field of external relations, COTER devoted much time and attention to implementing the Strategy, but was confronted with some setbacks.

6. If the European Union wishes to supplement Member States' efforts in the field of prevention, then fresh ideas for implementation of the Strategy for Combating Radicalisation and Recruitment need to be developed. An assessment of the implementation of the EU Strategy for Combating Radicalisation and Recruitment, as well as some suggestions for improvement, are proffered in the Coordinator's overall assessment of the implementation of the various counter-terrorism Action Plans.[1] Furthermore, the Coordinator looks forward to the Commission communication planned for mid-2008 which will, inter alia, identify good practice as regards addressing violent radicalisation within the EU and make specific recommendations to the Member States. That communication will in principle be based on various studies the Commission has contracted out in recent years, as well as on a questionnaire sent to the Member States and a conference the Commission organised on the role of education in preventing violent radicalisation.

[1] 15448/07

Disrupting the Activities of Networks and Individuals who Draw People into Terrorism

Developments Within the EU

7. Consecutive Presidencies have continued to work on the German "Check the Web" initiative, aimed at intensifying EU cooperation on monitoring and analysing Internet sites in the context of counter-terrorism. Council

conclusions on cooperation to combat terrorist use of the Internet and "Check the Web" were adopted at the meeting of the JHA Council on 12 and 13 June 2007. The information portal at Europol was further developed. In October 2007, five Member States were using the portal on a regular basis, while twenty others had requested accounts. Work is ongoing to implement the second phase (to be completed by the end of 2008), which will allow for the uploading of more data, including restricted materials, and access for a greater number of users. In addition, at the end of the German Presidency a handbook of "Check the Web" expert meetings was distributed to Member States, giving a detailed overview of various expert meetings held in the framework of the Check the Web initiative.

8. The Commission is studying non-legislative measures to prevent the distribution of violent radical content on the Internet, including possible notice and take-down procedures and cooperation between NGOs and law enforcement authorities. The Commission plans to contract out a study analysing to what extent the methods applied to counter the dissemination of child pornography over the Internet are applicable to content promoting terrorism.

9. The new Audiovisual Media Service directive, to be adopted by the end of the year and to be implemented within two years, will extend the prohibition of incitement to hatred to all audiovisual media services, including on-demand services.

10. Member States' actions to address radicalisation at other vulnerable places, such as educational institutions and places of worship, include training of local authorities (including police), and outreach of central governments to grass-roots organisations to detect and deal with the phenomenon.

11. Several Member States report that they have devised policies to prevent radicalisation of prison inmates. Reported measures are aimed at the collection of information, enhanced prisoner management, the presence of qualified mainstream religious teachers in prisons, and training of penitentiary staff to recognise and address radicalisation. Austria, Germany and France have submitted a project for funding by the Commission, aimed at the enhancement of the capacity of prison staff to recognise and address radicalisation within penitentiary institutions. The project has been selected for award but the actual grant agreement is yet to be signed.

12. A strategic cooperation agreement between the European Police College (CEPOL) and Europol has been signed. The purpose of this agreement is to enhance cooperation between Europol and CEPOL in strengthening the training of senior police officers, in particular by organising courses, seminars and conferences and developing and implementing common curricula and course material.

13. A CEPOL expert course on counter-terrorism was held from 3-7 September 2007, focusing on current threats from "home-grown terrorism" and terrorist networks. Various cases as well as current strategies to detect and to investigate threats in Germany, Spain, the UK and the Netherlands were analysed. A psychologist shared views on the mindset of extremists.

14. SitCen regularly draws up assessments of radicalisation and recruitment on the basis of contributions from Member States and Europol. Europol continued to analyse various themes related to radicalisation and recruitment, such as extremists returning from armed struggle in conflict zones, terrorist organisations, the role of religious converts and women with regard to radicalisation, training venues in the EU, and "home-grown terrorism".

External Action

15. In 2006 the EU launched a multi-pronged exercise of counter-terrorism technical assistance to Morocco and Algeria. This programme contains various strands of work, each carried out by an EU Member State. The Netherlands has developed a programme of cooperation with Morocco in the field of radicalisation and recruitment. The programme covers, in particular, the prevention of radicalisation among prison inmates and measures to counter radicalisation and recruitment through the Internet. In the course of 2006 and 2007, its implementation met with a number of difficulties. From 15–20 July 2007 the Netherlands and Morocco held a successful bilateral conference on counter-terrorism that sought to foster dialogue between the two countries and explore the potential for cooperation. The conference addressed some of the administrative hurdles for cooperation in the programme for the prevention of radicalisation. Both sides undertook to cooperate in the area of training for prison staff to deal with radicalisation (recognition of the personality of incarcerated extremists, gathering of information on their behaviour and possibilities for intervention). They also agreed to hold a number of seminars/workshops for experts on the recognition and prevention of radicalisation on the Internet and on ways to proactively use the Internet to foster tolerance and moderation.

16. COTER plans to include the fight against radicalisation and recruitment in its future technical assistance programme for Indonesia. At the request of Indonesia, rehabilitation of convicted terrorists in prisons was an important theme in an EU-Indonesian seminar (4–5 September 2007), organised to facilitate the identification of themes for future EU technical assistance.

Ensuring that Voices of Mainstream Opinion Prevail over those of Extremism

Working with Civil Society

17. Mainstream Islamic voices are often best placed to provide a credible alternative to the ideology of terrorists. COTER agreed two project proposals in this area: a UK proposal on the establishment of a network of mainstream voices to counter extremist networks and a German proposal on the promotion of dialogue among mainstream Muslims.

18. The German proposal would provide for an exchange programme whereby influential Muslim civil society, media, popular culture and academic and religious leaders from EU Member States and third countries are brought together to engage in dialogue on ways to counter terrorism. Implementation of the project would be entrusted to the Indonesian NGO Lib for All, which has developed innovative ways to counter radicalisation. Germany has submitted its proposal for financing under the Commission's call for proposals in the field of prevention and the fight against crime. At this stage, the procedure for the selection of projects submitted in response to this call is still ongoing but a decision is expected in early 2008.

19. The UK proposal suggests a network of civil society groups which could provide an alternative message to that of extremism and radicalisation. The intention is that this would be formed initially in Europe and neighbouring countries and eventually become a global grouping. No funding for this project was available in 2007, but it may be submitted anew (probably somewhat adapted) for Community funding in January 2008.

20. The Commission has contracted out a study on best practices in cooperation efforts between public authorities and civil society with a view to the prevention of violent radicalisation. The study will guide and support the Commission's future policy-making in this field.

21. Furthermore, the Commission has issued two calls for proposals which allow applicants (both private organisations and public bodies) to submit project proposals in the field of prevention of, and response to, violent radicalisation. Grants amounting to almost EUR 750 000 from the budget under the Pilot Project 2006 "Fight against Terrorism" have already been awarded under the first call. The grant agreements have not yet been signed however. By the end of the year more grants will be awarded on the issue of addressing violent radicalisation under the new Crime Prevention Programme (ISEC). This means that the Commission will allocate an estimated two million euros to support selected projects.

Intercultural Dialogue

22. Intercultural dialogue represents a long-term, strategic goal for the European Union. It has become one of the main priorities of the Culture programme 2007–2013, managed by the European Commission, and is mainstreamed in many other Community programmes. In addition, most reporting Member States indicate that intercultural dialogue is a priority for their governments, but the way in which they address this issue tends to vary.

23. On 15 May 2007, European Commission President José Manuel Barroso co-hosted a meeting attended by 20 leading representatives of the Christian, Jewish and Islamic faiths in Europe on the theme of "Building a Europe Based on Human Dignity". This was the third such meeting (previous ones took place in 2005 and 2006) and the first co-hosted by the Council and Parliament Presidents. This dialogue should not be seen as a form of inter-faith dialogue as such, but as a dialogue between the EU and various religious institutions.

24. On the basis of a proposal from the Commission, the European Parliament and the Council have decided to make 2008 the European Year of Intercultural Dialogue. The objectives of this project will be to promote intercultural dialogue as a process in which all those living in the EU can improve their ability to deal with a cultural environment in which different identities and beliefs coexist, to highlight intercultural dialogue as an opportunity to contribute to and benefit from a diverse society, not only in Europe but world-wide, to promote European citizenship and to highlight the contribution of different cultures to European societies. The Year will be developed around three types of action: actions on a Community scale, including an information campaign promoting the objectives of the European Year, surveys and studies, grants for emblematic actions at Community level aimed at promoting inter-cultural dialogue and raising awareness, particularly among young people, of the objectives of the European Year and co-financing of actions on national level. The budget for the European Year is ten million euro.

25. The participation of civil society will ensure that the discussions and activities held in the context of the Year are anchored in existing experiences. A contact group for the Year has been established, consisting of members of the Civil Society Platform for Intercultural Dialogue, the Social Platform and the European Youth Forum. This group is consulted on various steps in the implementation of the Year and circulates information to the numerous civil society groups involved in this matter. The Civil Society Platform has launched a consultation process with a view to the drafting of a "Rainbow Paper" identifying best practices in the field of intercultural dialogue and formulating policy recommendations.

26. The European Commission has developed a wide range of programmes that promote intercultural understanding. Of particular relevance in this context are projects in the areas of education, youth and culture. The Erasmus Mundus programme offers third-country students and scholars the opportunity to participate in selected courses at European universities. The Tempus programme funds projects for cooperation between universities in the EU and its ENP partners, in order to facilitate educational reform, mutual learning and intercultural understanding. The Youth in Action programme 2007–2013 has set respect for cultural diversity and the fight against racism and xenophobia as priorities. Intercultural dialogue is a priority of the Youth in Action programme for 2007 and 2008. The programme runs projects to support intercultural dialogue, tolerance and citizenship. The Commission also fosters intercultural dialogue at national level in third countries. The Philippine interfaith and multicultural dialogues are a good example. In addition, the Commission has issued a communication on a European Agenda for Culture in a Globalising World, proposing the first ever European strategy for culture. The strategy outlines a number of policy objectives, including the promotion of cultural diversity and intercultural dialogue, both internally and in the Union's external relations.

27. The Euro-Mediterranean partnership constitutes the most advanced structure for multinational intercultural cooperation available to the European Union. Through the Barcelona process, Europe and its Mediterranean neighbours cooperate in the fields of education, the fight against discrimination, and the promotion of democracy.

28. The Anna Lindh Euro-Mediterranean Foundation for the Dialogue between Cultures (ALF) promotes exchanges between the civil societies of EU countries and their Mediterranean partners. The ALF has launched programmes in the fields of media, education, women and youth. The themes for the first round of calls for proposals for programmes and projects for the period 2005–2008 include EuroMed music (workshops and compilation of samplers) and cultural/artistic creation, the EuroMed schools magazine and schools programme, EuroMed teams of young researchers, summer schools and exchange programmes, libraries, the promotion of books and reading, translation, and intercultural exchanges for women in civil society organisations. The European Year for Intercultural Dialogue 2008 will encompass all of the Euro-Mediterranean area. In the course of the Year, the ALF will launch a specific call for proposals on intercultural dialogue and organise a campaign named "1001 Actions for Intercultural Dialogue".

29. At the invitation of Euromed Ministers for Foreign Affairs, the Irish Department of Foreign Affairs and the European Commission co-organised a regional Euromed conference on "Preventing Incitement to Terrorism and Radicalisation: What Role for the Media ?" (Dublin, 21 May 2007).

Media practitioners from the Euro-Mediterranean area, government officials and the OSCE agreed a number of recommendations. These cover enhanced training for media practitioners, upgrading of educational standards in schools for journalism, and the promotion of networking and exchange between media in area. The recommendations have been submitted to the 9th Euromed Meeting of Ministers of Foreign Affairs with a view to follow-up at appropriate level.

30. The European Commission supported the organisation of the first meeting of the Euro-Mediterranean Youth Parliament under the German Presidency. This initiative brought together around 100 young people from both sides of the Mediterranean, who had the opportunity to discuss their views about the region and the prospects for future cooperation.

31. ASEM (Asia-Europe Meeting) organised thematic meetings and symposia, involving students, civil society, and the business and academic communities from Asia and the European Union. The Fifth ASEF (Asia-Europe Foundation) and the first Asia-Europe Youth Interfaith Dialogue took place back to back in Javier, Spain, in November 2006. In addition, ASEM continued its recent tradition of dedicated intercultural and interfaith dialogue meetings. After meetings in Bali (July 2005) and Larnaca, Cyprus (July 2006), the third ASEM interfaith dialogue, co-hosted by China and Italy, was held from 19–21 June 2007 in Nanjing. The meeting resulted in the Nanjing statement on interfaith dialogue, which addressed interfaith dialogue in relation to globalisation; world peace; social cohesion and development; and cultural and educational cooperation. Radicalisation was discussed at the fifth ASEM Conference on Counter-Terrorism (Tokyo, 15–16 May 2007) where the Commission was invited to present the EU counter-radicalisation policy at the event.

32. The 5th ASEAN Regional Forum (ARF) Inter-Sessional Meeting on Counter-Terrorism and Transnational Crime (Singapore, 2–4 May 2007) was devoted to "inter-civilisational dialogue". The EU gave presentations on the role of the media in enhancing the dialogue between people of different cultural backgrounds and the role international and regional organisations could play in this field. A statement on "Inter-civilisational Dialogue", originally tabled by Russia at the Inter-Sessional Meeting on CT, was adopted by the ARF on 2 August.

33. The EU continued to reach out to the Organisation of the Islamic Conference (OIC). During a Troika meeting with the OIC in the margins of the opening of the 62nd UN General Assembly, the EU voiced its support for a joint approach for the promotion of tolerance, dialogue and respect among people of all religion and beliefs.

34. The EU is a strong supporter of the Alliance of Civilisations initiative. The gist of the Alliance of Civilisations project is in line with a number of

EU initiatives in the field of promoting intercultural dialogue and understanding. The EU has supported the Alliance from its outset and is committed to backing Mr Sampaio in putting into practice the implementation plan following the recommendations of the report of the High Level Group. Several Member States have joined the group of friends of the Alliance and are devising national strategies for advancing the objectives of the Alliance.

Communication Through the Media

35. In July 2006, the Council adopted a Media Communication Strategy, covering both JHA and External Relations. The Strategy contains a series of key messages, suggestions for delivery of these messages, and a "common lexicon". The key messages enable EU officials to stay "on message" when explaining EU policies that could have a bearing on processes of radicalisation within and outside the EU. The "common lexicon" contextualises certain terms and thus contributes to a better understanding of how a certain use of language may be perceived. Since the last implementation review of the Strategy for Combating Radicalisation and Recruitment, the lexicon has been expanded.

36. Consecutive Presidencies have worked to ensure that the Media Communication Strategy is implemented. In the course of the year, COTER discussed a number of recommendations presented by government communications experts. Arabic translations of the Strategy's key messages were circulated to the Commission and the Member States, for use by their representations in the Arab world. Contacts were established with the Council's Information Working Party (IWP) Secretariat with a view to mainstreaming the implementation of the Media Communication Strategy, but no real cooperation with the IWP could be developed in 2007. COTER plans to continue to reach out to the IWP.

37. Over the last 18 months, the Press Service of the Council Secretariat has made active use of the Media Communication Strategy and the key messages therein. The Commission communicated the Media Communication Strategy to relevant departments in Brussels as well as some of its representations overseas with a request to make use of it. While its representatives have taken care to use appropriate language and to convey the essence of the key messages in their communication, the Commission reports that the Media Communication Strategy as such has not had a great impact on its external communication. Most Member States report that they have circulated the key messages and lexicon among spokespeople in relevant government services. In addition, a number of Member States report specific actions related to the implementation of the Strategy. It remains, however, difficult to gauge the real impact of the Media Communication Strategy on

the way in which they communicate on subjects that may have a bearing on radicalisation processes.

Promoting Security, Justice, Democracy and Opportunity for All

The UN Counter-Terrorism Framework

38. The Union continued its efforts to enhance the legitimacy of its counter-terrorism efforts by strengthening the international legal framework for the fight against terrorism. Through its Master Messages, COTER worked to include counter-terrorism on the agenda of EU meetings with third countries. These Master Messages promoted respect for human rights and rule of law in the context of national and multilateral counter-terrorism efforts. The EU also continued to encourage partners to ratify and implement the 16 UN Conventions and Protocols pertaining to the fight against terrorism and to carry out the provisions of the UN's Global Counter-Terrorism Strategy. The Portuguese EU Presidency undertook a first stock-taking of EU implementation of the Global CT Strategy with a view to the first informal review in New York, scheduled for December 2007. The EU plans to examine further possibilities to cooperate with relevant UN agencies and share its experiences and best practices with partners.

Education

39. A joint COTER-TWP seminar on the prevention of radicalisation of youth in the context of education was held on 11 September 2007. Follow-up to the seminar is discussed in COTER. On 16 and 17 October 2007, the Commission organised a conference on the role of education in the prevention of violent radicalisation. Experts from various backgrounds exchanged views on issues such as the distortion of Islamic texts, partnerships with academia for developing training programmes for religious leaders, provision of religious care in prisons. Among participants were several imams in need of a platform for expressing their views, representatives of NGOs, Member State officials working in the educational and the security field, and experts on radicalisation.

40. In order to strengthen equal opportunity for all, the European Union continued to assist third countries to create and reinforce comprehensive education systems. The Tempus programme constitutes the Union's main instrument to promote higher education cooperation. The programme supports the reform and modernisation of higher education systems in the partner countries in Eastern Europe, Central Asia, the Western Balkans and the Mediterranean region. Morocco, Algeria, Tunisia, Egypt, Syria, Lebanon, Jordan and the Palestinian Authority have been participating in the Tempus programme since June 2002. The annual budget allocation for

the MEDA countries amounts to EUR 20 million per year, which allows the Commission to fund around 40 joint European projects and 20 structural measures per year. Joint projects between higher education institutions in the EU and the MEDA countries fall into the areas of curriculum development, university management and institution-building. Structural measures directly support reform processes in higher education. The Tempus programme will be continued for a fourth phase over the period 2007–2013.

41. The Erasmus Mundus programme (2004–2008) is a scholarship scheme for students and scholars from third countries allowing them to participate in Erasmus Mundus master courses in the EU. Erasmus Mundus also supports the establishment of partnerships with institutions of third countries in the context of these courses. Thus far, more than 100 students and scholars from the Mediterranean countries have received scholarships to participate in master courses inside the EU. In addition, approximately 270 scholarships have been awarded to students from countries such as Pakistan, Indonesia and Iran. A new initiative—the Erasmus Mundus "External Cooperation Window"—was launched in 2006 to promote the creation of large partnerships between higher education institutions in the EU and specific regions. Nine partnerships projects have been selected thus far. These partnerships include Erasmus-style cooperation mechanisms for students, academic staff mobility and transfer of know-how.

Democratisation and Equal Opportunities for All

42. The Commission continued to make full use of its powers to adopt concrete measures to fight racism, xenophobia and anti-Semitism. It issued a report on the implementation of the Race Equality Directive and undertook an impact assessment on the possible enlargement of the scope of the Employment Directive. On 19 and 20 April 2007 the Council reached a general approach on the draft Framework Decision on Combating Racism and Xenophobia. In order to improve data collection on racism, in the first quarter of 2007 the Commission established an expert group to implement its five-year action plan on a comprehensive and coherent EU strategy to measure crime and criminal justice. In addition, the Commission and the Finnish Presidency developed a handbook on data collection which will shortly be distributed. The Commission's new Fundamental Rights and Citizenship Programme will allow for the support of projects aimed at fighting racism and xenophobia.

43. The promotion of democracy and equal opportunities remains a priority for the EU's political dialogue with the authorities of third countries. EU assistance programmes continued to address the development of appropriate work skills for young people as well as respect for democratic values and human rights. The activities supported by the Youth in Action and the Euro-Med Youth programmes help young people in third countries

to develop active citizenship, solidarity and mutual understanding as well as intercultural dialogue. They also contribute significantly to their acquisition of skills by providing informal learning opportunities.

44. The partnership between the European Commission and the Council of Europe has a strong focus on democratic values and human rights. The Partnership aims to reinforce citizenship, participation, human rights education and intercultural dialogue; social cohesion, inclusion and equal opportunities; recognition, quality and visibility of youth work and training; and understanding and knowledge of youth and youth policy development. Within the framework of the partnership, the European Commission contributed in 2006 and 2007 to the Council of Europe's campaign "All different—all equal" on diversity, human rights and participation. The Partnership's Euro-Med activities focus specifically on the training of trainers in the context of citizenship education.

45. Apart from the partnership activities, recurrent topics in the events the European Commission organises in cooperation with the Presidency's government department responsible for youth policy have been diversity and the participation of young people in democratic life. These Presidency events typically last a few days and involve 150 to 200 young people.

46. Within the context of the so-called 'Structured Dialogue' with young people, the Commission, Member States and regions have been using a series of events and meetings to focus on diversity and social inclusion. In 2008, a major focus of the Structured Dialogue will be on intercultural dialogue.

Deepening our Understanding and Reviewing our Approach

47. The German Presidency organised a number of expert meetings on radicalisation and recruitment. An international expert meeting "Monitoring Terrorism/Extremism—Prospects for Phenomena Monitoring at European Level" was held on 20–22 June in Wiesbaden. A meeting of experts on "The Recruitment of Islamist terrorists in Europe" was held on 30–31 May in Berlin. On 15 May, the Terrorism Working Group (TWG) held a thematic session on home-grown terrorism with contributions from several delegations as well as SitCen. On the basis of these meetings, the German Presidency proposed a number of amendments to the Radicalisation and Recruitment Action Plan in order to draw attention to the phenomenon of home-grown terrorism.

48. In September 2005, the European Commission issued a communication entitled "Terrorist Recruitment: Addressing the Factors Contributing to Violent Radicalisation", constituting its initial contribution to the EU Strategy adopted in December 2005. The Commission set up a group of

academic experts on violent radicalisation to inform its policies in this area. The group is to issue a report on the state of play of academic research into the phenomenon of violent radicalisation.

49. In 2006 the Commission contracted out three studies on violent radicalisation that encourage a multi-disciplinary and comparative approach to analysis of the phenomenon, based on field-work. The studies cover (i) the factors that may trigger or affect violent radicalisation processes, particularly among youth; (ii) the beliefs, ideologies and narrative of violent radicals; and (iii) the methods through which violent radicals mobilise support for terrorism and find new recruits. The results of the studies are expected by December 2007.

50. In July 2007, the Commission sent a questionnaire to the Member States in order to gain insights into Member States' policies and extract good practices for the prevention of violent radicalisation. The questionnaire covers a variety of subjects, such as policy approaches to reduce violent radicalisation in prisons, quality supervision of religious schools, and educational approaches towards improving student awareness of world religions. The Commission will finalise a summary of the replies in January 2008.

51. Earlier this year, the Commission contracted out a study on best practices in cooperation efforts between public authorities and civil society with a view to the prevention of violent radicalisation. The study will guide the Commission's policy-making in this field.

52. The knowledge and expertise to be gained from all these Commission initiatives, together with the ideas generated during its conference on education and radicalisation in October this year, will feed into a communication to the Council and the European Parliament that the Commission plans to adopt by mid-2008. The communication will outline good practices and make specific recommendations for the prevention of violent radicalisation. The Commission intends its 2008 communication to encourage discussion on a possible amendment of the EU Action Plan for Combating Radicalisation and Recruitment.

F. SPECIAL TOPICS

DOCUMENT NO. 31

EXTERNAL DIMENSION OF THE FIGHT AGAINST INTERNATIONAL TERRORISM

European Parliament Resolution P6_TA(2007)0050

24 November 2007

The European Parliament,

– having regard to the Treaty establishing a Constitution for Europe,

– having regard to Articles 6 and 7 and Title V of the EU Treaty,

– having regard to the Universal Declaration of Human Rights of 10 December 1948,

– having regard to the European Convention for the Protection of Human Rights and Fundamental Freedoms, signed in Rome on 4 November 1950,

– having regard to the European Convention on the Suppression of Terrorism of the Council of Europe, signed in Strasbourg on 27 January 1977,

– having regard to the thirteen United Nations instruments currently in force and to the four instruments adopted in 2005 but not yet in force relating to the prevention and eradication of international terrorism, to Security Council Resolutions 1368 and 1373 (2001) and 1267 (1999) and to General Assembly Resolution A/RES/60/288 of 8 September 2006 on the United Nations Global Counter-Terrorism Strategy and the Plan of Action annexed thereto,

– having regard to UN Security Council Resolution 1267(1999), implemented at EU level by Council Regulation (EC) No 881/2002 of 27 May 2002, imposing certain specific restrictive measures directed against certain persons and entities associated with Usama bin Laden, the Al-Qaida network and the Taleban,[1]

[1] OJ L 139, 29.5.2002, p. 9. Regulation as last amended by Regulation (EC) No 14/2007 (OJ L 6, 11.1.2007, p. 6).

- having regard to the 2005 UN World Summit Outcome on terrorism (General Assembly Resolution A/RES/60/1),
- having regard to the report of the High-Level Group entitled "Alliance of Civilisations", presented to the UN Secretary-General on 13 November 2006,
- having regard to the mutual defence clause contained in Article 5 of the Washington Treaty, invoked by the NATO members on 12 September 2001, thereby defining the terrorist attack on the World Trade Centre of 11 September 2001 as an outside attack against the United States,
- having regard to the European Security Strategy (ESS)—"A Secure Europe in a Better World"—approved by the European Council on 12 December 2003, and the EU Strategy Against Proliferation of Weapons of Mass Destruction of the same date,
- having regard to the report entitled "A Human Security Doctrine for Europe—The Barcelona Report of the Study Group on Europe's Security Capabilities", presented to the EU High Representative for Common Foreign and Security Policy (CFSP) on 15 September 2004,
- having regard to the conclusions of the Brussels European Council of 25 and 26 March 2004, in particular the European Council Declaration on Combating Terrorism of 25 March 2004, which included a solidarity clause,
- having regard to the Plan of Action against Terrorism, approved by the European Council on 21 September 2001, and the Council's revised Action Plan/Roadmap of 15 June 2004, endorsed by the European Council at its meeting on 17 and 18 June 2004,
- having regard to the European Union Counter-Terrorism Strategy, adopted by the European Council at its meeting of 14 and 15 December 2005, and the European Union Strategy for Combating Radicalisation and Recruitment to Terrorism, adopted by the European Council on the same date,
- having regard to the conclusions of the International Summit on Democracy, Terrorism and Security held in Madrid from 8 to 11 March 2005,
- having regard to the report of the Secretary-General of the United Nations of 27 April 2006 entitled "Uniting Against terrorism: recommendations for a global counter-terrorism strategy" (A/60/825),
- having regard to the report of the United Nations High-level Panel of Eminent Persons on Threats, Challenges and Change, "A more secure world: our shared responsibility", of 2 December 2004, and the report of the UN Secretary-General of 21 March 2005, prepared for the 2005 reform

summit and entitled "In larger freedom: towards development, security and human rights for all",

- having regard to the Euro-Mediterranean Code of Conduct on Countering Terrorism, adopted at the Euro-Mediterranean Summit of 27 and 28 November 2005 in Barcelona,
- having regard to the EU-US declarations of 26 June 2004 on Combating Terrorism, of 20 June 2005 on Enhancing Cooperation in the Field of Non Proliferation and the Fight Against Terrorism and of 21 June 2006 issued at the Vienna Summit, and noting with great concern the CIA's secret detention programme the existence of which was confirmed by President Bush on 6 September 2006,
- having regard to the European Union-Russia Road Map for the Common Space of External Security signed on 10 May 2005 on the occasion of the 15th EU-Russia Summit,
- having regard to the recently discovered existence of highly dangerous terrorist organisations in Italy and France,
- having regard to the Joint EU-ASEAN (Association of Southeast Asian Nations) Declaration on Terrorism signed on 27 January 2003 on the occasion of the 14th EU-ASEAN Ministerial Meeting,
- having regard to the Joint EU-OAU (Organization of African Unity) Declaration on Terrorism, signed on 11 October 2001,
- having regard to the Rome Statute of the International Criminal Court (ICC) adopted on 17 July 1998 by the United Nations Diplomatic Conference of Plenipotentiaries,
- having regard to the Communication from the Commission to the Council, the European Parliament and the European Economic and Social Committee of 29 November 2005 entitled "The Prevention of and Fight against Terrorist Financing through enhanced national level coordination and greater transparency of the non-profit sector", including a Recommendation to the Member States (COM(2005)0620) and the Commission's memorandum of 1 December 2005 entitled "Financing of terrorism: new guidelines for Member States on national level coordination structures and vulnerabilities of the non-profit sector" (MEMO/05/460),
- having regard to its Recommendation of 7 June 2005 to the European Council and the Council on the EU anti-terrorism Action Plan,[2]
- having regard to Rule 45 of its Rules of Procedure,

[2] OJ C 124 E, 25.5.2006, p. 241.

– having regard to the report of the Committee on Foreign Affairs and the opinions of the Committee on Development and the Committee on Civil Liberties, Justice and Home Affairs (A6-0441/2006),

A. whereas international terrorism (including its ideology) now constitutes one of the greatest threats to security, peace, stability and the democratic values of the international community and in particular a direct threat to European citizens, EU Member States, democracy and the rule of law, values on which the European Union is founded,

B. conscious of the diverse nature of terrorism, of the organisations which practise it and of the States and non-state agents which sponsor it, finance it and practise it for their own ends; conscious also of the emerging and unpredictable nature of a phenomenon which presupposes an obvious sense of opportunity (particularly in the case of the terrorism practised by radical groups which claim to be defending Islam) and the need for the European Union to pursue a proactive (and not just a reactive) policy in order to combat it,

C. whereas Europe, from being mainly a platform for logistical support, has turned into a major target of planned attacks,

D. whereas, pursuant to the ESS, the fight against terrorism constitutes a priority for the European Union and a key element in its external action,

E. whereas the pursuit of security beyond the EU's borders should be guided by the principles of the human security doctrine, namely the primacy of human rights, the imperatives of multilateralism, a bottom-up approach based on knowledge of the local situation, a regional focus and the establishment of a clear and legitimate political authority,

F. whereas the European Union has its own strategy for combating terrorism which must be integrated in a multilateral strategy and be firmly based on the unconditional respect of human rights and of the principles underlying states governed by the rule of law, whereas terrorism constitutes precisely a direct attack on both, and whereas any action outside that framework constitutes a failure of democracy,

G. whereas terrorism is always criminal and unjustifiable, in any circumstance, wherever and by whomsoever it is practised, and whereas it may never be used in the pursuit of political objectives,

H. whereas the victims of terrorism are a moral reference point for our societies and for democracy and whereas the public authorities should listen to their voice and ensure that they are taken into account whenever decisions are taken with a view to combating those who made them unwilling protagonists,

I. whereas terrorist groups exploit extreme poverty, the failure to uphold human rights and constitutional government, collective frustration, the lack of access to training and social exclusion in pursuit of their capture and infiltration strategies,

J. whereas societies which suffer from high levels of political, social, economic, ethnic, religious and other discrimination and from a lack of democracy and human rights constitute an ideal breeding ground for terrorism,

K. whereas, in order for terrorism to be fought effectively, a detailed knowledge is required of the terrorist group which is being fought, of that group's ideology and of the social, political, economic and religious context from which it emerges and on which its perpetrators and supporters feed,

L. whereas specific action should be taken in order to combat each terrorist organisation, in view of the fact that each one has its own objectives, organisation and modus operandi, and whereas, in particular, specific action should be taken against the Al-Qaeda organisation,

M. whereas the threat of terrorism is not restricted to specific geographic zones and whereas terrorist organisations are to be found both within and outside the Union's borders and have provided ample proof of their ability to carry out attacks and acts of violence in any continent and against various countries simultaneously,

N. whereas the Member States individually and the European Union and its institutions have already been or may be direct targets of international terrorism,

O. whereas the painful experiences to date show that no Member State can on its own successfully face terrorism and whereas it is therefore of fundamental importance that there be, first, a common Union policy to combat terrorism, making use of all the instruments and resources at the disposal of states governed by the rule of law and of the Union itself, and, second, effective and democratically controlled international cooperation in the fight against international terrorism,

P. whereas essential requirements in an effective fight against terrorism are an enhancement of transatlantic cooperation and coordination and full implementation of the above-mentioned EU-US declarations on Combating Terrorism and on Enhancing Cooperation in the field of Non-Proliferation and the Fight Against Terrorism, and the EU-US declaration issued at the Vienna Summit,

Q. whereas the fight against international terrorism calls for a strong linkage between internal and external aspects of security and whereas the EU must aim for a holistic, coherent and cross-pillar approach to this challenge,

R. aware that the global dimension of terrorism also requires a global response, tackling terrorism in all its dimensions, including the security, political, economic social and cultural aspects,

S. whereas the European Union is founded on a set of values, as expressed, for instance, in the Copenhagen criteria, and whereas those values should be promoted all over the world as the only way to prevent terrorism in the long term,

T. aware that the external and internal dimensions of the fight against terrorism are interlinked and inseparable,

U. whereas prevention, and hence the need for exhaustive consideration of intelligence reports, are basic elements in the fight against terrorism, as evidenced by some of the attacks which have recurred,

V. whereas in order for the actions of the Union in the fight against terrorism to be effective, close cooperation and an enhanced exchange of information between the institutions of the Union, the Member States and their respective intelligence services, and the Union's specialised agencies (such as Europol and Eurojust) are vital,

W. whereas the EU Counter-Terrorism Coordinator has an essential role to play and whereas he must be given more powers and resources,

X. whereas the Union must develop a proactive, rather than merely reactive, prevention, protection and suppression policy to combat international terrorism effectively,

Y. whereas, in order to be effective, the fight against international terrorism and its ideology must be backed by real conviction and determination within the Union and the Member States and have the backing of an aware and well-informed public,

Z. whereas the Member States must not delay implementation of all commitments associated with the fight against terrorism, based on counter-terrorism cooperation both within the Union and at the international level,

AA. convinced that demonising any culture, civilisation or religion in the name of combating terrorism is a mistake which may have counter-productive effects,

AB. whereas Muslims are themselves among the victims of Islamist terrorism, which is linked in turn to inherent conflicts within the Muslim world and to struggles for power and natural resources, including oil,

Fundamental Principles of the External Dimension of the Fight Against International Terrorism

1. Supports the need for a strategic objective of combating terrorism globally, respecting human rights, with the ultimate aim of achieving a

more secure European Union, and allowing its citizens to enjoy a true area of freedom, security and justice; shares the view of the Council that, other forms of terrorism notwithstanding, the most serious threat to Europe at the moment is posed by violent radical groups claiming to defend Islam, such as the criminal Al-Qaeda network and the groups which are affiliated to it or are inspired by its ideology;

2. Emphasises the need for the European Union, its Member States and its partner countries to base their global counter-terrorism strategy on the fundamental principles which also serve to guide the actions of the United Nations, on a constructive and serious dialogue between peoples and nations, as well as between cultures, religions and civilisations, taking account of the respective perceptions and concerns, and on respect for international law;

3. Calls on the Commission and the Member States to ensure that certain groups of people from various diasporas living in Europe are not stigmatised, in particular by supporting policies to combat xenophobia and human rights violations against immigrant and refugee communities, as well as development aid projects undertaken by migrants or migrants' associations;

4. Expresses its regret at the failure of the UN World Summit in 2005 to reach an agreement on a comprehensive definition of terrorism, and stresses the need to arrive at a generally accepted definition of international terrorism; therefore calls on the Council to adopt a common position establishing a definition of terrorism on the basis of Council Framework Decision 2002/475/JHA of 13 June 2002 on combating terrorism[3] and taking into account the definition proposed by the former Secretary-General of the United Nations, Kofi Annan;[4]

5. Stresses the urgent need fully and properly to implement all the political measures adopted at the highest political level in the European Union Counter-Terrorism Strategy, the Action Plan and the Strategy for Combating Radicalisation and Recruitment to Terrorism, so that the ambitious mechanisms and proposals set out in those documents result as soon as possible in specific and effective practical measures to combat terrorism;

6. Welcomes the adoption by the General Assembly of the United Nations Global Counter-Terrorism Strategy and its annexed Plan of Action on 8 September 2006; stresses the need for terrorism in all its forms and

[3] OJ L 164, 22.6.2002, p. 3.

[4] "In addition to actions already proscribed by existing conventions, any action constitutes terrorism if it is intended to cause death or serious bodily harm to civilians or non-combatants with the purpose of intimidating a population or compelling a Government or an international organization to do or abstain from doing any act." (definition as originally proposed by the High-level Panel on Threats, Challenges and Change in its report of 2 December 2004).

manifestations to be combated by all available means, pursuant to the UN Charter as reflected in the Security Council's Resolution 1624 (2005); expresses concern at the delay in the adoption of the global convention on international terrorism; encourages the Institutions of the European Union and the various Member States to continue working unstintingly to achieve an international consensus permitting, on the one hand, the adoption of the global convention and, on the other, the effective implementation of the measures set out in the said Strategy and Plan of Action;

7. Regrets the fact that, despite evidence of the terrorist threat, some Member States have not yet signed and/or ratified some of the 17 United Nations universal instruments on combating terrorism; notes that as yet only two countries have ratified 13 conventions and 78 other countries have ratified or acceded to 12 of them; considers it particularly worrying, however, that 33 other countries have ratified or acceded to only 6 or fewer such international conventions;

8. Calls on those Member States of the European Union and their partners which have not already done so to adopt swiftly the national legislation necessary for the effective implementation of those conventions and to inform the relevant bodies of the United Nations thereof in good time;

9. Recommends that, in its external actions, the European Union should make use of appropriate means in order to encourage countries to become parties to all universal instruments against terrorism and to enact, as appropriate, the domestic legislation necessary to implement the provisions of those conventions and protocols, also benefiting from the UN's technical expertise;

10. Emphasises that the European Union's external actions to combat international terrorism should in the first place be aimed at prevention, in order to ensure that radical or extremist groups, and also States, do not resort to terrorism and do not support it as a strategy in the pursuit of their objectives; urges the Member States to acquire greater institutional capacity for combating terrorism; considers that in broad terms the objectives relating to prevention set out in the European Union Counter-Terrorism Strategy are in keeping with that objective;

11. Calls on the EU to ensure that measures taken with a view to fighting terrorism do not lead to curbs on the ability of the media in countries in the South to deal in an independent way with issues relating to the rights of poor, vulnerable people and to publish information that is essential when it comes to determining the specific aid to be provided to those countries;

12. Calls on the countries with which the EU has commenced accession negotiations or which have expressed their intention of joining the EU to take immediate measures to disband nationalistic and fanatical organisations

which are directly opposed to the democratic principles of the Union and which stir up animosities and racial hatred;

13. Reiterates the need at all times to drive home the message that terrorism is unacceptable and unjustifiable by all state and non-state actors in all circumstances and in all cultures, whatever the considerations of a political, philosophical, ideological, racial, ethnic, religious or any other nature that may be invoked to justify it, and to eliminate all factors which may be exploited by terrorists, such as the dehumanisation of victims, the outbreak and persistence of violent conflicts, bad governance, the lack of civil rights and violation of human rights, religious and ethnic discrimination, political exclusion and socio-economic marginalisation;

14. Considers it likewise fundamental that the European Union's external actions to combat international terrorism, while complying with the relevant case law of the Court of Justice of the European Communities and the European Court of Human Rights, should aim to prevent terrorists from gaining access to the means for carrying out their attacks, for example by depriving them of the opportunity to travel, to gain access to means of communication and to proselytise, to use the Internet for their purposes, to receive financial support, to engage in money laundering, to gain access to arms, be they conventional, nuclear, biological, chemical or radiological, and to easily attain their objectives and achieve their aims;

15. Considers that the protective measures included in the European Union Counter-Terrorism Strategy are in line with this objective but that their actual effectiveness varies greatly and that there are various other options in terms of the Union's external action;

16. Reiterates the need to fight against flows of illicit capital and money laundering within the Union (through the implementation by December 2007 of Directive 2005/60/EC of the European Parliament and of the Council of 26 October 2005 on the prevention of the use of the financial system for the purpose of money laundering and terrorist financing[5]) and elsewhere, and to exercise effective control over various Islamic charities;

17. Notes that Member States have an obligation to exercise vigilance and recommends that determined use be made of the instruments at the disposal of the Union in its external actions in order to make countries which support terrorist groups and which organise, finance, encourage or support terrorist activities by any other means desist from doing so, if necessary through the imposition of sanctions or through coercive measures;

18. Supports unreservedly the development of the capacity of States to prevent terrorism through the promotion of the rule of law, respect for human

[5] OJ L 309, 25.11.2005, p. 15.

rights and the establishment of effective criminal justice systems as well as through the promotion of high-quality education and religious and cultural tolerance; to that end, urges all the States within the international community to ensure that incitement to commit terrorist acts is banned by law and to prevent such conduct, as called for in the United Nations Global Counter-Terrorism Strategy of 8 September 2006;

19. Considers that the development of a preventative capacity also requires States to directly oppose the financing of terrorist organisations by practical means, to seek to ensure that transport is safe (as stipulated in the European Programme for Critical Infrastructure Protection (EPCIP) (COM(2004)0702)), to make use of the possibilities offered by the Internet to combat terrorism, to improve the protection of potential terrorist targets and the capacity to respond to attacks, and to improve their capacity to prevent terrorists from acquiring conventional weapons or nuclear, biologic, chemical or radiological materials;

20. Emphasises the need to continue defending human rights and fundamental freedoms in the fight against terrorism by means of the international instruments available, taking account of the fact that human rights are a universal value and an integral part of European external action but also of the fact that their violation clearly jeopardises the fight against terrorism and constitutes a failure of democracy; considers, therefore, that the only effective instruments employed in the fight against international terrorism are legal means and that all activities that escape independent international scrutiny, such as extraordinary renditions or prisons that operate outside the international legal framework, should be prohibited under international law;

21. Considers it fundamental to have sufficient human and budgetary resources available to combat terrorism; supports the various proposals of the Commission in this regard; proposes that, in the event of a European Security and Defence Policy (ESDP) operation to combat terrorism, the cost of the common expenditure be charged to the budget of the European Union; supports the setting-up of an international fund to provide economic assistance to States with fewer resources in order that they may successfully assume their responsibilities in the fight against terrorism;

22. Considers that including financial support for a range of activities connected with preventing and fighting terrorism in ODA can only further undermine the concept of official development assistance and its primary aim, namely to eliminate poverty;

23. Stresses that any EU programme designed to foster cooperation on counter-terrorism, surveillance technology and exchanges of information should include a financial clause setting aside part of the budget for fundamental rights issues as well as for a subsequent independent impact assessment;

24. Strongly stresses to the Member States that nothing can justify diverting aid away from countries that are devoting themselves to reducing poverty and achieving the MDGs and towards countries directly involved in the war on terror;

25. Stresses that additional financial resources released via the implementation of innovative financial instruments cannot replace commitments already entered into in terms of ODA, and considers that, when those new resources become available, they should not be used to finance measures to prevent or fight terrorism at the expense of measures for fighting poverty, into which it is essential that the new resources be channelled;

26. Draws attention to the fact the development of a common approach to the management of the European Union's external frontiers could constitute one element of the fight against terrorism, and consequently is concerned that the technical equipment at the disposal of the authorities responsible for controlling the borders is not of a uniformly high standard;

27. Underlines the crucial role played by civil society and NGOs in the promotion of cross- cultural and inter-religious understanding through constructive dialogue;

28. Considers that it is essential to develop intercultural dialogue and other confidence-building measures within and outside the EU, the first requirement being to reach a common understanding of the concept of "intercultural dialogue" inside the EU; also considers it essential to examine the contributory factors leading to the radicalisation and recruitment of Muslims inside and outside Europe;

Means Available to the European Union in the Area of its External Action to Combat Terrorism

29. Emphasises the many-faceted nature of the responses available to the European Union in the area of external action to combat terrorism and the need for Member States to bring together and use in a coherent manner their political, preventive and suppressive instruments involving police and judicial cooperation, intelligence and communication, and all other types of responses called for and endorsed by the United Nations and forming part of a multilateral strategy;

30. Draws attention to the recommendations contained in its resolution of 28 September 2006,[6] and stresses in particular that if, with a view to implementing development cooperation, a large number of objectives are pursued that are only indirectly linked, or not linked at all, to the strategy laid down in the European Consensus on Development and the achievement of

[6] *Texts Adopted*, P6_TA(2006)0382.

the Millennium Development Goals (MDGs) (for which the UN believes additional annual aid of USD 50 billion is needed), it will become significantly more difficult to take effective action against poverty;

31. Calls on the Commission and the Member States to pursue an anti-terrorism policy that is careful not to undermine the contribution made by European development cooperation to drawing up and implementing strategies aimed at effectively combating poverty and at preventing—increasingly prolonged—violent conflicts, particularly in Africa;

32. Stresses that the response adopted by the EU in the face of terrorism must be proportionate and properly targeted on the fight against terrorism, bearing in mind that, until proved otherwise, the most productive measures in the fight against new forms of terrorism are effective intelligence and police services, in other words activities which, however legitimate, do not come within development cooperation policy or the fight against poverty;

33. Reiterates, therefore, its proposal to render the Union's anti-terrorist policy more coherent and effective in its relations with third countries through:

(a) the enhancement of political dialogue in this regard, in particular with those countries with which the European Union and/or its Member States have concluded or are negotiating Association or Cooperation Agreements;

(b) political and commercial support and development aid to moderate Islamic countries, relating both to the fight against terrorism and to the political, economic and social reforms implemented in those countries;

(c) a stepping-up of the dialogue on and cooperation in the fight against terrorism with the major partners of the Union (Israel, Japan, Australia, Canada, Russia, etc.) and, in particular, the United States, which is in the front line in the fight against terrorism, without affecting under any circumstances the level of protection afforded to human rights;

(d) the promotion of international consensus for the adoption of the Global Convention on International Terrorism and the development of the United Nations Global Counter-Terrorism Strategy of 8 September 2006, including a common definition of terrorism;

(e) the requirement that all third countries with which the Union maintains relations sign and ratify the 17 United Nations universal instruments on combating terrorism, as well as the optional Protocol to the UN Convention against Torture or Other Cruel, Inhumane or Degrading Treatment or Punishment;

(f) the strict implementation of the anti-terrorism clause as well as application of the human rights clause included in agreements with third countries, without any "ad hoc" modifications which detract from their substance;

(g) the suspension of political and trade relations with States which persistently fail to comply with their obligations to provide information to the Counter-Terrorism Committee of the United Nations;

(h) the establishment of an interinstitutional Code of Conduct for external relations of the Union as proposed by the European Parliament in its resolution of 25 April 2002 on the Communication from the Commission to the Council and the European Parliament on the European Union's role in promoting human rights and democratisation in third countries;[7]

(i) the strengthening of cooperation with international and regional organisations playing a key role in peacekeeping and global security, first and foremost the United Nations (in particular the Security Council and its Counter-Terrorism Committee and the United Nations Office on Drugs and Crime) the OSCE, the Council of Europe and NATO;

(j) the promotion and strict implementation of United Nations Security Council Resolution 1540 (2004), with the aim of preventing non-state actors and States which are not party to the Nuclear Non-Proliferation Treaty from acquiring nuclear, chemical or biological weapons, in pursuit of the EU strategy against the proliferation of weapons of mass destruction, support for and the development of new initiatives on nuclear disarmament and the revitalisation of the UN Conference on Disarmament;

(k) the stepping-up of cooperation as regards the exchange of information and cooperation between security and intelligence services including military intelligence, and police, judicial and customs authorities of the Member States, including with the Joint Situation Centre (SitCen), the European Agency for the Management of Operational Cooperation at the External Borders (Frontex), Europol, Interpol and Eurojust and the various competent authorities at European level, the Counter-Terrorism Coordinator, Gijs de Vries and the Commissioner with responsibility for justice, freedom and security, Franco Frattini; the enhancing of security protocols and interoperability, by keeping the activities of intelligence and law-enforcement agencies strictly separate as stipulated in numerous

[7] OJ C 131 E, 5.6.2003, p. 147.

national constitutions and on the condition that parliamentary and judicial scrutiny are provided;

(l) the organisation of regular meetings (held at least once a year) to be attended by the relevant ministers from the Member States, by the Commissioner responsible for freedom, security and justice, by the EU Counter-Terrorism Coordinator and by the heads of Europol, Eurojust, SitCen and Frontex, and to be devoted solely to the topic of combating international terrorism;

(m) the promotion of a global consensus about the need to put an end to off-shore banking and other forms of opaque fiscal paradises used by terrorists to conceal their financial transactions;

(n) the implementation of the Protocol against the Illicit Manufacturing of and Trafficking in Firearms, Their Parts and Components and Ammunition, supplementing the United Nations Convention against Transnational Organized Crime, and the UN Programme of Action to Prevent, Combat and Eradicate the Illicit Trade in Small Arms and Light Weapons in All Its Aspects;

(o) the strengthening of counter-terrorist military forces through training and other measures;

(p) an increase in Europol's powers in order to ensure that the role it plays in the fight against terrorism is an effective one;

(q) the enhancement of cooperation with the United States as regards exchanges of information and cooperation between security and intelligence services as well as police, judicial and customs authorities;

(r) the enhancement of cooperation between Member States' special forces and those of third countries;

34. Commends the various initiatives to promote dialogue, tolerance and understanding among different cultures, civilisations and religions; regards the idea of creating a "Euro-Med citizenship" as an example of a broad and concrete initiative that can help bring forward views of the region's common future;

35. Emphasises the need for greater cooperation and coordination with the United States in the fight against international terrorism, while stressing the need to protect the fundamental principles of human rights;

36. Emphasises the need for an increase in the powers and the resources available to the EU Counter-Terrorism Coordinator (with particular reference to the inadequate resources made available to him), so that his work can have a greater impact and assume a higher profile;

37. Calls on the Commission and the Council, in their external relations, to insist on the signature and the ratification of the Rome Statute and, consequently, on the universal recognition by all third countries of the binding nature of the jurisdiction of the International Criminal Court;

38. Calls on the Council, the Commission and the governments of the Member States to take effective practical action to bring about the proscription of terrorist organisations;

39. Considers it essential to encourage greater stability outside the Union through the use of all available instruments, programmes and means in the ambit of external action, including:

(a) the new Instrument for Stability established by Regulation (EC) No 1717/2006 of the European Parliament and of the Council of 15 November 2006,[8] which provides a new legal basis for long-term aid in such areas as the fight against terrorism, the non-proliferation of weapons of mass destruction, the fight against organised crime, conventional disarmament and human security; recalls the declaration by the Commission on anti-terror measures, annexed to the Instrument for Stability, in which the Commission undertakes that all anti-terrorism measures financed under that instrument will respect human rights obligations and related humanitarian law and that the Commission will monitor compliance with that principle by the recipient countries;

(b) the support, once the said Instrument enters into force, of the aid strategy designed by the Commission to help third countries face the terrorist threat through both the European Neighbourhood and Partnership Instrument (ENPI) established by Regulation (EC) No 1638/2006 of the European Parliament and of the Council of 24 October 2006[9] and the Instrument for Stability, and through the mainstreaming of counter-terrorist assistance into all its assistance programmes as requested by the European Council;

(c) the extension of the said aid strategy to all areas of the Union's external action and to all the major development aid programmes except for those relating to humanitarian aid, which are by their very nature unconditional;

(d) the strengthening of the use of the Civilian and Military Rapid Reaction Mechanism;

(e) the Council and the Commission ensuring that attention for the victims of terrorism becomes a cornerstone of the Union's policy in

[8] OJ L 327, 24.11.2006, p. 1.
[9] OJ L 310, 9.11.2006, p. 1.

this field, thus ensuring full regard for them so that they are listened to, kept informed and given every assistance;

(f) the creation of a similar office in the context of the new United Nations Counter-Terrorism Strategy of 8 September 2006, aimed at providing assistance to all victims of terrorism regardless of their citizenship;

40. Calls on the Commission to present as soon as possible a communication setting out the existing assistance mechanisms and programmes to reduce and face up to the threats to the security of the Union and its citizens, including in particular proposals and recommendations to improve the effectiveness and coherence of the Union's assistance programmes;

41. Calls on Member States to contribute more to an integrated EU-wide threat assessment by increasing the flow of information to SitCen in the Secretariat of the Council of the EU; calls on Member States to increase staff and resources at the disposal of the Situation Centre and to make increasing use of its combined terrorism assessments, which include information on external threats and information from internal security services and Europol;

42. Recommends the adoption of measures leading to establishment of a new configuration for meetings of the Council, involving the participation of Foreign Ministers and Interior Ministers when dealing with the fight against terrorism;

43. Recommends implementation of the provisions of the EU Treaty concerning the ESDP applied to the fight against terrorism and also of the Declaration on Combating Terrorism of 25 March 2004, the Plan of Action adopted by the European Council on 21 September 2001 and the Counter-Terrorism Strategy of 14 and 15 December 2005, through the adoption of measures such as:

(a) the joint elaboration of contingency plans to render effective the mutual-assistance solidarity clause in the Declaration on Combating Terrorism;

(b) recourse, where necessary, to specific police and/or military operations under the ESDP as part of the Union's response to terrorism;

(c) the adaptation to the new tasks of the permanent structured cooperation and the combat units provided for in Protocol 23 to the Treaty establishing a Constitution for Europe;

(d) derogation from the unanimity rule in certain areas of police and judicial cooperation in criminal matters;

Parliamentary Control of the Fight Against International Terrorism by the

Institutions of the Union

44. Highlights the vital importance of prevention in the fight against international terrorism and the need to share in real time with the other Member States and Institutions of the Union all information obtained through reliable and efficient information systems and for a rigorous and professional assessment of the reports drawn up by the various police and intelligence services;

45. Asks the Council for the Interinstitutional Agreement of 20 November 2002 between the European Parliament and the Council concerning access by the European Parliament to sensitive information of the Council in the field of security and defence policy[10] to be reviewed and brought up-to-date in order to improve the current system for the transmission of classified information and to guarantee the transmission to the European Parliament of all available information relating to the fight against international terrorism, without its being under any circumstances denied information which, in the internal sphere, has been or should be transmitted to national parliaments by the respective governments of the Member States or the international organisations of which they form part;

46. Calls on the Council not to limit itself in its annual report on the CFSP to describing the activities of the Union in the area of the fight against terrorism, but rather, on the basis of Article 21 of the Treaty on European Union, to really consult the European Parliament as regards the principal aspects and basic options of that fight, which constitutes a priority under the ESS, the Union's external action and the CFSP as a whole; considers it indispensable that it be informed and consulted in the event of a large-scale terrorist attack, where necessary through the Special Committee provided for in the above-mentioned Interinstitutional Agreement of 20 November 2002;

47. Considers the High Level Political Dialogue on Counter-Terrorism, which brings the European Parliament, the Council and the Commission together on a six-monthly basis, to be a good example of the possibilities available for the indispensable interinstitutional cooperation needed in the fight against terrorism; proposes that such meetings be held at least on a quarterly basis and that the European Parliament Delegation also include the chairmen of the permanent committees on the three main areas of external action (foreign affairs, international trade and development cooperation);

48. Asks for the reports drawn up by SitCen for the Council of the Union to be transmitted regularly to the European Parliament, if necessary pursuant

---

[10] OJ C 298, 30.11.2002, p. 1.

to the modalities provided for in the above-mentioned Interinstitutional Agreement;

49. Considers it of fundamental importance that the European Parliament be closely involved in the mechanism for implementing the solidarity clause (the introduction of which was approved in the Declaration on Combating Terrorism), essentially in cases where the decisions adopted have implications as regards the ESDP;

50. Calls on the Commission and on the European Counter-Terrorism Coordinator to submit an annual report to the European Parliament on their activities in the fight against terrorism and to take due account of Parliament's observations and recommendations in that regard;

51. Calls on the Council anew to inform Parliament on the regular updating of Council Common Position 2001/931/CFSP of 27 December 2001 on the application of specific measures to combat terrorism[11] (list of terrorist organisations and groups) and on developments since 2001;

52. Pledges to establish an enhanced dialogue with the national parliaments on the fight against terrorism with a view to guaranteeing joint parliamentary control of the activities of the various security and intelligence services, given that, in its capacity as representative of the peoples of the European Union, it is incumbent upon the European Parliament to exercise public and transparent control over the measures adopted by the Union in relation to the fight against terrorism, including the activities of the European Counter-Terrorism Coordinator and of the various bodies dedicated to that task;

53. Instructs its President to forward this resolution to the European Council, the Council, the Commission, the governments and parliaments of the Member States, the Council of Europe, the United Nations and its specialised agencies.

[11] OJ L 344, 28.12.2001, p. 93.

DOCUMENT NO. 32

DRAFT COUNCIL CONCLUSIONS ADOPTING STRATEGIC ORIENTATIONS AND PRIORITIES ON THE SECURITY ENHANCEMENT OF EXPLOSIVES

Report 15618/07
Council of the European Union

Brussels, 23 November 2007

from:	Presidency
to:	Coreper
No. prev. doc.:	14959/07 CATS 121 ENFOPOL 184 TRANS 357 MI 287 EEE 69
	15081/07 CATS 125 ENFOPOL 186
	15271/07 CATS 127 ENFOPOL 190
No. Cion prop.:	COM(2007)° 651 final
Subject:	Draft Council Conclusions adopting Strategic Orientations and Priorities on the security enhancement of explosives

1. On 6 November 2007, the European Commission adopted a Communication on Enhancing the Security of explosives containing a proposal for a comprehensive Action Plan on the subject.[1] This proposal draws notably on the work undertaken in late 2006 and early 2007 by a dedicated Public Private Task Force, as well as on the workings of an ensuing European Conference which took place in Braga, Portugal on 16 and 17 July 2007.

2. At its meetings of 5 September and 3–4 October, the Police Cooperation Working Party (PCWP) already analysed in detail the recommendations provided by the Task Force and discussed in the referred Conference.

[1] COM(2007) 651 final, of 6 November 2007

It drew for the effect on detailed contributions from the Commission on the work underway. Likewise, the Terrorism Working Party discussed proposed recommendations specifically related to the use of explosives by terrorists at its meetings of 4 July, 10 September and 15 October.

3. Given its comprehensive nature, the Commission proposal for the Action Plan will require detailed analysis and extensive horizontal coordination. The Presidency considers, however, also bearing in mind work undertaken by the Article 36 Committee in May 2007 and the procedure proposed in October 2007, that sufficient consensus can been registered in regard of key strategic objectives and orientations in the area of security of explosives to warrant the adoption of "Strategic Orientations on Explosive Security" as well as of a set of "Priority Measures on Explosive Security".

4. The PCWP examined and endorsed, subject to some amendments and study reservations, the draft Council conclusions adopting Strategic Orientations and Priorities on the security enhancement of explosives, as proposed by the Presidency in document 15081/07 CATS 125 ENFOPOL 186.

5. The Article 36 Committee in its meeting of 22 November 2007 further examined the draft Council conclusions and endorsed these, subject to some minor amendments.

6. The draft Council Conclusions in annex have been amended and are submitted to Coreper for examination and approval, with a view to their transmission to the Council of 6–7 December 2007.

Annex

Proposal for

Council Conclusions

Adopting Strategic Orientations and Priority Measures on Enhancing the Security of Explosives in the European Union

THE COUNCIL OF THE EUROPEAN UNION,

bearing in mind that the illegal acquisition and use of explosives poses a serious threat to the citizens of the European Union, and that terrorists and other criminals take advantage of the devastating effects of explosives to carry out attacks intended to kill and injure persons, destroy property and disrupt societal functions;

believing that it is important *"to ensure terrorist organizations and groups are starved of the components of their trade " and "to ensure greater security of firearms, explosives, bomb-making equipment, and the technologies that contribute to the perpetration of terrorist outrages"*, as the European Council pointed out in its Declaration of 25 March 2004;

noting that numerous relevant activities are already under way at EU and at national levels, e.g. to further limit the availability of explosives to terrorists and other criminals including through the adaptation of conventional legal instruments; by building on safety measures to address security concerns, by developing control, security, information and monitoring mechanisms dealing also with substances and products which can be used to make explosives;

1. WELCOMES the Communication addressed by the European Commission to the European Parliament and Council on Enhancing the Security of Explosives and the preparatory work conducted by the Explosives Security Experts Task Force and in the two European conferences on the Security of explosives held respectively in Brussels, in November 2006, and in Braga, Portugal, in July 2007;
2. WELCOMES the high level of commitment shown by economic actors and civil society, during the preparatory work, and in particular the high level of corporate responsibility shown by the explosive manufacture, transport and end user industries as well as related commerce.
3. APPROVES the enclosed **Strategic Orientations** and **Priority Measures** on Enhancing the Security of Explosives in the European Union.
4. CALLS UPON its preparatory bodies/the relevant Council Working Groups to rapidly complete work on the establishment of the EU Action Plan on Enhancing the Security of Explosives in accordance with the referred **Strategic Orientations** and to promptly implement these **Priority Measures;**

5. EXPRESSES ITS INTENTION to approve the EU Action Plan on Enhancing the Security of Explosives under the Slovenian Presidency;

6. INSTRUCTS Coreper, supported by the competent Council Working Party/ies, to monitor the implementation of these conclusions.

Strategic Orientations on Enhancing the Security of Explosives in the European Union

1. Explosive devices remain the weapons most frequently used by terrorists both in the Union and in the world at large. Explosives have also often been used by other forms of criminality, including organised crime.

2. In the wake of the Madrid terrorist attacks of 11 March 2004 attacks, the European Council, in its Declaration on Combating Terrorism adopted on 25 March designated as a priority the need *"to ensure terrorist organisations and groups are starved of the components of their trade ", noting* that *"there is a need to ensure greater security of firearms, explosives, bomb-making equipment and the technologies that contribute to the perpetration of terrorist outrages".*

3. On 6 November 2007, the Commission adopted a Communication on Enhancing the Security of Explosives setting out the Commission's views concerning the strategic approach to explosives security in the European Union, putting forward an Action Plan developed through a multi-stakeholder dialogue, and identifying key priorities for immediate action.

4. The Council reaffirms therefore that enhancing the security of explosives, detonators, precursors and related technologies is a key priority for the European Union.

The Challenge

4. The types, origin and manufacture methods of explosives used by terrorists and other criminals are very diverse:

- ➢ They include both legally manufactured explosives, either stolen or otherwise illegally obtained, as well as illicitly produced ones - the so-called "home made or improvised explosives devices";
- ➢ They may include explosives originating both within and from outside the EU, including demilitarised ones.
- ➢ They include both high yield explosives, used *per se* or as primary charges in improvised devices as well as lower yield explosives which can nevertheless be very dangerous when used in large quantities, often as secondary charges.

- The methods used in the assembly of explosive devices differ too and they may also include improperly acquired industrial systems and improvised explosive devices (IEDs) including Vehicle borne Improvised Explosive Devices.
- The *modi operandi* used by terrorists and other criminals may include various types of remote or time delayed detonation as well as direct detonation by suicide bombers. As protective and detection measures improve, criminals tend to look for new approaches such as the attempted use of liquid or gel explosives.

The Union needs to consider responses addressing all the above while prioritising them in accordance with the related risks.

5. The potential exists for conventional explosives to be used in conjunction notably with Chemical, Biological and Radiological materials to commit non-conventional attacks which could have an even more devastating effect both in terms of human lives as, especially of disruption of economic and social activities.

6. Given the generally high level of awareness and protection of industrial explosives there is a marked trend towards the use by terrorists of illicitly manufactured explosive substances, including high yield ones. Therefore, without neglecting the deepening and strengthening of preventive and protective measures applying to industrial explosives, the Union and its Member States must tackle with great determination the very significant challenges posed by availability in commerce of a broad range of substances, some of which of diverse and indispensable use in daily activities and industrial ones which can be used as precursors for the manufacture of explosives. It must equally address the large and growing availability, notably through the internet, of instructions regarding the illicit manufacture of explosives.

7. Measures to address the above challenges need do so without unnecessarily hindering social and economic activities or burdening citizens and enterprises. They must respect the principles of subsidiarity and proportionality, avoid duplication and as much as possible the creation of new legislative instruments and structures.

The Strategic Objective

8. The Union's strategic objective as regards enhancing the security of explosives is to combat the acquisition, production and use of explosive devices by terrorists and other criminals within the EU, thereby protecting society from the threat of attacks using explosive devices while taking full account of the multiple areas of economic activity in which explosives and their precursors are used for the benefit of all.

The Strategic Orientations

9. The European Action Plan on Enhancing the Security of Explosives will be the corner stone for the Union in addressing the above challenges and meeting the Strategic Objective.

10. The Action Plan will address the "Prevention" of access to explosives and its components, its "Detection" as well as the "Preparedness and Response" to attacks using explosives, including as regards the pursuit, apprehension and prosecution of the terrorists or other criminals responsible. It will also comprehend cross-cutting and horizontal measures relevant for several of these dimensions.

11. With a view to ensuring the proportionality and cost effectiveness of required measures, the Union will seek to develop and adapt its policy on explosive security on the basis of high quality threat and risk assessments regarding the types, origins, forms of production and weaponisation and *modi operandi* and will endeavour to improve related exchange of information and to develop analytical capacity;

12. This Plan will enable further efforts to intensify cross-border police cooperation in combating crime related to explosives and to facilitate the exchange of relevant information between police authorities. It will, as appropriate, aim at integrating capacity and developing common tools.

13. It will aim at joint and coordinated action by Member States and EU institutions, with a view to developing a uniform level of explosive security across the EU, facilitating cooperation between authorities and other actors, while acknowledging existing differences and, in some cases, multiple best practices;

14. It will seek to develop intelligent and flexible control, information and monitoring mechanisms for substances and products which may be misused by terrorists and criminals to produce explosives, drawing on appropriate *and proportionate* technological solutions. These systems can be effective only if they are implemented in and uniformly applied by all Member States, notably through the development and use of common standards, and need to avoid the distortion of competition caused by different costs to businesses and citizens;

15. In meeting the above challenges the Union will seek to make optimal use of science and technology, seeking thus both to enhance security and diminishing associated costs. To this effect the EU and Member States will seek to ensure the complementarity and, where appropriate coordination of their research and development strategies and activities, exchange their findings;

16. Throughout the completion and implementation of the Action Plan, Member States and Commission will continue to ensure the involvement of public and private stakeholders, as appropriate.

17. The Union will aim to ensure dialogue and cooperation with external partners, aiming at fostering an increase of respective levels of security of explosives and their components, facilitating the development of relevant exchange of information - in particular on explosives stolen in neighbouring countries - and developing international standards which avoid barriers to trade while ensuring appropriate levels of security and protecting EU industry from unfair competition.

Priority Measures with a View to Enhancing the Security of Explosives in the European Union

The Council designates within each of the areas of "Prevention", "Detection", "Preparedness and Response" and "Horizontal Measures" of the proposed Action Plan, the following measures as constituting priorities for the enhancement of the security of explosives in the EU:

1) The Establishment of an Early Warning System Concerning Explosives, *Based on Existing Systems*[2]

Such a system will be used in order to exchange information concerning, in particular, immediate threats, theft of explosives, detonators and precursors, suspicious transactions and the identification of new *modi operandi.* The system should be available in particular to Member States public security authorities, responsible for the inspection of manufacturing, production, transportation and usage of explosives and Europol and all operational Explosive Ordnance disposal units. In developing such system due account should be taken of existing information exchange networks *and, if necessary, it should be examined whether a similar system should be extended to other issues, such as CBRN.*

2) The Creation of a Network of Explosives Ordnance Disposal Units Active in the Civilian Context[3]

This system will facilitate information sharing and trust building and contribute to the identification of best practice and the organisation of joint training exercises, while keeping EOD units up to date concerning the latest developments of relevance to the sector. The network will be made available to all *competent* EOD-Units dealing with explosives within a civilian context in the Member States.

[2] Horizontal measure 1.1.1 in Commission Proposal, Task Force Recommendations nr 39 and 40
[3] Preparedness and response measure 4.1.1 in Commission Proposal, Task Force Recommendations nr 38

3) Security Within the Entire Supply Chain (Storage, Transport, Traceability)

The manufacturing, storage, transport and traceability of explosives is crucial to decrease the likelihood or reduce the effects of diversion, misappropriation and theft of explosive material and devices. A number of measures already exist in this field.

Governments, public security and administrative authorities responsible for the inspection of this activity and private sector should exchange information and take preventive measures in several key areas: staff awareness concerning precursors, regulation of explosives precursors available on the market, transactions involving precursors, control over explosives and pyrotechnic articles on the market, security of explosives facilities, security vetting of personnel, security of the transport of explosives.

4) Standing Committee of Experts Concerning Precursors[4]

With a view to developing a system to consider measures and prepare recommendations concerning the regulation of explosives precursors available on the market, a Standing Committee of Experts will be created at the Commission, tasked with identifying the risks associated with various precursors and recommending appropriate actions.

5) Establishing an Ad Hoc Group on Detection of Explosives[5]

This ad hoc group, to be composed of Member State, Commission and as appropriate Europol and other relevant EU agency representatives, will be tasked with developing and discussing in a secure environment detection related scenarios, and then identifying detection technology requirements for the scenarios.

6) Cooperation With a View to Assessing and Fighting the Spread of Bomb-making Information Over the Internet[6]

Member State authorities will cooperate to assess and combat the spread of bomb-making information over the Internet, thereby fully respecting the liberty of press, freedom of speech and freedom of information. The relevant authorities will exchange information about national rules and good practices concerning (the possibility of) the monitoring of specific websites, the cooperation with Internet providers and international partners, the education of children and awareness-raising of parents, the notification of contact points etc.

---

[4] Preventive measure 2.2.1. in Commission Proposal, Task Force Recommendation nr. 4
[5] Detection Measure 3.1.1. in Commission Proposal, Task Force Recommendations nr 23
[6] Preventive measures 2.8.1. and 2.8.2. in Commission Proposal, Task Force Recommendation nr. 41

7) Creating a European Bomb Data System[7]

This system should provide a common EU instrument enabling authorised governmental bodies at EU and Member States level to have 24/7 access to relevant information on incidents involving explosive devices. At least all operational EOD units in the Member States should have *a secure* access to the database, while access by other competent authorities in the Member States need be considered in accordance with national law. Competent units or bodies of the Member States will provide the required information for inclusion in the database.

The Council *welcomes* the decision by Europol to rapidly set up a central database for storing data on EU-wide offences involving explosives and arson. It *notes* that in a first phase, to be completed in December 2007, Europol is developing new categories within its Information System allowing the storage of information regarding offences involving explosives and arson, the technical development of which will already enable competent authorities to exchange data on offences without delay via the Europol National Units. It *notes* also that in a second phase, which will start in early 2008, Europol will assess the extent to which the alterations made to its information System meet the needs of the practitioners and consider options for the completion of the European Bomb Data System.

To facilitate progress, Europol and the Commission will look into the possibilities of using the funding available under the Financial Programme "Prevention of and Fight against Crime" for this measure.

[7] Horizontal measure 1.1.2 in Commission Proposal, Task Force Recommendations nr 35, 36 and 37

DOCUMENT NO. 33

EC COUNCIL JOINT ACTION 2007/753/CFSP OF 19 NOVEMBER 2007 ON SUPPORT FOR IAEA MONITORING AND VERIFICATION ACTIVITIES IN THE DEMOCRATIC PEOPLE'S REPUBLIC OF KOREA

(*Council Joint Action 2007/753/CFSP of 19 November 2007 on Support for IAEA Monitoring and Verification Activities in the Democratic People's Republic of Korea in the Framework of the Implementation of the EU Strategy Against the Proliferation of Weapons of Mass Destruction*)

THE COUNCIL OF THE EUROPEAN UNION,

Having regard to the Treaty on European Union, and in particular Article 14 thereof,

Whereas:

(1) On 12 December 2003, the European Council adopted the EU Strategy against the Proliferation of Weapons of Mass Destruction; Chapter III of the Strategy contains a list of measures to combat such proliferation which need to be taken both within the European Union and in third countries.

(2) The European Union is actively implementing the Strategy and is giving effect to the measures listed in Chapter III thereof, in particular by releasing financial resources to support specific projects conducted by multilateral institutions, such as the International Atomic Energy Agency (IAEA).

(3) The European Union has repeatedly called on the Democratic People's Republic of Korea (DPRK) to comply with its obligations under the Treaty on the Non-Proliferation of Nuclear Weapons (NPT) and to implement its comprehensive safeguards agreement in full cooperation with the IAEA.

(4) The European Union has continuously supported efforts in the framework of the six-party talks, aimed at finding a diplomatic solution to the nuclear situation on the Korean peninsula, including through political and financial support for the Korean Peninsula Energy

Development Organisation (KEDO). In the same spirit, the European Union welcomed the Joint Statement of 19 September 2005 and the Initial Actions of 13 February 2007.

(5) On 9 July 2007, the Board of Governors of the IAEA authorised its Director-General to implement ad hoc arrangements for monitoring and verifying the shutdown of nuclear installations in the DPRK, in accordance with the recommendations contained in the IAEA report to the Board of Governors.

(6) In accordance with the Initial Actions of 13 February 2007, the DPRK proceeded in July 2007 with the shutdown of nuclear installations and has invited the IAEA to monitor the shutdown. Subsequently, this shutdown has been confirmed by the IAEA.

(7) The European Union has welcomed this action carried out by the DPRK as a very important first step on the way to the dismantlement of the DPRK's nuclear programmes and the denuclearisation of the Korean peninsula.

(8) Since the costs incurred by the implementation of the ad hoc arrangements can currently not be covered by the regular safeguards budget of the IAEA, there is a need to make sufficient extra-budgetary contributions in order to allow for the implementation of the ad hoc arrangements, as long as there is no provision in the regular IAEA budget,

HAS ADOPTED THIS JOINT ACTION:

Article 1

For the purposes of giving immediate and practical implementation to some elements of the EU Strategy against the Proliferation of Weapons of Mass Destruction, the European Union shall support the IAEA monitoring and verification activities, which are carried out in accordance with existing arrangements for monitoring and verification, as agreed between the DPRK and the IAEA, in order to further the following objectives:

(a) to contribute to the confidence-building process aimed at the elimination of the DPRK's nuclear programme, through the continuation of monitoring and verification of the shutdown of DPRK nuclear facilities;

(b) to assure the European Union's continued active involvement in efforts to develop a diplomatic solution to the Korean nuclear issue;

(c) to make sure that the IAEA has available sufficient financial resources to carry out monitoring and verification activities relating to the implementation of the Initial Actions of 13 February 2007, agreed in the framework of the six-party talks.

The contribution by the EU will be used for the financing of staff resources and travel, equipment and transportation, rental of premises in the DPRK and related expenditure, as well as costs for communications and acquisition of information technology.

A detailed description of these activities is set out in the Annex.

Article 2

1. The Presidency, assisted by the Secretary-General of the Council/High Representative for the CFSP (SG/HR), shall be responsible for the implementation of this Joint Action. The Commission shall be fully associated.

2. The technical implementation of the activities referred to in Article 1 shall be carried out by the IAEA. It shall perform this task under the control of the SG/HR, assisting the Presidency. For this purpose, the SG/HR shall enter into the necessary arrangements with IAEA.

3. The Presidency, the SG/HR and the Commission shall keep each other regularly informed about the implementation of this Joint Action, in conformity with their respective competences.

Article 3

1. The financial reference amount for the implementation of the activities referred to in Article 1 shall be EUR 1 780 000 to be funded from the general budget of the European Union.

2. The expenditure financed by the amount stipulated in paragraph 1 shall be managed in accordance with the Community procedures and rules applicable to the general budget of the European Union.

3. The Commission shall supervise the proper management of the expenditure referred to in paragraph 2, which shall take the form of a grant. For this purpose, it shall conclude a financing agreement with the IAEA. The financing agreement shall stipulate that the IAEA is to ensure visibility of the EU contribution, appropriate to its size.

4. The Commission shall endeavour to conclude the financing agreement referred to in paragraph 3 within three months after the entry into force of this Joint Action. It shall inform the Council of any difficulties in that process and of the date of conclusion of the financing agreement.

Article 4

The Presidency, assisted by the SG/HR, shall report to the Council on the implementation of this Joint Action on the basis of reports prepared by the IAEA Secretariat for the IAEA Board of Governors, which will be submitted to the Presidency, assisted by the SG/HR. The Commission shall be fully associated. It shall report on the financial aspects of the implementation of this Joint Action.

Article 5

This Joint Action shall enter into force on the day of its adoption.

It shall expire 18 months after its adoption.

Article 6

This Joint Action shall be published in the *Official Journal of the European Union.*

Done at Brussels, 19 November 2007.

For the Council

The President

L. AMADO

Annex

EU Support for IAEA Monitoring and Verification Activities in the Democratic People's Republic of Korea (DPRK) in the Framework of the Implementation of the EU Strategy Against the Proliferation of Weapons of Mass Destruction

1. Description of IAEA Monitoring and Verification Activities in the DPRK

In March 2007, the Director-General of the IAEA informed its Board of Governors that on 13 February 2007 the Parties to the Six-Party Talks agreed in Beijing, China, on Initial Actions for the implementation of the Joint Statement issued by them on 19 September 2005. He also informed the Board of Governors that on 23 February 2007 he had received an invitation from the DPRK to visit the DPRK to 'develop the relations between the DPRK and the IAEA, as well as to discuss problems of mutual concerns'. In the Initial Actions the Parties agreed, *inter alia,* that the DPRK 'will shut down and seal, for the purpose of eventual abandonment, the Yongbyon nuclear facility, including the reprocessing facility, and invite back IAEA personnel to conduct all necessary monitoring and verifications as agreed between IAEA and the DPRK'. The Board of Governors welcomed the agreement on the Initial Actions and expressed the view that a successfully negotiated settlement of this long-standing issue, maintaining the essential verification role of the IAEA, would be a significant accomplishment for international peace and security. In this regard, the Board of Governors welcomed the invitation extended to the Director-General by the DPRK to visit the DPRK.

The Director-General visited the DPRK on 13 and 14 March 2007 and reported to the Board of Governors in June 2007 on the results of his visit. The Board of Governors, while emphasising the importance of continued dialogue for achieving a peaceful and comprehensive resolution of the DPRK nuclear issue and early denuclearisation of the Korean Peninsula, welcomed the Director-General's visit to the DPRK and his discussions with DPRK officials which had focused on re-establishing the relationship between the DPRK and the IAEA.

On 16 June 2007 the Director-General received an invitation from the DPRK to send an IAEA team to discuss procedural matters related to the monitoring and verification arrangement on the shutdown of the Yongbyon nuclear facility. This letter and the Director-General's reply thereto, dated 18 June 2007, were circulated to the Board of Governors.

An IAEA team, headed by the Deputy Director-General for Safeguards, visited the DPRK during the period 26 to 29 June 2007. The team visited the Nuclear Fuel Fabrication Plant, the 5 MW(e) Experimental Nuclear Power Plant, the Radiochemical Laboratory (reprocessing plant) and the 50 MW(e) Nuclear Power Plant (under construction), all of which are located at

Yongbyon. The DPRK informed the team that these facilities, and the 200 MW(e) Nuclear Power Plant (under construction), which is located in Taechon, would be shut down and sealed pursuant to the Initial Actions.

During the visit of the IAEA team to the DPRK, understanding was reached on the following arrangement:

(a) the IAEA will receive from the DPRK a list of facilities that have been shut down and/or sealed, and subsequently the IAEA will be kept informed of their status with a view to monitoring and verifying the shutdown and/or sealing of the declared facilities;

(b) the IAEA will have access to all facilities and equipment that have been shut down and/or sealed for the purpose of its monitoring and verification activities;

(c) the IAEA will install, and service as necessary, appropriate containment and surveillance and other devices to monitor and verify the status of the shutdown and/or sealed facilities and equipment. If containment and surveillance measures cannot be applied for practical reasons, the IAEA and the DPRK will agree on the implementation of other appropriate verification measures;

(d) the IAEA will examine and verify information on the design of the shutdown and/or sealed facilities and document the status of these facilities photographically or through video recordings. Re-verification of such information will be performed periodically;

(e) the IAEA will be informed in advance if the DPRK intends to change the design and/or status of facilities and equipment, so that consultations can be held with the DPRK about the impact such changes may have on the IAEA's monitoring and verification work;

(f) the IAEA will be informed in advance if the DPRK intends to move or remove any nuclear-related equipment or other essential equipment or components from the shutdown nuclear facilities or decommission any of these facilities. The IAEA will be provided appropriate access to verify such equipment, components, and/or activities;

(g) the DPRK will maintain all records relevant to the IAEA's monitoring and verification activities;

(h) the IAEA will be provided with the necessary visas for IAEA personnel, and will be extended the same privileges and immunities as those set out in the relevant provisions of the Agreement on the Privileges and Immunities of the International Atomic Energy Agency (INFCIRC/9/Rev.2) for IAEA property, funds and assets, its personnel and other officials in exercising their functions under this arrangement;

(i) the IAEA will be provided with full information on the health and safety procedures at the relevant facilities;

(j) the IAEA and the DPRK will consult on issues related to the costs of implementation;

(k) the above measures will be subject to periodic review by the DPRK and the IAEA.

The IAEA is authorised in accordance with Article III.A.5 of its Statute to '. . . apply safeguards, at the request of the parties, to any bilateral or multilateral arrangement, or at the request of a State, to any of that State's activities in the field of atomic energy'. This authorisation does not require the State to be a member of the IAEA and does not prescribe a particular form or substance for safeguards arrangements. The monitoring and verification in the DPRK will therefore be consistent with the Statute. At this stage such monitoring and verification will be implemented in accordance with the ad hoc arrangements referred to in recital (5) of the Joint Action.

The monitoring and verification activities in the DPRK were not foreseen and therefore there is no provision for the conduct of such monitoring and verification in the IAEA's current budget or the proposed budgets for the 2008–2009 biennium. The estimated costs to cover these activities are EUR 2,2 million for 2007 and 2008, respectively, based on the current arrangements for monitoring and verification between DPRK and IAEA. However, in the light of progress made in the six-party-talks process and a possible increased role for the IAEA in the monitoring and verification of understandings reached, the need for additional financial means could arise in the future.

2. Objectives

IAEA monitoring and verification remains an indispensable tool for building confidence among States with regard to nuclear non-proliferation undertakings, and for advancing the peaceful use of nuclear material.

Overall objective and project purpose:

— to contribute to the implementation of monitoring and verification activities in the DPRK, in accordance with the Initial Actions of 13 February 2007, as agreed in the framework of the six-party-talks.

Project results:

— continued monitoring and verification by the IAEA of the shutdown of the abovementioned nuclear installations in the DPRK.

3. Duration

The total estimated duration for the implementation of this Joint Action is 18 months.

4. Beneficiaries

The beneficiary of this Joint Action is the IAEA.

5. Implementing Entity

The IAEA will be entrusted with the implementation of the project. The project will be implemented directly by the IAEA, namely by the staff from the IAEA Department of Safeguards. In the case of contractors, the procurement of any goods, works or services by the IAEA in the context of this Joint Action will be carried out in accordance with the applicable rules and procedures of the IAEA, as detailed in the European Community Contribution Agreement with the IAEA.

The implementing entity will prepare reports on the basis of information provided to the IAEA Board of Governors. These reports will be submitted to the Presidency, assisted by the SG/HR for the CFSP.

6. Third-Party Participants

There will be no third party participants.

DOCUMENT NO. 34

DRAFT COUNCIL CONCLUSIONS ON ADDRESSING CHEMICAL, BIOLOGICAL, RADIOLOGICAL AND NUCLEAR RISKS AND ON BIO-PREPAREDNESS

Document 15127/07
Council of the European Union

Brussels, 16 November 2007

from:	General Secretariat
to:	delegations, CATS, PSC
No. prev. doc.:	14744/07 JAI 551 PROCIV 184 ENFOPOL 181 SAN 194 AGRI 360 AGRILEG 162 CODUN 32 COSDP 886 COTER 77 DENLEG 106 ENV 584 PHARM 5 RECH 334 VETER 24
No. Cion doc.:	11951/07 JAI 392 PROCIV 125 ENFOPOL 139 SAN 156 AGRI 241 AGRILEG 110 CODUN 23 COSDP 615 COTER 63 DENLEG 66 ENV 416 PHARM 2 RECH 213 VETER 12
Subject:	Draft Council Conclusions on addressing Chemical, Biological, Radiological and Nuclear Risks and on Bio-preparedness

The Commission submitted to the Council, on 11 July 2007, a Green Paper on bio-preparedness which aimed at protecting the populations, life and the environment against all biological hazards such as diseases, accidents, crimes and terrorism, in particular in case of multiple incidents.

This can be achieved by stimulating an active safety culture in a public-private partnership and using existing EU tools.[1]

This Green Paper was examined in multi-sectoral meetings of *Counsellors/ Attachés on bio-preparedness* convened by the Presidency.

[1] 11951/07

On the basis of several drafts submitted by *the Presidency*, the Counsellors/Attachés established, at their meeting on 5 November 2007 and following a subsequent silent approval procedure,[2] the draft Council conclusions contained in *the Annex*. This draft not only concerns bio-preparedness but also non-conventional (CBRN) risks in general.

The Counsellors/Attachés also took into account the first results deriving from the consultations undertaken by the Commission on the Green Paper and the lessons learned from a table-top exercise on a bio-terrorist scenario held within the EU-institutions in October 2007. In addition, the Counsellors/Attachés heard an exposé by the office of the SG/HR's personal representative for non-proliferation.

The draft conclusions are to be read together with the future Inventory of instruments on bio-preparedness, a draft of which contained in doc. 14802/07.

These draft conclusions are/were submitted to other Council bodies (TWG, ProCiv . . .) for information and to *CATS* and *PSC* for endorsement as regards matters falling within their remits.

The draft conclusions will then be submitted to *the Permanent Representatives Committee* and *the Council* for approval/adoption under the I/A-items of their agendas.

[2] *DK/DE/UK/Cion and the SG/HR's personal representative on non-proliferation* made suggestions on the text. Since they appeared to be technical or uncontroversial, it was not considered necessary to restart the silent approval procedure.

Annex

Draft[3] Council Conclusions on Addressing Chemical, Biological, Radiological and Nuclear Risks and on Bio-preparedness

The Council of the European Union:

(a) *Considering* that the growing complexity of modern civilisation has created increased threats and risks of non-conventional chemical, biological radiological or nuclear (CBRN) disasters of an accidental, pandemic or intentional origin, including terrorism; *noting* that the Commission Green Paper on Bio-Preparedness of July 2007,[4] that was based on an all-hazards approach, made a similar analysis **of** biological threats and risks;

(b) *Recalling,* in particular, that tackling terrorist access to weapons and explosives, ranging from components for homemade explosives to CBRN material is a key priority under the European Union Counter-Terrorism Strategy adopted by Council on 1 December 2005 [5] and under the EU Strategy against proliferation of weapons of mass destruction **(WMD) adopted by the European Council on 12 December 2003;**[6] *recalling* the obligations under the Chemical Weapons Convention (CWC), the Biological and Toxin Weapons Convention (BTWC) and the Nuclear Non-Proliferation Treaty (NPT), as well as the need to work with partners and international organisations on the non-proliferation of CBRN materials, as highlighted by the **abovementioned EU strategies;**

(c) *Recalling* that the EU Action Plan on Combating Terrorism establishes, in its latest revision of 29 March 2007,[7] the importance of ensuring full implementation of the Programme of cooperation on preparedness and response to biological and chemical agent attacks (Health Security Programme) adopted by the Health Security Committee (HSC) on 17 December 2001 and of the EU Solidarity Programme on the consequences of terrorist threats and attacks (Solidarity Programme) adopted by the Council on 2 December 2004,[8] as well as the need to adapt the

[3] Changes to 14744/07 are in bold.
[4] 11951/07.
[5] 14469/4/05, paras 20 and 31.
[6] 15708/03 and SN 400/03, no 68.
[7] 7233/1/07 REV 1, actions 2.3.4, 4.1.12 and 4.2.1.
[8] The Solidarity Programme (15480/04) **was the successor** to the Council and Commission Programme of 20 December 2002 to improve cooperation in the European Union for preventing and limiting the consequences of chemical, biological, radiological or nuclear terrorist threats (CBRN Programme)

database of military assets and capabilities relevant to the protection of civilian populations against the effects of terrorist attacks, including CBRN,[9] to reflect its expansion to all types of natural and man-made disasters; Recalling that the Council of 22 February 2007 temporarily prolonged the mandate in the areas of information, preparedness and coordination of response, that had been given to the HSC in 2001, extending it to cover also pandemic influenza and generic preparedness and response planning.[10]

(d) *Recalling* the two EU Radiological Risk Reduction seminars held on 23–24 November 2006 and on 21–22 June 2007 and the **keen** interest shown by the Member States in continuing and stepping up work in the radiological risk reduction field; recalling the two seminars on Bio-preparedness of 24–25 July 2006 and of 15–16 November 2006, and the workshop on Transportation and Traceability of Bio-Materials of 7 November 2006, which led to the elaboration of the Commission Green Paper on Bio-Preparedness of 18 July 2007;

(e) *Noting* the existence of an extensive arsenal of instruments aiming at avoiding accidents in the handling of CBRN substances or technologies (CBRN-safety) and *convinced* of the need to use and, where necessary, develop those instruments with a view to preventing and responding to a voluntary abuse of those substances or technologies (CBRN-security);[11]

(f) Noting the relevant work under way in the **subordinate bodies** of the Council with a view to strengthening the security of critical infrastructures in the EU;

(g) *Recalling* the importance of further enhancing the quality of *risk assessment* and analysis by making better use of *threat assessments* and by improving the methodological quality and the information on cross-border risks as highlighted in the Solidarity Programme;

(14627/02). The elements of the Solidarity Programme were included in the Action Plan on Combating Terrorism.

[9] 6644/4/04 REV 4.

[10] 5862/07.

[11] *OECD* defines "Biosecurity" as "Measures to protect against the malicious use of pathogens, parts of them, or their toxins in direct or indirect acts against humans, livestock or crops."
OECDE also defines "Biosafety" as "The safe handling practices, procedures and proper use of containment facilities to prevent accidental harm caused by living organisms either directly or indirectly to individuals within laboratories or to the environment."
http://www.biosecuritycodes.org/gloss.htm#biosec
WHO describes these terms as follows :
"Laboratory biosecurity describes the protection, control and accountability for valuable biological materials within laboratories, in order to prevent their unauthorized access, loss, theft, misuse, diversion or intentional release."
"Laboratory biosafety describes the containment principles, technologies and practices that are implemented to prevent the unintentional exposure to pathogens and toxins, or their accidental release."
http://www.who.int/csr/resources/publications/biosafety/WHO_ CDS EPR 2006 6.pdf.

(h) *Recalling* the importance of improving and interlinking the mechanisms for the *detection* and identification of terrorist threats and for alerting the professionals and the public, as also highlighted in the EU Solidarity Programme;

(i) *Recalling* the importance given in the Solidarity Programme to strengthening the *preparedness* and capabilities for consequence management by improved mutual assistance, by increased learning, training and exercises and by better coordination;

(j) *Noting* that that the EU Action Plan on Combating Terrorism identifies the need for the Civil Protection assistance Mechanism to be able to *respond* in **the event** of major terrorist attack in the EU[12] **and that the Mechanism includes** the ability to pool and compile, in the event of **a major emergency (such as** a bio-terrorist attack), information on necessary medical resources and on the stocks thereof which might be available for intervention;[13]

(k) *Recalling* that the Council's conclusions of 12 June 2007 on preparedness for the decontamination of casualties following chemical, biological, radiological and nuclear incidents (CBRN)[14] advocate, in the framework of the Civil Protection Financial Instrument[15] and of the Civil Protection Mechanism, precautionary measures to avoid primary or secondary contamination, exercises, training and the spread of best practices;

(l) *Recalling* the importance given by the EU Action Plan on Combating Terrorism to *scientific support* to bio-security policies, including research on biological agents, risk assessment and on the modeling of the propagation of biological agents that could be used by terrorists,[16]

Adopts the Following Conclusions:

A. Regarding Chemical, Biological, Radiological and Nuclear (CBRN) Risks, the Council:

1. *Considers* that, as the Union **takes** forward its work on developing a comprehensive approach to the security enhancement of explosives, detonators, precursors and related technologies, it must **continue addressing** with equal determination the non-conventional risks, in particular those posed by Chemical, Biological, Radiological and Nuclear substances,

---

[12] 7233/1/07 REV 1,actions 4.1.1, 4.1.3 and 4.1.6.

[13] Council Decision *2007/..* /EC, Euratom of 8 November 2007 establishing a Community Civil Protection Mechanism (Recast), 11163/1/07 REV 1 + COR 1 (ro); see Article 5, paragraph 6).

[14] 10015/07.

[15] Council Decision 2007/162/EC, Euratom of 5 March 2007 establishing a Civil Protection Financial Instrument, OJ L 71, **10.3.2007,** p. 9.

[16] See actions 4.1.3. and 2.7.2.

including those related to their potential terrorist use, **as recognized and addressed by the EU Strategies on counter-terrorism and against the proliferation of WMD;**

2. *Considers* that it is first and foremost the responsibility of each Member State to protect its populations against such disasters and that the EU intervenes in this area mainly in a supportive role in accordance with the principles of subsidiarity and proportionality, giving preference where possible to non-legislative solutions;
3. *Considers* that effective policies to address CBRN risks should be **further** developed in close consultation with national authorities and, as appropriate, the industrial sectors concerned, academic institutions and other relevant stakeholders, notably with a view to ensuring the viability and proportionality of measures which may be required, and *welcomes* the increasing security awareness and commitment shown, notably during the consultation process on the Commission Green Paper on Bio-Preparedness of 18 July 2007[17] and during the seminars referred to in Recital d), by private sector and civil society actors and their willingness to be actively involved;
4. *Calls on the Commission and the Member States* to implement, each for the areas within their responsibility, the Health Security Programme, the Solidarity Programme and other relevant programmes such as the Framework Programme for Research,[18] the Instrument for Stability[19] **and the relevant CFSP instruments and international obligations;**
5. *Requests* the Commission and the Secretariat General of the Council to update by mid-April 2008 the CBRN inventory of 2002[20] which outlined the many EU instruments that can be used to counter CBRN risks and threats so that the Council can, on this basis, take stock of the capabilities and needs in this area in the course of 2008; *requests* the Commission and the Council Secretariat General to update this inventory biennially;
6. Notes that the Joint Situation Centre of the Council Secretariat and, as appropriate EUROPOL, continue assessing the threats of CBRN-terrorism and of the spread of WMD; also restates the importance of assess-

---

17 11951/07, COM (2007) 399 final.

18 Seventh Framework Programme of the European Community for Research, Technological Development and Demonstration Activities (2007 to 2013), OJ L 54, 22.2.2007, p. 30, in particular the specific programme "Security", Council Decision 2006/971/EC of 19 December 2006 concerning the specific programme "Security" implementing the Seventh Framework Programme of the European Community for research, technological development and demonstration activities (2007 to 2013), OJ L 54, 22.2.2007, p. 30.

19 Regulation (EC) No 1717/2006 of the European Parliament and of the Council of 15 November 2006 establishing an Instrument for Stability, OJ L 327, 24.11.2006, p. 1.

20 Inventory of the EU instruments relevant for the Council and Commission Programme of 20 December 2002 to improve cooperation in the European Union for preventing and limiting the consequences of chemical, biological, radiological or nuclear terrorist threats (CBRN Programme), 15873/02.

ments and analyses of the risks caused by those threats to their possible targets such as persons, society, the economy and the environment; therefore calls upon the Commission and the Member States to reinforce work on risk assessment, notably looking into the mid-term future;

7. *Invites* the Commission, in accordance with its competences, to continue its work in the CBRN field together with the Member States and relevant stakeholders, avoiding duplications and building on good practices across Member States, and *notes* the Commission's intention to propose relevant policy measures in 2009;

8. *Invites the Counter-Terrorism Coordinator* and the *SG/HR's Personal Representative for non-proliferation* to work together and with Member States and the Commission, in accordance with their respective competences, with a view to identifying ways and means to mitigate the risk that terrorists might in the future obtain, directly or indirectly, CBRN materials;

9. *Considers* that regular training and exercises are of paramount importance in strengthening the *preparedness* and capability for consequence management; *calls for* due account to be taken of the lessons learned from several European exercises held in the CBRN-preparedness area such as EURATOX (France, October 2002), COMMON CAUSE (Denmark, October 2002), EU Response/FLORIVAL II (Belgium, February 2003), EUDREX (Austria, October 2004), EURATECH (France, June 2005), EUROSOT (Italy, October 2005), NEW WATCHMANN (SANCO, EU-wide, October 2007) and EULUX (Luxembourg, June 2007) and, most recently, CCAEX07 (EU Council September 2007) and invites the Commission and the Member States to continue to organise regular exercises addressing CBRN risks;

B. Regarding Bio-Preparedness in Particular, the Council:

10. *Encourages* Member States and the Commission, without prejudice to and in parallel with the broader work on addressing non-conventional risks, to address as a matter of priority the area of bio-preparedness with a view to addressing biological risks and threats through appropriate actions and activities in the relevant policy areas;

11. *Welcomes* the Commission's Green Paper on Bio-Preparedness of 18 July 2007[21] aimed at stimulating debate and at launching a process of consultation at European level on how to reduce biological risks and to enhance preparedness and response **in the context of an all-hazards approach;** *invites* the Commission to provide the Council with an analysis of the responses received to the Green Paper by mid-April 2008;

[21] 11951/07, COM (2007) 399 final.

12. *Welcomes* the broad interest raised by the subject and the active participation of private sector, civil society, international bodies and third countries in the two European seminars on bio-preparedness held on 24–25 July and 15–16 November 2006, in the workshop on Transportation and Traceability of Bio-Materials of 7 November 2006 which led to the Green Paper and in the public consultations on the Green Paper;

13. *Notes* the inventory of **EU** instruments **in the area of bio-preparedness** relevant **to the present conclusions, which addresses** prevention, preparedness and response to biological risks existing in the areas of in human, animal and plant health, police, research, environment, civil protection, etc. **and which was** established on the basis of the relevant sections of the 2002 CBRN inventory;[22]

14. *Notes* the existence of *many monitoring, notification and Rapid Alert Systems* which can provide early warnings in **the event** of pandemics or biological contamination, such as the Rapid Alert System for Biological **and** Chemical Agents and Threats (RAS-BICHAT) with a specific pillar on chemicals in development (RAS-CHEM), the Early Warning and Response System **for communicable diseases** (EWRS), the Medical Intelligence System (MEDISYS), the Rapid Alert System for Food and Feed (RASFF), the Animal Disease Notification System (ADNS), the Trade Control and Expert System (TRACES), the European Plant Health notification scheme (EUROPHYT), **the Customs Information System (CIS), the Community Customs Risk Management System (CRMS) with the RIF module for the rapid exchange of risk information and the Rapid Alert System for Non-Food Products (RAPEX);**

15. Notes the existence of several bodies which can provide *assistance and analysis* in **the event** of biological incidents, notably the European Centre **for** Disease Control (ECDC), the European Food Safety Agency (EFSA), the Civil Protection Monitoring and Information Centre (MIC), the Joint Research Centre (JRC), Europol, the Joint Situation Centre of the Council (Sitcen) etc.;

16. *Notes* the existence of *crisis response* systems and bodies in the EU such as the EU Crisis Coordination Arrangements (CCA), the Commission's overall alert network ARGUS,[23] the Civil Protection Mechanism, the Health Emergency Operations Facility (HEOF) with the Health Emergency & Disease Information System (HEDIS) as a situational awareness tool, the Health Security Committee, the Standing Committee on the Food Chain and Animal Health (SCOFCAH) **and the Standing Committee on Plant Health (SCPH);** with a view to testing and rein-

[22] Present draft in 14802/07.
[23] OJL19, 24.1.2006, p. 20.

forcing their interoperability, *invites* the Commission and **the** Council Secretariat to check, each for the instruments within their competence, the adequacy of those systems for bio-risks;

17. *Encourages the Commission, the Member States and the Council Secretariat* to strengthen, within the framework of their respective competences, interoperability, and to improve **the** exchange of information between the systems and structures referred to in 14, 15 and 16 while taking due care to preserve their specificity and effectiveness;

18. *Notes* the intention of the Commission, in the follow-up to the consultations on the Green Paper on bio-preparedness and in the work to be carried out in 2008, to continue to ensure the involvement of public and private stakeholders;

C. In conclusion, the Council:

19. Expresses its intention to remain seized of the matter;

20. *Considers* that the EU should carefully analyse the instruments that exist, make the best possible use of them—avoiding their duplication and seeking synergies with existing national, EU, regional and global mechanisms—and not create new instruments, systems or structures unless proven necessary;

21. *Calls upon* the Commission, the Member States and the Council Secretariat to implement the above conclusions, in accordance with their respective competences as laid down in the Treaties;

22. *Instructs* Coreper, supported by the competent Council Working Party/ies, to monitor the implementation of these conclusions.

DOCUMENT NO. 35

EC REGULATION NO 305/2006 OF 21 FEBRUARY 2006 IMPOSING SPECIFIC RESTRICTIVE MEASURES AGAINST CERTAIN PERSONS SUSPECTED OF INVOLVEMENT IN THE ASSASSINATION OF FORMER LEBANESE PRIME MINISTER RAFIQ HARIRI

THE COUNCIL OF THE EUROPEAN UNION,

Having regard to the Treaty establishing the European Community, and in particular Articles 60, 301 and 308 thereof,

Having regard to Council Common Position 2005/888/CFSP of 12 December 2005 concerning specific restrictive measures against certain persons suspected of involvement in the assassination of former Lebanese Prime Minister Rafiq Hariri,[1]

Having regard to the proposal from the Commission,

Having regard to the opinion of the European Parliament,[2]

Whereas:

(1) On 31 October 2005, the Security Council of the United Nations adopted Resolution 1636 (2005) noting the conclusion of the report of the International Investigation Commission into the 14 February 2005 terrorist bombing in Beirut, Lebanon, that killed 23 people, including former Lebanese Prime Minister Rafiq Hariri, and caused injury to dozens of people.

(2) The Security Council noted with extreme concern the International Investigation Commission's conclusion that there is converging evidence pointing at the involvement of both Lebanese and Syrian officials in this terrorist act, and acting under Chapter VII of the Charter of the United Nations, decided, as a step to assist in the investigation of this crime and without prejudice to the ultimate

[1] OJ L 327, 14.12.2005, p. 26.
[2] Not yet published in the Official Journal.

judicial determination of the guilt or innocence of any individual, to impose measures against all individuals suspected of involvement in the planning, sponsoring, organizing or perpetrating of this terrorist act.

(3) Common Position 2005/888/CFSP provides for implementation of the measures set out in UNSCR 1636 (2005) and, in particular, the freezing of funds and economic resources of persons registered by the Committee of the Security Council established by paragraph 3(b) of UNSCR 1636 (2005) as suspected of involvement in the planning, sponsoring, organising or perpetrating of the assassination of former Lebanese Prime Minister Rafiq Hariri and others on 14 February 2005.

(4) These measures fall within the scope of the Treaty and, therefore, notably with a view to ensuring their uniform application by economic operators in all Member States, Community legislation is necessary to implement them as far as the Community is concerned.

(5) For reasons of expediency, the Commission should be empowered to amend the Annexes to this Regulation, on the basis of notification or information by the relevant Sanctions Committee and Member States, as appropriate.

(6) Member States should determine the penalties applicable to infringements of the provisions of this Regulation. The penalties provided for should be proportionate, effective and dissuasive.

(7) In order to ensure that the measures provided for in this Regulation are effective, it should enter into force on the day of its publication,

HAS ADOPTED THIS REGULATION:

Article 1

For the purposes of this Regulation, the following definitions shall apply:

1. 'Sanctions Committee' means the Committee of the Security Council of the United Nations which was established pursuant to paragraph 3(b) of UNSCR 1636 (2005);

2. 'funds' means financial assets and benefits of every kind, including but not limited to:

   (a) cash, cheques, claims on money, drafts, money orders and other payment instruments;

   (b) deposits with financial institutions or other entities, balances on accounts, debts and debt obligations;

(c) publicly and privately traded securities and debt instruments, including stocks and shares, certificates representing securities, bonds, notes, warrants, debentures and derivatives contracts;

(d) interest, dividends or other income on or value accruing from or generated by assets;

(e) credit, right of set-off, guarantees, performance bonds or other financial commitments;

(f) letters of credit, bills of lading, bills of sale;

(g) documents evidencing an interest in funds or financial resources;

3. 'freezing of funds' means preventing any move, transfer, alteration, use of, access to, or dealing with funds in any way that would result in any change in their volume, amount, location, ownership, possession, character, destination or other change that would enable the funds to be used, including portfolio management;

4. 'economic resources' means assets of every kind, whether tangible or intangible, movable or immovable, which are not funds but can be used to obtain funds, goods or services;

5. 'freezing of economic resources' means preventing the use of economic resources to obtain funds, goods or services in any way, including, but not limited to, the selling, hiring or mortgaging of them;

6. 'territory of the Community' means the territories of the Member States to which the Treaty is applicable, under the conditions laid down in that Treaty.

Article 2

1. All funds and economic resources belonging to, owned, held or controlled by the natural or legal persons, entities or bodies listed in Annex I shall be frozen.

2. No funds or economic resources shall be made available, directly or indirectly, to or for the benefit of the natural or legal persons, entities or bodies listed in Annex I.

3. The participation, knowingly and intentionally, in activities the object or effect of which is, directly or indirectly, to circumvent the measures referred to in paragraphs 1 and 2 shall be prohibited.

Article 3

1. By way of derogation from Article 2, the competent authorities of the Member States, as listed in Annex II, may authorise, under such conditions

as they deem appropriate, the release of certain frozen funds or economic resources or the making available of certain funds or economic resources, having determined that the funds or economic resources concerned are:

(a) necessary for basic expenses, including payments for foodstuffs, rent or mortgage, medicines and medical treatment, taxes, insurance premiums, and public utility charges;

(b) intended exclusively for payment of reasonable professional fees and reimbursement of incurred expenses associated with the provision of legal services; or

(c) intended exclusively for payment of fees or service charges for routine holding or maintenance of frozen funds or economic resources;

provided that the Member State concerned has notified the Sanctions Committee of that determination and that the determination has been approved by that Committee.

2. The relevant competent authority shall inform the competent authorities of the other Member States and the Commission of any authorisation granted under paragraph 1.

3. Article 2(2) shall not apply to the addition to frozen accounts of interest or other earnings on those accounts provided that any such interest or other earnings are frozen in accordance with Article 2(1).

Article 4

Article 2(2) shall not prevent the crediting of the frozen accounts by financial institutions that receive funds transferred by third parties to the account of a listed person, entity or body, provided that any such crediting to such accounts is also frozen in accordance with Article 2(1). The financial institution shall inform the competent authorities of such transactions without delay.

Article 5

1. Without prejudice to the applicable rules concerning reporting, confidentiality and professional secrecy and to the provisions of Article 284 of the Treaty, natural and legal persons, entities and bodies shall:

(a) supply immediately any information which would facilitate compliance with this Regulation, such as accounts and amounts frozen in accordance with Article 2, to the competent authorities of the Member States listed in Annex II where they are resident or located, and shall transmit such information, directly or through these competent authorities, to the Commission;

(b) cooperate with the competent authorities listed in Annex II in any verification of this information.

2. Any additional information directly received by the Commission shall be made available to the competent authorities of the Member State concerned.

3. Any information provided or received in accordance with this Article shall be used only for the purposes for which it was provided or received. Such purposes shall be deemed to include cooperation with any international investigation related to the assets or financial transactions of the natural and legal persons, bodies and entities listed in Annex I.

Article 6

The freezing of funds and economic resources or the refusal to make funds or economic resources available, carried out in good faith that such action is in accordance with this Regulation, shall not give rise to liability of any kind on the part of the natural or legal person, entity or body implementing it, or its directors or employees, unless it is proved that the funds and economic resources were frozen as result of negligence.

Article 7

The Commission and Member States shall immediately inform each other of the measures taken under this Regulation and shall supply each other with any other relevant information at their disposal in connection with this Regulation, in particular information in respect of violation and enforcement problems and judgments handed down by national courts.

Article 8

1. The Commission shall be empowered to:

   (a) amend Annex I on the basis of determinations made by the Sanctions Committee; and

   (b) amend Annex II on the basis of information supplied by Member States.

2. Without prejudice to the rights and obligations of the Member States under the Charter of the United Nations, the Commission shall maintain all necessary contacts with the Sanctions Committee for the purpose of the effective implementation of this Regulation.

Article 9

Member States shall lay down the rules on penalties applicable to infringements of the provisions of this Regulation and shall take all measures necessary to ensure that they are implemented. The penalties provided for must be effective, proportionate and dissuasive.

Member States shall notify the Commission of those rules without delay after the entry into force of this Regulation and shall notify it of any subsequent amendment to them.

Article 10

This Regulation shall apply:

(a) within the territory of the Community, including its airspace;

(b) on board any aircraft or any vessel under the jurisdiction of a Member State;

(c) to any person inside or outside the territory of the Community who is a national of a Member State;

(d) to any legal person, entity or body which is incorporated or constituted under the law of a Member State;

(e) to any legal person, entity or body in respect of any business done in whole or in part within the Community.

Article 11

This Regulation shall enter into force on the day of its publication in the *Official Journal of* the *European Union*.

This Regulation shall be binding in its entirety and directly applicable in all Member States.

Done at Brussels, 21 February 2006.

For the Council

The President

K. GASTINGER

Annex I

List of Natural and Legal Persons, Entities and Bodies Referred to in Article 2

(Annex to be completed after the persons and entities have been registered by the Committee established by paragraph 3 (b) of UNSCR 1636 (2005))

Annex II

List of Competent Authorities Referred to in Articles 3, 4 and 5

BELGIUM

Federale Overheidsdienst Financiën Thesaurie
Kunstlaan 30
B-1040 Brussel
Fax: (32-2) 233 74 65
E-mail: Quesfinvragen.tf@minfin.fed.be

Service Public Fédéral des Finances
Trésorerie
30 Avenue des Arts
B-1040 Bruxelles
Fax: 00 32 2 233 74 65
E-mail: Quesfinvragen.tf@minfin.fed.be

CZECH REPUBLIC

Ministerstvo financí
Finanční anaytický útvar
P.O. BOX 675
Jindřišská 14
111 21 Praha 1
Tel.: +420 2 5704 4501
Fax: +420 2 5704 4502

Ministerstvo zahraničních věcí
Odbor společné zahraniční a bezpečnostní politiky EU
Loretánské nám. 5
118 00 Praha 1
Tel.: +420 2 2418 2987
Fax: +420 2 2418 4080

DENMARK

Erhvervs- og Byggestyrelsen
Langelinie Allé 17
DK-2100 København K
Tlf. (45) 35 46 62 81
Fax (45) 35 46 62 03

Udenrigsministeriet
Asiatisk Plads 2
DK-1448 København K
Tlf. (45) 33 92 00 00
Fax (45) 32 54 05 33

Justitsministeriet
Slotholmsgade 10
DK-1216 København K
Tlf. (45) 33 92 33 40
Fax (45) 33 93 35 10

GERMANY

Concerning funds:
Deutsche Bundesbank
Servicezentrum Finanzsanktionen
Postfach
D-80281 München
Tel.: (49) 89 28 89 3800
Fax: (49) 69 709097 3800

Concerning economic resources

—for information in accordance with Art. 5:

Bundesministerium für Wirtschaft und Technologie
Referat V B 2
Scharnhorststr. 34–37
D-10115 Berlin
Tel.: 01888-615-9
Fax: 01888-615-5358
Email: BUERO-VB2@bmwi.bund.de

—for granting of exemptions in accordance with Art. 3:

Bundesamt für Wirtschaft und Ausfuhrkontrolle (BAFA)
Frankfurter Straße 29–35
D-65760 Eschborn

Tel.: (49) 6196 908-0
Fax: (49) 6196 908-800

ESTONIA

Eesti Välisministeerium
Islandi väljak 1
15049 Tallinn
Tel.: + 372 6317 100
Faks: + 372 6317 199

Finantsinspektsioon
Sakala 4
15030 Tallinn
Tel.: + 372 6680 500
Faks: + 372 6680 501

GREECE

A. *Freezing of Assets*

Ministry of Economy and Finance
General Directory of Economic Policy
Address: 5 Nikis Str.
10 563 Athens—Greece
Tel.: + 30 210 3332786
Fax: + 30 210 3332810

A. Δέσμενση κεφαλαίων

Υπονργείο Οικονομίας και Οικονομικών
Γενική Δ/νση Οικονομικής Πολιτικής
Δ/νοη: Νίκης 5
10 563 Αθήνα
Τηλ.: + 30 210 3332786
Φαξ: + 30 210 3332810

B. *Import-Export restrictions*

Ministry of Economy and Finance
General Directorate for Policy Planning and Management
Address: Kornarou Str. 1
10 563 Athens
Tel.: + 30 210 3286401-3
Fax: + 30 210 3286404

Β. Περιορισμοί εισαγωγών — εξαγωγών

Υπουργείο Οικονομίας και Οικονομικών
Γενική Δ/νση Σχεδιασμού και Διαχείρισης
Δ/νση: Κορνάρου 1
Τ.Κ. 10 563 Αθήνα—Ελλάς
Τηλ.: + 30 210 3286401-3
Φαξ: + 30 210 3286404

SPAIN

Dirección General del Tesoro y Política Financiera
Subdirección General de Inspección y Control de Movimientos de Capitales
Ministerio de Economía
Paseo del Prado, 6
E-28014 Madrid
Tel.: (34) 912 09 95 11

Dirección General de Comercio e Inversiones
Subdirección General de Inversiones Exteriores
Ministerio de Industria, Comercio y Turismo
Paseo de la Castellana, 162
E-28046 Madrid
Tel.: (34) 913 49 39 83

FRANCE

Ministère de l'économie, des finances et de l'industrie
Direction générale du Trésor et de la politique économique
Service des affaires multilatérales et du développement
Sous-direction Politique commerciale et investissements
Service Services, Investissements et Propriété intellectuelle
139, rue de Bercy
75572 Paris Cedex 12
Tél.: (33) 1 44 87 72 85
Télécopieur: (33) 1 53 18 96 55

Ministère des affaires étrangères
Direction générale des affaires politiques et de sécurité
Service de la politique étrangère et de sécurité commune
37, Quai d'Orsay
75007 Paris
Tél.: (33) 1 43 17 45 16
Télécopieur: (33) 1 43 17 45 84

IRELAND

United Nations Section
Department of Foreign Affairs
Iveagh House
79-80 Saint Stephen's Green
Dublin 2
Tel.: + 353 1 478 0822
Fax: + 353 1 408 2165

Central Bank and Financial Services Authority of Ireland
Financial Markets Department
Dame Street
Dublin 2
Tel.: + 353 1 671 6666
Fax: + 353 1 679 8882

ITALY

Ministero degli Affari Esteri
Piazzale della Farnesina, 1
I-00194 Roma
D.G.M.M.—Ufficio II
Tel.: (39) 06 3691 2296
Fax: (39) 06 3691 3567

Ministero dell'Economia e delle Finanze
Dipartimento del Tesoro
Comitato di Sicurezza Finanziaria
Via XX Settembre, 97
I-00187 Roma
Tel.: (39) 06 4761 3942
Fax: (39) 06 4761 3032

CYPRUS

Ministry of Commerce, Industry and Tourism
6 Andrea Araouzou
1421 Nicosia
Tel: + 357 22 86 71 00
Fax: + 357 22 31 60 71

Central Bank of Cyprus
80 Kennedy Avenue
1076 Nicosia

Tel: + 357 22 71 41 00
Fax: + 357 22 37 81 53

Ministry of Finance (Department of Customs)
M. Karaoli
1096 Nicosia
Tel: + 357 22 60 11 06
Fax: + 357 22 60 27 41/47

LATVIA

Latvijas Republikas Prokuratūra
Noziedzīgi iegūtu līdzekļu legalizācijas novēršanas dienests
Kalpaka bulvāris 6
Rīga, LV-1801
Tel.: (371) 70144431
Fax: (371) 7044804

Latvijas Republikas Ārlietu ministrija
Brīvības bulvāris 36
Rīga, LV-1395
Tel.: (371) 7016201
Fax: (371) 7828121

LITHUANIA

Saugumo politikos departamentas
Lietuvos Respublikos užsienio reikalų ministerija
J. Tumo-Vaižganto 2
LT-01511 Vilnius
Lithuania
Tel. +370 5 236 25 16
Fax. +370 5 231 30 90

LUXEMBOURG

Ministère des Affaires étrangères et de l'Immigration
Direction des Relations économiques internationales
5, rue Notre-Dame
L-2240 Luxembourg
Tél.: (352) 478 2346
Fax: (352) 22 20 48

Ministère des Finances
3, rue de la Congrégation

L-1352 Luxembourg
Tél.: (352) 478 2712
Fax: (352) 47 52 41

HUNGARY

Hungarian National Police Headquarters
Teve u. 4–6.
H-1139 Budapest
Hungary
Tel./fax: +36-1-443-5554

Országos Rendőrfőkapitányság
1139 Budapest, Teve u. 4–6.
Magyarország
Tel./fax: +36-1-443-5554

Ministry of Finance
József nádor tér. 2–4.
H-1051 Budapest
Hungary
Postbox: 1139 Pf.: 481
Tel.: +36-1-318-2066, +36-1-327-2100
Fax: +36-1-318-2570, +36-1-327-2749

Pénzügyminisztérium
1051 Budapest, József nádor tér. 2–4.
Magyarország
Postafiók: 1139 Pf.: 481
Tel.: +36-1-318-2066, +36-1-327-2100
Fax: +36-1-318-2570, +36-1-327-2749

MALTA

Bord ta' Sorveljanza dwar is-Sanzjonijiet
Ministeru ta' l-Affarijiet Barranin
Palazzo Parisio
Triq il-Merkanti
Valletta CMR 02
Tel.: + 356 21 24 28 53
Fax: + 356 21 25 15 20

NETHERLANDS

De Minister van Financiën
Directie Financiële Markten/Afdeling Integriteit
Postbus 20201
NL-2500 EE
Den Haag
Tel.: (31-70) 342 89 97
Fax: (31-70) 342 79 84

AUSTRIA

A. *Freezing of Assets*

Österreichische Nationalbank
(Austrian National Bank)
Otto-Wagner-Platz 3
A-1090 Wien
Tel. (+ 43-1) 404 20-0
Fax (+ 43-1) 404 20-7399

B. *Import-Export restrictions and all other restrictions*

Bundesministerium für Wirtschaft und Arbeit
(Federal Ministry of Economics and Labour)
Abteilung C2/2 (Ausfuhrkontrolle)
Stubenring 1
A-1010 Wien
Tel. (+ 43-1) 711 00-0
Fax (+ 43-1) 711 00-8386

POLAND

Ministerstwo Finansów
Generalny Inspektor Informacji Finansowej (GIIF)
ul. Świętokrzyska 12
00-916 Warszawa
Poland
Tel. (+48 22) 694 59 70
Faks (+48 22) 694 54 50

PORTUGAL

Ministério dos Negócios Estrangeiros
Direcção-Geral dos Assuntos Multilaterais
Largo do Rilvas
P-1350-179 Lisboa

Tel.: (351) 21 394 67 02
Fax: (351) 21 394 60 73

Ministério das Finanças
Direcção-Geral dos Assuntos Europeus e Relações Internacionais
Avenida Infante D. Henrique n.° 1, C, 2.°
P-1100 Lisboa
Tel.: (351) 21 882 3390/8
Fax: (351) 21 882 3399

SLOVENIA

Ministry of Foreign Affairs
Prešernova 25
SI-1000 Ljubljana
Tel.: 00386 1 478 2000
Faks: 00386 1 478 2341

Ministry of the Economy
Kotnikova 5
SI-1000 Ljubljana
Tel.: 00386 1 478 3311
Faks: 00386 1 433 1031

Ministry of Defence
Kardeljeva pl. 25
SI-1000 Ljubljana
Tel.: 00386 1 471 2211
Faks: 00386 1 431 8164

SLOVAKIA

Ministerstvo financií Slovenskej republiky
Štefanovičova 5
P.O. BOX 82
817 82 Bratislava
Tel.: 00421 2 5958 1111
Fax: 00421 2 5249 3048

FINLAND

Ulkoasiainministeriö/Utrikesministeriet
PL/PB 176
FIN-00161 Helsinki/Helsingfors

Tel (358-9) 16 00 5
Fax (358-9) 16 05 57 07

SWEDEN

Article 3:

Försäkringskassan
SV-103 51 Stockholm
Tfn +46 (0) 8 786 90 00
Fax +46 (0) 8 411 27 89

Articles 4 and 5:

Finansinspektionen
Box 6750
SV-113 85 Stockholm
Tfn +46 (0) 8 787 80 00
Fax +46 (0) 8 24 13 35

UNITED KINGDOM

HM Treasury
Financial Systems and International Standards
1, Horse Guards Road
London SW1A 2HQ
United Kingdom
Tel. + 44 (0) 20 7270 4901
Fax + 44 (0) 20 7270 5430

Bank of England
Financial Sanctions Unit
Threadneedle Street
London EC2R 8AH
United Kingdom
Tel. + 44 (0) 20 7601 4768
Fax + 44 (0) 20 7601 4309

EUROPEAN COMMUNITY

Commission of the European Communities
Directorate-General for External Relations
Directorate Common Foreign and Security Policy
(CFSP) and European Security and Defence Policy
(ESDP): Commission Coordination and Contribution
Legal and institutional matters, CFSP Joint Actions, Sanctions, Kimberley
Process
CHAR 12/163
B-1049 Bruxelles/Brussel
Tel. (32-2) 295 55 85/299 11 76
Fax (32-2) 296 75 63
E-mail: relex-sanctions@cec.eu.int

DOCUMENT NO. 36

EUROPEAN PROGRAMME FOR CRITICAL INFRASTRUCTURE PROTECTION

Green Paper COM(2005) 576
Commission of the European Communities

Brussels, 17 November 2005

1. Background

Critical infrastructure (CI) can be damaged, destroyed or disrupted by deliberate acts of terrorism, natural disasters, negligence, accidents or computer hacking, criminal activity and malicious behaviour. To save the lives and property of people at risk in the EU from terrorism, natural disasters and accidents, any disruptions or manipulations of CI should, to the extent possible, be brief, infrequent, manageable, geographically isolated and minimally detrimental to the welfare of the Member States (MS), their citizens and the European Union. The recent terrorist attacks in Madrid and London have highlighted the risk of terrorist attacks against European infrastructure. The EU's response must be swift, coordinated and efficient.

The European Council of June 2004 asked the Commission to prepare an overall strategy to protect critical infrastructure. In response, the Commission adopted on 20 October 2004 a Communication "Critical Infrastructure Protection in the Fight Against Terrorism" putting forward clear suggestions on what would enhance European prevention, preparedness and response to terrorist attacks involving critical infrastructures.

The Council conclusions on "Prevention, Preparedness and Response to Terrorist Attacks" and the "EU Solidarity Programme on the Consequences of Terrorist Threats and Attacks" adopted by Council in December 2004 endorsed the intention of the Commission to propose a European Programme for Critical Infrastructure Protection (EPCIP) and agreed to the set-up by the Commission of a Critical Infrastructure Warning Information Network (CIWIN).

The Commission has organized two seminars and invited the submission of ideas and comments by MS. The 1st EU Critical Infrastructure Protection Seminar was held on 6–7 June 2005 with the MS participation. Following this seminar, the MS provided the Commission with relevant background papers concerning their approach to CIP and commented on the ideas discussed at the seminar. Submissions were received in June and July, and formed the basis for further CIP development. The 2nd EU CIP seminar was held on 12–13 September in order to advance the discussion on CIP issues. Both MS and industry associations participated in this Seminar. As a result the Commission has decided to put forward this green paper outlining the options for EPCIP.

2. Objective of the Green Paper

The main objective of the green paper is to receive feedback concerning possible EPCIP policy options by involving a broad number of stakeholders. The effective protection of critical infrastructure requires communication, coordination, and cooperation nationally and at EU level among all interested parties—the owners and operators of infrastructure, regulators, professional bodies and industry associations in cooperation with all levels of government, and the public.

The Green Paper provides options on how the Commission may respond to the Council's request to establish EPCIP and CIWIN and constitutes the second phase of a consultation process concerning the establishment of a European Programme for Critical Infrastructure Protection. The Commission expect that by presenting this green paper, it will receive concrete feedback concerning the policy options outlined in this document. Depending on the outcome of the consultation process, an EPCIP policy package could be put forward during 2006.

3. Purpose and Scope of EPCIP

3.1. The Overall Goal of EPCIP

The goal of EPCIP would be to ensure that there are adequate and equal levels of protective security on critical infrastructure, minimal single points of failure and rapid, tested recovery arrangements throughout the Union. The level of protection may not be equal for all CIs and may depend on the impact caused by the failure of the CI. EPCIP would be an ongoing process and regular review will be required to keep abreast of new issues and concerns.

EPCIP should minimise as much as possible any negative impact that increased security investments might have on the competitiveness of a particular industry. In calculating the proportionality of the cost, one must not lose sight of the need to maintain stability of markets that is crucial for long-term investment, the influence security has on the evolution of stock markets and on the macro-economic dimension.

Question

Is this an appropriate goal for EPCIP? If not, what should the goal be?

3.2. What Should EPCIP Protect Against

Although consequence management measures are identical or similar for most disruptions, protection measures may differ depending on the nature of the threat. Threats that would significantly diminish abilities to ensure the essential needs and safety of the population, to maintain order and to deliver minimum essential public services or the orderly functioning of the economy, may include intentional attacks and natural disasters. The options are:

a) **an all-hazards approach for everything**—This would be a comprehensive approach taking into account both the threat from intentional attacks as well as natural disasters. It would ensure that synergies between protection measures are exploited to the maximum, but it would not give any particular emphasis to terrorism;

b) **an all-hazards approach with a terrorism priority**—This would be a flexible approach that ensures a link with other types of hazards such as the threat from intentional attacks as well as natural disasters but with terrorism being a priority. If the level of protection measures in a particular industry sector were found to be adequate, stakeholders would concentrate on those threats for which they are still vulnerable.

c) **a terrorism hazards approach**—This would be a terrorism focused approach that would not pay any particular attention to more common threats.

Question

Which approach should EPCIP take? Why?

4. Suggested Key Principles

The following key principles are suggested to form the basis of EPCIP:

- **Subsidiarity**—Subsidiarity would be at the heart of EPCIP, with the protection of critical infrastructure being first and foremost a national responsibility. The prime responsibility for protecting critical infrastructure would fall on the MS and owners/operators acting under a common framework. The Commission would in turn concentrate on aspects related to the protection of critical infrastructures having an EU cross border effect. The responsibility and accountability of owners and operators to make their own decisions and plans for protecting their own assets should not change.

- **Complementarity**—The common EPCIP framework would be complementary to existing measures. Where community mechanisms are already in place, they should continue to be used and will help guarantee the overall implementation of EPCIP.
- **Confidentiality**—Information sharing regarding critical infrastructure protection would take place in an environment of trust and confidentiality. This is a necessity bearing in mind that specific facts about a critical infrastructure asset can be used to cause failure or unacceptable consequences for critical infrastructure installations. Both at EU level and MS level CIP information would be classified and access granted only on a need-to-know basis.
- **Stakeholder Cooperation**—All stakeholders including MS, Commission, industry/business associations, standardisation bodies and owners, operators and users ('users' being defined as organizations that exploit and use the infrastructure for business and service provision purposes) have a role to play in protecting CI. All stakeholders should cooperate and contribute to the development and implementation of EPCIP according to their specific roles and responsibilities. MS authorities would provide leadership and coordination in developing and implementing a nationally consistent approach to the protection of critical infrastructure within their jurisdictions. The owners, operators and users would be actively involved at both the national and EU level. Where sectoral standards do not exist or where international norms have not yet been established, standardisation organisations could adopt common standards where appropriate.
- **Proportionality**—Protection strategies and measures would be proportionate to the level of risk involved as not all infrastructures can be protected from all threats (for example, electricity transmission networks are too large to fence or guard). By applying appropriate risk management techniques, attention would be focused on areas of greatest risk, taking into account the threat, relative criticality, cost-benefit ratio, the level of protective security and the effectiveness of available mitigation strategies.

Question

Are these key principles acceptable? Are some superfluous? Are there additional ones that should be considered?

Do you agree that protection measures should be proportionate to the level of risk involved as not all infrastructures can be protected from all threats?

5. A Common EPCIP Framework

The damage or loss of a piece of infrastructure in one MS may have negative effects on several others and on the European economy as a whole. This is becoming increasingly likely as new technologies (e.g. the Internet) and market liberalisation (e.g. in electricity and gas supply) mean that much infrastructure is part of a larger network. In such a situation protection measures are only as strong as their weakest link. This means that a common level of protection may be necessary.

Effective protection requires communication, coordination, and cooperation nationally, at EU level (where relevant) and internationally among all stakeholders. A common EU level framework for the protection of critical infrastructure in Europe could be put in place in order to make sure that each MS is providing adequate and equal levels of protection concerning their critical infrastructure and that the rules of competition within the internal market are not distorted. With a view to supporting the activities of the MS, the Commission would facilitate the identification, exchange and dissemination of best practices on CIP related issues by providing a common framework for the protection of critical infrastructure. The scope of this general framework needs to be considered.

The common EPCIP framework would contain horizontal measures that define the competence and responsibilities of all critical infrastructure protection (CIP) stakeholders, as well as laying the foundation for sector specific approaches. The common framework is meant to complement existing sectoral measures at Community level and in MS in order to provide the maximum possible level of security of critical infrastructure present in the European Union. Work on reaching agreement on a common list of definitions and CI sectors should be prioritised.

As the different sectors containing critical infrastructure are very diverse, it would be difficult to prescribe exactly what criteria should be used to identify and protect all of them in a horizontal framework; this should be carried out on a sector-by-sector basis. Nevertheless, there is a need for a common understanding on certain cross-cutting issues.

It is therefore suggested that the strengthening of CI in the EU is achieved by the setting of a common EPCIP framework, (common objectives, methodologies e.g. for comparisons, interdependencies) exchanging best practices and compliance monitoring mechanisms. Some of the elements which would form part of the common framework would include:

- common CIP principles;
- commonly agreed codes/standards
- common definitions on the basis of which sector specific definitions can be agreed (an indicative list of definitions is included in Annex 1);
- common list of CI sectors (an indicative list of sectors is included in Annex 2);
- CIP priority areas;
- description of the responsibilities of the stakeholders involved;
- agreed benchmarks;
- methodologies to compare and prioritise infrastructure in different sectors.

Such a common framework would also minimise potential distorting effects on the internal market.

The common EPCIP framework could be voluntary or mandatory—or a mixture depending on the issue. Both types of framework could complement existing sectoral and horizontal measures at Community and MS level; however, only a legal framework would provide a strong and enforceable legal basis for a coherent and uniform implementation of measures to protect ECI, as well as defining clearly the respective responsibilities of MS and the Commission. Non-binding voluntary measures, while flexible, would not provide clarity on who does what.

Depending on the outcome of a careful analysis and paying due regard to the proportionality of proposed measures, the Commission may make use of a number of instruments, including legislation, in its EPCIP proposal. Impact assessments will accompany proposals for specific measures, where relevant.

Questions

Would a common framework be effective in strengthening CIP?

If a legislative framework is required, what elements should it contain?

Do you agree that the criteria for identifying different types of ECI, and the protection measures considered necessary, should be identified sector-by-sector?

Would a common framework be helpful in clarifying the responsibilities of the stakeholders concerned? To what extent should such a common framework be obligatory and to what extent voluntary?

What should be the scope of the common framework? Do you agree with the list of indicative terms and definitions in annex I on the basis of which, sector specific definitions (where relevant) can be created? Do you agree with the list of indicative CI sectors in annex II?

6. EU Critical Infrastructures (ECI)

6.1. Definition of EU Critical Infrastructure

The definition of what constitutes an EU critical infrastructure would be determined by its cross border effect which ascertains whether an incident could have a serious impact beyond the territory of a MS where the installation is located. Another element to take into account here is the fact that bilateral CIP cooperation schemes between MS constitute a well established and efficient means of dealing with CI between the borders of two MS. Such cooperation would be complementary to EPCIP.

ECI could include those physical resources, services, information technology facilities, networks and infrastructure assets, which, if disrupted or destroyed would have a serious impact on the health, safety, security, economic or social well-being of either:

(a) two or more MS—**this would include certain bilateral CI (where relevant);**

(b) involve three or more MS—**this would exclude all bilateral CI;**

When considering the respective merits of these options it is important to bear the following points in mind:

- the fact that a piece of infrastructure would be designated as ECI, does not mean that it would necessarily require any additional protection measures. The existing protection measures, which could include bilateral agreements between MS, may be perfectly adequate and hence unchanged by a designation as ECI;
- option (a) may involve a higher number of designations;
- option (b) may mean that for infrastructure of concern to only two MS, there would be no Community role even if the level of protection was considered inadequate by one of those two MS and the other MS refused to take action. Option (b) could also lead to a multitude of bilateral agreements or disagreements between MS. Industry, which often operates at a pan-European level, may have to work with a diverse patchwork of different agreements, which may introduce additional costs.

Moreover, it is acknowledged that, CI originating or existing outside of the EU, but interconnected or having a potential direct effect on EU MS should also be considered.

> **Question**
>
> Should ECI be infrastructure that has a potentially serious cross-border impact with two or more MS, or three or more MS? Why?

6.2. Interdependencies

It is suggested that the progressive identification of all ECI in particular take into account interdependencies. Studies in interdependencies would contribute to assessing the potential impact of threats against specific CI and in particular to identify which MS would be affected in case of a major CI related incident.

Full consideration would be given to interdependencies within and between businesses, industry sectors, geographical jurisdictions and MS authorities in particular those enabled by Information and Communications Technologies (ICTs). The Commission, the MS and the owners/operators of critical infrastructures would work together to identify these interdependencies and apply appropriate strategies to reduce risk where possible.

> **Question**
>
> How can interdependencies be taken into account?
>
> Do you know of any suitable methodologies for analysing interdependencies?
>
> At what level should the identification of interdependencies take place—at EU and/or MS level?

6.3. Implementing Steps for ECI

The Commission would suggest the following implementing steps for ECI:

(1) The Commission together with the MS draw up the specific criteria which would be used to identify ECI on a sector-specific basis;

(2) Progressive identification and verification on a sector-by-sector basis of ECI by MS and Commission. The decision on designating particular CI as ECI will be taken at the European level[1] due to the cross border nature of the infrastructure concerned.;

[1] With the exception of defence-related infrastructures.

(3) MS and Commission analyse existing security gaps in relation to ECI on a sector-by-sector basis;

(4) MS and Commission agree on priority sectors/infrastructure for action, taking into account interdependencies;

(5) Where relevant, for each sector, the Commission and MS key stakeholders agree on proposals for minimum protection measures, which could include standards;

(6) Following the adoption of the proposals by the Council, these measures are then implemented;

(7) Regular monitoring is ensured by the MS and the Commission. Revisions (measures and identification of CI) are made when and where appropriate.

Questions

Is the list of steps concerning the implementation of the ECI acceptable?

How do you suggest the Commission and the MS designate together ECI—MS have expertise, Commission has overview of European interest? Should this be a legal decision?

Is there a need for an arbitration mechanism if a particular MS do not agree to designate an infrastructure under its jurisdiction as ECI?

Is there a need for verification of designations? Who should be responsible?

Should MS be able to designate infrastructure in other MS or third countries as being critical for them? What should happen if a MS, a third country or an industry considers a piece of infrastructure in a MS to be critical for them?

What should happen if that MS then does not identify it? Is there a need for an appeals mechanism? If so what?

Should an operator have the possibility of appealing, if they do not agree with their designation or non-designation. If so, to whom?

What methodologies would need to be developed for setting priority sectors/infrastructure for action? Do suitable methodologies already exist that can be adapted to the European-level?

How can the Commission be involved in analysing the security gaps in relation to ECI?

7. National Critical Infrastructures (NCI)

7.1. The NCI Role in EPCIP

Many European companies operate across borders and as such are subject to differing obligations for NCI. It is therefore suggested in the interests of the MS and the EU as a whole that each MS protects its NCI under a common framework so that owners and operators throughout Europe would benefit from not being subject to a varied puzzle of frameworks resulting in a multitude of methodologies and additional costs. To that extent the Commission suggests that EPCIP—while focusing primarily on EU Critical Infrastructure—cannot leave out altogether National Critical Infrastructure. Nevertheless, three options could be envisaged:

a) NCI is fully integrated within EPCIP

b) NCI is outside the scope of EPCIP

c) MS may use parts of EPCIP at their own volition in relation to NCI, but are under no obligation to do so.

Question

The efficient protection of critical infrastructure in the European Union would seem to require the identification of both ECI and NCI. Do you agree that although EPCIP should focus on ECI, NCI cannot altogether be left out?

Which of these options do you feel is the most appropriate for EPCIP?

7.2. National CIP Programmes

Based on a common EPCIP framework, MS could develop National CIP Programmes for its NCI. The MS would be able to apply more stringent measures than those provided for under EPCIP.

Question

Is it desirable that each MS adopts a National CIP Programme based on EPCIP?

7.3. Single Overseeing Body

The need for efficiency and coherency suggests the necessity of designation by each MS of a single overseeing body dealing with the overall implementation of EPCIP. Two options could be envisaged:

(a) A single CIP overseeing body;

(b) A national contact point with no authority, leaving it to the MS to organise themselves.

Such a body could coordinate, monitor and oversee the implementation of EPCIP within its jurisdiction and could serve as the main institutional contact point on CIP matters with the Commission, other MS and CIP owners and operators. This body could form the basis for national representation in expert groups dealing with CIP issues and could be connected to the Critical Infrastructure Warning Information Network (CIWIN). The National CIP Coordination Body (NCCB) could coordinate national CIP issues notwithstanding that other bodies or entities within a MS that may already be involved in CIP matters.

The progressive identification of NCI could be achieved by obliging infrastructure owners and operators to notify the NCCB about any relevant CIP related business activity.

The NCCB could be responsible for the legal decision on designating an infrastructure under its jurisdiction as a NCI. This information would remain at the sole disposal of the MS concerned.

Specific competences could include:

a) Coordination, monitoring and overseeing the overall implementation of EPCIP in a MS;

b) Serving as the main institutional contact point on CIP matters with:

  i. the Commission

  ii. other MS

  iii. CIP owners and operators

c) Participate in the designation of EU Critical Infrastructure (ECI);

d) Taking the legal decision on designating an infrastructure under its jurisdiction as a National Critical Infrastructure;

e) Serve as an authority of legal recourse for owners/operators who do not agree that their infrastructure is designated "critical infrastructure";

f) Participate in the elaboration of the National Critical Infrastructure Protection Programme and the sector specific CIP programmes;

g) Identify interdependencies between specific CI sectors;

h) Contribute to sector-specific approaches to CIP through participation in expert groups. Owners and operators representatives could be invited in order to contribute to the discussions. Regular meetings could be held;

i) Supervise the process of drawing-up CI related contingency plans;

Questions

Do you agree that MS would alone be responsible for designating and managing NCI under a common EPCIP framework?

Is it desirable to designate a CIP coordination body within each MS having overall coordination responsibility for CIP related measures while respecting existing sector based responsibilities (civil aviation authorities, Seveso Directive etc.)?

Would the suggested competences of such a coordination body be appropriate? Are there others that are necessary?

7.4. Implementing Steps for NCI

The Commission would suggest the following implementing steps for NCI:

(1) Using EPCIP, the MS draw up the specific criteria which would be used to identify NCI;

(2) Progressive identification and verification on a sector-by-sector basis of NCI by MS;

(3) MS analyse existing security gaps in relation to NCI on a sector-by-sector basis;

(4) MS set-up priority sectors for action, taking into account interdependencies and EU level agreed priorities where relevant;

(5) Where relevant, for each sector, the MS agree minimum protection measures;

(6) MS are responsible for ensuring that the owners/operators under their jurisdiction carry out the necessary implementation measures;

(7) Regular monitoring is ensured by the MS. Revisions (measures and identification of CI) are made when and where appropriate.

Question

Is the list of steps concerning the implementation of the NCI appropriate? Are any steps superfluous? Should any steps be added?

8. Role of CI Owners, Operators and Users

8.1. Responsibilities of CI Owners, Operators and Users

Designation as a CI suggests certain responsibilities for owners and operators. Four responsibilities could be envisaged for owners and operators designated as NCI or ECI:

(1) **Notification to the relevant MS CIP body of the fact that an infrastructure may be of a critical nature;**

(2) **Designation of a senior representative(s) to act as Security Liaison Officer (SLO) between the owner/operator and the relevant MS CIP authority.** The SLO would take part in the development of security and contingency plans. The SLO would be the main liaison officer with the relevant CIP sector body in the MS and where relevant with the law enforcement authorities;

(3) **Establishment, implementation and updating of an Operator Security Plan (OSP).** A suggested OSP template is attached in Annex 3.

(4) **Participation in the development of a contingency plan** relative to the CI with relevant MS civil protection and law enforcement authorities where requested.

The OSP could be submitted for approval to the relevant MS CIP sector authority under the overall supervision of the NCCB regardless if it is a NCI or ECI which would guarantee the consistency of security measures taken by specific owners and operators and the relevant sectors in general. In return owners and operators could be given relevant feedback and support as to relevant threats, development of best practices and where appropriate help in assessing interdependencies and vulnerabilities through the NCCB and where relevant by the Commission.

Each MS could set a time limit for the creation of the OSP by the owners and operators of NCI and ECI (in the case of ECI the Commission would also be involved) and could set administrative fines for situations when these deadlines are not respected.

It is suggested that the Operator Security Plan (OSP) would identify the owner's/operator's critical infrastructure assets and establish relevant security solutions for their protection. The OSP would describe the methods and procedure which are to be followed to ensure compliance with EPCIP, National CIP Programmes and relevant sector specific CIP programmes. The OSP could represent a vehicle for a bottom up approach in regulating CIP that gives stronger leeway (and also more responsibility) to the private sector.

In particular situations when it comes to certain infrastructure such as electricity grid networks and information networks it would be unrealistic (from a practical and financial point of view) to expect the owners and operators to provide equal levels of security to all their assets. In such cases, it is suggested that the owners and operators could, together with the relevant authorities identify the critical points (nodes) of a physical or information network on which security protective measures could be concentrated.

The OSP could contain security measures arranged around two headings:

- **permanent security measures,** which would identify indispensable security investment and means, which cannot be installed by the owner/operator at short notice. The owner/operator would maintain a standing alertness against potential threats, which would not disturb its regular economic, administrative and social activities.
- **graduated security measures,** which could be activated according to varying threat levels. The OSP would therefore foresee various security regimes adapted to possible threat levels existing in the MS where the infrastructure is located.

It is suggested that failure on behalf of a CI owner and operator to adhere to the obligation of developing an OSP, contribute to the development of contingency plans and designating an SLO could entail the possibility to impose a financial penalty.

Questions

Are the potential responsibilities for owners/operators of critical infrastructure acceptable in terms of increasing the security of critical infrastructure? What would be their likely cost?

Should owners and operators be obliged to notify the fact that their infrastructure may be of a critical nature?Do you think the OSP concept is useful? Why?

Are the suggested obligations proportional to the costs involved?

What rights could the CI owners and operators be given by the MS authorities and Commission?

8.2. Dialogue with CI Owners, Operators and Users

EPCIP could engage the owners and operators in partnerships. The success of any protection programme depends on the cooperation and level of involvement that can be achieved with the owners and operators. Within the MS, the CIP owners and operators could be closely involved in CIP developments through regular contacts with the NCCB.

At EU level, forums could be created in order to facilitate exchanges of views on general and sector specific CIP issues. A common approach on private sector engagement on CIP related issues to bring together all stakeholders in the public and private sphere would provide the MS, Commission and the industry with an important platform through which to communicate on whichever new CIP issue arise. The owners, operators and users of CI could assist in the development of common guidelines, best practice standards and where relevant information sharing. Such dialogue would help shape future revisions of EPCIP.

Where relevant the Commission could encourage the creation of EU CIP related industry /business associations. The two ultimate objectives would be to ensure that European industry retains its competitiveness and that the security of EU citizens is enhanced.

Question

How should the dialogue with the owners, operators and users of CI be structured?

Who should represent the owners, operators and users in the public private dialogue?

9. EPCIP Supporting Measures

9.1. The Critical Infrastructure Warning Information Network (CIWIN)

The Commission has developed a number of rapid alert systems allowing for the concrete, coordinated and effective response in case of emergencies, including those of a terrorist origin. On 20 October 2004, the Commission announced the creation of a central network in the Commission ensuring rapid information flows between all Commission rapid alert systems and concerned Commission services (ARGUS).

The Commission is suggesting creating CIWIN which could stimulate the development of appropriate protection measures by facilitating an exchange of best practices in a secure manner as well as being a vehicle for transmission of immediate threats and alerts. The system would ensure that the right people have the right information at the right time.

The following three options are possible for the development of CIWIN:

(1) **CIWIN would be in the shape of a forum limited to the exchange of CIP ideas and best practices** in support of the CI owners and operators. Such a forum could take the form of a network of experts and an electronic platform for the exchange of relevant information in a secure environment. The Commission would play an important

role in gathering and disseminating such information. This option would not provide the necessary rapid alerts on imminent threats. However there could be scope for the broadening of CIWIN in the future.

(2) **CIWIN would be a rapid alert system (RAS) linking MS with the Commission**. This option would increase the security of critical infrastructure by providing warnings limited to immediate threats and alerts. The objective here would be to facilitate a rapid exchange of information about potential threats to CI owners and operators. The RAS would not involve the sharing of long-term intelligence. It would be used for the rapid sharing of information on imminent threats to specific infrastructure.

(3) **CIWIN would be a multi-level communication/alert system composed of two distinct functions:** a) a rapid alert system (RAS) linking MS with the Commission and b) a forum for the exchange of CIP ideas and best practices in support of the CI owners and operators composed of a network of experts and an electronic data exchange platform.

Regardless of the option chosen, CIWIN would complement existing networks and due care taken to avoid duplication. In the long-term, CIWIN could be linked to all relevant CI owners and operators in each MS through for instance the NCCB. Alerts and best practices could be channelled through this body which would be the only service directly connected to the Commission and thereby to all other MS. MS would be able to utilize their existing information systems for the establishment of their national CIWIN capacity linking the authorities to specific owners and operators. Importantly, these national networks could be used by the relevant MS CIP bodies and the owners and operators as a two way communication system.

A study will be launched to determine the scope and technical specifications necessary for CIWIN's future interface with the MS.

Questions

What form should the CIWIN network take in order to support the objectives of EPCIP?

Should CI owners and operators be connected to CIWIN?

9.2. Common methodologies

Different MS have different alert levels corresponding to different situations. At the present time there is no way of knowing whether, for example, a "high" in one MS, is the same as a "high" in another. This may make it difficult for trans-national companies to prioritise their expenditure on protection measures. It may be beneficial, therefore to attempt to harmonise or calibrate the different levels.

For every level of threat, there could be a level of preparedness whereby common security measures may be triggered in general and, where appropriate, the use of graduated security measures in particular. MS not wishing to deploy a certain measure would be able to address a specific threat by alternative security measures.

A common methodology of identifying and classifying threats, capabilities, risks, and vulnerabilities and drawing conclusions about the possibility, probability, and degree of severity posed by a threat to disrupt an infrastructure installation could be considered. This would include risk rating and prioritization in which risk events could be defined in terms of their probability of occurrence, impact, and relationship to other risk areas or processes.

Questions

To what extent is it desirable and feasible to harmonise or calibrate different alert levels?

Should there be a common methodology of identifying and classifying threats, capabilities, risks, and vulnerabilities and drawing conclusions about the possibility, probability, and degree of severity posed by a threat?

9.3. Funding

Following an initiative of the European Parliament (creation of a new budget line—pilot project « Fight against terrorism"—in the 2005 budget), the Commission took the decision on 15th September to allocate 7 Mio€ to finance a set of actions which will enhance European prevention, preparedness and response to terrorist attacks, including consequence management, critical infrastructure protection, terrorist financing, explosives and violent radicalisation. More than two thirds of this budget is consecrated to the preparation of the future European Programme for Critical Infrastructure protection, to the integration and development of capabilities required for the management of Crises of trans-national significance resulting from possible terrorist attacks and to emergency measures which may be required to address a significant threat or occurrence of such an attack. It is expected that this funding will continue in 2006.

From 2007 to 2013 funding will be taken over by the Framework programme on Security and Safeguarding Liberties. This will include a Specific Programme on "Prevention, Preparedness and Consequence Management of Terrorism"; the Commission's proposal allocated an amount of € 137,4 million designed to identify the relevant needs and to develop common technical standards to protect critical infrastructure.

The programme will provide Community funding to projects presented by national, regional and local authorities for the protection of critical infrastructures. The programme focuses on identifying protection needs and at providing information in view of developing common standards, threat and risk assessments, in order to protect critical infrastructure, or develop specific contingency plans. The Commission would make use of its existing expertise or could help finance studies concerning interdependencies in specific sectors. It is then mainly the responsibility of the MS or the owners and operators to upgrade the security of their infrastructure according to the identified needs. The programme itself does not fund the upgrading of critical infrastructure protection. Loans from financial institutions could be used for upgrading the security of infrastructure in the MS according to the needs identified through the programme, and to implement common standards. The Commission would be willing to support sector based studies to assess financial impacts the upgrading of security of infrastructure may have on the industry.

The Commission is funding research projects in support of critical infrastructure protection in the Preparatory Action for Security Research[2] (2004–2006), and has planned more substantial activities in the area of security research in its proposal for a Decision of the Council and the European Parliament concerning the 7th EC Research Framework Programme (COM(2005)119 final)[3] and its proposal for a Council Decision concerning the Specific programme "Cooperation" implementing the Seventh Framework Programme (COM(2005)440 final). Targeted research which aims to provide practical strategies or tools for risk mitigation is of prime importance to securing EC's critical infrastructure in the medium to long-term. All Security Research, including in this area, will be submitted to ethical review to ensure compatibility with the Charter of Fundamental Rights. The demand for research will only increase as the number of infrastructure dependencies increase.

Questions

How would you estimate the cost and impact of the implementation of the measures put forward in this green paper for administrations and industry? Would you find it proportionate?

[2] The total sum of credits in the 2004 and 2005 budgets amounted to €30 million. For 2006, the Commission has proposed the sum of €24 million, which is being examined by the budget authority.

[3] The budget proposal of the Commission for security and space related research activities under the 7th RTD framework programme amounts to €570 million (COM(2005)119 final)

9.4. Evaluation and Monitoring

Evaluation and monitoring of the implementation of EPCIP suggests a multi-level process which requires the involvement of all stakeholders:

- **at EU level, a peer evaluation mechanism could be established,** in which MS and the Commission would work together on assessing the overall level of implementation of EPCIP in each MS. Commission annual progress reports concerning the implementation of EPCIP could be prepared.
- **the Commission would report progress to MS and other institutions each calendar year** in a Commission staff working paper.
- **at MS level, the NCCB in each MS could monitor the overall EPCIP implementation under its jurisdiction ensuring the compliance with National CIP Programme(s) and sector specific CIP programmes,** to ensure that they are effectively implemented through yearly reports to Council and Commission.

EPCIP implementation would be a dynamic process, constantly evolving and evaluated both to keep pace with the changing world and to build on lessons learnt. Peer review evaluations and MS monitoring reports could be part of the instruments used to review EPCIP and suggest new measures to strengthen the protection of critical infrastructure.

Relevant information by the MS concerning ECI could be made available to the Commission for the development of common vulnerability assessments, consequence management plans, common standards for the protection of CI, prioritising research activities and, where necessary, regulation and harmonisation. Such information would be classified and kept strictly confidential.

The Commission could monitor various MS initiatives, including those that foresee financial consequences for owners and operators incapable of resuming essential services to citizens within a specified maximum timeframe.

Question

What type of evaluation mechanism would be needed for EPCIP? Would the above mentioned mechanism be sufficient?

The responses should be sent electronically by 15 January 2006 to the following e-mail address: **jls-epcip@cec.eu.int.** These will be kept confidential unless the responder explicitly states that they want it made public, in which case they will be placed on the Commission's internet site.

Annex

Annex 1

Cip Terms and Definitions

This indicative list of definitions could be further built upon depending on the individual sectors for the purpose of identification and protection of Critical Infrastructure (CI).

Alert

Notification that a potential disaster situation will occur, exists or has occurred. Direction for recipient to stand by for possible escalation or activation of appropriate measures.

Critical Infrastructure Protection (CIP)

The ability to prepare for, protect against, mitigate, respond to, and recover from critical infrastructure disruptions or destruction.

Critical Information Infrastructure (CII):

ICT systems that are critical infrastructures for themselves or that are essential for the operation of critical infrastructures (telecommunications, computers/software, Internet, satellites, etc.).

Critical Information Infrastructure Protection (CIIP)

The programs and activities of infrastructure owners, operators, manufacturers, users, and regulatory authorities which aim at keeping the performance of critical information infrastructures in case of failures, attacks or accidents above a defined minimum level of services and aim at minimising the recovery time and damage.

CIIP should therefore be viewed as a cross-sector phenomenon rather than being limited to specific sectors. CIIP should be closely coordinated with Critical Infrastructure Protection from a holistic perspective.

Contingency Plan

A plan used by a MS and critical infrastructure owner/operator on how to respond to a specific systems failure or disruption of essential service.

Contingency plans would typically include the development, coordination, and execution of service—and site-restoration plans; the reconstitution of government operations and services; individual, private-sector, nongovernmental and public-assistance programs to promote restoration; long-term care and treatment of affected persons; additional measures for social, political, environmental, and economic restoration as well as development of initiatives to mitigate the effects of future incidents.

Critical Information

Specific facts about a critical infrastructure asset, vitally needed to plan and act effectively so as to guarantee failure or cause unacceptable consequences for critical infrastructure installations.

Critical Infrastructure (CI)

Critical infrastructure include those physical resources, services, and information technology facilities, networks and infrastructure assets which, if disrupted or destroyed, would have a serious impact on the health, safety, security or economic well-being of Citizens or the effective functioning of governments.

There are three types of infrastructure assets:

- Public, private and governmental infrastructure assets and interdependent cyber & physical networks.
- Procedures and where relevant individuals that exert control over critical infrastructure functions.
- Objects having cultural or political significance as well as "soft targets" which include mass events (i.e. sports, leisure and cultural).

Essential Service

Often applied to utilities (water, gas, electricity, etc.) it may also include standby power systems, environmental control systems or communication networks that if interrupted puts at risk public safety and confidence, threatens economic security, or impedes the continuity of a MS government and its services.

European Critical Infrastructure (ECI)

European critical infrastructure include those physical resources, services, and information technology facilities, networks and infrastructure assets, which, if disrupted or destroyed would have a serious impact on the health, safety, security, economic or social well-being of two or more MS.

The definition of what constitutes an EU critical infrastructure is determined by its cross border effect which ascertains whether an incident could have a serious impact beyond two or more MS national territories. This is defined as the loss of a critical infrastructure element and is rated by the:

- extent of the geographic area which could be affected by the loss or unavailability of a critical infrastructure element beyond three or more Member State's national territories;

- effect of time (i.e. the fact that a for example a radiological cloud might, with time, cross a border);
- level of interdependency (i.e. electricity network failure in one MS effecting another);

Impact

Impacts are the total sum of the different effects of an incident. This needs to take into account at least the following qualitative and quantitative effects:

- *Scope*—The loss of a critical infrastructure element is rated by the extent of the geographic area which could be affected by its loss or unavailability—international, national, regional or local.
- *Severity*—The degree of the loss can be assessed as None, Minimal, Moderate or Major. Among the criteria which can be used to assess impact are:
  - Public (number of population affected, loss of life, medical illness, serious injury, evacuation);
  - Economic (GDP effect, significance of economic loss and/or degradation of products or services, interruption of transport or energy services, water or food shortages);
  - Environment (effect on the public and surrounding location);
  - Interdependency (between other critical infrastructure elements).
  - Political effects (confidence in the ability of government);
  - Psychological effects (may escalate otherwise minor events). both during and after the incident and at different spatial levels (e.g. local, regional, national and international)
- *Effects of time*—This criteria ascertains at what point the loss of an element could have a serious impact (i.e. immediate, 24–48 hours, one week, other).

Interdependency

Identified connections or lack thereof between and within infrastructure sectors with essential systems and assets.

Occurrence

The term "occurrence" in the CIP context is defined as an event (either human caused or by natural phenomena) that requires a serious emergency response to protect life or property or puts at risk public safety and confidence, seriously disrupts the economy, or impedes the continuity of a MS government and its services. Occurrences include negligence, accidents, deliberate acts of terrorism, computer hacking, criminal activity and malicious damage, major disasters, urban fires, floods, hazardous materials spills, nuclear accidents, aircraft accidents, earthquakes, storms, public health and medical emergencies and other occurrences requiring a major emergency response.

Operator Security Plan

The Operator Security Plan (OSP) identifies all of the operator's critical infrastructure assets and establishes relevant security solutions for their protection. The OSP describes the methods and procedures which are to be followed by the owner/operator.

Prevention

The range of deliberate, critical tasks and activities necessary to build, sustain, and improve the operational capability to prevent, protect against, respond to, and recover from an incident. Prevention involves efforts to identify threats, determine vulnerabilities and identify required resources.

Prevention involves actions to protect lives and property. It involves applying intelligence and other information to a range of activities that may include such countermeasures as deterrence operations; heightened inspections; improved surveillance and security operations; investigations to determine the full nature and source of the threat; public health and agricultural surveillance and testing processes; immunizations, isolation, or quarantine; and as appropriate specific law enforcement operations aimed at deterring, pre-empting, interdicting, or disrupting illegal activity, and apprehending potential perpetrators and bringing them to justice. Prevention involves the stopping of an incident before it happens with effective processes, guidelines, standards and certification. Seamless interactive systems, and comprehensive threat—and vulnerability analysis.

Prevention is a continuous process of ongoing actions to reduce exposure to, probability of, or potential loss from hazards.

Response

Activities that address the short-term direct effects of an incident. Response includes immediate actions to save lives, protect property, and meet basic human needs. As indicated by the situation, response activities include applying intelligence and other information to lessen the effects or consequences of an incident; increased security operations; continuing investigations into nature and source of the threat; ongoing public health and agricultural surveillance and testing processes; immunizations, isolation, or quarantine; and specific law enforcement operations aimed at pre-empting, interdicting, or disrupting illegal activity, and apprehending actual perpetrators and bringing them to justice.

Risk

The possibility of loss, damage or injury. The level of risk is a condition of two factors: (1) the value placed on the asset by its owner/operator and the impact of loss or change to the asset, and (2) the likelihood that a specific vulnerability will be exploited by a particular threat.

Threat

Any indication, circumstance, or event with the potential to disrupt or destroy critical infrastructure, or any element thereof. An all-hazards approach to threat includes accidents, natural hazards as well as deliberate attacks. It can also be defined as the intention and capability of an adversary to undertake actions that would be detrimental to critical assets.

Vulnerability

A characteristic of an element of the critical infrastructure's design, implementation, or operation that renders it susceptible to destruction or incapacitation by a threat.

Annex 2

Indicative List of Critical Infrastructure Sectors

Sector	Product or service
I Energy	1 Oil and gas production, refining, treatment and storage, including pipelines 2 Electricity generation 3 Transmission of electricity, gas and oil 4 Distribution of electricity, gas and oil
II Information, Communication Technologies, ICT	5 Information system and network protection 6 Instrumentation automation and control systems (SCADA etc.) 7 Internet 8 Provision of fixed telecommunications 9 Provision of mobile telecommunications 10 Radio communication and navigation 11 Satellite communication 12 Broadcasting
III Water	13 Provision of drinking water 14 Control of water quality 15 Stemming and control of water quantity
IV Food	16 Provision of food and safeguarding food safety and security
V Health	17 Medical and hospital care 18 Medicines, serums, vaccines and pharmaceuticals 19 Bio-laboratories and bio-agents
VI Financial	20 Payment services/payment structures (private) 21 Government financial assignment
VII Public & Legal Order and Safety	22 Maintaining public & legal order, safety and security 23 Administration of justice and detention
VIII Civil administration	24 Government functions 25 Armed forces 26 Civil administration services 27 Emergency services 28 Postal and courier services
IX Transport	29 Road transport 30 Rail transport 31 Air traffic 32 Inland waterways transport 33 Ocean and short-sea shipping
X Chemical and nuclear industry	34 Production and storage/processing of chemical and nuclear substances 35 Pipelines of dangerous goods (chemical substances)
XI Space and Research	36 Space 37 Research

Annex 3

Operator Security Plan

The possible contents of the OSP should include an introduction and a classified detail part (not accessible outside the relevant MS authorities). The classified part would begin with a presentation of the operator and describe the legal context of its CI activities. The OSP would then go on to presenting the details on the criticality of the infrastructure concerned, taking into consideration the operator's objectives and the Member State's interests. The critical points of the infrastructure would be identified and their security requirements presented. A risk analysis based on major threat scenarios, vulnerability of each critical point, and potential impact would be conducted. Based on this risk analysis, relevant protection measures should be foreseen.

Introduction

Contains information concerning the pursued objectives and the main organisational and protection principles.

Detailed part (classified)

– Presentation of the operator

Contains a description of the operator's activities, organization and connections with the public authorities. The details of the operator's Security Liaison Office (SLO) are given.

– Legal context

The operator addresses the requirements of the National CIP Programme and the sector specific CIP programme where relevant.

– Description of the criticality of the infrastructure

The operator describes in detail the critical services/products he provides and how particular elements of the infrastructure come together to create an end-product. Details should be provided concerning:

- material elements;
- non-material elements (sensors, command, information systems);
- human elements (decision-maker, expert);
- access to information (databases, reference systems);
- dependence on other systems (energy, telecoms);
- specific procedures (organisation, management of malfunctions, etc.).

– Formalisation of security requirements

The operator identifies the critical points in the infrastructure, which could not be easily replaced and whose destruction or malfunctioning could significantly disrupt the operation of the activity or seriously endanger the safety of users, customers or employees or result in essential public needs not being satisfied. The security of these critical points is then addressed.

The owners, operators and users ('users' being defined as organizations that exploit and use the infrastructure for business and service provision purposes) of critical infrastructure would have to identify the critical points of their infrastructure, which would be deemed restricted areas. Access to restricted areas should be monitored in order to ensure than no unauthorised persons and vehicles enter such areas. Access would only be granted to security cleared personnel. The relevant background security checks (if deemed necessary by a MS CIP sector authority) should be carried out by the Member State in which the critical infrastructure is located.

– Risk analysis and management

The operator conducts and risk analysis concerning each critical point.

– Security measures

The operator presents the security measures arranged around two headings:

- Permanent security measures, which will identify indispensable security investment and means, which cannot be installed by the owner/operator in a hurry. The owner/operator will maintain a standing alertness against potential threats, which will not disturb its regular economic, administrative and social activities. This heading will include information concerning general measures; technical measures (including installation of detection, access control, protection and prevention means); organizational measures (including procedures for alerts and crisis management); control and verification measures; communication; awareness raising and training; and security of information systems.
- Graduated security measures, which may be activated according to varying threat levels. The OSP will therefore foresee various security regimes adapted to possible threat levels existing in the Member State.

– Presentation and application

The operator will prepare detailed information sheets and instructions on how to react to various situations.

– Monitoring and updating

The operator sets out the relevant monitoring and updating mechanisms which will be used.

SUBJECT INDEX

Doc/Pg

Biological Terrorism

Border Security

Chemical Terrorism

Civil Liberties – Protection of

Counterterrorism

Doc/Pg

Cyber Security

European Union

Extradition

Germany

Doc/Pg

Human Rights

Immigration

Intelligence

Terrorism – Domestic

Terrorism – Financing of

Doc/Pg

Terrorism – Policy

Terrorist Incidents

Terrorist Organizations

www.ingramcontent.com/pod-product-compliance
Ingram Content Group UK Ltd.
Pitfield, Milton Keynes, MK11 3LW, UK
UKHW051224160926
475595UK00022B/168

9 780195 376913